COMPUTER-BASED INFORMATION SYSTEMS:
A Management Approach

COMPUTER-BASED INFORMATION SYSTEMS:
A Management Approach

Second Edition

Donald W. Kroeber
Radford University

Hugh J. Watson
The University of Georgia

Macmillan Publishing Company

New York

Collier Macmillan Publishers

London

Macmillan Publishing Company
866 Third Avenue, New York, New York 10022

Collier Macmillan Canada, Inc.

Library of Congress Cataloging in Publication Data

Kroeber, Donald W.
  Computer-based information systems.

  Includes bibliographies and index.
  1. Management information systems.   I. Watson, Hugh J.
II. Title.
T58.6.K757   1987   658.4′038   85-23711
ISBN 0-02-366870-9

Printing: 1 2 3 4 5 6 7 8   Year: 7 8 9 0 1 2 3 4 5

ISBN   0-02-366870-9

To David and Eric
DWK

Preface

The study of computer-related subjects changes almost as rapidly as the technology it addresses. Only a decade has passed since texts and courses in *management information systems* (MIS) were introduced, and already we find that term inadequate to describe the full range of information systems available to managers today. This book recognizes some of the changes by treating MIS as only one of several distinctly different *computer-based information systems* (CBIS) found in contemporary organizations. The others are *transaction processing systems* (TPS), *office automation systems* (OAS), *decision support systems* (DSS), *executive information systems* (EIS), and *expert systems* (ES).

CBIS can be viewed in a variety of ways. Certainly, the high-technology computer component of CBIS provides a fascinating viewpoint. But we have chosen instead a *management approach* to CBIS. That is, we are addressing an audience that is more interested in *what* CBIS do than in *how* they do it. An understanding of the information flows and requirements in organizations today is basic to both functional managers and information systems specialists. Students majoring in management, marketing, finance, accounting, and other business disciplines will find the material presented at a level that they can understand and relate to their majors. Information systems majors will learn what functional managers expect of them, but the technical skills for producing those results must come from more specialized courses in programming, systems analysis, and data base management.

Because we are addressing a broad audience and because we recognize the interdisciplinary nature of CBIS, we have included material on computer technology (both hardware and software), management and organizational principles, and the theories of decision making. Although the individual chapters dealing with these subjects are important to a full understanding of CBIS, they may be omitted if the material is covered elsewhere, as it generally is in undergraduate business curricula, or, if necessary, to resolve differences between quarter and semester calendars.

Revised Material in the Second Edition

Although only two years have passed since the introduction of the first edition, much has changed in the field of CBIS, and we have added and revised material accordingly. The original chapter on hardware and software has been split into two chapters (one on hardware; one on software) and updated to include more material on microcomputers, packaged software, and new developments in programming languages. The material on functional applications of MIS has also been expanded from one chapter to two with additional emphasis given to examples of commercially available software packages in the fields of manufacturing, marketing, finance, and human resource management. The text now concludes with a chapter on trends and developments in CBIS that includes material on robotics, executive information systems, expert systems, and other topics. Finally, in response to the suggestions of users of the first edition, we have added eight new end-of-chapter cases.

Instructor's Manual

An instructor's manual is available for this book. The instructor's manual contains the solutions to the end-of-chapter assignments, a test bank, and transparency masters.

Acknowledgments

Many debts of gratitude are incurred during the writing of a book, and this book is no exception. It is impossible to acknowledge everyone who contributed in some fashion—colleagues who offered suggestions, friends and family who provided support, and students who acted (unwittingly) as sounding boards for much of the material presented here—but some deserve special recognition: Bill Shrode (Florida State University), Mehdi Beheshtian (University of Missouri–St. Louis), Denise Nitterhouse (University of Illinois at Urbana–Champaign), Alan Wheeler (Clemson University), Claude Simpson (College of Boca Raton), William Van Dongen (University of Wisconsin–Oshkosh), Charles Woodruff (Winthrop College), Diane Hineline (Glassboro State College), Joseph Troxell (LaSalle College), Yao Chu (C. W. Post Center of Long Island University), and Gordon Pierce (Bryant College), who offered many helpful comments on the first edition in preparation for the second.

D. W. K.
H. J. W.

Contents

Chapter 14   Building a DSS   397

Chapter 15   Applications of DSS   434

PART I
INTRODUCTION

You are about to embark on a study of one of the most dynamic subjects in your college curriculum. But like many subjects, the study of computer-based information systems (CBIS) poses a certain "chicken versus egg" dilemma. Which topic should come first? How are these systems developed? How are they used? What are their components? What is their role in organizations? Each of these (and many other) issues is important to an understanding of the others. Our approach, therefore, is to begin this book with a single chapter that gives a broad overview of CBIS. We will define the various CBIS, offer some theories on the emergence of different CBIS to serve different organizational needs, explain the importance of CBIS, and describe the career opportunities for those of you who may choose to major in CBIS or a related topic.

Because this is an overview, you may find that it raises almost as many questions as it answers. Good. It is also our purpose here to whet your appetite, to arouse your interest in CBIS. Once you are familiar with the general subject matter, we will take you on an in-depth tour of this exciting subject and, we hope, answer these questions.

Chapter 1

Introduction to CBIS

Learning Objectives

After studying this chapter, you will be able to:

1. Identify different types of CBIS.
2. Explain the effect of evolution and hierarchy on the development of CBIS.
3. Justify the study of CBIS in terms of the changing environment.
4. Consider three career paths in CBIS.
5. Define the following terms:

   transaction processing system
   management information system
   office automation system
   decision support system
   executive information system
   expert system
   programmable decision

   nonprogrammable decision
   evolutionary view (of CBIS
      development)
   hierarchical view (of CBIS
      development)
   contingency view (of CBIS
      development)

3

Although we live in a constantly changing world, all changes do not take place at a constant pace. Perhaps you have taken a course in philosophy. If so, you studied much of the same material that your grandparents might have read had they taken a similar course at your age. But if you go to the library and browse through a 1955 catalog for your university, you will find no mention of computers. Even a 1970 catalog is unlikely to show a course in information systems.

The subject of computer-based information systems (CBIS) is both new and rapidly changing. Not only did courses on the subject not exist ten or fifteen years ago, the material in such courses when they were introduced was substantially different from today's subject matter. And in another fifteen years, you may look back on this course and this textbook and marvel at the additional changes that have taken place.

The changing nature of the subject matter makes it advisable to stop and take stock of our current position before moving on to specific topics in CBIS. The course in which you are enrolled is probably not even *called* CBIS. How does the material in this book relate to the study of, say, management information systems? Where do the computers come in? Whatever happened to data processing? And just what is a CBIS, anyway?

Types of CBIS

The term *CBIS* is generic; that is, there is a class of systems known collectively as CBIS. Just as highway systems, railway systems, and airline systems are different types of *transportation* systems, so there are several types of CBIS. And just as all railway systems are not alike, we expect to find differences *within* types of CBIS as well as *between* types. In this book, we consider four major types of CBIS: *transaction processing systems* (TPS), *management information systems* (MIS), *office automation systems* (OAS), and *decision support systems* (DSS). We also consider two lesser, more specialized CBIS: *executive information systems* (EIS) and *expert systems* (ES). The differences among these six types of CBIS are summarized in Table 1-1 and the following sections; the functions of the four major types of CBIS in an organizational context are depicted in Figure 1-1.

Transaction Processing Systems

Transaction processing systems are the outgrowth of the original CBIS: the *data processing* (DP) systems of the late 1950s. Data processing was concerned primarily with record keeping and the automation of routine clerical processes, such as payroll and billing. Although TPS are also concerned with

TABLE 1-1 Characteristics of CBIS Types

CBIS Type	Inputs	Processes	Outputs
TPS	Transaction data	Classifying, sorting, adding, deleting, updating	Detail reports, processed transaction data
MIS	Processed transaction data, some management-originated data, preprogrammed models	Report generation, data management, simple modeling, statistical methods, query response	Summary and exception reports, routine decisions, replies to management queries
OAS	Appointments, documents, address lists	Scheduling, word processing, data storage and retrieval	Schedules, memoranda, bulk mail, administrative reports
DSS	Some processed transaction data, mostly management-originated data, unique models	Query response, management science/operations research (MS/OR) modeling, simulation	Special reports, input to difficult decisions, replies to management queries
EIS	Processed transaction data, reports, and data analyses	Information retrieval, personalized analysis	Current status, projected trends, revised information
ES	Facts and production rules	Inferential responses to queries	Solutions to problems which usually require the skills of experts

record maintenance, the term *transaction* processing implies something more. It suggests that the TPS has something to do with the fundamental activities—the transactions—of an organization. The TPS captures data that reflect transactions—sales, receipts, expenditures, changes to inventory levels, and so on—and makes them available for use by other CBIS as well as for the original DP functions.

The role of furnishing data to other types of CBIS makes transaction processing systems somewhat different from data processing systems. We ordinarily think of a DP system as "standing alone," in an environment devoid of other organizational CBIS. In contrast, a TPS is just one of several CBIS in an organization that coexist in a symbiotic fashion, each dependent to some extent on the others both for inputs and for demand for its outputs. For example, MIS are dependent on TPS for processed transaction data (total sales volume, gross receipts, periodic expenditures, and so on), and TPS are partially justified by these requirements.

The dual role of transaction processing in an overall CBIS environment leads to this abbreviated definition of a TPS:

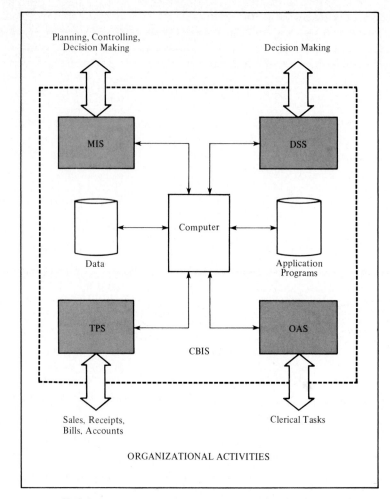

FIGURE 1-1 CBIS in an organizational context.

A transaction processing system is a computer-based system that captures, classifies, stores, maintains, updates, and retrieves transaction data for record keeping and for input to other types of CBIS.

Transaction processing systems are discussed in greater detail in Chapter 8.

Management Information Systems

Management information systems are also related to DP systems. By the mid-1960s, as the demand for business computer services grew, it soon became clear that the *clerical* orientation of DP would not satisfy the *management* orientation of the new users. Managers wished to use computers for planning, controlling, and decision making. In some organizations, DP capabilities were merely upgraded to include management-oriented reports. In other instances, a new system—an MIS—was formed to satisfy both needs. The introduction of MIS was more of an evolutionary process than a dramatic, overnight change. Today it is still common to find the DP/TPS function incorporated into MIS, but it is there mainly to satisfy the information needs of management.

Because MIS evolved from DP, there is a lingering confusion over the difference between DP and MIS. Early MIS bore much resemblance to DP, and many current DP systems do more for management than did the first MIS. As in other evolutionary processes, the higher form exists side-by-side with the lower form for a while before replacing it completely. We are not quite ready to announce the final demise of data processing; there are still too many would-be MIS that do not qualify. But even where MIS exist, there is a need for the clerical process associated with DP. To avoid the question of whether these processes are carried out in an MIS or a DP system, we attribute them to *transaction* processing, a function that is generally recognized as necessary in *both* DP and MIS.

To further clarify the nature of MIS, we offer this definition, synthesized from the works of various scholars in the field:

> *A management information system is an organized set of processes that provides information to managers to support the operations and decision making within an organization.*

A much more extensive explanation of MIS is provided in Chapter 9.

Office Automation Systems

Office automation systems (or, simply, "the automated office") are among the newest and most rapidly expanding CBIS. They are being ushered into organizations with the hopes and expectations that they will increase the productivity of office workers—typists, secretaries, administrative assistants, staff professionals, managers, and the like. Until their appearance, the office had been relatively unaffected by advances in computer technology.

Many organizations have taken the first step toward automating their offices. Often this step involves *word processing* equipment to facilitate the typing, storing, revising, and printing of textual materials. Another common development is a computer-based communications system such as *electronic mail,* which allows people to communicate in an electronic mode through computer terminals. The growing number of executives who are using personal computers in the office is also well documented. These developments point to offices that are increasingly turning to the use of computers and computer-related equipment to support a variety of office activities.

Not long ago, and still in many of today's offices, components of the automated office functioned as stand-alone systems. This circumstance is changing rapidly as communications technology is tying the various components together. For example, word processing equipment can also be used for electronic mail. Personal computers can communicate with mainframes. What is emerging, then, is a concept of the automated office that can be described by the following definition:

> An automated office is a multifunction, integrated computer-based system that allows many office activities to be performed in an electronic mode.

Not only are office automation systems evolving in the ways described, but they are also becoming increasingly linked to other types of CBIS. For example, because word processors are basically microcomputers, some organizations are using them for transaction processing applications. The same microcomputer, equipped to function as a terminal, gives office workers access to corporate data files and the use of the organization's MIS. And finally, some decision support systems are being developed on microcomputers by managers and other professionals.

The picture of the office of the future is becoming clearer. It will support a variety of office activities, be integrated, and have relationships to other CBIS. This subject is addressed in greater detail in Chapter 12.

Decision Support Systems

The relationship between DSS and MIS is somewhat similar to the relationship between MIS and DP. Just as MIS have expanded and built on one feature of DP (information for management), so DSS have refined and enhanced one aspect of MIS: decision-making support. At the moment, in the minds of some people, there is some confusion about the differences between MIS and DSS. After all, they argue, do not MIS support decision making? Are they not, then, by definition, DSS?

Well, no. At least not if you draw a distinction, as we do, between different kinds of decisions and decision processes. Much more is said on this subject in Chapter 13, but for now, let us merely say that many problems are routine and highly structured—they can be *programmed* for solution with little or no human intervention. These are decisions normally supported by MIS. Other problems are unique or unstructured and are *nonprogrammable*—they cannot be solved by a CBIS, but the CBIS can furnish valuable aid to the human who does solve them. These are the decisions normally supported by DSS.

Executive Information Systems

Although the classic research on what executives actually do shows them to be verbally oriented, there is increasing evidence that executives have very real needs for the analytical information retrieval capabilities of CBIS—

provided those systems satisfy the executives' rather special requirements. These requirements center around access to the current status and projected trends of the business.[1] In one sense, EIS seem to be fulfilling the early promise of DSS–CBIS support to upper levels of management. It now appears that DSS are used more by *middle* management and skilled professionals. The little interaction that does exist between CBIS and top management is more likely to result from EIS. EIS are discussed in greater detail in Chapter 19.

Expert Systems

There are a number of decision-making tasks performed by professionals who develop their skills through years of training and experience. A growing number of organizations see the potential value of capturing the facts and decision rules used by these experts in a computer program. These applications are referred to as expert systems.[2] They are developed by a *knowledge engineer* who is a specialist in working with an expert to learn how decisions are made and then encoding the expert's decision-making process in a computer program. A new set of software development tools based on artificial intelligence research is facilitating the creation of expert systems. More is said about expert systems in Chapter 19.

Relationships Among CBIS

Although there is growing acceptance of the concept of different types of CBIS, there is not yet agreement on their relationships to one another and their role in contemporary organizations. One school of thought, hinted at in our earlier discussion of MIS and DP systems, holds that CBIS *evolve* from lower to higher types, and a second maintains that there are different types of CBIS to serve different *hierarchical* levels in organizations. Let us look briefly at these two interpretations before proposing a third, a *contingency approach*.

The Evolutionary View

When changes occur periodically, after successive intervals of time, it is tempting to describe them as evolutionary, whether or not a linkage has been established. For example, heat pumps are more recent heating devices than

---

[1] John F. Rockart and Michael E. Treacy, "The CEO Goes On-Line," *Harvard Business Review*, January–February 1982: 82–88.
[2] Elisabeth Horwitt, "Exploring Expert Systems," *Business Computer Systems*, March 1985: 48–57.

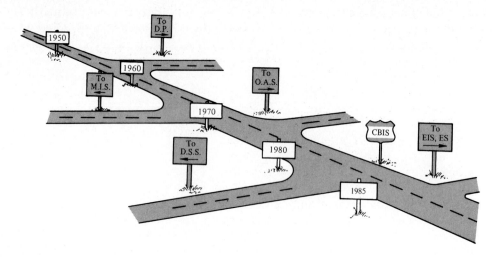

FIGURE 1-2   The evolutionary path of CBIS.

coal furnaces, but the totally different concepts and principles involved in each should preclude our saying that heat pumps *evolved* from coal furnaces. By contrast, the most recent automobiles employ the same basic design and theory as, say, automobiles of the 1930s, but with greater precision and efficiency. It is proper, then, to speak of the evolution of the automobile. Now the question becomes, "Are CBIS more like heating devices or automobiles with respect to their developmental progress?"

The evolutionary view of CBIS presented in Figure 1-2 has a strong logical basis. First, there is a clear-cut sequence through time: DP systems appeared in the mid-1950s, MIS followed in the 1960s, OAS are a product of the 1970s, DSS became available in the early 1980s, and now, in the late 1980s, we are witnessing the emergence of EIS and ES. Second, there is a common technology linking the various types of CBIS: the computer, which itself has evolved considerably over the period. And third, there are systemic linkages in the manner in which each processes data into information.

There are also some problems with this view. The more recent CBIS incorporate many features that did not evolve from earlier CBIS but originated in other disciplines, for other purposes. For example, DSS are not merely improved DP systems using bigger, faster, and more reliable computers. They serve a different clientele, perform different organizational functions, and take a different approach to problem solution.

Another problem with the evolutionary view is that there is an implicit assumption that higher forms of CBIS will *replace* lower forms, and that concurrent systems are merely a temporary condition. We can accept this assumption in some cases, as in the DP–MIS example; it is difficult, however, to view DSS as systems that will eventually take over TPS and OAS functions. Clearly, there must be other, nonevolutionary forces that shape the development of CBIS.

The Hierarchical View

As we shall see in Chapter 3, and again in Chapter 9, there are basic differences in responsibilities and the manner in which those responsibilities are discharged at different levels within an organization. Top management has problems different from those at the supervisory management level and requires different kinds of information in order to solve them. For our purposes, the key difference lies in the information requirements. Do CBIS provide different kinds of information because of evolutionary processes or because they are designed to serve different organizational levels? The hierarchical view, depicted in Figure 1-3, claims the latter.

There is a certain intuitive appeal to the hierarchical view. First, it explains the simultaneous existence of several substantially different CBIS within the same organization. Although it may seem like a small matter in this academic discussion, there is a very important difference between viewing one type of CBIS—an MIS, for example—as a dying dinosaur and treating it as a viable system with a future. Second, the hierarchical view allows for nonevolutionary influences (with respect to CBIS), such as management sci-

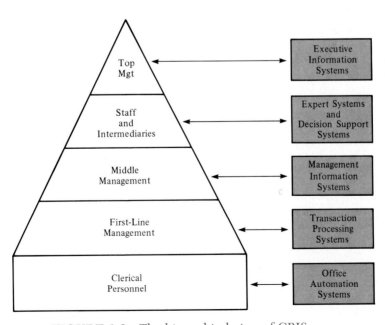

FIGURE 1-3   The hierarchical view of CBIS.

ence and operations research, to play a role in the design and operation of CBIS.

Theories, in order to gain acceptance, must hold in all cases. And this one does not adequately explain the gradual disappearance of DP systems or the overlap among organizational users of the various CBIS. Neither the evolutionary nor the hierarchical view accounts for all the changes in CBIS in the past thirty years, but each has its good points. This is a dilemma easily solved: We will simply form a new theory from the valid portions of the old ones.

The Contingency View

A contingency view is one that says, in effect, "It all depends on the situation." So it is with CBIS. Sometimes, it is convenient to view them as evolving; at other times, it is more convenient to view them hierarchically. The contingency view combining these two approaches is shown in Figure 1-4.

In addition to the evolutionary and hierarchical concepts conveyed by Figure 1-4, two other features of the contingency view are worthy of mention. First, different types of CBIS overlap, but not always to the same degree in different organizations. The overlap shown here is not necessarily

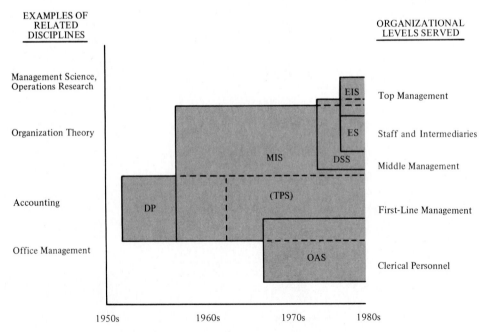

FIGURE 1-4 The contingency view of CBIS.

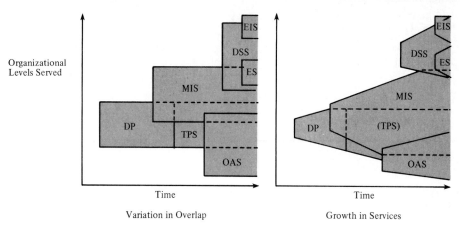

FIGURE 1-5   Variations in the contingency view.

the same in all CBIS; in some organizations, middle management may have a requirement for certain OAS capabilities, such as word processing, whereas in other organizations only clerical personnel may have such requirements. Demand for other CBIS services will vary similarly. Second, the scope of services offered by each system (represented in the vertical dimension) may change over a period of time. Typically, services will expand until a new system is introduced, at which point growth in the old system usually stops. Variations of the contingency view that accommodate these phenomena are shown in Figure 1-5.

Why CBIS Are Important

We began this discussion of CBIS with the assertion that something as new and rapidly changing as CBIS needed some preliminary clarification before a detailed examination could ensue. But although *computer-based* information systems certainly are new, information systems without computers have been around for a long, long time. For example, managers have always had systems to provide themselves information, although they tended not to call them "management information systems." Some of the oldest known examples of written language are on clay tablets that preserve the transactions of ancient Mediterranean merchants. When these records are deciphered by archaeologists, their similarity to modern management information is almost eerie: There are the equivalent of inventory records, accounting statements, receivables, and even what appear to be production records for piece-rate workers.

The use of information systems has not been restricted to commerce and industry. In the public sector, governments have felt obliged to collect and

TABLE 1-2 Why CBIS Are Important

Computers	Computers give CBIS capabilities not possible in other information systems.
Modern organization	The size, diversity, geographic dispersion, and complex production processes found in modern organizations demand sophisticated information management.
Legal and social environment	Government record-keeping and reporting requirements are facilitated by CBIS.
Advancing technology	High-technology industries require greater precision in monitoring production processes.
Expanding role of management	Managers today use CBIS to perform industry-independent, multifunctional, and decision-making tasks not required of their pre-CBIS predecessors.

maintain information on their operations, finances, and citizenry for as long as there have been governments. And there is no sign that government's appetite for information will be diminished in the future.

Clearly, organizations in government and business have survived with traditional, even primitive, information systems. But recently, a great deal has been written and said on this apparently old subject of information systems. What now makes information systems, particularly CBIS, so important? Why are time-proven methods no longer adequate? In short, why all the fuss about CBIS?

Growth has a way of sneaking up on us. For hundreds of thousands of years, the earth accommodated its human tenants with ease. Now, suddenly, we seem to be taxing the resources of our planet to their very limits. So it has been with organizations. Changes that once took place at an evolutionary pace now seem more revolutionary in their impact on the way we conduct the affairs of business and government. Specifically, computers, the nature of modern organizations, the current legal and social environment, advancing technology, and the expanding role of management have created an environment that renders traditional information-handling techniques obsolete. A closer examination of these five areas will underscore the demand for more sophisticated information systems. (See Table 1-2.)

Computers

There certainly was no computer in the information system of ancient Mediterranean merchants, nor, for that matter, in any information system before the mid-1950s. Yet now there is a reference to computers in almost every mention of an information system. Is a computer an indispensable part of an information system? If so, were there really information systems before the introduction of computers?

The answer to both questions is an unequivocal "yes." If this seems to be a contradiction, it is one that is easily resolved: Like many things that have existed for a long time, information systems have changed so that they are similar to their forerunners only in the abstract. In the 1980s, and presumably for a long time to come, when one addresses information systems in specific terms, there is an implicit assumption that computers are involved, that the information system is, in fact, a CBIS. Indeed, the computer is undoubtedly the single most compelling reason for the current level of interest in CBIS and influences every other reason as well. A more detailed discussion of computers is found in Chapter 4.

Computer Anxiety

To many managers, the requirement of a computer in a modern information system is not particularly welcome news. Early business computers were limited in computational power and storage capacity; they were subject to frequent malfunctions and excessive maintenance; the benefits were primarily operational rather than managerial; and many employees viewed them as job threats. As a result, there still is some suspicion concerning the computer component of CBIS.

Computer people themselves must accept a large share of the blame for the early alienation of management. Computer experts, perhaps overly impressed with their special skills, did little to make computer operations understandable to managers. Those few conscientious managers who tried to gain an insight into computers were scared off by their complexity and the strange jargon that accompanied them. It is ironic that advancing computer technology makes the understanding of computers *less* important than before. Middle- and upper-level managers who use CBIS often need to know no more about how to program and operate a computer than they do about how to fly the jet plane that takes them to a business conference. Both the computer and the jet are modern marvels that ease business problems; the manager today who is apprehensive of CBIS is as handicapped as the one who fears to fly.

The Nature of Modern Organizations

We have already alluded to organizational changes as a reason for the increased interest in CBIS. Let us now take a closer look at four specific characteristics of modern organizations that argue for sophistication in information processing.

Size

Although only 5 percent of the ten million or so nonfarm businesses in the United States are classified as "large" (i.e., not small) by the Small Business Administration, that 5 percent accounts for over one half of the national output of goods and services and employs over 40 percent of the labor force.

As an indication of the size of modern organizations, AT&T before its breakup in 1984 had reached the one million employee level[3] and Exxon, as early as 1981, became the first U.S. "$100-billion sales firm."[4] When one envisions the volume of data associated with the operation of such firms, it is no surprise that the sheer size of many modern organizations led them to pioneer CBIS.

But although size motivated early development efforts, its is no longer a prerequisite for a CBIS. Indeed, the most recent developments in computer technology have contributed more to the establishment of CBIS in small organizations than in large ones. Minicomputers, microcomputers, data communications devices, vendor-prepared application programs, and user-oriented software have all served to bring CBIS within the budget and operating constraints of small businesses.

Diversity

Not only are many organizations large, they are also diverse—diverse in the variety of products they offer, in the number of subsidiary plants and offices they maintain, and in the number of other firms with which they deal. For example, the larger retail firms, particularly those with mail-order operations, maintain inventories of several hundred thousand different items. When variations in size and color are considered, there can be millions of different items in inventory. If a CBIS did nothing more than keep track of those items, it would be well worth the associated costs. CBIS are used to maintain inventory, of course, but they also refine inventory data for use in management decisions on pricing, ordering, advertising, or purging items from stock.

Geographic Dispersion

A CBIS is particularly useful when company operations are scattered geographically. Parts needed in one plant of a company may well be gathering dust on the shelves of another plant without a CBIS to make managers aware of their whereabouts. Automobile dealers frequently make use of such systems to share their inventories of spare parts and, sometimes, whole automobiles. Developments in teleprocessing and data communications have made information from remote locations as readily accessible as that in the next room.

Production Processes

It is a rare firm today that starts with only raw materials and manufactures a finished consumer product. As an extreme example, consider the automobile, which is *assembled* rather than *fabricated* in the plant from which it

---

[3]"The Dimensions of American Business: A Roster of the U.S.'s Biggest Corporations," *Forbes*, May 12, 1980: 262–301.

[4]Monci Jo Williams, "The 500: The 500 Largest Industrials," *Fortune*, May 3, 1982: 258–284.

emerges in final form. Hundreds of vendors supply components from tires to spark plugs to quartz clocks. The information on the specifications, price, availability, shipping time, and reliability of these components is even more critical and more difficult to maintain than information on "in-house" inventories. In fact, specialized CBIS, called *manufacturing resources planning (MRP II) systems*, have been developed for production processes that rely on components or subassemblies furnished by contractors. More is said on MRP II in Chapter 10.

The Legal and Social Environment

The U.S. government has almost sixty agencies with the power to regulate business activities, either directly or indirectly. The old, familiar ones, such as the Interstate Commerce Commission, the Federal Trade Commission, and the Federal Power Commission, have been joined by a host of newcomers, such as the Consumer Product Safety Commission, the Equal Employment Opportunity Commission, the Occupational Safety and Health Administration (OSHA), and the Environmental Protection Agency. Although there are great jurisdictional differences among agencies, all have one common impact on business: They require, explicitly or implicitly, the maintenance of records or the preparation of reports to show compliance with agency regulations. Whether the social benefit of these regulations is greater or less than the cost of monitoring compliance with them is moot. What is of immediate significance to managers is that many of the data required for these records and reports are routinely processed by the firm in other applications. For example, the reports for workman's compensation insurance include all the data required for the OSHA log of occupational injuries and illnesses. If the data for one report are captured and stored in such a way as to make them available for the second report, then the cost of preparing the second report is greatly reduced—perhaps to only a few seconds of computer time. One may still find fault with the extent of government regulation of business, and there are currently many both inside and outside government who do, but the associated information-processing costs can be minimized by a CBIS designed with regulatory requirements in mind.

Advancing Technology

To a large extent, methods of collecting and analyzing management information are driven by the technological sophistication of the production process. In the pre–Industrial Revolution cottage industries, handcrafted output was counted and visually inspected to satisfy management's need for quantity and quality data. For comparison, consider the high-technology industry that produces integrated circuit chips. In order to accommodate the 600,000 or so circuit elements represented on a single chip, the pattern of the chip is drawn using *computer-aided design* (CAD) and reproduced photographically onto a silicon wafer. Tolerances on the chip itself, which may be only one-quarter inch square, are measured in millionths of an inch. And in spite of the sterile production environment, stray dust particles and other imperfections render about 50 percent of work-in-process and 10 percent of the final products useless. Clearly, this industry needs sophisticated information-processing techniques to satisfy management that the production process is under control. No human eye can detect flaws in chips, nor can the human hand etch the delicate patterns on the surface of the semiconductor. Managers must rely on computers to control production as well as to furnish information on the quality of the final product.

The role of the computer is easily accepted in tasks that cannot be accomplished otherwise. The manufacture of integrated circuits is one example; the computation of midcourse corrections that guide astronauts safely into space and back is another. But managers in the past have been strangely reluctant to accept the help of computers in more common situations. It is one thing to entrust the lives of astronauts to a computer, but it apparently is quite another matter to entrust the cash flow budget to one. Today, managers can no longer ignore advancing technology when it comes to the management of information. The competitive edge gained by the innovative firms that first developed CBIS leaves little choice. To try to manage information without a computer today is about as practical as making an integrated circuit chip with a soldering iron.

The Expanding Role of Management

At one time, it was possible for a manager to achieve a considerable measure of success with only a rather narrow range of skills—foundry operations, for example. Today, we would expect that same manager to have a variety of skills relating to other industries, to other functions within his or her own industry, and to certain academic disciplines. The importance of CBIS in this expanded role is illustrated in the following discussion of these three areas of additional management skills.

Industry-Independent Functions

The functions of management are, for the most part, industry-independent (see Chapter 3). In other words, managers in the automobile industry have approximately the same responsibilities as managers in, say, the breakfast food industry. This interchangeability has given a great deal of mobility to American managers, of course, but more important, it lends a note of stability to the tasks of management and the information-producing processes that support those tasks. If managing an automobile manufacturing firm were unique, then so, too, would the automobile manufacturer's CBIS be unique—and the breakfast food manufacturer's CBIS, and the catalog sales firm's CBIS, and so on. Under such conditions, it is doubtful that CBIS could have risen to their current level of sophistication. Individual firms and industries simply could not have afforded the development costs of industry-unique CBIS. But just as management functions are transferable among industries within the private sector—and even between the private and public sectors—so are the concepts that underlie CBIS.

Multifunctional Aspects

No manager today operates in the vacuum of a single functional area. It is usually helpful to have had experience (practical or educational) in other functional areas. For example, a marketing decision may be based as much on production and financial information as on marketing information. Without some knowledge of how the production and finance departments operate, a manager cannot properly understand and use information from them. And the best way to give managers access to information from other departments is with a well-designed CBIS that cuts across departmental lines. The interdepartmental nature of CBIS is a theme that recurs throughout this book.

Decision-Making Responsibilities

Just as modern production processes have become more complicated with advancing technology, so have the decision-making tools available to modern managers. Regression analysis, linear programming, Monte Carlo simulation, and other management science/operations research methods are widely used throughout government and industry (see Chapter 7). Although the mathematical and statistical processes involved in these methods have been known for years, practical applications in management are fairly recent developments. Once again, it is the computer that has facilitated the application of technology. The sheer computational complexity of a realistic problem in, say, linear programming is so great and so error-prone as to preclude manual solution. The speed and accuracy of the computer, along with modern collegiate business school curricula that stress such subjects, have turned the mathematician's toys into everyday management tools.

Careers in CBIS

Many students come to college armed with a suggestion from their parents, a friend, or a high school counselor to "get into computers" but do not really understand the employment opportunities afforded by computer-related curricula. If you fall into this category, it may be worth a few moments of your time to review the career fields open to information systems majors (see Figure 1-6). Notice that the emphasis here is on "information systems," not computers per se. Graduates of four-year programs in CBIS, MIS, or whatever the information systems major is called at your school can expect to find employment in one of three areas: programming and systems analysis, consulting, or computer sales.

Information Systems Professionals

Career opportunities a[...]
the Information Services [...]
American Cyanamid's M[...]

Data Base Administ[...]

• Control development[...]
standards
[...]ntain data dictiona[...]
[...]rdinate data bas[...]
[...]lopment activities.
[...]irements include [...]
[...]lopment experienc[...]
[...]knowledge of TOT[...]
[...]ce preferred.

[...]nning Coordinat[...]

[...]nitor and update lo[...]
[...]ms, network config[...]
[...]mbine   high-level [...]
[...]ical/business skill[...]
[...]ach to systems dev[...]
[...]dvanced informati[...]
[...] history of succe[...]
[...]ntial. Previous e[...]
[...]rience preferred.

Computational Chemist/
Macromolecular Structures

Work with investigators to apply latest computer
technologies to development of new pharmaceutical
agents. Position demands experience in cor[...]
putational techniques, molecular graphics, ar[...]
macromolecular structural analysis. Background [...]
bio or medicinal chemistry desired.

Systems Programmer, DEC-10

Install, maintain, monitor and modify system sof[...]
[...]e of DEC system-10 TOPS-1[...]
[...] and/or VAX/VMS required; E[...]
[...] math or engineering.

[...]ort Analyst

[...]M programming, and performanc[...]
[...]c 90/30 or System 80 experienc[...]
[...]depth knowledge of OS/3 and IMS[...]
[...]to job responsibilities.
[...]benefits and career opportunities i[...]
[...]ea convenient to recreationa[...]
[...]cultural activities, only 30 mile[...]
[...]w York City. Please reply in cor[...]
[...] salary history and requirements t[...]
[...]ofessional Employment Coordinato[...]

DIRECTOR OF MIS

Atlanta based company has newly
created position of MIS Director.
Qualified candidates will demonstrate ability to operate IBM 34 to
accomodate growth including telecommunications and systems revi-
sion/design. Full programming
knowledge of RPG II required. Replies should include salary requirements.

Reply to CW-B4010
Computerworld
375 Cochituate Rd., Box 880
Framingham, Ma 01701

EDP PROFESSIONALS
career specialists
$25,000-$65,000

DATABASE, $35,000-$50,000 +. Well-
known vendor has several immediate
needs in DB area. Solid technical skills
in IMS, IDMS, ADABAS, TOTAL or other DB along w/well developed interpersonal skills are the keys. Call M. Feiger
(201/966-1571), Florham Park.

SR. SYSTEMS ENGR. to $50,000.
BSEE/MSEE w/10-15 yrs program
mgmt exp in data analog environment.
Will design/develop data comm networks, data links & satellite networking
system. Strong HW/SW skills needed.
Must be good manager, aggressive,
good image. Call J. Taylor (703/790-
1335), McLean.

SYSTEMS ANALYST to $40,000. MD
client has urgent need for systems analyst to participate in design, analysis &
investigation of E/W systems for Navy
submarine programs. Tech degree (
BSEE, BSME, BSCS, etc) + 6-8 yrs
exp desired. Call J. Taylor (703/790-
1335), McLean.

INFO. RESOURCE MFG. to $38,000.
Dynamic mfr in Baltimore seeks a manager. Will head a nation-wide data communications area. Position leads to
EDP planning area. Req's degree, IBM
bkgd. Call C. Newman (301/296-4500).
Baltimore.

DEVELOP NEW SYSTEMS to
$38,000. Div, "Fortune 100" co seeks
P/A to assist in design, dvlpmt & implementation of new on-line systems. IBM
mainframe, both OS & DOS. Exp in
data base along w/min 2 yrs CICS, coupled w/degree & strong analytical skills
req'd. Great career growth – all new
dvlpmt team. Call J. Domenick (201/
966-1571), Florham Park.

DATA BASE ADMINISTRATOR

Total management of DP operations & per-
sonnel. Responsibilities include hardware
specifications & selection, systems analysis,
design, programming & implementation.
Successful candidate must be experienced in
all phases of data processing, data base
management and posses a thorough
knowledge of ANSI 74 COBOL, 307/303X (or
equivalent) assembly language, Bisync/async
telecommunications, and VS systems. Bat-
chelors degree plus 3 years experience
required. Salary from high 20'S. Send resume
with salary history to:

The Navy Motion Picture Service
Flushing & Washington Avenues
Brooklyn, N.Y. 11251
An equal opportunity employer

System Analyst/
Programmer

New York City
Utilize your problem
solving ability to
your best advantage
with this major
financial institution

We have an immediate opening for a
data processing professional to
develop systems, write programs and
set-up JCL within our Data Processing
Department. Position involves heavy
users interfoce requiring good written
and oral skills.
The successful candidate should have
experience with MSA and WANG VS
in addition, experience in OS, COBOL
IBM 370, 3033 with TSO and APL is
required.
We offer a salary commensurate with
experience, a comprehensive benefits
package, high visibility and opportunity for advancement. Please
forward resume in confidence to:

BOX ME4122
MIS WEEK
An Equal Oppor. Employer

FIGURE 1-6 Career opportunities in data processing and information systems.

Programming and Systems Analysis

Most CBIS curricula contain sufficient course work in computer programming languages to permit graduates to find employment in that area, although that certainly is not the main thrust of CBIS. The CBIS major who
takes a position as a programmer or a systems analyst probably does so with

the intention of eventually moving into information systems management, perhaps as the data base administrator or the director of information services.

Although programmers and systems analysts are normally considered *data processing* personnel, this is a normal route to middle or top management in information services for the simple reason that there are very few entry-level positions in information services. It also presents the additional option of staying in programming and becoming a "lead" programmer or perhaps a data processing director. The additional hardware and software skills required for these upper-level DP positions can be acquired on the job or in training programs.

CBIS majors who find that they prefer programming over management may also find employment with software development firms. The proliferation of computers, particularly micros and personal computers, has brought computer technology to many would-be users with little or no programming skill. These users have created a considerable market for "ready-to-use" software, and the software vendors have been quick to recognize and try to satisfy this demand.

Consulting

Many organizations either do not require the full-time services of an information systems specialist or feel that they can obtain greater expertise and objectivity from outside the organization. Such organizations obtain the services of consultants to assist in the design and implementation of CBIS.

CBIS consultants are found primarily in accounting firms, management consulting groups, and university faculties. Joining a university faculty will take some additional formal education, but the other two are realistic opportunities for CBIS graduates who are from the better institutions and who stand high in their class. Even the fortunate few who are offered such positions will find themselves junior members of a consulting team, but it is nonetheless an excellent way to gain broad experience in a short time and usually leads to senior management positions more rapidly than do other career options.

Computer Sales

For most organizations, acquiring new computer equipment represents a major decision in terms of both the size of the investment and the long-term effect it is likely to have on operations. It is also a decision that is not made very often, and there may be little in the way of policy, precedent, or experience within the organization to guide the decision process. The purchaser frequently looks to the sales representative for guidance in hardware and software selection.

Computer manufacturers have found that the organizational background of information systems majors—their knowledge of management, functional areas, decision making, and human behavior—makes them excellent "customer representatives" or "systems engineers," as computer sales personnel are frequently called. Like consulting, computer sales exposes the information specialist to a variety of situations in a relatively short time and provides an excellent opportunity for higher level management positions either with the manufacturer or, as often happens, with a former client.

Summary

CBIS may be classified as *transaction processing systems* (TPS), *management information systems* (MIS), *office automation systems* (OAS), *decision support systems* (DSS), *executive information systems* (EIS), and *expert systems* (ES). TPS, MIS, OAS, and DSS are now the primary CBIS in an organization, but increasing attention is being given to the new CBIS, EIS, and ES.

Different types of CBIS perform different functions and serve different clientele: TPS store and maintain transaction data for record keeping and to provide a base of data for other CBIS; MIS provide reports and support routine decision making, primarily for middle and first-line managers; OAS use computer technology to perform routine office functions with greater speed and accuracy; DSS support moderately difficult decisions, primarily for staff, intermediaries, and middle management; EIS provide top managers access to information on the current status of the organization and projections for the future; finally, ES solve problems the way highly skilled experts do.

The presence of different types of CBIS may be explained by a *contingency* view of the *evolutionary* and *hierarchical* forces at work in CBIS development. In one sense, CBIS have evolved gradually, with more sophisticated systems replacing older systems. On the other hand, different CBIS, using tools and methods of other disciplines, have been developed to meet the varying needs of management and clerical personnel at different organizational levels. It is useful to consider some aspects of each view in explaining the present mix of CBIS.

Although managers have had and used information systems for centuries, there has been a marked increase in interest in information systems in recent years. The primary reason for this increased interest is the introduction of computer technology into information systems; other reasons include the complexity of modern organizations, the demands of the legal and social environment, other advances in technology (in addition to computers), and the expanding role of management.

Information system specialists today are in great demand in a variety of industries. Many graduates of MIS or CBIS programs become *programmers* or *systems analysts*, but because of their management background, they eventually become *directors of MIS* or *data base administrators*. Others find employment as *consultants* or as *sales representatives* of computer manufacturers.

Assignments

1-1. The first part of this chapter describes and defines different types of CBIS but does not define the term *CBIS* itself. How would you have defined *CBIS before* you read this chapter? How do you define it now? Do you think you will define it differently after completing this course?

1-2. Use the terms *TPS, MIS, OAS, DSS, EIS,* or *ES* to identify the system most likely to be used for the following tasks:

   a. The president of a firm wishes to review the monthly sales reports.
   b. The president's secretary wishes to notify the staff of a change in a scheduled meeting.
   c. An operations research staff person wishes to simulate the effect of closing one of the drive-up windows at a branch bank.
   d. A monthly report showing the total sales by product line is to be prepared.
   e. A physicist wishes to determine the optimum temperature for the operation of a blast furnace in order to reduce noxious emissions without changing the quality of the steel produced.
   f. The arrival of a shipment of raw material is to be recorded.
   g. The quarterly budget update is to be prepared and distributed.
   h. A production plan is to be prepared based on market forecasts, changes in the availability of raw materials, and the recent addition of industrial robots.
   i. Overdue notices are to be mailed to delinquent account holders.
   j. An income tax specialist wishes to find the best mix of investments to minimize the firm's tax liability.

1-3. A major computer manufacturer recently advertised a computer terminal with the slogan, "Now you can have your own MIS in your office." What is wrong with this statement?

1-4. Heating systems and automobiles were cited as respective examples of the results of nonevolutionary and evolutionary development. Are these really "pure" examples, or should they, too, be approached from a contingency view? Give another example of each type of development process. Are your examples "pure," or does a contingency view explain them better?

1-5. In the early 1800s, the French economist Jean Baptiste Say proposed a "law of markets" in which he claimed that supply created its own demand. Do information systems create a demand for computers, or does the output of the computer industry create its own demand, some of which is satisfied by information system use? Justify your answer.

1-6. Technology is often credited with making work easier and faster, thereby creating additional time for leisure, recreation, and artistic pursuits. Is this an additional reason for the importance of CBIS? To what extent would you consider this reason if you had to make a decision to commit vast company resources to the development of CBIS?

1-7. What are your own career objectives? Do they depend in any way on your knowledge of CBIS? Why are you taking this course?

CASE   The State Department of Education

The state department of education has commissioned a task force to make recommendations for incorporating the use of computers into the curriculum at various levels of the educational system. One of the board members expressed the opinion that computers were indeed an integral part of the business and scientific world, but that other applications, such as the video game craze and refrigerators that alerted their owners when the dust builds up underneath, were merely a fad. He feels that the novelty of computers will soon wear off and that there is no need to expand computer usage in the classroom.

Another board member feels that computers will soon be (if they are not already) an integral part of everyone's life at work and at home. However, he feels that with the rapidly advancing computer technology, any computer training in the early grades would soon become outdated and thus waste the board's already scarce resources.

A third board member noted that some universities are already requiring science and information systems majors to buy their own microcomputer systems, just as students were previously required to own their own slide rules or calculators. She feels that computers should be part of every classroom in every grade so that students will come to look on them as an ordinary part of their lives.

Questions

1. What recommendations would *you* make for integrating computers into the elementary and junior high grades? For what would they be used? Would their use be mandatory or optional?

2. In what high school courses would you suggest that computers be used? Should students learn how to program them or how to use packaged programs? Are there any high school courses in which computers *must* be introduced?

3. Which college and university majors require interaction with computers? For business majors, what specific recommendations would you make for computer-related education? Should it include computer programming, knowledge of computer hardware, use of

packaged programs, and so on? Should students majoring in any particular subject areas be required to own a microcomputer?

Other Readings

Driscoll, James W. "People and the Automated Office." *Datamation* 25, no. 16 (November 1979).

Gibson, Cyrus, and Richard L. Nolan. "Managing the Four Stages of EDP Growth," *Harvard Business Review* (January–February 1974).

Information Systems in the 1980s. Boston: Arthur D. Little, 1978.

Lucas, Henry C. "The Evolution of an Information System." *Sloan Management Review* (Winter 1978).

Sprague, Ralph H., Jr., and Eric D. Carlson. *Building Effective Decision Support Systems*. Englewood Cliffs, N.J.: Prentice-Hall, 1982.

Walsh, Myles E. "MIS—Where We Are, How Did We Get Here, and Where Are We Going?" *Journal of Systems Management* November 1978).

PART II

FOUNDATIONS OF CBIS

One of the things you will learn in Part II is that systems, including computer-based information systems, are interdisciplinary; that is, they are founded on a number of often unrelated fields of study. To understand CBIS fully, you must have some background in these other disciplines. You and we are both at the mercy of your curriculum in this respect. Many of you will have taken one or more courses in the topics presented in Part II. Others may be totally unfamiliar with them. Our approach is to provide just enough coverage of these topics here to enable those with no previous work to understand the material in the subsequent parts of this book.

Studying foundations can sometimes be frustrating. There is an understandable urge to "get on with it," to get straight to the heart of the subject—the CBIS themselves. Those who feel this way are reminded of the admonition of Euclid to the Egyptian king, Ptolemy I. When Ptolemy, who had sent for Euclid to teach him geometry, protested the length of the thirteen volumes of *The Elements*, Euclid reportedly replied, "There is no royal road to geometry." Neither is there a royal road to the understanding of CBIS.

Chapter 2

Systems Concepts and CBIS

Learning Objectives

After studying this chapter, you will be able to:

1. Describe a system using general systems theory terminology.
2. Use the systems design approach to solve systems-related problems.
3. Use the systems improvement approach to correct deficiencies in systems.
4. Describe a business organization as a system.
5. Define the following terms:

general systems theory	suprasystem
input	environment
output	entropy
process	open system
interdisciplinary	closed system
holistic and holism	feedback
differentiated	systems approach
synergistic and synergism	systems design
hierarchical	systems improvement
system	systems analysis
subsystem	

The word *system* is used rather loosely to define a variety of things. We speak of a social system, the solar system, transportation systems, political systems, and, of course, computer and information systems. What characteristics do these things share that makes us call them all *systems?* What *is* a system? And why are systems concepts important to the study of CBIS?

These and other questions concerning systems will all be answered in due course, but the last question merits an immediate answer. The study of systems is relatively new and postdates the notion of transportation, political, social, educational, and many other systems. Those systems evolved without a conscious effort on the part of developers and participants to incorporate systems concepts. But CBIS postdate the interest in systems concepts, and CBIS developers approach their task with a full awareness of what systems are and how they function. Systems concepts are more than just a convenience in explaining how CBIS work, they also provide a "blueprint" for the design and implementation of CBIS. Systems concepts are more fundamental to CBIS than to most other systems, and as a consequence, CBIS are more difficult to understand without some familiarity with current systems thinking.

General Systems Theory

There is not a clearly defined body of knowledge that is universally accepted as "systems science" in the manner that other disciplines—chemistry, economics, history, and so forth—are recognized. However, most of the systems concepts that are relevant to CBIS can be found in a collection of principles known as *general systems theory* (GST). GST reflects the ideas of the Society for General Systems Theory, which was formed in 1954 by biologist Ludwig von Bertalanffy, economist Kenneth Boulding, biomathematician Anatol Rapoport, and physiologist Ralph Gerard.[1] The society was formed out of a belief that scientific research had become too narrow and too specialized, and that the scientific disciplines had lost touch with one another. The society, it was felt, would foster communication among scientists, facilitate the sharing of scientific knowledge, and minimize the duplication of scientific research.

Characteristics of Systems

Although the original purpose of GST was to study the phenomenon of growth, many of the characteristics attributed to systems by GST can lead to an understanding of the systems nature of CBIS. A brief explanation of some

---

[1] Peter P. Schoderbek, Asterios G. Kefalas, and Charles G. Schoderbek, *Management Systems: Conceptual Considerations*, 2d ed. (Dallas: Business Publications, 1981).

FIGURE 2-1   Diagram of a system.

of these characteristics will illustrate the relationship between GST and CBIS.

Systems Transform Inputs into Outputs

If there is a single, familiar image of a system it is the one shown in Figure 2-1. For all of its simplicity, this representation of a system is fully accurate. A manufacturing firm can be viewed as a system that transforms raw material inputs into outputs of finished goods. Universities receive inputs of students, faculty, money, and other resources and transform them into graduates, scholarly research, wages for their employees, and other outputs. And CBIS, as Figure 2-1 illustrates, receive inputs of *data* and transform or *process* them into *information*.

Systems Are Interdisciplinary

One of the main concerns of the authors of GST was the tendency of scientists to overspecialize, thus isolating themselves from developments in other fields that might apply to their own. For example, light-weight, corrosion-resistant servomechanisms developed for space exploration have advanced the design of prosthetic devices and industrial robots. The application of space technology to medicine and industrial engineering is typical of the kind of interdisciplinary exchange of information envisioned in GST.

The fact that managers in one industry can benefit from the experience of managers in another industry did not originate in GST, of course. Management theorists of the early 1900s recognized that. But many managers do not fully appreciate the extent to which they are crossing traditional disciplinary lines when they use CBIS.

First, the physical components of CBIS are the products of disciplines far removed from management. Computers, telecommunications terminals, high-speed printers, data storage devices, and other peripherals commonly used in CBIS have grown out of developments in physics and electrical engineering. Nor would these components have been developed solely to meet the information processing needs of managers. What is now CBIS hardware evolved from equipment originally designed for purely mathematical operations.[2] Second, many of the modern management tools facilitated

---

[2] Donald W. Kroeber, "The History of Computer Technology," *Computers for Business: A Book of Readings*, Hugh J. Watson and Archie B. Carroll, eds. (Dallas: Business Publications, 1980).

by computer hardware were also developed without management applications in mind. Linear programming, regression analysis, and other operations research methods are mathematical in origin but have been adapted to management purposes.

Finally, CBIS users not only draw on methods and techniques of other disciplines, they also share them among branches of their own profession. Thus, we may find the same linear regression model being used to forecast both sales for marketing managers and the cost of capital for financial managers. Or the same queuing model may be used to plan for the number of pumps needed at a gas station and the number of beds needed by a hospital.

Systems Are Holistic

The proper functioning of a system is a result of the interdependence of its parts. Therefore, a system must be viewed as a whole, with all parts considered, even though only one may be of immediate concern. This emphasis on the whole is known as *holism*, and systems that exhibit holism are said to be *holistic*.

The value of a holistic approach to systems is particularly evident in environmental matters. An entomologist, for example, must consider the whole ecosystem when developing a pesticide. The entomologist may discover that a certain chemical spray effectively kills potato bugs. But what are its long-term effects on the soil, the streams that receive runoff from the potato fields, and, most important, the people who eat the treated potatoes? These and other questions must be answered satisfactorily before the spray can be used.

Interdependencies in CBIS are less dramatic, of course, but are still important enough to warrant a holistic view. In a manufacturing organization, market research information has implications for product design and production scheduling as well as for purely marketing activities. Information on production scheduling, in turn, is useful in determining personnel requirements. And personnel actions, such as hiring or training, create financial obligations. These relationships are much easier to incorporate into the information flows if CBIS are viewed in their entirety. Many CBIS are now designed from a holistic point of view; it has not always been so, and directly or indirectly, we have GST to thank for holistic insights.

Systems Are Differentiated

Although it is important to view systems holistically, one must not lose sight of the fact that systems consist of a number of different parts. In fact, one of the simpler definitions of a system is that it is a "set of interrelated parts." Although it is appropriate to view the transportation system, for example, as a whole, there are times when it is equally important to consider just railroads or only airlines.

There are also parts to a CBIS. At a minimum, the kind of CBIS addressed in this book has a computer, input and output devices, data storage facilities, personnel to manage and operate the computer and its associated equipment, procedures for operating and using the system, programs for processing data into information, provisions for the dissemination of output, instructions for the interpretation of output, and, of course, managers who use the output.

Systems Are Synergistic

The property of *synergism* is sometimes defined as the quality of the "whole exceeding the sum of its parts." This statement should not be taken literally, of course, but in the figurative sense that a system is capable of results not possible from the individual efforts of its parts. The various parts of a communications system—telephones, cables, switches, relays, and so forth—are of little value by themselves, but they are of immense value when joined together in a specified manner. Even a small, inexpensive part such as a telephone book can add value to the system far beyond its intrinsic worth.

The synergistic effect of CBIS is somewhat more subtle and is much easier to ignore than the more obvious effect in the communications system example. If some parts in a CBIS do not work together, it may not be readily apparent that the system is operating at less than its full potential. This is particularly true in the application program area, where programs may be designed to serve a very narrow, specific information need without regard to other, related needs. For example, sales data may be maintained to satisfy billing requirements, but these data can also be used for inventory control, marketing management, and personnel evaluation. The CBIS that combines information needs and satisfies several with one set of data exhibits greater synergism than the CBIS that duplicates data for each application or, worse, ignores additional uses for data.

Systems Are Hierarchical

Parts of systems may themselves be small systems, and systems may, in turn, be parts of even larger systems. This ordering of systems is referred to as a *hierarchy*, a term that reflects the relative size or rank of the systems involved. Levels in the hierarchy of systems are usually identified with descriptive prefixes to prevent confusion over what is a part of what. Parts of systems that are systems in their own right are called *subsystems*, and the level above the original system is called the *suprasystem*. The level above the suprasystem is called the *environment*. In a sense, the environment is a sort of suprasuprasystem in that it contains other systems and suprasystems.

The terminology of the systems hierarchy can be confusing. Often, the hierarchical term used is dependent on one's point of view. For example, if the General Motors Corporation is viewed as a system, then the Chevrolet Motor Division is a subsystem, the automobile industry is the suprasystem, and the environment contains the legal system, the social system, and other industries. This view is illustrated in Figure 2-2. But if the object of interest is Chevrolet, then we would consider it the system, Chevrolet's St. Louis assembly plant a subsystem, General Motors the suprasystem, and the auto-

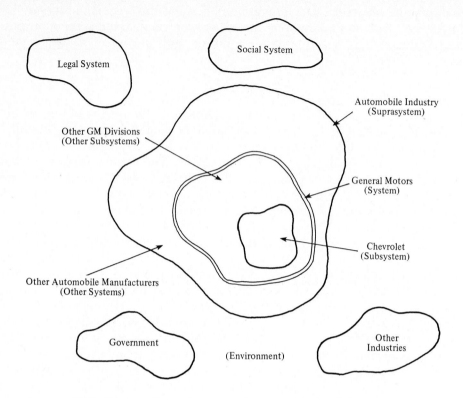

FIGURE 2-2   Chevrolet as a subsystem of General Motors.

mobile industry and other systems and suprasystems a part of the environment. This interpretation is shown in Figure 2-3.

The same hierarchy also applies to CBIS. When we are considering a CBIS, we think of it as a system and of the organization it serves as the suprasystem. There are a number of ways to classify the subsystems of a CBIS. In this book, we consider four principal types of CBIS—transaction processing systems (TPS), management information systems (MIS), office automation systems (OAS), and decision support systems (DSS)—and they could properly be called subsystems of CBIS. However, when MIS are discussed, they are the focus of attention and are referred to as *systems* and we treat functional applications—production, marketing, finance, and personnel—as *subsystems*.

One final note must be added on the subject of subsystems: They can extend for many levels below the systems level. This possibility gives rise to some awkward terminology: *subsubsystems*, *subsubsubsystems*, and so on. An anonymous poet might well have had the hierarchy of systems in mind when he (or she, perhaps?) wrote:

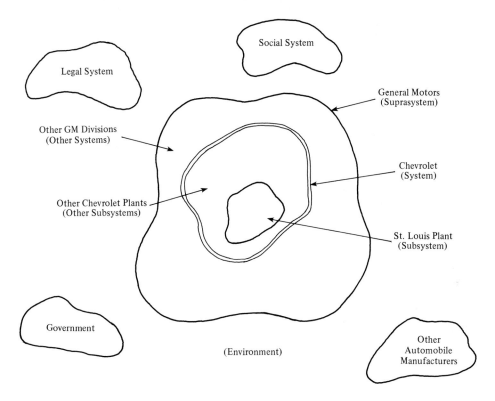

FIGURE 2-3   Chevrolet as a system.

Great fleas have little fleas
Upon their backs to bite 'em.
Little fleas have lesser fleas
And so on, ad infinitum.

Systems Must Be Regulated

In keeping with the interdisciplinary nature of systems and GST, this characteristic can be explained with a concept borrowed from physics: *entropy*. Entropy is a state of randomness or disorder. Left untended, systems tend toward maximum entropy; that is, they run down and become disorganized.

The tendency of a system to gain entropy can be explained in terms of its relationship with its environment. *Closed systems*, those that do not exchange inputs and outputs with their environment, constantly gain entropy and inevitably run down. In theory, even the universe, as the ultimate closed system, will eventually be reduced to a random collection of cold, energyless particles. (Present readers need not fear—the universe is quite safe for a long time to come!)

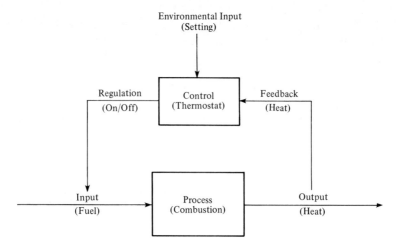

FIGURE 2-4   Control in a heating system.

On the other hand, *open systems*, those that *do* exchange inputs and outputs with their environment, can avoid entropy, at least for a reasonable time. To continue the astronomical example, many scientists believe that stars not only radiate energy (an output) into their environments, they also accumulate additional mass in the form of hydrogen atoms (an input) as they move through space, thus slowing the buildup of entropy and forestalling their eventual demise.

CBIS are not immune from entropy and the need for regulation. A CBIS left untended and out of touch with its environment quickly breaks down. As information needs change, as government regulations are imposed, as competition increases, and as the organization itself changes, an unregulated CBIS becomes less and less efficient in its purpose.

Regulation in a system is achieved by a control subsystem. Inputs into this subsystem may be from the environment or in the form of *feedback* from the system's own output. Outputs of the control subsystem, in turn, regulate system inputs. These concepts are illustrated in Figure 2-4 for the familiar home heating system in which fuel is converted into heat through a process of combustion under the control of a thermostat.

Systems Are Goal-Oriented

The earlier, simple definition of a system as a set of related parts does not adequately recognize the *purpose* of a system. We should now amend that definition to read, "A system is a set of related parts *working together to achieve some goal or objective.*"

The importance of goals and objectives to the successful operation of an organization is well established. Goals give direction to an organization and serve to initiate the management process, a subject that is discussed in greater detail in the following chapter. What may need some comment, however, is the fact that those organizational goals and objectives also guide the CBIS. To be sure, CBIS managers have certain unique goals pertaining to the CBIS—goals that set standards for the accuracy of information, the timeliness of reports, physical security, and the like. It is all too easy for CBIS managers to become totally absorbed in these goals and to forget that the purpose of the CBIS is to serve management. If a mail-order house has as an objective the filling of all orders within forty-eight hours of receipt, then the efforts of the CBIS and its managers, as well as the order-processing department and its managers, should be directed toward the accomplishment of that objective. Much of the suspicion and hostility toward CBIS today can be traced to early data processing systems that placed demands on functional managers that were greater than the value of the services rendered. Many managers felt that they were supporting the data processing function, rather than the reverse—and in many cases they were right! CBIS personnel are *still* trying to convert those turned-off managers.

Criticism of GST

Before moving on, it should be noted that GST has its detractors. Not all scientists agree, for example, that specialization is bad. Many would argue that science and technology today are so advanced and so complex that it is impossible to consider all facets of a single discipline (say, chemistry), let alone to consider the implications in related disciplines, such as physics and biology. Nor are all impressed by the implied benefits of sharing knowledge among disciplines. For example, the fact that the growth of both bacteria in a culture and money in a savings account can be explained by the same exponential equation is greeted with an unenthusiastic, "So what?"[3] Biologists and bankers discovered the fact of exponential growth independently, without any help from GST, and other potential beneficiaries of GST are equally likely to develop insights into their disciplines on their own. One criticism that is particularly relevant to the subject of CBIS concerns the appropriateness of a holistic approach. Just as no scientist can be expected to know everything about his or her discipline, the argument goes, neither can any one researcher be expected to comprehend an entire system in its totality. It is better, say the critics, to examine a system in small, manageable parts. In other words, critics of GST would trade general knowledge of the whole for specific knowledge of its parts.

This last criticism has had a considerable impact on approaches to the design of CBIS. Should CBIS be designed as total, integrated systems or as a collection of semi-independent, but related, parts? We are going to tease you a bit at this point and not provide an answer to this question; instead we encourage you to think about the advantages and disadvantages of the two

[3] See Chapter 1 of Schoderbek et al. for a more complete discussion of the "so what" criticism of GST.

approaches as you learn more about the foundations and structure of CBIS in the succeeding chapters. Of course, if you can't stand the suspense, you can always look ahead, at Chapter 17, where CBIS development is discussed in detail.

Systems Approaches

The term *systems approach* is used rather loosely to describe a number of theories, techniques, and methodologies that can be traced to GST. To avoid the implication that there is a single, rigid, universally accepted definition of the systems approach, we use the term in the plural and present not one, but several systems approaches that are useful in the study of CBIS: *systems design, systems improvement,* and *systems analysis.*

Systems Design

Although systems approaches are rooted in GST, in some instances the lineage can be traced back even further, particularly in the case of systems design, which, as shown in Figure 2-5, has origins in the ancient scientific method. There have been many variations on the scientific method, of course, but its influence on systems design can be observed by a brief look at a few of the more popular interpretations.

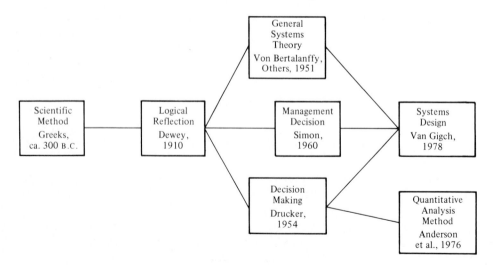

FIGURE 2-5   The evolution of systems design.

The Scientific Method

The systematic approach to problem solving called the *scientific method* is frequently attributed to Aristotle. More likely, the scientific method does not have a single author, although it does seem to have originated with the Greeks around 300 B.C., during the lifetime of Aristotle. The scientific method consists of five steps:

1. State the problem.
2. Form a hypothesis.
3. Observe and experiment.
4. Interpret the observations.
5. Draw a conclusion.

The Decision-Making Process

Over eighteen hundred years later, in 1910, Dewey[4] used five similar steps to describe a process of "logical reflection," which led, in 1954, to Drucker's five-step process for making management decisions:[5]

1. Define the problem.
2. Analyze the problem.
3. Develop alternative solutions.
4. Select the best solution.
5. Convert the decision into effective action.

Management Decision

The applicability of the scientific method to management decision making was reiterated by Simon in 1960 in his now popular "phases of decision making":

1. Search for problems and data.
2. Generate and analyze alternatives.
3. Select the best alternative.

These phases of decision making, which Simon called *intelligence, design,* and *choice,* are especially helpful in explaining decision-support processes in CBIS and are reintroduced in Chapter 13.[6]

[4] John Dewey, *How We Think* (Boston: D. C. Heath, 1910).
[5] Peter F. Drucker, *The Practice of Management* (New York: Harper & Row, 1954).
[6] Herbert A. Simon, *The New Science of Management Decision* (New York: Harper & Row, 1960).

The Quantitative Analysis Process

Another descendant of the scientific method of interest in the study of CBIS is the *quantitative analysis process* as defined by Anderson, Sweeney, and Williams in 1976:[7]

1. Define the problem.
2. Develop a model.
3. Prepare data.
4. Solve the model.
5. Generate reports.

The use of models in CBIS-assisted decision making is so well established that the library of software programs associated with some CBIS is referred to as the *model base*. The use of quantitative analysis in decision making is discussed in Chapter 7.

Systems Design

Systems design, as an approach to solving problems associated with systems, is simply one more extension of the scientific method, but one that also incorporates the principles of GST. Just as there is no universal agreement on a systems approach, neither is there agreement on the nature of systems design. The version offered here is itself the result of a systems approach: it is synthesized from different interpretations of systems design, but it draws most heavily on the work of van Gigch:[8]

1. Define the problem.
2. Identify systems boundaries, the suprasystem, and relevant environmental systems.
3. Establish systems objectives.
4. Search for and generate alternatives.
5. Identify outputs of the alternatives.
6. Evaluate alternatives by comparing outputs with objectives.
7. Choose the best alternative.
8. Implement the decision.

Systems design is said to be *extrospective*, because it looks outward, from the system to the environment. It is an *inductive* process, one that proceeds from the particular to the general. Systems design synthesizes individual parts of the system into a whole that satisfies the systems objectives imposed by the environment. A simple example will serve to illustrate this process.

Suppose a faculty committee is faced with the problem of designing an

---

[7] David R. Anderson, Dennis J. Sweeney, and Thomas A. Williams, *An Introduction to Management Sciences: Quantitative Approaches to Decision Making*, 3d ed. (New York: West Publishing, 1982).

[8] John P. van Gigch, *Applied General Systems Theory* (New York: Harper & Row, 1978).

information systems curriculum. The committee might apply the steps in systems design in the following manner:

1. What should be the requirements for a BBA degree with a major in information systems?

2. (a) The system is the school of business; (b) the suprasystem is the university; (c) in the environment are firms that hire graduates, accrediting societies, other universities, the state board of regents, and prospective students.

3. The objectives of the school of business are to meet accreditation standards, to serve the community, to establish a reputation for academic excellence, and to operate within budget constraints.

4. Various professional organizations, such as the Association of Computing Machinery (ACM) and the Data Processing Management Association (DPMA), have endorsed standard curricula, and a faculty subcommittee has prepared its own recommended curriculum.

5. Each curriculum has a slightly different mix of course requirements.

6. Does each curriculum meet the standards of the business accrediting society—the American Assembly of Collegiate Schools of Business (AACSB)? Which curriculum best provides the type of graduate sought by the prospective employers? Which curriculum best utilizes the current resources of faculty, equipment, and course offerings? Are the curricula likely to be recognized as innovative and to be emulated by other institutions?

7. The curriculum developed by the faculty, with some substitutions from the ACM curriculum, is judged to be the best.

8. The recommended curriculum is sent to the university administration for approval; course proposals are prepared; requests are submitted for the necessary computer hardware and software; new faculty are recruited; and the program is publicized among high school counselors and prospective employers.

Systems Improvement

In contrast to systems design, systems improvement is *introspective* and *deductive*. Systems improvement looks inward and proceeds from the general to the specific. Whereas systems design is future-oriented and attempts to predict what *will* happen (what kind of graduates will be in demand, for example), systems improvement looks to the past and attempts to remedy deviations from systems objectives. Once again, a synthesized version, drawn primarily from van Gigch, will serve as the model:

1. Define the problem.
2. Define the subsystems.
3. Observe the behavior of the subsystems.
4. Compare the observed behavior with the objectives.

    5. Reduce the problems to subproblems.

    6. Restore the system by correcting the subproblems.

We can illustrate the systems improvement process by continuing the information systems curriculum example. Let us assume that the recommended curriculum was adopted and has been in effect for several years. The feedback from recent graduates indicates that a number of them have had difficulty gaining admission to the graduate schools of their choice in spite of above average grades and aptitude test scores. Following the steps of the systems improvement approach, the problems might be viewed in the following way:

    1. The graduates are not receiving the desired recognition.

    2. The subsystems include the faculty, the students, and the academic courses.

    3. The faculty are active in scholarly research and receive student evaluations well above the university average. The students rank well above average in high school class rank and SAT scores. Several elective courses in data base management and simulation have not been offered in recent years. Increased enrollment has forced the faculty to concentrate on the required courses and only those electives that can be used by all business majors.

    4. The curriculum falls short of the "academic excellence" objective.

    5. The subproblems include excessive enrollments and a shortage of faculty.

    6. The enrollments in business courses can be restricted to business majors; graduate assistants can be used to teach some introductory courses; and funding can be sought to hire additional full-time faculty.

Systems Analysis

The term *systems analysis* has come to be used in a rather narrow sense to describe a systems approach to the development of CBIS. Literally, *analysis* is the opposite of *synthesis*. A synthetic process builds the whole out of parts, whereas an analytic process identifies the parts of the whole. Chemical analysis, for example, is the process of determining the type and quantity of the chemical constituents of a compound. By contrast, systems analysis deals with the identification of the components of a system.

But surely CBIS managers know the parts of their CBIS! Why is systems analysis so important in CBIS development? The answer is that systems analysis is applied not to the system under development, but to the system being replaced. The existing information system, perhaps a manual system or one that is only partially automated, is reduced to its component parts to present a clearer picture of what the new system must achieve. The analysis focuses on the information needs of the managers served by the CBIS—both those needs satisfied by the existing system and those unfilled needs that must also be satisfied by the new system.

In the development of CBIS, systems analysis is a necessary prelude to systems design. When systems design is applied to CBIS, the problem identified in the first step is actually the need for information revealed by systems analysis. Because of the sequential relationship between systems analysis and systems design in CBIS development, *systems analysis* may occasionally be used to describe *both* systems analysis and systems design. In fact, if you take a course in systems analysis, it will almost certainly include techniques of systems design. In order to avoid confusion over the use of these two terms, we refer to the combined process as *systems development.* Systems development and related topics are discussed in Chapter 17.

The Organization as a System

From the examples used to illustrate systems characteristics in the first part of this chapter, it should be clear that organizations are systems. The systems nature of an organization—its inputs, outputs, processes, control mechanisms, and so forth—is reflected in the organization's CBIS. It is particularly important, therefore, for us to view organizations as systems in order to understand CBIS better.

To further demonstrate the systems nature of organizations, let us consider the manufacturing firm diagrammed as a system in Figure 2-6. (Organizations that produce *goods* usually make better illustrations of systems concepts than organizations that produce *services*, although later in the book, when you are more familiar with systems and CBIS, we will use examples of each type.)

Inputs

Inputs into a manufacturing firm consist of plant and equipment, labor, raw materials, energy, money, data, and information. Suppose, for example, that the firm we are describing manufactures shoes. At a minimum, the plant and the equipment would consist of a factory building, tanning vats, lasts, molds, sewing machines, leather punches, and cutting machinery. Although the term *labor* is ordinarily used to mean blue-collar workers, in this instance we should also include the efforts of managers. The raw materials used to make shoes consist of leather, rubber, thread, nails, die, tanning fluids, and perhaps some miscellaneous hardware, such as eyelets for the laces. The energy used may be in the form of electricity or fuel. The important input of money is acquired by borrowing, investing, or selling stocks, bonds, and, of course, shoes.

These first few inputs are fairly obvious and need little explanation or justification. The inputs of data and information, however, are less apparent and warrant further discussion.

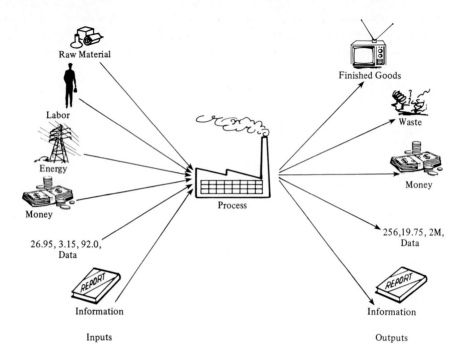

FIGURE 2-6   A manufacturing firm as a system.

Data

First, a distinction is made between data and information. The data input is a collection of facts about environmental elements: consumers, suppliers, competitors, government, and the like. As data, these facts are relatively unprocessed, although they may have been sorted, classified, or summarized as an adjunct to the collection process. Data collected by the using organization are called *primary*, whereas data collected by other agencies are called *secondary*. The Bureau of Labor Statistics, the National Association of Manufacturers, and similar organizations are common sources of secondary data for manufacturing firms.

A shoe manufacturer might collect primary data about consumer tastes and preferences in certain target markets, the sources and costs of raw materials in its geographic area, or the prices charged by its competitors. Some or all of these data may also be available from secondary sources, as would be tax rates, withholding schedules, the distribution of shoe sizes for different age groups, shipping costs, and similar data.

Information

Information, which is usually considered an *output* of an information system, is also an input into the organization. The explanation of this apparent contradiction lies in the fact that there are many information systems in the environment and that output from some of them serves as input into the organization. Government agencies, consulting firms, consumers' groups, and business journals are just a few examples of environmental systems that are sources of information of interest to a manufacturing organization.

Our shoe manufacturer might obtain U.S. Department of Agriculture information on the grading and tanning of leather, Small Business Administration information on how to obtain financial assistance, or trade journal information on fashion trends in footwear.

Data inputs into an organization generally must be processed by the CBIS before they are useful to managers, but information inputs may be used directly by any concerned manager. Much information received as input will be reprocessed, however, so that it is compatible with the CBIS and more accessible for further use.

Outputs

Outputs from a manufacturing firm include finished goods, money, waste and byproducts, data, and information. In our example of a shoe manufacturer, there is an obvious finished goods output of shoes. Money is an output in a number of ways: as wages and salaries to employees, dividends on stocks, interest on loans and bonds, investments, taxes, payment for inputs, and the repayment of borrowed funds. Typical byproducts of shoe manufacturing include scrap leather and rubber, used dye and tanning fluids, smoke, and other discharges.

Once again, the role of data and information is less clear and requires extra attention.

Data

Normally we think of data as inputs into a system that converts them into information. Some data, however, exit the system untransformed. Just as a manufacturing firm receives inputs of data from environmental systems, it also produces data that become inputs into environmental systems. The federal government is probably the largest single recipient of such data outputs, but other organizations, such as the manufacturing associations or the trade journals mentioned earlier, may also receive them.

In the case of the shoe manufacturer, data outputs would reflect the wages paid, the taxes withheld, the materials and energy consumed, the number of shoes produced, and similar matters.

Information

Most of the information produced within a system is used internally, by managers, and does not appear as a system output. After all, the information-producing part of the system—the CBIS—is really a *subsystem* of the organi-

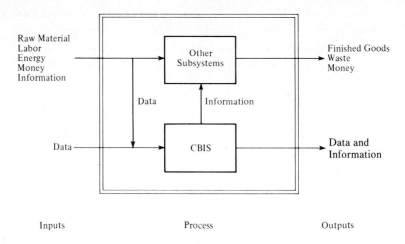

FIGURE 2-7 CBIS as a subsystem.

zation and interfaces with *its* environment—the other departments of the firm—and not necessarily with the environment of the system. The subsystem role of a CBIS is shown in Figure 2-7.

But Figure 2-7 also shows that some information finds its way out of the system. In a manufacturing firm, information outputs usually take the form of reports to stockholders, government agencies, or trade associations. In the example of the shoe manufacturer, annual accounting statements would be distributed to stockholders and would be made public in accordance with Securities and Exchange Commission regulations; corporate income tax reports would be made to the Internal Revenue Service; and hiring practices might be reported to the U.S. Department of Labor.

Processes

Processes in a manufacturing firm, as in any other system, transform inputs into outputs. Raw material is converted into finished goods by means of labor and machines—leather into shoes, in the example at hand. The "processing" of money is somewhat more subtle. In a business system, money changes *ownership* rather than *form*, for example, consumers' money used to purchase shoes eventually becomes the wages of employees. Energy, too, merely changes form—electricity into light and the mechanical action of machinery, or the potential energy of fuel into heat, and so on. And data, was we have already noted, are transformed into information. This last process is really the topic of this book and will be covered in much detail in subsequent chapters.

Regulation

Manufacturing firms, like other organizations, are controlled by managers. Managers are organizational thermostats. The setting on a thermostat is the heating system's goal or objective, and feedback in the form of heat is compared with the setting as a basis for further instructions to the heating unit. Managers receive goals and objectives from the firm's environment, and they use feedback from the firm's input, processes, and output to make similar comparisons and to issue appropriate instructions.

This analogy soon begins to break down, however. Heating systems are fairly simple and easy to regulate, but organizations may be very complex and difficult to regulate. The thermostat receives *actual* output—heat—as feedback, but we would not expect managers in the shoe-manufacturing firm to make a personal examination of the leather, sewing, and finished shoes in order to make decisions and develop plans for future production. Instead, managers rely on *information* concerning inputs, processes, and outputs. The use of information in this manner suggests a CBIS that parallels the physical organization, easing the task of control for managers by providing them with

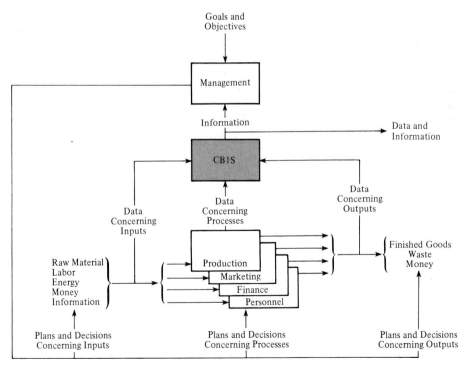

FIGURE 2-8   The role of CBIS in management control.

information concerning organizational activities. This role of CBIS in control is shown in Figure 2-8; the management function of control is discussed further in the following chapter.

Other Systems Characteristics

Although the roles of inputs, outputs, processes, and regulation certainly have the highest priority in any systems view of an organization, that view is really not complete without at least a perfunctory glance at how other systems characteristics help describe organizations. We will complete our discussion of systems by applying some of these additional characteristics to the example of the shoe manufacturer.

Organizations Are Interdisciplinary

Although there is a natural tendency to think of organizations primarily in terms of the discipline of their principal output, a closer examination almost always reveals another two or three related disciplines. The shoe manufacturer, for example, makes us think of chemistry because of the tanning processes required to prepare leather. But the leather comes from animal hides, which are dependent to some extent on agriculture and the environmental sciences. And this organization, like every other one, has a human element, the understanding of which is based on psychology. Also, the organization is a member of society, and its role in that capacity is understood more clearly through the contributions of sociology. The machines used in the shoe-making process operate according to principles of physics and are the products of an engineering technology. Even the physical layout of the plant and the operation of the assembly line are based on industrial engineering principles. We could extend the list of related disciplines, but the point has been made: organizations amply reflect the interdisciplinary nature of systems.

Organizations Are Holistic

Every organization has certain parts that are more glamorous and that attract more attention than others. When someone mentions a space shuttle, we immediately think of astronauts and a rocket rising on a magnificent tail of fire. We do not think a great deal about the mechanics, security guards, factory workers, computer programmers, and others who have made important, but not highly visible contributions. Yet all of them are necessary to the organizational system responsible for the space shuttle project. You can be sure that the project manager thinks about them, even if we do not.

It is as important to shoe factory managers to think holistically—to consider all parts of their organization—as it is to the space-shuttle project manager. The actions of the personnel, purchasing, marketing, accounting, and information systems departments are just as essential to the successful operation of the firm as is the actual production of shoes.

Organizations Are Differentiated

There are a variety of ways to slice the organizational pie. Some organizations are spread over a large geographic area and find it convenient to differentiate on that basis. The Federal Reserve System, for example, is organized into twelve geographic districts. Where organizational activities are less homogeneous, differentiation may be along product or service lines. An insurance firm, for example, many have automobile, life, and homeowners' divisions to handle different kinds of policies.

Perhaps the most common practice, and one that we shall use later to describe the subsystems of management information systems, is to differentiate along *functional* lines. Here we refer to the common business functions of finance, accounting, marketing, production, and personnel. It is along these lines that we would expect our shoe-manufacturing firm to be organized.

Organizations Are Synergistic

Many systems have no choice in the matter of trying to achieve synergism. Living organisms, for example, have certain subsystems—respiratory, circulatory, nervous, and so on—and can live with neither more nor fewer of them. But organizations do have such a choice. It is not necessary to have an integral CBIS, for example—you can subcontract your data processing work if you wish. Nor is it necessary for our shoe manufacturing firm to tan its own leather—one can buy leather already tanned. Every organization must evaluate alternative sets of subsystems to find the most synergistic combination for its situation. It is unlikely that organizational planners will think of their task in those terms, of course, but that is what they actually are, or should be, doing.

Organizations Are Hierarchical

Hierarchy refers to organizational levels, of which there may be any number in practice, but usually only three or four in theory. The four we consider in this book are patterned after Anthony's three categories of management activity: strategic planning, management control, and operational control.[9] To avoid confusion between the general category of management *activities* and the specific category of management *control*, we can simply refer to *top*, *middle*, and *first-line*, or *supervisory*, management levels. To these we add a fourth category of organizational personnel who have no management responsibilities. The hierarchy based on management activity (or the lack of it) is the basis for one dimension of the MIS model presented in Chapter 9.

Organizations Are Goal-Oriented

Reference has already been made to organizational goals and their importance to CBIS, but the subject is so important that attention should be called to it again. We all have goals as individuals: to graduate from college, to make

---

[9]Robert N. Anthony, *Planning and Control Systems: A Framework for Analysis* (Boston: Harvard University Graduate School of Business Administration, 1965).

the basketball team, to be elected to an honor society, and so on. Most of us probably also belong to organizations that have stated goals and objectives: churches that have fund-raising goals, clubs that have membership objectives, or intramural teams that have performance objectives.

The primary objective of a business organization is survival. The Chrysler Corporation gave evidence of this objective in the early 1980s when there was some real danger that the company would fail. Other, secondary objectives, such as profit, market share, dividends, stock value, and the like, were subordinated to survival.

The shoe company in our example is no different. It must make plans and take actions that will ensure its survival. Then it can consider appropriate profit, market share, and other objectives. The role of CBIS in meeting organizational objectives is to provide accurate information about past, current, and projected events to the managers responsible for accomplishing these objectives.

Summary

A *system* is a set of related parts working together to achieve some goal or objective. CBIS developers and other managers often turn to *general systems theory* for an understanding of how systems work. GST tells us that systems process inputs into outputs, integrate knowledge from many academic disciplines, have different parts but are best viewed in their entirety, and must be regulated to achieve the goals toward which they are oriented.

Although GST helps us to understand systems, not everyone agrees that it is a valid scientific or problem-solving theory. Critics of GST claim that a holistic approach may not be practicable in complex, high-technology systems and that the specialization repudiated by GST may be necessary after all.

Problems concerning systems call for systems solutions. Three approaches to solving systems problems are *systems design*, *systems improvement*, and *systems analysis*. Systems design, which draws on both the *scientific method* and GST, is useful in planning for new systems, and systems improvement is a good approach to correcting deficiencies in existing systems. Systems analysis is a systems approach to the development of CBIS that combines systems improvement (of the old or manual system) and systems design (of the new or automated system).

CBIS are subsystems of organizations. CBIS use data and information to reflect the physical parts of the organizational system. In order to understand CBIS, one must first recognize and understand the systems nature of the physical organization it reflects.

Assignments

2-1. Think of the class in which you are using this book as a system. What are its parts? Is it more helpful to view the class holistically or in terms of its parts? In what ways does the class exhibit synergism?

2-2. Describe your university as a system. What are its subsystems? What is its suprasystem? What other systems or suprasystems are in its environment? What insights into the functioning of the university are gained from this view?

2-3. "A holistic view is okay for top management, but first-line managers need not concern themselves with other activities in the firm." Is this statement true or false? Explain your answer. Would your answer be different if you were the president of a firm instead of a newly hired first-line manager? Why or why not?

2-4. Synergism is a difficult concept to understand and illustrate. Explain how synergism is demonstrated by a football team, in a management class, in a college curriculum.

2-5. Use Drucker's five-step process for decision making to show how a high school senior could decide which college to attend. Did you use such a process in selecting your college or university? Do you think your choice would have been different if you had?

2-6. Your dormitory frequently has parties sponsored by the residents. Use the systems design approach to develop a fair system of assessing the residents for the expenses associated with the parties.

2-7. Consider the class registration system at your university. Use the systems improvement approach to recommend changes that would correct any deficiencies you have detected. (If your registration system has *no* deficiencies, please contact the Guiness Book of Records at once!)

2-8. The organization as a system was illustrated in this chapter by the example of a shoe manufacturer. Make a similar analysis using a fast-food restaurant.

2-9. Some highway traffic signals are activated by an electrical current generated when an automobile passes through a magnetic field. The left-turn arrow, for example, does not come on unless a car is in the left-turn lane. Explain this process in terms of system regulation. What is the system? What are the inputs and outputs? Is the feedback actual or informational?

CASE   Hill Manufacturing—Part I

Debbie Cather, head of inventory control at Hill Manufacturing Company, is meeting with Dave Andrews from the Information Systems department. They are discussing the new materials requirements planning (MRP) system that is soon to be implemented in the firm. MRP is a computer-based information system that handles inventory and scheduling decisions for all the component parts of the exercise equipment that the company manufactures.

There are three major inputs into an MRP system:

1. The *master schedule* states how many of each item that the firm manufactures are needed during each week of a twelve-week planning horizon. These data come from orders that have already been placed by customers as well as from forecasted orders.
2. The *bill-of-materials file* lists all the assemblies, subassemblies, parts, and raw materials that comprise each of the company's products.
3. The *inventory records file* contains information about the inventory of materials on hand or on order, the lead time required to manufacture or purchase the materials, and information about vendors who supply the materials.

The MRP program takes the quantities specified in the master schedule and the information in the bill-of-materials and inventory records files and "explodes" it into the time-phased requirements for each assembly, subassembly, part, or raw material.

The major output of the MRP system specifies how much of each component item is needed and when it is needed. This information is given in (1) purchase orders to vendors for those items that are purchased and (2) shop-floor orders for component items that are manufactured by the firm. Other output includes various reports about the performance of the system.

The MRP system is illustrated in the following figure:

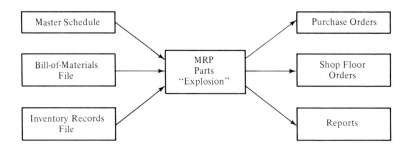

Ms. Cather is aware that some firms have met with limited success (or failure) in the implementation of MRP systems and wants to ensure that the new system will be successful. She has found that the following problems have caused other MRP systems to fail:

1. The master schedule was overstated and may have reflected quantities that the firm "hoped" would be needed instead of realistic quantities of finished products.

2. The bills-of-materials were inaccurate.
3. The workers ignored output from the system and continued to rely on informal methods to decide what to work on.
4. The computer support was inadequate.
5. Top management did not support the use of the MRP system.

Questions

1. With regard to each of these potential problem areas, what other organizational subsystems are involved?

2. In what ways does an MRP system exhibit synergism? What other departments might use some of the same information that is needed by the MRP system?

3. Explain how the MRP system could experience entropy if left untended. What types of information feedback should be incorporated into the system in order to regulate it?

Other Readings

Ackoff, Russell L. "Toward a System of Systems Concepts." *Management Science* (July 1971).

Bertalanffy, Ludwig von. "General Systems Theory: A New Approach to Unity of Science." *Human Biology* (December 1951).

Boulding, Kenneth E. "General Systems Theory—The Skeleton of Science." *Management Science* (April 1956).

Churchman, C. West. *The Systems Approach.* New York: Delacorte Press, 1968.

Cleland, D. I., and W. R. King. *Management: A Systems Approach.* New York: McGraw-Hill, 1972.

Gigch, John P. van. *Applied General Systems Theory* (2d ed.). New York: Harper & Row, 1978.

Johnson, Richard A., Fremont E. Kast, and James E. Rosenzweig. "Systems Theory and Management." *Management Science* (January 1964).

Kast, Fremont, E., and James E. Rosenzweig. "General Systems Theory: Applications for Organization and Management." *Academy of Management Journal* (December 1972).

Mockler, Robert J. "The Systems Approach to Business Organization and Decision Making." *California Management Review* 10, no. 2 (1968).

Schoderbek, Peter P., Asterios G. Kefalas, and Charles G. Schoderbek. *Management Systems: Conceptual Considerations* (2d ed.). Dallas: Business Publications, 1981.

Young, Stanley. "Organization as a Total System." *California Management Review* 10, no. 3 (1968).

Chapter 3

Management Concepts and CBIS

Learning Objectives

After studying this chapter, you will be able to:
1. Understand how CBIS aid the performance of management functions.
2. Relate different CBIS capabilities to levels of management.
3. Explain how CBIS affect the nature of management.
4. Define the following terms:

management process	scheduled reports
planning	on-call reports
organizing	special reports
staffing	detail reports
coordinating	summary reports
controlling	exception reports
management hierarchy	inquiry processing
planning horizon	data analysis

There are two important management implications of CBIS: the *role* of CBIS in management and the *impact* of CBIS on management. The role of CBIS is to serve managers, that is, to help them discharge their managerial responsibilities with greater efficiency and productivity. But in doing so, CBIS alter the techniques and methods used by managers and, invariably, alter the nature of management itself. This is the impact of CBIS.

The Nature of Management

The management implications of CBIS are so broad that it is helpful to have some framework for organizing and analyzing them. There are two common approaches to explaining management that serve this need rather well: the *process* view, which describes management as a cycle of job-independent functions common to all managers, and the *hierarchical* view, which considers differences in responsibility based on organizational levels. If you have taken an introductory course in management, you may be familiar with these approaches already, but a brief review will help you to place them in a CBIS context.

The Management Process

Although management scholars do not agree on the exact numbers or definition of functions in the management process, Figure 3-1 is representative of the responsibilities usually attributed to management.

Planning

The management process is guided by goals and objectives that originate with owners, government, society, or management itself. In the planning function, managers translate these goals and objectives into specific courses of action. For example, the board of directors' goal of increasing a firm's market share may result in plans to expand production capacity, to intensify promotional activities, or to improve product design. Similarly, the federal government's objective of reducing air pollution may require plans to modify the production process in a steel mill. And management's own goal of reducing the amount of returned merchandise may lead to plans for new quality control procedures.

By definition, planning is a future-oriented function. For organizations to survive in a constantly changing environment, managers must anticipate changes and plan accordingly. Some automobile manufacturers in the 1970s failed to anticipate decreased fuel supplies, higher fuel prices, consumer preferences for small cars, and government regulations for safety and fuel economy. The difficulties of these companies in the early 1980s was a direct reflection of their poor planning in the 1970s.

FIGURE 3-1 The management function.

Organizing

In a narrow sense, *organizing* refers to a structuring of resources—the establishment of divisions, departments, sections, and so forth—in order to carry out organizational plans in the most efficient manner. The body of knowledge on how best to accomplish this structuring is known as *organization theory*. The *classical school* of organization theory considers purely structural factors such as *span of control, chain of command*, and *specialization of labor*. The *behavioral school* adds human considerations and the very important concept of the *informal organization*. A more contemporary view, the *systems school*, considers the flow of resources—capital and labor—through the organization.

In the broader context of the management process, "organizing" also includes the identification of the other resources needed to carry out the plans developed in the planning function. A plan to introduce a new product line, for example, may require the formation of a new division in the company, but it may also require the identification of appropriately skilled labor by personnel managers, of material and equipment by production managers, of sources of capital by financial managers, and of potential markets by marketing managers.

Staffing

Although *staffing* is a term generally used to describe the acquisition of only human resources, in the management process it is also used generically to include the acquisition of all of the resources identified during the organizing function. Managers in the various functional areas of an organization discharge their staffing responsibilities by recruiting personnel, purchasing material, raising capital, and acquiring other necessary goods and services.

Coordinating

Coordinating is sometimes called *leading, activating, directing,* or even *communicating.* By any name, it refers to the actual execution of the plans made earlier in the management process. As coordinators, managers ensure that organizational resources are utilized in an efficient, cooperative manner. The alternate terms for this function reflect the need of managers to communicate instructions to subordinates and to motivate those subordinates to accomplish the goals and objectives on which the plans are based.

Controlling

Managers control organizational activities by comparing actual performance to planned performance and initiating corrective action to remedy any variances. Favorable variances, which occur when actual performance exceeds the planned performance, merit managerial attention as well as the more obvious situation in which actual performance falls short of that planned and creates an unfavorable variance. In the first instance, the standards should be reexamined to make sure they are not artificially low; if they are not, the reason for the exceptional performance should still be identified for possible extension to other activities in the organization. In the second case, the standards must also be reexamined to make sure they are not artificially high, and if they are not, the reason for the substandard performance must be isolated and corrected.

Although the part of controlling that involves the comparison of actual with planned performance takes place in the final phase of the management process, there are other, equally important controlling activities that occur in other phases. For example, the standards against which actual performance is compared are developed from goals and objectives during the planning function and should be incorporated into the written plans. Quality and performance standards for personnel, equipment, and material provide guidelines for identifying those resources during the organizing function and for acquiring them during the staffing function. Finally, the actual data that will be compared with the standards are collected as part of the coordinating function. And, of course, when the comparison indicates the need for corrective action, that action is initiated by the formation (or modification) of plans in— you guessed it—the planning function!

The Management Cycle

The formation of new or modified plans as a result of controlling illustrates the cyclical nature of management. Indeed, controlling can easily be thought of as the *first* function of management as well as the last. Figure 3-2 shows the natural flow of management actions (in terms of the five functions of the

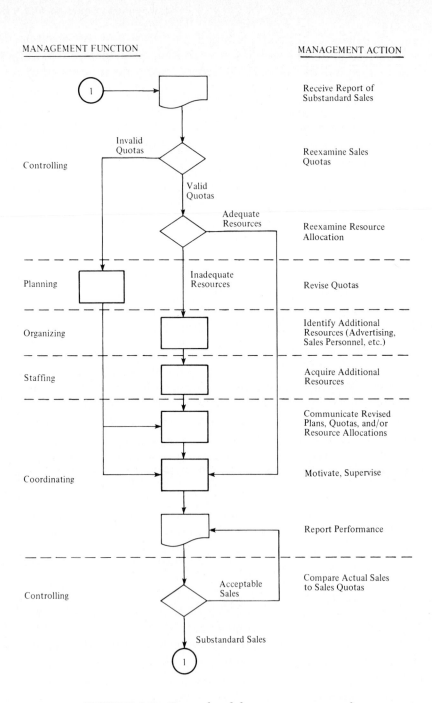

MANAGEMENT FUNCTION

MANAGEMENT ACTION

Receive Report of
Substandard Sales

Invalid
Quotas

Controlling

Reexamine Sales
Quotas

Valid
Quotas

Adequate
Resources

Reexamine Resource
Allocation

Planning

Inadequate
Resources

Revise Quotas

Organizing

Identify Additional
Resources (Advertising,
Sales Personnel, etc.)

Staffing

Acquire Additional
Resources

Communicate Revised
Plans, Quotas, and/or
Resource Allocations

Coordinating

Motivate, Supervise

Report Performance

Controlling

Acceptable
Sales

Compare Actual Sales
to Sales Quotas

Substandard Sales

FIGURE 3-2   Example of the management cycle.

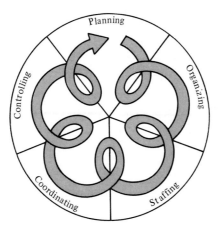

FIGURE 3-3 Cycles among management functions.

management process) that result when sales in a retail operation fall short of projections.

In addition to complete cycles through the five functions of the management process, there are often shorter cycles within and between functions. For example, a common planning tool is the *milestone chart* (see Chapter 17), which shows the expected completion dates for key events, such as the hiring of new personnel and the testing of new equipment. However, many of these events are first identified during the organizing function. Clearly, managers must "back up" and complete the plans after some initial work on organizing. And staffing, the acquisition of resources, often reveals flaws in organizing (the identification of resources) that require remedial work in that function. And so it is with other functions as well. The management process is never really completed but, as shown in Figure 3-3, cycles endlessly through and between its various functions.

The Hierarchy of Management

A second approach to viewing the nature of management is based on the hierarchy of organizational levels from which managers operate. Although an organization may have any number of hierarchical levels, traditionally we consider just three levels of management: *top, middle,* and *supervisory* or *first-line.* As shown in Figure 3-4, these levels are usually depicted as a pyramid to reflect the relative proportion of managers at each level.

Figure 3-4 also shows a relationship between the levels of management and management *activities.* In general, top managers are concerned with *strategic planning,* middle managers exercise *management control,* and su-

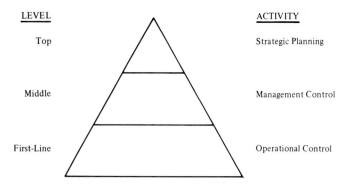

FIGURE 3-4   The hierarchy of management.

pervisory managers are involved in *operational control*.[1] We will explore these relationships further in Chapter 9 when we place the activities of management in a CBIS context.

The level of a manager is more a function of his or her activities than it is of the number of higher or lower hierarchical levels. For example, the organization chart of an automobile manufacturer may show 20 or more levels. If the managers at the first five levels are primarily involved in strategic planning, we would classify them as "top" managers. Another organization, say a large bank, may also have 20 organizational levels but only two or three levels that meet the definition of top management. At the other extreme, a sole proprietor, as the only manager in the firm, must engage in all three management activities and therefore represents all three levels of management.

The Relationship Between Process and Hierarchy

The hierarchical view of management is important for two reasons: information needs tend to be different at different levels of management, and the amount of time devoted to any given function varies considerably with the level or the planning horizon of management. The difference in information needs is described in Chapter 9; the way managers allocate their time to different functions is shown in Figure 3-5. When the management functions are shown in approximate proportion to the time that managers spend on them, it can be seen that there are differences both among functions and among management levels. These differences can be interpreted by CBIS planners in at least two ways.

First, a strong case can be made for allocating CBIS resources in proportion to the importance of the supported function at each management level.

[1] Robert N. Anthony, *Planning and Control Systems: A Framework for Analysis* (Cambridge, Mass.: Harvard University Graduate School of Business Administration, 1965).

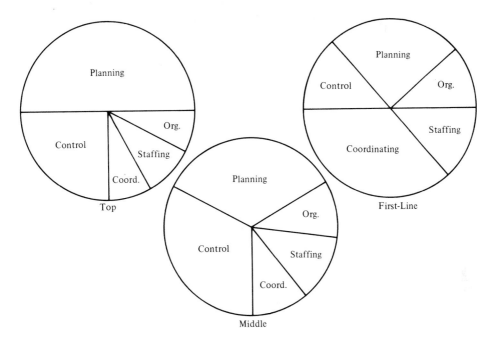

FIGURE 3-5 The allocation of managers' time. [Source: Raymond McLeod, Jr., *Instructors Guide to Management Information Systems* (Chicago: Science Research Associates, Inc., 1979).]

According to this line of thinking, which equates the importance of a function to the amount of time spent on it, one half of the CBIS resources allocated to serving top management's information needs should be in support of strategic planning. Yet planning, and strategic planning in particular, is the most innovative and creative of all the management functions. But computers, and therefore CBIS, are literally incapable of innovation or creativity.[2] This fact poses an interesting dilemma for CBIS designers: Should CBIS be directed into a role in which they do not perform well, or should they be restricted to areas of proven success?

Many designers opt for the second choice on the theory that freeing managers from mundane or highly structured responsibilities, which can be accomplished within the CBIS framework, gives them more time to devote to creative activities such as planning. Managers and CBIS in such organizations coexist in a symbiotic relationship: each performs independent but equally important tasks for their mutual well-being.

Current computer and CBIS design suggests that a third, compromise

---

[2] It must be conceded that there have been a number of "successful" experiments involving computer-generated art and poetry. Although these experiments give some evidence of creativity on the part of computers, the authors know of little success in applying this capability to normal management functions.

approach is now possible. There will always be requirement human creativity: a *person* must first recognize the potential of a corporate merger, a change in consumer tastes, an impending political situation, or any of the hundreds of other strategic planning considerations. But the fact that such creative activities must be initiated by humans does not completely rule out participation by CBIS. Once a manager has proposed, say, a merger, he or she can use the CBIS to collect facts, analyze alternative financing schemes, select the optimal course of action, and simulate the merged activities before actually entering the merger. For sophisticated decision making of this type, many organizations are now developing special CBIS known as *decision support systems* (DSS). DSS are discussed in Part VI of this book.

The Role of CBIS in Management

Three basic CBIS capabilities are involved in support of the management process: report generation, inquiry processing, and data analysis. All CBIS capabilities support all the functions of management to some degree, but certain capabilities are of greater importance in some functions than in others. Figure 3-6 shows the most common interactions between CBIS capabilities and management functions.

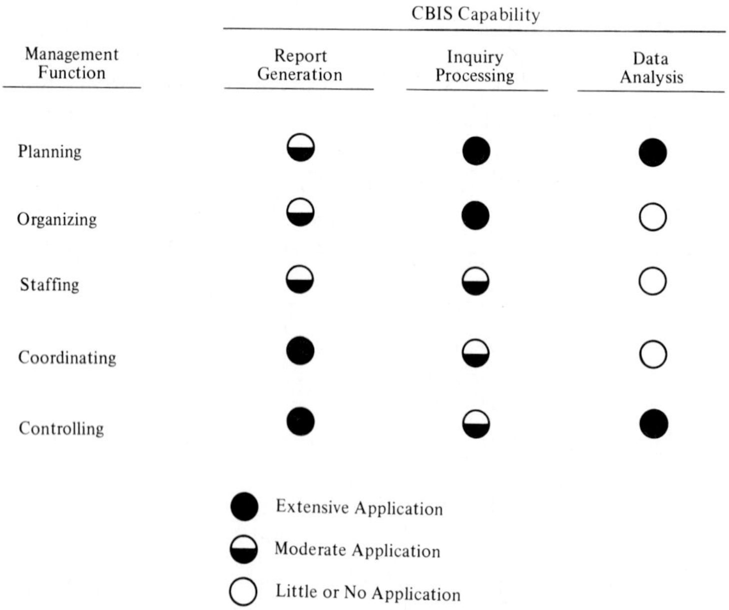

FIGURE 3-6 Management functions and CBIS capabilities.

Report Generation

Reports are the primary means of disseminating information in a CBIS. Reports are usually classified according to their frequency, their level of detail, and the degree to which they anticipate an information need.

Scheduled Reports

Scheduled reports are produced at regular intervals (daily, weekly, monthly, and so on) to satisfy recurring needs that were fully anticipated at the time that the CBIS was designed. Periodic sales reports, financial statements, inventory records, and other such reports fall into this category. Scheduled reports are distributed routinely and require no initiative on the part of the managers who receive them.

Often, the value of scheduled reports is diminished simply because they are routine. Familiarity may not necessarily breed contempt, but in this instance, neither does it stimulate interest. Many managers become so used to ignoring frequent, bulky, scheduled reports, which contain much information that they do not need, that they do not bother to use such reports to find information that they do need. CBIS personnel may not be able to change managers' attitudes toward scheduled reports, but they can at least review report content with interested managers periodically to confirm the need and applicability of the information provided.

On-Call Reports

On-call reports also satisfy anticipated needs, but they are not produced unless called for. For example, a computer program that generates a listing of employees' job skills would have been prepared during CBIS development, but the listing itself is not needed unless the personnel department is trying to fill a vacancy. When the need arises, the report can be requested and provided within a very short time—hours, perhaps.

The responsibility for the success of on-call reports rests primarily with the managers who need the information that the reports provide. Obviously, if a manager is unaware or forgets that a certain on-call report is available, he or she will not request it. CBIS personnel can help by circulating lists of available reports and by briefing new managers on the kinds of reports and other services offered by the CBIS.

Special Reports

Special reports are prepared to satisfy unanticipated information needs. For example, the discovery of a hazardous substance in a manufacturing process might prompt a request for a report on absenteeism and medical insurance claims by the personnel who work with the substance. In all probability, no program exists to prepare such a report, and one must be designed, programmed, coded, tested, and debugged (corrected) before the report can be produced. Depending on the availability of the data, the complexity of the programming task, and the urgency of the information need, the preparation of a special report can take days or even weeks.

Of course, once a program to produce a special report has been prepared it is kept on file and can be run again as requested to produce an on-call report, or it can be run routinely to produce a scheduled report. In the example just noted, employees' medical claims would probably be monitored for some time after the hazardous substance had been eliminated, and the report would be produced on a regular schedule as long as necessary and then would be placed in an on-call status.

Report Detail

Reports can also be classified by their level of detail. Reports that give all available information, such as every sale made by each member of the sales force, are called *detail reports*. It is rare for managers to need this kind of information, although it is quite common for CBIS to produce it. More often, management needs are served better by *summary reports*, which use statistical summary measures (totals, averages, ranges, deviations, and so on) to reduce report volume. Sales data, for example, might be summarized by listing only the monthly totals for each sales person or the mean dollar value of sales in each of several sales regions. Still better for most management needs are *exception reports*, which list only information that falls outside certain management-defined parameters, say, only those sales persons whose actual sales vary more than plus or minus 10 percent from their quotas. Examples of these kinds of reports are shown in Table 3-1.

Management Use of Reports

As the primary means of disseminating information in a CBIS, report generation can be expected to have broad application to the functions of management. Although this is generally true, in practice the greatest need for disseminating information occurs in coordination and controlling, and it is here that reports are employed most advantageously.

The significance of report generation in coordinating is more apparent when it is recalled that coordinating includes the function of communicating. Reports are often the means of communicating the nature of a task to be performed, the type of materials to be used, the destination of the goods to be produced, or the recipient of the services to be provided. This use of reports is particularly significant at the lower organizational levels, where coordinating occupies such a large proportion of the manager's time.

Coordinating reports flow downward in an organization, conveying top management's instructions for implementing plans to lower levels of management. By contrast, reports in support of the controlling function tend to flow upward as supervisory managers report the consumption of resources, the

TABLE 3-1a Example of a Detail Report

ACME Heating and Plumbing
463 Industrial Park Road
Richmond, Virginia 23279

Sales for July, 1983

Date	Description	Quant.	Unit Cost	Total Cost	Customer	Salesperson
07-01-83	Hydrant, 1″	25	3.50	87.50	Ace Constr.	Jones
07-01-83	Sink, SN 4367	1	175.00	175.00	Harris & Sons	Thompson
07-02-83	Drain pipe	200 ft.	.83	166.00	Ward's Constr.	Garcia
07-02-83	Sealant, can	5	2.89	14.45	Cash	Franklin
. . .	. . .	. . .	. . .	. . .	. . .	. . .

TABLE 3-1b Example of a Summary Report

ACME PLUMBING AND HEATING
463 Industrial Park Road
Richmond, Virginia 23279

Total Sales by Item, 2nd Quarter, 1983

Item	Quantity
Drain pipe, 2″ dia.	2305 ft.
Drain pipe, 4″ dia.	840 ft.
Furnace, gas, H-320	1 ea.
Furnace, elec., J47L	3 ea.
Heater, elec., baseboard	12 ea.
Heater, kerosene, sm.	19 ea.
. . .	. . .

TABLE 3-1c Example of an Exception Report

ACME HEATING AND PLUMBING
463 Industrial Park Road
Richmond, Virginia 23279

Items on Back Order over 30 Days as of July 1, 1983

Item	Quantity	Date Ordered	Supplier	Customer
P-250	6	05-23-83	Zeus Inc.	Inventory
G4RH Shower Head	2	04-17-83	Modern Baths	Ace Constr.
. . .	. . .	. . .	. . .	. . .

output of goods and services, and the results of quality inspections. Middle-level managers, who tend to spend more time on controlling than on any other function, compare these reports of actual performance with the standards established during planning.

Reports are of more limited use, but still helpful, in the management function of planning. Although plans are future-oriented, they are often based on data derived from past events. For example, an automobile insurance firm may plan for claim-settlement expenses on the basis of past trends in the number of policy holders, accident rates, and the cost of repairs. These data are undoubtedly available in historical reports, but if they are still in a machine-readable medium, special reports can be prepared in a format more convenient to the planners, or the data can be retrieved directly through inquiry processing.

Organizing may also be facilitated by historical data. Although it is unlikely that a plan will call for an exact duplicate of some previous mix of resources, most organizational activities can be broken down into tasks similar or even identical to some performed in the past. In such cases, the resource requirements of the planned activity can be synthesized from data on the actual expenditures for those past tasks. Many manufacturing processes can be organized in this fashion. Hand-held calculators, for example, may be unique in appearance and in their range of mathematical functions, but they are made up of more-or-less standard components and are assembled by similar production methods. The resource requirements for a new model of a calculator can be determined quite accurately from old production reports. Once again, the required information may be presented instead in a special report, or it may be obtained directly by an inquiry.

Staffing is difficult to support with any CBIS activity because it so often requires data from sources external to the organization. Although an organization may maintain data (and thus be capable of reports) on vendors, employment agencies, financial institutions, and other resource suppliers with which it has dealt in the past, there are usually no data in the CBIS on the thousands of other suppliers with which the organization has not dealt. Although it is appropriate for managers to choose from among former suppliers on the basis of their history of timeliness, quality, service, and price, it would be inappropriate to exclude completely other, perhaps equally dependable, suppliers simply for lack of CBIS-furnished data. This is an example of a situation in which managers must supplement the CBIS with professional knowledge in their area of expertise.

Not all resources are acquired externally. In the case of human resources, personnel managers often seek to fill vacancies from within the organization. In such a situation, the CBIS-generated job-skill listing suggested earlier would be extremely helpful. Of course, the promotion of in-house personnel simply creates an opening elsewhere in the organization, but usually at a lower level where the personnel selection decision is easier and less critical.

Inquiry Processing

Inquiries have already been mentioned as alternatives to special reports. Indeed, inquiries, as the term is used here, can be thought of as special reports that are "programmed" by the end user—usually a manager who can access an on-line, direct-access storage device via a computer terminal. The use of data base management systems (DBMS) greatly enhances inquiry processing. With a DBMS, managers can generate special reports on virtually any subject with a few simple commands. Of course, the basic data needed to produce these reports, usually captured during transaction processing, must already be in the data base. More is said on transaction processing in Chapter 8; DBMS are covered in Chapter 6.

Because inquiries are alternatives to special reports, managers should consider the advantages and disadvantages of each before deciding which to use. Three factors influence the choice: the ability of the user to process an inquiry, the urgency of the information need, and the volume of the expected output.

User Ability

Special reports require no data processing skills or equipment on the part of the user, whereas inquiries require some familiarity with the CBIS and the DBMS and access to a terminal. Managers who already fear or mistrust CBIS and are uncomfortable with computer equipment tend to opt for special reports.

Urgency

Inquiries produce results in seconds or minutes as opposed to the days or even weeks that may be required to obtain a special report. Even when time itself is not a critical factor, the administrative process of obtaining a special report may "turn off" many managers. A request for a special report must be thought out in great detail, with particular attention given to the content and the format of the information desired. In most organizations, a special report request must be made in writing and must be approved by a responsible person or a committee. If the requested information turns out not to satisfy the information need completely, many managers are reluctant to make a second request that tends to call attention to their original mistake. Inquiry processing permits managers to experiment with different data formats, to follow up interesting results with additional inquiries, and to rearrange data to facilitate analytical processes.

Output Volume

Inquiries tend to be limited in the volume of output that they can yield. Cathode ray tube (CRT) terminals can display perhaps one page of material at a time, and typewriter terminals are very slow. If the output is voluminous or very specialized (hard-copy graphs, multiple copies, wide-paper format, and so on), special reports may be more appropriate in spite of their other disadvantages. Of course, in many CBIS, inquiry output can be sent to a more versatile output device from the terminal keyboard, but the interactive nature of inquiry processing is sacrificed in the process.

Management Use of Inquiry Processing

Figure 3-6 shows that inquiry processing is used primarily in support of planning and organizing, although it certainly is the most flexible of all CBIS activities and can support *any* function of management. One reason that inquiry processing is not used more in support of coordinating and controlling is that those functions are already supported well by report generation. This situation may change, however. As managers develop inquiry processing skills for planning and organizing, they become dissatisfied with the restrictions inherent in report generation and seek to apply their new skills to more traditionally supported functions, such as coordinating and controlling. But although the use of inquiry processing is increasing dramatically with the proliferation of computer terminals, it is doubtful that it will ever completely replace report generation.

The ability to pose follow-up inquiries—that is, to have interactive access—is especially beneficial in the planning function. For planning is the least structured of all the management functions, and it is a rare planner who completely anticipates all the information needed to complete a plan. More likely, as the plans begin to take shape, additional information needs arise. The planning function would be seriously impaired if information were available only in reports or, worse, if planners failed to consider some information because it took too long to process it.

Searching large volumes of data and selecting elements that meet certain criteria is extremely difficult to do manually and equally easy to do by inquiry processing. And this is precisely what is required in the organizing function: Managers must review uncounted previous operations in search of activities similar to those planned for the future. It is like trying to find an entry in a telephone directory when you know only the telephone number. Yet this would be a relatively simple task—to associate a subscriber with a telephone number—for a terminal user accessing a telephone data base. It is also easy for a manager organizing the production of a new model of automobile to query a data base for previous examples of, say, front-wheel disc-brake assembly operations.

When information requirements for staffing, coordinating, or controlling are brief, inquiry processing may be the best way to obtain the information. Questions such as "Do we have an employee who speaks Spanish and has a degree in mechanical engineering?" or "What is the status of job number P4702-C?" or "What percentage of the allocated funds has been expended on advertising to date?" may be answered readily—provided the data have been captured and stored in an accessible device in some structured manner.

Data Analysis

In Chapter 1, it was noted that some transformation processes are more sophisticated than others. Storing, retrieving, sorting, duplicating, and classifying are important, but simple, processes. They make data available in a convenient form, but they do not add new information. They expand quantitative limits to handling data, but they do not qualitatively add to the information conveyed by the data. By contrast, processes such as calculating and summarizing improve data management quantitatively *and* qualitatively. There is a synergistic effect by which processed data convey more information than that contained in the individual, unprocessed data elements. Data analysis is the application of these more sophisticated transformation processes to increase the information content.

In scientific usage, *analysis* means to break down and examine in detail. For example, the chemical analysis of a substance reveals the type and amounts of its chemical components, often with unexpected (for the layperson) results. The fact that water, a liquid, is made up of oxygen and hydrogen, two gases, is certainly not apparent from a superficial examination of water. Similarly, data analysis is used to identify subsets of data that might convey hidden information to managers. For example, automobile sales data are a mass of numbers representing sales by model, color, year, geographic region, options, and so forth. One analytical approach to such data would be to isolate and examine the sales of, say, four-door sedans. If the sales of four-door sedans for the past six years have been .53, .62, .71, .69, .74, and .80 million, a *trend analysis* could be used to predict next year's sales to be approximately .85 million.[3] Additional analyses may refine this estimate by considering the effects of exogenous factors such as trends in family size, the age of automobile buyers, economic activity, and other relevant variables. Mathematical models form the basis of data analysis. The more commonly used models— trend analysis, linear regression, linear programming, and inventory analysis—may be kept in a *model base* on an on-line storage device. Computer programs that require one of these models simply call the appropriate model out of storage when it is needed to analyze data.

The model base can also be accessed interactively from a terminal. In a logical extension of inquiry processing, a manager not only can tailor reports to specific information needs, he or she can also call up a mathematical model to perform a detailed analysis of those reports without ever leaving the terminal. For example, many manufacturing firms determine an optimum mix of products from an analysis of the costs of the resources involved and the profit margin for each product. An inquiry can identify those costs that are changing, and the production manager can use a linear programming model to determine a new mix based on the revised data.

Not all models can be preprogrammed and stored in the model base—

---

[3]Trend analysis and similar techniques are discussed in Chapter 7.

any more than all reports can be anticipated. Some situations call for unique models, just as some information requirements call for special reports. When managers themselves possess the skill to develop such models—as they frequently do in research and development or engineering departments—it is a good idea to provide them microcomputers or "smart" terminals with which to program their own models.

Of course, just as special reports can evolve into scheduled or on-call reports, a "unique" model might have subsequent applications. The developer of a unique model may keep it on a cassette or diskette compatible with the terminal or microcomputer used as an input device, but if it appears that there are organization-wide applications of the model, it should be turned over to the information systems department for documentation and inclusion in the model bank. Models incorporated into the CBIS in this manner are still readily available to the developer. The development and use of unique models is a particularly important feature of decision support systems.

Management Use of Data Analysis

Figure 3-6 shows that data analysis is most useful in the management functions of planning and controlling. As the most creative function of management, planning is the most likely to require information that is not readily apparent in raw data but that must be developed by analytical methods. The future orientation of planning also demands a CBIS capability to forecast— one of the primary applications of mathematical models, such as regression analysis, usually found in the model base. Some of the other common uses of data analysis in planning include scheduling production, selecting facility locations, choosing from among alternative investment opportunities, and developing marketing strategies.

The controlling function is often facilitated by CBIS-supported project-management tools such as PERT (program evaluation and review technique) and CPM (critical path method). These models can also be used in the planning function. Indeed, many management theorists regard controlling as one end of a continuum, with planning at the other end. In this sense, controlling can be thought of as *very* short-range planning, and it is not surprising to find an extensive application of data analysis activities in both planning and controlling activities.

Of the other management functions, only staffing is supported to any significant degree by data analysis, and then only moderately. Certain financial models—those that determine net present values or internal rates of return—may be helpful in evaluating equipment or other resources acquired during the staffing function. These and several other decision-making methods used in data analysis are discussed in Chapter 7.

The Impact of CBIS on Management

The specter of a computer takeover has been a real concern to blue-collar and clerical workers for some time. Although it has received less attention, a similar concern exists among managers who view CBIS as a threat to their jobs. Are managers threatened by CBIS? Certainly, computers *do* replace some workers. Do managers face the same fate? CBIS have been with us long enough so that we need no longer speculate on these questions—the evidence now exists to determine just what impact CBIS have had on management.

Early Predictions

The first studies of the impact of computers (the term *CBIS* had not yet been coined) on management, conducted in the late 1950s, predicted a reduction in the responsibilities of middle management.[4] This prediction was based on an assumption that first-line managers would use computers to perform many of middle management's programmable duties and that top management would take over many of middle management's nonprogrammable tasks.

By the early 1960s, however, predictions were beginning to take on a different tone. It became apparent that, for the moment at least, computers were not *replacing* managers but were being *used* by managers. Instead of changing the number or organizational level of managers, computers seemed to be changing the way managers performed their jobs. This situation led to predictions that computers and MIS (a new term for that time) would result in a new elite class of managers skilled in computer operations and the quantitative methods typical of computer-supported decision making.

Current Observations

Management research in the 1970s revealed that early predictions of a reduction in middle management simply did not materialize. By 1973, it was seen that there had been no reduction in either the total number of managers (corrected for growth) or the number of middle managers.[5] But if this was comforting news at first, it soon began to raise doubts. After all, computers are expensive, and if the same number of managers was still required to get the job done, why have computers? How many times did managers hear "A

[4] Harold J. Leavitt and Thomas L. Whistler, "Management in the 1980s," *Harvard Business Review* (Nov.–Dec. 1958): 41–48.

[5] J. L. Gibson et al., *Organizations: Structure, Process, and Behavior* (Dallas: Business Publications, 1973).

computer will save time and money," only to find later that they still had the same number of employees (or even more) and that it was costing more to get the job done?

There were two responses to this charge. First, much of what managers did was not affected by computers. Attending conferences, meeting with clients, inspecting operations, and other similar duties had not changed.[6] Second, the quality and quantity of work accomplished had improved. It was true that the number of managers had not decreased, but they were now basing their decisions on a more thorough and accurate analysis of data than was previously possible. And if these decisions did not result in immediate, dramatic increases in profits or decreases in costs, it was because the environment had changed. The legal and social environment had placed ever-increasing demands on managerial resources. The competition, too, was making decisions based on more thorough and more accurate, computer-assisted analyses. A modern management needed CBIS not so much to get ahead as merely to hold its own in a changing environment. Although the erosion of middle management did not materialize, the predictions of changes in the scope of management did. There *was* a new elite of innovative, creative, mathematically oriented managers, and, ironically, they were *middle* managers—the very group that was supposed to be replaced by computers! As predicted, first-line managers (and in some cases, computers themselves) did assume responsibility for programmable decisions, but this process merely relieved middle management of routine tasks and freed it for more creative activities, such as planning.

Another reason for the lack of any decrease in total or middle management numbers is that computer and CBIS facilities themselves had to be managed. Every organization had a few managers, usually *middle* managers, to look after its data processing and CBIS activities. So although the *net* change in the number of managers was insignificant, it may have been the result of an increase in the information management function at the expense of decreases in more traditional areas of management. The numbers involved were small, however, and the losses were absorbed through attrition rather than by some wholesale firing of "replaced" managers.

The introduction of a new management responsibility—that of managing the CBIS—raises more questions than those concerning the number of managers. It also poses an organizational problem: where to place the equipment and personnel, managers included, associated with CBIS. These and related organizational questions are discussed in Part VII.

Research in the 1980s is again raising the spectre of middle-management reductions, however. A 1983 survey of 1200 major companies by Louis Harris Associates for *Business Week* indicated that over 40 percent had cut their middle-management staffs in 1982.[7] But it is not clear that computers or

---

[6] Henry Mintzberg, "The Manager's Job: Folklore and Fact," *Harvard Business Review* (July–Aug., 1975): 54.

[7] "The Shrinking of Middle Management," *Business Week* (April 25, 1983): 54–86.

information systems are to blame. 1982 was a recession year, and there has been a general concern in U.S. industry to increase productivity to meet foreign competition—by a variety of methods, to include cutting staff and other overhead. It remains to be seen if the current middle-management reductions are just a temporary aberration or if the predictions of the 1950s are finally coming to pass.

Conclusions

The impact of CBIS on management can be summarized in terms of the kind of decisions made at different levels of management and the extent to which these decisions can be supported by CBIS. Figure 3-7 shows that top management tends to make decisions that are, for the most part, nonprogrammable and not well supported by CBIS, although DSS are changing this situation somewhat. Many of the data required for top-management decisions deal with the environment and are not readily available in CBIS data bases.

Middle managers become involved in programmable and nonprogrammable decisions in roughly equal numbers, and they use CBIS extensively to support their decision-making responsibilities. Many decisions made at this level involve the analysis of organizational data using mathematical models—a task to which the CBIS, with its data base and model base, is particularly well suited.

The kind of decisions made by middle managers requires a greater degree of interaction with CBIS than the decisions of other management levels. CBIS do not yet have the environmental data required by top management, and once programmed, first-line managerial decisions continue to be made more or less automatically. Indeed, recent studies reveal middle manage-

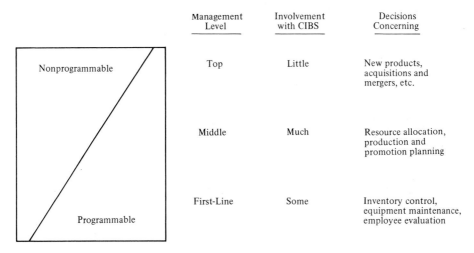

	Management Level	Involvement with CIBS	Decisions Concerning
Nonprogrammable	Top	Little	New products, acquisitions and mergers, etc.
	Middle	Much	Resource allocation, production and promotion planning
Programmable	First-Line	Some	Inventory control, equipment maintenance, employee evaluation

FIGURE 3-7   Management levels and decision making.

ment to be the single largest user of CBIS, and the authors' own study of over 150 business and government organizations in the late 1970s revealed that 58.2 percent considered middle management the principal beneficiary of CBIS (22.2 percent named top management, and the remaining 19.6 percent picked first-line management).[8] Although the proportion of programmable decisions faced by first-line management is great and would suggest considerable involvement with CBIS, the total number of decisions left to first-line management is not large, and there is only moderate involvement at this level. Also, as noted earlier, many programmable decisions can be made without *any* management intervention; this circumstance, too, reduces first-line management's involvement with CBIS.

These conclusions must be qualified. They are, of course, broad generalizations; the exact impact of CBIS on the different levels of management varies considerably from organization to organization.

Summary

Management can be viewed as a cyclical process of planning, organizing, staffing, coordinating, controlling, planning . . . and so on. It is also possible to think of management as a pyramid with relatively few, strategically oriented managers at the top; a larger number of tactically oriented managers in the middle; and a still larger number of operationally oriented managers at the base. All managers are involved in all functions to some extent, but top managers are concerned mostly with planning, middle managers mostly with controlling, and lower managers mostly with coordinating.

CBIS capabilities in support of management can be divided into categories of report generation, inquiry processing, and data analysis. Although all CBIS capabilities support all management functions to some degree, report generation is best suited to coordinating and controlling, inquiry processing supports planning and organizing particularly well, and data analysis is most helpful in planning and controlling.

It was thought, in the 1950s, that computers would erode the responsibilities of middle management. Recent studies have shown, however, that the proportion of middle managers has remained about the same, although there has been a change in the way that managers (middle managers, in particular) now discharge their duties. Managers are more likely to use computers and quantitative decision methods than previously and have more time for creative activities now that computers perform many routine tasks.

[8] Donald W. Kroeber, "An Empirical Study of the Current State of Information Systems Evolution" (doctoral dissertation, The University of Georgia, 1976).

Assignments

3-1. Top managers are less likely to use CBIS than are managers at other levels, and CBIS personnel are frequently critical of top managers for their lack of appreciation of the problems involved in designing, operating, and maintaining a CBIS. Who or what is to blame for these attitudes? Can you think of any ways to make top management and CBIS more tolerant of one another?

3-2. It has been suggested that managers should exercise control when actual performance *exceeds* the planned performance. Can you think of a situation in which management would actually want to *lower* the quality of output?

3-3. Think of a business or an industry with which you are familiar (perhaps one in which you have held a summer job). Do the managers there divide their time as shown in Figure 3-5? Give examples of planning, organizing, staffing, coordinating, and controlling in the organization you are thinking of.

3-4. Indicate the type of report—scheduled, on-call, or special—in which the following information would most likely appear:

    a. Names of patients regularly seen by a doctor about to leave on vacation (hospital report).

    b. The mileage logged on each vehicle in a truck rental agency.

    c. The inventory level of spare parts in an aircraft maintenance plant.

    d. The construction costs, adjusted for inflation, of a six-year-old warehouse that just burned down.

    e. The owners of automobiles manufactured between March 3, 1983, and May 16, 1983 (manufacturer's recall).

3-5. How (by report, inquiry, or data analysis) would the registrar of a university be most likely to obtain the following information from the student records file?

    a. The telephone number of a student who is late to a job interview.

    b. All the students currently enrolled in DP324 and majoring in management.

    c. The status of Mary Smith's unpaid library fine (she can't graduate until it is paid!).

    d. The projected grade-point average of a South Springfield High graduate who has a 3.4 high school GPA and a 670 math SAT score, and who plans to major in computer science.

    e. The names of the students eligible for spring graduation.

3-6. If you were a manager in the marketing department of a textile manufacturing firm, would your information needs be served better by a stand-alone microcomputer (such as an Apple Macintosh or an IBM PC) or a terminal connected to the main computer of the company CBIS? Would your answer be the same if you were in the engineering department? Explain the reasons for answering as you did.

3-7. Billions of dollars are spent on computers and information systems each year in the United States. Do you think these expenditures are worth it *from management's point of view?* What would be the impact on the management of a single firm if it suddenly lost all of its computer support? What would be the impact on management in general if *all* organizations suddenly lost the use of their computers?

3-8. It is now generally conceded that computers and CBIS have not drastically altered the structure of management. Is it safe to assume that this stability of the management structure will continue into the future? Justify your answer.

3-9. Students today are exposed to computer hardware as early as the elementary grades. Colleges and universities are modifying their curricula to accommodate the computer literacy of entering students. Should the companies that hire college graduates modify their management techniques similarly to accommodate the computer skills of today's graduates? Do they? What are the arguments for and against such modifications?

CASE   The Flower Pot

The Flower Pot is a chain of florist shops owned by Tom Appa. There are twenty-five shops in the metropolitan area, and all of them are supplied by two greenhouses. The manager of each store is responsible for ordering the appropriate quantities of cut flowers and plants. Each Friday, he or she submits orders to the central office for delivery during the following week. The flowers and plants are delivered from the greenhouse to each outlet two or three times per week.

Mr. Appa has had no computer support in his business but has decided to have a computer-based information system implemented as soon as possible, and he has been discussing his information needs with various hardware and software vendors. He has decided that if each store has a terminal connected to the main computer in his office, the result will be better record keeping, forecasting, and coordination of orders. Managers will also be able to change their orders in the middle of the week—something they are not currently permitted to do.

The store managers are all at least high school graduates; ten of them have attended college and two of them are college graduates. Three managers have taken an introductory computer course in which they wrote simple computer programs and submitted them on punched cards.

Questions

1. Which of the management functions are the most important for the store managers to perform? What are Mr. Appa's most important functions?

2. What kind of reports might Mr. Appa want generated? Classify your examples by frequency and level of detail.

3. Should he include an inquiry-processing capability for himself and/or the store managers? For what might it be used?

4. What kinds of data analysis might be beneficial in this business?

5. Do you foresee any implementation problems with Mr. Appa's store managers? How might he prepare for the changeover?

Other Readings

Alter, Steven L. "How Effective Managers Use Information Systems." *Harvard Business Review*, (November–December 1976).

Bittel, Lester R., ed. *Encyclopedia of Professional Management* (2d ed.). New York: McGraw-Hill, 1985.

Drucker, Peter F. *Management: Tasks, Responsibilities, Practices.* New York: Harper & Row, 1974.

Fredericks, Ward A. "A Manager's Perspective of Management Information Systems." *MSU Business Topics* (Spring 1971).

Koontz, Harold, and Cyril O'Donnell. *Management* (6th ed.). New York: McGraw-Hill, 1978.

Murdick, Robert G. "Managerial Control: Concepts and Practice." *Advanced Management* (January 1970).

Ross, Joel E. *Modern Management and Information Systems.* Reston, Va.: Reston, 1976.

Schendel, Dan E., and Charles W. Hofer, eds. *Strategic Management.* Boston: Little, Brown, 1979.

Schoderbek, Peter P., Asterios G. Kefalas, and Charles G. Schoderbek. *Management Systems: Conceptual Considerations* (2d ed.). Dallas: Business Publications, 1981.

Smith, H. R., A. B. Carroll, A. G. Kefalas, and H. J. Watson, *Management: Making Organizations Perform.* New York: Macmillan, 1980.

Wren, Daniel A. *The Evolution of Management Thought* (2d ed.). New York: Wiley, 1979.

Zachman, John A. "The Information Systems Management System: A Framework for Planning." *Data Base* (Winter 1978).

Chapter 4

Computer Hardware

Learning Objectives

After studying this chapter, you will be able to:

1. Name and briefly describe the hardware components of a computer.
2. Associate input and output media with their respective hardware devices.
3. Classify computers by their size, cost, application, and physical characteristics.
4. Define the following terms:

hardware
software
central processing unit
arithmetic and logic unit
control unit
microprogramming
firmware
on-line
off-line
sequential access storage device
direct access storage device
diskette
floppy disk
hard disk
interpretation
intelligent terminal
magnetic ink character
  recognition

remote job entry station
mark-sense reader
optical scanner
optical character reader
universal product code
character printer
line printer
page printer
typewriter terminal
CRT terminal
cardpunch
data communications
ring-distributed system
star-distributed system
microcomputer
minicomputer
mainframe
supercomputer

The first electronic computer was constructed only forty years ago, in 1946. ENIAC (for *electronic numerical integrator and calculator*), shown in Figure 4-1, covered 15,000 square feet and weighed over 30 tons. At the time, one expert felt that six or seven such machines would satisfy the entire U.S. computer market. And as late as 1954 it was estimated that perhaps fifty companies in the country "could eventually use electronic brains"—an estimate that was raised to 1,000 by *Dun's Review* in 1957. But by 1960 there were 6,000 computer installations in the United States. Eight years later, in 1968, that figure had increased tenfold, to 60,000.[1] Today it is almost impossible to count the millions of computers found in businesses, schools, laboratories, homes, automobiles, industrial robots, and other locations, but as a measure of the proliferation of computers, consider that during 1984 alone, 4.13 million microcomputers—each with many times the computational power of ENIAC—were sold.[2] It is no wonder that people speak of the "computer revolution!"

Hardware Components

Given the number of computers in operation and their broad range of size and application, it is not surprising that there is no such thing as a typical computer hardware configuration. Nonetheless, for our purposes, some extreme configurations can be eliminated, and we can describe the kind of computer hardware that you are likely to encounter in CBIS.

A typical CBIS computer has a CPU (for *central processing unit*) and one or more devices each for the external storage, input, and output of data.[3] These hardware components, shown schematically in Figure 4-2, play an important role in determining CBIS capabilities. Even if you do not intend to pursue a career in CBIS, you will find that some knowledge of hardware will help you to understand the numerous computer-supported activities to which we are increasingly exposed in our daily lives. And if you *are* a future CBIS professional, you need to know how computers can help satisfy the growing need for information in modern organizations.

The Central Processing Unit

The CPU is the heart of any computer. The characteristics of the CPU—its storage capacity, its speed of operation, the number of peripheral devices it can accommodate, and so on—establish the limits of the computational

[1] *Notes on the Data Processing Industry* (Armonk, N.Y.: IBM, 1969), 2–5.
[2] "Computers, '85," *Richmond Times-Dispatch*, March 10, 1985, K-3.
[3] Many smaller computers, not generally found in CBIS, may incorporate all of these hardware functions into a single desktop-sized device.

FIGURE 4-1 The ENIAC computer. (Courtesy of the Sperry Corporation.)

power available in the computer. It is convenient to view the CPU as having three parts: *storage*, an *arithmetic and logic unit*, and a *control unit*— although these parts may not occupy distinctly separate physical locations in a contemporary computer.

Storage
Data are stored in a computer in a binary code; that is, words and numbers are expressed in combinations of electrical pulses instead of letters and digits. In writing, we usually express the presence of a pulse with a 1 and the absence of a pulse with a 0. Any letter or number can be coded using these

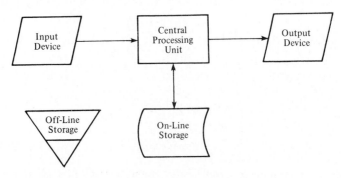

FIGURE 4-2 Hardware components of a computer.

two characters. For example, the American Standard Code for Information Interchange (ASCII) for the letter *A* is 0100 0001; it is 0011 0101 for the digit 5. These 1's and 0's are called *bits* (for *binary digits*). It is possible to code 256 different characters by using eight bits; a ninth bit is usually added to facilitate an internal computer check for errors during data transfer. The grouping of eight bits is called a *byte*. Because one byte is normally used to code one character, we will use the two terms interchangeably.

The use of a binary code greatly simplifies storage in the CPU. The two binary characters can be represented by the presence or absence of a magnetic field, the off–on positions of a switch, or any other two-state condition. Until recently, most CPU storage consisted of a three-dimensional grid of tiny ferrite rings, or *cores*, strung on a network of wires. Magnetic fields were induced in the cores by passing an electric current through a wire. When a core was magnetized in one direction, it represented a 1; when magnetized in the other direction, a 0. Consequently, each core represented a bit. More recently, integrated circuit chips, such as those shown in Figure 4-3, have been used for CPU storage. The most commonly used chip, such as those found in all but a few microcomputers, contains the circuitry to represent approximately 64,000 bits, but the latest IBM mainframe computer, the Sierra series model 200, uses chips with a capacity of approximately 288,000 bits. Some advanced computer equipment represents bits with magnetic "bubbles," and still more exotic devices are under development.

In the jargon of computer technology, memory capacity is measured in either *K* (for *kilo*, or *thousand*) or *M* (for *mega*, or *million*). Although *K* means 1,000 in metric usage, in computer usage it means 2^{10}, or 1,024. Similarly, *M* means 1,000,000 or 1000K. Thus, the 64K chip referred to earlier actually can accommodate 65,536 bits and the 288K chip can accommodate 294,912 bits. Storage in the CPU is usually expressed in *bytes* (as opposed to bits) and ranges from 4K (4,096) in the smallest microcomputers to 32M (32,768,000) in the largest supercomputers. Storage capacity is important because many CBIS applications require very large amounts of storage. Data base management systems in particular place heavy demands on CPU storage.

Access time (the time it takes to retrieve data from storage and make them available for processing) is also a key characteristic of storage. Access time varies with the storage medium—core, integrated circuit, bubble, and so on—but a typical late-model CPU has access times on the order of 50 billionths of a second or so. Again, to use computer jargon, a billionth of a second is called a *nanosecond* and a millionth of a second, abbreviated μsec, is called a *microsecond*. Current access times, then, are around .05 μsec, or 50 nanoseconds.

The Arithmetic and Logic Unit

The arithmetic and logic unit (ALU) contains the electronic circuitry that performs the data transformation operations conducted in the CPU. It also contains a few storage locations, called *registers*, to which data are moved for the actual operation. As suggested by the word *arithmetic*, many of the

FIGURE 4-3 Metal oxide semiconductor chips. (Photo courtesy of the IBM Corporation.)

operations are purely mathematical—adding, subtracting, multiplying, dividing, finding logarithms, and the like. These operations are carried out in binary numbers, of course, which are quite cumbersome for hand manipulation but are extremely efficient in computers.

The *logic* part of the ALU is based on the comparison of one data element with another and circuitry that initiates one operation if they are the same and another if they are different. This seemingly simple operation is a very powerful tool that facilitates much of what computers are able to do. Logical comparisons ensure that your bank deposit is credited to your account instead of to someone else's, that inventory is reordered at the proper time, that the grade of A is awarded four quality points, and so forth.

The Control Unit

The control unit contains electronic circuitry that reads coded instructions in software and initiates appropriate activity in other hardware components of the computer. The control unit, in conjunction with operating system software, brings programs and data into CPU storage from an input device or an external storage device, routes data to the ALU for transformation, restores the transformed data, and finally sends the transformed data to an output device or back to external storage.

The electronic circuitry that carries out these operations is usually built into the control unit, which somewhat restricts the choice of compatible software. Recently, some additional software flexibility has been gained by incorporating control unit-like instructions in small storage facilities within the CPU. The technique of substituting coded instructions (software) for electronic circuitry (hardware) is called *microprogramming*. The microprogrammed instructions are frequently stored on interchangeable circuit boards that permit the computer to accommodate different programming languages, to interface with different peripheral devices, or even to act like a different model computer. An interchangeable circuit board used in a microcomputer is shown in Figure 4-4. This blurring of the traditional lines between software and hardware has given rise to the term *firmware* to describe microprograms fixed on circuit boards.

External Storage Devices

CPU storage, even in supercomputers with megabyte capacities, is rarely adequate to store all the programs and data associated with CBIS. When they are not actually required by the CPU, additional programs and data are maintained in external storage devices. External storage devices are said to be *on-line* when they have an electronic data linkage to the CPU; otherwise, they are *off-line*. Some storage media are always off-line. Punched cards, optically scanned documents, and similar media require human intervention to make them available to the CPU. Other media, such as magnetic tape and

FIGURE 4-4   Microcomputer circuit board.

magnetic disks, are on-line when mounted on storage devices connected to the CPU but are off-line when stored in the data processing library.

External storage devices can also be classified by the mode of access—either *sequential* or *direct*. Two of the media suggested previously, tape and disk, will serve to illustrate these two modes of access.

Sequential Access Storage Devices

A sequential access storage device (SASD) is one in which data can be accessed only in the sequence in which they are stored. It is somewhat analogous to a dial telephone: To dial the number 9, the dial must rotate through the numbers 1, 2, 3, and so on until 9 is reached. It takes longer to dial 9 than, say, 5.

If your bank records are stored on an SASD, they can be accessed only by "rotating" through the device until your account number is reached. Of course, there are many more accounts than there are digits on a telephone dial, and such a search is correspondingly longer.

The most common SASD is the *magnetic tape drive* (see Figure 4-5). Computer magnetic tape is similar to audio recording tape. Most tape drives use 2,400-foot reels of tape, although some input terminals and microcomputers are designed to use audio-style tape cassettes.

Data are recorded on magnetic tape in binary code, with a magnetized area corresponding to a 1 and an unmagnetized area corresponding to a 0.

FIGURE 4-5   Magnetic tape drive. (Photo courtesy of Telex Computer Products, Inc.)

Heads positioned over the tape "write" by inducing magnetic fields in the magnetic oxide coating on the tape. Other heads "read" the tape by sensing these areas. There are usually nine read and nine write heads on a tape drive to accommodate an eight-bit byte and one check or *parity* bit. Figure 4-6 shows how data—in this case, the words *Management Information System* (*MIS*)—are represented on a nine-track tape.

The storage capacity of a tape is a function of its length and the recording density. One common recording density is 800 characters per inch (CPI), which gives a 2,400-foot reel a capacity of over 20,000,000 characters—the equivalent of about ten books the length of this one.

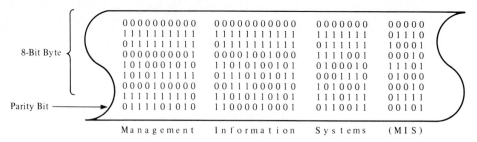

FIGURE 4-6   Magnetic tape.

Direct Access Storage Devices

A direct access storage device (DASD) is one in which data can be accessed directly without regard to the sequence or order in which they are stored. To continue the telephone analogy, a DASD is similar to a push-button telephone: Any digit can be "dialed" directly with one touch of the proper button. The total "dialing" time is reduced, and the telephone company imposes a slightly higher service charge for this convenience.

If your bank records are on a DASD, they can be accessed with equal ease—perhaps even by a clerk who keys in your account number in much the same fashion as one keys in a telephone number on a push-button telephone. And the bank pays the computer hardware vendor more for a DASD than for a SASD, just as you have to pay more for a push-button than a rotary telephone.

The most common DASD is the *magnetic disk drive.* Magnetic disks are similar in appearance to phonograph records, but they are more like magnetic tape in the way in which data are recorded on them. Disks do differ from tape, however, in the number of tracks used to record data. Instead of recording a byte *across* parallel tracks, bits are recorded *along* the tracks on a disk. The method of recording data on disk is shown in Figure 4-7.

There is a great variety in the way different manufacturers design disk drives. The disks may be used singly, as they frequently are in minicomputers and microcomputers, or they may be arranged in *disk packs* of six to twenty disks. Disks in packs may also vary in diameter (from 12 to 18 inches), the number of tracks per disk (from 100 to over 5,000), the speed at which they rotate (from 800 to 2,000 rpm), and recording densities. All of these factors combine to give disk packs storage capacities that range from 1 million bytes to over 700 million bytes. Figure 4-8 shows a modern disk pack in a sliding drawer.

The single disks used with small computers look more like 45-rpm records or compact audio disks. Most are either 5¼ or 8 inches in diameter, although the Sony Corporation has developed a 3½-inch disk now used with the Apple Macintosh and the portable Data General One. These small disks are called *diskettes* or, because they are somewhat flexible, *floppy disks.*

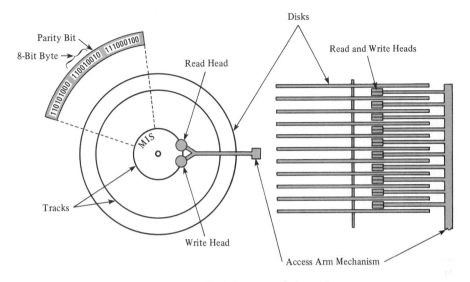

FIGURE 4-7 Magnetic disk pack.

FIGURE 4-8 Magnetic disk drive. (Photo courtesy of the IBM Corporation.)

FIGURE 4-9   Eight-inch diskette used in minicomputer. (Photo courtesy of the IBM Corporation.)

Diskettes typically hold 140K to 200K bytes of information per side and may be read on one or both sides, depending on the design of the disk drive. An 8-inch diskette used with a minicomputer is shown in Figure 4-9. A 5¼-inch diskette used with a microcomputer is shown in Figure 4-10. Figure 4-11 shows an Apple Macintosh microcomputer with its built-in 3½-inch disk drive (the size of the opening may be compared to the screen, which measures 9 inches diagonally).

The term *floppy disk* also serves to distinguish flexible disks from *hard* disks. Hard disks are mounted permanently in the disk drive unit and have exceptionally large storage capacity for their size. Hard-disk drives, also known as *Winchester drives,* generally have capacities of from 5M to 100M bytes and cost from $1,000 to $5,000, although at least one 5¼-inch Winchester drive with a storage capacity of up to 700M and a price approaching $25,000 is on the market. Some microcomputers, such as the IBM PC-XT and the Apple Macintosh XL, have built-in 10M-byte hard-disk drives.

Direct access to storage locations on a disk pack is achieved by a combination of electronic and electromechanical action. Read and write heads mounted on movable arms float a few millionths of an inch above and below the disks, as shown in Figure 4-7. An address code identifies the surface of the pack on which the data are stored as well as the track on which they are

FIGURE 4-10   Five- and one-quarter-inch diskette used in microcomputer.

located. The surface is selected by completing the electronic circuit to the appropriate head, and the arm is moved by electromechanical action to position the head over the appropriate track. The head then senses the magnetized areas on the disk in the same manner in which magnetized spots on tape are sensed.

Although there are other external storage media and devices—magnetic drums and magnetic tape cartridges, to name the most popular ones—we will use punched cards, magnetic tape, and magnetic disks to represent off-line, on-line sequential access, and on-line direct access devices, respectively, throughout this book. You should have no trouble understanding the other media you may encounter in the future if you have a good working knowledge of these three.

Input Devices

An input device is a computer hardware component that converts input data into a machine-readable binary code and transmits them to the CPU, where they may be used in processing or may be sent to storage for later use. In a sense, input devices "digest" data for the computer. But input devices have

FIGURE 4-11   Three- and one-half-inch disk drive built into the Apple Macintosh microcomputer. (Photo courtesy of Apple Computer.)

very restrictive diets. In most cases, there first must be an off-line auxiliary operation to convert source data (documents, transactions, and so on) into a form or medium that is acceptable to the input device. This process is shown for punched cards in Figure 4-12 and is explained in the following discussion of the card reader. Other media and data preparation devices are included in the discussions of their respective input devices.

Card Reader
A card reader is used to input data recorded on punched cards. Punched cards were one of the first computer input and storage media and remain an important one still. The most common cards have eighty columns and twelve

rows. Each column represents a character or a space according to a code of rectangular holes punched in the various row positions. These cards are called *Hollerith* cards after Herman Hollerith, who invented punched-card machines and developed the coding system. A smaller card, used with the IBM System 3 minicomputer, has only thirty-two columns, but it uses a smaller, round hole and only six rows to define a character. Three sets of rows give this card a potential of ninety-six characters or spaces. A card reader is shown in Figure 4-13 and examples of the Hollerith and System 3 cards are shown in Figure 4-14.

Punched cards are prepared off-line on a device called a *keypunch* machine, such as the one shown in Figure 4-15. In addition to punching holes in cards when keys on the typewriter-like keyboard are struck, a keypunch machine also prints the characters across the top of the card. The process of printing characters, called *interpretation*, aids in visual verification of the data punched on the cards. Cards may also be verified mechanically on a machine called a *verifier*. A verifier is similar to a keypunch machine in appearance, but it does not actually punch holes. Instead, it compares keystrokes with holes already punched. Any difference is signaled to the operator, who must then make a visual comparison of the card with the source document and, if necessary, repunch the card.

The card reader converts the holes in the cards to electrical pulses. Early card readers used a series of metal brushes that completed an electrical circuit when they passed over a hole, but kept the circuit open when no hole was present. Current card readers use photocells to detect the presence of holes. A card reader using the photocell method can read as many as 2,000 cards per minute. Although the potential of 160,000 characters per minute (2,000 cards times 80 columns) may seem impressive, card readers are among the very slowest of data input devices.

Tape Drives

Although magnetic tape is ordinarily considered a storage medium, it plays an important role in data entry. CPU operations are invariably faster than input operations, and the result is a bottleneck in which the CPU must wait for input. One solution to this problem is to speed up input. As in input device, a magnetic tape drive is about sixty times faster than a card reader. That is, the 20 million characters on a magnetic tape can be read into the CPU in about two minutes—a rate of over 165,000 characters per second. If

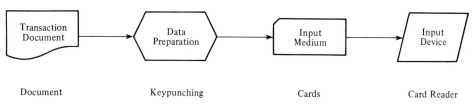

FIGURE 4-12 Preparation of data for card input.

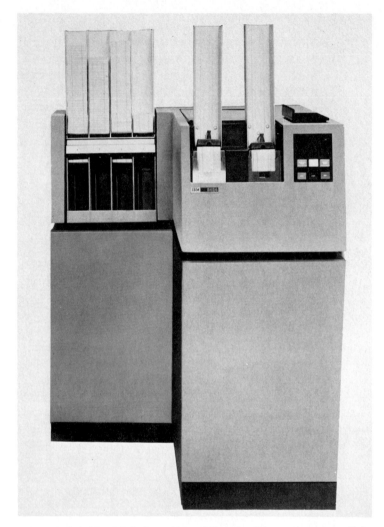

FIGURE 4-13   Multifunction card unit. (Photo courtesy of the
IBM Corporation.)

you have difficulty in comprehending characters per second, you can think in
terms of the length of time it would take to read the equivalent of this book:
about ten seconds!

Magnetic tape can be prepared off-line on a *key-to-tape* machine. A key-
to-tape machine also has a typewriter-like keyboard, but the keystrokes result
in magnetic impressions on the tape instead of holes. Keystroked data are
temporarily held in a small buffer storage area and are written onto the tape
in short bursts. This procedure is followed to simplify the problem of matching tape speed to keystroking speed as the tape passes through the machine.

Magnetic tape can also be prepared on-line. Many card-oriented systems

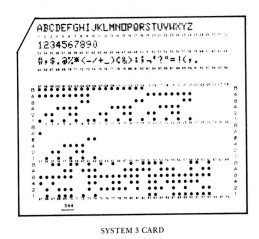

HOLLERITH CARD

SYSTEM 3 CARD

FIGURE 4-14   Punched cards.

use tape as an input device but retain cards for their convenience as documents in payroll, inventory, billing, and similar applications. In these systems, it is more efficient to convert cards to tape in a separate computer operation and then to conduct processing using taped input. In large-scale operations, a small computer may be dedicated to tape preparation while the larger computer performs the actual processing tasks.

Disk Drives
The use of disks as an input medium is exactly parallel to the use of magnetic tape in that role, even to the use of a *key-to-disk* device for off-line data preparation. Disk input is particularly popular in small computers using diskettes or floppy disks.

FIGURE 4-15   Keypunch machine. (Photo courtesy of the IBM Corporation.)

Disks have several advantages over tape in an input role. First, because the disk drive is a direct access device, input can be selective. That is, only those data actually required for an operation need be input. (Theoretically, this can also be done with tape, but it would be very inefficient.) Second, disk drives are usually faster than tape in an input role, further alleviating the input bottleneck. Because of the variety in disk-drive design mentioned earlier, there is no fixed rate of input for disk drives, but the range is from 80,000 characters per second to over 650,000 characters per second. The smaller floppy disks have an input rate of about 8,000 characters per second.

Terminals

Terminals are sometimes referred to as *direct input devices* because they do not require off-line data preparation, nor do they use an intermediate data medium. Instead, terminals generate machine-readable electrical pulses directly from keystrokes or other operator actions and transmit them to the CPU. *General-purpose* terminals, such as the portable model shown in Figure 4-16, usually have a typewriter-like keyboard on which the operator types data or program statements. *Special-purpose* terminals are designed to collect data from a specific activity, such as a manufacturing process, a retail store sale, or a hospital patient's vital life functions. Special-purpose terminals capture data via sensors or special, application-oriented keyboards.

When terminals have a limited processing capability, they are referred to as *intelligent* or *smart* terminals. Processing at a smart terminal is usually restricted to editing input and performing simple arithmetic operations prior to input. Many computer personnel include minicomputers or microcomputers in the definition of smart terminals, in which case much more extensive processing is possible.

Keyboard terminals are limited in input speed to the rate at which the operator can type—perhaps seven or eight characters per second. Why, then, would anyone choose a terminal over, say, a disk drive, which can input as much as 100,000 times faster? One reason is the lack of any requirement for off-line preparation, but a more important reason is that most terminals are also *output* devices. The capability of acting as both an input and an output device, on-line, permits the terminal user to operate *interactively* with the computer. That is, input can be processed and the output can be returned to the user in time to be considered before the next input. This

FIGURE 4-16   Portable terminal. (Photo courtesy of Texas Instruments, Inc.)

makes terminals particularly useful in the decision-making process, where data recovery and analysis might otherwise be prohibitively time-consuming.

Other Input Devices

The input devices, media, and data-preparation devices just described are those most commonly used in CBIS applications. Other input devices have a limited use in CBIS but are important in scientific or other specialized applications.

Magnetic ink characters are used almost exclusively by the banking industry. The stylized type font is limited to ten digits (0 to 9) and four special characters that identify routing through the Federal Reserve System banks, account numbers, and the number and amount of each check. The characters are printed in magnetic ink when the checks are produced, except for the amount of the check, which is added by a *magnetic ink character recognition (MICR) encoder* at the bank when the check is returned for processing. An *MICR reader–sorter* arranges the checks in numerical sequence by account number and transfers the data to the CPU at about three thousand characters per second. A processed check showing magnetic ink characters is shown in Figure 4-17.

Remote job entry (RJE) stations differ from the terminals described earlier in that they *do* require off-line data preparation. A typical RJE station may incorporate a card reader for input and a line printer for output. This combination permits much higher volumes of input and output than a keyboard terminal, but it also precludes interactive use in most instances.

Some data-input devices read directly from source documents. A *mark-sense reader* picks up electrographic pencil marks made with ordinary pencils

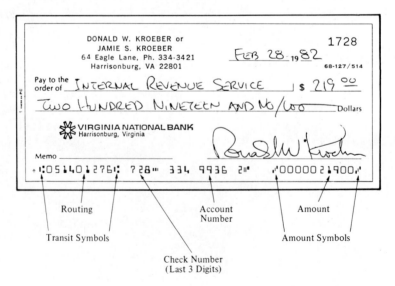

FIGURE 4-17   Magnetic ink characters.

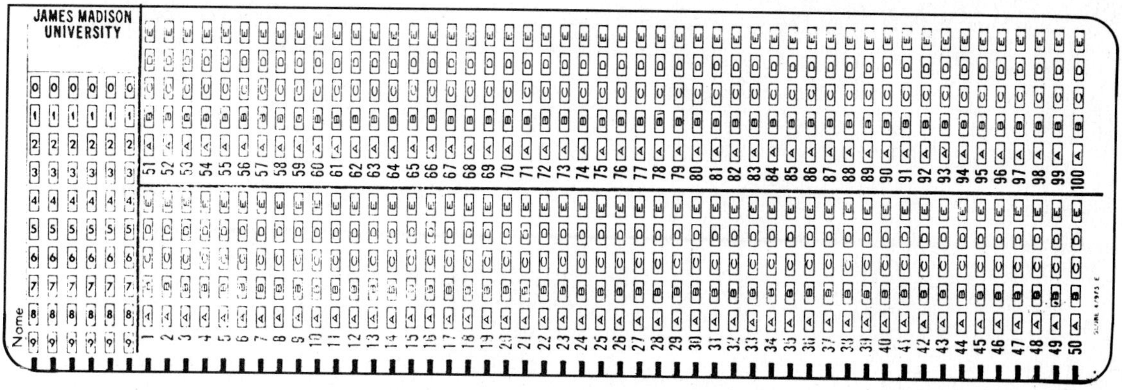

FIGURE 4-18   Optical scan form.

on carefully formatted forms, such as the one shown in Figure 4-18. Both mark-sense cards and optically scanned forms can be used to collect limited responses (true–false, multiple choice) in customer surveys, student testing, and similar applications. Where a greater variety of data is needed, an *optical character reader*, such as the one shown in Figure 4-19, may be more appropriate. One form of optical character reader, commonly incorporated into *point-of-sale terminals* in large retailing operations, reads the 26 capital letters of the alphabet, the 10 digits, and 6 special characters—provided they are printed in the special type font shown in Figure 4-20, called *OCR-A*. Another type of optical character reader can read hand-printed characters— if they are printed neatly and according to specified rules, such as crossing a Z to distinguish it from a 2 and so on.

The *universal product code* (UPC), illustrated in Figure 4-21, provides another means of reading data optically. The UPC, which uses a series of vertical lines to identify products, is particularly popular among retail grocers, although it has been opposed by some consumer groups. Advocates of UPC point to the increased accuracy of billing and record keeping, whereas its detractors argue that it could be used to deceive consumers with respect to prices.

Considerations in Choosing an Input Device
Most computer installations have a variety of input devices. The considerations in selecting one or more such devices include input speed, cost, convenience, and the nature of the application. These considerations are summarized for various input devices in Table 4-1.

Output Devices

Output devices accept processed data in binary-coded form and record them on various output media. Some output is stored externally for additional processing at a later date or for record-keeping purposes. Such output is most

FIGURE 4-19   Optical character reader. (Photo courtesy of the IBM Corporation.)

conveniently stored on a machine-readable medium such as tape, disks, or even cards. Other output, particularly in CBIS, is used to provide information to humans and must be recorded or displayed in letters, numbers, and other easily recognized characters. Paper and video displays are the best media for this purpose. Printed output on paper can be produced by either a printer or a typewriter terminal, whereas CRT (or *cathode ray tube*) terminals are used for video displays. Each device has distinguishing characteristics that make it suitable for certain applications.

```
A B C D E F G H I J K L M N O P Q R S T U
V W X Y Z , . $ / * - 1 2 3 4 5 6 7 8 9 0
```

FIGURE 4-20   OCR-A type font.

FIGURE 4-21   Universal product code markings. (Photo courtesy of the NCR Corporation.)

Printers

There are perhaps more approaches to printer design than to any other peripheral computer device. These design differences result in printing speeds that vary from 10 characters per second to over 90,000 characters per second.

The lower speeds (10 to 600 characters per second) are representative of *character printers*, such as the one shown in Figure 4-22, which print a single character at a time. Many character printers are of the *dot matrix* design,

TABLE 4-1   Computer Input Devices

Device	Characteristics	Applications
Card reader	Low cost, slow speed, inconvenient medium	Inventory, billing, payroll where card doubles as document
Tape drive	Average cost, high speed, sequential access	High-volume, periodic processing such as payroll or billing
Disk drive	High cost, high speed, direct access	High-volume, continuous processing such as airline reservation or database management
Terminals	Low cost, very slow speed, interactive access	Remote data entry, management queries
MICR reader	Average cost, slow speed	Check processing
Mark-sense reader	Low cost, slow speed	Student testing, customer surveys
Optical character reader	Average cost, slow speed	Retail store sales, credit card billing
Remote job entry station	Average cost, speed varies with medium	High-volume remote processing, such as branch office payroll

which forms characters by striking stiff metal wires through a typewriter-style ribbon. In a 5-by-7 matrix, a column of 7 wires moves across the page, striking selected wires in groups of 5 columns per character. The patterns formed are somewhat similar to the lights on many outdoor advertising signs. The addition of eighth and ninth wires gives greater realism to lower-case letters, as shown in Figure 4-23.

Other low-speed printers use a *daisy wheel*—so called because the characters are set on arms that radiate from a hub in a fashion resembling the petals of a daisy—to achieve "letter quality" (comparable to a good typewriter) at a speed of 10 to 50 characters per second. And many dot matrix printers now offer a compromise between speed and quality by providing a "correspondence" or "near-letter-quality" mode. These printers can output "draft" quality at 160 to 200 characters per second or, by making additional passes to fill in the spaces between the dots, correspondence quality at 40 to 50 characters per second. The more advanced dot matrix printers, such as the Epson LQ-1500, achieve correspondence quality by using a print head with up to 24 wires to give higher resolution to the printed characters.

Higher speeds (200 to 2,000 lines per minute) are achieved by *line printers,* which print an entire line of 120 to 144 characters at a time. Some line printers align print wheels in each position to print the line; others strike through rotating bands or chains of characters to achieve the same effect. Line printers are the most common type of printer found in CBIS today.

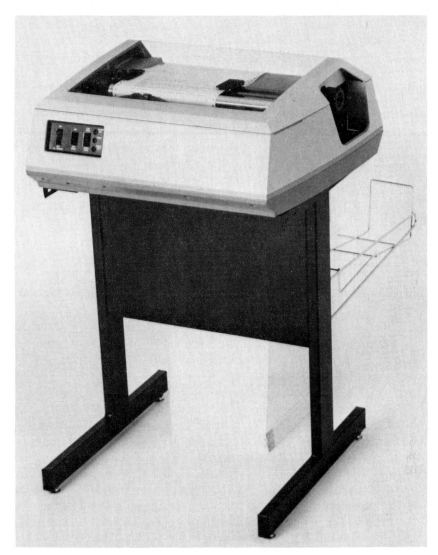

FIGURE 4-22   Character printer. (Photo courtesy of Mannesmann Tally.)

Some advanced printers are so fast (5,000 to 20,000 lines per minute) that they have been described as *page printers*, although they may still print only one character or line at a time. These speeds are necessary in high-volume operations where output bottlenecks may be just as troublesome as the input bottlenecks discussed earlier. Page printers use ink jet, laser, or electrostatic processes to avoid the mechanical action that limits other printers. Because the printer hardware does not physically touch the paper in these printers, they are also called *nonimpact* printers to distinguish them further from line printers, which typically use *impact* processes. A page printer that uses laser technology is shown in Figure 4-24.

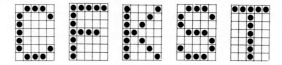

5-by 7 Uppercase Letters

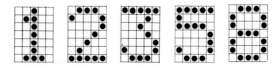

5-by-7 Numerals

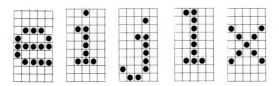

5-by-9 Lowercase Letters

FIGURE 4-23   Dot matrix characters.

Terminals

It was noted earlier that many terminals are also output devices. *Typewriter* terminals may use an electric typewriter-style ball or a wire-dot matrix to strike through a ribbon, although some ribbonless typewriter terminals heat the wires in the matrix to form characters on special heat-sensitive paper. Typewriter terminals print one character at a time and have print speeds similar to those of character printers.

CRT terminals have small television-like screens instead of typewriter mechanisms. CRT terminals are faster (250 to 5,000 characters per second) but do not leave the user with a hard copy of the output. CRT terminals are also better than typewriter terminals for graphic displays. Graphics can even be modified on some CRT terminals through the use of a *light pen*, shown in Figure 4-25, which can "erase" and originate lines on the CRT display. And some terminals, like the one shown in Figure 4-26, combine the features of CRT and typewriter terminals by including a limited print capability— usually just what is shown on the screen at the time of printing.

Even though the upper limits of output speeds on a CRT terminal are quite high, terminals should be used only for limited volumes of input and/or output. There are more efficient devices for high volumes, and in many systems, these other devices can be activated from a terminal, which has the additional benefit of making the terminal available for other use.

FIGURE 4-24 Laser page printer. (Photo courtesy of Datagraphix, Inc.)

Cardpunch

There are not many card-oriented applications remaining in CBIS, but when they do occur, there may also be a requirement of producing output in the form of punched cards. The device to produce this output is called a *cardpunch* (not to be confused with the *keypunch*, an off-line data preparation device). A cardpunch can turn out between 80 and 650 cards per minute, depending on the model and the number of columns used per card.

Other Output Devices

The focus on output devices thus far has been on those that produce documents or other output readable by humans. A great deal of computer output goes directly into storage and is never seen by humans. For example, master files and data bases are almost never printed in their entirety; they are

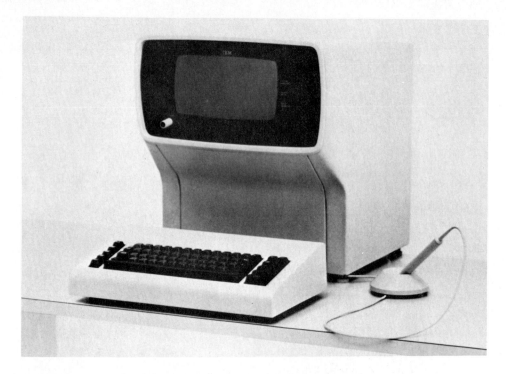

FIGURE 4-25 CRT terminal with light pen. (Photo courtesy of the IBM Corporation.)

maintained in external storage as the basis for further processing. When output goes directly to storage, the storage device itself is also the output device. Any on-line storage device, such as the tape drive or the disk drive described earlier, can serve as an output device. Output speeds for these external storage devices are approximately the same as their respective input speeds.

Considerations in Selecting an Output Device

Computer systems serving CBIS have a variety of output devices to satisfy the different needs of the many functional applications found in modern information systems. The characteristics to be considered when one is selecting an appropriate mix of such devices—cost, speed, and the nature of the applications—are summarized for the most common output devices in Table 4-2.

Data Communications

One of the more interesting recent trends in computer hardware is the increased use of data communications to link widely separated hardware components. It is now quite common for input and output devices, particu-

FIGURE 4-26 CRT terminal with print capability. (Photo courtesy of Hewlett-Packard.)

larly terminals, to be located some distance from the CPU. For short distances (say, within the same building), terminals may be connected directly to the CPU simply by the use of longer cabling. In this case, data to and from the terminal are transmitted in the same digital form used within the CPU.

For greater distances, it is usually better to convert digital data to another form for ease of transmission. When the communications channel is a telephone line, a *modem* (for *modulator/demodulator*) at the terminal converts the binary pulses of the digital code to an audio frequency that can be transmitted over telephone lines. A standard telephone handset may be fitted into the modem for this purpose. Because only a narrow frequency band is needed to code a binary signal, there is sufficient space in the tele-

TABLE 4-2   Computer Output Devices

Device	Characteristics	Applications
Character printer	Low cost, slow speed, limited capabilities	Small business, microcomputers
Line printer	Medium cost, high speed, very versatile	High volume hard copy output, report generation
Page printer	High cost, very high speed, very high quality output	Very high volume; personalized documents to customers, stockholders, etc.
Terminals	Low cost, very slow speed, limited volume	Real-time processing, management queries
Cardpunch	Low cost, slow speed, inconvenient medium	Card-only systems such as payroll or billing

phone frequency range to accommodate a number of channels on one line. At the CPU end of the channel, a second modem converts the audio signal back to binary pulses, and the communications link is completed.

The audio signal produced by a modem is an *analog* of digital data; that is, it is analogous to, but not exactly the same as, digital data. A system developed by Bell Telephone, DDS (for *dataphone digital service*), permits the direct transmission of digital data, without the use of modems, between selected cities in the United States. Maximum transmission rates over DDS are about six times faster than over regular telephone lines (56,000 bits per second compared with 9,600 bits per second), but DDS is somewhat limited in scope and is more expensive than regular telephone use.

Data can also be communicated over other channels. Microwave transmission uses a radio frequency analog of digital data. However, microwaves are "line-of-sight" and require frequent relay stations to follow the curvature of the earth. This drawback of microwave communication has been alleviated somewhat through the use of satellites, which require only a few retransmissions to achieve intercontinental distances.

Even more promising than microwave transmission are the experiments using light analogs of the digital data. Both visible and infrared light can be used as communications channels. Light has great speed, but it, too, is line-of-sight and is subject to weather conditions, although these disadvantages can be overcome by transmitting the light signals through extremely fine glass fibers.

Distributed Systems

Input and output devices are not the only computer hardware with data communications capabilities. CPUs can also be linked together. Two or more CPUs joined by data communications networks form what is called a *distributed system*. Figure 4-27 shows two different types of distributed systems.

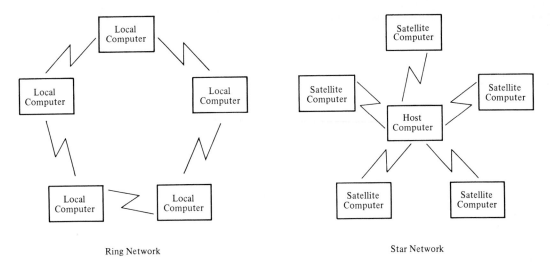

Ring Network   Star Network

FIGURE 4-27 Distributed systems.

A *star system* has a large *host computer* connected to smaller computers known as *satellites* (not to be confused with the *space* satellites used in microwave retransmission). Data communication is possible between any two computers in a star system by going through the host computer, but the communications network is predicated on the assumption that most communication will be between the host and its satellites.

Star systems often reflect organizational structure, with the host at the company headquarters and the satellites at branch locations. Centralized applications, such as financial planning and market analysis, are performed on the host computer, but the satellites can draw on the programs and files for local applications in those areas. Similarly, the files of branch applications in production sheduling, inventory management, or other local concerns can be tapped by the host computer for organization-wide analyses.

A *ring system* has no host computer. Instead, each CPU in the system is linked to its neighbors. Ring systems are common in very homogeneous organizations, such as banks, where a number of branches have identical computing requirements. In a ring system, each computer maintains a share of the files and programs, which can be made available to any other computer. In the banking example, each branch maintains files for its own customers, but a customer can initiate a transaction from any branch. Some ring systems can also link CPUs to create the effect of a single larger computer for certain applications.

Hardware Classification

No discussion of computer hardware is complete without some discussion on the classification of computers according to their cost and capabilities. At one time, computers were classified by *scale:* large, medium, and small. The lines between classes never were very distinct, and they are less so now. Today it is more common to speak of *microcomputers, minicomputers, mainframes,* and *supercomputers.* The lines between these classes are also somewhat blurred and change constantly as computer manufacturers package more and

TABLE 4-3   Classification of Computers

Common Name	CPU Storage (Bytes)	Cost	Characteristics	Examples
Microcomputer*	64K to 1M	$500 to $10,000	Desktop size, slow operating speeds, limited peripherals and applications, BASIC programming, home and small-business use	Apple IIe, Macintosh IBM PC Tandy 2000
Minicomputer*	256K to 8M	$10,000 to $500,000	Desksize; medium operating speeds; broad range of peripherals, applications, and programming languages; data processing in small businesses; ring-distributed processing	HP 3000 IBM System 34, 36, 38 VAX 11/782, 11/785
Mainframe	2M to 16M	$250,000 to $5,000,000	Room size; high operating speeds; full range of peripherals, applications, and programming languages; multiprogramming; multiprocessing; data base management systems; host computer in star-distributed systems; government and large-business use	Amdahl 470 Control Data Cyber 170 IBM-Model 200,3033
Supercomputer	32M to 2,000M	$5,000,000 to $25,000,000	Similar to mainframe, but with extremely high operating speeds	Control Data Cyber 205 Cray X-MP, 2

*Some extreme examples of micro- and minicomputers were not considered in compiling this table to avoid distortion of the data.
Source: *Data Sources,* Ziff-Davis Publishing Company, January, 1985.

more computational power into smaller and smaller machines. Nonetheless, because CBIS users and other managers frequently encounter computer classification terms, a rough classification guide is presented in Table 4-3 and the following paragraphs.

Microcomputers

Microcomputers are also known as *personal* computers—not so much because they are personally *owned*, although many are, but because they are used in personal tasks. These personal tasks may be in the home—correspondence, budgeting, record keeping, and recreation—or in the office—data analysis, report writing, and file maintenance.

Microcomputers typically are used with one or more disk drives, a video-display monitor, and a dot matrix printer. Internally, the microprocessor that forms the heart of the microcomputer uses 8-, 16-, or 32-bit words. Greater word length generally produces faster processing times. The Apple II computers use an 8-bit processor, the Motorola 6502; the IBM PCs use a 16-bit processor, the Intel 8088; and the Apple Macintosh uses a 32-bit processor, the Motorola 68000. An Apple IIc microcomputer is shown in Figure 4-28.

Microcomputers have between 64K and 1M bytes of internal storage and may cost as little as $500. A complete system with the peripherals just mentioned may cost between $1,500 and $5,000, or up to $10,000 with a letter-quality printer and hard-disk drive.

A new class of microcomputers that seems to defy these standards is called *supermicros* or *high-end micros*. These machines usually employ 32-bit microprocessors and can have as much as 16M bytes of internal storage. They frequently are networked to accommodate many users who wish to share software or data. Supermicros compete with minicomputers in terms of processing power but trade some of the versatility and networking capability of minis for the lower cost achieved by using the standard components commonly found in microcomputers. The use of standard components also facilitates the use of proprietory operating systems and software packages. The Hewlett-Packard HP 9000, with up to 2.5M bytes, Ethernet networking capability, and a price in the $25,000 range, is typical of the new class of supermicros.

Minicomputers

Minicomputers tend to use 12-, 16-, or 24-bit words in processing and rarely have more than a 2M-byte internal storage capability. They are very popular in small business applications or as remote processors in a distributed network. The cost of a typical minicomputer installation, with a line printer and disk drive, is around $25,000.

As with microcomputers, there are also *high-end* minicomputers (other, non-high-end minis are sometimes called *traditional* to distinguish them

FIGURE 4-28   An Apple IIc microcomputer. (Photo courtesy of Apple Computer.)

from their larger, more powerful siblings). High-end minis use 32-bit or even 64-bit processors and may have as much as 16M bytes of internal storage. High-end minis are more like mainframe computers, especially in their capacity to support a large number—96 or more—of remote users. This latter capability makes high-end minis, such as the Digital Equipment Corporation VAX 11/785, very popular for academic computing centers in colleges and universities. An IBM System 34 minicomputer is shown in Figure 4-29.

Mainframe Computers

Mainframe computers are the mainstay of corporate computing. They generally use 32-bit or higher processors and can support many peripheral devices—disk drives, tape drives, printers, terminals, and, when used as the host computer in a star-distributed network, other computers. Mainframe computers are characterized by very high processing speeds—up to 25 million instructions per second (MIPS). The great range of capabilities of main-

FIGURE 4-29 IBM System 34 minicomputer. (Photo courtesy of the IBM Corporation.)

frame computers makes it difficult to describe a "typical" system, but an IBM Model 3033 system would cost between $1.5 and $2 million. Figure 4-30 shows an IBM Model 200 mainframe computer.

Supercomputers

The "high-end" mainframe computers are so unique that they are generally considered in a class by themselves and are called *supercomputers*. There are only a few manufacturers of supercomputers, and they all use 64-bit processors and are capable of up to 32M bytes of internal storage. It is the extraordinary processing speed, however—up to 1,200 MIPS for the new Cray 2—that distinguishes supercomputers from ordinary mainframe computers. Very few applications have need of such speed, but you might be surprised to learn of those that do. Computer-generated graphics, such as those found in the movie *Tron*, require hundreds of thousands of computations per frame. Since motion pictures are run at 64 or more frames per second, it is easy to see how the graphics would fall behind in an ordinary computer. Hollywood, consequently, has become one of the principal users of supercomputers. At the other end of the intellectual and geographic spectrum, some scientific research also has need for such speed, and approxi-

FIGURE 4-30   IBM Model 200 "Sierra" mainframe computer.

mately ten universities now have supercomputers. Supercomputers are also used by the U.S. Department of Defense, the U.S. Weather Service, and NASA. A Cray 1 supercomputer is shown in Figure 4-31.

Summary

Computers have *hardware* and *software* components. Hardware components are further classified as the *central processing unit, input devices, output devices,* and devices for *external storage.*

The central processing unit consists of the *arithmetic and logic unit,* the *control unit,* and *internal storage.* External storage is most commonly on *cards, tape,* or *disks.* These three media are input through *card readers, tape drives,* and *disk drives,* respectively. Tape and disk drives are also output devices, and cards are output through a *cardpunch. Printers* and *terminals* provide output readable by humans; terminals also double as input devices.

External storage devices are classified as *sequential access* or *direct access.* Sequential access devices read data in the order in which they are stored; direct access devices can read in any order. Additionally, external storage devices are said to be *on-line* when they are directly accessible by the CPU and *off-line* when they are not.

Computers are classified as *microcomputers, minicomputers, mainframes,* or *supercomputers.* Micros are found in homes, in businesses, and as personal computers in professions such as engineering and education. Minis are used in distributed systems or in medium-sized businesses. Mainframes

FIGURE 4-31   Cray-1 supercomputer. (Photo courtesy of Cray Research, Inc.)

are found typically in large organizations, and supercomputers are appropriate for research and other high-speed applications.

Assignments

4-1. The popular hand-held calculator is an extreme example of a microcomputer. Identify the major components of a computer as they may exist in a calculator. Are any missing? What effect do the missing components have on the usefulness of your calculator?

4-2. External storage devices were classified as sequential access or direct access, but no reference was made to the method of accessing internal storage. Do you think internal storage is direct or sequential? Why?

4-3. It is recommended that punched cards be verified by someone other than the person who punched them. Why might this be important?

4-4. Special-purpose terminals are becoming increasingly popular in retail operations such as fast-food restaurants. Can you cite an example of such usage? What are the advantages and disadvantages of such terminals?

4-5. Identify the type of computer (micro, mini, mainframe, or super) and the configuration (stand-alone or distributed processing) you feel is appropriate for the following:

    a. A chain of discount stores.
    b. The Internal Revenue Service.
    c. The National Severe Weather Alert Center.
    d. The authors of this textbook.
    e. The registrar at a medium-sized college.
    f. A small tax accounting firm.
    g. Your own use.

4-6. The evolution of storage media has progressed from cards to tape to disk and now, possibly, to magnetic bubbles or other exotic devices. Other than the obvious technological advances, can you explain why the evolution followed these steps?

CASE   Hill Manufacturing—Part II

Preparations are continuing for the installation of the new MRP system at Hill Manufacturing Company. The topic of this afternoon's meeting is the shop flow-control subsystem. This subsystem manages the shop-floor orders that are output from the MPR "parts explosion" as they move throughout the factory. It enables the firm to keep track of the location of special orders and the amount of work completed at each work station. It also reports all of the unplanned complications that are an ordinary part of the typical work day, such as the breakdown of machinery, the absenteeism of workers, and the loss of parts or raw materials. These reports allow the managers to establish priorities and to make appropriate changes in schedules for the next day and beyond.

There are three options under consideration to provide feedback from the shop floor:

1. Each employee has a worksheet on which he or she records the order number being worked on, the time of beginning and ending work on that order, and the number of parts or raw materials used. At the end of each work shift, the worksheets are collected from the employees and are taken to the data processing department. Here

the data are put on magnetic tape and read into the computer to update the appropriate files and to generate the appropriate reports.

2. When each order is released to the shop, a set of punched cards is made that accompanies the order throughout its route. There is one card per operation. When an employee finishes working on a particular order, he or she removes the appropriate card from the envelope and adds information regarding how long the job took and how many materials were used. At the end of the work shift, the cards are collected and read into the computer to update the files and to generate reports.

3. Each work station has its own portable terminal, which is linked to the firm's main computer. As the employee finishes each job, he or she types the pertinent information onto the terminal in order to update files and generate reports.

Questions

1. For each of these options, what computer hardware would be required?

2. What advantages and disadvantages would each of the options present? Include in your discussion accuracy of information and worker reaction to each option.

3. What other options might be considered for collecting and inputting the data?

4. What factors or criteria should be used in making this decision?

Other Readings

Data Sources, published quarterly by Ziff-Davis Publishing Company. New York.

Elliot, David J. *Integrated Circuit Fabrication Technology.* New York: McGraw-Hill, 1982.

Leeson, Marjorie M. *Computer Information: A Modular System.* Chicago: Science Research Associates, 1985.

Schadewald, Robert. "Devices That Count." *Technology Illustrated* (October/November 1981).

Turn, Rein. *Computers in the 1980s.* New York: Columbia University Press, 1974.

Unger, E. A., and Ahmed Nasir. *Computer Science Fundamentals.* Columbus, Ohio: Charles E. Merrill, 1979.

Recent issues of the following journals: *Computer World, Datamation, Data Management, Data Processor.*

Chapter 5

Computer Software

Learning Objectives

After studying this chapter, you will be able to:

1. Distinguish between systems and application software.
2. Identify the four generations of computer languages.
3. Understand the capabilities of packaged software.
4. Define the following terms:

systems software	Ada
application software	APL
operating system	BASIC
programming language	COBOL
transparent (operation)	FORTRAN
control programs	Pascal
service programs	PL/1
logic errors	GPSS
syntax errors	RPG
machine language	fourth generation (language)
assembler language	multiprogramming
high-level language	multiprocessing
language translator	personal computing
macroinstruction	word processing
compiled (language)	spreadsheet
interpreted (language)	DBMS
source program	filing system
object program	integrated package
procedure-oriented (language)	windowing
problem-oriented (language)	

In Chapter 4, we noted that a computer system includes both hardware and software and that software consists of the coded instructions that direct the operation of the hardware. In this chapter, we shall take a closer look at the software component of a computer system.

Software can be divided into two broad categories: *systems software* and *application software*. Systems software is oriented to the general control of computer hardware components, whereas application software contains specific instructions for the transformation of data. The classification of software into these two major categories and further subdivisions is shown in Figure 5-1 and discussed in the following sections.

Systems Software

The purpose of systems software is to simplify the control of a computer. Systems software functions as an intermediary between the application programmer or user, who communicates in words and numbers, and the computer, which responds to electrical impulses. In order to control a computer, two different kinds of systems software are needed—an *operating system* and a *programming language*. Other systems capabilities, such as *time sharing* or *data communications*, also may be required, depending on the application and the hardware configuration. Let us look at these components of systems software more closely.

Operating Systems

Each different computer, or, in the case of microcomputers, each different microprocessor, requires a unique set of binary codes to make it function. Operating systems convert more or less standard instructions into these unique codes to make the operation *transparent* to the programmer or user. That is, the programmer or user is unaware of the peculiar requirements of the computer. For example, *Control Program/Microcomputers* (CP/M) is a popular microcomputer operating system. You may purchase CP/M for an Apple IIe or for a Tandy TRS-80 Model 4. Although these two microcomputers use different microprocessors, an application program written for CP/M will run on either machine. The Apple CP/M will translate the application program into a code understood by its 6502 microprocessor, and the Tandy CP/M will translate the same program into a code understood by its Z80A microprocessor. The compatibility problem is not quite as simple as this example might indicate, however, since there are often several versions of an operating system.

The purpose of an operating system is to make the job of the application-software programmer easier. This is especially evident in the one function of operating systems just discussed—that of translating application programs

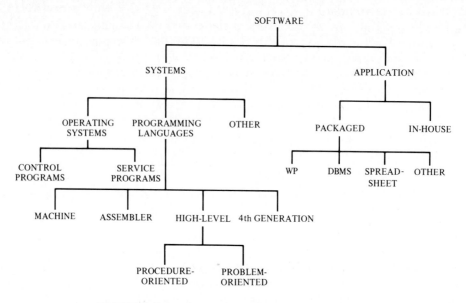

FIGURE 5-1 Computer software classification.

into binary code. The operating system also includes programs that relieve programmers of the responsibility of including routine, repetitive, or purely "housekeeping" functions in application programs. *Control programs* and *service programs* are two types of such systems software.

Control Programs

Control programs manage the input, output, and storage of data required by application programs. These programs are concerned with the actual physical location of data as well as with the logical and hierarchical relationships (data elements, records, and files) that determine the organization of data in storage. Control programs schedule input and output according to assigned priorities or standing instructions. They also maintain logs on the machine and peripheral time required for various applications and/or accounts. This latter function is especially important when the computer center is operated as a profit center and must "bill" other departments for services rendered. Control programs account for one-third to one-half of the processing required for a typical business application.

Service Programs

Service programs provide commonly used routines that might otherwise have to be included in the application software. For example, it is often necessary to sort data according to alphabetical or numerical sequence or to merge two sorted data sets into a single sequential list. Many operating systems permit the application programmer to call up a service program to perform these tasks with only one or two statements.

There are also service programs in operating systems to reformat data for a different medium (e.g., from tape to disk) and to detect errors in application programs. System software can detect only *syntax* errors—misspellings, incomplete statements, and other violations of programming rules. It cannot detect *logical* errors—programming statements that follow all the rules but have not been used in a manner that will produce the desired output.

Programming Languages

It has already been noted that systems software provides an interface between the words and numbers used by programmers and the binary code used by the computer. The systematic set of procedures and rules governing the use of such words and numbers is called a *programming language*. Programming languages are classified as *machine, assembler,* or *high-level.* These classes are also called *first, second,* and *third generation,* respectively, to acknowledge both their relative age and sophistication. In this vein, some recent, very sophisticated high-level languages are called *fourth generation* in recognition of the advances they represent over other, third-generation, high-level languages.

Machine Languages

The first generation of computer languages is called *machine language* because they use the binary code—1's and 0's—understood directly by the computer and do not, in fact, require the services of an operating system. Machine language instructions are typically in two 4- and 5-bit parts: an *operation code*, which tells what is to be done, and an *operand*, which tells where to store the results. For example, a machine language code to "store a value called X in register 11011" might be written 1100 11011. Although, technically speaking, machine languages are in binary code, most computers accept the decimal (base 10) or hexadecimal (base 16) equivalents of these codes. Languages using nonbinary equivalents are still referred to as machine languages.

Every computer has its own more or less unique machine language, which is determined by the ALU circuitry. All computers ultimately operate in machine language, but almost none still require the programmer to use one. Instead, system software translates other, easier-to-use languages into machine language.

Assembler Languages

The second generation of computer languages freed the programmer from the tedious, error-prone binary instructions and was the first to require an operating system. This generation is called *assembler,* or sometimes, *symbolic languages.* Assembler languages substitute short alphabetic expressions for the operation code. For example, ADD X means "add the variable previously defined as X to the value currently stored in an accumulator register."

Although not strictly a machine language, most assembler languages are nonetheless machine-oriented. That is, each computer has unique assembler language symbolic expressions that correspond to machine language instructions on a one-to-one basis. A portion of the operating system known as a *language translator* performs the conversion of symbolic instructions into machine language instructions.

Some assembler languages use *macroinstructions* that generate two or more machine language instructions from a single assembler language statement. For example, the macroinstruction ADD A, B, C, which means, "add the variable A to the variable B and call the result C," replaces three simple instructions to load A into a register, add B to it, and store the result.

Assembler languages trade ease of programming for greater efficiency in execution. They are most appropriate when program operations are simple, but the volume of data may require long processing times. A knowledge of assembler languages also enhances one's understanding of high-level languages. Many CBIS curricula require an assembly language course for this reason.

An exception to the general rule of unique assembler languages is found in the very recent (1983) language C. The C language is sometimes described as a "portable" assembler language because there are versions of it available for many computers, from micros to supercomputers. C is a very powerful language used most often by systems programmers for writing systems software or by application programmers in very specialized applications, such as computer-generated animation in motion pictures, where the speed of processing is more important than the ease of programming.

High-Level Languages

The third generation of computer languages is called *high-level* and was the first to free programmers from specific hardware requirements, although there were (and often still are) minor differences in high-level languages among the various makes and models of computers.

High level languages use English-like statements to code instructions. Each statement requires many, possibly hundreds, of machine language instructions. A statement such as IF (HOURS.GT.40.0) GO TO 180, which means, "if the value of a variable called HOURS is greater than 40, program statement number 180 should be executed next," involves the evaluation of a variable, a logical comparison, a move within the program, and the execution of statement number 180 and all those that follow. The conversion of high-level programs into the appropriate machine language instructions may be accomplished in one of two ways: They may be *compiled* or *interpreted*.

In compiling, the high-level or *source* program is translated in its entirety into a machine language or *object* program prior to execution. Interpreters translate and execute one program statement at a time. Until recently, most high-level languages were compiled for more efficient use of CPU time. Now, however, the extremely high speeds of the latest computer hardware and certain inherent advantages to interpreting have spurred a renewed interest in interpretive languages. Many fourth-generation languages are of the interpretive variety.

High-level languages may also be classified as *procedure-oriented* or *problem-oriented.*

Procedure-Oriented Languages Most third-generation, high-level languages are *procedure-oriented;* that is, they are designed to apply certain fixed procedures to the appropriate data. For example, the BASIC instructions FOR I = 1 to N . . . NEXT I will perform the operations specified between the two instructions to the first through the Nth value of some variable. Some of the more popular procedure-oriented languages are described here and summarized in Table 5-1.

Ada Named after Ada Augusta, the Countess of Lovelace, who assisted Charles Babbage in the development of early computing devices and who is considered to have been the first programmer, Ada was developed under the direction of the Department of Defense as a potential replacement for COBOL. Ada has not gained the expected popularity, however, and only a few Defense agencies, notably those in the U.S. Navy, have adopted Ada. The mathematical and scientific capabilities of Ada are very good, but it is less adept at handling typical business functions involving data management and report generation.

TABLE 5-1 Procedure-Oriented Languages

Language	Type	Strengths	Weaknesses	Extent of Use
Ada	Compiler	Mathematical, scientific applications	Data management	Very limited
APL	Compiler	Data retrieval	Requires special keyboard	Primarily IBM users
BASIC	Compiler/ interpreter	Easy to learn, good mathematical capabilities	Not standardized	Widespread among micro users
COBOL	Compiler	Data management, report generation	Mathematical capabilities	Widespread, business mainframes
FORTRAN	Compiler	Mathematical, scientific capabilities	Data management	Widespread, business and research
Pascal	Compiler	Mathematical, scientific capabilities	Limited to smaller computers	Moderate, science and education
PL/1	Compiler	General purpose	Few non-IBM versions	Primarily IBM users

APL   *A Programming Language* (APL) is an interactive language developed at Harvard and introduced by IBM in the late 1960s. Although APL is a third-generation language, it gave an indication of some of the developments that were to come in fourth-generation languages, in this case, specialization to make certain tasks very easy. Unfortunately, the task that APL does very well—data retrieval—requires special keys that are not found on every keyboard. Partially for this reason, and perhaps also because APL did not represent a sufficient improvement over COBOL to warrant the change, APL has not achieved the success it might have.

BASIC   The *Beginner's All-Purpose Symbolic Instruction Code* (BASIC) was developed in the early 1960s by John Kemeny as a simple language suitable for use by college students (not that college students are unable to understand more complex languages, but because the learning of the language was thought to be subordinate to its use in other academic endeavors). BASIC is not a standardized language; that is, there is no single, universally accepted version of BASIC. There is an American National Standards Institute (ANSI) version of BASIC, which contains certain minimum features found in almost every other version, but most versions of BASIC go well beyond the ANSI standards.

Computer manufacturers either use an available version of BASIC or develop their own version. For example, there are versions of Microsoft BASIC available for the Apple Macintosh, IBM PC and PC compatibles, and computers that use the CP/M, MSDOS, and XENIX operating systems. Microsoft BASIC is also available in both compiler and interpreter versions. Apple is an example of a company that has written its own version of BASIC, Applesoft, which is built into the operating system of the Apple II series of microcomputers.

BASIC is by far the most widely used language to program microcomputers. It is both simple and powerful. The success of BASIC in microcomputers and the renewed interest in interpretive languages has led to the development of even more powerful, mainframe versions of BASIC. These advanced versions of BASIC have mathematical capabilities comparable to those of FORTRAN as well as excellent file management capabilities. With the apparent failure of Ada as the next universal business programming language, there is some speculation in the computer industry that this mantle may fall to BASIC.

COBOL   The *Common Business-Oriented Language* (COBOL) was developed by the Conference on Data Systems Languages (CODASYL)—a committee of representatives from business, government, and computer manufacturers gathered under the leadership of the U.S. Department of Defense—in the early 1960s. COBOL quickly became an industry standard when the Defense Department, then the largest single user of computer equipment in the world, announced it would purchase only computers with a COBOL capability. COBOL is by far the most popular language for programming mainframe computers for business applications. Unlike BASIC, there *is* a standard version of COBOL, so that a COBOL program written for one computer will (perhaps with a few minor modifications) run on another computer. Although the major features of COBOL are now 25 years old, there have been revisions. The most recent revision occurred in 1981, giving rise to the version called, logically enough, COBOL-81.

COBOL has excellent file management capabilities and was extremely well suited to early DP and MIS applications, which featured transaction processing and report generation. COBOL is less well suited to the data-analysis tasks typical of contemporary MIS and DSS. COBOL is also very much a programmers' language. Its tedious rules and lack of an interactive capability make COBOL inappropriate for users. These are precisely the shortcomings information systems professionals hope to overcome in fourth-generation languages.

FORTRAN The *FORmula TRANslation* language (FORTRAN) was the first high-level language. It was introduced in the mid-1950s and quickly became the standard for scientific programming—a position it still holds. Since FORTRAN is not very effective at handling alphabetic data, it initially found little use in business applications. As data analysis became more common in MIS, however, FORTRAN gained in popularity among business users. Although information systems professionals have long sought a single, multipurpose language to manage both numerical and alphabetic data, most CBIS today will have some COBOL programs for file management and report generation and some FORTRAN programs for data analysis. Like COBOL, FORTRAN has been standardized and periodically revised. The early revisions carried Roman numerals, but the most recent, FORTRAN-77, reflects the year of revision.

Pascal Pascal is named after the seventeenth-century mathematician, Blaise Pascal, who, in 1642, developed a mechanical calculator that is frequently mentioned as one of the precursors of computers. Since its introduction in the early 1970s, Pascal has become the second most popular (next to BASIC) language for programming microcomputers and is frequently found in college-level computer science curricula. The mathematical abilities of Pascal are somewhat superior to BASIC, and its file-handling capabilities are better than those of FORTRAN. The multipurpose nature of Pascal makes it very attractive as a general-purpose business language. In this respect, Pascal is to microcomputers what Ada was to have been to mainframes. Pascal compilers are available for all but the smaller microcomputers, including the various models of Apples, IBM PCs, and the larger Tandy micros.

PL/1 Perhaps the most successful attempt to combine mathematical and data management capabilities, *Programming Language One* (PL/1), was developed by IBM and introduced in the mid-1960s. PL/1 is often described as a blend of COBOL and FORTRAN. However, in spite of the enormous popularity of IBM hardware and the apparent demand for a multipurpose programming language, the use of PL/1 remains restricted to a small core of IBM users.

Problem-Oriented Languages Problem-oriented languages are created with a specific type of task or problem in mind. Although these languages are somewhat less versatile than procedure-oriented languages, they are very convenient for programming the types of applications for which they were designed. Two third-generation problem-oriented languages are described here.

    GPSS The *General Purpose System Simulator* (GPSS) is used to simulate the behavior of queuing (waiting line) systems. Although this sounds like a very narrow range of applications, many business functions—inventory, cash flow, and production processes, as well as the classic waiting lines found in banks and grocery stores—can be described as queues and simulated with GPSS. Simulation, which is described in greater detail in Chapter 7, is a very powerful management science tool used extensively in decision support systems. Features of GPSS that make it attractive for business applications include automatic time advance, data collection, statistical analyses, graphics, and report generation.

    RPG The *Report Program Generator* (RPG) was introduced by IBM in the mid-1960s and quickly became popular among small business users. Although RPG is not very efficient in mathematical operations, it is very convenient to use for its designed purpose of systematically updating files and producing formatted reports. There are not many versions of RPG available for non-IBM computers, but there are more than enough IBM computers—especially the Systems 3, 34, 36, and 38—currently using RPG to make it one of the most common minicomputer languages. The most recent version of RPG, RPG III, is especially well suited for time-sharing and, when used with a computer such as the IBM System 38, a data base management system environment.

Fourth-Generation Languages

There is a tradeoff, shown in Figure 5-2, between application programming and systems programming and, to a lesser extent, hardware. Systems programming and hardware circuitry can be minimized if one is willing to place the full software burden on the application programmer. Early computers did just that. Programmers worked directly in binary-coded machine languages without the benefit of systems software. Whatever control or service program requirements existed were incorporated directly into the application program. Needless to say, application programmers had to be highly skilled and intimately familiar with the computers they programmed. They were also hard to find, but as there were not many computers about, this did not

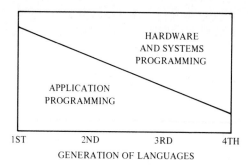

FIGURE 5-2 Distribution of programming effort.

present much of a problem. There was never any thought given to the possibility that a manager or other nonprogrammer might use a computer directly.

As computers proliferated, it became apparent that programming had to be simplified. Assembler languages satisfied this requirement to some degree, but their machine orientation still presented problems in training and retraining programmers as hardware was upgraded or programmers changed jobs.

Third-generation languages such as COBOL and FORTRAN made programming easier and allowed applications to be moved from one machine to another with only minor modifications. In general, however, these languages were used by professional programmers for application development. Managers and other non-DP personnel rarely developed their own applications.

With the introduction of fourth-generation languages (and personal computers) there was a new phenomenon—hands-on application development by non-DP personnel. Fourth-generation languages are sufficiently easy to use that with just a little training and help, many end users can develop their own applications. This is referred to as *end user computing* and is one of the CBIS trends discussed in Chapter 19. This does not imply that *all* applications should be developed by end users. In many instances that would be inappropriate use of precious managerial and staff time. Rather, it suggests that *some* applications are appropriately developed by end users.

Fourth-generation languages are too new and too dissimilar for the kind of generalization used to describe the first, second, and third generations, but some patterns are emerging. Fourth-generation languages tend to be:

1. Faster than the third generation in the time required to write a program. Author and programming language expert James Martin uses a factor of 10 as a rule of thumb for the increase in speed over the third generation. Some so-called fourth-generation languages fall short by this criterion, but others, such as FOCUS, exceed it.
2. Interpretive. Compiled programs tend to be more efficient than interpreted programs when relatively short, simple operations are being

performed on large volumes of data—as they generally are in transaction processing with COBOL. When the data volume is small and the operations are long and complex, as they frequently are in decision support system applications, interpreted programs may be more efficient. Interpretive languages are often easier to debug and to extend by defining new words or functions.

3. Nonprocedural. Fourth-generation languages may permit the use of familiar English verbs, nouns, and modifiers, such as, "Tell me the names of all customers who have ordered J-79 robots."

4. Interactive. In the third example, there would follow an exchange between the computer and the user to confirm the correct interpretation of the request. The request may not be understood in its initial form, but at least a correct form will be reached in the ensuing dialog instead of leaving the user staring at a screen with the message "SYNTAX ERROR."

5. Oriented toward decision support functions, where nonprogrammers are more likely to be the users.

6. Inefficient in the use of computer resources. This is the price paid for "friendliness." The good news is that current technology is more than adequate for the support of fourth-generation languages and, in many cases, can run a program written in a fourth-generation language with less cost than a computer of 10 years ago could run a similar program written in a third-generation language.

7. Easy to learn. The rule of thumb here is that a nonprogrammer should be able to learn a fourth-generation language in two days. Contrast that with the time it took you or your classmates to learn COBOL!

8. Faster to program. An MIS developed for an agency of the U.S. Navy using FOCUS is reported to have used only 10 percent of the program statements and 20 percent of the programming time required for a comparable set of COBOL programs.

The introduction of fourth-generation languages may bring about some dramatic changes in the traditional relationships between user and information specialist. As it becomes more convenient for the user to develop his or her own applications, CBIS personnel will take on an advisory and planning role. There will still be many programming and analysis tasks—especially in transaction processing and management information systems—in which users will not be involved, but many users will prefer to do their own programming for selected applications. Organizations will also be forced to make critical decisions concerning the responsibility—budgeting, maintenance, revision, and so on—for user-developed systems. More is said on these organizational issues in Part VII.

The names of fourth-generation languages are as varied and exotic as the languages themselves: SAS (a statistical analysis language), FOCUS (a data retrieval language), IFPS (a financial modeling language discussed in Chapter 14), RENDEZVOUS (a conversational data retrieval language), PROLOG (an inferential, expert system language), as well as CUPID, FLORAL, SQUARE, COLINGO, and others.

Other Capabilities

System software can aid application programming in other ways. *Job processing* schedules application programs and the input–output devices to be used with each job. The application programmer provides input through statements in a special programming language called JCL (for *Job Control Language*). The operating system converts these statements to machine language for actual execution. JCL is also used to initiate and terminate processing, to specify the application language, and to identify the user for accounting purposes.

System software can also be used to achieve *time-sharing*—the processing of two or more programs concurrently. There are many ways of sharing time in the CPU: Statements in several programs can be run alternately; small increments of time can be allotted to programs on an alternating basis; programs can be assigned processing priorities; storage space can be partitioned to accommodate several programs; or some combination of these methods can be employed. Time-sharing is desirable because the CPU is so much faster than the input or output devices and the CPU is often idle during input and output. Time-sharing converts time idle with respect to one program into productive time for other programs. Time-sharing through software technique is called *multiprogramming* and should not be confused with the hardware technique of *multiprocessing*, in which the CPU is made to act like two or more units to permit the simultaneous execution of application programs.

Another powerful capability of system software is *virtual storage*. This term refers to the ability of an operating system to make CPU storage appear virtually unlimited by moving data back and forth between CPU storage and external storage with exceptional speed. Virtual storage enhances time-sharing and permits the use on small or medium-sized computers of programs that ordinarily would require a very large computer.

Application Software

Application software is usually referred to simply as *programs* or *code*. CBIS may use hundreds of different programs to process pay, maintain inventory records, schedule production, analyze sales, aid decision making, and otherwise support the managerial and operational activities in an organization. Application software may be developed uniquely for the using organization by *in-house* (or contractual) personnel or it may be purchased in ready-to-use *packages*.

In-House Development

Large organizations or those with unique applications often develop their own application software. In the case of a very large organization, the cost of revising, say, the accounts receivable system to conform to a standard package may be greater than the cost of developing software that conforms to the existing system. This situation often arises in student records and class registration applications, where standard packages are available, but the conversion process involves more effort than that required to write new application software.

Unique or nearly unique applications give the using organization little choice; the application programs must be developed in-house. The airline industry has a unique scheduling and reservation function, which airline companies have tended to develop and maintain themselves ever since the introduction of SABRE by American Airlines in the mid-1960s. This system has now been extended to other airlines, travel agencies, hotels, and other organizations with a reservation function. Major users still do their own application program development, however, using a special programming language called SABRETALK.

Packaged Software

At one time, in-house development was the normal approach to the automation of standard business applications. However, as competition in the computer industry grew, manufacturers began to offer application software and other services to make their products more attractive. And as the number of computer users grew, they soon constituted so large a market that "third-party" (other than the manufacturer or the user) firms found it profitable to develop and market application software. Today a user who wishes to purchase a software package can choose from among thousands of programs written for dozens of different application areas and virtually every make, model, and size of computer. Table 5-2 shows some of the categories of application software available for non-industry-specific functions; Table 5-3 shows a similar listing for industry-specific functions.

Microcomputer Packages

The advent of the microcomputer has accelerated the movement toward packaged software. Microcomputers are much more likely to be used by individuals or organizations who lack the skills and/or the inclination to develop their own software. Also, the number of microcomputers in use—there were over four million sales in 1984 alone—provides an attractive market for microcomputer software.

A small organization that uses a microcomputer-based information system has many of the same information needs as a large firm using a mainframe-based system, and it is not surprising to find microcomputer versions

TABLE 5-2 Non-Industry-Specific Application Software

Accounting	Marketing
Accounts payable	Direct marketing
Accounts receivable	Research and survey analysis
Billing/invoicing	Sales analysis/reporting
Costing	Office automation
Fixed assets	Electronic mail
General ledger	Personnel management
Payroll	Word processing
Tax preparation and reporting	Physical distribution
Facilities management	Distribution management
Energy management	Freight/trucking
Equipment maintenance	Inventory control
Financial analysis	Warehousing
Financial planning	Technical support/engineering
Forecasting and econometrics	Computer-aided design
Spreadsheets	Statistics and mathematics
Manufacturing	
Bill of materials	
Computer-aided manufacturing	
Material requirements	
Numerical control	
Process control	
Production control	
Purchasing	
Shop floor control	

Source: *Data Sources* (*Software*), Ziff-Davis Publishing Company, 1st Quarter, 1985.

of most of the applications listed in Tables 5-2 and 5-3. But microcomputers, both inside and outside of CBIS, are frequently used to support *personal* computing, which requires a somewhat different approach to packaging software.

Personal computing refers to the way a computer is used rather than to the nature of the task. That is, the task may well be a normal part of one's job, as it is when a bank loan officer makes a decision to grant a loan to a customer. If the loan officer actually operates a microcomputer in his or her workspace, enters data about the applicant, maintains records of the output, and bases the decision on the analysis performed by the micro, we would characterize the process as personal computing. In contrast, if the loan officer fills out a form and turns it over to the information systems office for processing, we would not call it personal computing. Of course, many home applications are personal in both respects; that is, they involve personal finances, correspondence, and entertainment or other similar subjects, as well as being performed personally by the user.

Much personal computing can be accomplished by one of three types of

TABLE 5-3   Industry-Specific Application Software

Agriculture	Insurance
Associations/membership	Agency management
organizations	Claims processing
Fund raising	Medical claims processing
Political/nonprofit organizations	Policy management
Religious organizations	Legal services
Banking/finance	Docket scheduling
Brokerage houses	Practice management
Credit and collections	Manufacturing/processing
Credit union management	Automotive
Deposits and accounts	Chemical
Electronic funds transfer	Food and beverage
General banking	Fuel distribution
Investment management	Lumber industries
Loans and mortgages	Metal industries
Communications/media	Petroleum and gas
Circulation/subscriptions	Printing and typesetting
Newspaper industry	Textiles and clothing
Publishing	Mining and minerals
Radio/TV/entertainment industry	Professional services
Telecommunications	Advertising and public relations
Construction/contractor management	CPA services
Education	Real estate and service industries
Administration	Employment agencies
Library services	Hotel/restaurant management
Student services	Recreational clubs and services
Government	Tickets and reservations
Law enforcement	Travel agencies
Social services	Trade
Health services	Import/export trade
Diagnosis/treatment	Retail trade
Hospital/nursing home	Wholesale trade/distributors
administration	Transportation industries
Laboratory systems	Utilities (Public)
Pharmacy management	
Practice management	

Source: *Data Sources* (*Software*), Ziff-Davis Publishing Company, 1st Quarter, 1985.

application software—*word processing, electronic spreadsheets,* or *data base management systems.* Many microcomputer software packages combine these and other functions into an integrated management package, such as Lotus 1-2-3, Lotus Symphony, Framework, Appleworks, and others. The three primary functions of microcomputer software are described here; examples of integrated packages are shown in Table 5-4.

TABLE 5-4   Integrated Software Packages

Product	Vendor	Functions	Compatibility	Approximate Price
Appleworks	Apple Computer	WP, ES, DB	Apple IIc, IIe	$250
Corporate MBA	Context Management Systems	WP, ES, DB, GR	IBM PC and compatibles	$375
Decision Manager	Peachtree Software	WP, ES, DB, GR	IBM PC and compatibles	$900
Framework	Ashton-Tate	WP, ES, DB, GR	IBM PC and compatibles	$700
Lotus 1-2-3	Lotus Development Corporation	ES, DB, GR	IBM PC and compatibles, DEC Rainbow, TI, Wang, Zenith, and others	$500
Lotus Symphony	Lotus Development Corporation	WP, ES, DB, GR, COMM	IBM PC and compatibles	$700
3-Plus-1	Commodore Business Machines	WP, ES, DB, GR	Commodore 64	$200

WP = Word processing
ES = Electronic spreadsheet
DB = Data base management
GR = Graphics
COMM = Data communications
Source: *Data Sources*, Ziff-Davis Publishing Co., 1st Qtr., 1985.

Word Processing   In its simplest form, word processing can be thought of as a method of typing in which the typist has the opportunity to view and correct a draft on a CRT screen before printing the final document. In more complete forms, word processing permits the user to move portions of the document to new locations, conduct "global" searches and corrections of errors, automatically insert footnotes, merge address files and text to generate form letters, print repetitious words or phrases with a single keystroke, and perform many other functions that reduce the workload and result in more attractive output.

Word processing is the single most popular microcomputer application (in terms of software *sales*—no one is quite sure how much various software packages are actually used *after* they are sold). In a recent monthly survey, the three top-selling software packages for Apple computers were all word processors, and for IBM personal computers, one was a pure word processor and the other two were integrated packages that included word processing.[1] Word-processing software for a microcomputer costs from $50 to $500 if

[1]*FutureViews*, Vol. 84-3, Future Computing, Inc.

purchased separately or from $200 to $900 if part of an integrated package. More is said on the specific capabilities of word processing in Chapter 12.

Electronic Spreadsheets   An electronic spreadsheet is a matrix of rows and columns in which the cells can be filled with text, numerical values, or formulas based on numerical values found in other cells. The largest spreadsheets, such as SMART, can accommodate up to 9,999 rows and 999 columns, although the 255 rows and 63 columns of *Multiplan* are more representative. Figure 5-3 shows a spreadsheet *template* based on the integrated package *Appleworks*. The example is that of a proforma cash-flow budget, greatly simplified to illustrate a few basic spreadsheet functions. The entries in this example are explained as follows:

Row 1. Labels, not subject to computation.
Row 2. Sales estimates, entered by the analyst as shown.
Row 3. Interest income of .85 percent per month times a starting amount of $35,000, thereafter times the amount available for investment (row 18).
Row 5. Total income is the row 2 value plus the row 3 value.
Row 8. Cost of goods is 25 percent of sales for this firm.
Row 9. The cost of labor is 10 percent of sales for this firm.
Row 10. A $100,000 loan payment is due in February.
Row 11. Interest on the loan is 1 percent per month.
Row 12. Overhead must be estimated by the analyst.
Row 14. Total expenses are the sum of rows 8 to 12.
Row 16. The net is total income minus total expenses.
Row 18. This function is interpreted as follows: If the value computed for C18 is positive, enter 35 (the starting cash balance) plus the net income from row 16; otherwise, enter 0. For subsequent months, 35 is replaced by the previous amount available for investment.
Row 20. If the amount available for investment in row 18 is negative, that amount must be borrowed.

A six-month projection using the spreadsheet just described is shown in Figure 5-4. The boxed values are those that were computed; the other values were entered by the analyst.

Spreadsheets became popular with the introduction of VisiCalc in 1979 and remain among the most widely used microcomputer software packages. It is now more common to purchase a spreadsheet as part of an integrated package rather than as a separate piece of software. Spreadsheet software for microcomputers costs from $100 to $500 if purchased separately or from $200 to $900 if part of an integrated package.

Data Base Management Systems   Data base management systems (DBMS) provide a means for organizing, storing, and retrieving data in formats and/or

```
File:    TEMPLATE                                                        Page   1

                A                              B                          C

  1    INCOME                                 JAN                        FEB
  2       SALES
  3       INTEREST                         35*.0085                  +B18*.0085
  4
  5       TOTAL                            +B2+B3                    +C2+C3
  6
  7    EXPENSES
  8       COST OF GOODS                    +B2*.25                   +C2*.25
  9       PAYROLL                          +B2*.10                   +C2*.10
 10       LOAN PAYMENT                                                 100.0
 11       LOAN INTEREST                    +C10*.01
 12       OVERHEAD
 13
 14       TOTAL                        @SUM(B8...B12)             @SUM(C8...C12)
 15
 16    NET                                 +B5-B14                   +C5-C14
 17
 18    AVAIL TO INVEST     @IF(35+B16)0,35+B16,0)    @IF(B18+C16)0,B18+C16,0)
 19
 20    NEED TO BORROW      @IF(35+B16<0,B16-35,0)    @IF(C18=0,-C16-B20,0)
```

```
File:    TEMPLATE

        . . .                                G

        . . .                               JUN

        . . .                            +F18*.0085

        . . .                            +G2+G3


        . . .                            +G2*.25
        . . .                            +G2*.10
        . . .
        . . .
        . . .

        . . .                         @SUM(G8...G12)

        . . .                            +G5-G14

    . . .  @IF(F18+G16)0,F18+G16,0)

        . . .              IF(G18=0,-G16-G20,0)
```

FIGURE 5-3 Template for cash-flow application.

categories specified by the user. DBMS for microcomputers are sometimes
referred to as *filing systems* to distinguish them from larger, more powerful
DBMS found on mainframe computers. Some microcomputer DBMS, such
as PC/FOCUS and dBASE III, bring full DBMS power to micros, but most
others, such as PFS-File and Quick File II, are more limited. The smaller
microcomputer DBMS can maintain at most a few thousand records with
perhaps twenty elements of data per record and cost from $100 to $400. The
DBMS portions of integrated packages have similar capabilities.

```
File:    CASH.FLOW                                                   Page   1
```

INCOME	JAN	FEB	MAR	APR	MAY	JUN
SALES	52.0	47.0	51.0	55.0	60.0	58.0
INTEREST	.3	.5	0.0	.2	.4	.7
TOTAL	52.3	47.5	51.0	55.2	60.4	58.7
EXPENSES						
COST OF GOODS	13.0	11.8	12.8	13.8	15.0	14.5
PAYROLL	5.2	4.7	5.1	5.5	6.0	5.8
LOAN PAYMENT		100.0				
LOAN INTEREST	1.0					
OVERHEAD	10.0	9.5	9.0	9.0	8.5	8.5
TOTAL	29.2	126.0	26.9	28.2	29.5	28.8
NET	23.1	-78.5	24.1	27.0	30.9	29.9
AVAIL TO INVEST	58.1	0.0	24.1	51.1	82.0	111.9
NEED TO BORROW	0.0	20.4	0.0	0.0	0.0	0.0

FIGURE 5-4 Cash-flow application on spreadsheet.

The larger microcomputer DBMS have truly enormous capacities—dBASE III is capable of up to 2 billion records per file and up to 10 files—but can become awkward to use without very large external storage devices such as Winchester drives. These DBMS cost from $700 to $1500 dollars and, although they are not found in integrated packages per se, many are designed to interface with the more popular integrated packages. Much more is said on the subject of DBMS in Chapter 6.

Integrated Packages   Software packages that incorporate two or more of the primary microcomputer applications are called *integrated* when there is a capability to use data from one application in a second or third application. For example, a customer file maintained in the DBMS portion of an integrated package could be used to furnish the names and addresses for a form letter prepared with the word-processing portion. Or the volume of sales to the various customers in the DBMS file could be tabulated by product and month of sale to use in a spreadsheet analysis of sales.

Many integrated packages permit the user to view the displays of several applications simultaneously through a process called *windowing*. Figure 5-5 shows the windows (clockwise from the upper left) of MacWrite (word processing), MacGraph (graphics), and MacCalc (electronic spreadsheet) as they appear on the Apple Macintosh XL. Integrated packages are quickly becoming the most popular form of personal-use microcomputer software, with Appleworks leading the way for the Apple II family and Lotus 1-2-3 and Lotus Symphony holding a similar position among IBM and IBM-compatible users. A windowed display of Lotus Symphony showing word processing

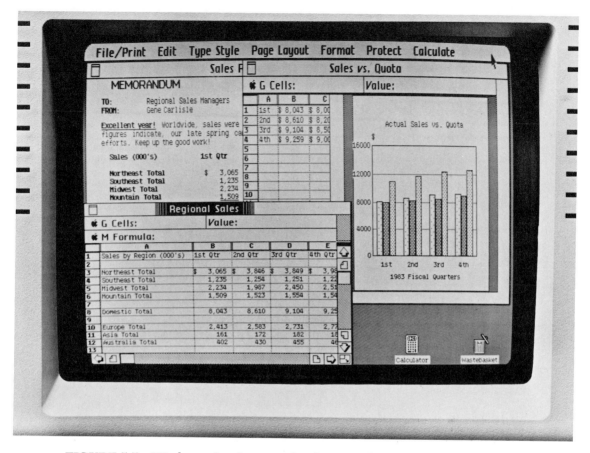

FIGURE 5-5 Windows of an Integrated Software Package for an Apple Microcomputer. (Photo courtesy of Apple Computer.)

(top), spreadsheets (lower left), and graphics (lower right) is pictured in Figure 5-6.

Summary

Software consists of the coded instructions that direct the operation of computer hardware. Software is generally classified as *systems*—software that controls hardware directly—and *application*—software that contains specific instructions for the transformation of data. Application software controls hardware indirectly through systems software.

The *operating system* is a type of systems software that consists of *control programs* to manage the input, output, and storage of data and *service pro-*

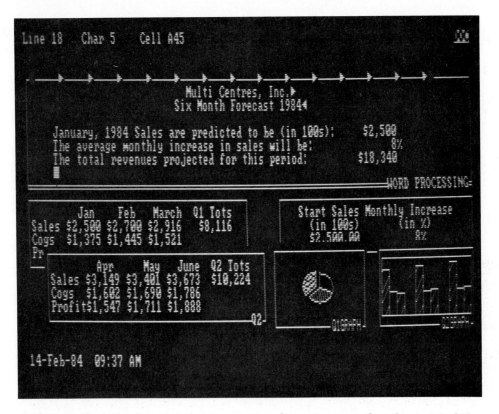

FIGURE 5-6 Windows of the Lotus Symphony Integrated Software Package. (Photo courtesy of Lotus Development Corp.)

grams, which make commonly used routines available to application programs.

Programming languages are used to write application programs. The first generation of languages consisted of *machine languages* and used a code of 1's and 0's. The second generation consisted of *assembler languages*, which used short alphabetic expressions. *High-level languages* introduced the third generation and used English-like instructions. The fourth generation is also high-level but is faster, easier to learn, and usually more specialized than the third generation. *Procedure-oriented* languages emphasize general procedures that can be applied to a variety of tasks. *Problem-oriented* (nonprocedural) languages emphasize specific tasks, such as report generation or financial analysis.

Application programs can be developed *in-house* by organizational personnel or purchased in ready-to-use *packages*. Microcomputer users usually purchase packages for *word processing, electronic spreadsheets*, and *data base management (filing) systems*. These capabilities are often combined, sometimes with graphics or data communications, into *integrated packages*.

Assignments

5-1. Listed here are five computer programs. Identify each as application or systems and, if systems, whether it is a service or control program.

    a. A program that recognizes a password and grants access to a terminal user.

    b. The program that generates your end-of-term grade reports.

    c. A program that generates random numbers for a Monte Carlo simulation.

    d. The program that allocates disk space to a terminal user.

    e. A program that uses random numbers to simulate the demand for electricity.

5-2. There is a brief reference to expert systems in Chapter 1. What kind of programming language, procedure-oriented or problem-oriented, would be most appropriate for the following experts?

    a. A financial analyst.

    b. A mathematician.

    c. An automobile designer.

    d. A marketing research specialist.

    e. A data base manager.

    f. An application programmer.

5-3. The fourth generation of languages is just now entering into use, and already a *fifth* generation is under development. What characteristics would *you* like to see in the next generation?

5-4. *Friendly* and *user-friendly* are terms often used in the advertising of computer hardware and software. Can computers or software be friendly? How? In your experience, are they? Why is friendliness considered so important by these advertisers?

5-5. Computers in which processing is delayed while data are being entered or output are said to be "input/output bound." Can multiprogramming alleviate this condition? Can multiprocessing alleviate it?

5-6. It is ironic that when application programmers had to work in machine languages, almost all program development was in-house. Now, with the availability of third- and fourth-generation languages, literally thousands of application packages are available. How do you explain this apparent contradiction?

5-7. A professor has a university-owned microcomputer at her desk to use for research, the preparation of classroom material, and other similar tasks. Is it appropriate to call the machine a *personal* computer or what she does with it *personal* computing? Why or why not?

5-8. If you are a business major, you probably have taken—or certainly will take—coursework in accounting. What are the advantages and disadvantages in using an electronic spreadsheet or similar tool in the teaching of elementary accounting?

5-9. Now that you have answered assignment 5-3, consider that many experts feel that artificial intelligence and fifth-generation languages are linked together. Does this change your answer? What do you think the term *artificial intelligence* means?

CASE   Collegiate Software

As their term project in a course on entrepreneurship, Bridgette, Kevin, and Mike helped the owner of a newly established gift shop set up a small, microcomputer-based information system. The shop owner had an IBM PC with a correspondence-quality dot matrix printer; an integrated software package consisting of a word processor, a filing system, graphics, and a spreadsheet (*Framework* by Ashton-Tate); and a general ledger accounting package (*General Ledger* by Peachtree Software, Inc.). Bridgette is an accounting major, Kevin is an MIS major, and Mike is a marketing major. All three will graduate in May.

The project was so successful and the three students so compatible that they have decided to start a small-business information-system consulting firm and call it "Collegiate Computing." They have agreed to use the upcoming summer for a trial run and, if successful, to continue the business on a full-time basis starting in the fall. Although their initial investment will not be large, the project is not without risk: Each partner has declined a good job offer because he or she will not be available for a summer starting date.

Now that they are committed, at least for the summer, a few cracks are beginning to develop in their heretofore harmonious relationship. Bridgette feels that they should specialize in installing packages (like the gift-shop project) and training their clients to use the system. Kevin argues that this is a shortsighted approach and that they should develop their own software to eventually market nationally. Mike likes the national marketing idea but wants to build a local reputation and some working capital first.

Questions

1. What is the best course of action on the packaged vs. developed-software issue?

2. What long-term strategy could make the best use of the diverse majors of the three partners?

3. What are the hardware and software requirements of Collegiate Computing? How are these requirements affected by the packaged vs. developed-software issue?

4. Is it realistic for three new graduates to enter a market in which they will compete with seasoned professionals and, to some extent, corporate giants such as IBM?

Other Readings

Arthur, Jay. "Software Quality and Measurement." *Datamation* (December 15, 1984).

Bernstein, Amy. "Defining Integrated Software." *Business Computer Systems* (June 1984).

Horwitt, Elizabeth. "A New Language for Managers." *Business Computer Systems* (January 1985).

Martin, James. *Application Development Without Programmers.* Englewood Cliffs, N.J.: Prentice-Hall, 1982.

Moreland, D. Verne. "The Evolution of Software Architecture." *Datamation* (February 1, 1985).

Sammett, Jean. "An Overview of High-Level Languages." In Marshall C. Yovits, ed. *Advances in Computers.* New York: Academic Press, 1981.

Verity, John W. "Bridging the Software Gap." *Datamation* (February 15, 1985).

Walden, Jeff. "A New Formula for Spreadsheets." *Business Computer Systems* (October 1984).

Recent issues of the following journals: *Business Computer Systems, Byte, Computer World, Datamation, Data Management, Data Processor, Infosystems,* and *MIS World.*

Chapter 6

Data Management

Learning Objectives

After studying this chapter, you will be able to:

1. Organize data into a hierarchy of elements, records, and files.
2. Distinguish among the major approaches to organizing data.
3. Name and describe different types of data files.
4. Discuss the use of data languages in data base management systems.
5. Explain three approaches to structuring data in a data base management system.
6. List the advantages and disadvantages of a data base approach.
7. Define the following terms:

data element	bucket
data record	application-oriented file
data file	data base management system
data base	data management routines
key element (record key)	device media control language
master file	data description language
transaction file	data manipulation language
sequential file	query language
random file	schema
serial file	subschema
physical order	logical entry
logical order	tree (hierarchical) structure
hashing (key transformation)	network (plex) structure
synonym	relational structure

In very simple terms, to *manage* data means to make data readily accessible for authorized use while storing them in an orderly, efficient, and secure manner. In this sense, data management is not much different from inventory management, records management, or the management of other resources. But data are, in many respects, different from other resources: data tend to be far more numerous than most other resources; they are subject to more frequent change; and they are more easily lost or damaged. Consequently, data management methods are also different. In this chapter, we examine two broad approaches to data management: the use of *application-oriented files* and the *data base* approach. But first, let us look at a framework for organizing data.

The Organization of Data

Proper data management requires the structuring of data according to very precise rules. Data must be organized in specified formats, with the right number and kind of characters, and in the proper storage location; if not, the CBIS transformation processes will not yield correct output or may not take place at all. The specific rules of data organization in any given application are defined by systems analysts and programmers during system design and development; the general rules follow an established hierarchy of data relationships.

The Hierarchy of Data

The conventional terms used to describe the hierarchical levels of data are *data element, data record*, and *data file*. The relationships among these levels are shown in Figure 6-1. Those of you who have had an introductory programming course should be familiar with these terms already, but we will review them briefly to refresh your memory and to bring the other students up to your level.

Data Elements
The collection of *bits* into *bytes* to represent characters was described in Chapter 4. When a number of characters are grouped together, the result is a data element. Data elements represent basic facts that describe some entity involved in processing. An employee's name, social security number, address, and job code are all data elements that might be used in a personnel administration application. The number and type (numeric and/or alphabetic) of characters in a data element can vary, although there are usually upper limits to the length imposed by the application program, the programming language, or the computer itself.

141

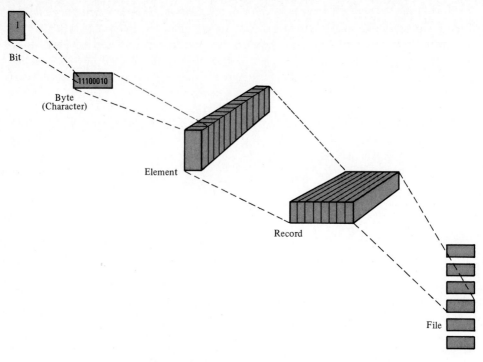

FIGURE 6-1   The hierarchy of data.

Data Records

A group of related data elements is called a data record. Data records can contain any number of elements, as long as the programmer has established their association with the record. We shall see shortly how this association is made.

In order to distinguish among similar records, one or more elements are usually designated the *key element* or *record key*. As shown in Figure 6-2, a personnel record consisting of all of the elements related to one employee might use the elements for the social security number as the record key. Numerical elements are generally preferred as record keys because they are less subject to duplication (there may be two or more Mary Smiths in an organization, for example, but their social security numbers will be different); they are less susceptible to quirks of spelling (a computer will not recognize "Smyth" as "Smith" if you happen to misspell it); and they have a convenient use in random files (see the discussion of random files later in this chapter).

Data Files

Finally, related records may be grouped to form a data file. For example, the personnel records of all of the employees in an organization constitute the personnel file. Files, too, vary in length, with the maximum number of

FIGURE 6-2 The key element.

records in a file dependent on the record length and the available storage space.

Files differ according to their content, their use, and the length of time they are maintained. A *master file* is a permanent file that contains complete records and is the primary source of data in any application. *Transaction files* are temporary and contain records of the firm's basic activities, such as accepting orders and withdrawing items from inventory. Records in transaction files need contain only those elements necessary to identify and update a record in the master file. For example, as shown in Figure 6-3, a transaction that changes an employee's address needs only the social security number (the key element used to identify the record) and the new address. Of course, if the nature of the transaction is to add a new employee, there will be no existing record in the master file, and the transaction file must contain all the data elements necessary to establish a new record.

Data Bases

There is a fourth term that is sometimes associated with the hierarchy of data: *data base*. However, while the other hierarchical terms have precise, generally accepted definitions, *data base* may be used in several different and sometimes confusing ways. First, the term may be used in a very general sense to refer to *all* organizational data, including those found on documents and in other media not related to computers. Second, *data base* may be used to describe a collection of computer-related files in an organization, in which

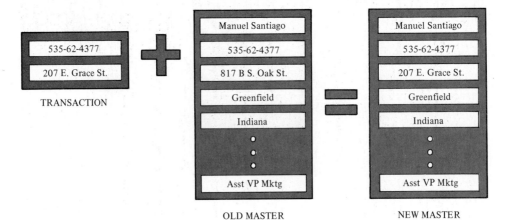

FIGURE 6-3   Updating a master file.

case it is literally a fourth hierarchical level. Finally, *data base* can be defined in a rather narrow sense as the repository of data in a *data base management system* (DBMS). Because DBMS play an integral role in the view of CBIS taken in this book, we use the last definition and, to prevent misunderstanding, hereafter avoid using *data base* in other contexts.

Application-Oriented Files

The traditional data processing approach to managing data involves the establishment of a unique file for each application program. This one-to-one relationship between programs and files gives rise to the term *application-oriented file*. With such files, application programs are limited by the format of the file, and the file, in turn, may be restricted by the sequence of operations followed by the program. Much flexibility in programming additional applications is lost, and any expansion or revision of the basic format of records in the file may preclude the use of existing application programs.

Although there are disadvantages to an application-oriented approach to data management, there are also certain advantages: application-oriented files are easy to establish and maintain; they require no special hardware or software; and they are relatively secure from inadvertent destruction or alteration by other users. Application-oriented files are time-proven methods of information processing for organizations with stable, independent applications and limited CBIS resources.

The nature of processing with application-oriented files is addressed in subsequent chapters. At this point, we are concerned primarily with the data management aspects of application-oriented files: how such files are *described* and how they are *organized*.

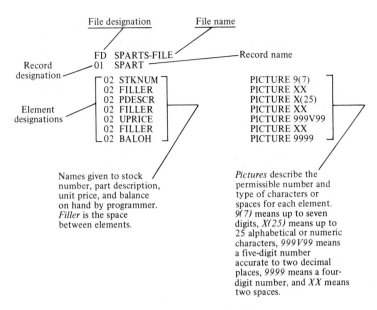

FIGURE 6-4   A COBOL file description.

File Description

The way in which a programmer describes a data file is fixed by the rules of the application programming language. In most cases, short names are assigned to the file, the records, and each data element. Data elements are also formatted for length and character composition. The file–record–element hierarchy is established by the order in which the names are listed in the program, the use of alphabetic or numeric codes, and indentation. An example of the file description of a spare parts inventory, using the COBOL programming language, is shown in Figure 6-4.

There is an important distinction between the *names* used to designate the file, records, and elements in Figure 6-4 and the *values* associated with the elements. For example, a SPART (Spare *PART*) record has no value. It can be identified only by its key element, probably STKNUM (the *STocK NUMber*). The actual stock number for a given spare part is the *value* of STKNUM—a seven-digit number according to the *picture* defined for that element. The stock number uniquely identifies the spare part and distinguishes that spare part's record from all the other records in the file.

File Organization

File organization refers to the *physical* order of records on the storage medium. Records also have a logical order—the order in which they are normally processed—which may or may not be the same as the physical

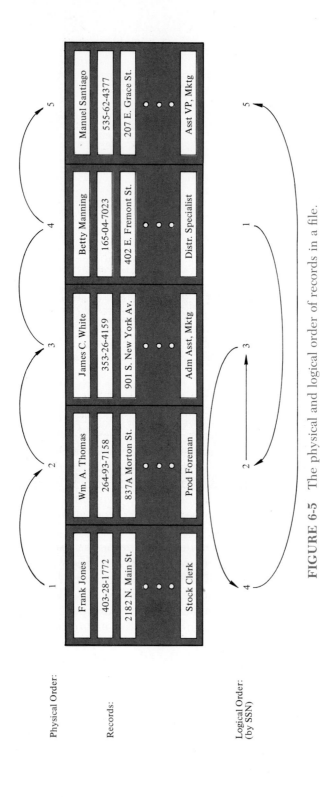

FIGURE 6-5 The physical and logical order of records in a file.

order, as shown in Figure 6-5. File organization is described as being *sequential, random,* or *serial.*

Sequential Files

A sequential file is one in which the physical order and the logical order are the same. For example, in a billing application, the logical order might be by account number, in which case a sequential billing file would be arranged in account number sequence.

Files are always sequential when using a sequential access storage device, such as a tape drive. Files may also be organized sequentially on a direct access storage device, such as a disk drive, if other factors so dictate. When sequential files are stored on disks, records can be "packed" into every available storage location. This is in marked contrast to the storage of random files on disks, where, as we shall see, certain inefficiencies are encountered when the disk is more than 70 or 80 percent full. Sequential files on tape and disk are shown in Figure 6-6.

Random Files

Records in a random file are distributed about the storage medium according to a process that selects storage locations randomly. Often, some data element in the record itself, usually the record key if it is numerical, is used to

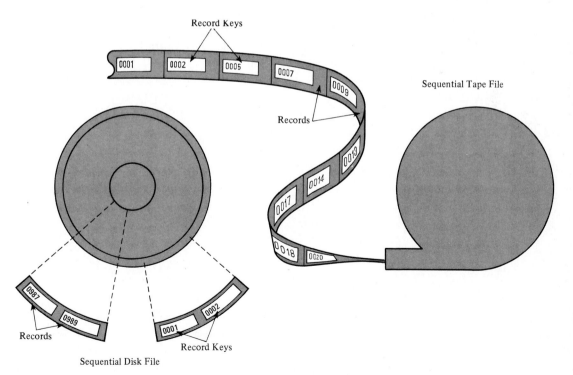

FIGURE 6-6   Sequential files on tape and disk.

determine the storage location. The process of this determination is called *hashing* or *key transformation*.

There are many ways to transform a key element into a storage location; one example will serve to illustrate the kinds of processes involved. Suppose a personnel file is to be stored randomly and there are 12,685 storage locations available. The key element in each record is the social security number of the employee represented by the record. Each social security number is divided by 12,685, and the remainder is the address of the storage location for that record. (Using a divisor equal to the number of storage locations ensures maximum utilization of the storage space—the remainder can be any number from zero up to one less than the divisor, which is the total number of storage locations available.) Thus, the storage location for the record of the person whose social security number is 535-62-4377 is 252, because 535,624,377 divided by 12,685 is 42,225, *remainder 252*. This process is illustrated in Figure 6-7.

It is possible for key transformation to produce the same storage location for more than one record. In the example just given, key transformation would also direct the record with social security number 403-28-1772 to location 252, because 403,281,772 divided by 12,685 equals 31,792, *remainder 252*. Records with the same storage location are called *synonyms*. When key transformations produce synonyms, the synonymous records following the original are placed in an overflow storage area called a *bucket*.

A subsequent process that locates a record in a random file may use the same key transformation procedure or may refer to an *index* at the front of the file. If key transformation is used, the record in the addressed storage location must be checked for the correct record key; if the key is not the one desired, the process must be diverted to the overflow area to search for the correct record.

As more and more records are added to a random file, the possibility of synonyms increases. The extra time spent searching an overflow area for the desired record soon begins to offset the speed and efficiency normally associated with random files. This is the reason for restricting random files to approximately 70 or 80 percent of the available storage space. Thus, the 12,685 locations allocated to the personnel file in this example would probably be used to accommodate not more than 10,000 records.

Although sequential files can be stored on either direct access or sequential access storage devices, random files can be used only in conjunction with DASD. Figure 6-8 shows the random location of records on one such medium, a disk.

Serial Files

A serial file is a special case of a sequential file in which the sequence is the order in which records in the file have been created. Sales, bank deposits, orders, and other similar transactions may be collected into a file in this fashion. Although it is common for transaction files to be stored serially, it would be most unusual to find a serial master file.

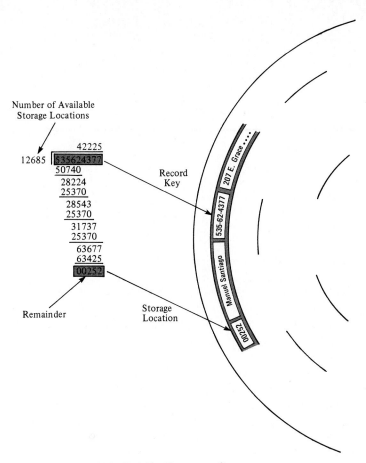

Number of Available
Storage Locations

42225
12685 | 535624377 |
50740
28224
25370
28543
25370
31737
25370
63677
63425
| 00252 |

Record
Key

Remainder

Storage
Location

FIGURE 6-7   Key transformation.

Serial transaction files may be used to update random master files, but
they are normally converted to sequential transaction files in order to update
a sequential master file. The sequential transaction file created for this purpose is sometimes called a *sort file*. More is said on the conditions under
which a serial transaction file is sorted into a sequential file in the discussion
of transaction-processing modes in Chapter 8.

The Data Base Approach

The alternative to the use of application-oriented files is to follow a *data base*
approach. A data base may be thought of as a large, application-*independent*
file. Data are entered into the data base in a certain format, of course, but
that format is not fixed. It can be varied to meet the needs of any application

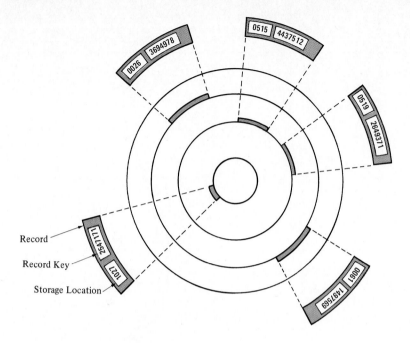

Record

Record Key

Storage Location

FIGURE 6-8 Random file on disk.

program that requires the data. Files for individual application programs are not maintained permanently; they are created on an ad hoc or temporary basis as they are required for processing. After processing, the updated elements are returned to the data base until required again—whether for the same or a different program.

TABLE 6-1 Mainframe Data Base Management Systems

DBMS	Type	Vendor	Compatibility	Cost	Host Languages
ADABAS	Relational	Software AG	IBM 360, 370, 30-, 43-Series	$100,000+	COBOL, FORTRAN, PL/1, Assembler
DMS-II	Plex	Burroughs	Burroughs B1000, B7000	$15,000–$30,000	COBOL, PL/1, ALGOL
FOCUS	Relational	Information Builders	IBM 370, 30-, 43-Series	$66,000–$120,000	COBOL, FORTRAN, Assembler
IDMS	Relational	Cullinet	IBM 360, 370, 30-, 43-Series	$55,000	COBOL, FORTRAN, PL/1, Assembler
System 2000	Tree	Intel	IBM 360, 370, 30-, 43-Series; CDC 6000, Cyber; UNIVAC 1100	$50,000–$100,000	COBOL, FORTRAN, PL/1, Assembler

TABLE 6-2 Microcomputer Data Base Management Systems

DBMS	Type	Vendor	Compatibility	Cost	Operating System
Database Manager II	Index	Alpha Software	IBM PC, XT, compatibles	$300	PC-DOS, MS-DOS
DataEase	Relational	Software Solutions	IBM PC, XT, compatibles; DEC Rainbow; TI, Wang, Victor	$600	PC-DOS, MS-DOS
dBase III	Relational	Ashton-Tate	IBM PC, XT, compatibles	$700	CP/M-80, CP/M-85
DB Master	Index	Stoneware	Apple II +, IIe	$350	DOS 3.3
filePro	Relational	The Small Computer Co.	Apple II with CP/M, other CP/M systems	$200	CP/M
Information Management	Tree	BPI Systems	IBM PC, XT; Compac	$425	PC-DOS, MS-DOS
R:base	Relational	MicroRIM	IBM PC or compatible, DEC Rainbow, HP 150	$500	PC-DOS, MS-DOS, CP/M-80

On the surface, the data base approach is appealingly simple: one merely dumps all the relevant data into an accessible container and retrieves those that are needed at the appropriate time. The process is roughly analogous to a filing cabinet that, instead of containing neatly alphabetized file folders (comparable to application-oriented files), is filled with scraps of paper on which are written individual names, account numbers, inventory balances, and every other element of organizational data. All of the data are present in both cases, but it is difficult to imagine how an organization could function in the latter instance. Clearly, there must be some structure to the data in the data base and an organized set of procedures to facilitate their recovery. The data base management system satisfies both requirements.

Data Base Management Systems

A data base management system (DBMS) is primarily a software component—a set of computer programs that manages data.[1] The original DBMS were developed by user organizations that found application-oriented files inadequate for their special data management needs, but it is now more common to purchase one of the many commercially available DBMS. Some of the more popular DBMS designed for mainframe computers are shown in Table 6-1; a similar list for microcomputer DBMS is shown in Table 6-2. It

---

[1] Some DBMS also make use of hardware or "firmware" components. The IBM System 38 is an example of DBMS-oriented hardware.

should be recalled that many integrated packages for microcomputers also contain filing or data base management capabilities.

Although it is only an adjunct to the primary CBIS, a DBMS is nonetheless a full-fledged system with inputs, outputs, interrelated parts, and other systems characteristics. The various parts and the systems nature of DBMS are shown in Figure 6-9, which views a DBMS as a set of special programming languages and a software management package that completes the interface with the hardware and software of the host CBIS. A brief description of these components is helpful in understanding how a DBMS works.

Data Management Routines

Every DBMS has an integral software or combination software/hardware package to interpret statements in the special programming languages for the operating system of the host computer. In this book, that package is called *data management routines* (DMR).[2] It will be recalled that, among other tasks, the operating system of a computer links the various hardware components. Because the data base is maintained in external storage, the operating system must provide the route to and from the storage device. The DMR converts storage and retrieval instructions in DBMS languages into commands that the operating system understands.

Device Media Control Language

Whether in a data base or in more conventional files, data must be structured both physically and logically. *Physical structure* refers to the relationships among physical storage locations: disk surfaces, sectors, drives, and so on. In a DBMS, the assignment of physical storage space to data is accomplished through a *device media control language* (DMCL). Although the overall allocation of storage space in a DBMS is the responsibility of the data base administrator (DBA), the actual programming in DMCL is generally delegated to a systems programmer.

DMCL are also exceptions to the general rule that DBMS programming languages interface with the operating system through DMR. As shown in Figure 6-9, the DMCL interfaces directly with the operating system of the host computer.

Data Description Language

The logical relationships between data elements in a DBMS collectively are called the *schema* and are defined by a *data description language* (DDL). A schema shows element and record formats similar to those in a conventional file. For example, Figure 6-10 shows the schema for a data base on the customers of a computer manufacturer. The schema is organized by sales representatives, who have various customers, who, in turn, have various

---

[2]The DMR package is also called the *data base manager* (DBM), a term avoided here because *manager* is used throughout this book to refer to a person rather than to a software or software/hardware combination.

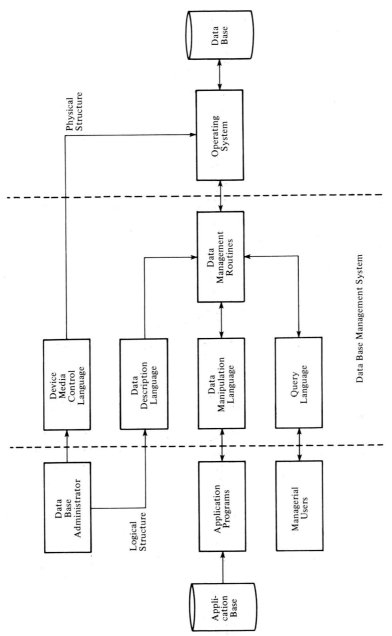

FIGURE 6-9　Components of a data base management system.

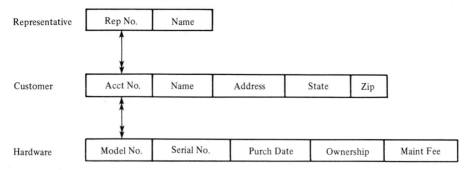

FIGURE 6-10   Schema for a data base on computer customers.

hardware components. The relationships among the representatives, customers, and hardware are shown by arrows connecting the *key elements* at each level. The number of arrowheads on the arrows further defines the relationship: the single arrowhead from "ACCT NO" to "REP NO" means that each customer can have only one representative, whereas the double arrowhead in the opposite direction means that a representative may service more than one account. This schema is greatly simplified, of course, to serve our illustrative purposes. An actual schema for such a data base would have many more elements pertaining to each level (representative, customers, and hardware) as well as to additional levels.

Every DBMS has its own more or less unique data description language, although there have been attempts to standardize DBMS languages. In the late 1960s, the Conference on Data Systems Languages (CODASYL) formed a Data Base Task Group (DBTG), which developed DBMS language specifications, but the industry has been slow to adopt them. We have selected one DDL—that used in the System 2000 DBMS—to show, in Figure 6-11, how a DDL is used to describe a schema. The schema described in this figure is the same one illustrated in Figure 6-10.

The description of the schema in DDL is similar to the COBOL file description illustrated earlier, with the exception that the DDL incorporates more detail. For example, there are different types of elements (integers, names, dates, and decimals) and a provision for multiple customers and hardware components through the use of *repeating groups* (designated by *RG*). The technique for defining the picture of each element is similar to that used in COBOL. The asterisks, colons, and indenting are formatting methods used by this DDL. Because this is a very limited example, it does not illustrate all of the special terms and notational conventions used in the System 2000 DDL.

The schema differs from the format of conventional files in that it merely establishes an overall logical structure; it does not restrict processing to any particular format. Processing formats are defined, also by the DDL, in a *subschema*. A subschema is often described as the *user's* view of data (as opposed to the *DBA's* view, the schema). The subschema contains only those

```
 1*  Representative (Key Integer 9(5)):
 2*  Representative Name (Non-key Name X(25)):
 3*  Customer (RG):
 4*  Account Number (Key Integer 9(7) in 3):
 5*  Customer Name (Non-key Name X(20) in 3):
 6*  Address (Non-key Name X(25) in 3):
 7*  State (Non-key Name XX in 3):
 8*  Zip Code (Non-key Name X(5) in 3):
 9*  Hardware Component (RG in 3):
10*  Model Number (Key Name X(5) in 9):
11*  Serial Number (Non-key Name X(10) in 9):
12*  Purchase Date (Non-key Date in 9):
13*  Ownership (Non-key Name X in 9):
14*  Maintenance Fee (Non-key Decimal 9(4).9(2) in 9):
```

FIGURE 6-11 Schema description in System 2000 DDL.

elements needed for a particular application. For example, if the computer manufacturer has an application program that analyzes maintenance fees by the state in which leased hardware components are located, only the data elements in the subschema shown in Figure 6-12 would be necessary.[3]

In an analogy made popular by James Martin, the schema can be compared to a city map, such as the one in Figure 6-13, which shows how *all* parts of the city are connected by streets, rail lines, and other physical features. This is comparable to describing the overall relationships of the data in the data base. By contrast, the subschema is more like a route map, such as the one in Figure 6-14, which shows only the streets traveled and the key landmarks found between two points—say, the high school and the northside park. This is analogous to identifying only the relationships among the few data elements necessary for a particular application.

Loading the Data Base   Once the schema of a data base is described, there still remains the very important function of entering or *loading* the initial data before any application programs can be run. The data description language performs this function as well. Figure 6-15 shows a partial *logical entry* (analogous to a record in an application-oriented file) for the data base on computer customers—partial because only one customer is shown for the

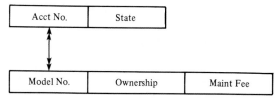

FIGURE 6-12 Subschema for maintenance fees of leased hardware, by state.

[3] Notice that "ACCT NO" and "MODEL NO" have no direct bearing on this analysis, but they provide access to "STATE," "OWNERSHIP," and "MAINT FEE," which cannot be accessed directly because they are not key elements.

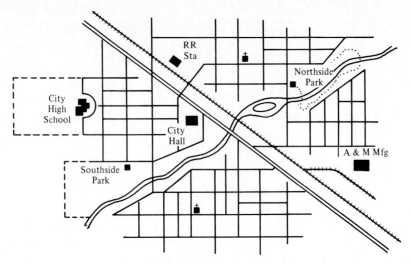

FIGURE 6-13   A city map.

representative when, in reality, each representative would have many customers. This figure also illustrates the repeating group concept, by which
multiple data sets for hardware can be associated with a single customer.

The representation of data in the format of the schema is merely an aid to
understanding the transition from data description to data loading. Data are
not actually entered onto a form that reflects the schema, of course; they are
incorporated into data statements as shown in Figure 6-16. These statements,
which are also in the System 2000 DDL, combine the schema description in
Figure 6-11 with the partial logical entry in Figure 6-15. The use of repeating
groups is even more clearly illustrated here by the repetition of line number
9 (the hardware repeating group) under line number 3 (the customer repeating group). Asterisks in each line separate component numbers (see Figure
6-11) from the actual value for each component[4] (see Figure 6-15).

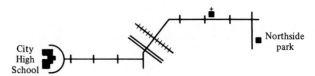

FIGURE 6-14   Route map from the high school to
northside park.

---

[4] System 2000 uses the term *component* generically to include *elements* (components that
contain data) and *repeating groups* (components that designate the name of a group of elements that may occur repeatedly). In this illustration, components 3 and 9 are repeating
groups and are never assigned data values. The other components are elements and have the
values following the asterisk after each element number in Figure 6-16.

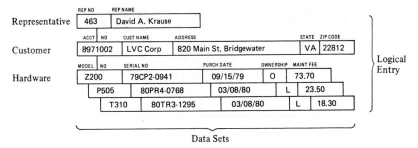

FIGURE 6-15 Partial logical entry for a computer customer data base.

Data Manipulation Language

Application programs communicate with the data base through a *data manip-ulation language* (DML). Although, like other DBMS languages, there are no universally accepted standards for DML, most DML are now compatible with standard programming languages such as COBOL and FORTRAN (see Table 6-1). DBMS that use such DML are referred to as *host-language* systems, as opposed to *self-contained* systems, in which the DBMS is a unique application programming language, as well as an interface between applications and the data base.

In a host-language system, DML statements are inserted in appropriate places in the application program to identify the schema and the subschema required for the application. Records as defined by the subschema are created as needed and are moved to working storage for processing. When processing is completed, updated elements are returned to the data base by other DML statements. Only slight modifications to programming rules—such as starting the DML statements in a different column than, say, COBOL statements—are necessary when a host-language system is used.

In self-contained DBMS, the application programming language and the DML are incorporated into a single language—usually a unique language

```
1*463*2* David A. Krause*
 3*4*8971002*5* LVC Corp*6*820 Main St, Bridgewater*7*Va*8*22812*
 9*10*Z200*11*79CP2-0941*12*09/15/79*13*O*14*73.70*
 9*10*P505*11*80PR5-0768*12*03/08/80*13*L*14*23.50*
 9*10*T310*11*80TR3-1295*12*03/08/80*13*L*14*18.30*
 3* (Additional customers of David A. Krause)
 9* (Hardware of additional customers)
 9* (Last hardware component of last cutomer of David A. Krause)*END*
1* (Additional representatives)
        :
 9* (Last hardware component of last customer of last representative)*END**
```

FIGURE 6-16 Data entry format for loading the data base in system 2000 DDL.

developed by the user for a highly specialized application. The early user-developed DBMS tended to be of the self-contained variety, but host-language systems are now far more numerous and can satisfy all but the most unusual requirements. Because they are falling into disuse, we will not discuss self-contained systems further in this book.

Query Language

One of the great advantages of DBMS is the opportunity afforded users to interface directly with the data base without the assistance of programmers and analysts. To facilitate user access to the data base, most DBMS have a *query language* (QL) designed to be used interactively via terminals. QL are characterized by a few simple, yet powerful, commands employed in an uncomplicated format. Nonprogrammers can usually be given a working familiarity with a QL in a few hours, and the basic sign-on, access, and data analysis procedures can be summarized on a pocket-sized reference card for the user's convenience. Of course, more extensive training and experience are helpful if the user wishes to become truly proficient in QL.

Data Structures

Data base management systems can be classified according to the manner in which data are logically structured in the data base. There are three major types of data structures: *tree, network,* and *relational.* In each case, pointers or indexes are used to establish relationships between data elements stored in a direct access storage device, but the logic of the different structures is easier to visualize in diagrams.

Tree Structures

Data trees are usually drawn "upside down" with respect to trees in nature; that is, the *root* node, from which the *branches* emanate, is at the top, and the *leaf* nodes are below. Additional branches lead to subsequent levels of leaves. The levels in tree structures are sometimes referred to as *grandparent* (root), *parent* (first level of leaves), *children* (second level of leaves), and so on. A leaf may have only one parent, but it may have many children. A tree illustrating the computer manufacturer's data base from the example given earlier is shown in Figure 6-17. The characteristic pyramid shape and the clearly defined levels of data also help explain the alternative term *hierarchical,* which is sometimes used to describe tree data structures.

The single-parent requirement for customers in this example is easy to maintain, because the schema (Figure 6-10) stipulates that a customer can have only one representative. But hardware presents a problem. No customer can expect to be the exclusive user of a particular model of computer equipment, yet the tree structure requires single parenthood. The solution to this dilemma is to repeat the hardware model in the diagram as often as

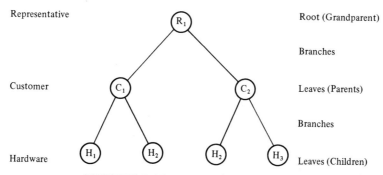

FIGURE 6-17   A tree data structure.

necessary. In this example, there are three types of hardware (H_1, H_2, and H_3), and Type 2 is used by both customers (C_1 and C_2). Therefore, H_2 must appear twice.

Another, more elegant way to show that more than one customer uses H_2 is to *invert* the tree and make H_2 the root, as shown in Figure 6-18. DBMS using a tree structure can usually invert on any key element. Figure 6-18 also shows an inversion placing C_1 at the root. Of course, the DBMS does not literally invert the data tree; the pointers or indexes are merely used in such a way as to create the effect of a schema based on a root of hardware models or customers rather than representatives.

DBMS using tree structures employ the inversion technique to define a subschema. This is one way in which DBMS avoid the duplication of data used in several applications. Data elements appear in the schema only once, but they may be in any number of subschema, subject only to the restrictions imposed when the relationships between elements were defined with the DDL. For example, an application program that lists all the customers using each type of hardware might employ a subschema based on an inverted tree like the first one shown in Figure 6-18, whereas a program that lists the hardware used by each customer would require a subschema more like the second version shown in Figure 6-18.

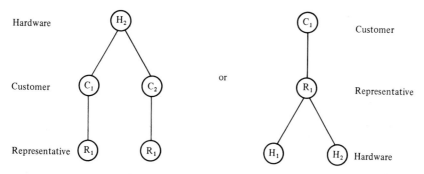

FIGURE 6-18   Inverted data trees.

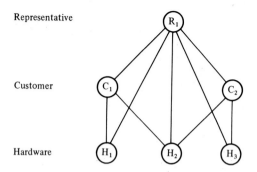

Representative

Customer

Hardware

FIGURE 6-19   A network data structure.

Network Structures

The logic of network data structures, sometimes referred to as *plex struc-tures*, is similar to that for tree structures, with the exception that the constraint on single parenthood is relaxed. "Children" in DBMS based on network logic may have more than one "parent" or "grandparent." In general, network data structures require more extensive systems of pointers or indexes, but they do not have to be inverted in order to describe a subschema. If the data concerning computer sales representatives, customers, and hardware were maintained in a DBMS using a network data structure, we could represent them in a diagram such as the one shown in Figure 6-19. This figure reflects exactly the same relationships described earlier, but in network logic. The network characteristic of multiple parenthood is illustrated by the lines joining H_2 (a "child") with two different "parents" (C_1 and C_2).

Relational Structures

The third approach to data structuring in DBMS can be viewed as a series of two-dimensional tables or *relations*. A relational structuring of data concerning the representatives, customers, and hardware in our hypothetical data base is depicted in Figure 6-20.

Representative	Customer
R	C
1	1
1	2

Representative	Hardware
R	H
1	1
1	2
1	3

Customer	Hardware
C	H
1	1
1	2
2	2
2	3

FIGURE 6-20   A relational data structure.

The rows in the tables are called *tuples* but can be treated as records, because they are made up of related elements. The columns in the tables represent the *attributes*, or different kinds of elements, that make up the tuples. For example, the first table, or relation, shows that Representative 1 (R_1) and Customer 1 (C_1) are related, as are Representative 1 (R_1) and Customer 2 (C_2). The relationships between representatives and hardware and between customers and hardware are shown in the second and third tables. Subschema are created by mathematical processes that form subsets of tuples with like attributes.

The relational data structure is more difficult to diagram and is based on more abstract principles than are tree and network structures. DBMS using relational data structures are, however, no less efficient nor more difficult to use than other DBMS.

Considerations in Adopting a Data Base Approach

The adoption of a data base approach to data management is a major decision that impacts on every facet of CBIS; it is one that should not be made lightly. For new CBIS, the decision dictates a virtually irreversible course of systems design, and for existing, file-oriented systems, the decision may involve some temporary disruption of services and no small risk to file integrity during the conversion process. How can CBIS planners make such a decision? What factors should they consider? We will examine some more sophisticated methods in the following chapter, but here, to evaluate the data base approach, we use a simple yet effective framework for decision making: a listing of advantages and disadvantages.

Advantages of the Data Base Approach

The advantages of the data base approach are summarized in Table 6-3. The first, and perhaps most obvious, advantage is that much redundancy in the storage of data is reduced. For example, the complete name, address, social security number, and other information pertaining to a student need not be stored in both an academic records file and a billing file. If all the data about the student are maintained in a data base, each application program can use those data to create a temporary file for its own use.

TABLE 6-3   Advantages of the
Data Base Approach

1. Redundancy in data storage is reduced.
2. Data maintenance is simplified.
3. Processing time is reduced.
4. Internal consistency among data is improved.
5. Data can be shared by many applications.

A second advantage is that the maintenance of data is simplified. If the student in the preceding example changes her home address, a single transaction updates the data base to the benefit of both applications. This advantage takes on major significance when data are voluminous or are subject to frequent change. For example, the prices of the thousands of parts used to manufacture automobiles are constantly changing. If each change had to be posted to a separate file for every application that uses those prices (cost accounting, accounts payable, purchasing, and so forth), the effort expended in data entry alone would justify a data base approach.

The use of a data base can also reduce processing time because only necessary data elements need be drawn from the data base for any given application. In general, shorter records take less time to process than do longer records, even though the number of elements actually changed may be the same in each case. In the case of the student data base, the billing application will need, for each student, a name, a permanent address, a status code (full-time or part-time, graduate or undergraduate), and the services covered by the bill (room, board, tuition, activities, and so on) for the preparation of the initial bills. A subsequent application for sending reminders to those with unpaid bills may need only the name, the address, and the amount due, and then only for those students with unpaid bills. Not only are the *records* created for this application shorter, the *file* itself is shorter because it contains fewer records.

A fourth advantage lies in the greater internal consistency among data within a data base. If both billing and student records must include the number of students enrolled for reports to the state board of regents, an examination of the respective application-oriented files may give different answers, depending on the currency of the files. But with a data base, the query for counting students is unrelated to applications and gives the same response to all parties. Of course, there is no guarantee that the common response will be correct, but at least all parties will work with the same data.

Finally, and perhaps most important, updated information in a data base is available immediately for other applications. To continue the student data base example, let us assume that a student who carries more than the normal course load will incur an additional tuition expense. If the extra course is added after the normal registration period, that information would be available to the billing application as soon as it is entered via the student records application. With application-oriented files, billing might normally learn of such changes through periodic reports and might be required to reenter the data in order to update its own files. Days or even weeks could pass, during which the bills would be prepared on the basis of incomplete data.

Disadvantages of a Data Base Approach

Organizational planners contemplating a new or substantially revised CBIS are frequently dazzled by the power and flexibility of contemporary hardware and software; they consider the *advantages* of new technology but not the

TABLE 6-4   Disadvantages of the
Data Base Approach

1. Costs are high.
2. Security is difficult to maintain.
3. Consequences of security breaches may be severe.
4. Greater control over data is required.

disadvantages. We believe that, for most organizations, a careful analysis of the advantages and disadvantages of a data base approach will lead to the decision to adopt a data base. This decision should not preclude performing the analysis, however, if for no other reason than to point out potential trouble spots in future operations. It is appropriate, therefore, to examine some disadvantages of the data base approach (summarized in Table 6-4).

Some data base management systems may be beyond the budgetary constraints of small businesses. System 2000, ADABAS, FOCUS, IDMS, and other large, mainframe-oriented DBMS cost thousands of dollars per month just to rent, or tens of thousands to purchase (see Table 6-1), and they may severely tax the internal memory capacity of the organizational computer.

Even if the benefits of a DBMS outweigh the costs, there are other disadvantages. Security, for example, is much more difficult to achieve under a data base concept than with application-oriented files. Data of a personal or confidential nature are more vulnerable simply because they are exposed to a greater number of users, and as part of the data base, they must be kept on-line for longer periods of time than the same data in an application-oriented file. More is said about security in Chapter 18.

Not only is security more difficult to achieve with a data base approach, but the *consequences* of a breach in security are more severe. If a disgruntled employee or a mischievous "data-diddler" succeeds in gaining unauthorized access to the data base, he or she could destroy virtually all of an organization's basic operating data. Such damage would be far more difficult to inflict on a large number of application-oriented files.

A data base approach also demands greater control over data codes and application programs. A production application cannot code a date as day–month–year while an accounting application uses month–day–year if both are to draw dates from a common data base. Of course, many CBIS managers see increased control as an *advantage* of a data base approach, although the functional users tend to disagree with this assessment. The adoption of a data base must be accompanied by a strong sales pitch to show users the benefits that they will receive and to convince them of the need to conform to rigidly defined standards.

Summary

Data management begins with the organization of data into a hierarchy of *elements*, *records*, and *files*. Files can be classified by their content as *master files*, which contain complete records reflecting the most recent changes, or *transaction files*, which contain data used to change or update master files. A fourth term, *data base*, is sometimes used to extend the hierarchy, but it is used in a more narrow sense here to describe the collection of data in a *data base management system* (DBMS).

The *application-oriented* approach to data management uses files that relate to application programs on a one-to-one basis. Statements in the application program describe the *names*, *pictures*, and *sequences* of elements in the records that constitute the file. The physical order of records in application-oriented files is described as *sequential, random*, or *serial*. Master files may be either sequential or random. Transaction files are usually serial, but they are normally sorted into sequence if the master file is sequential.

Data base management systems provide means for many application programs to access a single *application-independent* data base. DBMS use special data management languages to assign storage space (a *device media control language* or DMCL), to describe the logical relationships among data (a *data description language* or DDL), to move data back and forth between the data base and the application programs (a *data manipulation language* or DML), and to provide users direct access to the data base (a *query language* or QL).

The way in which DBMS establishes the logical relationships among data is a reflection of its *data structure*. The three major forms of data structure are *tree* or *hierarchical*, *network* or *plex*, and *relational*. The overall structure of data in the data base is referred to as the *schema*, and the more limited structure required for an application is called the *subschema*.

The major advantages of a data base approach to data management are the reduction of redundancies, the immediate availability of updated information to all applications, and the direct access afforded managers and other users. The disadvantages include more serious consequences when data are lost or destroyed, difficulty in establishing and maintaining security, and relatively high cost.

Assignments

6-1. The example of hashing in the text used a divisor equal to the number of storage locations available for the application. What is the effect of using a *smaller* divisor? What is the effect of using a *larger* divisor?

6-2. Many CBIS with a data base management system still use some application-oriented files. Can you think of some applications where this procedure might be appropriate? What are the advantages and/or disadvantages of mixing an application-oriented and a data base approach within a single family of CBIS?

6-3. In Chapter 4, we discussed different media (tape, cards, disk, and so on) used in CBIS. What role does the primary storage medium play in the decision to use an application-oriented or a data base approach to data management? Conversely, what role does the data management approach play in the selection of media? Which decision should be made first?

6-4. The CBIS for a university might well use a DBMS to maintain student records. Make a drawing similar to Figure 6-10 to describe the schema for such a system. Make two additional drawings similar to Figure 6-12 to describe the subschema for the registrar's grade-posting application and the treasurer's billing application. Were you able to describe the subschema without going back to alter the schema?

6-5. Using the schema prepared in assignment 6-4 and the format shown in Figure 6-15, prepare the logical entry pertaining to yourself.

6-6. Using Figure 6-11 as an example, write the System 2000 DDL statements to describe the student-record data base developed in assignment 6-4. Now use Figure 6-16 as an example and write the DDL statements to load your own logical entry (from assignment 6-5) into this data base.

6-7. Place yourself in the role of the director of information systems for a large, multibranch bank. How do the advantages and disadvantages of a data base approach apply to such an organization? How might they apply to a state welfare office? To a manufacturing firm?

6-8. There is currently a great deal of concern over an apparent conflict between the data-sharing capabilities of DBMS and the right to privacy of individuals whose records might be maintained by a DBMS. Is this conflict real or imagined? Should information systems managers give up such capabilities in the public interest, or is there a technological solution to this problem?

CASE   Hill Manufacturing—Part III

In conjunction with the implementation of the new materials-requirements-planning (MRP) system at Hill Manufacturing Company, a data base management system will be installed. This installation will make it easier for those in inventory control, production planning, and the purchasing departments to gain access to the information in the various files used in the system. The inventory status file is one such file; it is used by many individuals in different departments. Some of the data to be maintained will include:

- Part number.
- Part description.
- Standard cost.
- Raw material used (for manufactured parts).
- Purchase-order quantity or quantity discounts (for purchased parts).
- Quantity of item currently on hand.
- Vendor name, number, and address.
- Date and quantity ordered from vendors.
- Date of arrival of orders from vendors.

The departments will be performing numerous functions that involve these data. Four of these are as follows:

1. When an order arrives from a vendor, the quantity on order and the quantity on hand are adjusted, and the arrival data is acknowledged.
2. Inventory transactions must reduce the quantity on hand and generate a report if additional quantities of the part need to be ordered (after a check on any scheduled receipts). This report will also identify all vendors for that item.
3. The purchasing agent will indicate part number, vendor number, quantity, and date needed, and the system will generate an order to that vendor.
4. The purchasing department wants to maintain information for each vendor: what its delivery performance is or how well it meets the scheduled due dates.

Questions

1. Does a data base approach seem warranted in this situation? Could the system work as well without one?

2. Develop a schema for this data base that will facilitate all four of these applications. Designate the key element for each record you establish.

3. Illustrate a subschema for the first application described.

Other Readings

Cardenas, Alfonso F. *Data Base Management Systems.* Boston: Allyn and Bacon, 1981.

DeLong, David. "Demystifying Data Management." *Business Computer Systems* (February, March, and April 1983).

Kroenke, David. *Database Processing* (2d ed.). Chicago: Science Research Associates, 1983.

Martin, James. *An End User's Guide to Data Bases.* Englewood Cliffs, N.J.: Prentice-Hall, 1981.

Martin, James. *Principles of Data-Base Management.* Englewood Cliffs, N.J.: Prentice-Hall, 1976.

Martin, James. *Computer Data-Base Organization* (2d ed.). Englewood Cliffs, N.J.: Prentice-Hall, 1977.

Sweet, Frank. "What, If Anything, Is a Relational Database?" *Datamation* (July 15, 1984).

"Theme: Databases." *Byte* (October 1984). (Theme consisting of nine articles.)

Chapter 7

Decision-Making Concepts and Tools

Learning Objectives

After studying this chapter, you will be able to:

1. Identify the four decision environments according to the extent of knowledge of the future and the preference for outcomes.
2. Select the appropriate alternative according to strategies of decision making under uncertainty.
3. Apply the expected value criterion to decision making under risk.
4. Suggest appropriate decision models to apply to decision making under certainty.
5. Incorporate limited optimizing approaches into administrative behavior.
6. Appreciate the importance of CBIS in modern decision making.
7. Define the following terms:

computational decision	opportunity loss	present value
judgmental decision	minimax	satisfice
expert knowledge system	expected value	administrative behavior
compromise decision	decision tree	point estimate
inspirational decision	decision node	interval estimate
state of nature	chance node	trend analysis
uncertainty	optimizing model	regression analysis
risk	linear programming	simulation
certainty	feasible region	static model
payoff table	objective function	dynamic model
maximax	economic order quantity	process generator
maximin	deterministic model	descriptive model

In Chapter 1, an *MIS* was defined, in part, as "an organized set of processes . . . to support . . . decision making within an organization." Similarly, the definition of *DSS* included the "easy access to decision models . . . to support . . . decision-making tasks." The key to providing this support is an understanding of how decisions are made: Do managers pick the best possible solution or merely one that works? To what extent do managers analyze data, and to what extent do they rely on intuition? By what means are data manipulated to answer critical questions in the decision process? And how can decision making be enhanced by a computer-based information system?

Although these questions cannot be answered completely in the limited space available here, it is possible to survey the more important aspects of modern decision making by omitting the details of actual computational procedures. Those of you who have already taken a course in quantitative methods have some appreciation of these computations. In actual practice, managers without quantitative skills can seek advice from management science/operations research (MS/OR) specialists who can help with model selection, and the computer will perform the actual computations.

A Decision Environment Model

There is a tendency, on the part of CBIS specialists and other quantitatively oriented managers, to forget that not all decisions can be "programmed." Indeed, in planning for the support of organizational decision making, it is as important to recognize the limitations of computers as to know their capabilities. Figure 7-1 shows a model, originally suggested by J. D. Thompson, that combines managers' knowledge of cause–effect relationships and their preference for outcomes to create four different decision environments: *computational, judgmental, compromise,* and *inspirational.*[1]

Computational Decisions

When managers have a definite preference for specific outcomes—high profits over low profits, few production defects over many defects, and so on—*and* they have complete knowledge of the factors that cause these outcomes, they can literally *compute* the best course of action to follow. This is the environment in which computers and quantitative methods flourish. For example, there are numerous standard computer programs available that can compute the order quantity that minimizes inventory costs, the shipping routes that minimize transportation costs, the product mix that maximizes profits, the allocation of resources that minimizes project time, and the solutions to many other similar problems.

[1]James D. Thompson, *Organizations in Action* (New York: McGraw-Hill, 1967), 134.   **169**

Preference for Outcomes

		Clear	Unclear
Knowledge of Cause-Effect Relationships	Complete	Computational	Compromise
	Incomplete	Judgmental	Inspirational

FIGURE 7-1   Decision environments. [Adapted from J. D. Thompson, *Organization in Action* (New York: McGraw-Hill Book Company, 1967), p. 134.]

Judgmental Decisions

In other situations, the preference for an outcome may be equally clear, but the knowledge of how to achieve such an outcome is less than complete. Many personnel decisions fall into this category. The objective to hire a marketing manager who will increase sales may be abundantly clear, but the choice of the best person to fill that position cannot be computed. Instead, the decision makers exercise *judgment:* they consider the information available on each candidate and make their decision subjectively. CBIS are not excluded completely from such judgmental decision processes. CBIS may be used to locate candidates from among current personnel or to create files on other candidates who apply or who are suggested by placement services. Nor are such decisions always nonquantitative. Some highly structured organizations, notably the military, attempt to quantify personal and professional attributes and base personnel decisions on numerical scores.

More recently, there have been attempts to make judgmental decisions directly by the computer. Computer programs are written that approximate the thought process used by human decision makers. Applications of this type are frequently referred to as *expert knowledge systems* because they simulate the decisions made by experts in a particular field. Screening applicants for law school, processing overdrafts (bad checks), and processing charge card applications are all examples of judgmental decision-making tasks which are aided by computers.

Compromise Decisions

A particularly frustrating decision environment exists when managers know exactly how to achieve certain outcomes, but their preference for any given outcome is unclear. For example, in the 1960s, IBM undoubtedly possessed the knowledge—and the ability to apply it—of how to achieve monopolistic control of the computer industry. But did IBM prefer such an outcome?

Clearly, it had a preference for the high profits that accompany such control, but just as clearly, it had a distinct preference for avoiding the antitrust suits that would inevitably follow. The situation called for a *compromise:* a trade-off between market share and the tolerance of the federal government.

Compromise decisions are quite common in the public sector, where conflicting or unclear preferences are present in almost every situation. Individual freedom versus public safety, environmental concerns versus economic benefits, defense spending versus human services, and other such philosophical differences constantly face elected and appointed decision makers in government. The dispute over preferences cannot, of course, be resolved by CBIS, although CBIS may help gather and analyze data relevant to the issue. But once preferences are established, the decision environment shifts back to the computational quadrant, and CBIS become an important, almost dominating, factor in the decision process.

Inspirational Decisions

Pity the poor decision makers in the environment depicted in the lower right-hand corner of Figure 7-1. They are unsure of what they prefer and even if they did have a preference, they would not know how to achieve the desired outcome. Faced with such a decision, most of us simply raise our eyes heavenward and murmur, "Help," hoping for an *inspirational* answer to our problem. Once again, such situations are somewhat more common in the public sector. Should a friendly but totalitarian foreign regime be supported or not, and assuming that it should, how can it be kept in power? Should unemployment really be eliminated, and how can it be without excessive inflation? At present, CBIS are all but helpless in solving these and similar dilemmas. Human decision makers must resolve preferences to the extent that the environment shifts to the judgmental or the computational.

Limitations of the Model

The matrix of decision environments is a convenient model for explaining decision situations, but it has several shortcomings that should be mentioned. First, the scales of preferences and outcomes are not dichotomous, as shown in the figure. In reality, they are continuous. The matrix shows only the extreme end-points. There are many shades of gray between the black and white of "complete–incomplete" and "clear–unclear." Obviously, the extent of CBIS help in these inbetween situations also varies continuously from much to little or none. Second, the matrix gives no clue to the *frequency* of each decision environment. The organization—a bank, for instance—that habitually finds itself in a computational situation will undoubtedly make a heavier commitment to CBIS than, say, the U.S. State Department, which through no fault of its own is more likely to find itself in an inspirational environment. An organization's decision environment is a major factor in the design of its CBIS.

Decision Strategies

There is another dimension to the matrix of decision-making environments that is particularly relevant to the computational cell. The additional dimension, shown in Figure 7-2, describes the extent of a manager's knowledge of the external conditions that will prevail at the time the decision is carried out. This knowledge of the future—of the *state of nature* that will exist—ranges from *certainty* (perfect knowledge) to *uncertainty* (no knowledge whatsoever), with a middle ground of *risk* (probabilistic knowledge).

Decision Making Under Uncertainty

When managers have no knowledge of future environmental factors, they tend to be guided by their personal philosophy toward success and failure. For some, the rewards of success dominate the decision process, whereas others are more motivated by fear of failure. To illustrate, consider the case of an electronics manufacturing firm that wishes to enter the market for home computers. Three alternative courses of action have been proposed: (1) to manufacture its own brand of home computer; (2) to manufacture accessories to be used with the home computers of other manufacturers; and (3) to become a supplier of circuit boards and subassemblies used by other manufacturers.

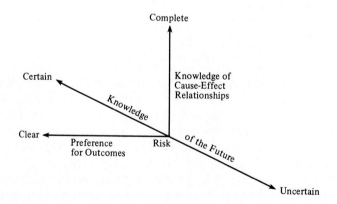

FIGURE 7-2 Dimensions of the decision environment.

TABLE 7-1 Payoff Table for an Electronics Firm

| | State of Nature | |
Alternative	1. Industry leader reenters market	2. Industry leader does not reenter market
1. Manufacture own home computer	($250,000)	$1,200,000
2. Manufacture home computer accessories	$600,000	$ 450,000
3. Supply subassemblies to other manufacturers	$400,000	$ 500,000

The states of nature that might prevail in the future are related to the possible actions of the computer industry leader, which has recently withdrawn from the home computer market. The management of the electronics firm believes that if the industry leader reenters the market, the sales of its own home computer would be low, but there would be a good market for accessories (for the industry leader's computer) and a fair market for subassemblies (for the computers and accessories of other manufacturers). However, if the industry leader does not reenter the market, the firm's own home computer would sell well, other firms would enter the market and boost the sale of subassemblies, but lower total sales of home computers would hurt the accessory market.

The electronics firm, of course, does not know what the industry leader will do, and its management feels that its decision must be made *before* the industry leader's plans become known. The estimated profits (or losses) from each combination of an alternative and a state of nature are shown in the form of a *payoff table* in Table 7-1. These estimates are largely subjective, but they may be based in part on a CBIS analysis of the historical performance of other products in similar competitive environments.

The Maximax Strategy
Maximax is an abbreviated expression for "*maximize the maximums*," that is, evaluate each alternative in terms of its maximum possible payoff and select the one with the highest maximum. A manager of the maximax philosophy would view the courses of action for the electronics firm as shown in Table 7-2. Such a manager would naturally favor the manufacture of home computers, because it is the alternative with the highest potential profit.

Maximax is often referred to as the strategy of the complete optimist. Only favorable outcomes are considered, even if they happen to require different states of nature. In order to achieve the maximum profits for the first and third alternatives, the maximax manager must assume that the industry

TABLE 7-2 Maximax View of Expected Profits

Alternative	Maximum Profit
1. Manufacture own home computer	$1,200,000
2. Manufacture home computer accessories	$ 600,000
3. Supply subassemblies to other manufacturers	$ 500,000

leader will *not* reenter the market; however, the maximum profit for the second alternative is based on an assumption that the industry leader *will* reenter the market. Such inconsistencies do not deter a true optimist, of course, but they may be bothersome to the information analyst trying to design a system to support this manager's decision making.

The Maximin Strategy
Maximin is a shortened version of "*maxi*mize the *min*imums." In this case, the decision maker considers only the worst possible outcome for each course of action and selects the one with the highest minimum. For the electronics firm, a maximin manager would consider only the outcomes shown in Table 7-3 and would elect to manufacture accessories for the home computers of other manufacturers.

If a maximax is a complete optimist, a maximin is obviously a complete pessimist. Maximin managers are no more or less logical than maximax managers—both require the state of nature to vary freely in order to support their payoff assumptions; they simply have a different philosophical outlook. There are, perhaps, more managers of the maximin persuasion (how many times have you heard, "If we do this, what is the worst thing that can happen?"), but our society tends to glorify the risk takers, the maximax managers who go for the big payoff. The football coach who calls for a long pass on a fourth-and-one from his own twenty-yard line (a maximax approach) is hailed for his

TABLE 7-3 Maximin View of Expected Profits

Alternative	Minimum Profit (Loss)
1. Manufacture own home computer	($250,000)
2. Manufacture home computer accessories	$450,000
3. Supply subassemblies to other manufacturers	$400,000

courage—especially if the pass is successful—but the coach who punts in the same situation (a maximin attitude) is more likely to enjoy a long career.

The Opportunity-Loss Criterion

Some decision makers prefer to view alternatives in terms of their *opportunity loss* instead of their payoffs. Opportunity loss is the difference between the best payoff for a given alternative under a specified state of nature and the payoff for each other alternative under that same state of nature. For the electronics firm, Table 7-4 shows that if the industry leader reenters the market and the firm manufactures accessories (alternative 2), there is no opportunity for higher profit and the opportunity loss is zero. However, if the firm decides to manufacture its own home computer and the industry leader reenters the market, it loses $250,000 when it could have made $600,000 by manufacturing accessories—an opportunity loss of $850,000. Finally, the opportunity lost by the decision to become a subassembly supplier is the $600,000 of alternative 2 less the $400,000 of alternative 3, or $200,000. Opportunity losses when the industry leader does not reenter the market are computed similarly as differences between the best payoff ($1,200,000 for making the firm's own home computer) and the payoffs for the other alternatives.

The use of opportunity loss to evaluate alternatives is often called *minimax*, which stands for "*mini*mize *max*imum opportunity loss." For the electronics firm, the maximum opportunity loss for each alternative is shown in Table 7-5. A minimax strategist would select the third alternative because of its low opportunity loss.

The minimax strategy often turns out to be a compromise (as in this example) between the completely optimistic and the completely pessimistic

TABLE 7-4   Opportunity Loss for an Electronics Firm

	State of Nature	
Alternative	**1. Industry leader reenters market**	**2. Industry leader does not reenter market**
1. Manufacture own home computer	600,000 − (250,000)	1,200,000 −1,200,000
	850,000	0
2. Manufacture home computer accessories	600,000 − 600,000	1,200,000 − 450,000
	0	750,000
3. Supply subassemblies to other manufacturers	600,000 − 400,000	1,200,000 − 500,000
	200,000	700,000

TABLE 7-5   Minimax View of Opportunity Loss

Alternative	Maximum Opportunity Loss
1. Manufacture own home computer	$850,000
2. Manufacture home computer accessories	$750,000
3. Supply subassemblies to other manufacturers	$700,000

outlooks. The philosophical foundation of minimax is still somewhat pessimistic, however, in that it seeks to minimize loss.

Decision Making Under Risk

The quality of decision making can be improved by additional information about the possible states of nature. Indeed, one of the major objectives of decision makers is to reduce or eliminate uncertainty. Uncertainty is reduced when probabilities can be assigned to the occurrence of each state of nature. For example, in the electronics firm case, it may be determined that the probability that the industry leader will reenter the market is .6 (six chances out of ten), which implies a probability of .4 (the remaining four chances out of ten) that it will not reenter the market. In this case, the probabilities represent the subjective estimate of the decision maker based on an evaluation of the industry leader's historical market activity and, perhaps, indications found in its current activities.

Expected-Value Criterion

When probabilities can be assigned to the states of nature, the appropriate decision criterion—irrespective of the decision maker's personal philosophy—is the *expected value* of each alternative. An expected value is the weighted average of the payoffs for a given alternative under the various states of nature. For alternative 1, the expected value is the payoff when the industry leader reenters the market, weighted (multiplied) by the probability that the leader will enter the market, plus the payoff when the leader does not enter the market, weighted by that probability. In numbers, the expected value is

$$(-250,000)(.6) + (1,200,000)(.4) = -150,000 + 480,000 = \$330,000$$

This and other expected values for the alternatives under consideration by the electronics firm are shown in Table 7-6.

The three alternatives now represent expected profits of $330,000,

TABLE 7-6   Payoff Table with Expected Values

	State of Nature		
	1. Industry leader reenters market. Probability = .6	2. Industry leader does not reenter market. Probability = .4	Expected Value
Alternative			
1. Manufacture own home computer	−250,000 × .6 −150,000	1,200,000 × .4 480,000	= 330,000
2. Manufacture home computer accessories	600,000 × .6 360,000	450,000 × .4 180,000	= 540,000
3. Supply subassemblies to other manufacturers	400,000 × .6 240,000	500,000 × .4 200,000	= 440,000

$540,000, and $440,000, respectively. The best decision, of course, is the one with the highest expected value: to manufacture home computer accessories.

Decision Trees

In its simplest form, a decision tree is merely a graphic representation of a payoff table. Figure 7-3, for example, shows exactly the same information included in Table 7-6. In keeping with conventional decision tree notation,

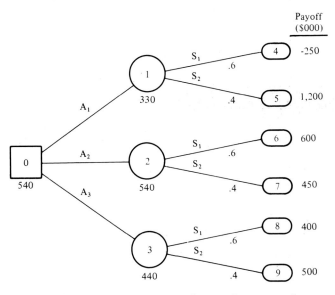

FIGURE 7-3   Decision tree for an electronics firm.

the alternatives are shown as arcs (lines) designated with an A, subscripted to identify specific alternatives (A_1 is the first alternative, A_2 the second, and so on). Similarly, states of nature are shown by arcs with a subscripted S. When probabilities are assigned to states of nature, they are shown on or near the arc; in this example, they appear under the arc, just below the identifying S. The shape of the nodes is also governed by convention: Squares represent *decision nodes* (where the decision maker has a choice of alternatives to follow), and circles represent *chance nodes* (where probability determines which state of nature will occur). A third type of node—a rectangle with rounded ends—has been borrowed from flow-charting conventions to represent the ends, or *terminals*, of the state-of-nature arcs. Terminal nodes are normally omitted when drawing decision trees, but they are useful in computer analyses that tend to use nodal designations to identify the beginnings and endings of arcs. The home-computer decision has been diagrammed in this fashion in Figure 7-3, with the nodes numbered according to the rules of a specific software package. The numbers below or to the right of the nodes show the value of the alternative that ends in that node. For terminal nodes, the value is the payoff; for chance nodes, it is the expected value of the subsequent payoffs; and for decision nodes, it is the largest of the subsequent values. A decision is reached by looking forward from a position at each decision node and selecting the alternative that leads to the highest expected value. The number below the decision node represents the expected value of that alternative. In this decision tree for the electronics firm, the number 540 below the decision node means that alternative 2, with an expected value of $540,000, should be selected.

Software for decision-tree analysis may now be found as a supplement to college texts in management science. One such package[2] was used to analyze the example just described and to produce the output shown in Figure 7-4. In this analysis, as in most decision-tree software, the user must have the layout of the decision tree well in mind before entering the data. The software will not actually draw the decision tree, but it will perform the arithmetic operations involved and display the solution. Decision-tree software is most helpful when the solution requires present values or other computations more complex than those illustrated here.

Decision trees can become quite complex, especially when they reflect a number of sequential decisions or when indicators suggest a need to systematically revise the initial probability assessments for the states of nature. The technique for revising probabilities is an application of *Bayes' law* and is beyond the scope of this chapter. You may find an explanation of it in most college-level statistics books.

CBIS can enhance decision tree analysis in several ways. First, revised probabilities and expected values can be computed automatically. Second,

---

[2] Warren Erikson and Owen Hall, Jr., *Computer Models for Management Science* (Reading, Mass.: Addison-Wesley Publishing Company, Inc.).

```
       ** INFORMATION ENTERED **

DECISION NODES

                        ALTERNATIVE   ENDING
   NODE     BRANCHES      NUMBER        NODE

    0          3            1            1
                           2            2
                           3            3

CHANCE NODES

                                       ENDING
   NODE     BRANCHES   PROBABILITY      NODE

    1          2          .6            4
                          .4            5

    2          2          .6            6
                          .4            7

    3          2          .6            8
                          .4            9


TERMINAL NODES

   NODE          PAYOFF

    4            -250
    5            1200
    6             600
    7             450
    8             400
    9             500


      ** RESULTS **

SELECTED ALTERNATIVES:   2

EXPECTED PAYOFF:   540

      ** END OF ANALYSIS **
```

FIGURE 7-4   Computer analysis of decision tree.

and perhaps more important, some commercially available decision-tree programs incorporate discounting techniques (discussed later in this chapter) that express expected values in present values. This feature is particularly important when payoffs will occur over differing periods of time and when, as now, interest rates are high.

Decision-tree analysis has wide application, especially in marketing, where the indicators predict consumer attitudes toward a product. Decision trees help justify (or reject) decisions to conduct market research by showing the effect that such additional information will have on the profits expected from marketing different products.

Decision Making Under Certainty

When the state of nature is known with certainty, the emphasis shifts from the selection of an alternative to the computation of outcomes. The decision itself is usually obvious under certainty; the challenge comes in developing a model that will yield the answer. When the decision situation is unique, management scientists or operations researchers may be required to develop an appropriate model. Fortunately, many decisions can be supported with standard models that require only brief familiarization and a little practice on a computer terminal. A few examples of commonly used modeling techniques will serve to illustrate the process of decision making under certainty.

Linear Programming

The term *linear programming* refers to the formulation (programming) of a decision situation with first-order (linear) equations expressed in terms of certain decision variables. The equations are solved simultaneously to give not just the best of two or three proposed alternatives, but the *best of all possible solutions* to the problem. Models that yield a best possible solution directly are called *optimization models*. It has been estimated that 15 to 20 percent of all businesses use linear programming, which makes it one of the most popular of all optimization techniques.

Linear programming can be used to find the optimum mix of products to manufacture under certain production constraints, the most profitable combination of investments that meets a client's investment philosophy, the least expensive shipping plan for a distribution network, and the solutions to many other typical problems. Most such problems involve numerous variables and constraint equations and, for all practical purposes, must be solved by computer. It is possible, however, to make a graphical analog of the way problems are solved by linear programming if the problem is restricted to only two variables and a few constraints. One such problem is presented in Table 7-7.

TABLE 7-7   A Product Mix Problem

Process	Requirement (Minutes)		Available Time (Minutes)
	Lens A	Lens B	
Grinding	2	3	940
Polishing	10	6	3,080

Profit: $15 for each A lens, $12 for each B lens

Maximum demand for A lenses is 275/week. All B lenses made can be sold.

Problem: How many of each type of lens should be made in order to maximize profits?

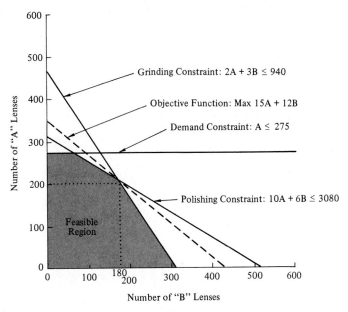

FIGURE 7-5   Linear programming graph.

The production manager of an optical company has some idle time available each week on the grinding and polishing machines. The company wishes to use this time to produce camera lenses. A type A lens yields a profit of $15 and requires two minutes of grinding time and ten minutes of polishing time. The type B lens brings a profit of $12 and requires three minutes of grinding and six of polishing. The firm can sell all the type B lenses it can make, but the demand for type A lenses is only 275 per week. Based on the limited grinding and polishing time available and the limited demand for type A lenses, how many of each type should be manufactured to maximize profits? The graphical solution to this problem is shown in Figure 7-5.

The constraint on grinding time is expressed as $2A + 3B \leq 940$, meaning that 2 (minutes) times A (the number of A lenses made) plus 3 (minutes) times B (the number of B lenses made) must be less than or equal to 940 (minutes of grinding time available). The line from 470 on the A axis to 313 on the B axis represents combinations of A and B lens quantities that will require *exactly* 940 minutes of grinding. The area below the line represents combinations that use *less than* 940 minutes. The polishing constraint and the A lens demand constraint are plotted similarly. The shaded area defined by the overlap of the three constraints is known as the *feasible region*—the combinations of A and B quantities that meet all three constraints. Somewhere in this region is the optimum combination.

Profit for this problem is given by $15A + 12B$, or 15 (dollars) times the number of A lenses plus 12 (dollars) times the number of B lenses. The objective is to maximize this expression; hence this expression is called the *objective function* and is written as MAXIMIZE 15A + 12B.

The optimum combination is found by plotting the slope of the objective function and moving it as far from the origin (the lower left-hand corner of the graph) as possible while staying within the feasible region. For this problem, the optimum combination is where the objective function, shown by a dashed line, just touches the corner of the feasible region at A = 200, B = 180. The solution to the problem, therefore, is to manufacture 200 type A lenses and 180 type B lenses for a profit of $5,160. No other combination of A and B lenses will bring as much profit.

Linear programming software is also available in supplements to college texts as well as in many commercial packages, such as *Linear Programming*, by Computer Software Technology, or *Linear Programmer*, by Dynacomp, Inc. The ouput of a computer analysis of the lens problem is shown in Figure 7-6. This analysis shows the same optimal quantities of A and B lenses as well as how *sensitive* the solution is to the input variables.[3] For example, the objective function coefficient of A can range from 8 to 20 without changing the solution. Similarly, the right-hand-side constant for the first constraint can vary from 715 to 1,540 without changing the solution. Sensitivity analysis is a very powerful element of linear programming.

Inventory Analysis

Every organization that maintains inventory faces the problem of striking a balance between certain *ordering* and *carrying* costs associated with inventory. Ordering costs are administrative expenses generated by the placing of an order and are largely independent of order size. Ordering costs argue for very large orders that would have to be placed only infrequently. Carrying costs are based on insurance, taxes, storage fees, and other costs directly related to the quantity of inventory maintained. Carrying costs argue for very small orders, which obviously would occur more frequently than large orders.

Figure 7-7 shows that carrying cost is a straight line function that increases constantly with order size. It costs twice as much to carry, say, 100 units as 50; three times as much to carry 150; and so on. Ordering costs follow a curve that decreases more and more gradually as order size increases. In the extremes, one could place very small orders every day or one very large order once a year. The *total* cost curve represents the sum of the annual ordering and carrying costs for any given order size. The optimum order size is the quantity that minimizes total cost.

The relationships shown in Figure 7-7 have been expressed mathematically in the following equation:

$$Q^* = \sqrt{\frac{2\,DC_o}{C_k}}$$

[3] Erikson and Hall.

```
        ** INFORMATION ENTERED **

NUMBER OF CONSTRAINTS          3
NUMBER OF VARIABLES            2
NUMBER OF <= CONSTRAINTS       3
NUMBER OF  = CONSTRAINTS       0
NUMBER OF >= CONSTRAINTS       0

MAXIMIZATION PROBLEM

   15A   +   12B

SUBJECT TO

    2A   +    2B   <=    940
   10A   +    6B   <=   3080
    1A   +    0B   <=    275

       ** RESULTS **

              VARIABLE    ORIGINAL     COEFF.
VARIABLE        VALUE      COEFF.       SENS.

    A            200        15            0
    B            180        12            0


CONSTRAINT   ORIGINAL    SLACK OR     SHADOW
 NUMBER        RHS       SURPLUS      PRICE

    1           940         0          1.67
    2          3080         0          1.17
    3           275        75          0


OBJECTIVE FUNCTION VALUE:    5160


             SENSITIVITY ANALYSIS

       OBJECTIVE FUNCTION COEFFICIENTS

              LOWER     ORIGINAL      UPPER
VARIABLE      LIMIT    COEFFICIENT    LIMIT

    A           8          15          20
    B           9          12          22.5

               RIGHT-HAND SIDE

CONSTRAINT    LOWER     ORIGINAL      UPPER
 NUMBER       LIMIT    COEFFICIENT    LIMIT

    1          715        940         1540
    2         1880       3080         3530
    3          200        275       NO LIMIT


      ** END OF ANALYSIS **
```

FIGURE 7-6 Computer analysis of linear programming.

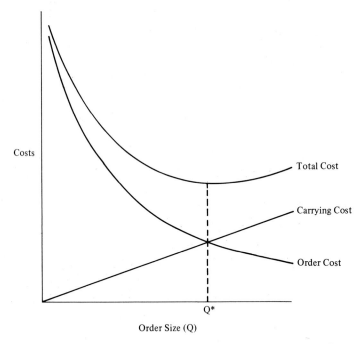

FIGURE 7-7   Minimizing annual inventory costs.

where $Q*$ is the economic order quantity (EOQ)
    D is the annual demand for the item
    C_o is the cost of placing an order for items
    C_k is the cost of carrying one item in inventory for one year

The optimum order size, usually called the *economic order quantity*, or *EOQ*, is given by the square root of two times the annual demand for the item, times the cost of placing an order, divided by the cost of carrying one item in inventory for one year. This formula can be used by anyone who is certain of the demand and the costs and who has a pocket calculator.

The basic EOQ model is *deterministic;* that is, the variables involved are known with certainty and can assume only one specific value each in the computation of the EOQ. More sophisticated analyses of inventory introduce *probabilistic* values for some variables. Such factors as the shipping time and the demand during shipping time may vary from period to period. If shipping time exceeds the expected time or if demand suddenly increases while the firm is waiting for an order to arrive, the inventory may not be sufficient to satisfy the demand and a stock-out will occur. Stock-outs result in back orders, loss of goodwill, possibly the loss of the order, or, at worst, the loss of the customer. In order to avoid these losses, inventory managers carry some additional number of items called *safety stock*. The optimum level of safety stock can be determined from an analysis of the probability distributions for demand and shipping time, the penalty perceived for a stock-out, and the cost of carrying safety stock.

The EOQ model is valid only when certain assumptions are met, principally, that the demand function is linear throughout the period under analysis. When demand is seasonal or follows no predictable pattern, order size may be based on periodic demand, modified by a "smoothing constant" to dampen oscillations in order size that tend to appear in this method. This latter technique is a particularly good CBIS application, especially when many different items are carried in inventory, because it is so tedious in a manual system to monitor inventory balances constantly and to revise the order size from period to period. EOQ, by contrast, is easy to apply even in manual systems, although it is still worthwhile to incorporate EOQ into a CBIS inventory application when the underlying assumptions are met.

Present-Value Techniques

It would seem that when future costs and revenues are known with certainty, the choice between competing investment opportunities would be simple. Surprisingly, it is not, and many poor financial decisions are made because of a lack of knowledge of the appropriate decision techniques. For example, consider the two projects shown in Figure 7-8. Project 1 involves fairly high start-up costs but low maintenance costs over the life of the project. Project 2 is exactly opposite, having low start-up costs and high maintenance costs. Both projects produce identical yearly revenues, including the salvage value of capital investments received in the final year.

From a superficial review of the data presented in Figure 7-8, it would seem that project 1 is the more profitable by $25,000. After all, the total revenues are the same, but the total costs are $25,000 higher in project 2. But this reasoning ignores the *time value* of money. We know that a dollar in hand today is of more value than a dollar payable one year from now. But how much more? Assuming that one could invest today's dollar at 15 percent, it would be worth $1.15 in one year. Conversely, the dollar payable in one year is worth the amount that, if invested today at 15 percent, would yield exactly one dollar a year from now. That amount is known as the *present value*. The present value of one dollar payable one year from now, at an interest rate of 15 percent, is 86.9565 cents. It can also be said that this is the value of one dollar *discounted to the present* at the rate of 15 percent.[4]

When the revenues and costs of the two projects shown in Figure 7-8 are expressed as present values, the cash-flow chart appears as shown in Figure 7-9. Total profit is still the relevant criterion, but profit is now expressed as

---

[4]This value is obtained by $P = F(1 + i)^n$, where P is the present value, F is the future sum, i is the annual interest rate, and n is the number of years. For this example, $P = 1/(1.15)^1 = .869565$. This formula can be modified to take into consideration periodic compounding of interest, which has been omitted here for the sake of simplicity.

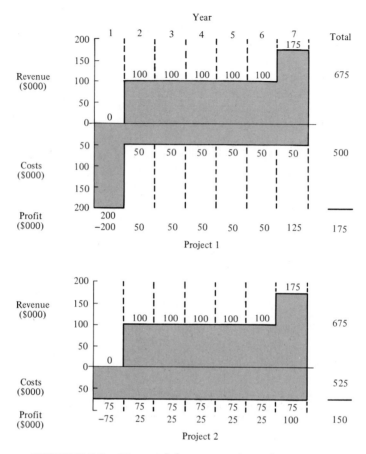

FIGURE 7-8   Financial decision without discounting.

the difference between the present value of revenues and the present value of costs—a difference referred to as the *net present value.*

Two facts are apparent in Figure 7-9. First, neither project is nearly as profitable as first imagined, and second, our superficial analysis led to the wrong decision—we should have picked project 2!

Present values are now so universally accepted and so simple to use that they have been programmed into many hand-held calculators. They are, of course, also incorporated into the model base of CBIS for the convenience of terminal users and for use as subroutines in applications such as the decision-tree model described earlier. Electronic spreadsheets, either as separate software or as part of an integrated package, are very convenient to use for financial analyses involving present values. Figure 7-10 shows a spreadsheet solution to the financial decision just described. The format or *template* for this solution requires only the entry of yearly revenues and costs. Formulae

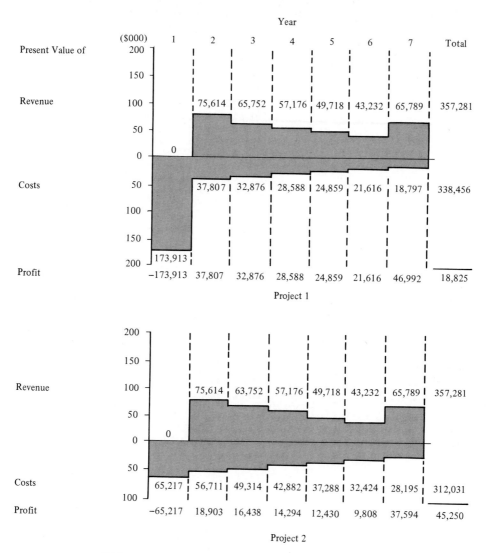

FIGURE 7-9   Financial decision with discounting.

entered into other cells compute profit (revenue minus cost) and totals. The NPV (net present value) column is found by a command similar to NPV (.15,B5 . . . H5), which means, "Discount at 15 percent the values in column B (the YEAR-1 column), row 5 (the REVENUE row) through column H (the YEAR-7 column), row 5." The attractiveness of spreadsheet analysis lies in the ease with which changes or "what if" situations can be applied to the original data without triggering a complete reworking of the problem by the analyst.

DISCOUNTED CASH FLOW ANALYSIS

YEAR

	1	2	3	4	5	6	7	TOTAL	NPV
PROJECT 1									
REVENUE	0	100000	100000	100000	100000	100000	175000	675000	357280.72
COST	200000	50000	50000	50000	50000	50000	50000	500000	338455.76
PROFIT	−200000	50000	50000	50000	50000	50000	125000	175000	18824.96
PROJECT 2									
REVENUE	0	100000	100000	100000	100000	100000	175000	675000	357280.72
COST	75000	75000	75000	75000	75000	75000	75000	525000	312031.48
PROFIT	−75000	25000	25000	25000	25000	25000	100000	150000	45249.25

FIGURE 7-10   Computer analysis of discounted cash flow.

Administrative Behavior

Before we leave the subject of decision strategies, it should be pointed out that the objective of choosing the one best alternative is considerably easier to achieve in the closed environment of a textbook than in the open environment of the real world. In the real world, the combinations of alternatives and states of nature may be too numerous to consider. Certainty and deterministic conditions also occur much less frequently in the real world than we are sometimes led to believe. And many variables are difficult or impossible to express in the quantitative terms required by these analyses. How would you, for example, estimate the value of goodwill created by landscaping the physical plant of a firm?

The result is that many managers prefer intuitive methods over the more analytical methods presented here. It can be argued, of course, that intuition *is* an analytical process—we simply are not yet able to discern the steps involved.

There is also evidence that managers do not really attempt to optimize, to find the best solution. Instead, it is argued, they *satisfice;* that is, they accept the first solution that satisfies certain acceptance criteria. Personnel managers, for example, cannot possibly consider every potential candidate for a job opening. Rather, they establish criteria for experience, education, and other relevant attributes and then hire the first candidate who qualifies.

The tendency to satisfice instead of optimize is called *administrative behavior* by behavioral scientists. Administrative behavior unquestionably occurs, but certainly not to the exclusion of quantitative techniques. The current popularity of quantitative topics in business school curricula and the increasing availability of computational power, of both the hardware and the software variety, tend to relegate satisficing to a "second-choice" role behind optimizing. Even when satisficing is appropriate, as in the personnel example, many managers compromise by selecting a number of satisfactory alternatives and then optimizing from among those selections.

Most of us tend to satisfice in personal decisions as well. For example, did you consider *every* possible college or university before selecting the one you now attend? Or did you set certain criteria—tuition cost, distance from home, majors offered, coed dorms, and so on—and then narrow the field down to a reasonable number? If you did the latter, then you, too, satisfice rather than optimize.

Other Decision Tools

In addition to those decision methods selected to illustrate decision making under uncertainty, risk, and certainty, two other decision tools merit discussion because of their widespread use and their great value in the support of decision making. They are *statistical methods* and *simulation.*

Statistical Methods

Some of you may also have taken a course in statistics, in which case you are familiar with the kind of decision support offered by statistical methods. For those of you less familiar with this subject, we offer a brief explanation, without computational detail, of how statistical routines in the CBIS model base can aid managerial decision making.

In conversational English, most of us use the term *statistics* to refer to numerical data—as in labor statistics, population statistics, baseball statistics, and so on. To the management scientist, however, *statistics* refers to the branch of mathematics concerned with probabilistic concepts. The decision-tree analysis discussed earlier, for example, is based on probability and is properly included in the field of statistics.

Other statistical tools enable managers to predict future events and thus reduce uncertainty about the state of nature. For example, a marketing manager may hypothesize several levels of demand for a product as possible states of nature. With no way of knowing just which state will exist, the selection of an alternative must be guided by maximax, maximin, or some other philosophical approach to decision making under uncertainty. However, if a single level of demand can be predicted using statistical methods, then the decision can be made, under certainty, by a method such as linear programming.

It is obvious that the quality of any decision based on a prediction is directly dependent on the accuracy of that prediction. Accuracy, in turn, is dependent on the quality and the quantity of the data collected, chance, and the method of prediction. One such method of statistical prediction is the process of *estimation.*

Estimation

In statistics, estimates are made of some population characteristic based on knowledge gained from a sample of that population. For example, the estimated mean age of household heads within an insurance sales region could be estimated from a survey of a few hundred households. A few *thousand* households would improve the precision of the estimate, but, as the number of households surveyed increases, the cost of the survey also increases. There are statistical methods of determining the appropriate sample size based on the maximum allowable error of the estimate.

An estimate expressed as a single value is called a *point estimate.* Thus, to continue the example above, if a survey of 200 households indicated a mean age of 41 years for the head of the household, then the point estimate for the mean age of the heads of all households in the region would also be 41 years. Point estimates are convenient for use in deterministic models where a single value must be substituted for an unknown, but they are also risky in that they give no indication of possible deviation from the estimated value.

A more informative form of an estimate, but one that is more difficult to incorporate into analytical models, is the *interval estimate.* Thus, one might say that the mean age of all heads of households in the region is 41 years *plus or minus,* say, 1.7 years. The amount added and subtracted to give the interval is based on three things: the size of the sample, the inherent variability of the population as exhibited in the sample, and the degree of confidence desired by the decision maker. Small samples, much variability, and high levels of confidence all contribute to large intervals. Large samples, little variability, and a willingness to accept a lesser degree of confidence all tend to reduce the interval. Sample size, as noted earlier, can be computed; variability is expressed by a statistical measure called the *standard deviation,* which can be computed from the sample data; and confidence is usually expressed as 90, 95, or 99 percent. A 95 percent confidence level for an interval estimate means that the decision maker is 95 percent certain that the population mean falls within the stated interval about the sample mean.

Estimation is usually based on *current* observations of the variable to be estimated. It is also possible to make predictions based on *past* observations of the variable under examination. This form of prediction is called trend analysis.

Trend Analysis

Trend analysis is appropriate for predictions into the future when there is evidence that the future will be at least partially determined by the past. Population growth, for example, can be reasonably predicted on the basis of the past, but one might be less willing to predict next year's snowfall based on historical data. Annual gross sales, the number of people who participate in

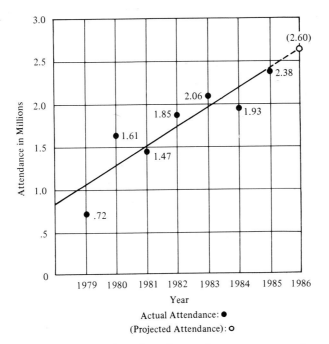

FIGURE 7-11 Trend analysis of amusement park attendance.

various recreational activities, the number of computer systems in use, and other similar facts of interest can be predicted fairly well by trend analysis.

In trend analysis, a decision maker seeks to "fit" a line to a plot of data. For simplicity, an example using a straight line will be used, although many trends are explained better by curved lines. "Curve-fit" programs in the CBIS model base can determine the type of line that best fits the data at hand. Figure 7-11 shows how a straight line has been fitted to a plot of attendance at an amusement park.[5] Based on a straight-line projection of attendance, the park management could expect 2.6 million visitors in 1986.

Trend analysis is easy to understand and to use, but it is very susceptible to sudden environmental changes that may make the estimate totally wrong. For example, consider the net earnings of the Polaroid Corporation for the years 1975 to 1978. Figure 7-12 shows that a linear trend analysis of net earnings would have predicted a 1979 figure of $132.5 million. Yet Polaroid's actual net earnings for 1979 were around $37 million! Clearly, the conditions that led to the steady increases between 1975 and 1978 had changed and should have been incorporated into any models used to predict 1979 net earnings.

[5]The exact placement of the line in Figure 7-11 is determined by the "least-squares" method, which minimizes the sum of the squared deviations of each plotted point from the line.

Regression Analysis

Regression analysis is closely related to trend analysis in that it also makes predictions on the basis of historical data. But where trend analysis relies on the past performance of the *predicted* variable, regression analysis uses other, related variables to make the prediction. In this way, sales of television sets might be predicted on the basis of total population, disposable income, interest rates, and other such variables. Like trend analysis, regression analysis is not restricted to straight-line, or linear, relationships. But unlike trend analysis, there may be more than two variables involved in regression analysis. Again, for the sake of simplicity, a linear example is used and, to permit a graphical solution, only two variables are considered. Neither of these conditions poses a serious problem in computer applications of regression analysis, which can accommodate a variety of curvilinear relationships and do not use graphical solution methods.

Table 7-8 shows the number of hot dogs sold at a major-league baseball park and the home team's winning percentage as of that date. Regression analysis permits the concessions manager to predict the number of hot dogs to be prepared for each game (the *dependent* variable) on the basis of the team's current winning percentage (the *independent* variable). The results of such an analysis are shown in Figure 7-13.

A *regression line* fitted to the hot dog/winning percentage data shows that if the team's current percentage is .450, past performance suggests the sale of approximately 12.1 thousand hot dogs. This is called *simple* regression because it employs only one independent variable. Of course, there are other variables that affect hot dog sales—such as the weather, the opponent, the team's involvement in the pennant race, and so on—as evidenced by the fact that all the plotted points do not lie exactly on the regression line. The inclusion of such additional independent variables requires a form of analysis called *multiple regression*, which, as suggested earlier, is difficult to portray graphically, but that is not particularly demanding of a computer analysis.

The examples of regression and trend analysis presented here are comparable to the point estimates discussed previously. It is also possible to con-

TABLE 7-8   Hot Dog Sales and Winning Percentages

Date	Winning Percentage	Sales (in Thousands)
April 15, 1984	.250	9.9
June 1, 1984	.375	11.4
August 1, 1984	.533	12.8
September 15, 1984	.482	11.5
April 15, 1985	.667	13.9
June 1, 1985	.571	13.5
August 1, 1985	.510	13.4
September 15, 1985	.425	12.4

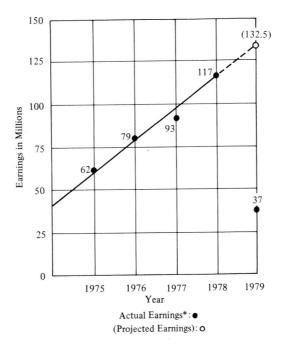

*From *Business Week,* March 2, 1981.

FIGURE 7-12   Trend analysis of Polaroid's annual net earnings.

struct intervals about regression and trend analysis predictions. In the hot dog example, the concessions manager might wish to operate at the upper end of a 95 percent confidence interval to reduce the chance of running out of hot dogs. The refinement of the prediction by including additional independent variables and the use of a confidence interval would greatly reduce uncertainty over the demand for hot dogs.

Multiple regression, or even simple regression with a large number of data points, involves a complexity of computations beyond that normally conducted by hand. For complex regression problems, a computer analysis, such as the one shown in Figure 7-14, is virtually a necessity.[6] The computer analysis shows the parameters of the *regression equation, correlation data,* and *standard deviations* as well as other information about the analysis. For this problem, the regression equation is

$$Y = \text{constant plus coefficient times } X$$
$$Y = 7.70757 + 9.74022X$$

[6] Donald W. Kroeber, *Forecasting: A Computer-Assisted Instruction Approach* (Charlottesville, Va.: Ivy Publishing, 1985).

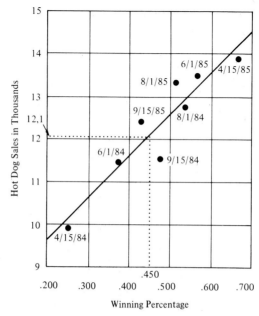

FIGURE 7-13 Regression analysis of hot dog sales.

so that the winning percentage of .450 results in

$$7.70757 + 9.74022(.450)$$
$$7.70757 + 4.38310 = 12.09067$$

or approximately 12.1 thousand hot dogs. The *coefficient of determination* shows that slightly over 85 percent of the variation in hot dog sales can be explained by variation in the team's winning percentage. An interval estimate of plus and minus two *standard errors of the estimate* would result in a prediction that hot dog sales will be 12.1 ± (2)(.55700) or, roughly, between 11.0 and 13.2 thousand.

Simulation

The models described up to this point are more or less standard mathematical or statistical techniques. They can be included in the model base and used in a variety of situations with little effort other than entering data according to a specified format. They also are *static;* that is, they show a final solution with little attention given to what may have transpired en route to the solution. There are many decision situations in which no standard model applies or in which a *dynamic* model—one that shows and considers intermediate results—is necessary. The technique of *simulation* is particularly appropriate in these cases.

```
CORELATION MATRIX
------------------
1               .92356
.92356          1

VARIABLE        MEAN        STANDARD DEVIATION
--------        ------      ------------------
WIN PCT         .47662          .12752
HOT DOGS        12.35           1.34483

REGRESSION EQUATION
-------------------------------------------------
DEPENDENT VARIABLE: HOT DOGS
-------------------------------------------------
INDEPENDENT                 STANDARD
 VARIABLE       COEFFICIENT  DEVIATION   T-RATIO
-----------     -----------  ---------   -------
WIN PCT          9.74022     1.65099     5.89963
-------------------------------------------------
CONSTANT         7.70757      .81117     9.5018
-------------------------------------------------
COEFFICIENT OF DETERMINATION   =    .85296
COEFFICIENT OF CORRELATION     =    .92356
DEGREES OF FREEDOM             =   6
STANDARD ERROR OF ESTIMATE     =    .557
-------------------------------------------------
TABLE OF RESIDUALS
-----------------------------------------
ACTUAL          PREDICTED    RESIDUAL
------          ---------    --------
  9.9           10.14262     -.24262
 11.4           11.36015      .03985
 12.8           12.8991      -.0991
 11.5           12.40235     -.90235
 13.9           14.20429     -.30429
 13.5           13.26923      .23077
 13.4           12.67508      .72492
 12.4           11.84716      .55284
-----------------------------------------
```

FIGURE 7-14   Computer analysis of linear regression.

Simulation imitates the activities in an organization. A simulation of inventory, for example, might consider the depletion of inventory each day as orders are filled, the reordering of stock, the delay while awaiting replacement stock, the daily costs of carrying inventory, and the daily starting and closing stock levels. Annual costs and average stock levels would be determined from the daily figures. On the average, the results of this simulation would be the same as the resullts of the EOQ inventory analysis described earlier, but the simulation would point out more clearly the peaks and valleys of inventory over the course of the year.

Simulation is particularly helpful in unstructured decisions such as those encountered in financial planning. A static financial plan might ensure annual receipts that will cover annual expenditures, but financial managers must also be assured of adequate funds to meet day-by-day demands. The simulation of daily receipts and expenditures will show the requirement for cash reserves and how much money can be placed in term investments.

The key to simulation is the determination of these daily figures—demand on inventory, receipts, expenditures, and so on. The average values are probably known, but they have the same disadvantage as static models: they do not reflect daily fluctuations. Simulation solves this problem by generating a value for each variable as the variable occurs. If daily demand on inventory has been found to vary from fifteen to sixty units, then the simulation model will generate a number between fifteen and sixty to subtract from the previous day's balance.

The mechanism for assigning values to a variable in simulation is called a *process generator.* The inputs into a process generator are *random numbers,* and the ouputs are the values of the variable to be simulated. A simulation that uses random numbers in this fashion is referred to as *Monte Carlo simulation*—in recognition of the element of chance that is introduced into the model.

Once again, the computer application for simulation is mathematical, but the process can be explained in simpler terms graphically. Figure 7-15 shows how random numbers between zero and one can be converted to the daily demand for inventory when the demand varies from fifteen to sixty. In this example, a random number of .63 results in a demand for thirty-two items. As many different variables as necessary may be simulated in this way and incorporated into the model.

Of course, it is unlikely that demand for inventory on the day in question really will be thirty-two. The value of simulation lies not in its ability to predict specific outcomes but in the way in which it shows the results of the interaction of a number of probabilistic variables. Because no single iteration of the simulation model is likely to reflect the actual situation, it is common to run hundreds or even thousands of iterations. The resultant hundreds or thousands of answers indicate the likelihood of specific outcomes. Perhaps a simulation of a certain inventory policy (the level of safety stock, the reorder point, and the order size) shows that the level of inventory never falls below fifty-two items. The inventory manager may wish to simulate different policies until a lower minimum is reached and stock-outs are still held to an acceptable level. Notice that simulation does not lead directly to a *best* solution. Simulation is not an optimization model like linear programming. It is merely *descriptive:* it describes the situation defined by the decision maker. It is up to the decision maker to alter the situation in order to improve the solution.

Although there are many computer software packages for simulating general business situations, many analysts prefer to write their own simulation programs because it enables them to tailor the model to the specific conditions of the situation they wish to simulate. The results of one such "home-made" program, as they appear on the screen of a microcomputer monitor, are shown in Figure 7-16. This program simulates the cost of inventory for the parameters entered by the user in response to *prompts* that appear on the screen when the program is run. Unlike the diagram in Figure

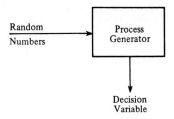

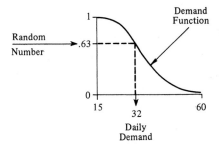

FIGURE 7-15 Process generator for demand on inventory.

7-16, the process generators in this model use *straight-line* functions for demand and lead time.

Readers with some familiarity with BASIC will be able to follow the program listing for this model shown in Figure 7-17. Statements 90 through 190 generate the prompts for the input data. The actual simulation, starting with the random number seed, runs from statement 200 to 420. Statements 440 to 480 print the results. Although this program is written in Applesoft BASIC for an Apple II microcomputer, it can be modified easily for any other version of BASIC.

CBIS and Decision Making

Many of the decision tools discussed in this chapter can be used without computers or a CBIS. The techniques involved have been known for years and years and are all described in standard textbooks on statistics and management science. But like the examples used here, textbook examples are invariably simple and admittedly unrealistic in comparison with real-world situations. A linear programming solution for a real optical company might involve dozens of product variables and hundreds of constraint equations. Although it is theoretically possible to solve such a problem manually, the

```
ENTER STARTING INVENTORY:  10

ENTER REORDER POINT:  12

ENTER UNIT CARRYING COST:  .50

ENTER ORDER COST:  25.00

ENTER ORDER SIZE:  35

ENTER STOCKOUT COST:  10.00

ENTER MINIMUM DEMAND PER PERIOD:  5

ENTER MAXIMUM DEMAND PER PERIOD:  20

ENTER MINIMUM LEAD TIME IN PERIODS:  2

EMTER MAXIMUM LEAD TIME IN PERIODS:  5

ENTER NUMBER OF ITERATIONS:  200


        STAND BY - SIMULATING INVENTORY.

TOTAL CARRY COST:  753.5

TOTAL ORDERING COST:  1075

TOTAL STOCKOUT COST:  80

TOTAL COST:  1908.5

TOTAL DEMAND FOR 200 PERIODS:  2448
```

FIGURE 7-16 Computer analysis of inventory simulation.

hundreds of thousands of individual calculations involved would take so long and would be so error-prone as to preclude any manual attempt.

Other decision tools increase in complexity similarly when employed in the real world. One iteration of a simulation model may require values for ten or twenty variables. And it is not uncommon to run through several hundred iterations just to get a *starting point* for the model. Even the daily interval mentioned here is an oversimplification; a production simulation can use intervals of only a few seconds—and then simulate a monthly period! The present-value model explained here used an *annual* compounding period. But we know that most financial institutions now compound *daily* or even continuously—for perhaps thousands of accounts! Clearly, these models too are impractical in a manual mode.

It is the computer that has raised management science models from the level of theoretical curiosities to the practical decision-support tools they represent today. And it is the CBIS, which collects these models into a readily accessible model base, that makes management science techniques available for organizational decision making. And as we shall see in the following chapter, it is the manager who is ultimately responsible for applying these techniques.

```
10 FLAG = 0: REM    SET ORDER FLAG TO ZERO
20 TCC = 0: REM    SET TOTAL CARRYING COST TO ZERO
30 OCT = 0: REM    SET ORDER COST TOTAL TO ZERO
40 TSC = 0: REM    SET TOTAL STOCKOUT COST TO ZERO
50 TT = 0: REM    SET TOTAL COST TO ZERO
60 DD = 0: REM    SET TOTAL DEMAND TO ZERO
70 ARR = 0: REM    SET ARRIVAL TIME TO ZERO
80 HOME
90 INPUT "ENTER STARTING INVENTORY: ";SI
100    PRINT : INPUT "ENTER REORDER POINT: ";RP
110    PRINT : INPUT "ENTER UNIT CARRYING COST: ";UCC
120    PRINT : INPUT "ENTER ORDER COST: ";CO
130    PRINT : INPUT "ENTER ORDER SIZE: ";Q
140    PRINT : INPUT "ENTER STOCKOUT COST: ";SC
150    PRINT : INPUT "ENTER MINIMUM DEMAND PER PERIOD: ";D1
160    PRINT : INPUT "ENTER MAXIMUM DEMAND PER PERIOD: ";D2
170    PRINT : INPUT "ENTER MINIMUM LEAD TIME IN PERIODS: ";L1
180    PRINT : INPUT "ENTER MAXIMUM LEAD TIME IN PERIODS: ";L2
190    PRINT : INPUT "ENTER NUMBER OF ITERATIONS: ";N
200 X = 12345
210    HOME : VTAB 11: HTAB 5: PRINT "STAND BY - SIMULATING INVENTORY."
220    FOR I = 1 TO N
230    IF I < > ARR THEN 260
240 SI = SI + Q
250 FLAG = 0
260 D =  INT (D1 +  RND (X) * (D2 - D1) + .5)
270 EI = SI - D
280    IF EI >  = 0 THEN 310
290 TSC =  ABS (TSC + EI * SC)
300 EI = 0
310 TCC = TCC + EI * UCC
320 SI = EI
330    IF EI > RP THEN 400
340    IF FLAG = 0 THEN 360
350    GOTO 400
360 LT =  INT (L1 +  RND (X) * (L2 - L1) + .5)
370 ARR = I + LT
380 OCT = OCT + CO
390 FLAG = 1
400 TT = TCC + OCT + TSC
410 DD = DD + D
420    NEXT I
430    HOME
440    PRINT : PRINT "TOTAL CARRYING COST: ";TCC
450    PRINT : PRINT "TOTAL ORDERING COST: ";OCT
460    PRINT : PRINT "TOTAL STOCKOUT COST: ";TSC
470    PRINT : PRINT "TOTAL COST:          ";TT
480    PRINT : PRINT "TOTAL DEMAND FOR ";N;" PERIODS: ";DD
```

FIGURE 7-17 Inventory simulation program in BASIC.

Summary

A decision maker's preference for outcomes and his or her knowledge of cause–effect relationships define the *environment* of a decision. Because the *computational* environment is commonly associated with CBIS, we tend to forget that many, if not most, decisions are made in an environment better described as *judgmental*, *compromise*, or *inspirational*. When these other environments are encountered, decision makers often try to quantify subjective data or restrict their alternatives to make better use of CBIS capabilities.

Decision strategies also depend on the decision maker's knowledge of the future states of nature. When knowledge of the future is perfect, decisions are made under *certainty;* when it is probabilistic, decisions are made under *risk;* and when there is no knowledge of future events, decisions must be made under *uncertainty.*

Under uncertainty, the manager's philosophical outlook determines the strategy: optimists tend to follow a *maximax* strategy and pessimists tend to follow a *maximin* strategy. Under risk, the relevant decision criterion is the *expected value* of the alternatives under consideration. And under certainty, managers can choose from a variety of management science/operations research models to aid in decision making.

Although decision makers obviously prefer an *optimum* solution to a problem, optimization is frequently impracticable or impossible, and the problem must be resolved through the *administrative behavior* of *satisficing.* Decision makers satisfice when they choose the first acceptable solution to a problem.

Decision making is not new to management, nor are most of the techniques discussed in this chapter. What is relatively new is the incorporation of these techniques into CBIS and their availability to managers for decision support at all organizational levels. More than any other feature, decision support distinguishes contemporary CBIS from older data processing systems.

Assignments

7-1. Identify the environment of the following decisions as computational, judgmental, compromise, or inspirational:

    a. Reducing the size of a luxury automobile will improve fuel economy but may damage the luxury image. What should the manufacturer do?

    b. The EOQ for a certain item is 236, but you can get a 5 percent discount if you order in lots of 500. What order size should you use?

    c. The data base course is difficult and the instructor has a reputation for giving low grades. The family planning course is a sure "A." Either will satisfy an elective requirement. Which should you take?

    d. If State beats Tech and A & M beats Normal, your team will go to the NCAA tournament. But if Normal beats A & M, you will go only if Tech beats State. You do not know who won the A & M versus Normal game; for whom should you cheer in the State versus Tech game?

7-2. You are the buyer for a chain of department stores and wish to purchase dresses with a rather radical hem length. You must choose between two styles of dress: A and B. If the hem length is popular, the stores will net $10,000 on dress A and $6,000 on dress B. But if the hem length does not catch on, dress A will lose $7,500 and dress B will lose $3,500. Which dress would *you* buy?

7-3. Analyze your response to the previous question. Are you a maximax or a maximin? Is your answer consistent with the way you view yourself as either an optimist or a pessimist?

7-4. You have just discovered that a poll of fashion experts shows 60 percent in favor of the hemline in problem 7-2. Will this change your decision? Explain your answer.

7-5. Classify the following models as either optimizing or descriptive:

    a. The EOQ model.
    b. Linear programming.
    c. Present value.
    d. Monte Carlo simulation.
    e. A model that gives the mean length of a waiting line at a bank teller's window.

7-6. In the past, many managers made financial decisions by selecting the alternative with the shortest *payback* period (the initial cost of an investment divided by the expected annual return). What is wrong with this method? Why are present value techniques superior? Which method makes better use of CBIS? Why do you think some managers still use payback?

7-7. We have discussed some of the *present* techniques of supporting decisions with CBIS. What kind of decision support do you think CBIS will furnish in the future? What kind of decisions in government or business would you like to see given better CBIS support?

CASE   To Compute or Not to Compute

At Regional State University, textbooks for the core courses in the Bachelor of Business Administration degree program are selected by a committee of faculty from the various departments in the college of business administration. The core course in management science is taught by faculty from the department of decision sciences, but other faculty are represented on the textbook selection committee and some have rather definite ideas on how management science should be taught.

    "You guys cannot see the forest of business decision making for the trees of mathematical modeling," complains the management representative. "Who cares how to solve linear programming by simplex? No one does that anymore anyway. Teach the students a good LP package and spend your time more profitably by showing them how to enter data and interpret the results of realistic problems—not the ridiculously simple ones you work by hand. I vote for the case-study book that comes with the diskette of models and data. That's all our students need."

"You cannot fully understand the output of a computer model without an understanding of how the model works," responds the decision science representative. "Only by working through simplex do you gain an adequate understanding of the capabilities and limitations of the algorithm as well as a feel for the meaning of the results. We are *educating* students, not *training* them to be data entry clerks. We want to motivate the better ones to go on to graduate programs in operations research. Besides, they won't always have access to a computer. I want to stay with the traditional management science text."

"I understand your feelings and I admire your love of your discipline," replies the management representative. "I have an idea that this discussion has taken place before—perhaps when a Chinese professor tried to introduce an abacus into the classroom 20 centuries ago. By the way, does anyone here still know how to find a square root by hand?"

There was an awkward silence, finally broken when the decision science professor huffed that taking square roots had nothing to do with the matter at hand.

What kind of textbook do *you* think Regional State University should adopt for its management science course?

Other Readings

Anderson, David A., Dennis J. Sweeney, and Thomas A. Williams. *An Introduction to Management Science: Quantitative Approaches to Decision Making* (4th ed.). New York: West Publishing, 1985.

Austin, Larry M., and James R. Burns. *Management Science: An Aid for Managerial Decision Making.* New York: Macmillan, 1985.

————. *Management Science Models for the Microcomputer.* New York: Macmillan, 1985.

Biermann, Harold, Jr., Charles P. Bonini, and Warren H. Hausman. *Quantitative Analysis for Business Decisions* (6th ed.). Homewood, Ill.: Richard D. Irwin, 1981.

Erikson, Warren J., and Owen P. Hall, Jr. *Computer Models for Management Science.* Reading, Mass.: Addison-Wesley, 1983.

Kroeber, Donald W., and R. Lawrence LaForge. *The Managers' Guide to Statistics and Quantitative Methods.* New York: McGraw-Hill, 1980.

Levin, Richard I. *Statistics for Management* (2d ed.). Englewood Cliffs, N.J.: Prentice-Hall, 1981.

Raiffa, Howard. *Decision Analysis.* Reading, Mass.: Addison Wesley, 1968.

Schull, Fremont A., Jr., André L. Debecq, and L. L. Cummings. *Organizational Decision Making.* New York: McGraw-Hill, 1970.

Simon, Herbert A. *Administrative Behavior*. New York: Harper & Row, 1957.

Simon, Herbert A. *The New Science of Management Decision*. New York: Harper & Row, 1960.

Thompson, James D. *Organizations in Action*. New York: McGraw-Hill, 1967.

Recent issues of the following journals: *Decision Sciences, Interfaces, Management Science, Omega*.

PART III

TRANSACTION PROCESSING SYSTEMS

In Part II, we addressed CBIS generically; that is, the discussion of foundations did not distinguish among the different types of CBIS. We are now ready to abandon this broad approach in favor of a more specific one, one that examines the structure and applications of individual CBIS in their organizational context. Part III begins that examination with a discussion of a fundamental CBIS, the transaction processing system.

Transaction processing systems are direct descendants of the original data processing systems and, as such, are of interest to us as examples of the evolutionary forces at work in CBIS. But they are also essential components of the CBIS family in their role as input systems to other CBIS. This role should be kept in mind as we examine the specific techniques of transaction processing described in Chapter 8.

Chapter 8

Transaction Processing

Learning Objectives

After studying this chapter, you will be able to:

1. Describe the organizational role and objectives of transaction processing systems (TPS).
2. Name and describe the steps involved in TPS data input.
3. List and explain typical TPS processes.
4. Identify the types and uses of TPS output.
5. Specify the appropriate medium and file organization for different transaction processing applications.
6. Discuss the techniques of transaction processing in different approaches to data management.
7. Select an appropriate mode of processing to be used in transaction processing.
8. Define the following terms:

transaction	mode (of processing)
storage	batch processing
retrieval	transactional processing
classification (of data)	pointer
sorting (of data)	real time
update	on-line/real-time
interface	binary search
serial system	

It was suggested in Chapter 2 that CBIS transform or *process* data into information. This function gave rise to the term *data processing* (DP) used to describe early CBIS. CBIS still process data into information, of course, but the information and many of the processes are now so different that it is almost misleading to refer to a contemporary CBIS as a DP system. Instead, we speak of *management information systems* (MIS), *decision support systems* (DSS), *executive information systems* (EIS), and *expert systems* (ES) to recognize the need for more sophisticated CBIS. But there is still a need for some of the basic transformation processes that once were the mainstay of data processing. Storing, retrieving, classifying, sorting, and updating data are still necessary activities in CBIS. In order to distinguish these processes in a CBIS environment, from the same or similar processes in a DP environment, we now refer to them as *transaction processing* and to the CBIS in which they are conducted as *transaction processing systems* (TPS).

You will recall from Chapter 1 that TPS perform the basic record-keeping in organizations and also are a source of processed data for other CBIS. In order to understand this dual role better, we will examine in detail some of the mechanics of transaction processing: the approach to data management, the use of different media, and the mode or timing of processing. But first, it is helpful to take an overview of TPS, to define TPS more clearly, and to examine their role in contemporary organizations.

An Overview of TPS

If you were to visit the reception desk of a modern organization and inquire about its TPS, you might be met with a blank stare. Other CBIS are relatively independent in function, staffing, and sometimes even in hardware. But in many organizations, transaction processing is so well integrated with other CBIS activities that it is not associated with a unique system. Management information systems in particular, as you shall see in Part IV, depend on transaction processing. Nonetheless, there are certain information systems activities that cannot properly be attributed to other CBIS, and whether or not there is formal recognition of a TPS, it is much easier to understand these activities in the context of a separate, a *transaction processing*, CBIS.

Transactions and Transaction Data

In every organization, there are certain fundamental activities that form a foundation for the primary role and mission of the organization. For example, manufacturing firms are based on processes that transform labor and raw materials into finished goods. Charitable organizations collect the contributions of donors and transfer them directly or indirectly to those in need. And educational institutions transform human and material resources into instruc-

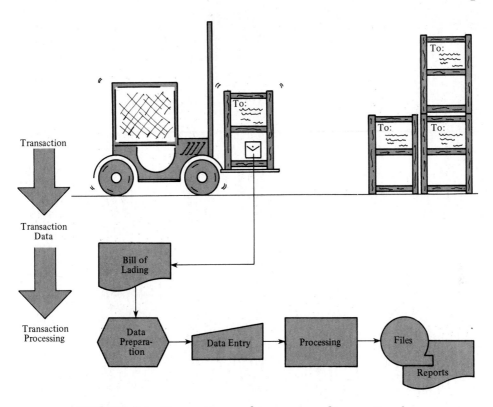

FIGURE 8-1 Transactions and processing of transaction data.

tion, housing, and food services for students. Collectively, we refer to these and other such transformation processes as *transactions*.

The objective of transaction processing systems is not to process actual transactions but to process *data* that reflect or describe those transactions. There is a subtle difference between the two. As shown in Figure 8-1, a transaction may consist of an addition to the goods in inventory, but the corresponding TPS activities deal with the creation of transaction files and reports about inventory transactions. The transaction itself involves material and material-handling equipment—a forklift in this example. The TPS activities involve data and data-handling equipment—computer hardware and software.

Functions of TPS

If there is a "mainstream" in CBIS evolution, it is reflected in transaction processing systems. Whereas other CBIS have evolved to accommodate special needs, TPS by and large still perform the functions for which the earliest data processing systems were developed. These functions are carried out

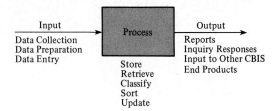

FIGURE 8-2   Functions of transaction processing systems.

faster, more accurately, more thoroughly, and at much less cost in modern TPS, but conceptually they are not much different from DP functions. It is not surprising, therefore, that we can use the old, but accurate, model shown in Figure 8-2 to examine the functions of TPS: *input, processing,* and *output.*

TPS Input

Various input media and devices were discussed in Chapter 4 and will be considered again later in this chapter. However, to examine input as a function of TPS, it is more appropriate to look at the operational steps that must be performed to make transaction data available for processing. There are three such steps: *data collection, data preparation,* and *data entry.*

Data Collection   TPS input may be either *direct* or *indirect.* Direct input implies that the transaction itself generates the data inputs for the TPS. For example, the act of an automobile passing through a toll gate is a service transaction—the use of the toll road—and also may activate a counter that provides input for financial and usage records maintained by the tollway authority. When TPS input is direct, the steps of data collection, data preparation, and data entry are combined with the transaction into a single function. This combination, as well as other combinations of data collection, data preparation, and data entry, is shown in Table 8-1.

In indirect data input, the steps of data collection and preparation are distinctly different, although entry may still be combined with preparation. Data are generated at the point of the transaction, but they are maintained in an intermediate form, usually a document, and prepared later. Data pertaining to many business and government transactions are collected in this fashion. Industrial orders and sales, income tax returns, claims for unemployment benefits, and consumer credit card purchases are all recorded on documents at the time of the transaction and held for subsequent data preparation. The transaction document for this last example, the familiar credit card charge slip, is shown in Figure 8-3.

Data Preparation   Data preparation, as noted in Chapter 4, is the conversion of data into a form and/or format consistent with the data entry procedures. Just as direct data input eliminates the need for data preparation,

TABLE 8-1 Transaction Processing Input

Transaction	Data Collection	Data Preparation	Data Entry
Hours worked	Employee records time on time card	Payroll clerk transfers time to OCR form	Data entry clerk feeds forms into optical scanner
End-of-course evaluations	Students enter multiple-choice responses on mark-sense card		Data entry clerk feeds cards into mark-sense reader
Savings account deposit	Customer fills out deposit slip	Bank teller keys account number and amount into terminal	
Purchase in supermarket	Clerk passes bar-code label over scanner, price is read from file and added to total, other data are recorded for management purposes		

some data preparation techniques also include data entry. For example, data on credit card charge slips may be keyed into terminals, or they may be optically scanned at the credit card company. This procedure *prepares* the data and also enters them into the TPS for immediate or subsequent processing.

In other cases, data from transaction documents are rerecorded on a

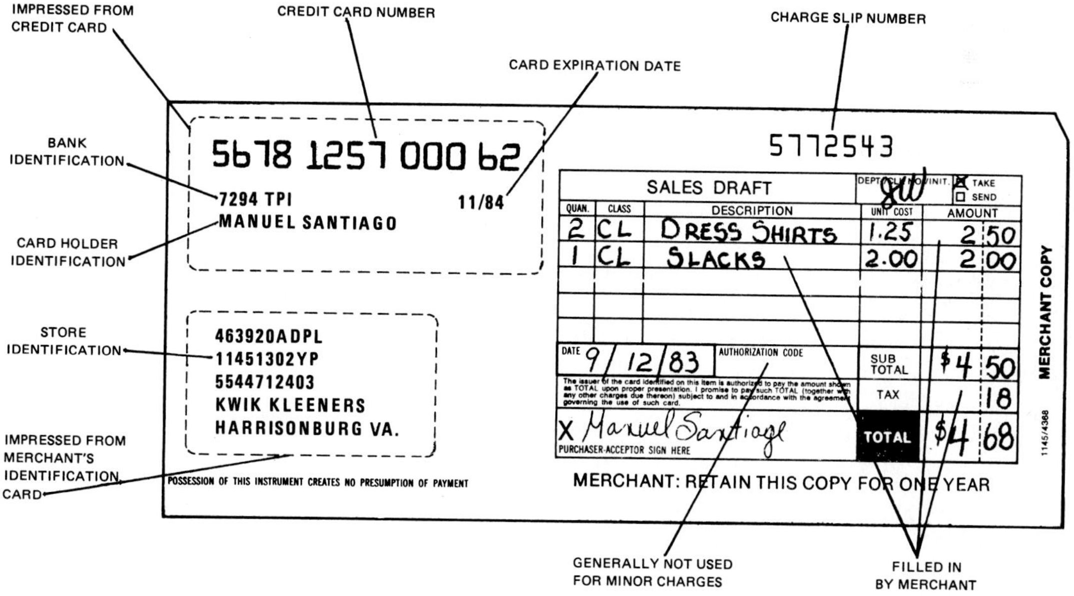

FIGURE 8-3 Transaction document for credit card transaction.

second document or other medium prior to entry. For example, if punched cards or optically scanned documents are the input medium for an inventory file, they must be prepared from the original bills of lading or "picking tickets." In still other cases, the second document may be used simply to provide greater clarity and to reduce the possibility of input error. Figure 8-4 shows how such a document is used to prepare data from a personal check for a banking application.

Data Entry   Data entry is the step that makes transaction data available for processing. As explained above, it may occur automatically with data collection or data preparation, or it may be a separate, final step in the input function. The mechanics of data entry are dictated by the input medium and devices. For example, card input is entered through a card reader, magnetic ink characters are read through a magnetic ink character recognition (MICR) reader, data on other documents may be read optically or keyed in by a terminal operator, and so on.

Data entry also differs by the timing of the input. Some transaction data are saved and entered periodically, and others are entered as they occur (or at least as they are prepared for entry). Both the medium and the timing orientation of TPS are discussed in greater detail later in this chapter.

TPS Processing

Two characteristics that distinguish TPS from more sophisticated CBIS such as MIS and DSS are the relative simplicity of the transformation processes and the high volume of data. TPS tend to involve large numbers of simple, repetitive operations, whereas DSS, for example, are more likely to use complex operations involving small volumes of data. There are exceptions in each case, of course. A transaction process could involve a small number of data (reflecting a single transaction), and some DSS processes, such as simulation, often involve thousands of simple, repetitive operations. These exceptions aside, let us look at some typical TPS processes.

Storage   One of the most basic capabilities of TPS is that of *storing* data. In one sense, TPS act as superefficient, electronic filing cabinets that can accommodate the equivalent of hundreds of thousands or even millions of documents. Although TPS storage is accomplished with a fraction of the space and cost normally associated with a manual storage medium, such as hard-copy files, it is not of itself a sufficient reason to develop and maintain TPS.

Retrieval   Any capability of storing data must, of course, be complemented by the ability to *retrieve* them when needed. The comparative advantage of TPS over manual methods is even greater in the retrieval process than it is in storage, primarily because of the speed of computer-driven search methods. It simply is easier and faster to find specified data in a TPS than it is in a manual system. Retrieval is also the process that makes data in a TPS available to other CBIS.

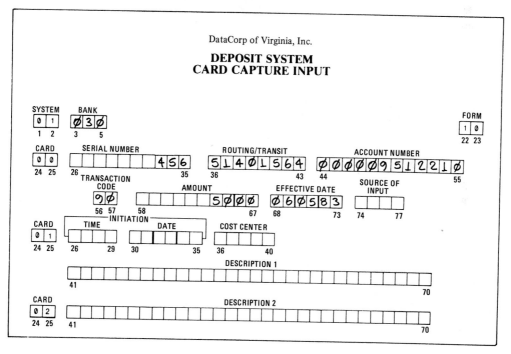

FIGURE 8-4   Transcribing data to improve clarity.

Classification   To classify data means to group them according to some common characteristic. The characteristic may be an existing data element, as it is in the classification of sales by customer shown in Figure 8-5, or it may be a new element derived from one or more existing elements. The "aging" of accounts, by grouping them into categories of "under 30 days," "between 30 and 60 days," and "over 60 days," illustrates the derivation of a new element

Unclassified Data

Stock Number	Description	Unit	Amt	Unit Cost	Extended Cost	Sold To	Date
1-7934	Bumper Jack	Ea	1	17.95	17.95	Ace Parts	6/11/83
1-1865	Spark Plug	Box	4	15.50	62.00	Acme Auto	7/04/83
3-0427	10W-40 Oil	Case	2	8.95	17.90	City Olds	5/23/83
3-8110	Anti Freeze	Case	1	6.75	6.75	Ace Parts	8/15/83
1-1865	Spark Plug	Box	6	15.50	93.00	City Olds	6/09/83
2-1974	Wiper Blade	Ea	8	1.25	10.00	Acme Auto	7/16/83
.	.	.	.	.	.	.	.
3-0427	10W-40 Oil	Case	1	8.95	8.95	Ace Parts	6/12/83

CLASSIFY BY CUSTOMER

Data Classified by Customer

Sold To	Stock Number	Date
City Olds	3-0427	5/23/83
City Olds	1-1865	6/09/83
Ace Parts	1-7934	6/11/83
Ace Parts	3-8110	8/15/83
Ace Parts	3-0427	6/12/83
.	.	.
Acme Auto	1-1865	7/04/83
Acme Auto	2-1974	7/16/83

FIGURE 8-5 The classification of data.

214

Student Data Classified by Major   Classified Data Sorted by Social Security Number

Major	Name	SSN		SSN	Name	Major
History	Jones, Thomas J.	414-29-8365				
.	.	.		.	.	.
.	.	.		.	.	.
.	.	.		.	.	.
Marketing	Smith, Mary L.	259-74-9432		103-36-6305	Abrams, Paul P.	Marketing
Marketing	Sanchez, Miguel S.	747-02-6810		259-74-9432	Smith, Mary L.	Marketing
Marketing	Wilson Frank M.	319-48-6165	SORT BY	312-73-1520	Barker, Susan P.	Marketing
Marketing	Barker, Susan P.	312-73-1520	SOCIAL	319-48-6165	Wilson, Frank M.	Marketing
Marketing	Diaz, Juan S.	454-83-1927	SECURITY	454-83-1927	Diaz, Juan S.	Marketing
Marketing	Chinotti, Sophia A.	522-66-8394	NUMBER	522-66-8394	Chinotti, Sophia A.	Marketing
Marketing	Abrams, Paul P.	103-36-6305		747-02-6810	Sanchez, Miguel S.	Marketing
.	.	.		.	.	.
.	.	.		.	.	.
.	.	.		.	.	.
Physics	Nelson, Charles H.	824-91-8365				

FIGURE 8-6   The sorting of data.

("age") from an existing one ("payment due date"). Classification may be carried out in any data management environment, but it is particularly efficient when one is using a data base management system.

Sorting   A process somewhat related to classifying is *sorting*—the arranging of data into a specified sequence, such as numerical or alphabetical order. Sorting may be a separate process, as it is when addresses are sorted by zip code to facilitate bulk mailing, or it may be combined with classifying, as shown in Figure 8-6, to produce a list of students in social security number sequence, classified by their academic major. Sorting also is carried out with greater efficiency in a data base environment.

Update   The term *update* is used generically to describe various processes that maintain the currency of data. TPS are used to *add* new data to existing records or files, to *delete* obsolete or irrelevant data, and to *change* incorrect or outdated values. The process of updating is described more completely later in this chapter.

TPS Output

TPS processes result in a variety of output, which, for our purposes, can be grouped into four categories: *reports*, responses to *inquiries*, *input* to other CBIS, and *end products*.

Report Generation   The preparation or *generation* of reports is a special form of retrieval that frequently follows the updating process. Of the different types of reports described in Chapter 3, TPS are most likely to produce *scheduled* and *detail* reports. A weekly report showing the balance on hand for all items in inventory or an end-of-semester report showing the grades of each student in a class illustrates the concept of both scheduled and detailed reporting.

The term *report* usually evokes an image of a document—information printed on paper. Reports can be printed on other media as well. For example, the inventory report suggested above could be very bulky and inconvenient to use if printed on paper. Many organizations now output such reports on *microfilm* (rolls of film somewhat larger than 35mm camera film) or *microfiche* (sheets of film about 5 inches square). These media require special readers to illuminate and enlarge the printed matter, but they are more convenient to use, more durable, and easier to store than reports printed on paper. Your library probably maintains back issues of periodicals on microfilm or college catalogs on microfiche.

Inquiry Response   Although the data maintained in TPS are usually made available to users in bulk, via reports, they often are required individually or in small volumes on short notice. The technique for outputting data on this basis is the *inquiry response*. Inquiries are handled best when operating in a data base environment where the *query language* (see Chapter 6) of the data base management system provides the user ready access to data. An airline reservation clerk confirming the availability of a seat on a specified flight, a sales representative checking the status of an unfilled order, and a university registrar looking up a student's grade point average all illustrate the use of inquiry response output in TPS.

Input to Other CBIS   Up to this point, we have considered transaction processing for the sake of transaction processing—a not altogether bad idea for organizations with very large volumes of data to process, but one that does not fully consider the synergistic effect of several CBIS working in concert. One simple way in which TPS interact with other CBIS is in the role of an *input system*—a serial relationship, as shown in Figure 8-7, in which the output of one system (the TPS) becomes the input for another system (an MIS, in this example).

Other CBIS can use TPS output more readily when there is a common or *corporate* data base maintained by a data base management system.[1] Data in the data base are structured according to an overall *schema* and may be restructured for any given application by an appropriate *subschema*. But when data are maintained in application-oriented files, the applications of

---

[1]The term *corporate data base* is used to describe the general-purpose data bases available to application programs in different CBIS. Most use of this data base is by TPS and MIS. DSS usually can access the corporate data base but may also have unique data bases.

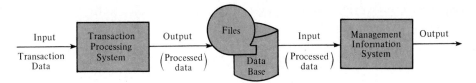

FIGURE 8-7   Serial relationship between TPS and MIS.

those other CBIS must be designed to use the existing TPS output file. This constraint severely limits the interface between TPS and other CBIS.

End Products
Although TPS process *data* about transactions, they occasionally produce output that has some functional use in addition to the data it reflects. We refer to this kind of output as an *end product*, since it is, in fact, a product of the transaction. For example, a paycheck, which is an output of a TPS, has more significance than the data it conveys about payroll processing. And an airline ticket, which is also the product of TPS, has some intrinsic value in addition to the data printed on it. In many cases, including the two examples given here, TPS processing results both in end products and other forms of output. Payroll processing yields reports as well as paychecks and the response to an inquiry in an airline reservation system may be accompanied by a printed ticket, if that is what the customer wants.

Manual TPS
Because this is a book on *computer*-based information systems, we have assumed that the TPS in Figure 8-7 is also a CBIS. This may not be true in every case. Much transaction processing is still done manually. For example, most medical facilities—hospitals, clinics, doctors' offices, and the like—still maintain patients' records in file folders and update them with handwritten entries. We will not deal specifically with manual TPS here, but it is important to be aware that such systems do exist and that they pose a serious limitation on those other CBIS that depend on TPS for input data.

Interface with Other Organizational Subsystems

In a CBIS context, to *interface* with a subsystem is to exchange inputs and outputs with it. We have already seen that TPS interface with other CBIS by providing them data—either directly in the form of application-oriented files or indirectly by furnishing data to the corporate data base.

TPS also interface with other, non-CBIS subsystems. Transactions occur throughout organizations, and where they do, there is interface with the TPS, in the form of either inputs or outputs. It is impossible to list every way in which such interfaces can occur, but a few examples will serve to illustrate how this interface is achieved with the major functional subsystems of an organization.[2]

Production Subsystem

The production subsystem in an organization is where the input resources of labor and capital are transformed into the output of goods and services. And production processes are rich sources of transaction data! The production subsystem furnishes TPS inputs concerning the acquisition and consumption of raw materials and components, the amount of labor used, the quantity and quality of the output, and other basic activities. To a lesser extent, the production subsystem is also a recipient of TPS output concerning these same processes.

Production inputs also provide additional examples of direct and indirect data input. Some data—such as the active and idle time of machinery, the number of items that pass through a work station, or even the presence of defects in material as it is processed—can be input directly by sensors attached to equipment used in the production process. In other cases, data may be collected separately but prepared and entered in a single step. For example, one may record the amount of direct labor involved in production by punching buttons on special-purpose terminals at the work station as work is begun and ended. Or punched cards attached to raw material shipments may be removed at the receipt station and used to enter data for an inventory application. In still other cases, all three data input steps may be necessary, as they are when the volume of production is recorded manually in a log, transcribed onto a mark-sense form, and entered for processing through an optical scanner.

Marketing Subsystem

To most of us, marketing transactions are quite familiar because we often participate in them as consumers. But our purchases (sales, from the organization's point of view) are only the tip of the marketing iceberg. The acquisition, transportation, storage, and promotion of goods are equally important both to the marketing subsystem and to the operation of the TPS.

The interface between marketing and TPS is also input-oriented, but not to the same extent as that between production and TPS. Although there are relatively few outputs to production at the TPS level (there are more from other CBIS), many marketing transactions result in both TPS input and TPS output. For example, orders for goods result in TPS inputs concerning item identification, quantity, price, and destination. Data from those same orders are reflected in outputs of invoices, bills, and sales reports.

Like production data, marketing data may also be input directly, as they

---

[2]Not every organization is structured according to the functions identified here (governmental organizations, for example, do not have a marketing function), but the functions of production, marketing, personnel, and finance are generally representative of typical business operations.

are when sales are transacted at point-of-sale terminals. It is more common, however, for transactions in marketing to be collected separately—on order forms, shipping orders, invoices, receipts, and other documents—for subsequent data preparation and entry into the TPS.

Personnel Subsystem

Although we do not normally think in terms of *transactions* concerning personnel—except perhaps when a professional athlete is traded from one team to another—there are certain fundamental personnel *actions* that are reflected in transaction data and are maintained and processed in much the same way as production or marketing data. The applications of those looking for jobs, the hiring of those selected, training, promotion, sick leave or vacation time, and discharge or retirement are just a few examples of such actions.

As a general rule, there is less urgency over personnel transactions than those of, say, production. As a result, there is less emphasis on sophisticated data collection and entry methods. Personnel matters tend to be recorded on traditional forms and to be prepared later for data entry, even where personnel clerks have access to remote terminals and could input data directly if necessary. An additional reason for maintaining manual personnel records is the legal requirement of making personnel records available to the individual concerned. Manual records are easier to submit to individual examination and also preclude access to data concerning other individuals whose privacy must be assured.

Financial Subsystem

Financial data occupy a unique position in TPS. First, as has been observed elsewhere, financial transactions were among the earliest to be subjected to data processing and now enjoy a user acceptance not always found for other TPS applications. Second, financial data are likely to cut across traditional functional lines and are themselves something of an integrative force within organizations and organizational CBIS.

Many financial transactions are familiar to us because of their obvious involvement with money. Wages, salary, payment for materials, rent, loan payments, interest and dividend payments, and revenue from sales fall into this category. Other transactions, particularly those associated with cost accounting, have a more subtle relationship to monetary matters and are less obvious.

Because financial data are closely related to the transactions of other functional departments, we often find a close relationship in data inputs as well. For example, the point-of-sale terminal, mentioned earlier, records financial data as well as marketing data. And material usage recorded in the production process can easily be converted to dollar amounts for cost accounting purposes. The same relationship exists among outputs based on financial data. Invoices, for example, are both the output of a marketing transaction (the acknowledgment of an order) and a financial transaction (a request for payment). Other integrative characteristics of transaction data are illustrated in Part IV in the discussion of management information systems.

Data Management Techniques in TPS

In Chapter 6, we defined two major approaches to data management: the use of application-oriented files and a data base approach. Let us now examine the ways in which these approaches influence and, in some cases, *dictate* the techniques of transaction processing.

Transaction Processing with Application-Oriented Files

You should recall that an *application-oriented* file is structured according to the processing requirements of a specific application and is normally used exclusively with its corresponding application program. In fact, it is common to store the application program at the beginning of the master file so both are readily accessible at processing time. This is the way data were managed in traditional DP systems and are still managed in many contemporary TPS.

Application-oriented files may be on punched cards, magnetic tape, magnetic disks, or some combination of these three media.[3] Combinations can occur when different media are used in different stages of processing. For example, a billing application could use punched cards as transaction documents, transfer the data on cards to tape to use as a transaction file, and then use the tape to update a master file on disk. This is a rather extreme example, however, and in those that follow, it will be assumed that the transaction and master files, at least, are on similar media.

Even if a single medium were always used throughout an application, differences among applications would necessitate a combination of media within a TPS. Most TPS have facilities for cards, tape, disks, and perhaps other media. The exact proportion of work carried out on the various media is determined by the mix of applications.

Card Systems
Card systems date back to the earliest days of data processing and represent something of an intermediate stage between manual and automated information systems. On one hand, cards can be read visually, sorted, filed, and handled like conventional transaction documents. On the other hand, they can also be read, sorted, merged, collated, and otherwise processed by ma-

---

[3] Cards, tape, and disks are used here, as earlier, as the representative media of off-line, on-line sequential access, and on-line direct access storage. Substitutions can be made as necessary for TPS that use different media.

chines. These characteristics give rise to a curious blend of manual and computer operations in transaction processing with cards.

Card systems are being phased out of CBIS at a rapid pace, and it is unlikely that current users of this text will ever encounter a pure card system. The purpose in describing a card system here, therefore, is not to prepare students for future involvement with cards, but to use them as an example of the most simple form of transaction processing. Then, following the evolutionary development of CBIS media, we will proceed on to tape and disk systems.

Updating a Master File A pure card system, such as the one shown in Figure 8-8, does not use files in on-line storage. Instead, all data necessary for processing—the program, master file, and transaction file—are maintained off-line, in *decks* until the time for updating. Because most card systems use a single card reader, some provision must be made for bringing the appropriate transaction record and master record into internal memory simultaneously. This is done off-line by first sorting both files into identical sequence and then *merging* the two decks into a single data deck in record key sequence. If every master record is to be updated, there will be alternate transaction and master records, but there may be consecutive transactions or master records if some master records need not be updated or if some new master records are to be opened.

The application program contains the logic for comparing transaction and master record keys to determine the appropriate updating process. For example, if the first two cards are a transaction and a master record, and if their record keys are the same, the master record is updated with the transaction. If both are master records, it is an indication that the first one is not to be changed; it is copied as is and the next card is read and compared with the remaining master record. In general, the logic for updating master records on cards now follows the logic for tape updating, which is explained in greater detail in the following section.

Part of the output of a card system, in addition to any reports generated, is a new master file on cards. In the next processing cycle, this file, along with the program deck and a new deck of transactions, serves as input. The old transaction and master file may be saved as historical records or as backup material to re-create a new master file should something happen to the current one.

Advantages and Disadvantages Card systems are simple and somewhat reassuring to laypeople because of the built-in backup capability and the fact that cards can double as *turnaround documents;* that is, they are the output of one cycle that is "turned around" by a user or customer and becomes the input for a subsequent cycle. These were distinct advantages in early data processing applications, particularly in finance and accounting, when computers were less reliable and auditors were inexperienced in computer operations. It is still common to use card systems in payroll and billing applications

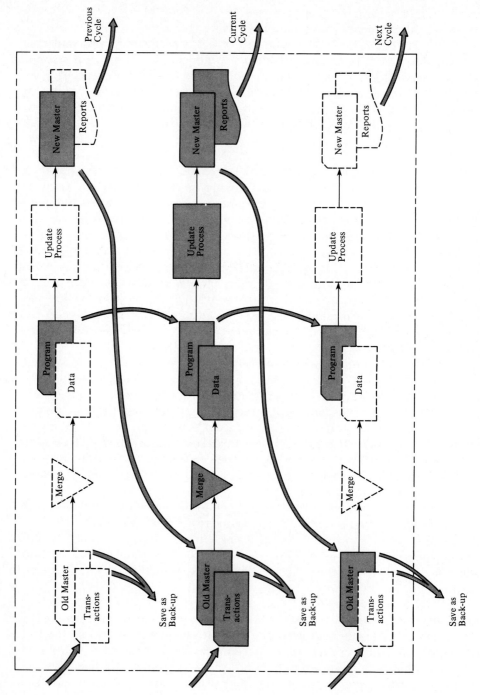

FIGURE 8-8 Updating a master file in a card system.

(look at your last paycheck or utility bill), but cards are slowly and surely being replaced by other media.[4]

One reason for the decline of card systems is, of course, the slow speed of card readers and card punches and the consequential underutilization of the CPU. But cards are also bulky and difficult to use when damp (from humidity, for example) or dog-eared. Cards also require extensive off-line operations in the form of keypunching, verifying, sorting, merging, collating, duplicating, and the like—most of which can be done in the CPU or are unnecessary with other media. These off-line operations also involve special pieces of equipment that are increasingly idle as card usage declines, thereby creating further pressure to eliminate cards and their associated equipment.

Tape Systems

Tape represents a transition from cards to more sophisticated media, such as disks, in the same way that cards were a transition from manual to computer operations. To a certain extent, tape systems merely emulate the operation of card systems, but they use technology (magnetic impressions on an oxide of iron) like that of disks. Files in tape systems tend to be magnetic versions of card decks, but they can be read and written at speeds approaching those associated with disks. Like card systems, they preserve the old master file intact, and like disk systems, they use on-line storage and can accommodate very large files. For these and other reasons, tape systems have enjoyed a great deal of success and popularity in transaction processing and still carry a large share of the processing work load in TPS.

Updating a Master File   In a typical tape operation, such as the one shown in Figure 8-9, the program and the master file are stored on one tape, and the transaction file, organized into the same sequence as the master file, is on a second tape. After the program is read and rewritten onto a third tape (which will also hold the new master file), the first transaction is compared with the first record on the old master file.

If the record keys are the *same*, the transaction data and the master file data are combined to create an updated record for the new master file.

If the transaction record key is *greater* than the master record key, it is an indication that one or more master records are not to be updated, and the master file is advanced (with the unchanged records being copied onto the new master file) until the record keys match.

If the transaction record key is *less* than the master record key, it is an indication that no master record with that key exists, and a new record must be created from the transaction data and written onto the new master file. The next transaction record key is then compared with the same master

---

[4]The U.S. Treasury, which has been using punch-card checks since 1945 and which now issues over 600 million checks per year, began phasing into optically scanned checks in 1985. The transition is expected to take three years.

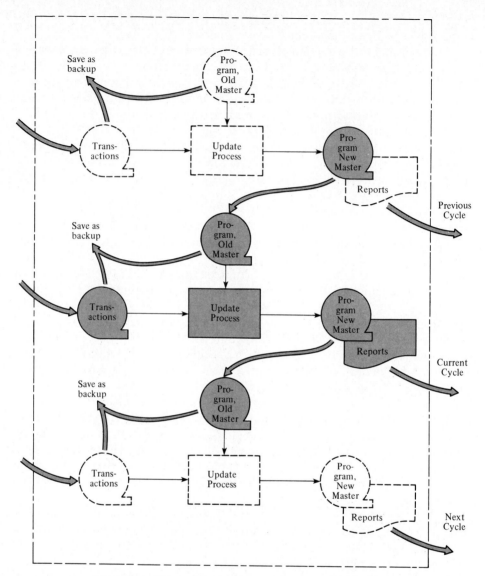

FIGURE 8-9 Updating a master file in a tape system.

record key used in the previous comparison. The logic of updating in a tape system is shown in flowchart form in Figure 8-10.

All of these rules are dependent on accurate sequencing of records in both transaction and master files and on the absence of errors. In practice, additional steps—such as editing the transaction file and adding a data element to indicate the required updating process (to add, delete, or change a master record)—are taken to ensure accuracy.

As records are updated, the data to be included in any printed output are

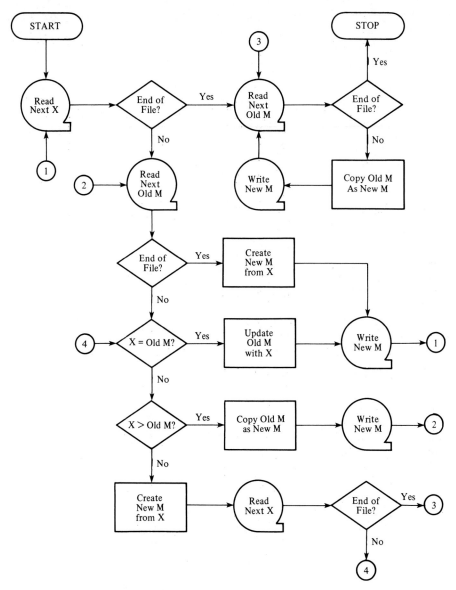

FIGURE 8-10 Logic of updating a tape system.

placed in a temporary storage area, either internal or external, until the updating process is completed and reports can be prepared according to program instructions. The new master file now becomes the basic source of data for the application, and the old master file and transaction file are stored, off-line, for a few cycles as backup in the event of loss or damage to the new master file. The relationship among the several master files is often explained in family terms: the backup file is called the *grandparent file*, the one used in processing is called the *parent*, and the new one, naturally, is called the *child*.

Advantages and Disadvantages   Tape systems have several distinct advantages over card systems: tapes can be read much faster than cards; they are less bulky for any given volume of data; and preliminary operations, such as sorting, can be performed by computer. But the biggest advantage of tapes is that they must be stored on-line, in quantity, subject only to limitations on the number of tape drives available and the capability of the CPU to support peripherals. Also, the creation of a completely new master file, while the transaction file and the old master file are preserved for backup purposes (a trait shared with card systems), is an advantage over the disk system described in the following section.

The biggest disadvantage of tape systems is that they are limited to sequential files. When many transactions are to be processed at once, as in the case of a monthly billing system or a payroll system, transactions can be sequenced as in the master file and processing with tape is quite efficient. However, if transactions must be processed serially, as they occur, tape systems are prohibitively slow.

A lesser disadvantage is that tape systems tie up a lot of equipment. In order to update a master file on tape with a tape transaction file, a minimum of three tape drives is required: one each for the transaction file, the old master file, and the new master file. If several tape applications are to be run concurrently, under time-sharing, the requirement for tape drives could easily exceed the number available.

Finally, pure tape systems cannot operate in a data base environment. It is possible, of course, for a tape–disk system to use a data base management system, but it is not possible to maintain a DBMS on a sequential access storage device.

Disk Systems

Disks are rapidly becoming the most popular medium for transaction processing. Disk drives, although somewhat more expensive than tape drives, are faster, have greater capacity, and offer more freedom in the choice of processing modes. Although disk drives are direct access storage devices and are most commonly used with random files, it is also possible to create sequential files on disks.

Updating a Sequential Master File   There are several reasons for using sequential files on disks. First, it will be recalled that random files become inefficient when the disk is more than 70 to 80 percent full; with sequential files, the disk can be filled to capacity without loss of efficiency. Second, there is a limited capability of updating a sequential master file on disk with a serial or other nonsequential transaction file (see the discussion of the transactional processing mode later in this chapter). Finally, if all or most of the other

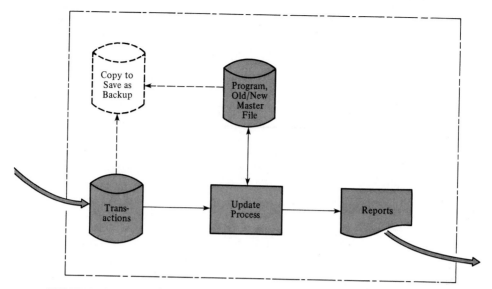

FIGURE 8-11   Updating in a disk system with a sequential master file.

applications in the TPS use random files, it may not be worth the bother to introduce tape just to support one or two sequential applications.

When both the master and the transaction files are sequential, processing is conducted almost exactly as in a tape system, with the obvious exception that disk drives are substituted for tape drives. The direct-access capability of the disk drive is lost, of course, but the system can access the next record in physical order in much the same way that tape systems can read the next record on a tape. The comparison of record keys is conducted exactly as with tape. The new master file is even created on a new disk—a departure from the more common random file procedures—although both old and new disks may be on the same drive, as shown in Figure 8-11.

Updating a Random Master File   When the master file is organized randomly, the sequence of the transaction file is unimportant. When a transaction is read, the master record can be found by the key transformation process described earlier, or by an index at the beginning of the file, and brought into the CPU for updating. In contrast to processing with sequential files, the new master record is returned to the same location on the same disk from which the older master record came. The process of rewriting the new record over the old record effectively erases the old one, although it does cut down on the total amount of storage space required for the application. A disk system using a randomly organized master file and a terminal for entering transaction data is diagrammed in Figure 8-12.

Advantages and Disadvantages   Disk systems are favored over tape or card systems because of their higher speeds, their direct access capabilities, and

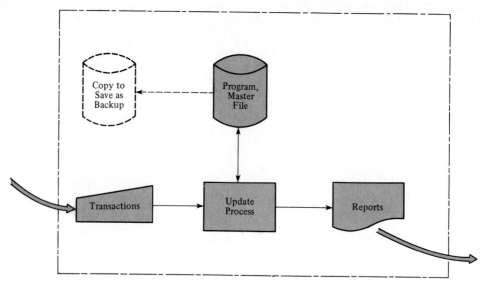

FIGURE 8-12 Updating in a disk system with a random master file.

their large on-line storage capacities. They also permit greater flexibility in the choice of file organization and processing modes, although it would be inefficient to use a disk system exclusively with sequential files and simply imitate a tape system.

The one major drawback of disk systems is the erasing of the old master file when a randomly organized file is updated. Disk drives are susceptible to "head crashes," although now rare, in which a read or write head makes contact with the magnetized surface of the disk, scoring it and destroying any data recorded there. In such cases, it is difficult to reconstruct a new master file without an old one. Also, certain financial and other applications have auditing requirements that are difficult to carry out without historical files. In these instances, the master and transaction files must be periodically transferred onto a second disk, a tape, or even a printout and held in the data library to satisfy legal or operational requirements.

Transaction Processing in a Data Base Environment

The data processing ancestors of transaction processing systems were all application oriented, and many TPS, even when they are part of a CBIS family that includes MIS and DSS, still use application-oriented files. But there is an ever-increasing trend to apply data base concepts and data base management systems concepts to transaction processing, especially where they are already incorporated into higher level CBIS. Since data base management systems were discussed in detail in Chapter 6, we will use a some-

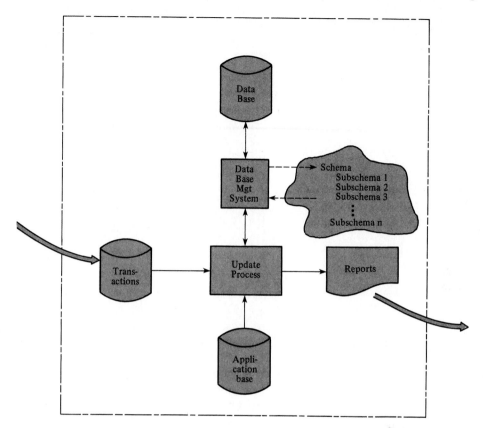

FIGURE 8-13   Updating in a data base environment.

what simplified model, as shown in Figure 8-13, to point out the major differences between transaction processing with application-oriented files and with a data base.

The use of the symbol for a direct-access storage device to depict the data base in Figure 8-13 is not arbitrary. Data *must* be stored on DASD if they are to be constantly structured and restructured according to the various sub-schema required by the application programs. It should be borne in mind, however, that it is not the DASD *per se* that determines the extent of file independence; many application-oriented files are on disks or other DASD. Instead, it is the DASD working in conjunction with a DBMS that creates the data base environment.

Updating a Data Base

Because the data base must be on a DASD, we expect the updating process to be somewhat similar to updating in a disk system with application-oriented files. It is, but as Figure 8-13 shows, there are several important differences.

First, there is no permanent master file. An equivalent of a master file is defined by a subschema and is assembled as needed for the application. Second, application programs obviously cannot be stored at the beginning of the master file as they are in application-oriented TPS. Instead, application programs are drawn from an *application base*, which is also maintained on a DASD.

The application base is the repository of application programs for all CBIS, although DSS often have a separate base of programs called a *model base*. This name derives from the fact that many programs used in DSS literally are mathematical or statistical models of the type discussed in Chapter 7. The programs normally used for transaction processing, however, are little different from those used with application-oriented files. All that is unique about these programs in a data base environment is the inclusion of program statements to identify the subschema by which the data are structured for the application.

At this point, the system has all the characteristics of the disk system described earlier, including the ability to update either a sequentially or a randomly organized master file. If the master file is sequential, the transaction file is usually sorted in like sequence, but if the master file is random, the transaction file may be in any sequence—just as in any other disk system. Updating then proceeds as in the comparable application-oriented disk system.

When the updating process is complete, a third difference is evident. The "new" master file is disbanded, and the individual data elements are returned, by the DBMS, to their original locations in the data base. For updated elements, the new values replace the former values and are the ones that will be used in any subsequent processing—even if it occurs only seconds later and involves a completely different application.

Advantages and Disadvantages

The advantages of transaction processing in a data base environment are similar to those listed for DBMS in Chapter 6: Redundancy is reduced, maintenance is simplified, processing time is shortened, consistency is improved, and data can be shared. For transaction processing, which tends to serve as the primary source of CBIS data, the major advantage lies in the reduction of redundancy in data input. Data collection, preparation, and entry are perhaps the most time-consuming and error-prone phase of CBIS operations. Any reduction in data input is bound to improve CBIS accuracy and efficiency.

The disadvantages of a data base environment for transaction processing are also similar to those for DBMS in general: DBMS are costly, security is more difficult, errors or breaches of security are more damaging, and greater control is required. No one of these disadvantages is more significant than the others in transaction processing; all must be considered in the decision to implement a DBMS.

Processing Modes

The *mode* of processing refers to the timing of the updating process with respect to the occurrence of transactions. Transaction data may be collected and processed periodically, say, at the end of each day, or as the transactions occur. In the first case, the mode is said to be *batch*, and in the second, it is called *transactional* or *on-line*.[5] In the special case in which a transactional system processes some data and returns output in time to influence the remainder of the transaction, it is further identified as being *real-time*. A few examples will serve to illustrate the processing modes.

Batch Processing

In most transaction processing applications, the updating interval is much greater than the interval between transactions. A payroll file, for example, may be updated weekly, although payroll transactions (the earning of pay) take place continuously. Credit card holders can charge purchases daily, but they are billed only monthly. In these and similar cases, transaction data are held until processing time, and all records on the master file are updated in a *batch*, in a single run through the master file.

With Sequential Master Files
As noted earlier, sequential files may be on cards, tape, or disks. Figure 8-14 shows how transactions on cards are saved over a period of time and then used to update a card master file. Figures 8-9 and 8-10, although presented to illustrate an application-oriented tape system, are also representative of batch processing with tape.

With Random Master Files
Random master files, of course, must be on a DASD, and although such files are normally associated with the transactional mode, there are two common approaches to using them in a batch mode. The choice depends on the number of master records to be updated.

For small numbers of transactions, usually fewer than half the number of master records, the updating occurs in the order in which the transactions are stored. As each transaction record is read, the corresponding master record is located and read into memory. After that record is updated, the next transaction is read, and so on, to the end of the transaction file. The location of the master record is determined from an index or by the techniques of key transformation described in Chapter 6.

---

[5]The term *transactional processing*, which means that transactions are processed as they occur, should not be confused with the similar term *transaction processing*, which literally means the processing of transactions and which may be either batch or transactional.

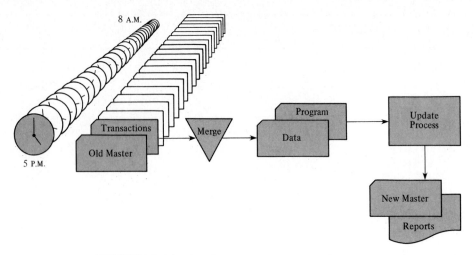

FIGURE 8-14   Batch processing in a card system.

If one half or more of the master records are to be updated, it is best to sort the transactions into logical order and to process them sequentially. Sequential processing in a randomly organized master file is aided by the use of *pointers*. A pointer is a data element that gives the storage location of the next record in logical order. An *external access pointer* at the beginning of the master file gives the location of the first logical record (i.e., the one with the lowest numerical record key). A pointer in that record gives the storage location of the second logical record, and so on. The slight disadvantage of adding an additional element to each record for the pointer is offset by the advantage of not having to search the index or to perform a key transformation for each record. Of course, if only a few records are to be updated, one would not wish to run through the entire master file in logical order. This is the rationale behind the rule of thumb of processing sequentially only when more than one half of the master records are involved. The use of pointers to establish logical order is depicted in Figure 8-15.

Transactional Processing

When output is required for each transaction—say, to give a receipt to a customer—or when the data collection process is on-line, it is more efficient to process transactions as they occur. Many retail sales applications now operate in a transactional mode. Instead of being punched on cards or being keyed onto tape or disk at the end of the day, transactions are recorded on point-of-sale terminals that double as cash registers. A typical point-of-sale terminal is shown in Figure 8-16. The operator may key in such data as the price, the quantity, the stock number, the department, the clerk identification, and the sales tax, or some of these data may be read optically by a *wand*.

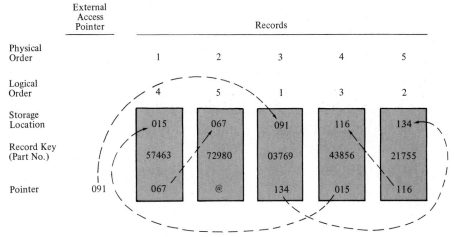

Note: @ is the symbol for the end of the file.

FIGURE 8-15 The use of pointers in random master files.

Processes not apparent to the customer and the clerk also post the sale to department accounts, deduct the quantity sold from inventory, debit charge accounts, and maintain records for sale and marketing analysis. These latter functions also illustrate the manner in which transaction processing supports higher level activities in other CBIS.

Transactional processing requires direct access storage devices such as disk drives. Figure 8-17 illustrates the continuous processing of transaction data with the use of terminals for input and disks for storge. Once again, the exact manner in which master records are updated is dictated by file organization.

With Sequential Master Files

It is possible to process transactionally even when the master file is sequential. As noted earlier, a disk drive cannot locate a *record* in a sequential file directly, but a disk drive can go directly to any given *storage location*. If a particular record in a sequential file is desired, one can find it by systematically halving the file in what is called a *binary search*. For example, as shown in Figure 8-18, if account number 535-62-4177 is needed for update and there are 3,143 accounts in the file, a check will be made of the 1,572nd storage location (one finds the mid-point by adding the first and last location values and dividing the result by 2). Because the account number there, 642-84-2138, is *greater* than 535-62-4177, then account 535-62-4177 must be somewhere among the first 1,571 locations. The next check is of location number 786 where the account number, 419-23-7781, is *less* than 535-62-4177. This means that account number 535-62-4177 is somewhere between location 787 and location 1571, so a check is made of location 1179. Eventually, although in less time than you might think, this process will find the

FIGURE 8-16 Point-of-sale terminal. (Photo courtesy of NCR.)

desired record. It can be shown that the *maximum* number of steps needed to find any record by binary search is n, where n is the first power of 2 that gives a value greater than the number of records. The *average* number of steps will be close to $n - 1$. Because 2^{12} is 4,096, the average number of steps needed to find any given record in a sequential file of 3,143 records is around 11, but it will never take more than 12. Of course, one might get lucky and find it much earlier—perhaps even on the first step.

With Random Master Files

The ability to process transactionally with a sequential disk file is merely a fringe benefit of disk drives. When the dominant processing mode is transactional, it is best to use a random file organization. The process of finding the master record is the same for transactional processing as it is for batch pro-

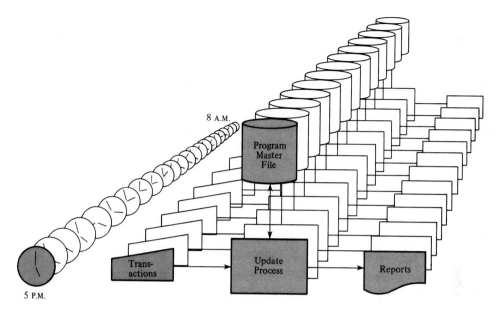

FIGURE 8-17   Transactional processing in a disk system.

cessing with random master files: the storage location is determined from an index or by key transformation. In a sense, transactional processing with a random master file can be thought of as a special case of batch processing in which the batch is very small—only one transaction!

Real-Time Processing

Real-time processing, the ability to influence a transaction while it is taking place, is one of the most powerful capabilities of transaction processing. The first real-time systems were developed by the U.S. Air Force for air defense missile control, where only fractions of a second could be tolerated between the detection of an approaching aircraft and the decision to launch a missile against it. This application led many to equate "real-time" with "instantaneous." This is not a bad definition for the air defense application, but in TPS, much slower systems can be considered real-time.

Real-time processing is interactive; that is, there is an exchange of inputs and outputs at the source of the transaction. Real-time applications in business typically use a CRT or a typewriter terminal to gain interactive access to a processor and a master file as shown in Figure 8-19.

Real-time systems are of necessity transactional or on-line. Indeed, such systems are often described as *on-line/real-time*, although that terminology is somewhat redundant. Airline ticket reservation systems are excellent examples that demonstrate both real-time and transactional capabilities in a business application.

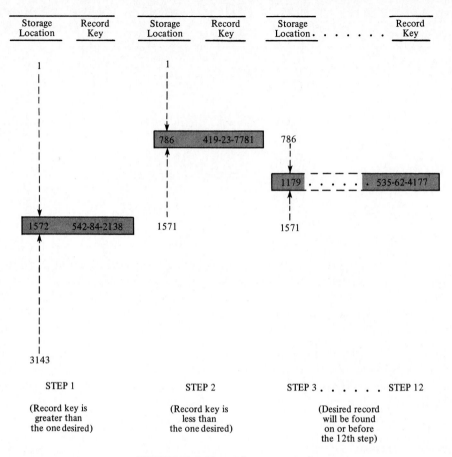

Storage Location	Record Key	Storage Location	Record Key	Storage Location • • • • • •	Record Key

1   1

786   419-23-7781   786

1179   • • • • • •   535-62-4177

1572   542-84-2138   1571   1571

3143

STEP 1	STEP 2	STEP 3 • • • • • • STEP 12
(Record key is greater than the one desired)	(Record key is less than the one desired)	(Desired record will be found on or before the 12th step)

FIGURE 8-18 A binary search.

The ticket reservation system is real-time because the initial processing of a request for an airline ticket influences the outcome of the transaction—whether a ticket is sold or not. When a ticket request is keyed into a terminal at the reservation counter, the master file record for that flight is checked for the availability of a seat. If a seat is available, it is temporarily "booked" to prevent its commitment to another reservation office, and that information is displayed on a CRT screen. A second input at the reservation terminal confirms the sale and makes the booking permanent. The entire process may take a few minutes, but that is real-time in ticket reservation if not in air defense!

The ticket reservation system is also transactional, because requests for tickets are processed individually, as they occur, instead of periodically, in a batch. Different versions of this system can also print tickets, bill customers for tickets purchased on credit, and provide data for scheduling and route optimization. Again, in these latter uses, we see the value of transaction data in decision support and management information.

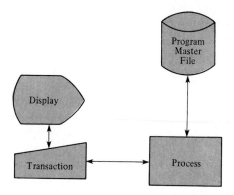

FIGURE 8-19 Real-time processing with a CRT terminal.

Computer booking on airlines often raises the question of overbooking. When more tickets are sold than there are seats on a flight, it is rarely because of a failure of the reservation system. More likely, it is a deliberate policy based on statistical evidence that a few ticket holders will not show up for the flight. This is an interesting example of another form of interface between the TPS and a higher level system such as a DSS: the TPS furnishes data for analysis by the DSS, and the DSS is the probable source of the criteria (overbooking) for processing transactions!

Summary

Transaction processing systems perform many of the functions originally associated with data processing, but in a CBIS environment, they are also a basic source of data for other CBIS.

In the TPS function of data input, data are *collected, prepared,* and *entered.* When data input is *direct*, all three functions are carried out in a single step. In *indirect* data input, collection is a separate step, but preparation and entry may still be combined.

Processing in TPS is typified by the *storage, retrieval, sorting, organizing,* and *updating* of transaction data. In general, these processes are less complex than those found in other CBIS.

The output of TPS is in the form of detail and scheduled *reports*, responses to *inquiries*, or *input* to other CBIS. The manner in which TPS output is made available to other CBIS depends on the approach to data management. A data base approach provides much greater access than do application-oriented files.

In addition to interfacing with other CBIS, TPS also interface with functional subsystems—production, marketing, personnel, and finance—of an organization. Interface is achieved by the exchange of inputs and outputs, although TPS tend to be more involved with data inputs, whereas other CBIS tend to be more output oriented.

Application-oriented TPS can use master files on cards, tape, or disk, but disk files are now the most popular. Application-oriented files are less costly and more secure, but they are less accessible to other CBIS applications and may result in duplication of data.

TPS operating in a data base environment must use master files on disk or other DSAD. Data bases and data base management systems are costly, but they reduce much redundancy in the TPS data input and storage.

Transactions may be processed as they occur, in a *transactional* mode, or saved and processed periodically, in a *batch* mode. The transactional mode is further classified as *real-time* when the initial output of the process is received in time to influence the outcome of the transaction. The nature of the transaction process, including the requirement for speed, determines the best combination of file organization, medium, and processing mode to use in any particular application.

Assignments

8-1. Describe the steps of data collection, preparation, and entry for each of the following transactions:

   a. Consumption of electricity by a home owner. The electric utility company uses an optical character reader for data entry.
   b. Completion of a college course. The university uses mark-sense grade report forms.
   c. Purchase of a hamburger at a fast food chain that uses point-of-sale terminals.
   d. Production of soft drinks. The counters on the bottling machines are electronically linked to a computer.

8-2. Airline ticket reservations are processed in a TPS. Give examples of the TPS processes of storage, retrieval, classification, organization, and updating as they may occur in such a system.

8-3. The TPS output of an inquiry response is accomplished best in a data base environment. How are inquiries handled with application-oriented files? (You may wish to refer to Chapter 3 to confirm your answer to this question.)

8-4. For each of the following transaction processing applications, select an appropriate file organization, medium, and processing mode. Assume that all options discussed in this chapter are available. Explain your choices:

a. Inventory record maintenance in a catalog mail-order firm.
b. Reservation booking in a motel chain.
c. Student record maintenance at your university.
d. Claim settlement in a medical insurance firm.

8-5. Refer to Figure 8-10. Trace the logic of the flowchart using the following "files" of transactions and master records:

a.   *File*   *Record Key*
   Transaction   1, 3, 4, @
     Master   1, 2, 3, 5, 6, @

b.   *File*   *Record Key*
   Transaction   1, 3, 4, 6, @
     Master   1, 2, 3, 5, @

(Note: @ is the symbol for the end of the file.)

8-6. Assume that you are an information systems consultant and have been asked to recommend an approach to processing administrative transactions (grade reporting, billing, automobile registration, and so on) at your university. Would you recommend application-oriented files or a data base approach? What are the advantages and disadvantages of each for this application?

8-7. A rather small sequential master file on disk has fifteen records. The storage locations and the key element of the record in each location are as follows:

Location	Key Element	Location	Key Element
1	029	9	479
2	083	10	503
3	129	11	542
4	165	12	588
5	215	13	613
6	374	14	721
7	398	15	793
8	426		

a. What is the theoretical maximum number of steps needed to find any record in this file by means of a binary search?
b. How many steps will it take, and in which locations will you look, to find the record with the key 215 by binary search?
c. Answer b above for the record with key number 721.
d. This will take a little time, but what is the exact average number of steps required to find a record in this file?

8-8. Think of an institution—for example, a bank—with voluminous transaction processing requirements. This bank acquired its first computer in 1958 and today has a modern family of CBIS. How do you think transaction processing in the bank has changed over the years? Are the changes due entirely to hardware advancements? To what other factors can the changes be attributed?

CASE   Hill Manufacturing—Part IV

At Hill Manufacturing Company, Debbie Cather is again meeting with Dave Andrews regarding the firm's new materials requirements planning (MRP) system. The topic of this meeting concerns updating the system, that is, processing changes such as new orders, canceled orders, receipts of ordered parts, and delays in ordered parts or on the shop floor. There are two basic approaches to updating MRP systems: a regenerative system or a net-change system.

A regenerative system accumulates all changes that occur over a time period (e.g., one or two weeks) and then periodically updates the system. Each regeneration or "explosion" of the master production schedule involves a replanning of requirements and an updating of the inventory status for all items that are part of the MRP system.

In a net-change system, changes are entered into the system as they occur. The entire production plan is not regenerated; "partial explosions" modify the portion of the plan that is affected.

The regenerative system is better suited to more stable environments, because there is a delay between the time that changes actually occur and when they are incorporated into the production plan. This time lag, though, does allow time for changes to "cancel each other." The net-change system gives managers the most current information available for planning and control purposes, but the system may exhibit what is called nervousness because many small changes keep modifying the production plan.

Questions

1. For each of the two types of systems, outline options for file organization, medium, and processing mode.

2. Which of the two types would most likely incur less processing costs? Why?

3. What criteria would be used to choose between these two ways of updating the MRP system?

Other Readings

Awad, Elias M. *Business Data Processing*. Englewood Cliffs, N.J.: Prentice-Hall, 1980.

Capron, H. L., and Brian K. Williams. *Computers and Data Processing*. Menlo Park, Calif.: Benjamin/Cummings Publishing Company, 1982.

Murach, Mike. *Business Data Processing with BASIC and FORTRAN* (2d ed.). Chicago: Science Research Associates, 1977.

Parker, Charles S. *Understanding Computers and Data Processing: Today and Tomorrow*. New York: Holt, Rinehart and Winston, 1984.

Spencer, Donald D. *Data Processing: An Introduction*. Columbus, Ohio: Charles E. Merrill, 1978.

Watson, Hugh J., and Archie B. Carroll. *Computers for Business* (2d ed.). Dallas: Business Publications, 1980.

PART IV

MANAGEMENT INFORMATION SYSTEMS

The second specific CBIS with which we shall deal is the *management information system*, or MIS. Not too many years ago, MIS might have been the topic of this *book* rather than this *part*. But recent developments, particularly those in decision support systems, tend to make us think in terms of CBIS instead. This change in emphasis does not diminish the importance of MIS; it merely recognizes the existence of other, equally important, business computer systems.

Even though MIS are now just one of several CBIS, they are, to many managers, *the* organizational CBIS. There are several reasons for this. First, many organizations include transaction processing in the MIS function. Second, many managers are aware of the presence of office automation systems but are not aware of the extent to which OAS are integrated into the CBIS. Finally, many organizations do not yet have decision support, executive information, or expert systems, and managers in these organizations may simply be unaware that new types of CBIS have emerged. As the dominant CBIS in many organizations, MIS serve as the basis for a general model to explain how organizational information needs are satisfied. Part IV presents such a model.

Chapter 9

An Overview
of MIS

Learning Objectives

After studying this chapter, you will be able to:

1. Discuss the effect of placing MIS in organizational environments with different combinations of CBIS.
2. Identify different types of models according to a taxonomy of models.
3. Describe the processing dimension of MIS.
4. Name the three management activities of MIS.
5. Illustrate the use of functional subsystems in MIS.
6. Use a three-dimensional model of MIS to explain information flows in an organization.
7. Define the following terms:

CBIS technology	mathematical model
CBIS applications	processing dimension (of MIS)
technology-intensive	management dimension (of MIS)
application-intensive	functional dimension (of MIS)
stand-alone MIS	calculation
physical model	summarization
symbolic model	communication
iconic model	strategic planning
analog model	management control
verbal model	operational control

The approach to the study of management information systems—MIS—presents an interesting contrast to the approach to TPS. We began our system-by-system discussion of CBIS with TPS for several reasons: a TPS is the first system in line when CBIS are related serially; TPS processes are simple and easy to understand; TPS can be used to demonstrate the full range of CBIS design characteristics—the use of different media, data management techniques, and processing modes; and there is general consensus on just what constitutes a TPS.

In comparison, MIS occupy an intermediate position in the CBIS family and may overlap other CBIS to a considerable degree. MIS are also more complex than TPS, and the model we will use to explain them is correspondingly complex. The greater complexity of MIS also restricts the design options—an MIS could not reasonably be based on batch processing with punched cards, for example. Finally, there are structural, philosophical, and technological differences that introduce great variety into the way MIS are designed, developed, and operated in different organizations. Let us look more closely at each of these points, beginning with the position of MIS in the CBIS family.

MIS and the CBIS Family

In Chapter 1, we examined some temporal relationships among CBIS with graphs and figures that showed how CBIS emerged over a period of time. Now we are more concerned with nontemporal relationships: how information processing responsibilities are distributed among CBIS, at what level of technology various CBIS function, and whether all types of CBIS are present in a given organization. To examine these relationships, let us consider just two aspects of CBIS: *technology* and *applications*.

The technology of a CBIS includes hardware, software, and processes. Technology has no universally accepted unit of measurement, but we can use a continuous scale ranging from *simple* to *complex*. For example, we can say that card readers, file-oriented programs, and the process of classification are simple, whereas touch-sensitive CRT displays, data base management systems, and nonlinear extrapolations are complex.

Applications of CBIS can be measured similarly. File maintenance, billing, and payroll preparation are simple applications, whereas sales forecasting, financial planning, and simulation are more complex.

Figure 9-1 shows the four possible combinations of technology and applications that can occur in CBIS. When complex technology is used to perform simple applications (say, a real-time system in a data base environment used to process a payroll), we say the CBIS is *technology-intensive*. At the other extreme, complex applications attempted with simple technology, such as an iterative forecasting application using a batch-mode card system, are indica-

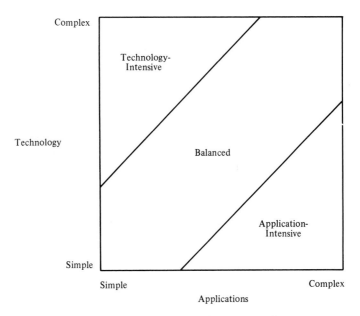

FIGURE 9-1 Combinations of technology and applications in CBIS.

tive of an *application-intensive* CBIS. The other two combinations—simple applications with simple technology and complex applications with complex technology—suggest a *balanced* CBIS.

Stand-Alone MIS

When an organization has only one CBIS, it is most likely to call that system an MIS. There is a typical scenario that leads to a single CBIS/MIS: over a number of years, the equipment in a data processing system is periodically upgraded; additional applications that support management are developed; perhaps a data base management system is installed; and at some point, the name is changed to *management information system.* We will refer to such systems as *stand-alone MIS.*

A stand-alone MIS is shown in Figure 9-2. Because the technology is geared to applications of moderate complexity, very simple applications (those normally found in TPS) fall into the technology-intensive area, and very complex applications (those typical of DSS) must be accomplished by application-intensive methods.

Transaction processing, office automation, and decision support still occur in organizations with stand-alone MIS, but they are seriously impaired by inappropriate technology and a management that does not fully appreciate the technological support required for these applications.

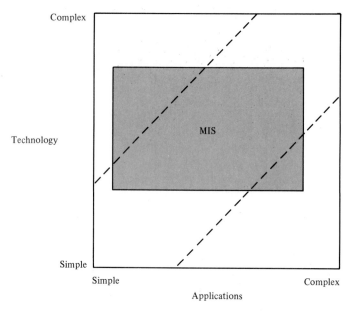

FIGURE 9-2   A "stand-alone" MIS.

MIS with TPS and OAS

When organizations do recognize the need for different CBIS, the exact mix is dictated by the nature of the information and processing needs. In those organizations with extensive transaction processing requirements—mail order firms, insurance companies, banks, and the like—the additional CBIS are most likely to be TPS or OAS, as shown in Figure 9-3.

The effect of additional CBIS on MIS is to narrow the range of MIS applications. In this case, pure TPS or OAS applications are performed in their respective systems, and the MIS can be tailored to the needs of managerial users. Some overlap among CBIS remains, however. There are still MIS applications of relative simplicity—exception reports, summary reports, and the like—and some TPS applications, such as airline reservations, require complex technology.

MIS with DSS, EIS, and ES

In other organizations, the pressure on MIS may be not for greater transaction processing capability but for greater decision support. This is particularly true in high-technology firms where rapidly changing environmental factors make planning decisions both difficult and critical. The lack of adequate decision support is especially frustrating because, as a general rule, an MIS adapts less readily to the specialized requirements of decision support than to

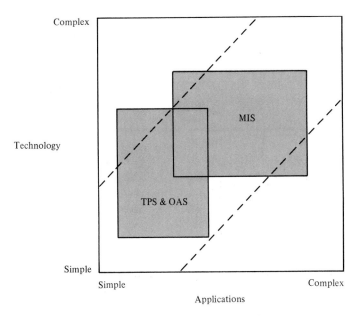

FIGURE 9-3   MIS with TPS and OAS.

those of transaction processing. Put another way, a technology-intensive approach (TPS applications with MIS technology) is more feasible than an application-intensive approach (DSS applications with MIS technology). Executive information systems (EIS) and expert systems (ES) also do not function well in an application-intensive environment and, like DSS, usually require more complex technology than that used to support MIS. Consequently, many organizations now find themselves moving toward the combination of CBIS shown in Figure 9-4.

The effect of an MIS/DSS/EIS/ES combination is much the same as that of MIS/TPS/OAS: The range of MIS applications is narrowed—but in a different direction. MIS technology—mainframe computers, corporate data bases, and report generating software—is no longer asked to perform DSS applications such as model building, statistical analysis, and graphical representations. The overlap area now represents applications and technology that may be common to both systems, for example, an inquiry processing capability that generates special or ad hoc reports.

MIS in a Total CBIS Environment

There are also organizations that have recognized the need for additional CBIS specialization in all three areas: transaction processing, office automation, and decision support. In these organizations, as shown in Figure 9-5, the range of MIS applications has been reduced at both ends, and there is good balance between technology and applications in all CBIS. This is the

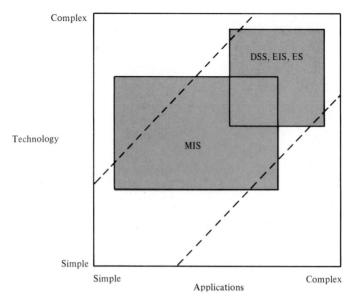

FIGURE 9-4   MIS with DSS, EIS, and ES.

CBIS environment we shall assume for the remainder of this book, and with the exception of TPS, we shall not directly refer to other CBIS in the discussion of MIS. It will aid your understanding of MIS, however, if you keep the relationships with other CBIS in mind as we develop the MIS model that follows.

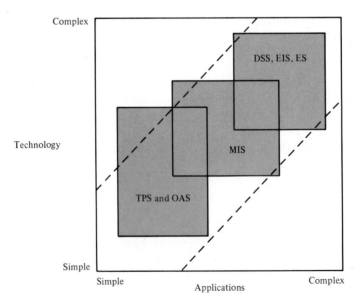

FIGURE 9-5   MIS in a total CBIS environment.

An MIS Model

It is difficult to describe an MIS in clear, unambiguous terms. Even with the assumptions we have just made regarding the presence of other specialized CBIS, MIS still differ from one organization to the next, taking on characteristics peculiar to the role of the organization, the information needs of managers, and the available technology. We would not expect the MIS of, for example, a large financial institution to be exactly like that of a department of the federal government.

An MIS is also difficult to describe because much of it is conceptual rather than physical. There is a certain security in dealing with physical components: they can be seen, handled, taken apart to reveal what makes them work, and sent out for repair when they are broken. Perhaps it is this security that causes many managers to think of MIS only in terms of their physical components—the computer hardware. The conceptual components of MIS—the information flows, the relationships between functional applications, and the managerial decision processes—are less understandable. Both difficulties can be overcome through the use of an appropriate *model*. Models are abstractions that help us to understand the real world when the real-world situation is too complex, too dangerous, too time consuming, or too expensive to examine firsthand. As shown in Figure 9-6, models can be classified as either *physical* or *symbolic*. Physical models are further classified as *iconic* (those models that look like the real-world objects they represent) or *analog* (those that act, but do not necessarily look, like the objects they represent). Symbolic models are usually classified as either *verbal* (consisting of words) or *mathematical* (consisting of numbers and mathematical symbols).

You are undoubtedly familiar with some iconic models, such as the non-working scale models used in aircraft and automobile design. You should also

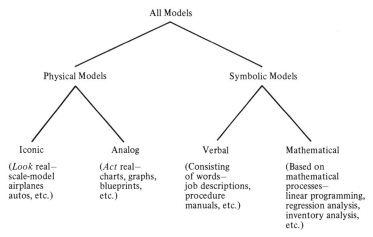

FIGURE 9-6   A taxonomy of models.

be familiar with analog models—such as graphs, charts, and maps. Verbal models are the most common of all—we all use verbal models when we describe something in speech or in writing. And in Chapter 7, we discussed a number of mathematical models used in decision making.

One reason for using models is that they simplify, often by leaving out unessential or minor elements. Little or no understanding would be gained from devising a model as complex as the real-world situation it represents. Economic models, for example, are understandable (to economists, at least) only because they omit much detail and embody many qualifying assumptions. So it must be with an MIS model. Once an MIS is stripped down to its essential parts and the interrelationships among key elements are understood, additional detail may be added to tailor it to the features of a particular organization.

The model that we shall develop here to explain MIS is something of a hybrid: it is an analog model in the sense that it is represented in drawings that reflect MIS processes (but certainly do not *look* like an MIS!), and it is also verbal because the drawings are accompanied by a detailed description in words. Let us take a closer look at this MIS model.

Dimensions of the MIS Model

Try to imagine a symbolic model of a machined part, such as the crankshaft of an automobile engine. A verbal description would soon become hopelessly bogged down; certainly, no machinist could make a crankshaft from such a model. Instead, the designer of the crankshaft conveys the shape and measurements with an analog model, a drawing in this case. But even the drawing has limitations. It is not possible to show all details of the crankshaft in any one perspective. The standard solution to this problem is to draw the part as it appears in three *dimensions*—from the top, the side, and the front. It still takes a certain amount of skill and experience to visualize the end product from these drawings, but the task is greatly simplified.

The crankshaft is comparatively easy to model—it, at least, is physical. An MIS, with its conceptual elements, is more complex, but it, too, can be simplified by being viewed one dimension at a time. Of course, the top, side, and front views of the crankshaft are physical dimensions, and we do not expect to visualize an MIS in that fashion. Instead, we will view it, conceptually, in a *processing* dimension, a *management* dimension, and a *functional* dimension.

The Processing Dimension

All CBIS transform or process data. In this respect, MIS processing is similar to the TPS processing described in the previous chapter. But as noted earlier, the complexity of MIS processes eliminate some options that were available for TPS. Whereas transaction processing can be based on either application-oriented files or a data base, in order to function in the total CBIS environ-

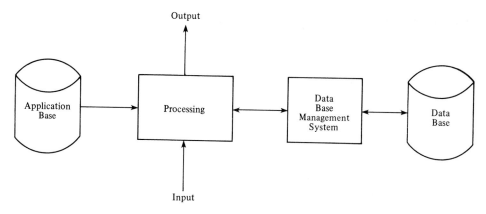

FIGURE 9-7 The processing dimension of MIS.

ment assumed here and to support the information needs of modern management, the processing in our MIS model uses the data base components shown in Figure 9-7.

The Application Base The application base is the repository of MIS application programs. The use of the symbol for a direct access storage device (DSAD) to represent the application base suggests that MIS applications are "on-line" and may be run at any time. Although this requirement exists for some applications—programs that display information to remote terminal users, for example—most MIS applications are not used in this fashion. This is also true of the TPS applications in the application base. All TPS applications may be in DASD, but only those used in a transactional processing mode really need to be.

The most common MIS applications involve the generation of reports and the support of structured decisions. To a lesser extent, MIS applications may also perform data analyses or furnish other support for semistructured decisions. In the data base environment depicted here, these applications do not use traditional files; they draw data from the data base with program statements that specify an appropriate subschema.

MIS Processing Many of the processes used in TPS—storing, retrieving, classifying, sorting, and updating—are used in MIS as well. But MIS also make use of additional processes such as *calculation, summarization,* and *communication.*

Calculation The term *calculation* refers to the mathematical manipulation of numerical data. Of course, simple arithmetic processes are carried out in transaction processing, too. The updating of inventory obviously requires addition and subtraction as items are added to and deleted from stock. The process of calculation that we attribute to MIS goes well beyond simple arithmetic, however. Calculations used in MIS applications may involve linear programming, trend analysis, exponential smoothing, or probabilistic methods.

Just as simple calculations are also found in TPS, more complex calculations are also found in DSS. The distinction lies in the manner of usage: MIS calculations are more likely to be incorporated into standard application programs, whereas DSS users may assemble unique combinations of calculating processes to solve a specific problem.

Summarization   The term *summarization* refers to the condensation of data to enhance the information it conveys. If you have had an introductory statistics course, you may already be familiar with the techniques of organizing and summarizing data. The use of frequency distributions, totals, means, medians, modes, variances, deviations, and other descriptive summary measures makes large volumes of numerical data easier to comprehend and compare.

Communication   The term *communication* is a process now more commonly found in OAS, but one that still plays an important role in MIS. In a very broad sense, reports, responses to inquiries, CRT displays—anything that conveys information from one part of an organization to another—are forms of communication. But in normal usage, we think of communication in a more limited context as a means of conveying short messages of immediate interest to only a few addresses. In OAS, these communications usually concern administrative matters—appointment schedules, meeting agenda, and the like. In MIS, the subject is more likely to concern operational matters—the sequencing of work in a job shop operation, the assignment of machines to jobs, or a change to the normal work schedule.

The Data Base Management System   The DBMS is a key component for the entire family of CBIS, but especially for the MIS. Without a DBMS, the integration of systems within the family of CBIS and the integration of applications within the MIS itself would be difficult if not impossible. DBMS promote data independence by freeing MIS from the format of transaction processing. Data can be provided in any format, subject only to the need to describe the format in a subschema. The details of how DBMS accomplish data independence were discussed in Chapter 6.

The Data Base   The last component in the processing dimension is the data base. The presence of a data base is implied by the DBMS, of course, and only a few words are necessary to put it in the context of this model. First, the data base shown in Figure 9-7 must be common to the TPS and MIS and may be common to other CBIS as well. That is, data generated and entered into the data base by the TPS are available at least to the MIS and possibly to some combination of OAS, DSS, EIS, and ES. We emphasize the commonality of data between TPS and MIS because MIS applications are usually based on transaction data. Other CBIS applications may also be based on transaction data, but they also use data from other sources, which may be stored in the common data base or in data bases unique to the system.

Second, the use of a single DASD symbol should not be construed to mean that there is just one disk drive to store all CBIS data. There may be dozens of DASD, all on-line and all available for use by the various CBIS. Nor does the single symbol convey a single, massive schema for all CBIS data. There are normally a number of functionally oriented data bases, but as long as they are managed by a common DBMS and are on-line, data from any one or a combination of them are available to the MIS. For example, a cost analysis may use one subschema to obtain data from a personnel data base and another to draw data from a purchasing data base to project the total costs of a proposed project.

The Management Dimension

The second dimension of our MIS model considers differences based primarily on the organizational levels served by MIS. There are two important factors to consider in analyzing MIS support to these levels: the basic thrust of managerial activity is different at each level, and the characteristics of information needed to support these activities changes with the level served. Let us examine first the activities of managers at each organizational level.

Managerial Activities The *levels* of management are usually classified, as shown in Table 9-1, as *top, middle,* and *first-line* or *supervisory*. However, as noted in Chapter 3, when we refer to the *activities* of managers at these levels, it is more common to use the terms *strategic planning, management control,* and *operational control*.

Operational Control Operational control is *task*-oriented. Operational control ensures that work will be performed according to accepted standards of quality and resource utilization. Standards at the operational level are imposed by higher levels of management and tend to be *absolute*—a minimum volume of output, a maximum number of defective parts, a final completion date, and so on. The contribution of MIS at this level is to collect

TABLE 9-1 Managerial Activities

Management Level	Management Activity	Activity Orientation
Top	Strategic planning	Goals and objectives
Middle	Management control	Resources
First-line	Operational control	Tasks

actual performance data and compare them with the standards. Managers then exercise control by taking the necessary action to correct deficiencies.

The exact nature of the tasks subject to operational control varies from organization to organization. When *goods* are produced, as in a manufacturing firm, the tasks involve positioning materials, setting up equipment, fabricating components, assembling end items, inspecting finished goods, and so on. In a *service* organization (an employment office, for example), they may include preparing job descriptions, interviewing applicants, maintaining records, visiting work sites, and the like. You probably can identify the basic operational tasks found in other organizations as well.

Management Control   Management control is *resource*-oriented. Managers at this level exercise control over the acquisition and use of the basic resources—materials, labor, time, and money—required to carry out operational tasks. As in operational control, standards (organizational goals and objectives, in this case) are imposed by a higher level of management, but, unlike operational control, the criteria tend to be more *relative*—ratios of resource inputs to outputs, comparative prices and quality of input resources, return on investment, and so on. MIS are used to compute the efficiency with which resources are used and to compare the results with the standards. Again, it is left to the human managers to take the necessary corrective action if the standards are not met.

Interactions between persons play a much more important role in management control than in operational control, which tends to be somewhat mechanistic. Management information systems do not support interpersonal relations well, but much of the slack in this area has been taken up by office automation systems, which are discussed in detail in Chapter 12.

Strategic Planning   For the final management activity we must make a subtle change from *control* to *planning*. Actually, the transition began, as shown in Figure 9-8, in the previous activity, where some *tactical* or short-range planning takes place. At this level, however, we are concerned with long-range or *strategic* planning.

Strategic planning is oriented to the establishment of organizational *goals*

FIGURE 9-8   Planning-control continuum.

and *objectives*. The issue is not the tasks to be performed or even the resources with which to perform them but the *purpose* of performing them.

Goals and objectives take many forms. They may define the scope of organizational activities—the products to be made, the services to be offered, the markets to be reached, and so on. Or they may establish performance standards—market share, profit, total sales, quality, and the like. Or in some other way, they may convey the future direction of the organization. MIS can provide and analyze historical data in support of strategic planning, but decision support systems are, perhaps, more useful in establishing goals and objectives.

In many organizations, goals and objectives are established *outside* the realm of management activity, by stockholders, boards of directors, legislative bodies, or other nonmanagement agencies. MIS rarely serve such bodies. This manner of establishing goals does create some downward slippage of management activities, however, and top managers may find themselves in a position of *implementing*, rather than *setting*, goals and objectives. MIS are of greater value in this environment but still must be complemented by DSS.

Information Characteristics If we were to try to identify the information needs of the various management activities, the list would be hopelessly long, as well as incomplete, simply because of the great variety of organizations served by MIS. However, if we look at the *characteristics* of information at each level, certain patterns emerge. Just knowing the activity level of an MIS application gives us an insight into the decisions involved, the data required, and the way the MIS will be used.

Decisions If you were to single out one characteristic that distinguishes managers from other organizational personnel it would probably be their decision-making responsibilities. Four properties of decisions—the *situations* in which they occur, the *processes* they employ, the *criteria* on which they are based, and the *support* furnished them by MIS—are shown for different management activities in Figure 9-9. Although there are many

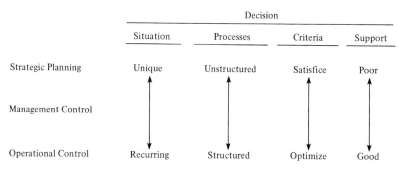

FIGURE 9-9 MIS decision support.

other ways to describe decisions, these properties are particularly useful in an MIS context.

In each case, strategic planning and operational control define the end points of a continuous scale for the properties of decisions, and management control occupies a middle ground. For example, decision situations range from *unique* to *recurring;* in between we expect to find decisions that have some characteristics in common or that recur only occasionally. Decision processes are defined as *unstructured*—that is, not conforming to standard models or solution methodologies—or as *structured.* Here the middle ground is referred to as *semistructured.* The criterion for decision making in strategic planning is usually the administrative behavior of *satisficing*— selecting the first acceptable alternative—whereas decision makers in operational control attempt to *optimize* by selecting the best possible alternative. Decisions in management control may require either criterion. Finally, it can be seen that MIS support diminishes toward the strategic planning end of the scale.

This analysis must be qualified because we have been dealing in generalities. You should not expect *all* operational control decisions to be recurring, structured, optimal, and well supported by MIS. There may be exceptions in each property, at each activity level.

Data Information can also be characterized by the *data* on which it is based. Four properties of data that are particularly relevant to MIS support of management activities are the *source,* the *accuracy,* the *currency,* and the extent of *aggregation.* As shown in Figure 9-10, data properties are also measured on continuous scales.

The source of data is primarily *external* for strategic planning and mainly *internal* for operational control. This, of course, is one reason that MIS do not support strategic planning well: MIS tend to rely on internal data developed from transaction processing; external data generally must be obtained by the user.

In strategic planning, where outputs may be subject to great variation, the accuracy requirements are not as high as they are in operational control.

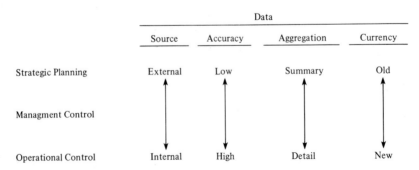

	Data			
	Source	Accuracy	Aggregation	Currency
Strategic Planning	External	Low	Summary	Old
Managment Control				
Operational Control	Internal	High	Detail	New

FIGURE 9-10   MIS data requirements.

For example, an estimate of next year's sales would be considered accurate if it is within 5 percent of the actual amount, but a shipment of television sets to a retailer is expected to be exactly as ordered.

It was noted earlier, in Chapter 3 and elsewhere, that the upper levels of management are more likely to require *summarized* information, whereas the lower levels have greater use for *detail*. This fact is reflected again in the aggregation of data for MIS applications at different activity levels.

The last property of data requires some explanation. As a general rule, we would always prefer to use current data. However, long-term trends, cycles, or other patterns may not manifest themselves over short periods of time. In such cases, and these cases are far more likely in strategic planning, it may be necessary to use *old* data simply to get *enough* data. Operational control, with its present orientation, is in a better position to use *new* data.

The properties of data used in management control lie between the extremes represented by strategic planning and operational control. Data may originate partially from internal sources and partially from external sources; accuracy requirements may be greater than in strategic planning but less than in operational control; some data may be summarized, whereas others are used in detail; and short-range planning suggests "middle-aged" data. Once again, the properties attributed to data for different management activities are generalizations.

Usage   The final characteristic of MIS support to management activities concerns the *use* of information. This is another characteristic that could be described in a great number of ways, but we will look at just three usage factors: the *frequency* of use, the *outlook* of the users, and the *purpose* of use. These factors are shown in Figure 9-11 in the familiar format of continuous scales.

Managers responsible for strategic planning tend to be infrequent users of MIS primarily because there are fewer MIS applications that deal with strategic planning. A second reason is that the time between strategic planning situations tends to be longer. In contrast, there are many operational control applications, and they are used at comparatively short intervals. For

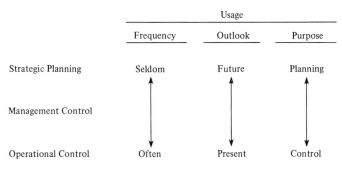

FIGURE 9-11   MIS usage.

example, an evaluation of the market for a new product line may be performed no more than once per year, but the scheduling of work may be done daily.

The outlook of MIS users mirrors their data requirements. Just as strategic planning must reach farther back in time for data, it also results in information dealing with the more distant *future*. In contrast, operational control, using current data, deals with the *present*. Management control, as you might expect, has an *intermediate*-range outlook.

Finally, the purposes for using MIS complete the circle of relationships between information characteristics and management activities. Those purposes can be described in the same terms that are used to explain the activities of management: a continuum running from *planning* at the top (strategic planning) to *control* at the bottom (operational control), with a mix of planning and control in the middle (management control).

The Management Dimension in Processing   Figure 9-12 shows the management dimension, with the addition of transaction processing as a fourth, nonmanagerial activity, superimposed on the processing dimension. Transaction processing is not conducted in MIS under the total CBIS environment assumed here, but there are very close ties between TPS and MIS and it is easy to see how an MIS could incorporate transaction processing if there were no separate TPS. MIS, particularly in operational control applications, are very dependent on TPS for data, even when, as shown here, the data are maintained in a common data base.

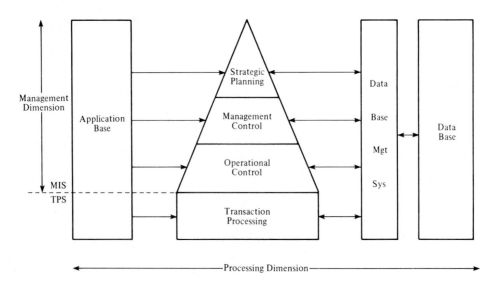

FIGURE 9-12   The management and processing dimensions of MIS.

The Management Dimension Illustrated The management dimension of MIS brings together a number of concepts that, up to this point, have been difficult to view holistically. Decision processes, the data base, the application base, transaction processing, internal data, external data, reports, inquiries, and data analyses have been discussed either individually or in relation to only one or two other system components. We will now attempt to illustrate how these components work together as a system.

It is not necessary to analyze every facet of an MIS to demonstrate its systems character. In fact, it is better not to do so. An example of a complete MIS would soon become hopelessly bogged down in detail. Instead, the example used here shows how a single transaction in a hypothetical automobile insurance firm eventually plays a role in decisions and other processes throughout the management dimension. A flowchart of those processes is shown in Figure 9-13.

Transaction Processing The MIS of the insurance firm is activated, for our purposes, when a policy holder files a claim arising out of an automobile accident ("START," at the left center of Figure 9-13). The claim is mailed to the firm and received by one of several claim clerks. The first action in processing this transaction is to inspect the claim document visually for errors in *form*—usually incomplete data. If errors are detected, the claim is returned to the policyholder with a form letter explaining what corrective action is required.

If the claim data appear to be complete and in proper form, the claim is temporarily entered into the data base via a terminal or other data entry device. The data entry routine calls an edit program out of the application base to check the claim for erros in *fact*—whether the data in the claim are confirmed by the data in the policyholder's records. The edit program also detects errors in *form* that may have been overlooked in the manual edit. Input errors on the part of the data entry clerk are easily resolved and the data reentered, but more serious errors must be referred back to the policyholder. When the data are error free, they are permanently admitted to the data base.

Operational Control The payment of a claim is a routine, programmable decision found in operational control. In this example, claims are processed in batches on a daily basis. A claim processing program is called out of the application base, and an ad hoc file of unprocessed claims is created from the data base. Checks are prepared and sent to policyholders for valid claims; invalid claims result in a letter explaining the reason for denying the claim.

The decision criteria are fairly simple in this case, consisting only of a series of questions that can be answered "yes" or "no." For example, if the claim has resulted from a collision, was the policyholder at fault? If so, does he or she have collision coverage? And so on. When all questions have been

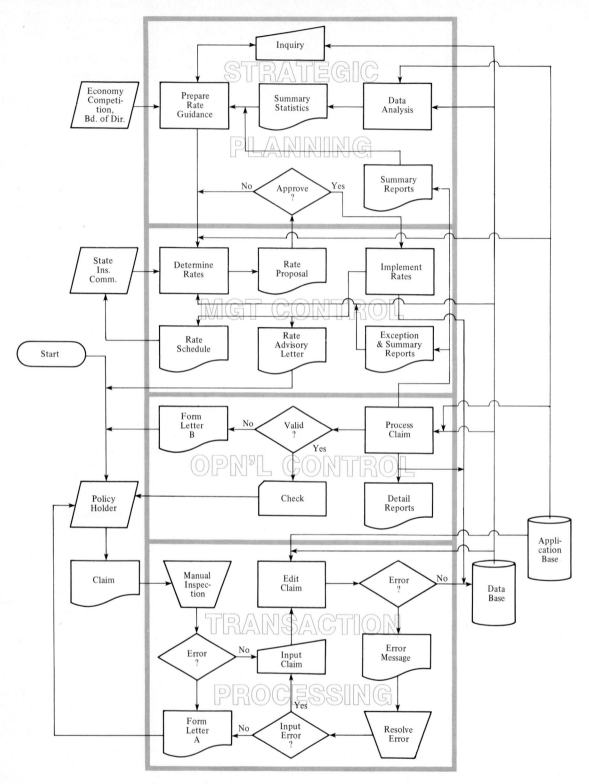

FIGURE 9-13 Management dimension in an automobile insurance company MIS.

answered satisfactorily, the settlement amount is computed by subtracting the deductible amount from the repair estimate.

Decisions that are usually programmable may sometimes turn out to be nonprogrammable. In this illustration, certain conditions may require human intervention in the decision process. For example, excessive estimates, repeated claims from the same policyholder, or other indications of fraud will cause the claim to be removed from the normal processing routine and referred to an investigator.

In addition to the check and the form letter, the claim process produces other output. The data base is updated with records of payment, accident statistics are recorded, penalty points are assigned to the policyholder, and so forth. A number of reports will also reflect data from this claim. At the operational control level, we would expect a *detail* report showing the policy number, the type of claim, the disposition of the claim, the amount paid, and other information relating to each claim processed in this cycle.

Management Control   Except in cases of fraud or extraordinary losses, middle management does not become involved in the processing of individual claims. Consequently, management control reports are of the exception or summary variety. Typical exceptions include referrals for cancellation when a policyholder meets management-defined "bad risk" criteria, when claims exceed a specified dollar amount, or when claims involve litigation. Summary reports might show the total numbers of claims processed, by category (collision, comprehensive, and personal liability), and the sum of payments dispersed. These data may be expressed "per thousand policyholders" to make them more comparable with historical data and industry averages.

The original claim, if we assume that it was an ordinary one that required no individual attention above the operational control level, is now absorbed into summary statistics, but it is not lost for management decision-making purposes. It contributes a proportional share of the information on which decisions in management control and strategic planning are based. One such decision involves the determination of the rates charged for various types of insurance coverage.

Rate determination is one of those hybrid programmable–nonprogrammable decisions peculiar to management control. The rates that will achieve certain profit objectives literally can be computed from actuarial data and the historical accident activity of the firm's own set of policyholders. But these rates are also influenced by regulations of the various state insurance commissions (which may or may not be incorporated into the basic rate model) and the professional judgment of the managers who prepare the rate proposals (which certainly cannot be programmed).

When the proposed rates are approved, a rate implementation program is called out of the application base to update the policy information in the data base with the new rates and to advise policyholders and the respective state commissions of the new rate schedule. This is just one of many organizational activities that may be influenced in part by the single claim that started this discussion.

Strategic Planning   It would be extremely unusual for top management to become involved in the processing of a single claim. Strategic planning in an insurance firm will more likely deal with investment policies, affiliations with firms of adjustors, or the extension of coverage to other losses—say, personal property. Yet claim data are available to top management for any or all of these decisions. The claim on which this example is based has already been incorporated into summary reports to top management and can be included in inquiries or data analyses as well. Inquiries can be satisfied directly through the use of a DBMS query language. Data analysis usually goes beyond the simple computational capability of a query language and may require the use of a decision support system if the manager wishes to perform the analysis personally.

One strategic planning activity in which claim data play an important role is the preparation of *rate guidance*. The formulation of such guidance is not programmable, and we do not expect to find a standard application program that actually outputs guidelines for determining rates. But we may find programs that help collect information—trends in the number of claims, amounts paid out to claimants, the extent of injuries in accidents, and so on— for the manager who does prepare these guidelines. Because the rate determination process is recurring—perhaps on an annual basis—these requirements have been anticipated and the reports are available *on-call* from the MIS. If this were a new or otherwise unique decision, managers desiring this information would have to ask for a *special* report or perform the analysis themselves, perhaps using an executive information system if one is available.

Although the preparation of rate guidance involves some highly distilled internal data, it is based more on external data. Top management depends on the environment for most of its data inputs. In this decision, strategic planners are influenced by economic factors, the rates of competitors, and guidance from *their* superiors—the board of directors of the firm. Many of these external data cannot be quantified for analytical purposes—the board of directors' instructions to "project an image of personal concern," for example. Other external data, such as rates of inflation and economic growth, may fit perfectly into multiple regression models that predict claims losses. This blending of internal and external and the mixture of programmable and nonprogrammable processes makes the use of MIS particularly difficult in strategic planning.

The Example in Perspective   The management dimension of an MIS is characterized by vertical flows: Progressively more refined data and information flow upward from the TPS through the three levels of management activity, and directives and guidance flow downward. These flows have been illustrated in one narrow application in an organization involved in the production of a service: automobile insurance. In the following section, we discuss some additional functions (other than production), and in the following chapters, we look at information flows in an organization involved in the production of *goods*.

The Functional Dimension

As you will see in Chapter 16, CBIS may be designed around a set of functional subsystems, but even if that design approach is not adopted, there is a certain inescapable functional role in every MIS. The primary purpose of an MIS is to support management, and all but a few top managers in any organization have a functional outlook. A production manager is unlikely to be swayed by the argument that she or he should "collect data this way because it is better for accounting." Nor will a marketing manager willingly forgo a certain report because its preparation places some burden on production, and so on. Middle and first-line managers are understandably parochial in viewing their responsibilities. MIS must satisfy the needs of these managers without degrading the integrative information needs of top managers.

The designation of functional subsystems is somewhat arbitrary and varies from organization to organization. For now, we shall assume the same four functions introduced in Chapter 8—production, marketing, finance, and personnel—although you can easily add or delete functions. For example, the MIS of a small organization is unlikely to have a personnel subsystem, and an organization with extensive shipping requirements may incorporate a transportation system.

Figure 9-14 shows the functional dimension of MIS added to the processing dimension. Application programs peculiar to the four functions are stored in the application base, although some applications, such as budgeting, may be used in several functional areas. The data base management system provides application-related data from the data base for processing and facilitates the return of updated values. The merging of the arrows into the DBMS suggests that data lose their application identity in the schema when they are returned to the data base, but the branching arrows back to the functional

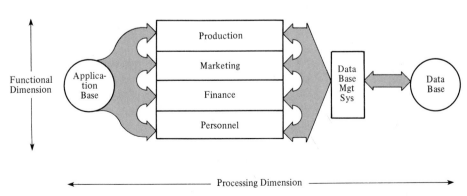

FIGURE 9-14   The functional and processing dimensions of MIS.

subsystems indicate that they can be made available again to any functional application through an appropriate subschema.

A Three-Dimensional View

This discussion of an MIS model began with an analogy to machine drawings of a crankshaft in each of three dimensions. Such drawings are usually supplemented by a three-dimensional view to aid visualization of the finished product. Although the dimensions of the conceptual MIS model—processing, management, and function—do not conform exactly to the physical dimensions of height, width, and depth, it is still possible to view MIS in all three dimensions. Figure 9-15 shows how an MIS and a TPS can be viewed in the three dimensions discussed here.

One advantage of a three-dimensional view is that it often reveals relationships that may not be apparent in individual views. One such relationship in this case is the combined effect of vertical (managerial) and horizontal (functional) integration. We have seen that data can be shared among applications and between TPS and MIS. The three-dimensional model suggests that there is a sharing of data in the functional dimension as well as an aggregation of data in the management dimension. Management control may require summarized or condensed information based on more than one operational function, and in strategic planning, data from several management applications may be further summarized or analyzed. Although MIS still do not support strategic planning well, it is only through this two-way integration that any such support can be offered.

Summary

Management information systems may exist in a variety of combinations with other CBIS. In one extreme, *stand-alone* MIS are the only CBIS in an organization and must support transaction processing and office automation with a *technology-intensive* approach and decision support with an *application-intensive* approach. In organizations with heavy transaction processing requirements, a multiple-CBIS configuration will most likely include TPS and OAS with MIS, but in high-technology organizations, a DSS/MIS combination is more probable. At the other extreme, some organizations will have all four CBIS. The MIS model in this chapter assumes this *total* CBIS environment.

MIS can be explained with a model that incorporates three dimensions.

The *processing* dimension includes the *application base;* all of the TPS processes plus *calculation, summarization,* and *communication;* the *DBMS;* and the *data base.*

The *management* dimension considers the *activities* of managers at different organizational levels and how the *characteristics* of information required by managers changes from level to level. The activity of *operational control* is

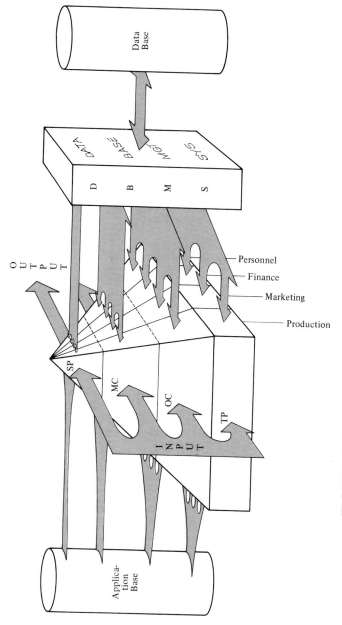

FIGURE 9-15 A three-dimensional view of MIS.

oriented to the accomplishment of *tasks; management control* deals mainly with *resources,* and *strategic planning* is primarily concerned with organizational goals and objectives. The MIS support of these activities can be explained through differences in *decisions, data requirements,* and the way MIS are *used* at each level.

The *functional* dimension acknowledges differences in MIS support and information needs among various organizational functions, such as *production, marketing, finance,* and *personnel.*

Assignments

9-1. A stand-alone MIS is likely to extend into both the technology-intensive and the application-intensive areas. Which poses the greater difficulty? How could you resolve this difficulty within the framework of a stand-alone MIS? How does your answer change if the stand-alone constraint is removed?

9-2. How do you think CBIS support will be allocated by different requirements—office automation, transaction processing, management support, and decision support—in organizations where MIS are complemented with TPS and OAS? Where they are complemented with only DSS?

9-3. It is theoretically possible for a single CBIS—call it anything you like—to span the full range of technology and application and to give reasonable support to all organizational users. What advantages and/or disadvantages would such a system have compared with the total CBIS environment depicted in Figure 9-5?

9-4. Assume for a moment that your MIS has no access—either through application-oriented files or the data base—to the output of your TPS. What problems might arise? How could you cope with these problems?

9-5. An MIS application analyzes the demand for automobile parts for a two-year period and then prepares a report of projected demand for each part for the next six months. What *processes,* explicit or implicit, do you think are necessary in this application? (Include any TPS processes that must take place prior to MIS processing.)

9-6. Identify each of the following management responsibilities as *operational control, management control,* or *strategic planning:*

  a. The decision (by American Motors) to manufacture the Renault Alliance.
  b. Rejecting faulty output on an assembly line.
  c. "Balancing" an assembly line to a specified number of workers.
  d. Producing a special order of football shoes for the Dallas Cowboys.

    e. Obtaining a shipment of goose down to use in the manufacture of ski jackets.

9-7. Use the function of hiring new personnel to describe the properties of decisions associated with management control (see Figure 9-9).

9-8. Use the task of reordering items for inventory to explain the properties of the data required for operational control (see Figure 9-10).

9-9. Use the requirement of raising $10 million for a new manufacturing plant to explain the MIS usage factors for strategic planning (see Figure 9-11).

9-10. The organizational functions used in the description of the functional dimension of MIS do not necessarily apply to all organizations. Develop a set of functions to serve as a basis for MIS subsystems in each of the following organizations:

    a. Your college or university.
    b. A commercial bank.
    c. A publishing house.
    d. A television network.
    e. A computer manufacturer.

CASE   Boomer Petroleum

Boomer Petroleum was founded in 1946, when Doug Fairley returned from World War II and decided to use his GI bonus to do some wildcatting in south central Oklahoma. The venture was more than successful, and Doug soon had a very profitable business selling crude oil to major refineries in Texas and Oklahoma. He considered opening his own refinery but decided that he did not have the necessary technical skills and used his profits to buy the mineral rights on surrounding lands instead.

    Boomer Petroleum acquired its first computer, an IBM 1410, in 1958 and located it in the accounting department, where it was used primarily for payroll and financial accounting applications. The company upgraded to an IBM 360-40 in 1964 and added some applications involving production reports to management. The 360 was replaced with a 370 in 1976, and the remaining tape operations were converted to disk. The data processing division, now called "information services," remained in the accounting department.

    Doug is contemplating retirement and has brought his son Dave, a 1979 graduate of Oklahoma University in petroleum engineering, into the firm as the Vice President for Operations with the hope that he will assume the presidency in a few years. Dave's experience includes three years as an operations analyst for a major oil refinery, which used computer modeling of seismographic data to predict the location and size of oil deposits. Dave would like to use similar techniques at Boomer, but the head of the accounting department, Fred "Tiny" Walker, argues that he does not have scientific programmers on his staff, nor is the hardware appropriate for the graphic displays and output of such an application. Doug has known Tiny since their World War II days and is reluctant to upset his old friend. He counsels Dave to go slowly, pointing out that the company has done quite well without "fancy computer graphs" in the past, and besides, "Tiny will probably retire shortly after I do and then you can bring in your own man."

Dave is discouraged because he knows new deposits are becoming increasingly difficult to find, and most of Boomer's competitors are using computer analyses of potential oil fields. He worries that by the time he becomes president, Boomer will have lost its competitive edge. The accounting department is not under Operations, so there is little he can do to force Tiny to develop an expert system for oil prospecting, and he does not wish to use his relationship with his father to force the issue.

Questions

1. Where does Boomer now stand in the CBIS–environment model illustrated in Figure 9-1?

2. Using Figure 9-9, analyze the decision-support requirements of the oil prospecting application Dave has in mind. Is it an appropriate application for an MIS? Are Tiny's arguments valid?

3. What should Dave do now?

Other Readings

Anthony, Robert N. *Planning and Control Systems: A Framework for Analysis.* Boston: Harvard University Graduate School of Business Administration, 1965.

Gorry, G. Anthony, and Michael S. Scott Morton. "A Framework for Management Information Systems." *Sloan Management Review* 13, no. 1 (Fall 1971).

Hicks, James O., Jr. *Management Information Systems: A User Perspective.* St. Paul, Minn.: West Publishing Co., 1984.

Hussain, Donna, and K. M. Hussain. *Information Processing Systems for Management* (2e). Homewood, Ill.: Richard D. Irwin, 1985.

Kroeber, Donald W. *Management Information Systems.* New York: Free Press, 1982.

Kroeber, Donald W., Hugh J. Watson, and Ralph H. Sprague. "An Empirical Investigation and Analysis of the Current State of Information Systems Evolution." *Information and Management* 3, no. 1 (February 1980).

Chapter 10

Functional Applications of MIS: Production and Marketing

Learning Objectives

After studying this chapter, you will be able to:

1. Describe the flow of information within and between the functional subsystems of an MIS.
2. Relate the information needs of functional managers to the three levels of management activity.
3. Discuss the input, processing, and output associated with subsystems based on the functions of production and marketing.
4. Define the following terms:

   module
   material requirements planning (MRP) module
   operations module
   engineering module
   shipping and receiving module
   purchasing module

   quality control module
   marketing research module
   product development module
   pricing module
   promotion module
   sales management module

A systems view of an organization permits several options for defining subsystems. One could, for example, construct a perfectly logical model using subsystems based on the flow of resources: labor, money, and raw materials. Levels of management or the approach to decision making, which were discussed in the previous chapter, are also legitimate bases for describing subsystems, as are geographical regions, markets, and product lines. Typical organizational structure and the scope of managerial responsibilities, however, argue for another approach: subsystems organized along *functional* lines.

In most organizations, departments are formed by the grouping of similar functions. An accounting department is made up of those individuals responsible for accounting functions, a marketing department consists of persons who carry out marketing activities, and so on. And managers in these departments, particularly *middle* managers, who tend to be the primary users of MIS, have few responsibilities that require information about the activities of the other functional departments.

There is also a historical precedent for functional subsystems in MIS. When data processing first expanded beyond the initial accounting department stage, computer technology could not support integrative applications, and new programs—even hardware, in some instances—were dedicated to very limited, functional information requirements. The resultant attitude of "marketing programs" or "production programs" still influences MIS design.

Not all organizations have the same functions, of course, but the principle of functional organization applies nonetheless. An MIS designed along traditional functional lines may be less threatening to managers, who are understandably parochial in their attitude toward information systems. It is much easier to win a manager's support for, say, a production subsystem than for a "middle management subsystem" or a "material resource subsystem."

Although the division of an MIS into functional subsystems may be convenient for middle or first-line managers, top-level managers are more likely to need information based on two or more functions. To serve these needs, an MIS must be able to exchange information among the functional subsystems and to integrate functional information for strategic planning. Figure 10-1 shows the information exchange among typical functional departments in an organization.

In manual systems, before the introduction of computers, information was exchanged informally (by observation or word of mouth) and formally (by written reports or in staff meetings). In the extreme, a sole proprietor had only to *think* about the various functions that he or she performed in order to make information from one functional area available to the others.

Ironically, the advent of data processing actually degraded the quality of this information exchange in some organizations by interrupting the informal communications channels and inundating management with detail reports. Single-function data processing applications tended to be too narrow and too specific for management in other functional areas, and there was no direct way to exchange information among applications.

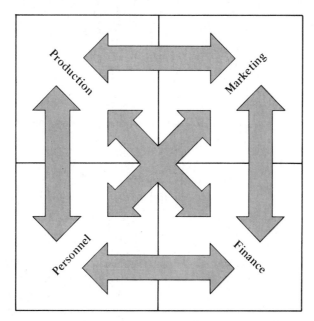

FIGURE 10-1   Information exchange among functional departments.

The modern MIS comes close to duplicating the sole proprietor's ability to make information from one function immediately available to other functions. The computer at the heart of an MIS does not nearly match the reasoning and associative powers of the human brain (although you have undoubtedly seen references to computers as "electronic brains" in the popular press), but it does—with the assistance of software—provide for better information exchange than any previous manual or data processing system.

Organizational functions represent only the first level of MIS subsystems. In large organizations, functional departments are further subdivided into more specialized sections or divisions. For example, a production department may have engineering, quality control, purchasing, and other divisions. These subunits have their own peculiar information needs and must share information with each other as well as with other functional departments and their respective subunits. An MIS can reflect this structure by incorporating specialized *modules* into the functional subsystems.[1] The inter- and intradepartmental information flows in such an MIS are illustrated in Figure 10-2. The departmental modules in this figure are merely examples and do not represent a universal MIS design any more than the four functional departments used in this model depict a universal organizational structure.

---

[1] As noted in Chapter 2, the systems hierarchy proceeds from the suprasystem to the system to subsystems to subsubsystems, ad infinitum. To avoid this sometimes confusing terminology, we use the term *modules* for the level below subsystem in this chapter.

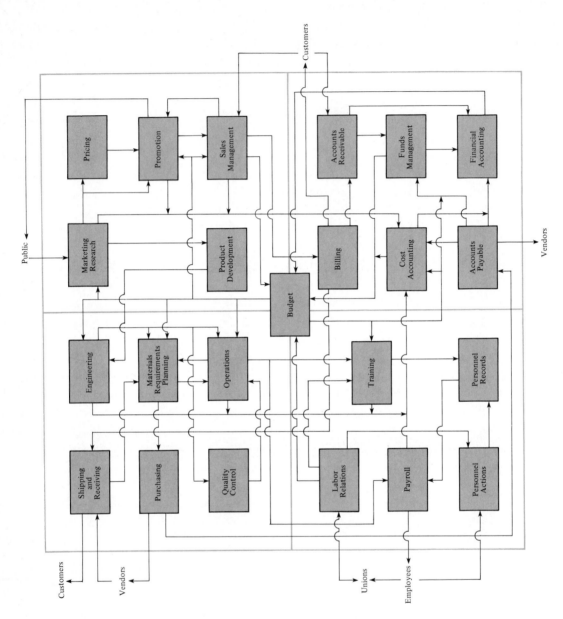

FIGURE 10-2 Application modules in functional subsystems.

It is possible, of course, to add additional levels of detail down to the specific application programs used in various modules. For the general purpose model presented here, however, it is sufficient to view the subsystems as consisting only of modules. Let us look at these functional subsystems and their component modules in greater detail.

The Production Subsystem

Production involves the conversion of resource inputs into goods and service outputs. Automobile manufacturers convert labor, capital, and raw material into finished automobiles. Law firms "produce" legal services with the time and the professional expertise of their partners. And military units provide national security using labor, ships, tanks, aircraft, and other military hardware. Although these examples show that a production function can be identified in a variety of organizations, it is more common to think of production in terms of the manufacture of *goods*. Manufacturing involves a number of activities not typically found in the production of services—inventory management, for example—and will serve as a more complete example of the production function. A diagram of the production subsystem of an MIS for a manufacturing firm is shown in Figure 10-3.

Production Subsystem Modules

Modules in the production subsystem reflect the organizational structure of the production department in the same manner as the subsystems reflect overall organizational structure. For example, a *purchasing* module reflects the presence of a purchasing section responsible for the acquisition of raw materials. Other production modules in this model include *shipping and receiving, engineering, material requirements planning, operations,* and quality control.

Material Requirements Planning
Material requirements planning (MRP) combines two of the most important activities in a manufacturing operation: scheduling and the control of materials. Scheduling can be viewed as very short term planning in which specific times are assigned for various production activities. MRP integrates material control with scheduling by making materials available for production in a timely manner, without undue inventory buildup or delays in the production schedule. MRP is most appropriate when the demand for a manufactured product is subject to a great deal of variation and the product is assembled from subcomponents.

There are three basic inputs to the MRP module: the *master production schedule, inventory status,* and the *bill of materials.* The master production

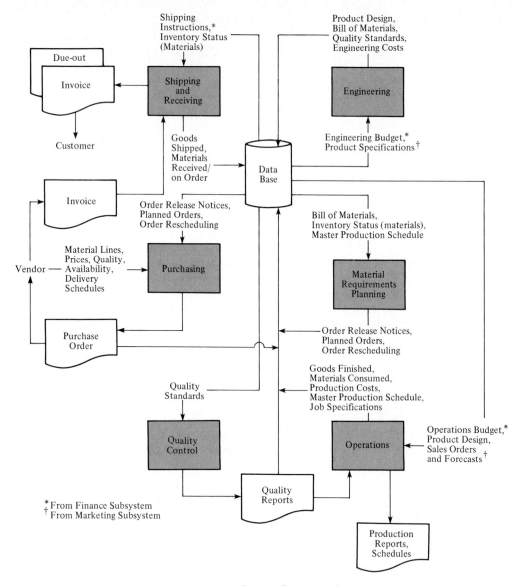

FIGURE 10-3 The production subsystem.

schedule defines what finished products are needed and when they are needed. It is based on orders and forecasts from the marketing department. The bill of materials is developed in engineering and is based on the product specifications (also from marketing) and engineering design principles. Inventory status shows both the quantity of materials and the finished products on hand or on order. MRP itself is not an inventory system, but it helps reduce inventory levels by resolving uncertainty over the demand for materials.

Processing in MRP involves a computation of the total material requirements for all finished products. A comparison of these requirements with on-hand or on-order quantities and the desired safety stock level gives the additional quantity to order. A further analysis involving the order and shipping time and the production schedule results in the output of an *order release notice*, which gives the purchasing section instructions to place the order. A second output, *planned orders*, serves as an early warning to alert the purchasing section of impending material requirements; and *order rescheduling* changes open orders as a result of expediting or deexpediting.

Operations

Operations involves the actual conversion of resources into goods or services. Although operations is "where the action is" in production, it is actually one of the simpler modules in this subsystem. Of course, many manufacturing processes are fully or partially automated and use computer-based methods such as numeric control or robotics. The computer applications in these processes are certainly not simple, but neither are they greatly involved in the creation of management information. For this reason, we will not consider further the role of computers in automation.

The operations module in this model receives *orders* and *demands forecasts* from the marketing subsystem, *budgetary* data from finance, and *product design* information from engineering. The operations module also receives a very important feedback input (from the quality control module) in the form of *quality reports*. Although these reports are shown as documents in Figure 10-3, quality information is also furnished in a more immediate form, verbally or by a mechanical signal, when deviations from quality standards require the cessation of production operations. Obviously, a manufacturing process cannot be permitted to continue out of control during the time it takes to prepare and deliver a printed report; it must be corrected as soon as possible after the problem is detected. The exact method of alerting operations personnel to quality discrepancies varies with different manufacturing processes and products. Some Japanese manufacturing firms have installed pull cords at work stations that permit any employee who discovers a quality problem to signal for the shutdown of the manufacturing process.

Many operations inputs are actually transaction data and reflect basic activities such as the consumption of materials, labor time, machine time, and quantities of output. What makes the inputs somewhat unusual in operations is the variety of data collection devices that may be employed. Sensors that record the starting and stopping of machines, special purpose terminals that log in the arrival and departure of employees, scanners that measure raw material usage, counters that record the volume of output, and similar devices are commonly used to collect data in operations.

Classification, summarization, computation, and other TPS and MIS processes convert operational data into management information that is used throughout the MIS. For example, information on resource consumption is made available to finance for cost accounting purposes, employee activities are reported to personnel for the payroll, finished goods production is reported to shipping and receiving so that orders may be filled, and so on. One of the more important outputs is not based on transaction data but is prepared on the basis of resource availability and marketing input: the master production schedule, which is used internally for scheduling operations and in the MRP module for planning material requirements.

Engineering

The engineering section—whether included in the production department, as it is in this model, or organized as a separate department, as it is in many large manufacturing firms—is chiefly responsible for the design of the product and the production facilities. Engineering works closely with marketing in product design and with other sections in the production department, notably operations, in facility design.

Engineering, especially when it has a research and development function, can be a very expensive activity if not closely controlled. Budget inputs are particularly important to engineering for this reason. Other than the budget and the *product specifications* developed in the marketing subsystem, the engineering module receives few MIS inputs. More likely, the engineering section will depend on environmental inputs relating to new developments in materials, health and safety standards, and basic research. Also, many engineering data are generated internally through product and materials testing.

The complexity of the processes found in engineering applications and the increased likelihood of external data suggest the use of decision support systems rather than MIS. DSS, or, at least, DSS technology—microcomputers, mathematical models, independent data bases, graphics displays, and the like—are used extensively in engineering, but many MIS implications remain. The bill of materials used by the MRP module is engineering-based, as are the product design followed by operations and the standards used in quality control. Although engineering may use independent hardware for many internal applications, it is still possible, through data communications, to make engineering output available to other modules and, in turn, to use MIS applications and/or data for DSS applications in engineering.

Shipping and Receiving

The dominant CBIS activity in the shipping and receiving section is transaction processing, but the MIS module is interesting nonetheless for its interface with two enormously important environmental elements: *vendors* and *customers*. The vendors are the suppliers of the raw material, components, and subassemblies used to manufacture finished products, and the customers, of course, are those who purchase the finished products. The customers of a manufacturing firm may be wholesalers, retailers, or other manufacturers and should not be confused with *consumers*, who are the ultimate users of manufactured goods.

In the absence of a separate inventory module in this model, we will assume that data on the inventory of both materials and finished goods are maintained by shipping and receiving. Inventory applications require inputs on the addition of raw materials (from receiving) and finished goods (from operations) as well as on the consumption of raw materials (by operations) and the shipping of finished goods (to customers). Because this model incorporates an MRP module, some of the more traditional inventory processes—the computation of EOQ, for example—are not required. The very important MRP input of inventory status replaces traditional inventory reports and is a major output of this module.

Two additional inputs to the shipping and receiving module are the *shipping instructions* from the finance subsystem and *invoices* from vendors. Shipping instructions give the authority to ship finished goods to customers, after billing actions have been initiated in finance, and invoices are notifications that raw materials or other physical resource inputs are in transit to the manufacturer. Other outputs of the shipping and receiving module include *invoices* from the manufacturer (which advise customers that goods have been shipped) and *due-out* notices (which inform customers of temporary delays in shipping).

The processing in these other shipping and receiving applications reflects the transaction processing orientation and consists largely of data maintenance. In particular, data on unfilled orders, for which due-out notices have been sent, must be maintained to ensure shipment when the inventory is replenished. Other data, such as the description and quantity of the goods shipped and received, are important to certain financial applications. Although the TPS processes in the shipping and receiving module, like those elsewhere, can be carried out in any data management environment, the dependence of MIS applications on the timeliness and the availability of these data require that they be stored and maintained in a data base.

Purchasing

The purchasing function in this model appears to be just an extension of MRP. Indeed, all of the internal inputs to purchasing shown in Figure 10-3 are MRP outputs: order release notices, planned orders, and rescheduled orders. These inputs are processed into purchase orders issued to the suppliers of raw materials or components used in production. But purchasing agents, in order to make intelligent decisions concerning the choice of vendors, must also have data on the type, quality, price, delivery schedules, and availability of raw material offered by various vendors. These data are not normally found in the MIS data base; they must be provided by the user from external sources. This is another situation in which a decision support system may be more appropriate than an MIS.

Quality Control

Quality control (QC) ensures that materials, work in process, and finished goods meet acceptable standards of quality. Although quality control is part of the production subsystem in this model, care must be exercised to avoid any conflict of interest between QC, which *measures* quality, and operations, which is responsible for quality. To a lesser extent, QC is also kept at arm's length from engineering, which may have some responsibility for establishing the standards against which quality is measured.

Inputs to quality control from the MIS include only the *quality standards*. However, as in some other modules we have discussed, there may be decision support applications. In this case, DSS models may be used to develop sampling plans for selecting items to be inspected, simulating the cost of various inspection plans for hypothetical quality levels, and performing statistical analyses on the results of quality inspections.

Output from the QC module is in the form of *quality reports*, with the provision, as noted earlier, that some more expeditious means may be necessary to call serious quality control problems to the attention of operations managers.

Management Activities in Production

In the previous chapter, we saw that activities at each level of management have a unique orientation: operational control is *task* oriented, management control is *resource* oriented, and strategic planning has a *goal* orientation. This orientation holds for individual functions as well as for the overall organization. In production, we find that operational control is concerned with tasks such as the assembly of finished goods from components or raw materials, the maintenance of inventory, and the shipment of goods to customers. Management control in production is exercised over the resources of equipment, materials, and personnel through scheduling, purchasing, and the preparation of job specifications, respectively. Strategic planning does not ordinarily deal with a single function, but typical production concerns in strategic planning include future levels of production, the quality image of the organization, and the extent of automation in the conversion process.

Different management activities call for different information needs. Table 10-1 shows representative information required by production managers at the three activity levels. Items in parentheses indicate needs that cannot be satisfied by MIS and that must come from external sources.

MRP II

The success of the MRP module in the production subsystem, particularly in those firms that manufacture products from components, has prompted the development of specialized *manufacturing systems* by software vendors. These systems go well beyond the functions of MRP and are usually referred to as *manufacturing resource planning* (MRP II) systems. The MRP II system of one vendor, Management Science America (MSA), Inc., is shown in Figure 10-4.

TABLE 10-1 Examples of Information Requirements in Production

Operational Control	Management Control	Strategic Planning
Production schedule	Budget	Sales forecasts
Bill of materials	Inventory status	Production reports
Shipping instructions	Planned orders	(Competition)
Order release notices	Order rescheduling	(The economy)
Quality standards	Sales orders	
	Product design	
	Quality reports	
	(Technology)	

Parentheses indicate that information must come from external sources.

The MSA manufacturing system consists of interrelated *components*, which are similar to the *modules* of the production subsystem described earlier in this chapter. The components are linked together to support the various management functions of planning, organizing, staffing, coordinating, and controlling as those functions relate to manufacturing. Systems like this are often described as *closed-loop* in recognition of the planning feedback derived from the control components. In this respect, MRP II and other closed-loop systems simply reflect the cyclical view of management discussed in Chapter 3.

Figure 10-4 also shows how the MSA manufacturing system may be linked to executive, human resource, and financial management systems. This version of MRP II, which is called an *extended closed-loop* system, approaches the total-MIS concept followed in this book. The inclusion of executive support in the extended closed loop is especially significant to an integrated CBIS model and is an indication of the narrowing gap between information system theory and practice.

Repetitive Manufacturing

MRP II systems are most useful in a repetitive manufacturing environment. Repetitive manufacturing is characterized by the production of a specific type of product or part, a flow of parts through sequentially arranged work centers, short production times, and relatively few transactions for the ordering of materials. Although these characteristics may seem restrictive, they still include a majority of the firms that produce consumer goods and many of those that produce commercial or industrial products.

Management Support

Although there is a temptation to view manufacturing information systems primarily as transaction processing systems, the components of MRP II also support all levels of management. For example, Figure 10-5 shows a *material*

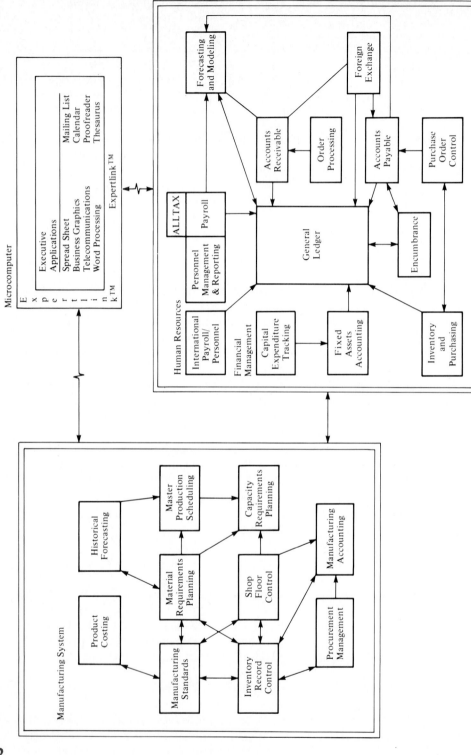

FIGURE 10-4 The MSA manufacturing system.

282

MSA The Software Company

MATERIAL REQUIREMENTS PLAN

PLANNER MK DATE 02/06/84 PAGE 14

PART NUMBER	BASIC DESCRIPTION	GROUP CODE	ITEM TYPE	PROD STAT	UNIT MEAS	ALT U/M	U/M CONV. FACT.	PRIME STOCK LOC.	BUYER	MAS SCH CD	LOW LEVEL CODE	SUBSTITUTE PART NUMBER	SHRINKAGE CODE	SHRINKAGE FACTOR	ABC	LEAD TIMES PURCH	LEAD TIMES CODE	LEAD TIMES PROD	STACKED	SIZE	DRAWING NUMBER
1000-2110	FRAME ASSEMBLY 21"	FAB	F	C	PC		1.00000	MULTIPLES		N	1		0	.010	A	0	F	15	55		3010-F

ON HAND	SCHEDULED RECEIPTS	REQUIREMENTS RELEASED	REQUIREMENTS TOTAL	LOT SIZING POLICY	LOT SIZING QUANTITY-TIME	LOT SIZING MODIFIERS MIN	LOT SIZING MODIFIERS MAX	LOT SIZING MODIFIERS MULT	SAFETY STOCK POLICY	SAFETY STOCK QUAN-TIME	PROCURE CODE	ANNUAL GROSS REQUIREMENTS	LAST ENGINEERING CHANGE NUMBER	LAST ENGINEERING CHANGE EFFECTIVE DATE	PENDING ENGINEERING CHANGE NUMBER	PENDING ENGINEERING CHANGE EFFECTIVE DATE
407	400		1000	DISC LOT				1	NONE			14000		02/06/84		

NON NET	PRIME VEND	ALT VEND	BLANKET ORDER RELEASE LEAD TIME	BLANKET ORDER RELEASE QUANTITY	PRICE BREAK 1 QUANTITY	PRICE BREAK 1 PRICE	PRICE BREAK 2 QUANTITY	PRICE BREAK 2 PRICE	PRICE BREAK 3 QUANTITY	PRICE BREAK 3 PRICE	MAD	MAX SERV ORDER	INVENTORY CARRYING RATE	NORMAL SELLING PRICE
												0		0.000

SETUP COST	TOTAL S.U. TIME	S.U. CONV. FACT	TOTAL RUN TIME	RUN CONV. FACT	TOTAL INTEROP TIME	INTEROP CONV FACT	CURRENT CYCLE	KEEP	LT	RUN TIME FILTERS NEED	IN	OUT	CANCEL	TOTAL COST	SUBCONTRACT COST	MATERIAL	LAST ACTUAL COST ABOR
0.00	0.00	1.00	0.00	1.00	0.00	1.00	2	0	0	156	0	0	156	16.7558	13.2753	0.0000	0.0000

ACTION MESSAGES

RESC OUT ORDER FOLLOWUP

INV CTL	REP CTL	SPECIAL INSTRUCTIONS	PERIOD OFFSET	PEG	LAST CYCLE COUNT DATE	LAST VARIANCE	NEXT CYCLE COUNT DATE
R			L			0	

WEEK	OVERDUE	02/13/4	02/21/4	02/27/4	03/05/4	03/12/4	03/19/4	03/26/4	04/02/4	04/09/4	04/16/4	04/23/4	04/30/4	05/07/4	05/14/4	05/21/4	WEEK
SERVICE	0	0	0	0	0	0	0	0	0	0	0	0	0	0	0	0	SERVICE
PRODUCTION	0	0	200	200	0	200	200	0	406	0	206	0	206	0	412	0	PRODUCTION
SCHEDULED RECEIPT	0	0	198	198	0	0	0	0	0	0	0	0	0	0	0	0	SCHEDULED RECEIPT
AVAILABLE	407	407	405	403	403	203	3	3	-403	-403	-609	-609	-815	-815	-1227	-1227	AVAILABLE
PLANNED ORD REL	0	0	0	0	0	407	0	208	208	0	417	0	0	208	0	417	PLANNED ORD REL

WEEK	05/29/4	06/04/4	06/11/4	06/18/4	06/25/4	07/02/4	07/09/4	07/16/4	07/23/4	07/30/4	08/06/4	08/13/4	08/20/4	08/27/4	09/04/4	09/10/4	WEEK
SERVICE	0	0	0	0	0	0	0	0	0	0	0	0	0	0	0	0	SERVICE
PRODUCTION	0	206	0	412	0	0	206	206	0	206	0	206	206	206	0	206	PRODUCTION
SCHEDULED RECEIPT	0	0	0	0	0	0	0	0	0	0	0	0	0	0	0	0	SCHEDULED RECEIPT
AVAILABLE	-1227	-1433	-1433	-1845	-1845	-1845	-2051	-2257	-2257	-2463	-2463	-2669	-2875	-3081	-3081	-3287	AVAILABLE
PLANNED ORD REL	0	0	208	208	0	0	208	0	208	208	208	208	0	208	0	0	PLANNED ORD REL

WEEK	09/17/4	10/15/4	11/12/4	12/10/4	01/07/5	02/04/5	03/04/5	04/01/5	04/29/5	05/28/5	06/24/5	07/22/5	08/19/5	09/16/5	10/14/5	11/11/5	WEEK
SERVICE	0	0	0	0	0	0	0	0	0	0	0	0	0	0	0	0	SERVICE
PRODUCTION	412	618	412	618	412	618	618	412	618	412	412	618	412	618	412	618	PRODUCTION
SCHEDULED RECEIPT	0	0	0	0	0	0	0	0	0	0	0	0	0	0	0	0	SCHEDULED RECEIPT
AVAILABLE	-3699	-4317	-4728	-5347	-5759	-6377	-6995	-7407	-8025	-8437	-8849	-9467	-9879	-10497	-10909	-11527	AVAILABLE
PLANNED ORD REL	624	624	624	208	832	416	624	416	416	416	416	624	416	416	832	416	PLANNED ORD REL

SCHEDULED RECEIPTS

START DATE	DUE DATE	ORDER NUMBER	LOT NO	QUANTITY DUE	TS YT
01/30	02/21	M1274 RESC OUT		200 031284	M4
02/03	02/27	M1275 RESC OUT		200 031984	M2

REQUIREMENTS

REQUIRED DATE	REQUIRED QUANTITY	REFERENCE NUMBER	ORDER NUMBER	LOT NO	PSSA GTRB
02/24	200	1000-2100	M1014		FP
02/27	200	1000-2100	M1012		FP
03/12	200	1000-2100	M1015		FP
03/19	200	1000-2100	M1016		FP
04/02	200	1000-2100	M1017		FP
04/06	206	1000-2100	PLAN		
04/19	206	1000-2100	PLAN		
04/30	206	1000-2100	PLAN		
05/14	206	1000-2100	PLAN		
05/18	206	1000-2100	PLAN		
06/04	206	1000-2100	PLAN		
06/18	206	1000-2100	PLAN		
06/22	206	1000-2100	PLAN		
07/09	206	1000-2100	PLAN		
07/16	206	1000-2100	PLAN		
07/30	206	1000-2100	PLAN		

REQUIRED DATE	REQUIRED QUANTITY	REFERENCE NUMBER	ORDER NUMBER	LOT NO	PSSA GTRB
08/13	206	1000-2100	PLAN		
08/20	206	1000-2100	PLAN		
08/31	206	1000-2100	PLAN		
09/10	206	1000-2100	PLAN		
09/24	206	1000-2100	PLAN		
10/08	206	1000-2100	PLAN		
10/15	206	1000-2100	PLAN		
10/29	206	1000-2100	PLAN		
11/05	206	1000-2100	PLAN		
11/16	206	1000-2100	PLAN		
12/05	206	1000-2100	PLAN		
12/11	206	1000-2100	PLAN		
12/19	206	1000-2100	PLAN		
12/27	206	1000-2100	PLAN		
01/14	206	1000-2100	PLAN		
01/28	206	1000-2100	PLAN		

FIGURE 10-5 The MSA material requirements plan.

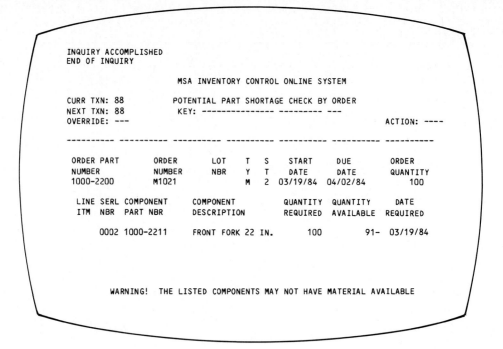

```
INQUIRY ACCOMPLISHED
END OF INQUIRY

                        MSA INVENTORY CONTROL ONLINE SYSTEM

CURR TXN: 88           POTENTIAL PART SHORTAGE CHECK BY ORDER
NEXT TXN: 88             KEY: -------------- --------- ---
OVERRIDE: ---                                               ACTION: ----


---------- ---------- ---------- ---------- ---------- ---------- ----------

ORDER PART      ORDER        LOT    T   S    START      DUE        ORDER
NUMBER          NUMBER       NBR    Y   T    DATE       DATE       QUANTITY
1000-2200       M1021               M   2    03/19/84   04/02/84        100

LINE SERL COMPONENT    COMPONENT            QUANTITY  QUANTITY   DATE
ITM  NBR  PART NBR     DESCRIPTION          REQUIRED  AVAILABLE  REQUIRED

     0002 1000-2211    FRONT FORK 22 IN.       100         91-  03/19/84




        WARNING!  THE LISTED COMPONENTS MAY NOT HAVE MATERIAL AVAILABLE
```

FIGURE 10-6 The MSA potential part shortage check.

requirements plan (MRP component) for tubeless tires used by a bicycle manufacturer. Information such as this on order release notices is characteristic of operational control. The representation of CRT output on *potential part shortages* (inventory record control component), shown in Figure 10-6, is more typical of management control. And strategic planning may be supported by the *forecast summary* (historical forecasting component) shown in Figure 10-7. The support levels of the other components vary similarly.

Make Versus Buy Options

The decision to develop one's own MIS, which is assumed throughout most of this book, or to install a vendor-supplied system is discussed in more detail in Part VII. It should be noted here, however, that certain industries and organizations are better suited than others to the use of packaged systems. Certainly organizations involved in repetitive manufacturing fall into this category. If a packaged system provides, or can be modified to provide, management's information needs, a great deal of time and development effort can be saved. For example, MSA uses 9 months as a typical implementation period for MRP II, whereas in-house development of a comparable system might take 2 or 3 years. Other factors to consider include the availability and skill of in-house personnel, the commitment and investment in an existing system, and the extent to which the organization is willing to modify its procedures to conform to the packaged system.

```
02/06/84                    MSA EXPERT INDUSTRIES MANUFACTURING              F030 FUNC
09:34:06                         FORECAST SUMMARY SCREEN                     FCT 02/06/84

LOC: LA              ITEM NBR: 1000-52000
CAT: CHILDS             SUB-CAT:
C/U: C                                 AT SELL PRICE

    MONTH          (-2)              (-1)            FCST                PLAN
    -----     ----------------  ----------------  ---------------    ---------------
    JULY           39,092            65,138            90,528             97,467
    AUG            41,972            84,102           104,697            114,972
    SEPT           44,316            86,361           103,346            114,026
    OCT            51,951            71,622            95,016            108,296
    NOV            42,976            64,626            97,821            124,711
    DEC            58,017            64,472           104,367            132,881
    JAN            54,972            86,617            98,402            110,741
    FEB            36,777            51,117            89,872             98,232
    MAR            47,971            63,371            97,011            100,981
    APR            61,091            99,196           109,351            118,389
    MAY            48,131            74,376           109,356            118,485
    JUNE           58,672            84,022           105,797            114,362
    TOTALS        585,938           895,000         1,205,564          1,353,543
```

FIGURE 10-7   The MSA forecast summary.

Other Uses of Computers in Manufacturing

Because this is a book on information systems, we sometimes tend to ignore other uses of computers. In the case of manufacturing, the other uses often are the more visible and more exotic application of computers. Two examples will serve to illustrate this point.

Robotics

A *robot* is a machine that can be programmed to do a variety of tasks. Welding, painting, transporting, and assembling are tasks typically assigned to robots in manufacturing. There are both advantages and disadvantages to the use of robots. Robots, of course, do not tire, get bored, take vacations, have "bad days," or suffer other afflictions that frequently impact on the quality and quantity of output by human workers. On the other hand, they are not capable of the judgment or modification of work that is required in many manufacturing situations. An industrial robot is pictured in Figure 10-8.

Computers, often microcomputers, are used to control the activities of robots. Robots are designed to respond to the digital output of a computer in much the same way in which a printer or other peripheral device is controlled by a computer. The arm or other articulated part of the robot interprets the

FIGURE 10-8   An industrial robot. (Courtesy of UNIMATION)

commands and translates them into movements. More is said on the role and functioning of robots in Chapter 19.

CAD/CAM

Computer-assisted design or *computer-aided design* (CAD) is more closely related to information systems technology, but still falls outside the usual definitions of CBIS. The more sophisticated CAD packages give the designer the capability to create a three-dimensional view of an object; rotate the view around its axes; edit or modify the view; zoom in for a close-up view of part of the object; use standard shapes from a library or data base; and perform calculations concerning the surface area, volume, or dimensions of the object. Hard-copy output of CAD can be used to replace architectural renderings, technical illustrations, engineering drawings, and other similar work. A typical CAD software package for an IBM PC, with the features just described, costs between $1,000 and $5,000. More powerful CAD software designed for mini- or mainframe computers can cost over $100,000. The screen display of a CAD package in use is shown in Figure 10-9.

Computer-assisted manufacturing or *computer-aided manufacturing* (CAM) is somewhat similar to the use of computers to control robots, with the exception that the devices controlled in CAM are less flexible than

FIGURE 10-9 A CAD screen display. (Courtesy of Computervision)

robots. Early applications of CAM were called *numerical control* and used punched cards or punched paper tape to control drill presses, milling machines, lathes, and other types of manufacturing equipment. Today, control is more likely to be exercised by a mini- or microcomputer programmed in a high-level language such as FORTRAN or a special CAM language such as AML (*A Manufacturing Language*). One computer can control several machines and can provide for a sequence of operations that vary within the capabilities of the machine. For example, a drill press can only drill holes, but the number and size of the holes drilled can be changed by CAM as different jobs are encountered. CAD software can cost up to $60,000 per installation.

The term *CAD/CAM* is often used to convey the idea of an integration of CAD and CAM, although, in practice, there are very few applications in which computer-assisted design is automatically executed by computer-assisted manufacturing. There are, however, a growing number of *local area networks* (LAN) in which CAD, CAM, computer-assisted design *and drafting* (CADD), *computer-assisted engineering* (CAE), MRP, and other manufacturing applications share hardware and data to form a *computer-integrated manufacturing* (CIM) system. It may well be that true integration of these functions to form an automated factory will be achieved in the near future.

The Marketing Subsystem

Traditionally, the marketing function has consisted of those activities designed to get finished goods from the manufacturer to the ultimate consumer. Since the early 1950s, however, the marketing function has grown in scope and importance to a point where many companies now speak of a "marketing orientation," a "total marketing concept," or "integrated marketing" as their principal organizational philosophy. In some prominent firms (General Electric, for example), the marketing function even includes inventory management, production scheduling, and the physical distribution of finished goods. Not surprisingly, there are also many MIS in which the *M* stands for *marketing*, rather than *management*.

Marketing Subsystem Modules

The scope of marketing activities assumed for this MIS model represents a compromise between the traditional and "total" roles. Inventory and production scheduling are assigned to the production subsystem, but some preproduction activities, such as *product development*, are carried out in marketing. Other activities included in the marketing function here are *pricing, promotion, sales*, and *marketing research*. Figure 10-10 shows how each of these activities is represented by an application module in the marketing subsystem of an MIS.

Marketing Research

An important contribution of the total marketing concept is the notion that marketing activities take place *before* production as well as *after* production. In other words, the marketing department does not merely sell what the production department produces; it also helps determine what those products will be. Marketing research contributes to this determination by ascertaining consumer needs, preferences, and behavior with respect to planned products.[2]

Inputs to the marketing research module are based almost exclusively on external data. Some secondary data, in the form of published institutional governmental research on consumer activities, are available, but most marketing research data are primary; that is, they are collected by the using

---

[2]The collection of similar data on *existing* products is called *market research*. A third, related term, *marketing intelligence*, refers to comparative data on competitive firms.

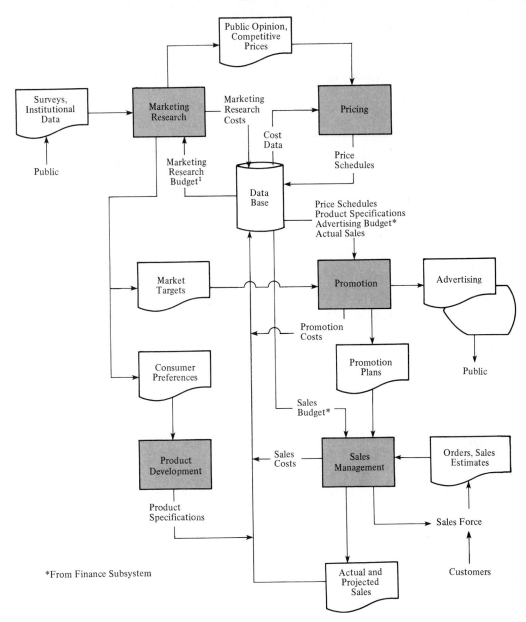

FIGURE 10-10 The marketing subsystem.

organization (or an agent of the organization) to meet specific information needs. Telephone or mail surveys, interviews, experiments, and direct observation are all means of obtaining data on consumer preferences and buying habits. Like engineering, marketing research is open-ended and is not limited by other organizational activities in the way that, for example, quality control is. There is a delicate balance between the cost of marketing research and the additional revenues that such information may bring. The concept of *expected value of sample information* (EVSI), used in decision theory, is useful in placing limits on marketing research expenditures.

Processes in marketing research rely heavily on statistical models. Much of the analysis is descriptive: tabulating findings, classifying data, constructing frequency distributions, preparing graphic displays, computing measures of central tendency, and so forth. But much of the analysis is also inferential: estimating population means from sample data, testing hypotheses about product success, and projecting consumer behavior from past activities (trend analysis) or from other, related variables (regression analysis). These latter processes are more typical of DSS, but because they are used in a structured, recurring manner in marketing research applications, it is appropriate to include them in the MIS.

Most marketing research output is used internally to prepare written reports on consumer preferences, market targets for promotional campaigns, and the value the public places on various products and services. In an automobile manufacturing firm, for example, marketing research may determine that small, fuel-efficient cars are desired; that "two-car" families represent the largest potential market; and that, for an extra $800, the average buyer would rather have velour upholstery and a stereo radio than airbags and crash-resistant bumpers. Information like this is rarely used by other MIS applications and need not be placed in the data base. It is of interest to planners, however, and is conveyed to them in document form.

Product Development

Product development is the second marketing module involved in the "front end" of production. The product development function is to translate consumer preferences (from the marketing research module) into *general* product specifications, which are refined into *detailed* product design and *material specifications* by the engineering section.

It is the responsibility of the product development section to provide information about the legality, exclusivity (patent rights), competition (similar products), performance, appearance, reliability, customer benefits, and company benefits of a proposed product. Although many of the inputs required to generate this information come from external sources—patent right information, for example—many others are made available by other MIS subsystems or modules: the engineering module of the production subsystem provides product performance and reliability data; the marketing research module can provide consumer reaction to the appearance of the product; the finance subsystem can furnish data on the profitability of similar products; and so on.

The primary outputs of the product development module are specifications for new products. Specifications developed by marketing personnel are concerned more with product *attributes* than with *design* characteristics. For example, product design may specify that a portable hair dryer be hand-held, fold to fit in a 6″ by 8″ by 3″ case, have variable fan and heat controls, use no more than 1,000 watts of electricity, and cost less than $3.75 to produce in quantities of 100,000 or more. An artist's conception of the finished product may accompany the specifications. These specifications may be changed to accommodate the working mechanisms, materials, and assembly processes proposed by engineering. The exchange of information between product development and engineering is particularly important when several products are under development concurrently or products require many cycles between these two sections. Graphic representations and the technology for producing them, which are characteristic of CAD, are very helpful in both product development and engineering.

Pricing

The role of the pricing module is to fix an appropriate price for each product made by the firm. In microeconomic theory, prices are determined in the marketplace and cannot be controlled by the seller alone. In practice, however, the underlying economic assumptions (rational behavior by consumers, perfect competition, no product differentiation, and so on) are not met, and the seller has considerable say in setting prices. Advertising, in particular, permits variances from the market price by modifying consumer preferences for a particular brand.

Prices are based on marketing research output on public opinion, the prices of competitive products, and the costs of production (from the production subsystem). The processes used to determine price can be as simple as a percentage markup on costs, or they may be based on a simulation of profit for various prices under assumed demand functions. Whatever the process, the output becomes an important input to the promotion module and the finance subsystem.

Promotion

The promotion of a firm's product, one of the most important functions of marketing, is based on creative activities—commercial art, script writing, radio and television production, and so forth—carried on outside the realm of MIS. Nevertheless, there are certain inputs and outputs of the promotion module integral to MIS. Promotion is another open-ended activity in which there are no inherent spending limits (such as some maximum amount of resources needed by, say, production, to manufacture a given volume of output) and that must be monitored closely to ensure that the firm will not become "promotion poor" any more than it can afford to become "engineering poor" or "marketing-research poor." The control mechanism, of course, is a promotion or advertising budget that establishes the standard data with which the actual cost data, a promotion module output, are compared.

Other inputs to the promotion module include *price schedules* (from the pricing module), *product specifications* (from the product development module), and feedback on *actual sales* performance (from the sales management module).

Although advertisements are not literally developed by programs from the MIS application base, the management of advertising activities is supported by the MIS. Linear programming models can be used to develop a "media mix" (analogous to the product mix used to illustrate LP in Chapter 7) that shows how to allocate limited advertising dollars among the various media in order to maximize sales.

Sales Management

The entire marketing effort ultimately culminates in sales, and the success or failure of marketing is often (unjustly, perhaps) attributed to sales personnel. In a typical manufacturing firm, where products are not sold directly to consumers, the sales personnel deal with the purchasing agents of other organizations and must rely more on a technical and professional knowledge of their products than on the stereotyped "sales pitch" frequently associated with consumer products. The sale of industrial products is much more compatible with an MIS sales management module.

Sales management is less open-ended than some other modules, but it is still subject to budget control and receives, from the finance subsystem, a *sales budget* input. Other inputs include the plans for the promotion of each product (from the promotion module) and *sales estimates* and *orders* (from the sales force).

As usual, budget constraints on the input side must be complemented by appropriate outputs. In this case, the actual cost and volume of sales complete the information needed for management control. The processing implied by the budget is relatively simple: expenditures, balances, and projected surpluses or deficits are computed for various accounts, and the results are conveyed to managers via reports.

Another important output of the sales management module is a projection of the sales volume for subsequent periods. Such projections often become the basis for organizational objectives, which may come back to haunt the sales management section. Overly optimistic projections cannot be met, and overly pessimistic ones reflect badly on the ability and/or the integrity of the manager who submits them. The techniques of developing sales projections range from the purely intuitive to the highly mathematical. Although there is much to be said for intuition, experience, "gut feelings," and other intangibles, they are not to be found in the MIS data base or application base. Instead, MIS can assist in projections of this type through multiple regression analysis, simulation, exponential smoothing, and other management science tools of forecasting. Economic conditions, historical sales data, performance evaluations of salespersons, and the promotion budget can all be incorporated into predictive models. And if Bayesian analysis is used, there are even ways to combine a manager's subjective, intuitive estimates with empirical data.

TABLE 10-2   Examples of Information Requirements in Marketing*

Operational Control	Management Control	Strategic Planning
Sales quotas	Consumer preferences	Sales projections
Price schedules	Actual sales	Public opinion
Orders	Market targets	(Competition)
	Budget data	
	Institutional data	

*Parentheses indicate that information must come from external sources.

Management Activities in Marketing

Like production, marketing involves different management activities at different organizational levels: operational control in marketing is concerned primarily with sales-oriented tasks; management control deals with the human and financial resources necessary to develop information on products and markets; and strategic planning is involved in the establishment of sales objectives and promotional strategy. The information needed to support these activities in marketing are shown in Table 10-2.

Marketing Information Systems

It was noted earlier that some information systems bear the descriptive modifier "marketing" in recognition of their orientation to the support of marketing functions. References to marketing information systems appeared in the literature as early as 1967, just a few years after the concept of management information systems gained acceptance.[3] By 1971, a survey of Fortune 500 firms indicated that 77 percent either had or were developing a marketing information system.[4] This figure remained remarkably constant through 1984, when a similar survey of Fortune 1000 companies revealed 76 percent with marketing information systems.[5] Some interesting findings of this most recent study are summarized here.

[3] D. F. Cox and R. E. Good, "How to Build a Marketing Information System," *Harvard Business Review*, May–June, 1967: 145–54.

[4] L. E. Boone and D. L. Kurtz, "Marketing Information Systems: Current Status in American Industry," *Marketing in Motion: Relevance in Marketing* (Minneapolis: American Marketing Association, 1971), pp. 163–67.

[5] R. G. McLeod Jr. and J. C. Rogers, "Marketing Information Systems: Their Current Status in Fortune 1000 Companies," *Journal of Management Information Systems*, Spring 1985: 57–75.

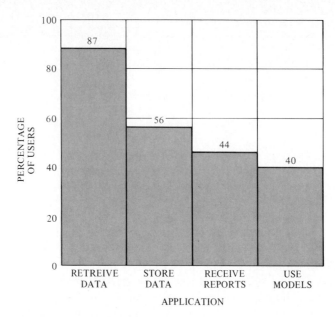

FIGURE 10-11 Marketing managers' use of terminals.

Marketing Managers' Use of Terminals

McLeod and Rogers found that "two-thirds" of marketing managers used terminals to gain access to a marketing information system, mostly, as shown in Figure 10-11, to retrieve data. This figure is up from the 10 percent found by Boone and Kurtz in 1971 and the 51 percent reported by McLeod and Rogers in an earlier 1980 study—a not unexpected trend given the advances in information systems technology over that period. It is more surprising to note that 40 percent use terminals for modeling—a function more associated with DSS than with MIS. It is quite possible, however, that the term *marketing information system* was interpreted by survey respondents to include marketing applications of DSS or, for that matter, the marketing module of an integrated MIS.

Internal Versus External Data

Managers' requirements for both internal and external data, as well as the ability of CBIS to satisfy those requirements, have been addressed already. We know, for example, that top-level managers tend to have greater needs for external or environmental information than do managers at the supervisory level. It may be less apparent, however, that these needs also vary according to function. Marketing managers, for example, tend to have greater need for environmental data than, say, managers in accounting. Figure 10-12 shows how computers are used to maintain the four major sources of environmental data, as defined by King and Cleland, used in marketing manage-

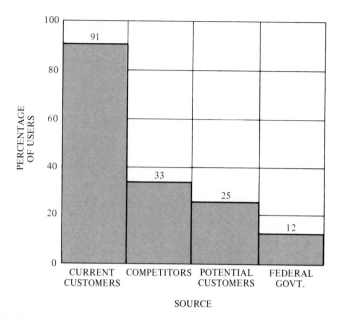

FIGURE 10-12   Sources of environmental data in marketing.

ment.[6] Of the four, only data on current customers is maintained to any great extent by computers.

Modeling

The McLeod and Rogers study further analyzed the use of models in marketing decisions and concluded that ". . . marketing management has embraced the mathematical model as a decision support tool." Some of the responses, such as "budgeting," "reorder point," and "economic order quantity," are in other functional areas as we have defined them. Decisions that fit more closely into the marketing subsystem of our integrated MIS, and the percentage of survey respondents using models to support those decisions, are shown in Figure 10-13. It is interesting to note that the percentage of respondents who use models to support decisions in, say, product evaluation (42 percent), is greater than the percentage that uses terminals for modeling (40 percent of two-thirds, or approximately 27 percent). This suggests that much of the modeling is not conducted in an interactive mode as we would expect in DSS, but is performed using routine application programs or special analyses performed by the information systems staff—a situation more typical of MIS.

Marketing Packages

Although the literature of marketing is rich with references to marketing information systems, it is interesting to note that software vendors have not offered integrated marketing packages to the extent that, say, manufacturing

[6]W. R. King and D. I. Cleland, "Environmental Information Systems for Strategic Marketing Planning," *Journal of Marketing*, April 1974: 35–40.

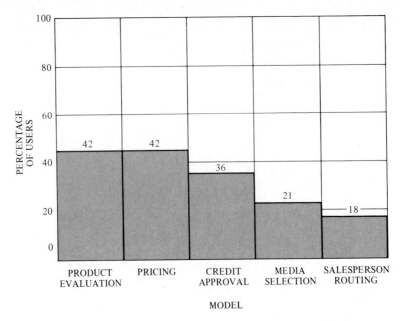

FIGURE 10-13   Use of models to support marketing decisions.

packages are offered. Software guides, such as *Data Sources*, list relatively few marketing applications outside of direct mail and other sales programs. One exception is the IBM mainframe-based *Marketing Information System* offered by Innovative Systems, Inc. This package provides the usual customer account information as well as statistical tools for market research, strategic planning, promotional program development, analysis of product penetration, and some related financial applications. *Data Sources* lists the price range of marketing packages from under $1,000 for some micro-based systems to over $40,000 for some mainframe-based systems.

Summary

The functions of a typical business organization—*production, marketing, finance,* and *personnel*—provide a basis for establishing the *subsystems* of an MIS. Within each subsystem, we can identify specific functional tasks that form a basis for *subsystems* or *modules*. The modules and subsystems share data through a data base management system.

The production subsystem in an organization that produces goods (as opposed to services) might have modules for *materials requirements planning, operations (MRP), engineering, shipping and receiving, purchasing,* and *quality control*.

The success of MRP in production applications has led to specialized manufacturing systems called *manufacturing resource planning (MRP II)*. These vendor-supplied systems, when integrated with financial and other functional applications, begin to approach the total-MIS concept. Other specialized uses of computers in manufacturing include the control of *robots* and *computer-assisted* (or computer-*aided*) *design* and *manufacturing*.

The marketing subsystem would have modules for activities in *marketing research, product development, pricing, promotion,* and *sales management.* Research over the past 15 years has revealed that many organizations have *marketing information systems* that perform the functions attributed to the marketing subsystem in our model as well as some functions attributed to other MIS subsystems or even other CBIS (such as DSS).

Assignments

10-1. The functional applications discussed in this chapter are representative of typical MIS, but they do not nearly cover all such applications. Go to your library and look through the information processing sections of journals such as *Business Week* and find additional examples of functional applications of MIS. Be prepared to report your findings to the class.

10-2. The production subsystem described in this chapter assumes the production of *goods.* In what ways would the production subsystem of a *service* organization—say, a bank—be different?

10-3. MRP is used when the end product of manufacturing has variable demand and is assembled from components. With what might you replace MRP if the demand is steady and the finished product is made directly from raw materials, as in the case of a ball bearing factory?

10-4. Suppose that the engineering section in your company has asked to have its terminals to the MIS mainframe computer replaced with stand-alone micros to be issued to each engineer. As the director of information services, how would you respond to this request?

10-5. The production operations manager has complained to you, the vice-president for production, that the quality control personnel are disrupting his operations with their continual testing. He wants the quality control section placed under his control. In general, the quality of output is very high. How would you respond to this request? What are the *information system* implications of the request?

10-6. Assignment 10-2 raises the question of MIS differences in service organizations. In what ways would the *marketing* subsystem of a bank's MIS be different from that found in a manufacturing company?

10-7. Both engineering (production subsystem) and product development (marketing subsystem) are concerned with the characteristics of new products. In what ways do these two modules work together? In what areas might they be in conflict?

10-8. One important decision made for every new product concerns the length and terms of any *warranty* it carries. Suppose you were responsible for preparing the warranty for a moped manufactured by your company. What information would you want to know? From which modules would you expect to receive that information? What needed information is not available from MIS sources?

CASE   Blue Ridge Communications Systems

Blue Ridge Communications Systems (BRCS) was formed in 1976 by Phil Jackson and Sal Dimensco as an office communications consulting group. Phil had been a three-year starter at quarterback for the regional state university and, with his pleasing personality and name recognition among the local sports fans, turned out to be an excellent salesperson. Phil had been a speech major in college, but he left without a degree when his eligibility ran out. Sal had his BBA in industrial management from the same institution but was almost the exact opposite of Phil in personality. It turned out to be a good combination: Phil got the customer's interest and Sal designed the communications system around standard products available from the phone company.

The breakup of AT&T and the variety of new communications products that appeared on the market in the early 1980s boosted BRCS sales and the company grew rapidly. Sal became President, Phil was Vice-President for Marketing, and a Vice-President for Finance, Sherry Hiller, was hired. Sal also looked after the production function and Phil took care of personnel, since most employees were in sales anyway.

By late 1985, BRCS could count among its clients almost every large- or medium-sized business in its natural geographic boundaries. Sal was beginning to feel that growth, if there was to be any, would have to come from expansion into new fields. He had always felt a little frustrated at not being able to apply his education in manufacturing and now thought that BRCS should move into the manufacture of communications equipment. Sal knew that most communications equipment was assembled from components available from electronics suppliers and that, for other than the plastic housings, BRCS would not be involved in the fabrication of parts. After some debate, the board of directors agreed and authorized the purchase of a plant for the manufacture of typewriter terminals that had recently been closed by a national electronics firm. Much of the equipment could be applied to the manufacture of telephones and other communications equipment in which Sal was interested.

At another board meeting in early 1986, the subject of an information system came up. Sherry said that she had known that they would need a computer system but that she had just assumed it would be primarily financial in nature and that her division would develop it. Sal replied that many studies had shown that information systems were more effective in high-level, independent locations, but he agreed that with BRCS's experience in systems design they should develop the system themselves, perhaps even with some of the new CAD/CAM and robotics applications; after all, the system was being introduced in response to BRCS's move into manufacturing. Everyone was surprised when Phil, who had had little to contribute in the planning meetings, spoke.

"I realize that we have some excellent systems expertise in BRCS, but it is in communications, not information. Most of us have been out of school for ten or more years and I can tell you that computer systems have changed considerably in that time. I have spent a lot of time on the road visiting our clients and I have seen some of the things they are doing with computers. Frankly, I don't think we should expend the resources developing applications that already exist. Some of our manufacturing clients are getting along just fine with packaged systems. I recommend that we form a committee to evaluate vendor-supplied manufacturing packages before we commit ourselves to developing a system in-house."

Questions

1. What fundamental issues have been raised at the latest BRCS meeting? Rank order the issues in importance and, if it is different, the order in which you think the issues should be resolved.

2. Comment on Phil's statement. Is it possible that he has a better perspective than Sal and Sherry, who, as a systems expert and a potential systems user, have more direct interest? What weight would you, as a board member, give to Phil's contribution?

3. How should the board resolve the issues you have identified?

Other Readings

Appleton, Daniel S. "The State of CIM." *Datamation* (December 15, 1985): 66–72.

Gold, Bela. "CAM Sets New Rules for Production." *Harvard Business Review* (November–December, 1982): 88–94.

Groover, Mikell P. *Automation, Production, and Computer-Aided Manufacturing.* Englewood Cliffs, N.J.: Prentice-Hall, 1980.

Hall, Robert W. "Production Control and Japanese Productivity, Parts I and II." *Inventories and Production Magazine* (September–October, 1981): 6–10 and (November–December, 1981): 6–12.

Hudson, C. A. "Computers in Manufacturing." *Science* (February 12, 1982): 818–25.

Hussain, Donna, and K. M. Hussain. *Information Processing Systems for Management.* Homewood, Ill.: Richard D. Irwin, 1985.

McLeod, Raymond, Jr., and John C. Rogers. "Marketing Information Systems." *Journal of Management Information Systems* (Spring 1985): 57–75.

Montgomery, David B., and Glen L. Urban. "Marketing Decision-Information Systems: An Emerging View." *Journal of Marketing Research* (May 1970).

Chapter 11

Functional Applications of MIS: Finance and Personnel

Learning Objectives

After studying this chapter, you will be able to:

1. Describe the flow of information within and between the functional subsystems of an MIS.
2. Relate the information needs of functional managers to the three levels of management activity.
3. Discuss the input, processing, and output associated with subsystems based on the functions of finance and personnel.
4. Define the following terms:

budget module	personnel records module
cost accounting module	training module
funds management module	payroll module
financial accounting module	personnel information system
billing module	behavioral information system
accounts receivable module	computer-based training
accounts payable module	computer-assisted instruction
accounting information systems	computer-managed instruction
labor relations module	authoring systems
personnel actions module	item analysis

In Chapter 10, we adopted an approach of defining subsystems along functional lines and examined two subsystems, production and marketing, in detail. We now conclude the discussion of functional subsystems with an examination of the *finance* and *personnel* subsystems.

The Finance Subsystem

Although we have chosen a functional approach to the definition of subsystems, other approaches are possible. For example, a strict systems view of an organization might argue for subsystems based on the flow of resources—material, people, and money. In one sense, the finance subsystem of this model fits into both approaches. It represents both an organizational entity responsible for financial matters and the cross-departmental flow of financial resources that takes place in every organization. Finance departments typically have interests and responsibilities that transcend departmental boundaries. The MIS subsystem for finance must reflect this expanded point of view.

The finance subsystem, as defined here, includes the function of accounting—the historical home of data processing. It is not surprising, therefore, to find extensive MIS application in the finance subsystem. But as might be expected in view of the data processing history, many of these applications are of the transaction processing variety and are of little *direct* interest to managers. These applications are the source of input data for much MIS financial information, however, and are of considerable *indirect* interest to finance and accounting managers.

Finance Subsystem Modules

One of the most obvious ways in which the finance department becomes involved in the activities of other departments is through the administration of the *budget,* a fact represented by the manner in which the budget module overlaps all four subsystems in Figure 10-2. Other finance modules, shown in Figure 11-1, include *cost accounting, funds management, financial accounting, billing, accounts receivable,* and *accounts payable.*

Budget
The budget provides control over an organization's financial resources, and because other resources can be expressed in monetary terms, the budget is a control measure over those resources as well. The budget is also a planning tool—a means of implementing plans by allocating resources (or the funds to acquire resources) to various activities in the organization for specific purposes. A plan to introduce a new product, for example, is implemented by a budget (and other directives) authorizing funds for research and develop-

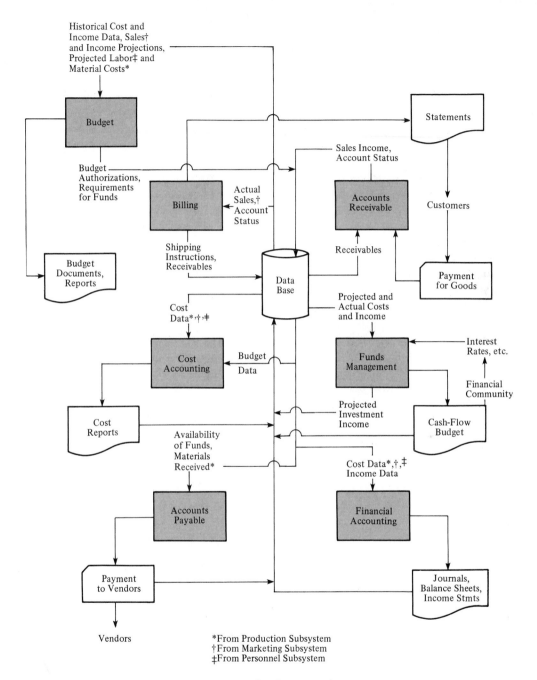

Historical Cost and Income Data, Sales† and Income Projections, Projected Labor‡ and Material Costs*

Budget

Statements

Budget Authorizations, Requirements for Funds

Sales Income, Account Status

Billing

Actual Sales,† Account Status

Accounts Receivable

Customers

Budget Documents, Reports

Shipping Instructions, Receivables

Data Base

Receivables

Payment for Goods

Cost Data*·†·‡

Projected and Actual Costs and Income

Interest Rates, etc.

Cost Accounting

Budget Data

Funds Management

Financial Community

Cost Reports

Projected Investment Income

Cash-Flow Budget

Availability of Funds, Materials Received*

Cost Data*,†,‡ Income Data

Accounts Payable

Financial Accounting

Payment to Vendors

Journals, Balance Sheets, Income Stmts

Vendors

*From Production Subsystem
†From Marketing Subsystem
‡From Personnel Subsystem

FIGURE 11-1 The finance subsystems.

303

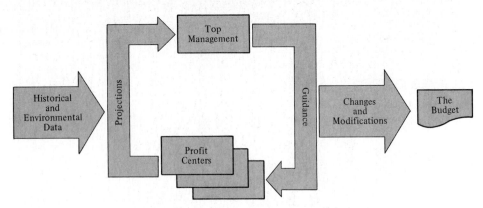

FIGURE 11-2 The budget cycle.

ment, the acquisition of new equipment and material, the hiring and training of production personnel, promotional campaigns, and so forth.

Budgeting is a cyclical process that starts with budget guidance from top management. The various profit centers in the organization then submit projected costs and incomes for the coming budget period. These inputs are refined during budget preparation as both the budget guidance and the expectations of functional managers are modified to approach a common level. As shown in Figure 11-2, inputs to this process are both internal (in the form of historical data) and external (environmental data).

The development of a budget involves some unstructured decision making, particularly on the part of top management. Electronic spread sheets, such as VisiCalc, can be of assistance in the budgeting process. The development of income and cost projections may require forecasting models. This capability may be provided by a DSS, although the recurring nature of the budget process may lead to the incorporation of such models into the MIS. The remaining processes by which data are exchanged between those who formulate guidance and those who prepare the projections, and by which the budget document itself is prepared are largely a matter of record keeping and report generation. In large organizations, however, the sheer volume of the data associated with the budget can make even these routine functions a challenging MIS application.

Although budgets are prepared and distributed as documents, the dynamic nature of the budget requires that it be maintained in the data base, where it is available to both planners and users. Planners must have the capability of modifying the budget as environmental conditions change, and users must have access to the current status of their accounts.

Cost Accounting

In financial control, the budget provides *projected* data, whereas *actual* data are furnished by the cost accounting module. As noted earlier, not all resource expenditures are measured in monetary terms, and some control—

over labor, machine time, and raw materials, for example—is exercised outside the finance subsystem. Even these resource expenditures, however, are converted to dollar amounts and serve as input data to the cost accounting module.

Processing in cost accounting involves the maintenance of cost data and the comparison of actual costs to standards. For example, if the standard time for performing a certain job is 3 hours at a standard wage of $6.50 an hour, an actual time of 3½ hours would result in a *labor variance* of ($6.50 × 3) − ($6.50 × 3.5), or − $3.25. If the criteria for an exception report is 10 percent over standard, this particular performance, which is (3.5 − 3)/3, or 16.67 percent, over standard, would be called to the attention of management for corrective action. Although this example results in a *negative* variance, management should also be made aware of large *positive* variances, which might indicate inappropriate standards, an unexpected learning curve effect, or an unusually efficient operation that could be adopted in other areas.

Funds Management

Another financial module with close ties to budgeting is funds management. The purpose of funds management is to ensure that funds will be available to meet the financial obligations of the organization while at the same time maximizing the returns on invested funds not needed to meet current obligations.

Funds management, also referred to as *capital budgeting*, is an upper-level management activity in an organization and, not unexpectedly, relies heavily on data from external, as well as internal, sources. External data for these applications come primarily from the financial community: investment opportunities, interest rates, bond ratings, and so on. Internal data center on projected *sources* (interest and dividends on investments, accounts receivable, borrowing, and so on) and *uses* (interest and principal on debt, dividends due, wages, accounts payable, and so on) of funds.

There are a number of management science tools that are useful in the management of funds. Linear programming can be used to develop an optimum mix of long- and short-term investments to meet constraints on acceptable risk and the availability of funds. Simulation can be used to determine the effects of various investment plans. And, of course, the ability to compute present values, internal rates of return, amortization schedules, and compound interest is now a common feature on hand-held calculators as well as being part of the financial planning models in the MIS application base. The combination of external data and management science models also suggests the use of DSS in funds management.

The basic output of the funds management module is a cash-flow budget of the type shown, in an abbreviated form, in Table 11-1. This budget shows the amount of cash that must be borrowed or is available for investment for each period of the budget. Although it is shown as a document, the cash-flow budget, like other budgets, is a dynamic tool and is maintained in the data base for convenience of revision and updating.

TABLE 11-1 Cash-Flow Budget (000's)

	January	February	March	April	...	December
Balance:	—	2	—	4	...	6
Income:						
Accounts receivable	52	49	65	56	...	50
Interest	8	8	7	7	...	10
Miscellaneous	6	5	7	10	...	9
Total	66	64	79	77	...	75
Expenses:						
Wages and salaries	28	28	29	29	...	30
Accounts payable	19	16	18	20	...	17
Interest	10	10	8	8	...	6
Dividends	—	—	15	—	...	15
Loan payment	—	14	—	—	...	—
Miscellaneous	7	3	5	6	...	8
Total	64	71	75	63	...	76
Balance	2	(7)	4	14		(1)
Available to invest	2		4	14		
Need to borrow		7				1

Financial Accounting

The classification, recording, and summarization of monetary transactions is referred to as *financial*—as opposed to *managerial*—accounting. Although there is some management information generated in financial accounting, the primary purpose is to paint a financial picture of the organization for investors and creditors and to satisfy legal requirements. This is in marked contrast to a purely managerial activity such as cost accounting, although financial and cost accounting may share certain input data.

Monetary transactions—receipts and expenditures of funds—are made available to the financial accounting module through the data base and are maintained in *journals*. Periodically, journal data are used to update basic financial statements, such as the *balance sheet* and the *income statement*. The processes involved in the preparation of these statements rarely go beyond simple calculation and report generation.

Although the accounting department is a traditional computer user, accounting applications have been somewhat constrained by longstanding "generally accepted accounting principles" (GAAP), some of which can be traced back to the fifteenth century! One particular problem facing automated accounting is the need for an *audit trail* to back up accounting entries. Random access files and data bases are particularly difficult to audit, and in many cases, processing and storage efficiencies must be sacrificed for compliance with GAAP.

Billing

The billing module receives input in the form of sales data (orders) from the marketing subsystem and sets in motion the process of filling those orders and obtaining payment for them. The first step in this process involves a *credit check* that compares the amount of the order with the limits imposed when the account was established and modified by account status feedback from the accounts receivable module. If credit can be extended, the order is further processed to generate output for the customer, the accounts receivable module, and the production subsystem. The customer receives a *statement* containing the amount and terms of the payment due; similar data are provided the accounts receivable module; and shipping instructions are sent to the shipping and receiving module of the production subsystem.

Billing is essentially a transaction processing activity, although some routine, structured decisions (such as the approval of credit) are made. Management information based on billing data is more likely to be reflected in reports from other modules—accounts receivable, for example—than from the billing module itself.

Accounts Receivable

The accounts receivable module is a logical extension of the billing module. At the transaction-processing level, inputs from the billing module are added to a customer's account balance, and payments are subtracted. Outputs from accounts receivable include sales income data for budgeting and financial accounting as well as account status feedback to billing.

At the MIS level, accounts are analyzed to provide information used in the determination of credit ratings and payment terms. For example, if an analysis shows that very few customers are taking advantage of discounts for early payment, consideration should be given to increasing the discount. Simulation or other techniques of financial analysis can weigh the loss of income from discounts against the benefits of receiving early payment and can help financial managers to make the discount decision. In the case of decisions regarding discounts, the MIS analysis is subject to modification on the basis of external data that are not found in the MIS data base, such as the general economic factors affecting payment, the discounting practices of competitors, and current interest rates. Other analyses *classify* accounts by risk, *age* accounts by their due dates, or compute *ratios* for *turnover* and *collection*.

Accounts Payable

The accounts payable module is the "cost counterpart" of the accounts receivable module. The purpose of accounts payable is to pay vendors for the materials ordered by the production subsystem and to settle other payable accounts—except the payroll—in the organization. For simplicity, only payments for materials are shown in Figure 11-1.

Payments are made on the basis of statement or invoice data entered into the data base by the shipping and receiving module of the production department, or on receipt of the material, depending on payment terms. The timing of payments is also influenced by discounts and the availability of funds. Discounts, such as "2–10, net 30" (which means, "2 percent discount if paid within ten days, or the full amount if paid between eleven and thirty days"), are usually taken if funds for the budget period have not been expended or can be made available from other sources.[1]

Accounts payable is also a good example of how legal requirements and generally accepted accounting practices complicate an MIS. Although payment data can be stored almost indefinitely in electronic media in relatively little physical space, state statutes of limitations require the maintenance of canceled checks for an average of six years. This is just one example of the legal requirements for retaining records that influence many modules within an MIS.

Management Activities in Finance

Operational control is concerned with *tasks*. In finance, those tasks include preparing billing documents, recording receipts, and making payments. Management control is exercised over *resources* and is especially important in finance, where the resource to be controlled is money. The preparation of the budget is the primary means of control, but it is followed closely in importance by funds management. Cost accounting provides a means of exercising control over other resources, such as time and materials, and the aging of accounts and other analyses help to control receivable resources. Strategic planning deals with *objectives*. In finance, those objectives establish criteria for funds management, discounting and collection policies, and budget guidance. The information needs of financial managers at different activity levels are shown in Table 11-2.

TABLE 11-2 Examples of Information Requirements in Finance*

Operational Control	Management Control	Strategic Planning
Actual cost data	Projected cost data	Cash flow budget
Actual income data	Projected income data	Income statements
Receivables	Funds requirements	(Interest rates)
	Account status	(Investment opportunities)
	Funds availability	
	Cost reports	

*Parentheses indicate that information must come from external sources.

[1] Not paying until the end of thirty days is, in effect, borrowing the amount of the payment at a rate of 2 percent per twenty days or 36 percent, uncompounded (about 43 percent, compounded), per annum!

Accounting Information Systems

Many current MIS grew out of data processing applications in accounting departments, but in some cases, those applications retained their accounting orientation and the subsequent generations became known as *accounting information systems*. Accounting information systems encompass the processes and procedures by which an organization's financial information is received, registered, recorded, handled, processed, stored, reported, and ultimately disposed of.[2]

Often, the difference between accounting and management information systems is one of semantics—the accounting information system also serves other functional areas and in another organization might well be called a management information system. These systems are merely MIS with an accounting *perspective*. That is, the focus is on costs and other monetary impact of transactions. Table 11-3 shows how subsystems in an MIS with an accounting perspective might be organized. This is the approach of many accounting information systems. It is a legitimate view, but one that is, perhaps, of greater importance to accountants than to managers in other functional areas. Accounting information systems of this type are not sufficiently different from the MIS described here to warrant further discussion.

In other instances, accounting information systems are dedicated solely

TABLE 11-3 Subsystems in an
MIS with an Accounting Perspective

The Expenditure Subsystem
    Procurement and vendor control
    Receiving and inspection
    Accounts payable
The Conversion Subsystem
    Inventory control
    Production control
    Payroll
The Revenue Subsystem
    Marketing
    Shipping and transportation
    Billing and collection
The Administrative Subsystem
    Cash receipts and disbursements
    Property control
    General ledger

Source: Robinson et al. p. 205.

[2]Leonard A. Robinson, James R. Davis, and C. Wayne Alderman, *Accounting Information Systems: A Cycle Approach* (New York: Harper & Row, 1982), p. 4.

to accounting and financial functions. For the purpose of this discussion, it is convenient to group such systems into three categories: traditional accounting systems, systems for accounting firms, and special-purpose systems.

Traditional Accounting Systems

Traditional accounting systems are similar to the accounting subsystem of our MIS model, in that they provide the traditional accounting services to an organization, with or without integration with other functional subsystems. Such accounting systems have been defined as "That portion of the formal information system concerned with the measurement and prediction of income, wealth, and other economic events of the organization and its subparts and entities."[3] Unlike fully integrated MIS, which are usually developed in-house, traditional accounting information systems are often available in packages from software vendors. Packaged accounting systems for mainframe computers cost up to $90,000, those for minicomputers up to $20,000, and those for microcomputers run from $500 to $5,000.

The *Corporate Financial System* (CFS), by American Management Systems, Incorporated, is one example of a packaged, traditional accounting system. CFS is designed for IBM mainframe computers and contains fully integrated modules for general ledger accounting, budgeting, accounts payable, accounts receivable, capital projects, and other accounting functions. Features include on-line updating and inquiry processing, a built-in data base, an audit trail capability, and data security measures.

A somewhat different approach to packaging accounting systems has been taken by American Software, Incorporated, in the design of the *Financial-8* package. Financial-8 consists of semi-independent modules that may stand alone, work with each other, or act as extensions to American's manufacturing and distribution systems. The modules are COBOL compatible for IBM mainframes and include accounts receivable, accounts payable, capital projects, fixed-asset accounting, inventory control, order processing, procurement, and purchasing. The concept of extending a manufacturing package with financial applications is similar to the MSA illustration in Chapter 10 and also approaches the total MIS concept.

Systems for Accounting Firms

Accounting firms offer accounting and other consultative services to clients and have somewhat different information systems needs. Although the information systems for accounting firms include traditional accounting applications, the fact that these applications are performed for many clients and must be maintained separately requires a greater degree of data management than that normally encountered. Consulting also involves some unique accounting applications such as the valuation of a firm, auditing, and the billing of clients for services.

---

[3]"Report of the Committee on Accounting and Information Systems," *The Accounting Review Supplement*, 1971: 289–90.

Large accounting firms usually develop accounting information systems in-house. Some, such as Arthur Andersen and Company, have taken advantage of the experience gained in developing their own systems and now offer *systems* as well as *accounting* consultation to their clients. Smaller accounting firms, which may have begun automated accounting only recently, are more likely to purchase or lease one of the many commercial packages designed to support accounting firms.

The *Management Information and Accounting System* (MIS), by Computer Utility Management, Limited, is one example of a package designed to support a multi-office accounting firm. In addition to providing the usual applications in accounts payable, accounts receivable, account aging, collections, financial statements, and forecasting, this package also furnishes job analysis, client statements, staff utilization reports, and other information unique to the management of a consulting firm. MIS is compatible with Honeywell mainframes and costs between $50,000 and $90,000. The fact that firms are willing to pay fees in this range is an indication of their view of the opportunity costs of in-house development.

Special-Purpose Systems

There are a number of accounting and financial applications that lie outside of the "mainstream" of accounting information systems, in that they are used only rarely or by a very limited number of users. For example, tax preparation is used only yearly by most firms or extensively only by income tax consultants. The frequency with which the tax laws change makes an income tax module impractical for any but the full-time tax consultant. Most tax programs are purchased from vendors who provide the basic software, supplements for the various state codes, and annual updates to accommodate changes in state and federal codes.

Investment analysis is another specialized area not normally represented in MIS. Investment analysis is actually a better DSS application because it represents a decision (which investment opportunity to pursue), it is based on personalized criteria (the investor's philosophy and goals), and it requires extensive external data (stock prices, interest rates, and so on). The availability of proprietary investment data bases, such as the *Dow Jones News Retrieval* service, have made investment analysis available to almost any microcomputer installation with access to a modem and compatible software. Some representative investment analysis packages designed for microcomputers are shown in Table 11-4.

The Personnel Subsystem

The management of personnel information is a subject that has received little attention in systems literature. One reason is that personnel applications tend to be routine record-keeping activities and make little use of the more inter-

TABLE 11-4   Investment Analysis Packages

Name	Vendor	Data Base Compatibility	Hardware Compatibility	Approximate Cost	Remarks
Compu Trac	Computrac	Dow Jones, others	Apple	$1,800	Analysis of stocks and commodities, programmable
Investment Master PC	ALRO		IBM PC	$200	Portfolio management
Market Analyst	Anidata	Dow Jones, Source, Compu-serve, Warner	Apple, IBM PC	$400– $500	Technical analysis, portlfolio management, quotes
Market Manager	Dow Jones	Dow Jones	Apple, IBM PC	$300	Portfolio management
Stockpak II	Standard and Poor's		Apple, IBM PC	$200	Monthly update of S&P data on 4500 firms
Value/Screen	Value Line	Value Line	Apple, IBM PC	$500	Stock selection by user-selected criteria

esting management science models applied to the production, marketing and finance functions. Another reason is that, unless the number of employees is very large, personnel records may be just as easy to maintain manually— easier, perhaps, within the constraints of freedom of information and privacy laws. Not only do large organizations achieve certain economies of scale in maintaining computerized personnel records, they are also more likely to look for appropriately skilled employees from within their own ranks when job openings occur. The capability of searching a personnel data base for, say, an electrical engineer who has an MBA and is fluent in Spanish is not particularly helpful if you have only twenty-five employees.

Personnel Subsystem Modules

To complete the MIS model we have been building, we will assign to the personnel department certain responsibilities that might normally reside elsewhere if we had additional subsystems. For example, the *labor relations* module could just as easily be in a legal subsystem, and the *training* module could be an independent subsystem. Also, the *payroll* module is sometimes found in the finance subsystem, but *personnel actions* and *personnel records* are traditional activities in a personnel department. Let us look at these modules, which are shown in Figure 11-3, more closely.

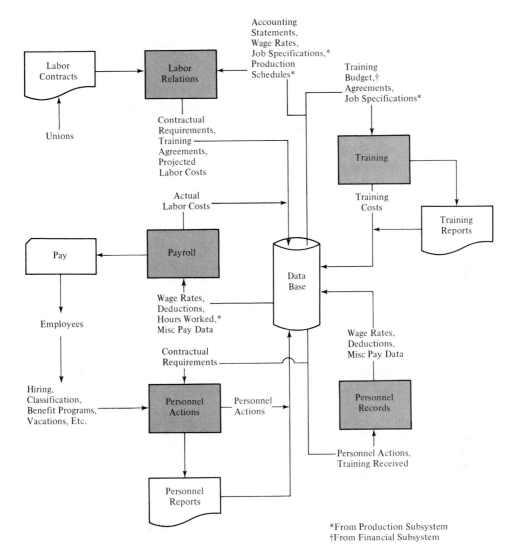

FIGURE 11-3   The personnel subsystem.

Labor Relations

Labor relations provide the interface between management and unions or other worker organizations. Although labor relations are not normally thought of as an MIS application, management representatives must have access to MIS data concerning wage rates, production schedules, job specifications, and other matters typically discussed in contract negotiations. Even accounting statements showing company profits or losses in the past can become a basis for negotiating wage packages. Access to this information and to the analytical tools of the MIS or a DSS gives management representatives the ability to determine quickly and accurately the effect of a proposal by either side.

The retrieval processes used by labor relations to obtain information for negotiations are mirrored by storage processes that make the results of negotiation available to other MIS users. Wage rates, fringe benefits, work conditions, provisions for training, and other such data are entered into the data base, where they may be accessed by other application modules. Wages, particularly as they may escalate during the term of the contract, are of great importance to the finance modules of budget and funds management, as well as to the personnel module of payroll. Work conditions—safety requirements, rest periods, shift schedules, and the like—are inputs to the production subsystem. And commitments to train or retrain employees are an important input to the budget module and, along with the requirements specified by operations, to the training module.

Personnel Actions

Personnel actions can be thought of as *transactions* involving personnel. Hiring, classification, promotion, taking vacation or sick leave, participation in group health and life insurance, transfers, and termination are all examples of personnel actions. Inputs to the personnel actions module include the labor contract, which often contains provisions or restrictions on personnel actions; organizational policies; requests from employees; and requests from supervisors. Outputs are in the form of summary or detail reports—summary to managers to show, for example, the number and percentage of employees participating in the health insurance program and detail to the personnel records and payroll modules to show that, for example, John Jones is participating.

Personnel Records

The maintenance of personnel records is still a manila-folder operation in many organizations, although it is well suited to MIS and data base management. There is a great deal of redundancy in personnel records that can be eliminated in a data base environment. If you were to examine the personnel records of a typical employee in a large organization (or the records of a typical student in a university, for that matter), you might find his or her name and social security number on eight or ten separate documents. An MIS personnel records module using a data base would need to state that information only once.

But you *can't* examine the personnel records of that employee. Or any but your own student records. Privacy laws prohibit it. This would not be a problem were it not for the freedom of information laws that require access to an individual's own records. Now the personnel and MIS managers must devise a way to let you see your own, but no one else's, records. It is difficult to give this assurance when individuals, some of whom may be quite knowledgeable about data base procedures, are allowed to sit at a terminal and scan their records. As a result, most personnel sections print out records when there is a request to examine them. Many organizations have adopted the attitude that it is just as easy to maintain "hardcopy" files in the first place and do not use computer files for personnel records.

Privacy and freedom of information requirements aside, personnel records require inputs on name, social security number, address, telephone number, next of kin, training, education, age, employment history, skills, job title, wage rate, and other similar data for every employee. In addition to maintaining and updating these data through normal transaction processing methods, the personnel records module outputs management reports summarizing relevant information, such as an age or educational profile of employees. Special reports may be used to find "in-house" candidates for job openings—such as the electrical engineering example cited at the beginning of this section on the personnel subsystem.

Training

In-house training in modern organizations can range from none at all to the operation of collegelike facilities. Programs of instruction also vary greatly from very specific, job-oriented skills to very general, management development programs. And much training is conducted by outside agencies on a contract basis or simply by the reimbursement of employees for educational expenses.

For MIS purposes, we are concerned not so much about the conduct of training but about the generation of training information. The training activity is normally a profit center. That is, other departments are "charged" for training services and have the option not to use them or to go elsewhere for training. The training section is motivated to provide high quality training at low cost and reasonable prices in order to show a profit. In this context, training is like production or marketing or any other profit center and has similar information needs.

The training module also has some unique MIS applications. Inputs are received on purely training matters, such as job specifications, management development requirements, contractual obligations to train or retrain employees, employee qualifications and skill levels, and the availability of instructors and training facilities. These data are used to develop and schedule programs of instruction in almost the same way that the production subsystem develops production schedules. In an integrated MIS, some of the same scheduling algorithms could be used for both applications.

Outputs from the training module include summary reports of training activities, detail reports for the updating of personnel records, cost data for cost accounting, and projections of future requirements for budget planning.

Payroll

The last module in this MIS module is also the first—or at least *one* of the first—business data processing application: the payroll. You are probably already familiar with payroll operations. The inputs consist of wage rates, hours of labor, deductions, withholdings, and other similar data, from which pay is computed, paychecks are printed, and reports are produced for state and federal tax agencies. Although the computation of pay is largely a transaction processing activity, the payroll represents so great a portion of the budget that even slight changes in pay must be considered in financial planning. In this regard, analyses of the payroll to show age, seniority, wage differentials, overtime, and other factors can be used to determine the effect of wage demands during labor negotiations, the burden of future retirement benefits, or the impact of changes in tax laws, such as a change in the employer's contribution to social security.

Management Activities in Personnel

Personnel operations are perhaps more dominated by operational control activities than any of the other functions considered in this model. The tasks over which operational control is exercised in personnel are those of maintaining records, processing pay, and conducting training. Management control is exercised over the very important human resource with which personnel activities deal, primarily through hiring and the management of training resources—instructors, equipment, and other facilities. At the strategic planning level, top managers establish policies and objectives for hiring, promotion, training, and other personnel activities. And although labor negotiations are technically a *task*, the importance and the long intervals between negotiations make them a strategic responsibility as well. Examples of the information needs of personnel managers at the three management activity levels are shown in Table 11-5.

TABLE 11-5   Examples of Information Requirements in Personnel*

Operational Control	Management Control	Strategic Planning
Training schedules	Training requirements	Projected labor costs
Wage rates	Labor costs	(Labor law)
Personnel actions	Personnel reports	
	Labor contracts	
	Labor markets	
	Training reports	
	(Privacy Acts)	
	(Freedom of Information Acts)	

*Parentheses indicate that information must come from external sources.

Personnel Information Systems

The fact that there are independent information systems for personnel functions should come as no surprise in light of our previous discussion of manufacturing, marketing, and accounting information systems. Information systems dedicated to personnel matters go by a variety of names, to include *Personnel Information Systems*, *Human Resource Information Systems*, and *Human Resource Management Systems*. Personnel information systems have been defined as ". . . a systematic data handling process that organizes, maintains, and reports personnel information needs to top management, the personnel staff, employees, and governmental agencies. The system is intended to facilitate the performance of regular personnel activities and to provide management with information for decisions."[4] Typical applications in personnel information systems include personnel record keeping, employment functions (recruiting, job matching, analysis of applicants, evaluation of recruiters, and interpretation of tests), wage and salary administration, performance appraisal, and training and development.

Once again, we see that independent functional information systems are similar to their counterpart subsystems in an integrated MIS. The primary difference, as before, lies in the availability of commercially prepared packages: In general, they are readily available for functions such as personnel and rarely available for fully integrated MIS.

Since it is not possible to examine in detail each of the many specialized applications found in personnel information systems, let us look briefly at three *categories* of systems: personnel software packages, behavioral information systems, and computer-based training.

Personnel Software Packages

A few representative personnel packages are described in Table 11-6. The Argonaut Information Systems, Inc. (AIS) *Human Resources System* is typical of a complete, stand-alone personnel information system. The AIS system is compatible with minicomputer and mainframes of DEC, IBM, and UNIVAC. It provides on-line access to data bases for employee skills, position and salary information, and other employee information. It is capable of time and attendance reporting, performance evaluation, attrition analysis, and generating other management information. One important feature is compliance with government reporting requirements. Government reporting, which was mentioned briefly in Chapter 1, is of particular significance in the personnel function. For example, 55 separate sections of the Equal Employment Opportunity Act (EEOA) of 1972 define reporting requirements, as do 19 sections of the Occupational Safety and Health Act (OSHA) of 1970 and various provisions of the 1974 Employee Retirement Income Security

---

[4]Sang M. Lee and Cary D. Thorp, Jr., *Personnel Management: A Computer-Based Approach* (New York: Petrocelli Books, Inc., 1978), p. 8.

TABLE 11-6 Human Resource Management Packages

Name	Vendor	Hardware Compatibility	Approximate Cost	Remarks
PRES	National Information Systems	DEC, VAX minis	$2,500–$15,000/module	Administration, affirmative action, compensation. On-line, interactive.
Human Resource Information Data Base System	Adalcar Group, Ltd.	IBM, TI, Burroughs, CDC mainframes	$15,000–$85,000	Administration, placement, position control, government compliance, benefits, payroll, planning. Interactive.
Interactive Personnel	IBM	IBM mainframes	$1,000–$1,500/mo. (lease)	EEO and OSHA reporting, benefits, other applications.
Computer-Assisted Job Interview	Adalcar Group, Ltd.	Apple, IBM, TI, Victor micros	$6,000	Interview screening.
Executive Resource	Customation	Datapoint micro	$4,000	Executive job-candidate information.

Act (ERISA).[5] Since all organizations covered by the acts have essentially identical reporting requirements, it makes a good deal of sense to purchase a package of proven reliability rather than "reinvent the wheel." The tradeoff, of course, is that the purchased package is not likely to be compatible with other MIS subsystems.

At the other extreme lie the many single-purpose packages for time and attendance reporting, pension systems, travel expenses, computer-assisted job interview, and the like. Many of these specialized applications are microcomputer-based and can be purchased for as little as a few hundred dollars—in contrast to the multipurpose packages that tend to be mainframe-based and often cost tens of thousands of dollars.

Behavioral Information Systems

Most data collected for MIS reflect transactions and can be expressed quantitatively. Even personnel data usually refer to "hard" facts concerning age, length of employment, wage rates, and so on. Only a few MIS applications, notably those dealing with the evaluation of products, vendors, or personnel are likely to contain subjective or "soft" data. Even then, the nature of information processing may require us to quantify our evaluations using a numerical scale. An interesting adjunct to personnel information systems, and one which is almost totally based on subjective data, is the *behavioral information system*. Behavioral information systems are designed to generate

---

[5] Lee and Thorp, pp. 225–227.

information about employee perceptions, preferences, and attitudes on important job-related issues such as pay, promotion, supervision, job content, and job satisfaction.[6] In order to evaluate the effect of policy changes and the attitudes workers bring with them to the job, data should be collected prior to employment (in entrance interviews), during employment (in periodic surveys), and after employment (in exit interviews). Maintaining data in a fashion to facilitate cross-tabulations by department, length of employment, sex, education, and age will also help to isolate differences based on those variables.

The intent of behavioral systems is to provide information for management actions designed to reduce the costs associated with turnover, absenteeism, and counterproductive behavior. Although there is some potential to integrate behavioral information systems with other personnel applications and other functional subsystems, most uses occur in a stand-alone mode. One reason for keeping behavioral applications separate is that raw data from the interviews and surveys can be very misleading and must be subjected to rigorous analysis and expert interpretation. Since many organizations do not have personnel with these skills, they rely on outside consultants not only to interpret the data but to collect it as well.

Computer-Based Training

Computer-based training (CBT) includes two separate and distinct capabilities: *computer-assisted instruction* (CAI) and *computer-managed instruction* (CMI). CAI refers to the use of a computer as a means, either primary or secondary, of delivering instruction. CMI software is used to create and score tests, maintain student grades, analyze test items, and perform other functions inherent in the management of training.

Computer-Assisted Instruction   Although we have in mind here a corporate training program administered by the personnel department of a company, there are many other applications of CAI with which you may be more familiar and that might help you to understand the basic concepts of CAI. For example, parts of the second edition of this text were written with the word-processing component of Appleworks—an integrated software package for Apple computers. The package comes with a *tutorial* disk, which demonstrates the various capabilities of the package and guides the user through some simple examples. The user can create a document, spreadsheet, or data base under the direction of the tutorial. Work is "critiqued" by the tutorial as it is performed and the user is not permitted to proceed until each step is done correctly. The tutorial is, in effect, computer-assisted instruction. Two frames from the Appleworks tutorial are shown in Figure 11-4; you may have encountered similar tutorials with other microcomputer software packages.

Formal training programs use CAI that differs from software tutorials primarily in scope and length, although they do not always use the same

---

[6] Lee and Thorp, p. 59.

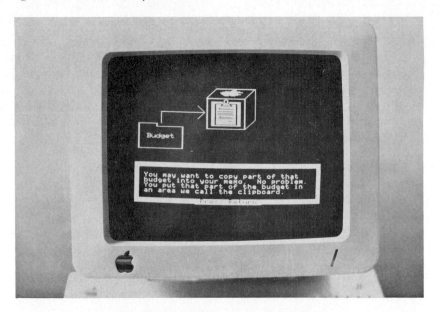

FIGURE 11-4   Appleworks tutorial.

dialog management techniques. Some CAI software communicates with students through *questions and answers*, some uses *menus*, some requires *joystick* movements, and others may use combinations of these techniques. CAI has been used successfully by Kodak to teach word processing, by the military to simulate flight instruction, and by IBM to give accounting instruction. Of course, there are also numerous examples in education where CAI uses range from spelling and arithmetic exercises in the primary grades through college instruction in chemistry.

Computer-assisted instruction has a number of advantages over the more traditional teacher–student method of presenting instruction. First, CAI is convenient to use. Students can select the time and length of the training session, the rate at which new material is introduced, or even the subject to be studied. Second, CAI can pace itself to the rate at which the student is learning. Mastery of elementary topics will cause CAI to move automatically to more advanced material, whereas errors or lack of retention will lead the student back through preliminary topics. Finally, CAI promotes greater student involvement in training than does the lecture method. It is a well-accepted principle of education that skills acquired by *doing* are retained longer than those learned merely by *listening*.

There are also some disadvantages to CAI. First, CAI is costly to develop. The time and special programming skills required to produce CAI software make it practicable only if it is to be used extensively. Second, CAI can be frustrating for students in some situations. CAI can respond only with programmed material and may not satisfy the curious student who wants in-depth explanations or who has questions beyond the scope of the lesson objectives. Finally, in contrast to the advantage of involvement cited earlier, involvement in some subjects may actually be *less* than that found in the alternative means. This is true in the case of flight simulation, where the alternative—actual flight in an aircraft—represents a higher level of involvement. In this example, however, one of the disadvantages—cost—is also reversed because flight simulation, particularly when it results in a simulated crash, is far less expensive than real flight. Clearly, there are tradeoffs involved that must be considered by the training manager before making a commitment to CAI.

Computer-Managed Instruction Although computer-assisted instruction holds great value to users and operational-level personnel, computer-managed instruction is often of more interest to managers and has greater information systems implications. One particularly powerful application of CMI, an *authoring system*, permits training managers to develop their own CAI rather than rely on standard, vendor-prepared packages. Authoring systems can be considered special-purpose programming languages that incorporate many of the looping, branching, graphics, and message-sending capabilities typical of CAI. The author merely selects a capability (branching, for example) and specifies the question or question sequence to be followed for each possible student response. In this manner, the author can provide immediate feedback to reinforce correct answers or provide the student additional instruction when the answer is incorrect. Authoring systems have helped reduce the initial CAI development costs and have made CAI available to many small or highly specialized users who previously could not find or afford applicable CAI software.

Trainer 3000, an authoring system developed by Computer Systems Research, Inc. (CSR), permits an author to construct questions by selecting menu items and keying in the appropriate text. There are provisions for giving hints in the event of an incorrect answer, branching to remedial instruction, highlighting the correct answer after an incorrect response, and giving the student an opportunity to enter comments—all in response to menus or prompts provided by the system. Some CMI capabilities, such as student performance evaluation, are also included. Trainer 3000 is designed to operate on IBM mainframe and microcomputers; it costs around $2,500.

As an example of the managerial implications of CBT, the U.S. military has developed an *adaptive testing* system that identifies the vocational aptitude of recruits.[7] Adaptive testing extends the branching concept to tailor every instance of testing to aptitudes suggested by the responses to early questions. For example, if early responses indicate greater mechanical than verbal skills, those portions of the test designed to show aptitude for jobs in public information or clerical fields will be skipped in order to focus on questions pertaining to vehicular maintenance or electronic equipment repair. This system not only saves time; it also promotes a more positive attitude on the part of the recruits by giving them questions more likely to be of interest to them.

CMI is also used to analyze the results of tests. For example, a score of 50 percent on a test seems to imply that the student knows about half of the subject matter. However, a CMI analysis may show that the student knows certain subjects quite well and has virtually no knowledge of others. Rather than force the student to take the entire course over, it may be possible to raise the score to a passing level by offering remedial instruction in only the deficient areas. This logic also applies to high grades, which seem to indicate an acceptable level of knowledge in all topics but may, in fact, conceal serious deficiencies in certain areas. Students or employees in this category should also receive remedial instruction, especially if the deficiency is in an area that could influence safety on the job or the quality of the company's product.

CMI can be used to evaluate the test itself as well. In a technique known as *item analysis,* individual questions and responses are analyzed to determine their contribution to identifying "good" students. For example, a question missed often by poor students (those with low scores on the entire test) and rarely by good students (those with high test scores) has a high level of *discrimination* and should be retained. Similarly, individual responses can be examined for their contribution. A distractor (an incorrect option on a multiple-choice test) that is never selected may be too obvious and should be rewritten to make it more attractive. Item analysis has been used successfully by the military to refine, over a period of years, the tests used to determine the eligibility for proficiency bonuses to pay in certain military occupational specialties.

---

[7]Vandra L. Huber and Geri Gay, "Channeling New Technology to Improve Training," *Personnel Administrator* (February 1985): 49–57.

Other, more conventional CMI applications are used to maintain employees' educational records, test scores, and attendance at training sessions. Software packages that perform these functions in a school environment are readily available in microcomputer versions for a few hundred to a few thousand dollars and could easily be adapted for use by companies that do not wish to expend the time and other resources necessary to integrate CMI into the personnel subsystem of their MIS.

Summary

The integrated MIS model portrayed in this text incorporates subsystems for *production, marketing, finance,* and *personnel.* The finance function, which includes accounting, is represented by a subsystem that contains modules for the *budget, cost accounting, funds management, financial accounting, billing, accounts receivable,* and *accounts payable.* The budget module is treated as a part of the finance subsystem, although it overlaps into each of the other functional departments.

Some organizations have specialized information systems called *accounting information systems.* In some cases, accounting information systems perform all or almost all of the functions normally attributed to MIS, but in other cases, they are more specialized. *Tax preparation, investment analysis,* and the management of accounting *consultative services* are specialized applications frequently developed outside the usual MIS boundaries.

The last subsystem of this MIS covers the personnel function. Personnel modules include *labor relations, personnel actions, personnel records, training,* and *payroll.* Specialized information systems in the personnel field deal with *human resource management, behavioral information,* and *computer-based training.*

Like production and marketing subsystems, finance and personnel subsystems retain a management dimension. Strategic planners use finance and personnel subsystems to formulate *goals* and *objectives,* management control is concerned with financial and personnel *resources,* and these subsystems provide information to facilitate operational control over financial and personnel matters.

Assignments

11-1. One of the finance subsystem modules, cost accounting, deals with cost variances. What advantages to cost accounting are realized in an *integrated* MIS over a stand-alone cost accounting software package?

11-2. Not all finance subsystem modules provide *management* information to the same degree. Identify those modules and their outputs that are particularly useful to managers.

11-3. "An accounting firm embraces only one functional area (accounting) and therefore does not need an integrated MIS but is better served by an accounting information system." Do you agree or disagree with this statement? Justify your answer.

11-4. What special difficulties do you think might be encountered in an attempt to integrate the special-purpose application of investment analysis into the funds management module?

11-5. The personnel subsystem has a considerable requirement for external data. Give examples of some external data requirements in personnel and explain how they can be satisfied.

11-6. Automated personnel applications sometimes raise the spectre of Orwell's *1984* Big Brother. Are there any serious threats to individual freedom posed by such systems? If so, how can they be avoided?

11-7. For each functional subsystem described here (Chapters 10 and 11), we have discussed the availability of vendor-supplied software packages. Why could not an organization simply piece together an MIS from these packages and save enormous development costs?

11-8. How could computer-assisted instruction be used in your field of study? Are the considerations for adopting CAI in college any different than those applicable to the training section of a corporate personnel office?

11-9. Are the CMI principles of test analysis applicable to testing in college? Should a college student be forced to repeat all of a failed course if it is a graduation requirement? Should a student be required to repeat failed portions of *passed* courses?

CASE Behavioral Systems, Incorporated

William Simpson and Eugene Nichols are professors at a major midwestern university. Simpson has a PhD. in industrial psychology from the University of Tennessee and Nichols has a PhD. in psychology from the University of Illinois. In 1979, the two conducted a nationwide survey of attitudes in the workplace, which resulted in a number of publications in scholarly journals. Although the recognition for their work was restricted to academic circles initially, Simpson and Nichols soon became known in industry when reprints of their articles were used in workshops and seminars for personnel managers.

The gratification of having the definitive work in a field is rewarding, but Simpson and Nichols felt that there was an income potential beyond an occasional merit raise and promotion to a higher faculty rank—especially since very profitable seminars had been organized around their work by others. Consequently, in 1983, they formed Behavioral Systems, Incorporated (BSI) and offered their services to companies interested in improving worker satisfaction. Their idea was to replicate their survey in individual companies and to analyze the results based on their original work. Each replication added to the data base and helped to ensure the currency of the data. The analysis resulted in a number of computer-generated tables and graphs as well as written recommendations and a briefing to the client.

Simpson and Nichols soon found that the business world is quite different from the academic world. Gone were the graduate assistants, the department secretarial support, and, most important, the university computer center with its extensive software library and professional staff. In addition, they had retained their faculty positions and were having increased difficulty in meeting their obligations to both clients and the university. It was particularly frustrating to know that, although they had designed the computer programs to maintain and analyze the data, the actual coding had been done by university computer service personnel and was no longer available to them for commercial endeavors—even if they had access to a Control Data mainframe such as the one used by the university.

A few successful jobs—analyzed manually and typed by hand—convinced Simpson and Nichols of two things: The potential they envisioned was real, and they needed computer support. They reaffirmed their committment to BSI in response to the first point and drew up the following list of options in response to the second:

1. Purchase their original software from the university and locate a service center to maintain their data base and run their programs on demand.
2. Purchase a microcomputer and recode (or hire someone to recode) the software. Simpson and Nichols believe an IBM PC-XT with a 10-megabyte hard-disk drive and dBase III can handle the data base. As an alternative to recoding the original software, a PC version of SPSS could perform the data analysis if some minor differences in methodology are acceptable.
3. Lease or purchase a minicomputer and hire a consultant—perhaps a colleague from the Information Systems Department in the College of Business and Economics—to develop an integrated information system to handle administrative functions in finance and marketing as well as the operational matters associated with the survey analyses. One of their smaller clients is upgrading and can offer Simpson and Nichols a very good price on a used, data base-oriented IBM System 38. This option would permit either recoding the original software or using a standard statistical package, as in option 2.

Questions

1. List the advantages and disadvantages of each option as you perceive them.
2. Which option would you pursue if you were Simpson and Nichols? Explain the rationale of your choice.
3. What additional problems do you foresee for Simpson and Nichols after they adopt the option you have selected?

Other Readings

Lederer, Albert L. "Planning and Developing a Human Resource Information System." *Personnel Administrator* (August 1984).

Lee, Sang M., and Gary D. Thorp, Jr. *Personnel Management: A Computer-Based System.* New York: Petrocelli, 1978.

Leitch, Robert A., and K. Roscoe Davis. *Accounting Information Systems.* Englewood Cliffs, N.J.: Prentice-Hall, 1983.

Schwade, Stephen. "Is It Time to Consider Computer-Based Training?" *Personnel Administrator* (February 1985).

Wu, Frederick H. *Accounting Information Systems: Theory and Practice.* New York: McGraw-Hill, 1983.

PART V

OFFICE AUTOMATION SYSTEMS

White-collar workers are a major part of our nation's labor force. By 1986 it is estimated that their numbers will be about 55 million and that employers will spend over one billion dollars on their salaries. Because of their numbers and the wages that they earn, these managers, nonmanagerial professionals, and clerical workers have become attractive targets for advances in computer and other computer-related technology.

The introduction of computer technology in the office has not been an overnight phenomenon. Word processing, which improves typing productivity, dates back to the 1960s. However, it was in the 1970s and 1980s that other advances such as electronic and voice mail, teleconferencing, and personal computers began to have a growing impact on how office work is conducted.

Office automation has now progressed to the point where it merits discussion along with transaction processing systems, management information systems, and decision support systems as a related yet unique type of CBIS. In this one-chapter part on office automation systems (OAS), we will explore the impetus for OAS, the various components of OAS, how to plan for and implement OAS, and some of the problems that are holding back further OAS advances.

Chapter 12

The Automated Office

Learning Objectives

After studying this chapter, you will be able to:
1. Describe an automated office.
2. Discuss the impetus for the automated office.
3. Explain planning for and implementing the automated office.
4. Describe word processing.
5. Discuss computer-based communications systems, including electronic mail, voice mail, facsimile, teleconferencing, and telecommuting.
6. Discuss personal computing.
7. Describe micrographics.
8. Describe communications networks in the automated office.
9. Discuss ergonomics.
10. Discuss the relationship of the automated office to other CBIS.
11. Describe office automation at the Continental Illinois Bank.
12. Discuss people in the automated office.
13. Explain the problems of automating the office.
14. Define the following terms:

automated office
prototype
pilot study
production stage
word processing
word wrap
automatic hyphenation
scrolling
search and replace
spelling check
electronic filing
electronic mail

electronic calendars and
   ticklers
voice mail
facsimile
teleconferencing
audio conferencing
audiographic conferencing
video conferencing
computer conferencing
telecommuting
personal computing
professional workstation

micrographics
computer output
   microfilming (COM)
computer-aided retrieval
   (CAR)
protocols
baseband
broadband
server
gateway
local area networks
ergonomics

For many years, office work remained largely the same. Letters were typed and mailed. Documents were filed. Executives traveled to meetings. Decisions were made based on experience and intuition. While many offices still function in these ways, changes are beginning to be seen. For example, documents are increasingly being prepared on word processing equipment. Mail is being sent electronically. Documents are being filed electronically. Meetings are being held via teleconferencing methods. And managers are receiving decision support from personal computers.

Office workers represent a significant portion of the total labor force. Over one third of all workers are employed in offices, and this proportion is growing. And these workers receive about two thirds of the wages that are paid to employees. Because of their number and the wages they receive, office workers have become targets for improved productivity through computer technology.

Changes in the office are being realized through advances in computers, computer-related equipment, and communications technology. Names such as the *automated office*, the *electronic office*, and the *office of the future* are associated with these changes. They connote a new way of doing office work.

Offices are being automated at an uneven pace. Some organizations are moving ahead much faster than others. Some components of the automated office, such as word processing, are being implemented quickly, whereas others, such as voice mail, are just beginning to appear. There can be no doubt, however, that the automated office is going to have a significant impact on office work and the employees who perform it.

The automated office does not appear magically in organizations. Management has important responsibilities for assessing the organization's office automation needs, for planning for the automated office, for evaluating the available office equipment, for seeing the equipment implemented, and for preparing organizational personnel for the inevitable changes that occur. This chapter should help you to prepare for this important managerial role.

A Definition of the Automated Office

What is an automated office? As the term is currently being used, it is many things. It is a new way of preparing documents. It is enhanced communications methods. It is placing the power of the computer in the hands of office workers. It is a new way of filing, storing, and retrieving documents.

Equipment is very much at the heart of the automated office. It includes *word processors* for the preparation, storage, revision, and printing of documents; computer-based communications systems such as *electronic mail*, *voice mail*, *facsimile*, *teleconferencing*, and *telecommuting* for electronic communications; *personal computers* that support the work of office workers; *computer terminals* that give office workers access to electronically filed documents and other forms of support; and *micrographics equipment* for the

TABLE 12-1   The Components of the Automated Office
and Their Major Function

Word processing	Facilitates the preparation of typed documents.
Electronic mail	Allows typed messages to be sent electronically.
Voice mail	Allows spoken messages to be sent electronically.
Facsimile	Allows any document to be sent electronically.
Teleconferencing	Electronically brings conference participants together without travel.
Telecommuting	Allows employees to work at home.
Personal computing	Places computational decision support at workers' fingertips.
Computer terminals	Provides access to electronically filed materials and other components of the automated office.
Micrographics	Stores documents on microfilm for easy retrieval.

efficient filing, storing, and retrieving of documents. Although many of these capabilities can and do exist on a stand-alone basis, increasingly they are becoming part of an integrated system, with the integration being provided by computer technology and communications networks.

For our purposes, the following definition of the automated office is appropriate:

> *An automated office is a multifunction, integrated, computer-based system that allows many office activities to be performed in an electronic mode.*

The components of the automated office and the major function that they serve are summarized in Table 12-1.

The Impetus for the Automated Office

Our nation as a whole has been experiencing a growing awareness of the importance of productivity. Our personal and national wealth and well-being depend on it. We need to be as efficient as possible in transforming inputs into goods and services. One way of accomplishing this objective is by augmenting or replacing human labor with equipment. Over the years, this approach has significantly increased the productivity of blue-collar workers. Until just recently, the average investment in equipment for white-collar workers was less than for their factory counterparts. Consequently, the productivity of office workers increased little. This is now changing as organizations recognize that a higher level of investment can result in productivity gains.

Office automation can result in productivity gains for secretaries, man-

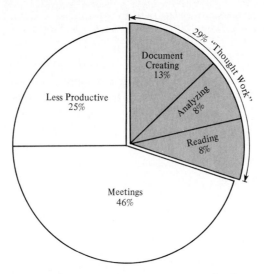

FIGURE 12-1 How managers and other professionals spend their time. (Source: Booz Allen & Hamilton.)

agers, and other professionals. As an illustration of this point, most secretaries and other clerical personnel spend a substantial portion of their time typing and revising documents. It is estimated that a good 60-word-per-minute typist actually produces only 10 to 14 words of finished typing per minute by the time all corrections are made. With the use of a word processor, that figure can be increased to 20 to 30 words per minute—a 100 percent increase in actual productivity.

In a 1980 study, the consulting firm of Booz Allen & Hamilton investigated the potential productivity gains of managers and other professionals from making full use of automated office tools.[1] The study probed the activities, output, working habits, and attitudes of some three hundred professionals in fifteen major U.S. manufacturing, banking, insurance, and government organizations. Figure 12-1 shows how typical knowledge workers spend their time creating documents, analyzing situations, reading, attending meetings, and being involved in less productive activities. The less productive activities include doing clerical tasks, finding and screening the "right information," waiting idle while traveling, expediting previously assigned tasks, and scheduling and organizing work. The study concluded that 15 percent of professionals' time could be saved if office automation systems were fully employed.

[1] "Office Tools Salvage 15% of Users' Time," *Computerworld*, September 29, 1980, SR/2, SR/4.

Planning for and Implementing the Automated Office

A growing number of organizations are benefiting from office automation, but a considerable amount of effort is required in order to receive the benefits. One report on office automation concluded that "the implementation of office automation in most large companies with multiple offices and plants will take 7 to 10 years. This requires a long-range plan and a careful choice of technologies."[2]

Office automation requires top management support and involvement. This group helps provide long-range directional guidance, lends the necessary organizational clout, and allocates the required resources.

Many companies planning for office automation utilize a steering committee. This group oversees the office automation effort. It consists of representatives from the various functional areas of the organization and upper management.

A department within the organization must be assigned the responsibility for office automation. Data processing, word processing, office systems, records management, and information systems are all possible candidates. However, many organizations choose to create a separate office automation department. This approach enhances the likelihood of a well-coordinated office automation effort. Members of the office automation department are normally drawn from other departments. It may also be necessary to hire new employees with specialized skills and experience.

Top management, the steering committee, and the office automation department should work together to create a flexible master plan. This plan should identify what components of the automated office are to be implemented, when, and where in the organization. Some organizations choose to implement the most frequently used components of the automated office first. This strategy might lead to early plans for word processing. Some organizations turn first to those components that will most help upper management, such as electronic mail. There is no single strategy that is best for all organizations. However, the first component should have the potential for being implemented quickly and successfully, so that it will help sustain high morale in the office automation department, generate interest in office automation throughout the organization, and reassure upper management that its decision to back the office automation effort was a good one.

Many organizations utilize a "Three P's" implementation approach: prototype, pilot, and production. *Prototypes* are used in an exploratory manner to assess the strengths and weaknesses of proposed office automation equipment and systems and to make any necessary adjustments. Frequently, they are tested in the office automation department. If initial prototypes prove

[2]Wayne L. Rhodes, Jr., "Office of the Future: Light Years Away?" *Infosystems*, March 1981: 40.

successful, a *pilot study* is conducted. Here the office automation equipment is actually implemented in a portion of the organization. This is the first full-scale test of the equipment with typical users. If reactions to the pilot test are positive, the office automation component enters the *production stage*, and it is implemented throughout the organization as planned. This Three P's approach maintains an inverse ratio of risk to expenditure. Relatively high risk at the outset is counterbalanced by low investment. Only when the risk becomes minimal is a high expenditure made.

We have described in general terms a commonly used approach to planning for and implementing office automation. The details of this process vary from organization to organization. Later in the chapter, you will see how the process was used at the Continental Illinois Bank. First, however, let us explore in greater detail the possible components of an automated office.

Word Processing

Typing is an important activity in most offices. A considerable amount of time and effort goes into preparing letters, reports, tables, proposals, and the like. Most fundamentally, *word processing* is used to improve typing productivity; however, modern word processing systems do even more. Table 12-2 gives several examples of how offices benefit from word processing.

Typing began its movement to word processing in 1964, when IBM introduced the Magnetic Tape/Selectric Typewriter in Germany. This typewriter allowed typists to prepare documents more quickly because errors could be removed easily. All the typist had to do was backspace and then type the correction. Having no name for this capability, the Germans called it *Textverarbeitung*, which loosely translates to "word processing," and the term has continued to be used.

Several years later, IBM's Magnetic Card/Selectric Typewriter was introduced. It allowed one page of text to be stored on a magnetic card about the size of a keypunch card, so that the text could be easily stored, located, and revised.

In the early 1970s, word processors with a visual display (CRT) screen appeared. Then, for the first time, the text of a document could be displayed on a screen and edited and, when correct, could be output by a printer. Initially, these word processors were *stand-alone systems*, in that each unit was self-contained. Later, *shared-resource systems* appeared. With these systems, multiple workstations share resources. Depending on the system, the shared resources might include software, central processor, storage, and printers.

In the mid 1970s, computer manufacturers began offering word process-

TABLE 12-2   Offices That Benefit from Word Processing

Law firms	Word processors type legal documents faster and more accurately. The "stored paragraph" feature of many word processors is ideal for producing standard documents such as wills.
Insurance firms	Word processors are used to quickly type prospect letters, renewal letters, and contract forms.
Medical offices	Medical practices and hospitals find word processors invaluable in preparing appointment letters, billing statements, and insurance applications.
Accounting firms	A word processor, especially one with math capabilities, can quickly and accurately prepare lengthy audit reports and financial statements.
Small businesses	A small business can employ a word processor as a total business system—to speed typing, handle inventory, prepare payroll, and keep the books—while minimizing personnel costs.
Large companies	A central word processor department can do the typing for an entire office, or individual departments can maintain autonomy with their own stand-alone word processors. Software can tailor word processors to suit the needs of accounting, inventory, engineering, or other departments, and communications packages can speed up paperwork flow between departments or offices.

Reprinted from "CPT Takes the Mystery Out of Word Processing," CPT Corporation, Minneapolis, Minnesota, p. 11.

ing software for their machines. This development brought data and word processing together in a single piece of equipment.

Currently, firms seeking a word processing capability have four major options: (1) text editing typewriters; (2) stand-alone display systems; (3) shared-resource systems; and (4) word processing software for micro, mini, and mainframe computers.

Text-Editing Typewriters

Text-editing typewriters, or *electronic typewriters*, as they are sometimes called, generally have fewer storage, editing, and printing capabilities than other word processors. However, they also cost less: Some of them sell for less than $1,000. Figure 12-2 shows the IBM Electronic Typewriter Model 60. Special function keys support the manipulation of textual material. All storage is internal to the typewriter. The typewriter serves as its own output device.

FIGURE 12-2 A text-editing typewriter. (Courtesy of IBM.)

Stand-Alone Display Systems

The next level of word processing capabilities, and also cost, is provided by *stand-alone display systems*. Each work station is self-contained and does not share any of its resources with other word processors. A CRT screen displays messages from the word processor to the user, as well as any text and instructions that are entered by the user. Special function keys facilitate the preparation of textual material. There is external storage, which is most commonly provided by floppy disks. A separate, attached printer is used for output. Figure 12-3 shows the Wangwriter, a stand-alone display system. In addition

FIGURE 12-3   A stand-alone display system. (Courtesy of Wang).

to serving as a word processor, it can be used for personal computing. It also has communications capabilities that support other automated office capabilities, such as electronic mail.

Shared-Resource Systems

The most expensive and sophisticated systems feature multiple workstations that *share resources*. The shared resources may include the central processor, software programs, external storage, and one or more printers. The advantages of a shared-resource system include more storage capacity (perhaps provided by hard disks), more sophisticated software, superior text handling capabilities, job sharing among workstations, and additional input/output options (e.g., Optical Character Reader (OCR) input). Figure 12-4 shows the IBM Displaywriter with keyboard, display screen, diskette unit, and printer. Multiple workstations can share the same printer. All other components are self-contained in such workstations.

Word Processing Software for Micro-, Mini-, and Mainframe Computers

Micro-, mini-, and mainframe computers have most of the component parts of a word processing system: visual display terminals, a central processing unit, storage, and printers. The only missing component is *word processing software*, and this is normally available from either the computer manufacturer or a software vendor. A computer with word processing software tends to have fewer capabilities than a dedicated word processing system because the entire system was not designed with word processing in mind. However, a computer has more flexibility in that word processing software can be easily replaced with software for other applications.

Figure 12-5 shows the IBM Datamaster, which combines data processing and word processing. It can accommodate four workstations, which permits four people to use the system simultaneously.

Word Processing System Capabilities

All word processing systems include input, editing, storage, and output capabilities. The exact nature and sophistication of the capabilities depend on the specific system. We will first describe the capabilities found on most word processors and then several advanced capabilities found on some systems.

Input
Instructions and text are generally input from a keyboard. Many word processors are menu-driven, with each menu requesting information about the application. For example, assume that a typist wants to create a new docu-

FIGURE 12-4 A shared-resource system. (Courtesy of IBM.)

FIGURE 12-5   A microcomputer with optional word processing capabilities. (Courtesy of IBM.)

ment. The first menu might be used to indicate the creation of a new document, the second menu to provide information about the document, and a third menu to format the document.

After the document has been formatted (or a previously defined format has been specified), typing begins. On most systems, a *word-wrap* feature automatically moves the text to the next line as the preceding line is completed. This process speeds up typing, as there is no need to watch (or listen) for the end of a line. Some systems *automatically hyphenate* words when the end of a line is reached. To aid the user, a *cursor*—in the form of a bar of light, a blinking character or symbol, or an underline—is provided. It indicates where in the text the system is pointing. Cursor-control keys allow the user to move the cursor to wherever he or she desires. *Scrolling* is another useful feature. It is the process in which an entire display is moved up and down (vertical scrolling) or right and left (horizontal scrolling). This capability allows the user to look at text that has been entered but is not currently displayed on the screen.

Editing

The editing capability facilitates making changes in documents. A user can *insert* spaces, characters, words, phrases, and blocks of text and can as easily *delete* spaces, characters, words, full and partial lines, paragraphs, and pages. Blocks of text can be marked and, once defined, can be copied, moved, deleted, printed, or placed in storage. *Search and replace* is another powerful editing capability. The user specifies a word or a phrase-length character string to be located by the word processor. For example, the word processor might be instructed to find every reference to a *CDC* 3081. Once these are found, the user can replace the previous character string with another string, such as with *IBM* 3081. Search and replace operations can be performed individually, repeated at the touch of a single key, or performed automatically any number of times.

Storage

Text can be input to a word processor, can be given a name by the user, and can be saved for future revision or output. The document can be stored as one long string, or it can be broken up into individual pages. The word processor automatically determines where to store the text and maintains a directory that includes the name, the location, and the length of each document. Floppy disks (3, 5¼, and 8 inches in diameter), and hard disks are most commonly used as the storage media.

Output

When a document is ready for output, the user formats it by filling in a checklist of formatting options. Page format specifications include right, left, top, and bottom margins; characters per inch; lines per inch; paragraph spacing; and physical page length. The user can request automatic page headings and page numbers printed in any location or alternating between right- and left-hand corners for "book style" arrangements. Right, left and right, and left justification of lines of text are almost universally available, as are line- and page-centering commands.

Word processors provide letter-quality output. Characters can be bold-faced, underlined, shadowed (double-struck), superscripted, subscripted, and printed in a second color by means of a two-color ribbon.

Advanced Capabilities

Advanced capabilities are available in many word processing systems. One feature is a *spelling check*. The word processor checks the spelling of all words typed against a master file of words. When a typed word does not match with a word in the master file, the typed word is highlighted on the display screen. The user can then either change the word or leave it if the spelling is correct. The master file contains predefined, commonly used words and words that are added by the user. This latter feature is helpful for documents that contain names of people or places or jargon unique to a particular profession.

Some word processors also allow *full function math*. The user specifies how calculations are to be performed, and the word processor makes the calculations automatically. This capability is very useful when one is preparing tables.

Some word processors do *basic accounting tasks*, such as payroll, general ledger, accounts receivable and payable, invoicing, and inventory control. This capability may serve all of the data processing needs of a small organization.

Electronic mail, which is discussed in greater detail later in the chapter, is possible on some word processors. A message is entered on one word processor and sent via cable, phone lines, or satellite to another word processor, where it is displayed or printed.

Sophisticated *electronic filing* capabilities are also available in some word processing systems. For example, in addition to filing and retrieving a document by a user-given name, some systems allow a search for documents written by specific authors during specific periods of time and containing specific words.

Computer-Based Communications Systems

It is important for organizational personnel to be able to communicate effectively and efficiently with others. Sometimes the other person is in the next room, and in other instances, the person may be thousands of miles away. Historically, letters, telegrams, phone calls, and meetings have been used for communications. These are important and useful ways of communicating, and they will continue to be so in the future. However, the arrival of the automated office is bringing with it a variety of alternative computer-based communications systems, including electronic mail, voice mail, facsimile, teleconferencing, and telecommuting.

Electronic Mail

The concept of *electronic mail* is quite old. The *telegraph*, which was developed by Samuel Morse in the 1840s, is a form of electronic mail. You may also be familiar with *mailgrams*. They involve an electronic mail system in which Western Union works in conjunction with the U.S. Postal Service to deliver messages quickly. The sender of a mailgram contacts Western Union and arranges to have a message sent. A Western Union operator uses a computer-based system to transmit the message to a post office near the recipient, from which the mailgram is then delivered. *Telex* and *TWX* machines can also be used to send mailgrams. These machines connect directly with a Western Union computer, which routes the message to the recipient.

Although telegrams and mailgrams are examples of electronic mail, there are newer systems that are creating much of the interest in electronic mail. In these systems, a sender uses a computer terminal to enter, store, and transmit a message to a recipient. The recipient, in turn, receives the message at a computer terminal. The advantages of electronic mail include:

1. *Faster communications.* Messages can be received almost as fast as they are entered into a terminal.
2. *Reduced typing and mailing costs.* Many communications no longer need to be typed and mailed.
3. *Streamlined communications.* There is less opportunity for messages to be lost or delayed.
4. *Instant access to messages.* The recipient can receive messages at any time from any connecting terminal.

There are a number of electronic mail systems. Some are extremely large and include many users and computers. For example, ARPANET is a computer network used by managers, scientists, and contractors associated with the U.S. Department of Defense Advanced Research Projects Agency. Currently, ARPANET is used daily by ten thousand people, includes two hundred computers on the network, and features twelve different electronic mail systems. Most electronic mail systems are smaller in scope. Frequently, they feature a single host computer and a network of terminals. The computer system may be especially designed for and dedicated to electronic mail, or more commonly, the electronic mail capability is provided by a software package that has been designed for use on specific computers. Many computer manufacturers and software vendors are now offering electronic mail software packages. Yet another alternative is to use the electronic mail services offered by national time-sharing vendors. These include GTE Telenet's Telemail and Tymnet's On-Tyme. They offer the potential advantages of (1) lower cost because they use their own nationwide networks for transmission; (2) the ability to accommodate many different types of terminals; and (3) the ability to communicate with other subscribers outside a company.

Let us now consider the use of a typical electronic mail system. The sender begins by specifying the recipient(s) of the message by entering a name, a terminal number, and/or a predefined group of users or terminals. For example, the system can be instructed to send the message to all senior-level marketing managers. After the system validates the destinations to ensure that all individuals and terminals can be located, a sending screen is displayed and a message is entered. The sender can then transmit the message immediately and/or store it in an "electronic file drawer." This is a personal storage location maintained on a magnetic disk for the user. Drafts of messages or permanent copies can be filed there. Messages that are sent are placed in the recipients' "electronic mailbox." This, too, is a storage location on a magnetic disk. Recipients can check for messages at their convenience or have them delivered automatically whenever there is a work pause at their terminal. Messages can be retrieved from any terminal that can be connected

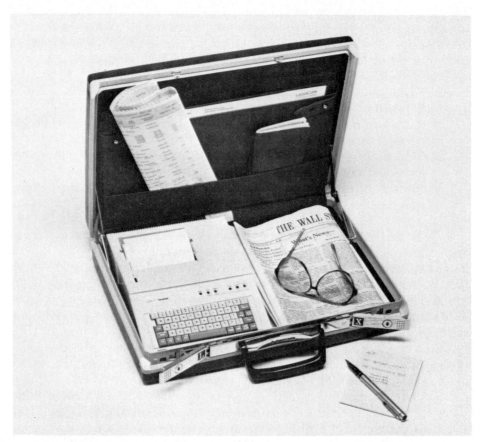

FIGURE 12-6   A portable computer terminal. (Courtesy of Lexicon.)

to the system, including terminals like the small, light LEX-21 portable terminal shown in Figure 12-6. A sender of a message can check at any time to see whether the message has been received.

Another common feature is the creation of archive files. All electronic mailboxes are periodically cleared of all canceled, delivered, and overage messages and are then stored in an archive file that can be accessed if needed. Messages stored in personal electronic file drawers are not affected by this procedure. The system typically also has built-in security features. Messages cannot get lost because they are stored in the computer as soon as they are entered. They are sent only to the specified electronic mailboxes. And they are filed in such a way that only the senders and the intended recipients have access to them.

Some electronic mail systems also include *electronic calendars and ticklers* (reminders) as substitutes for paper calendars, sequentially dated folders, notes on slips of paper, and the like. Electronic calendars are used to schedule daily activities such as meetings, a trip to the dentist, and an undisturbed afternoon for working on the budget. Ticklers are reminders of things that have to be done during the day, such as calling the West Coast office, picking up dinner on the way home, and working on a new promotional brochure. If one wants to place an activity such as a meeting on the calendar, its date, time, place, subject, and the anticipated attenders of the meeting are entered from a terminal. An automatic scheduler feature can be used to advise whether the meeting can be scheduled as requested by checking the other participants' calendars. To view a day's scheduled activities, the user enters the date and all activities for that day are displayed. Reminders in the tickler system are stored in electronic files until the specified date, when they are automatically displayed at the user's terminal.

Voice Mail

Telephones play an important role in our personal and professional lives. Unfortunately, however, especially in a business setting, a variety of problems tend to be associated with the use of telephones.

1. *Telephone tag.* The person called is not in, and a message is left to return the call. When the call is returned, the original caller may not be in.
2. *Interruptions.* The person called may be busy but takes the call as a courtesy to the calling party.
3. *Incomplete information exchange.* Because the person called is interrupted or is not prepared for the call, important information is miscommunicated or left out.
4. *Late information or lost opportunity.* When there is difficulty in completing a call, the information communicated may be received too late for full and effective use.
5. *Unproductive social exchange.* Because of social customs and habits, calls of a factual nature are often punctuated with obligatory chitchat.

Voice mail in the automated office is a flexible means of sending a spoken message. The caller talks into a telephone, and the message is stored and is communicated later to the recipient's voice mailbox. The recipient, at his or her choosing, can listen to the message, stop playing it if interrupted, skip ahead or back, or replay the message at will. Even if there is a need for a two-way exchange of information, voice mail can be helpful. For example, it can be used to schedule a telephone conversation and to set the agenda. Then, when the telephone conversation takes place, both parties are prepared and willing to give their full attention.

The power of a voice mail system is in its ability to relay commands to the voice mail computer. This is done through the standard twelve keys on a Touch-Tone phone. The keys generate tones that the computer interprets. Most systems have some kind of voice prompting to explain to the user which

FIGURE 12-7   A voice mail system. (Courtesy of Wang.)

key or keys should be pushed next. Many systems have a plastic template that fits neatly over the keyboard and explains the functions of each key. Using the keys, the user can record a message, listen to the message before transmitting it, change the message, and send it to one or more recipients, or even to a predefined group of people.

A growing number of companies are offering voice mail systems. Figure 12-7 shows a manager using the Wang Audio Workstation. The system allows a user to dictate, review, edit, and send voice messages.

Facsimile

Facsimile (or *fax*) equipment is for the electronic transmission of copies of documents from one location to another. It can be used to send photographs, charts, and even signatures, as well as text and data. At the sending end, there is a facsimile transceiver that scans the documents and converts the visual images into electronic signals. These images are then communicated via telephone lines to their destination, where a receiving unit decodes the information and prints out a copy (facsimile) of the original.

Facsimile equipment offers several advantages. First, it is very *accurate*. Whatever is sent and received is an exact copy of the original. Because the originals are kept by the sender, there is no danger of their being lost. Facsimile equipment is very *flexible*. It is possible to send and receive anything that is typed, handwritten, printed, or drawn. Facsimile transmissions can be very *confidential*. There is no need for a third party to be involved in either entering, transmitting, or receiving the document. And finally, facsimile equipment involves *simple installation and training*. It can be located anywhere a telephone and electrical output are available, and very little user training is required for equipment operation.

Both analog and digital facsimile equipment is currently being used. In an analog system, everything on a document is "read." Four to six minutes are required to read a single page. Digital systems read only images, eliminating white spaces. They are faster, being able to read an average 250-word business letter in about half a minute.

At the present time, facsimile is used primarily for intracompany communications. However, this is changing. A major reason for this change is that industry leaders have agreed on standards that make facsimile terminals compatible worldwide. This compatibility is leading to an increase in the use of facsimile for intercompany communications.

Figure 12-8 shows the Xerox Telecopier 495. It features digital compression to provide fast transmission rates, automatic document feed, automatic receiving of documents without operator intervention, and automatic transmission of documents to predefined locations at predefined times.

Teleconferencing

The time, difficulty, and cost of travel have continued to grow. Business travelers are experiencing less convenient airline schedules, increasing plane and ground transportation fares, and climbing hotel rates and meal costs. As a consequence, many organizations are using or considering alternatives to usual business travel. These alternatives, which eliminate the need for the physical movement of personnel to one common spot for the exchange of information, are collectively known as *electronic meetings* or *teleconferencing*. It exists whenever two or more people are communicating electronically from different locations. Current teleconferencing alternatives include audio conferencing, audiographic conferencing, video conferencing, and computer conferencing.

In *audio conferencing*, there is only voice communications. This is the familiar "conference call" concept. It can employ a variety of types of telephone equipment: individuals each using a standard telephone headset; large groups using special equipment that levels the voice volumes of all the people

FIGURE 12-8   A facsimile terminal. (Courtesy of Xerox.)

in the group; small groups using speakerphones; or specially equipped tele-conferencing rooms.

Figure 12-9 shows a Darome Conveners. It is a portable audio teleconferencing system that can be used anywhere that there is a telephone. Microphones pick up the words spoken by the participants in the meeting, and these words are transmitted to other meeting rooms, where they are amplified so that all can hear.

Audiographic conferencing combines audio transmissions with graphics capabilities, such as graphic display, facsimile, or freeze-frame (also called *slow-scan*) video, in which the image changes only once every few seconds. The graphics capability may allow conference participants to send or receive documents, view documents, and see one another.

Video conferencing uses two-way, full-motion video combined with two-way audio for a simulation of a face-to-face meeting. It is the most expensive of the teleconferencing methods because of the cost of the image and sound transmission system.

FIGURE 12-9 An audio conferencing system. (Courtesy of Darome.)

Video conferencing has not found wide acceptance in the business community. One reason for this is cost. Consider AT&T's Picturephone Meeting Service, which was recently dropped as a service. It was a network of public and private camera-equipped conference rooms providing two-way pictures and sound. Using public Picturephone rooms on each end, one hour cost $2,380 from New York to Los Angeles and $1,660 from New York to Washington. Using its own rooms, a company could cut that cost roughly in half, but private Picturephone rooms cost $117,000 to install and $11,000 a month to maintain, over and above transmission costs. Another problem is that video conferencing is not as rich an experience as being there in person. There is little opportunity for off-the-record conversations. It is not possible to get nonverbal reactions from people off-camera. Most people and organizations are not very skilled and experienced in video conferencing. We expect Dan Rather-type performances and get something far less. And finally, many executives do not mind travel, feel that it is important to meet in person with people, and believe that a broader perspective can be maintained by visiting regional locations. Despite the problems of video conferencing, however, it has current and future potential, especially as people and organizations learn how and when to use it.

Computer conferencing uses the computer to facilitate communications. Parties to the conference enter messages from a terminal that either are sent directly to one or more locations or are centrally stored for later access. The computer can also perform tasks such as keeping each participant up to date on messages since he or she last used the system, maintaining a transcript of the ongoing conference, providing voting capabilities, and so on. This approach to teleconferencing is relatively inexpensive, provides the opportunity for a hard copy of all discussion inputs, and allows the participants more time to prepare their contributions to the discussion.

Telecommunications are more appropriate for some types of meetings than for others. They are best used when the meetings are low in conflict and when the participants know one another. This is often the case with training sessions, ad hoc problem solving, policy dissemination, and emergency meetings. In general, telecommunications are less appropriate for first meetings, sales calls, delicate negotiations, the replacement of tours, or the signing of documents.

Telecommuting

For some people, commuting to a central office poses a variety of problems: It can be costly and time-consuming; it tends to limit where people can live; it can hinder the ability of women to combine family and career; and it can reduce the ability of handicapped people to find work. Some companies, such as Control Data Corporation, Digital Equipment Corporation, Data General Corporation, and the Continental Illinois Bank, are allowing selected employees to work from their homes using computer terminals. This mode of work is referred to as *telecommuting*. Telecommunications are used to replace commuting to work.

Telecommuting is not appropriate for all types of jobs and all people. Currently, most telecommuting is performed by people whose primary job is to move, manipulate, and/or transform information in some way. These include word processing operators, programmers, systems analysts, systems designers, and some types of researchers.

Telecommuting is not likely to become widespread even if the job allows it. Most people need and enjoy the personal contact provided by the work place. This sentiment is borne out by a study of over 700 knowledge workers conducted by the Honeywell Corporation.[3] The study found that only 7 percent of the workers would choose to work exclusively at home, 36 percent would work half at home and half at the office, and an overwhelming 56 percent said that they would go to the office every day even if it was not necessary.

Personal Computing

Microcomputers such as the IBM PC shown in Figure 12-10 have allowed office workers to gain direct control over a powerful computer resource. Easy-to-use microcomputers and supporting software have helped spawn a large group of first-time computer users who are increasingly developing their own computer applications. The major reason that managers and professionals are obtaining personal computers is to improve their productivity. White-collar workers are using microcomputers for a variety of applications,

FIGURE 12-10   A personal computer. (Courtesy of IBM.)

[3] Lee White, "You *Can* Get There from Here—OA Survey Shows How," *Computerworld Focus*, February 6, 1985: 26.

including preparing budgets, maintaining sales data, and evaluating production plans. Personal computers provide this support at an affordable price.

It should be recognized that not all managers want a personal computer. Some managers have been successful in the past without one and feel that they do not need a computer. For some managers, this is probably true. Other managers probably have less valid reasons. They may not be willing to commit themselves to the time and effort required to learn to use a computer. Even a lack of typing skills may be an obstacle. As one manager candidly admitted, "I don't want to look like a jerk!"

When microcomputers first became available, many data processing managers were less than enthusiastic about their introduction into the organization. Some of their concerns were more emotional than rational. They saw the personal computer as decreasing their power and control and acting as a drain on the dollars available for centralized computing. However, they also had a number of legitimate concerns. They worried about incompatible hardware and software, multiple maintenance contracts, data integrity and security, documentation for end-user-developed applications, providing users access to mainframe data, and training end users.

Despite the obstacles, the desire by office workers to have access to microcomputers was a force that could not be denied. Today, data processing managers still worry about the problems associated with personal computers, but they recognize that microcomputers have forever changed how computing is performed in organizations, and they have taken steps to bring the problems under better control. For example, many organizations now have an approved list of personal computers and software from which any purchase must be made. This has helped control incompatibility, maintenance, and training problems. Most large organizations now have information centers (discussed in Chapter 19) where users can go for help in developing their applications.

Chapters 4 and 5 provide comprehensive descriptions of personal computer hardware and software. A problem with these descriptions is that they become dated very quickly. Every year, personal computers become faster, have more memory, have better software, and cost less for the capabilities provided. There is a particular trend, however, that is less obvious and needs to be discussed in the context of the automated office.

An important development is the evolution of the personal computer as the hub of what is referred to as the *professional, executive,* or *universal workstation*. This workstation increasingly serves as a single place for a variety of automated office capabilities. Office workers can use the workstation for tasks such as word processing, electronic filing, electronic calendars, electronic mail, voice mail, document transmisssion, and personal computing. Let us consider just one example of the usefulness of an integrated set of capabilities. At the start of the day, a West coast manager arrives at work, to find an electronic mail message about a problem that has occurred on the East coast. The manager reads the message, adds a voice mail message, and sends it to an assistant to follow up on the problem. Before the day is done, the assistant has sent an electronic mail problem solution to the East coast. In arriving at the problem solution, the assistant used the computing capabilities of the professional workstation. The message was created using the workstation's word processing capabilities. By the end of the 1980s, easy-to-use professional workstations with integrated capabilities like the ones used in the example should be a reality in many organizations.

Micrographics

Some offices need to file, maintain, and retrieve large quantities of textual and graphic information. When the system for doing this involves paper documents, there are a number of problems:

1. *Cost.* It is expensive to file, maintain, and retrieve paper documents.
2. *Time.* It is time consuming to file and retrieve paper documents.
3. *Space.* Maintaining paper documents in filing cabinets requires considerable space.
4. *Errors.* Paper documents are easily lost, misplaced, or misfiled.
5. *Portability.* Paper documents are not easily moved from one place to another.
6. *Protection.* It is difficult to protect paper documents from illegal access or disasters such as fires and floods.

In some offices, *micrographics* provides a solution to these problems. It involves the use of microfilm for the capture, maintenance, retrieval, and display of textual and graphic materials.

A camera is used to capture a document on microfilm. The camera may film the hard-copy source document, or it may be part of a *computer output microfilming* (COM) system. In a COM system, computerized information is filmed without the generation of a hard-copy source document. Normally, this is accomplished by outputting the document on magnetic tape, displaying it on a high-resolution CRT, and photographing the document with a built-in camera.

Microfilmed materials are maintained either on rolls of film or as *microfiche*. With microfiche, the filmed information is recorded on separate 4" by 6" sheets.

Conventional retrieval systems have external indices for locating microfilmed documents. The user consults the index, inserts the microfilm roll or microfiche in a display unit, and views the document. In more advanced systems, *computer-aided retrieval* (CAR) is employed. In these systems, an index is maintained internally by a computer, and CAR provides the users with either partial or total retrieval assistance. In a partial retrieval system, the computer identifies where the document is located, and the user must then select and manually insert the microfilm roll or microfiche in the display

FIGURE 12-11   A micrographics system. (Courtesy of Minolta.)

unit. In a fully automatic system, the desired document is retrieved and displayed with no human intervention. Such a system is another example of electronic filing in the automated office.

Figure 12-11 shows the Minolta Automatic Retrieval System. It is used with microfilm rolls and provides computer-aided retrieval. Documents can be automatically searched out, retrieved, and printed.

Communications Networks in the Automated Office

Many office products were originally developed as stand-alone pieces of equipment. Many of the advantages of office automation, however, are realized only when the various pieces are able to communicate with one another. For example, there are instances when it is useful for a personal computer to be able to access data from a mainframe computer or to send files to another personal computer. While considerable progress is being made in connecting various office products, an accepted, comprehensive solution is still not here.

Solutions to portions of the communications problem are available in different forms. Some of the solutions, such as telephone systems, have been used for many years. Using private automatic branch exchanges (PABXs), messages are routed over telephone lines between senders and receivers. The telephone system is also being used increasingly to transmit data and images as well as voice messages. The data is coded by the sending device for transmission over telephone lines and then decoded by the receiving device. Facsimile works in this way. One of the reasons that facsimile has been broadly successful is because vendors of facsimile products have agreed on communications protocols or standards that allow various vendors' products to easily communicate with one another. *Protocols* are technical customs or guidelines that govern the exchange of signal transmission and reception between equipment. Each protocol specifies the exact order in which signals will be transferred, what signal will indicate that the opposite device has completed its transfer, and so forth. Currently there are no widely accepted communications standards for all office equipment, but IBM's approaches often serve as *de facto* standards because of its dominance in the market-place.

The telephone system cannot be used to connect all office equipment. It provides only a *baseband* communications capacity. Some office automation technologies, such as teleconferencing, require a *broadband* network. With broadband technology, the cable is divided into separate channels, with each channel acting as a separate line. This added capacity allows much more information to be communicated.

Currently there is considerable interest in being able to network personal computers. This not only allows personal computers to communicate but also permits them to share resources such as hard disk storage and printers. In order to share resources, it is necessary to include computers that act as *servers*. These can be either some of the existing personal computers or dedicated servers. *File servers* allow hard disk storage to be shared. *Print servers* permit the sharing of printers. *Communications servers* allow the personal computers in the network to communicate outside the network by acting as a *gateway* to other networks. Often, a single computer serves as a file, print, and communications server. Dozens of vendors offer systems for networking personal computers. IBM's PC Network is a broadband network for IBM PCs that moves data over a coaxial cable at 2M bits per second. It is a popular network because of the large number of IBM PCs that are installed.

Networks that connect a number of devices in a limited geographical area such as a building are referred to as a *local area network*. Figure 12-12 illustrates a local area network (LAN) that connects a wide variety of office products. Most LANs do not currently connect this many different types of

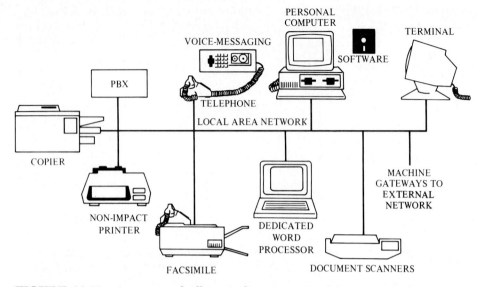

FIGURE 12-12 A variety of office products connected by a local area network. [Source: Jerry Borrell, "Strategy Debates Cloud Office Automation," *Mini-Micro Systems* (May 1985), p. 137.]

equipment. In fact, a network that connects only PCs can be referred to as a local area network.

Three important local area networks are Ethernet, offered by Xerox; Wangnet, offered by Wang; and DECnet, offered by Digital Equipment Corporation. Each requires a special coaxial cable in the building or buildings that it serves. Any office equipment that is designed for either Ethernet, Wangnet, or DECnet can be connected to the appropriate network. IBM is expected to introduce its comprehensive local area network product in 1987.

Offices typically need to communicate outside a limited geographical area. The telephone system is often used for voice messages, communicating low volumes of data, and for other types of baseband communications. Microwave and satellite-based communications are popular alternatives for other types of communications.

Ergonomics

Ergonomics is a term that is frequently heard when the automated office is discussed. It refers to the physiological interaction between humans and machines. With more and more office workers using office automation equipment, there is a growing awareness of the importance of designing equipment that is comfortable and easy to use.

A major focus of ergonomics has been on the *physical* design of CRT-

FIGURE 12-13 Ergonomically designed office furniture. (Courtesy of BIOTEC systems.)

based workstations. More than one secretary has complained, "My shoulders are sore, my back is killing me, and I've been staring at the tube so long my eyes won't focus right." Because of complaints like this, workstations are now being designed with the user more in mind. Some of the new features include height adjustment for both keyboard and display screen, and an adjustable chair with good back support. Figure 12-13 shows office furniture that has been ergonomically designed for a CRT-based workstation.

The *mental* aspects of man–machine interaction are also a concern of ergonomics, even though they have not received as much attention as the physical aspects. It is important to design office systems that minimize errors, mental fatigue, confusion, loss of patience, and frustration. For example, systems should be designed so that proficient users are given ways to bypass certain executional steps that may be needed by novices or casual users.

A number of concerns about CRT-based workstations have been raised by groups such as 9 to 5, the National Association of Working Women. Of particular importance is whether the low levels of radiation emitted by CRTs increase the likelihood of miscarriages and other reproductive problems. While many women in CRT environments believe this to be true, it has not been substantiated by current research studies. However, more long-term research will be needed before the issue is resolved.

There is no doubt that some CRT users experience high levels of stress.

One study by NIOSH (the National Institute for Occupational Safety and Health) found that full-time CRT operators had the highest stress levels among workers—more stress than air-traffic controllers. One reason for this is that the computer can monitor every keystroke, like an electronic supervisor standing beside the worker all day with a stopwatch. Rebecca Alford, a CRT operator with the Equitable Life Assurance Society, described it this way at a House Health and Safety Subcommittee hearing: "Electronic monitoring is one of the most pernicious aspects of our jobs. . . . We clock in at 7 A.M. and from then until the end of the day the visual display terminal is counting every keystroke. Managers have a complete readout from which productivity is determined and then averaged with subjective factors such as attitude to determine our rate of pay."[4]

In response to these potential problems with office automation equipment and systems, managers must select equipment that is comfortable to use, emphasize the design of systems that minimize frustration and stress, and monitor and respond to potential long-term health problems caused by office automation equipment.

The Relationship of the Automated Office to Other CBIS

In the beginning, there was little relationship between office automation and other computer-based information systems. Early office automation products, such as text editing typewriters and facsimile equipment, affected only clerical tasks in the office. In general, these tasks were unrelated to either TPS, MIS or DSS. Although this is still the case in most organizations, this situation is slowly changing and should continue to do so. A major reason for this change is that office automation products are being introduced for managers and professionals. Some of these products, such as personal computers, serve a complementary role to MIS and DSS. Consequently, there is a blending of certain aspects of office automation with TPS, MIS, and DSS.

Office automation is beginning to affect transaction processing in some organizations, especially in regard to word processors. In addition to helping prepare the documents that are associated with many transaction processing applications (e.g., preparing letters to customers who are overdue in paying their accounts), word processors are being used to perform entire transaction processing applications. This is not a surprising development because many word processors are basically microcomputers and can consequently be used for computational purposes. All that has been needed have been transaction processing software packages, and they are now becoming available. Of course, most organizations will not be doing their data processing on word

---

[4]"Are VDT's Health Hazards?" *Newsweek*, October 29, 1984: 123.

processors. Such use will be associated with very small firms that have limited transaction processing requirements and that do not have computerized transaction processing systems already in place.

An MIS has been characterized as being the most encompassing of CBIS. It includes transaction processing; structured information flows, especially in regard to supporting planning and controlling functions; decision support, especially through the ability to query a data base; and management science models to support decision-making tasks that tend to be structured and repetitive. In the 1970s, with the advent of terminals connecting to mainframe computers and the emergence of distributed minicomputer systems, managers and professionals received readily available MIS support in the office: corporate files could be searched for needed information; applications programs could be run; and reports for planning and controlling purposes could be generated.

Office automation equipment has extended and enhanced the possibility of MIS-type support. Of primary importance has been the personal computer. It can be used to provide more custom-tailored MIS support. Managers and professionals can develop programs and data that are especially appropriate for their organizational responsibilities. In the future, personal computers will be able to communicate better with other computers and data bases. This development will allow even more comprehensive decision support.

Office automation equipment can provide office workers with better access to documents, messages, and data through the concept of electronic filing: documents can be electronically filed by word processors; messages can be electronically filed in voice and electronic mail systems; and data can be electronically stored by personal computers.

Decision support systems are another type of CBIS, and they are discussed in the next three chapters of the book. At this point, it is appropriate to say only that they are user-initiated systems that make use of models, data, and sophisticated software interfaces to provide support for semistructured and unstructured decision-making tasks. Their primary relationship to office automation is through personal computers. Software products are available that facilitate the development of decision support systems on personal computers.

Office Automation at the Continental Illinois Bank

Now that we have discussed the possible components of office automation, it seems appropriate to describe how one large organization went about putting various components in place. The organization described is the Continental Illinois National Bank and Trust Company of Chicago, which in 1977 committed itself to the creation of an integrated automated office.[5] The impetus for the commitment was the realization that an unacceptable amount of managerial, staff, and clerical time and effort was going into the collection, processing, preparation, and dissemination of information.

In planning for office automation, Continental focused its attention on three categories of office work: text preparation and communication, acquisition of information, and voice communication. The office automation system was designed to meet the needs of organizational personnel in all three areas. It was also decided that a central library, a computerized stronghold of virtually every byte of data that had been captured and stored, would be placed on-line in the bank's mainframe computer and would be available to the automated office system components. Management also wanted a system in which any of the components could be used by someone with access to a terminal and a telephone. And finally, they wanted a system that utilized existing technology rather than waiting for products that were still on the drawing board to become available. The office automation system that evolved over the next three years contained four major components: word processing and remote dictation, electronic mail, an instantaneous retrieval and information system, and voice mail.

Word Processing and Remote Dictation

The first component put in place was word processing centers to support various work centers. Although these centers increased productivity, the turnaround times on text preparation were found to be highly related to the managers' proximity to the word processing center. Consequently, remote telephone-dictation facilities were established so that managers could use their telephones as dictation machines. This capability allowed managers at their desks, at the airport, or in a hotel room thousands of miles away to have text prepared.

Continental opened a satellite word processing center about twenty-five miles from downtown Chicago at a community college. One purpose of the center was to teach students how to operate various pieces of word processing equipment. When the center is not being used for teaching purposes, some of the students work for Continental, using the word processing skills they have acquired. The satellite word processing center has also been an experiment on whether selected support functions, such as word processing, can be located away from the main place of business. The preliminary findings indicate that this is indeed feasible, and perhaps even desirable, given the number of people who cannot or do not wish to travel to a downtown office.

---

[5]This description is based on Louis H. Mertes, "Doing Your Office Over— Electronically," *Harvard Business Review*, March–April 1981: 127–135, and an interview that Ann Dooley had with Douglas Bott, vice-president of information systems at Continental, which appeared in "A User's Perspective," *Computerworld OA*, June 23, 1982: 16–20.

Electronic Mail

In late 1977, the electronic mail system was begun. One of its features is the central library, which offers users a single depository for all communications. No longer is it necessary to archive certain types of paper documents. The system also includes a limited text editing function, which can be used to edit messages before sending them out. A multiple addressing capability makes it possible to send messages to a predefined list of recipients, such as "senior managers." Bank officers who are out of town can communicate with others in the system as long as they take along a portable terminal and have access to a telephone. From the early prototype systems, electronic mail has now grown to where it serves about five thousand users, who are predominantly professionals and managers.

Instantaneous Information Retrieval System

The instantaneous information retrieval system (IRIS) was developed to give users a simple means of drawing on vast amounts of data and text. Considerable flexibility already existed for drawing on data held in traditional data processing files. However, there was no general-purpose text and data file system that could handle requests in plain English. IRIS was designed to serve this purpose.

Over time, more and more text and data have been entered into IRIS. For example, customer data are easily accessed. It is easy to determine whether a check has been presented for payment. The bank's commercial lending department can obtain up-to-date interest rate quotations on various financial instruments such as treasury bills.

Currently, there are about four thousand authorized IRIS users, more than 120 data bases, with over twenty billion characters of data on file in the central library. Users operate more than eight hundred IRIS terminals, located throughout Continental's worldwide organization. Access to IRIS is not limited to the confines of Continental's offices; it extends to any authorized user with a portable terminal and a telephone.

Voice Mail

In 1978, Continental decided to add a voice mail capability. Rather than waiting for some of the products that were being developed to become commercially available (products with the capabilities described previously in this chapter), management decided to add ordinary telephone answering devices in the offices of Continental personnel who receive many calls each day. Some interesting findings emerged from Continental's experience. The first was the validation of the telephone tag problem. It was discovered that answering machines intercept 65 percent of the incoming calls, whereas the recipient handles only 35 percent. It was also discovered that although at first bank employees confronted with a recorded message often felt inclined to hang up, as time went on an increasing number began leaving short messages, and finally, they left longer, more complete messages. Today, more than three hundred telephone answering devices are being used at Continental. It is even possible for a user with a pocket-sized signaling device to call his or her answering machine to get messages that have come into the office.

People in the Automated Office

Automated office equipment has the potential for increasing office productivity; however, it must always be remembered that *people* are the most important part of any office system. Consequently, management must ensure that office automation will be accepted and used effectively by office employees in order for the desired productivity gains to be realized.

The introduction of office automation equipment results in change. There are changes in job functions, as well as work procedures, schedules, and environments. In some instances, these changes are welcomed. For example, many managers have purchased personal computers on their own initiative. In other instances, change is resisted. For example, a manager may still prefer to give dictation rather than using an electronic or voice mail system. Some resistance to change should be anticipated, and steps should be taken to minimize its effects.

Many companies have been very successful in handling potential user resistance. Jack Hammond of Market Wholesale Grocery Company has observed, "There are no tricks involved in getting people to accept advanced office technology. All you need is good communication."[6] This communication can take various forms. At Sunkist Growers, quality circles are held weekly to identify problems related to office automation and to discuss possible solutions. A major wholesaling firm has a public relations campaign that emphasizes the benefits, to the employees as well as to the company, of office automation.

Education has been a key to user acceptance in many firms. The Irving Trust Company has training programs that are designed to support particular office automation efforts. General Electric has a continuing series of training programs designed to familiarize people with advanced office systems. GE also has monthly roundtable discussions with users and publishes a newsletter that explains new systems and applications.

A key finding of behavioral research is that participative organizations not only motivate their members more effectively but also excel in achieving organizational goals.[7] In regard to office automation, this participation can be

[6]"A Business Puzzle—Today's Managers," *Today's Office*, January 1982: 40.

[7]James W. Driscoll, "People and the Automated Office," *Datamation*, November 1979: 106–112.

realized in a variety of ways, as a few examples will illustrate. One possibility is to allow the users to participate in the selection and implementation of the system. In the Department of Management at the University of Georgia, several different word processing systems were used on a trial basis. The departmental secretaries' evaluation of the systems was an important input to the final selection decision.

Though electronic mail systems are implemented to aid formal communications, users can be encouraged to use them for informal communications. It has been noted that in successful electronic mail systems, users have developed informal distribution lists to notify each other of social events and gossip. If employees are encouraged to use a new electronic mail system for informal as well as formal communications, potential resistance can be minimized.

Typists placed in a word processing center can become frustrated because of the physical and social distance between them and the originators of the materials to be typed. A number of successful word processing centers have overcome this frustration by encouraging face-to-face contact between the creators of the materials to be typed and the operators of the word processing equipment.

New groups do not typically work together well. It takes time for group members to answer such questions as: "Who's in charge here?" "What's in it for me?" and "What do people expect from me in this group?" Answering questions such as these and resolving other group problems and concerns are normally best achieved on a face-to-face basis. This characteristic of new groups has implications for teleconferencing. A new group should probably not use teleconferencing for its first session. Teleconferencing should be used only after the initial difficult social issues have been resolved.

Problems of Automating the Office

Despite all that has been written about the automated office and its potential for improving the productivity of white-collar workers, only a small cadre of leading-edge users—such as Atlantic Richfield, Aetna, Avon Products, and some branches of government, such as the Department of Transportation—have seriously committed themselves to automating the office. Other firms are holding back, moving at a slower pace, until more of the problems are worked out. The resolution of these problems will involve a combination of time enough to understand and assimilate the new technology that has come into the marketplace, a better understanding of the impact of office automation, new attitudes on the part of white-collar workers toward office automation equipment, and the ability to integrate the components of the automated office more easily.[8]

[8]These problems are discussed in Bro Uttal, "What's Detaining the Office of the Future," *Fortune*, May 3, 1982: 176–196.

So many new products are being introduced every month that it is not surprising that firms are confused about which products to purchase and which vendors to buy from. Within a thirty-day period in late 1981, Digital Equipment, Hewlett-Packard, and Data General all launched new office automation systems. A Hewlett-Packard manager joked, "So many companies have thrown their hats into the ring that the hats are landing on top of each other." Vendors often do not help the situation. As one information systems manager has said, "Watch out, vendors are there for one reason and one reason only. They are there to sell. They will sell as much as the floor will bear without collapsing."[9] Many managers feel that office automation decisions will be clearer after some shakeout in the marketplace has occurred.

Despite the claim of higher productivity through office automation, there are few hard data to support this contention. Unlike in a factory, where the effect of the substitution of machinery for human labor is readily apparent and easily measured, in the office the impact is less obvious and more difficult to measure. Office automation tends to reorganize the way that work is done and to impact the effectiveness of workers in the organization. Many managers are waiting to see whether office automation equipment justifies its cost in other organizations.

In 1982, it was estimated that about 500,000 secretaries had a word processor and that about as many more did enough typing to be logical prospects for getting one. Once trained on a word processor, secretaries tend to be lifelong converts. Managers and professionals, on the other hand, account for about 80 percent of white-collar salaries and have been less willing to accept and use office automation equipment. There are a variety of reasons for this: beliefs that using a keyboard is a clerical task; complicated-looking keyboards; embarrassment over poor typing skills; and fears of loss of status. Vendors are working hard on products that managers and professionals will feel comfortable using.

Related to managerial and professional resistance to employing automated office equipment is the difficulty of specifying exactly what steps managers and professionals go through in doing their jobs. Despite years of study, there is still much to learn about the nature of managerial work so that products that best meet the needs of managers can be developed. Vendors recognize this need and are actively investigating this area. Xerox is well along in this endeavor, thanks to over nine thousand man-years of experiments. Their studies have identified four major "professional" activities: the communication of data and ideas that are still in a pliable state and being worked on by groups of professionals; the creation of documents; the filing and retrieval of documents; and the distribution of written work. From investigations such as Xerox's, products should emerge that have greater appeal to upper-echelon workers.

Though integrating the components of an automated office is a desirable goal, the industry as a whole still has a way to go in realizing this goal. So far,

---

[9]Rhodes, p. 41.

equipment manufacturers have left users hanging—unable to communicate with other vendors' machines and sometimes within their own product lines. This condition is often referred to as a Tower of Babel because each vendor's products speak (communicate) in their own tongue. Because the advantages of having components of an automated office that are able to speak to one another are so great, some firms are hesitant to commit themselves to products that cannot guarantee this integration.

There are problems to be overcome before the fully automated office is realized in many firms. As we have seen, steps are being taken to eliminate or reduce the problems. The potential benefits for vendors and users alike are so great that we can count on substantial progress in the future.

Summary

Changes are taking place in how office work is conducted because of advances in computers, computer-related equipment, and communications technology. This new office environment is often referred to as the *automated office,* the *electronic office,* or the *office of the future.*

The automated office can be defined as a multifunction, integrated, computer-based system that allows many office activities to be performed in an electronic mode. It includes word processing, electronic mail, voice mail, facsimile, teleconferencing, telecommuting, personal computing, electronic filing, and micrographics.

Our nation is experiencing a growing awareness of the importance of productivity. Because of the increasing number of office workers and the potential for increased productivity in the office, it is not surprising that the automated office is receiving so much attention.

A considerable amount of time and effort is required in planning for and implementing an automated office. It calls for contributions from top management, steering committees, office automation specialists, and office workers. Components of the automated office are often implemented by means of the Three P's approach: prototype, pilot, and production.

Most fundamentally, word processing is used to improve typing productivity. With word processing equipment, it is relatively easy to enter, store, revise, and later print textual materials. Word processing capabilities are provided by text editing typewriters, stand-alone display systems, shared-resources systems, and word processing software for micro-, mini-, and mainframe computers.

Computer-based communications systems such as electronic mail, voice mail, facsimile, teleconferencing, and telecommuting are changing how office workers communicate. In electronic mail systems, a sender uses a computer terminal to enter, store, and transmit a message to a recipient. In a voice mail system, a caller talks into a telephone, and the message is stored and is communicated to the recipient's voice mailbox, where it is later heard by the recipient. Facsimile is used for the electronic transmission of copies of documents from one location to another. Teleconferencing is used to bring people together electronically without the cost, time, and inconvenience of travel. Telecommuting allows employees to do their work at home.

Personal computers are appearing on the desks of a growing number of executives. They are being used to provide personal decision support. Despite the potential value of personal computers, there are concerns about compatibility, data base, and security issues.

Micrographics has potential value, especially in offices that need to file, maintain, and retrieve large quantities of textual and graphic materials. Microfilm is used for this purpose.

A communications network is required to tie the various components of an automated office together. Many executives are experiencing difficulties in selecting the approaches that are best for their organization.

Office automation equipment is now being designed with greater attention to ergonomics. This attention is making office automation equipment more comfortable and easier to use.

Initially, office automation was largely unrelated to other CBIS activities. However, this is changing rapidly.

One organization that has moved aggressively into office automation is the Continental Illinois Bank. Since 1977, it has implemented word processing and remote dictation, electronic mail, an instantaneous information retrieval system, and voice mail.

Although office automation has the potential to increase white-collar productivity, it should be kept in mind that people are the most important element of any office system. Consequently, any movement toward office automation should consider the possible reactions of the people in the office.

Despite the progress in automating the office, problems remain that are causing some organizations to hold back. These problems include confusion over what products to buy, uncertainty over the impact of office automation, the negative attitudes toward office automation equipment held by some office workers, and concern about how best to integrate the components of the automated office.

Assignments

12-1. The automated office has been described in this chapter as being multifunctional and integrated. Is this perspective important? Why? Is it necessary to consider the integration of various components right from the start or can such consideration wait until after the initial components are in place?

12-2. Discuss why the automated office is receiving so much attention. What developments are making it possible?

12-3. Some organizations introduce office automation components using the Three P's approach: prototype, pilot, and production. Discuss each of the Three P's.

12-4. Distinguish among the following types of word processors:

    a. Text editing typewriters.
    b. Stand-alone display systems.
    c. Shared-resource systems.
    d. Word processing software for micro-, mini-, and mainframe computers.

12-5. Describe the following word processing capabilities:

    a. Word wrap.
    b. Scrolling.
    c. Search and replace.
    d. Spelling check.
    e. Full function math.

12-6. Assume that you are in charge of data processing in a small manufacturing firm and the president comes to you and wants you to investigate the pros and cons of purchasing word processing equipment. In exploring the pros, you decide to list the possible applications in various departments. What applications might you list in:

    a. Sales?
    b. Purchasing?
    c. Accounting?
    d. Manufacturing?

12-7. Assume that your boss is a "workaholic" but you are not one yourself. Might you ever regret the day that electronic mail was created? Discuss.

12-8. Discuss any advantage(s) that voice mail might have over electronic mail.

12-9. Discuss whether the following meetings would be appropriate for teleconferencing:

    a. Scientists meeting to discuss their research on potential cures for cancer.
    b. Division managers meeting to discuss how required budget cuts will be accomplished.
    c. A board of directors meeting to select a new Chief Executive Officer (CEO).
    d. Regional sales managers meeting to decide how to respond to a competitor's price cuts.
    e. A manager meeting with disgruntled employees.

12-10. Even if a job could be performed through telecommuting, would everyone want to use this method? Discuss.

12-11. This chapter has included personal computers as a component of the automated office. Would they be better classified as part of data processing? Discuss.

12-12. In regard to micrographics, what do computer output microfilming (COM) and computer-aided retrieval (CAR) refer to?

12-13. Consult trade publications such as *Computerworld* and *Datamation*, and prepare a report on the current status of local area networks such as Ethernet, Wangnet, and DECnet.

12-14. Talk with a secretary who uses word processing equipment, and briefly describe:

    a. What his or her initial reaction was to the implementation of word processing equipment.
    b. How the word processing equipment was selected.
    c. How long it took him or her to become proficient in using the word processing equipment.
    d. How well the word processing equipment is designed ergonomically.

12-15. Discuss how office automation is related to:

    a. TPS.
    b. MIS.
    c. DSS.

12-16. What components of the automated office are in place at the Continental Illinois Bank? Would you recommend that these be the initial components for any organization? Discuss.

12-17. What are some of the major obstacles standing in the way of office automation?

CASE   Miller and Associates*

Richard P. Miller is a CPA who worked many years in the Tax Division of a Big Eight accounting firm. He became well known for the quality of his opinions on complex tax issues. In the late 1960s, Miller gave up his partnership and started his own consulting firm, which specializes in researching and giving opinions on tax questions asked by the company's clients.

*From Mary A. Karon, "When It Doesn't Work," *Computerworld: OA*, March 31, 1982: 25, 76. Copyright 1982 by CW Communications, Inc., Framingham, MA 01701. Reprinted from *Computerworld Office Automation*.

Two important groups within Miller and Associates are the skilled typists and the research personnel. The typists must be able to type at least sixty words a minute accurately; must be well grounded in grammar, spelling, and punctuation; and must possess superior vocabularies. The research personnel are CPAs with specialized training in taxes who research tax questions. Upon conclusion of their studies, the researchers prepare extensive reports, ranging in length from 20 to 150 pages.

Throughout the 1970s, there was good rapport between the typists and the researchers. Typically the time between the conclusion of a study by the researchers and the production of a final report by the typists was two weeks. In the interim, two or three drafts were produced and revised. The typists took pride in their ability to produce clean, accurate copy of a high quality, and they enjoyed an esprit d'corps not only among themselves, but also with the authors of the reports.

In 1981, the decision was made to install word processing equipment. The features of particular interest were the capability of storing and recalling text and the ability to make the necessary revisions for another draft in a fraction of the time. Equipment vendors convinced the management that the reports would be produced faster and with fewer people. The vendors did warn, however, that it would take three to six months to train the operators fully and that there could be no staff reductions until after this training was completed.

Sixteen months later, the management of Miller and Associates was ready to throw out the word processing equipment and go back to typewriters. The following conditions existed:

- There had been no staff reductions and there was no indication of any to come.
- It took the same length of time as before for the operators and the authors to produce approximately the same volume of material.
- The elapsed time from the conclusion of a study to the production of the final report still remained at two weeks. However, the number of drafts required more than doubled, from two to three to an average of six to seven.
- The operators slackened off on the proofreading. As a result, the authors were annoyed because they had to make what they believed to be trivial and unnecessary corrections in the copy. They found more and more errors that they felt the operators should have caught, and friction ensued.
- As the anticipated savings in time and energy used failed to materialize, the researchers tended to blame the operators, and the operators blamed the researchers; the harmonious relationships that had characterized the pre-word processing era evaporated.

At this point the decision was made to bring in a management consulting firm specializing in work flow and operations analysis. After several weeks of study, the consulting firm reported on the nature and causes of the problem:

1. The training period had been trying for the typists. The equipment had not been introduced in stages, but all at once. While learning to use it, the staff had been held responsible for production of the same volume of work as before. No such extra effort was demanded of the research staff, which continued to produce reports at the usual pace. The typists, feeling the burden of integrating the new equipment was theirs alone, developed resentments that were subsequently compounded by other developments.

2. All parties—management, researchers, and typists—had nurtured unrealistic expectations about making corrections and changes. The authors seemed to believe that revisions did not require much more than the push of a button. They took less care in the writing of their reports and fell into a pattern of creating first drafts that were merely skeletal, so that the "revisions" became total rewrites.

3. Because of the skeletal quality of the first drafts, the typists were denied the exercise of their editorial functions; they came to believe that their only requirement was to produce some form of typed document, not to plug holes and correct errors, as they would have in serious, well-thought-out drafts. As the authors grew more careless, so did the typists; they no longer felt the compulsion to proofread carefully and to be responsible for the accuracy of typed materials.

4. For the reasons described, the number of drafts grew; the capabilities of the equipment were used to prepare more drafts in the same length of time, rather than the same number of drafts in decreased time. And without a realization of time savings, there could be no staff reductions nor any opportunity to increase volume with the current staff.

5. For these reasons, also, the typists and the authors drew apart; they no longer operated in concert, as a team, but worked almost as adversaries.

An unfortunate consequence of all this was that the typists, who had been highly skilled and effective prior to word processing, felt usurped by the equipment, angry with the researchers, and resentful of what they perceived to be their reduced status. In addition, they believed that management prized the sophisticated equipment more than their skills and performance, and so they lowered their standards to what they perceived to be the lower expectations of management, concentrating their efforts on the mechanics of operating the equipment, rather than on the applications of their skills in grammar, spelling, punctuation, and breadth of vocabulary.

Questions

1. Who is to blame for the problem at Miller and Associates? The vendor, the management, the researchers, and/or the typists?

2. Assume that you were part of the consulting group that studied the problem. What recommendations would you make to eliminate or reduce the problem? Develop a specific plan of action.

Other Readings

Barcomb, David. *Office Automation.* Bedford, Mass.: Digital Press, 1981.
Canning, Richard G. "Can Tele-communications Replace Travel?" *EDP Analyzer* (April 1982): 1–15.

Crawford, A. B., Jr. "Corporate Electronic Mail—A Communication Intensive Application of Information Technology." *MIS Quarterly* (September 1982): 1–13.

Doswell, Andrew. *Office Automation.* New York: Wiley, 1983.

Driscoll, James W. "People and the Automated Office." *Datamation* (November 1979): 106–112.

Glatzer, Hal. "Portables for the Mobile." *Computerworld Extra* (November 14, 1984): 33–36.

Katzan, Harry, Jr. *Office Automation.* New York: American Management Association, 1982.

McNurlin, Barbara C. "The Automated Office: Part I." *EDP Analyzer* (September 1978): 1–13.

Mertes, Louis H. "Doing Your Office Over—Electronically." *Harvard Business Review* (March–April 1981): 127–135.

Poppel, Harvey L. "Who Needs the Office of the Future?" *Harvard Business Review* (November–December 1982): 146–155.

Rifkin, Glenn. "Where Will Your Office Be?" *Computerworld OA* (June 15, 1983): 67–74.

Uttal, Bro. "What's Detaining the Office of the Future?" *Fortune* (May 3, 1982): 176–196.

PART VI

DECISION SUPPORT SYSTEMS

Throughout the 1970s there was growing interest in decision support systems (DSS); as we move deeper into the 1980s, this interest continues to intensify. This interest has been fostered by factors such as hardware and software advances that facilitate the creation and use of a DSS, executives who are better informed about the availability and capabilities of the new technology, and today's volatile competitive conditions that heighten the desire among managers for more timely information and analysis. DSS has become an important type of CBIS in many organizations, especially in the support of difficult decision-making tasks.

This part of the text provides three DSS chapters. A definition and the characteristics of a DSS are given. It will be seen why a DSS may be needed, how it is approved, the computer hardware and software that might be used, the possible structure and components of a DSS, and how it is operated and evolves. And, finally, detailed descriptions of four DSS applications are presented, including a financial planning system in use at the Louisiana National Bank; BRANDAID, a marketing-mix model; a computer-assisted dispatching system at Southern Railway; and a DSS for ski area design. This information should be of value to you whether you become an approver, user, or builder of a DSS.

Chapter 13

An Overview of Decision Support Systems

Learning Objectives

After studying this chapter, you will be able to:
1. Describe a DSS.
2. Identify the characteristics of a DSS.
3. Discuss the differences between MIS and DSS.
4. Explain the impetus for DSS.
5. Identify and explain the three DSS levels.
6. Discuss the development of a DSS.
7. Define the following terms:

decision support system (DSS) specific DSS
intelligence phase DSS generator
design phase DSS tools
choice phase manager (or user)
independent decisions intermediary
sequential interdependent DSS builder
  decisions technical supporter
pooled interdependent decisions toolsmith

You should now have the beginning of a good understanding of CBIS. It should be clear how transaction processing systems, management information systems, and office automation systems differ. Yet another type of CBIS is in use in organizations such as Northwest Industries, American Airlines, Sun Oil Company, Del Monte, First Chicago Corporation, and Dillingham Corporation.[1] These systems, known as decision support systems, are sufficiently important to merit considerable attention.

Decision support systems (DSS) are not revolutionary. They represent a natural evolution in the way that computers can be used. DSS progress has been described as "not a single, clean innovation that occurred overnight, but more like a tide moving in many currents and eddies over a period of time."[2]

As the name implies, a decision support system focuses on providing decision support. It combines data, models, a software interface, and the user into an effective decision-making system. A DSS provides decision support for some of the really tough decisions that managers face. A DSS is not a replacement for an organization's MIS. Rather, a DSS is an additional source of decision support for managers and other users.

A Definition of DSS

A logical beginning for our discussion of decision support systems is a definition. Though there is no universally accepted one, the following definition will be useful for our purposes:

> *A decision support system is an interactive system that provides the user with easy access to decision models and data in order to support semistructured and unstructured decision-making tasks.*

Several points in the DSS definition need further elaboration and discussion. A DSS is an interactive system. The decision maker or an intermediary sits at a terminal and directs the operation of the system. The system's use is initiated and controlled by the decision maker. The user has easy access to models and data. This access is provided by a sophisticated computer software system that provides flexibility when one is using the system. The user can create or access previously created models. These models are customized for the specific decision-making tasks being supported. Most typically, the decision-making tasks are semistructured or unstructured and demand managerial judgment in addition to analytic aids. Available to the decision maker and models are data that are collected and maintained with specific decision-making tasks in mind. The data include extractions from the organization's

[1] Ralph H. Sprague, Jr., "DSS Trends," *Computing Newsletter*, March 1981: 2.
[2] P. G. W. Keen and G. R. Wagner, "DSS: An Executive Mind-Support System," *Datamation*, November 1979: 117.

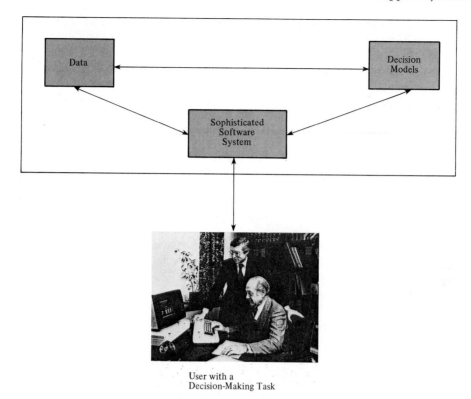

User with a
Decision-Making Task

FIGURE 13-1   The basic components of a decision support system.

TPS, but they also include other internal or external data that might be needed by the models or the decision maker.

Diagrammatically, a decision support system is shown in Figure 13-1. This is a very simple diagram, one that will need elaboration and enhancement as our understanding of DSS grows. It does, however, capture the essence of our DSS definition.

DSS Characteristics

From a decision-maker's perspective, a DSS should possess a number of characteristics. The following are of major importance:

1. A DSS should provide support for decision making, but with emphasis on semistructured and unstructured decisions.
2. A DSS should provide decision-making support for managers at all levels, assisting in integration among the levels whenever appropriate.

3. A DSS should support all phases of the decision-making process.
4. A DSS should support a variety of decision-making processes but should not be dependent on any one.
5. A DSS should support decisions that are *inter*dependent as well as those that are *in*dependent.
6. Finally, a DSS should be easy to use.[3]

These characteristics are important to the DSS concept and merit further discussion.

Support for Semistructured and Unstructured Decisions

In an earlier chapter, a distinction was made between structured and unstructured decisions. These terms mark the end points of a continuum of decision-making situations. *Structured decisions* are repetitive and routine. A definite procedure can be worked out so that they don't have to be treated anew each time they occur. *Unstructured decisions* are novel and consequential. There is no cut-and-dried method of making the decision. Because it is new, its precise nature and structure are elusive or complex, or it is so important that it deserves special treatment.[4]

Many TPS and all MIS make at least some contribution to supporting or automating the making of structured decisions. For example, out-of-stock reports are generated by most inventory control systems. This information is useful for decisions on expediting the placement of orders. Most MIS play at least some role in supporting semistructured and unstructured decisions. For example, cash flow models are often used to support short-term borrowing and investing decisions.

A decision support system is designed primarily to support semistructured and unstructured tasks. Although a DSS can be used to support structured decision making, it is implicitly assumed that these kinds of decisions are being accommodated by either the organization's TPS or its MIS.

Support for Decision Making at All Levels

Initially, a DSS may support only a limited number of decision-making tasks at a single organizational level. However, as a DSS evolves, it may provide decision-making support for all managerial levels. Not only can a DSS ultimately serve a variety of organizational levels, it can also serve as a mecha-

---

[3]Ralph H. Sprague, Jr., "Characteristics of Decision Support Systems," *Computing Newsletter*, February 1981: 1.
[4]These points are made in Herbert A. Simon, *The New Science of Management Decision* (New York: Harper & Row, 1960), 5–6.

nism for integrating decision making among levels. A DSS for banks can be used to illustrate this point.[5] At the *top* management level, a DSS might be used to assist in forecasting the amount of the funds that will be available to the bank from demand and time deposits. These forecasts can then be used by decision makers at the *middle* management level who are using the DSS to assist in deciding how the bank's funds should be invested. For example, how much should be made available for personal loans? Automobile loans? Treasury bills? The results of these decisions can then be used at *lower* organizational levels. For example, the amount of the funds available for personal loans might be used by a manager who is using the DSS in setting the cutoff score for the bank's credit-scoring model. Those applicants who score higher than the cutoff score receive a loan, and those who do not are denied a loan. The larger the quantity of the funds available, the lower the cutoff score, and vice versa.

Support for All Phases of the Decision-Making Process

Decision making involves more than selecting a course of action. A number of phases are involved. Simon calls these phases intelligence, design, and choice:[6]

> 1. *Intelligence* refers to searching the environment for conditions requiring decisions and for information that supports decision making.
> 2. *Design* refers to generating and analyzing alternatives.
> 3. *Choice* refers to selecting a particular alternative.

A DSS should provide some support for all of these phases.

A TPS makes some contributions to the intelligence phase. The summary reports sometimes point out conditions that require managerial action. An MIS provides even more help in the intelligence phase because of the enhanced reporting system and the query capabilities. To the extent that models are part of the MIS, an MIS supports the analysis portion of the design phase. Typically, however, little assistance is given in generating alternatives. The management science models of an MIS can make significant contributions to the choice phase. The objective of a DSS is to support all phases of decision making, even the difficult generation of alternatives in the design phase. In later chapters, we will see, through DSS examples, how this objective can be at least partially realized.

---

[5]See Ralph H. Sprague, Jr., and Hugh J. Watson, "A Decision Support System for Banks," *Omega: The International Journal of Management Science* 4 (June 1976): 657–671.
[6]Simon, pp. 1–3.

Support for a Variety of Decision-Making Processes

Managers differ in the process by which they arrive at decisions. Some managers tend to be highly *rationalistic*. They base their decisions on logical reasoning. Problems are analyzed in a straightforward, systematic manner. Structured methods of analysis are preferred.

Intuitive decision makers, on the other hand, tend to utilize a different decision-making process. They base their decisions on personal considerations—their feelings about a particular situation. They jump from one solution approach to another by being sensitive to cues that they may not be able to identify initially. Less structured and more flexible methods of analysis are preferred.

Decision-making processes are neither "good" nor "bad" in themselves; the best process, or combination of processes, depends on the decision maker and the decision-making task. In a DSS, differences in decision-making processes should be accommodated. The way that decisions are explored should be under the user's control rather than being dictated by the system. For example, a flexible DSS might lead a novice, rationalistic user through a series of menus, from which the user makes selections. On the other hand, an experienced, intuitive user might employ a command language to operate the DSS in a more flexible manner. In other words, the user operates the system in a way that reflects his or her experience and preferred method of using the system.

Support for Independent and Interdependent Decisions

Most organizational decisions are not made *independently*.[7] That is to say, they are not made by a decision maker acting in isolation. Rather, decisions are made *interdependently* with others in the organization.

Some decisions can be described as being *sequential interdependent*. A decision maker makes part of a decision, which is then passed on to others. This is frequently the case in production planning and scheduling. The broad outline of the production plan is worked out by one decision maker, who passes it on to another decision maker, who determines the master production schedule.

Other decision-making situations can be described as being *pooled interdependent*. In these cases, a decision results from negotiation and interaction within a group of decision makers. Many budgeting decisions are made this way.

---

[7]These decision-making situations are discussed in Peter G. W. Keen and Richard D. Hackathorn, "Decision Support Systems and Personal Computing," Department of Decision Sciences, The Wharton School, The University of Pennsylvania, Working Paper 79-01-03, (April 3, 1979).

Ease of Use

The final DSS characteristic is that it should be easy to use. As is frequently said, the system should be "user-friendly." This is especially important for a DSS, because a DSS often serves discretionary users. Use of the system is initiated by the decision maker, and unless the system is easy to use, it may not be used at all.

A Brief Example of a DSS

Having considered a definition and the performance characteristics of a DSS, let us now consider an actual example. Although the example is brief, it should add to your understanding of DSS.[8]

The Houston Oil and Minerals Corporation was interested in a proposed joint venture with a petrochemicals company to develop a chemical plant. The executive vice president who was responsible for the decision requested a simulation model to analyze the risks involved. David Sampson, manager of planning and administration, and his staff built a DSS in only a few days. The speed with which the model was developed was due to the availability of a sophisticated software package and the talents of Sampson and his staff. The executive vice president accepted the validity of the model and the value of the results but was worried by the risk of a catastrophic outcome. Sampson was told something like "I would like to see this in a different light. But I realize the amount of work you have already done, and I am ninety-nine percent confident with it. I know we are short on time and we have to get back to our partners with our yes-or-no decision." Sampson replied that he could provide the desired risk analysis in less than an hour's time. Within twenty minutes, the results of the "what if?" questions were being reviewed in the executive boardroom, and they led to the eventual dismissal of the project, which would probably have been accepted otherwise.

Some Differences Between MIS and DSS

From the DSS definition, the discussion of the performance characteristics of a DSS, and the brief DSS example, it should be clear that there are differences between a DSS and an MIS. These differences are real and merit our attention. Our approach here is to emphasize what can be expected from a DSS that is less typically possible with an MIS. This does not mean that an MIS cannot have these features; rather, these features are simply not com-

[8]This example was presented in Keen and Wagner, p. 118.

mon to most management information systems. The Houston Oil and Minerals Corporation example can be used to illustrate these differences.[9]

A DSS can be used to address ad hoc, unexpected problems. The proposed joint venture was possibly a once-in-a-lifetime decision-making situation. Most MIS decision support is supplied by structured information flows in the form of summary and exception reports. Structured reports are of limited value for unique problems. Either the needed information is not provided or it is in the wrong format.

A DSS can provide a valid representation of the real-world system. In our example, the decision maker accepted the validity of the model and the value of the results. The model builders were able to develop a model that could be trusted. The way in which many models are embedded in an MIS does not engender such trust. They are frequently built by the management science group and are left for the user as the management scientists move on to other projects. Over time, the models become out-of-date and either are not used or are used and provide potentially misleading information.

A DSS can supply decision support within the available time frame. A model for the proposed joint venture was completed and working within days. A request for risk analysis was satisfied within an hour. In an MIS, if the model is not already available, the lead time for writing programs and getting answers is often too long to help the decision maker.

A DSS can evolve as the decision maker learns more about the problem. In many cases, managers cannot specify in advance what they want from programmers and model builders. In our example, the request for risk analysis occurred after the model was built. The way in which many computerized applications are developed requires that detailed specifications be formalized in advance. This requirement is not reasonable for most semistructured and unstructured decision-making tasks.

A DSS is often developed by non-DP professionals. In our example, the planning and administration group created the model with no outside help. This was possible because of the software package that was available. Most MIS applications and systems must be developed by data processing professionals.

These distinguishing DSS features are summarized in Table 13-1. Keen

TABLE 13-1 Reasonable Expectations of a DSS

• A DSS can be used to address ad hoc, unexpected problems.
• A DSS can provide a valid representation of the real-world system.
• A DSS can provide decision support within the available time frame.
• A DSS can evolve as the decision maker learns more about the problem.
• A DSS can be developed by non-DP professionals.

[9]These differences are noted in Keen and Wagner, pp. 117–118.

TABLE 13-2   The Differences Among MIS, OR/MS, and DSS

Management Information Systems

- The main impact has been on *structured* tasks, where standard operating procedures, decision rules, and information flows can be reliably predefined.
- The main payoff has been in improving *efficiency* by reducing costs, turnaround time, and so on, and by *replacing* clerical personnel.
- The relevance for managers' decision making has mainly been indirect, for example, by providing reports and access to data.

Operations Research/Management Science

- The impact has mostly been on *structured* problems (rather than tasks), where the objective, data, and constraints can be prespecified.
- The payoff has been in generating better *solutions* for given types of problems.
- The relevance for managers has been the provision of detailed *recommendations* and new methodologies for handling complex problems.

Decision Support Systems

- The impact is on *decisions* in which there is sufficient structure for computer and analytic aids to be of value but where managers' judgment is essential.
- The payoff is in extending the range and capability of managers' decision processes to help them improve their *effectiveness*.
- The relevance for managers is the creation of a *supportive* tool, under *their own control,* which does not attempt to automate the decision process, predefine objectives, or impose solutions.

Reprinted by permission from Peter G. W. Keen and Michael S. Scott Morton, *Decision Support Systems* (Reading, Mass.: Addison-Wesley, 1978), 1–2.

and Scott Morton have also noted the distinctive nature of DSS, and Table 13-2 summarizes the differences that they see among MIS, operations research/management science (OR/MS), and DSS.

The Impetus for DSS

Technological advances are normally due to a number of factors. This is certainly true of DSS. Especially during the past fifteen years, there have been the following:

1. An increasingly complex decision-making environment for managers.
2. Significant advances in computer hardware and software technology.
3. A growing supply of personnel who are either managerially fluent and technically literate or technically fluent and managerially literate.

Greater Decision-Making Complexity

Many observers of the contemporary business world have noted that organizations are operating in increasingly complex, turbulent environments. This, in turn, has affected managerial decision making in ways that increase the need for decision support. A few examples should make this point clear.

After the 1973–1974 oil crisis, organizations will probably never again take the availability of raw materials for granted. Organizational planning must now include contingency planning for possible shortages of raw materials. This situation has created a need for enhanced analysis capabilities.

Many organizations are facing increased competition, especially from foreign competitors. If firms in this position are to survive and prosper, effective decisions must be made in the marketing, finance, research and development, and production areas.

There is increased economic uncertainty that must be considered in decision making. Inflation rates, interest rates, wage rates, and raw material costs exhibit a volatility that increases decision-making uncertainty. This uncertainty causes a greater need for risk analysis.

The federal government has placed unprecedented reporting requirements on business. The Occupational Safety and Health Administration (OSHA) wants a new report. The Internal Revenue Service wants more information. Management needs to be able to meet these requirements in cost effective ways.

Computer Hardware and Software Advances

It is not a coincidence that decision support systems have evolved hand in hand with advances in computer hardware and software technology. The first decision support systems were developed in the late 1960s, at about the same time that time-sharing using computer terminals became widespread. These terminals gave the user relatively easy access to data and the computer's computational power. Today it is interesting to read the description of one of the first decision support systems (it was then called a *management decision system*) and to note the amount of attention devoted to the computer terminals that were used.[10] Today we take terminals, even intelligent terminals, largely for granted.

In-house time-sharing is only one way in which computational power has been placed in the hands of users. Today many firms subscribe to large, nationwide time-sharing networks. Mini- and microcomputers are becoming increasingly prevalent as the concept of distributed processing spreads.

An obvious key to supporting decision making is having access to the relevant data. Evolving data base management technology is doing much to

[10] Michael S. Scott Morton, *Management Decision Systems: Support for Decision Making* (Cambridge, Mass.: Harvard University Graduate School of Business Administration, 1971).

facilitate entering, maintaining, analyzing, extracting, and reporting the data maintained in data bases.

New programming languages are appearing that make it easier to create and use models in support of decision making. As a result, functional area users are increasingly becoming model builders as well as users.

Diffusion of Modeling Expertise

Not only has computing become distributed, but there is a growing supply of organizational personnel who are trained, able, and ready to employ analytic aids in their work. In the not-so-distant past, nearly all of the organization's modeling expertise resided in the hands of management science professionals. If the end users have OR/MS skills, the likelihood that models will be used to support decision making is enhanced. As Francis F. Bradshaw, former president of the Society for the Advancement of Management, has said, "Most managers would rather live with a problem they can't solve than use a solution they don't understand."[11] Although this may be an overly strong statement, it does point out that managers are hesitant to put their managerial careers on the line if they do not understand the basis of a suggested decision.

Today's graduates of business schools are better trained to use, if not create, models than ever before. Most current business school graduates have been required to take coursework in mathematics, statistics, computer science, and management science and to apply these tools in courses in their area of specialization. These graduates entering the business world tend to be more technically literate than ever before.

Another change that has taken place in many organizations is the breaking up of large, centralized OR/MS departments and the dispersion of the personnel in these departments to functional areas.[12] This change places personnel with the greatest modeling skills close to the problems that need to be solved. And as a consequence, over time, the quantitative specialists become increasingly managerially literate.

DSS Levels

It is useful to think of decision support systems in terms of three different levels: *specific DSS*, *DSS generators*, and *DSS tools*.[13] Each has an important DSS role, and knowledge of these roles should help eliminate some of the misunderstanding that sometimes results from the use of the DSS term.

[11] Russell L. Ackoff, "Frontiers of Management Science," *The Bulletin (TIMS)*, February 1971: 20.

[12] George Thomas and Jo-Anne Da Costa, "A Sample Survey of Corporate Operations Research," *Interfaces*, August 1979: 103–111.

[13] These distinctions are made in Ralph H. Sprague, Jr., "A Framework for the Development of Decision Support Systems," *MIS Quarterly*, December 1980: 6–7.

Specific DSS

The discussion of decision support systems in this chapter thus far has been at the specific DSS level. This is the hardware and software system that is used to support a specific set of decision-making tasks. In the Houston Oil and Minerals Corporation example, the specific DSS was the system that provided information about the proposed joint venture to develop a chemical plant. From the decision maker's perspective, the specific DSS *is* the DSS.

DSS Generator

In recent years, there have been significant advances in DSS generators. These are hardware and software "packages" that can be used to develop a specific DSS. For example, Executive Information Services (EIS, offered by Boeing Computer Services), Interactive Financial Planning System (IFPS, available from Execucom Systems Corporation), and EXPRESS (marketed by Tymshare) are all examples of DSS generators. They typically possess capabilities such as data management, graphic display, financial and statistical analysis routines, risk analysis, and optimization analysis. These capabilities have been available separately for some time, but only recently as an integrated, easy-to-use package. In the Houston Oil and Minerals Corporation example, the specific DSS was developed with IFPS as the DSS generator. The speed with which a specific DSS can be developed usually increases with the availability of a DSS generator. It can be expected that DSS generators with enhanced capabilities will become increasingly available.

DSS Tools

DSS tools can be thought of as DSS building blocks. Either they can be used to create a specific DSS, or they are incorporated into DSS generators. Consider a net discounted present value routine as an example of a DSS tool. It might be (1) a callable subroutine in a simulation model or (2) a financial analysis capability in a DSS generator. Other examples of DSS tools are color graphics, Monte Carlo sampling routines, data base inquiry capabilities, and a linear programming package. The ease of performing the risk analysis in the proposed joint chemical plant venture was due to the risk analysis capability of IFPS.

Relationships Among DSS Levels

The relationships that exist among DSS levels are shown in Figure 13-2. The highest level is the specific DSS. A specific DSS can be created either from DSS tools, as at the left of the diagram, or from a DSS generator, as at the

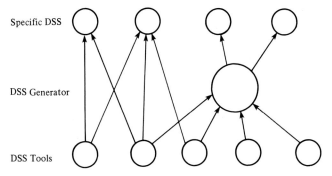

FIGURE 13-2 The various DSS levels. [This figure is patterned after Ralph H. Sprague, Jr., "A Framework for the Development of Decision Support Systems," *MIS Quarterly* (December 1980), p. 8.]

right. A DSS generator is a package of DSS tools. The lowest level contains DSS tools for building either a specific DSS or a DSS generator. Examples from each level are given in Table 13-3.

Institutional and Ad Hoc DSS

Decision support systems can vary in many ways: the type of application, the variety of decisions supported, the number of users of the system, the time required to develop the system, and so on. One way to understand this variation is to think of decision support systems as being either institutional or ad hoc.[14] An *institutional* DSS deals with decisions of a recurring nature, whereas an *ad hoc* DSS deals with specific problems that are usually not anticipated or recurring. The Houston Oil and Minerals example given earlier is an example of an ad hoc DSS. Chapter 15 provides several illustrations

TABLE 13-3 Examples of the DSS Levels

Specific DSS	DSS Generators	DSS Tools
Portfolio management	IFPS	Risk analysis
Marketing mix	EXPRESS	Color graphics
Capacity planning	SYSTEM W	APL
Venture analysis	EMPIRE	Trend analysis

[14]John J. Donovan and Stuart E. Madnick. "Institutional and Ad Hoc DSS and Their Effective Use," *Data Base*, Winter 1977: 79–88.

TABLE 13-4   A Comparison of Institutional and Ad Hoc DSS

Characteristic	Institutional	Ad Hoc
Number of decision occurrences	many	few
Number of people making decisions	many	few
Range of decisions supported	narrow	wide
Range of issues addressed	narrow	wide
Specific data needed known in advance	usually	rarely
Specific analysis needed known in advance	usually	rarely
Importance of operational efficiency	high	low
Duration of specific type of decision being addressed	long	short
Need for rapid development	low	high

This table is suggested by John J. Donovan and Stuart E. Madnick, "Institutional and Ad Hoc DSS and Their Effective Use," *Data Base* (Winter 1977), p. 82.

of institutional DSS, such as the financial planning system at the Louisiana National Bank.

In addition to whether the decision being supported is recurring or not, institutional and ad hoc DSS typically have several other distinguishing characteristics. An institutional DSS often supports many users, whereas an ad hoc DSS supports only a few. An institutional DSS is normally designed to support a narrow range of decisions and issues, whereas an ad hoc DSS may be varied to explore a wider range. The specific data and analysis requirements of institutional DSS usually become well defined over time, whereas the data and analysis requirements of an ad hoc DSS are rarely known in advance. An institutional DSS usually has a high level of operational efficiency, whereas the operational efficiency of an ad hoc DSS is often low. An institutional DSS normally supports a decision-making task that exists for a long period of time, whereas an ad hoc DSS typically supports a decision that exists for only a short time. An institutional DSS normally has a low need for rapid development, whereas a high need for rapid development often exists for an ad hoc DSS. These distinguishing characteristics are summarized in Table 13-4. They are helpful in understanding the differences that exist among decision support systems.

The Development of a DSS

Chapters 17 and 18 are devoted to the development of CBIS in general. However, the development of a DSS is significantly different and so much a part of the DSS concept that it needs to be discussed here. We will focus our attention on the roles filled by organizational personnel and on the developmental process that is followed.

Roles Filled by Organizational Personnel

Let us start by considering the personnel who might be involved in the creation of a DSS. The following possible roles for organizational personnel have been suggested:

1. The *manager or user* is the person faced with the problem or decision—the one who must take action and be responsible for the consequences.
2. The *intermediary* is the person who helps the user, perhaps merely as a clerical assistant who pushes the keys of the terminal, or perhaps as a more substantial "staff assistant" who interacts and makes suggestions.
3. The *DSS builder* assembles the necessary capabilities from DSS tools or a DSS generator to create the specific DSS with which the user or the intermediary interacts directly. This person must have some familiarity with the problem area and must also be comfortable with the information system technology components and capabilities.
4. The *technical supporter* provides additional specialized expertise that may be needed. This person may be an in-house employee, such as a systems programmer who places a newly purchased DSS generator on the organization's computer; or the person may not be an employee of the organization, such as an employee of a vendor of a DSS product who answers customers' questions on the "hotline." Technical supporters normally do not become involved with the DSS on a regular basis.
5. The *toolsmith* develops new technology, new languages, new hardware and software; improves the efficiency of linkages between subsystems; and so on.[15]

Several comments should be made about these roles. First, an individual may serve in more than one role. Some users are also the builders and operators of their DSS. Although this is not yet a common practice, as managers become more technically fluent and DSS generators become more user-friendly, it should be expected that the roles of user, intermediary, and builder will be increasingly assumed by the decision maker. Second, more than one person may be involved in a single role. The decision may be made by a group, or there may be several model builders involved in the creation of the DSS. And finally, not all of the roles may be required. Though intermediaries are very common, they are not always needed. The same is true for technical supporters and toolsmiths.

There is a relationship between the three DSS levels and the five DSS roles. This relationship is shown in Figure 13-3. The manager uses the

---

[15] Ralph H. Sprague, Jr., "Development of Decision Support Systems," *Computing Newsletter*, December 1980: 4.

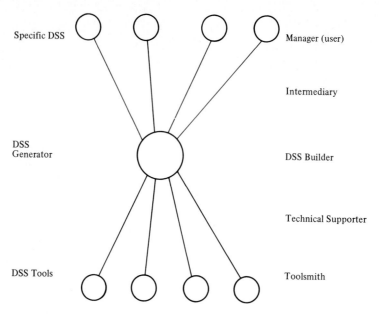

FIGURE 13-3 The relationship between DSS roles and levels. [Source: Ralph H. Sprague, Jr., "Development of Decision Support Systems," *Computing Newsletter* (December 1980), p. 4.]

specific DSS. The intermediary serves as a "chauffeur" for the user. The DSS builder works with the DSS generator. The technical supporter provides a link between the DSS generator and the DSS tools. The toolsmith develops DSS tools.

The Developmental Process

The need for management support and user involvement when one is developing computerized systems is well known, especially when one is dealing with decision-support-oriented systems. With decision support systems, this is even more true than is usually the case. Because a DSS is designed to support semistructured and unstructured decision making, it is imperative that the user play an active role in specifying the characteristics and the capabilities of the system. It is frequently only the decision maker who truly understands what type of decision support is needed. At a minimum, the user should be an active member of the development team. At the other extreme, as has already been suggested, the user may also assume the roles of intermediary and builder.

Another key concept in the development of decision support systems is that the developmental process should be evolutionary and iterative. Because the type of decision support needed is often initially uncertain, even to the

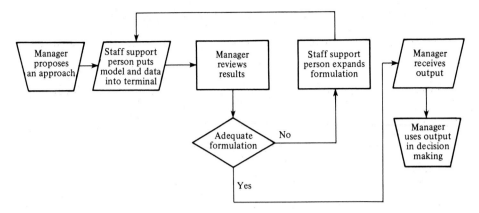

FIGURE 13-4   The developmental process for a DSS. [Source: This figure is suggested by G. R. Wagner, "Enhancing Creativity in Strategic Planning Through Computer Systems," *Managerial Planning* (July–August 1979), p. 13.]

decision maker, it is best to build small, tentative systems first. Such systems can be easily, quickly, and inexpensively modified as the needs of the user become better known to both the user and the builders. Such systems are also responsive to sudden changes in the decision-making environment. The availability of DSS generators has made this developmental approach possible. Figure 13-4 depicts this type of development. Note the iterative nature of the developmental process when the system does not fully meet the user's needs. Over time, the system evolves in terms of its features and capabilities and as its worthiness is demonstrated.

Summary

Decision support systems are the latest development on the CBIS scene. This chapter has provided an overview of DSS. The next chapter considers in detail the building of a DSS. The final chapter in this three-chapter part on DSS looks at DSS applications.

A DSS can be defined as an interactive system that provides the user with easy access to decision models and data in order to support semistructured and unstructured decision-making tasks.

A DSS has a number of characteristics. It should provide support for decision making, with an emphasis on semistructured and unstructured decisions. It should provide decision-making support for managers at all levels, assisting in integration among the levels whenever appropriate. A DSS should support all phases of the decision-making process: intelligence, design, and choice. It should support a variety of decision-making processes but should not be dependent on any one. It should support independent, sequential interdependent, and pooled interdependent decisions. And finally, a DSS should be easy to use.

A growing number of organizations are developing decision support systems. One of these is the Houston Oil and Minerals Corporation, which developed a DSS to analyze a proposed joint venture with a petrochemicals company.

A DSS differs from MIS and OR/MS. It can be used to address ad hoc, unexpected problems. It can provide a valid representation of the real-world system. A DSS can provide decision support within the available time frame. It can evolve as the decision maker learns more about the problem. It can also be developed by non-DP professionals.

Several factors have led to the development of decision support systems. Growing decision-making complexity has increased the need for decision support. Computer hardware and software advances have made DSS feasible. Also, there is a growing supply of personnel with modeling expertise.

Decision support systems can be conceptualized as existing on three levels. A specific DSS is used by a decision maker to support his or her decision-making tasks. A DSS generator is a hardware and/or software package that can be used to create a specific DSS. DSS tools either are elements of a DSS generator or are used independently to develop a specific DSS.

Decision support systems can be categorized as being either institutional or ad hoc. An institutional DSS is used to support recurring decisions, whereas an ad hoc DSS supports decisions that are usually not anticipated or recurring.

Personnel filling one or more roles may be needed in the development of a DSS. There is the manager or user, the intermediary, the DSS builder, the technical supporter, and the toolsmith.

The developmental process for a DSS differs from that for other types of CBIS. The end user must be an active member of the development team. The developmental process should be evolutionary and iterative. The personnel involved in the developmental effort should be managerially rather than technically oriented.

Assignments

13-1. It has been suggested that the term *executive mind support* is a suitable alternative term for DSS. How appropriate is this term? Discuss.

13-2. When thinking about a DSS, should the user be considered a part of the system? Why?

13-3. Decision-making tasks run on a continuum from structured to unstructured. Give examples of structured and unstructured decisions from the personnel, finance, production, and marketing areas.

13-4. Herbert A. Simon categorized the phases of decision making as intelligence, design, and choice. An alternative classification is:

   a. Definition of objectives.
   b. Collection of data.
   c. Generation of alternative courses of action.
   d. Analysis of the alternatives.
   e. The decision.
   f. Followup.

Compare these two classifications. Which do you prefer? Why?

13-5. Decision-making styles range from rationalistic to intuitive. Is a decision maker consistently one or the other? Give examples from your personal experiences.

13-6. Prepare a matrix similar to the one shown here and fill in the cells with examples.

Functional Area

		Marketing	Finance	Production
	Independent			
Decision-Making Environment	Sequential Interdependent			
	Pooled Interdependent			

13-7. The CBIS field is famous for its use of "buzzwords." Is DSS just another buzzword void of meaning, or is it a significant development? Discuss.

13-8. Has organizational decision making become more complex, or does it just seem that way, because we are closer to today's complexities? Discuss.

13-9. Identify the software and hardware advances that have helped to make decision support systems feasible.

13-10. Decision support systems can be conceptualized as existing on three levels: specific DSS, DSS generators, and DSS tools. Give examples not mentioned in the text for each level.

13-11. If you were designing a DSS generator, what capabilities and DSS tools would you include in it?

13-12. Some people have a difficult time distinguishing between sophisticated MIS applications and certain types of DSS. Is this difficulty more likely to occur with an institutional or an ad hoc DSS? Discuss.

13-13. It has been suggested that an ad hoc DSS often has low operational efficiency. Why is this the case? Is it a problem?

13-14. Possible DSS roles include manager or user, intermediary, DSS builder, technical supporter, and toolsmith. For each role, how important is it to be managerially fluent and/or technically fluent? On graduation, which role(s) would you like to assume? Why?

13-15. Discuss why the developmental process for a decision support system should differ from that for an order entry application.

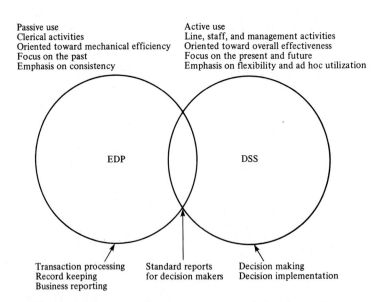

Passive use
Clerical activities
Oriented toward mechanical efficiency
Focus on the past
Emphasis on consistency

Active use
Line, staff, and management activities
Oriented toward overall effectiveness
Focus on the present and future
Emphasis on flexibility and ad hoc utilization

EDP   DSS

Transaction processing   Standard reports   Decision making
Record keeping   for decision makers Decision implementation
Business reporting

FIGURE 1   Electronic data processing systems versus decision support systems. [Source: Steven L. Alter, *Decision Support Systems: Current Practice and Continuing Challenges* (Reading, Mass.: Addison-Wesley, 1980), p. 2.]

13-16. Should organizations form separate groups to create decision support systems? Why? If your answer is yes, what personnel should be included in the group? Why?

13-17. Steven Alter is well known in decision support system circles. However, he discusses DSS in a way that differs considerably from that of most other people. To Alter's way of thinking, a CBIS is either an EDP system or a DSS. This dichotomy of CBIS is shown in Figure 1. Compare Alter's classification system with the TPS, MIS, and DSS taxonomy used in this text. Does Alter's use of the DSS term have any appeal? What is it? Are there any drawbacks to Alter's dichotomy? What are they?

CASE   Alpha Technology*

In the early 1960s, Alpha Technology was formed by a group of engineers who had left NASA. Because of the talents of its founders and the growth in the nation's space program, Alpha Technology prospered. Over the years, Alpha Technology has continued to conduct aerospace and defense industry related research.

Each time a government contract goes up for bid, Alpha Technology and its competitors go into what has been described as a "state of emergency." In a relatively short period of time, proposal teams must prepare their company's responses to government RFPs (requests for proposals), which are the life's blood of the government contractor.

During the early years at Alpha Technology, it was not unusual to find a highly paid manager running a copy machine on Sunday night or punching a calculator for hours on end. Computers were new to Alpha Technology and were used only for basic data processing applications, such as payroll, and for engineering-related tasks.

In the early 1970s, the proposal preparation process became a little less traumatic. The data needed in the preparation of proposals were stored in the company's data base and could be accessed by FORTRAN and COBOL programs. The difficulty was that the demands placed on the data processing department often exceeded its ability to respond in a timely fashion to new requests for information. This was a critical shortcoming in such a rapidly moving decision-making environment.

In 1980, the decision was made to open the data processing shop to users and to bring in two sophisticated software systems: IFPS, a financial planning system, and RAMIS, a report-writer/data-base management system. These decisions have been highly successful. Now, in a very short period of time, proposal teams can analyze various bid options. In a highly competitive industry, Alpha Technology is emerging as a leader, in part because of its proposal analysis and preparation capabilities.

*The facts in this case are patterned after the experiences of Vought Corporation, an aerospace subsidiary of the LTV Corporation, as described in "Automated Decision Support in the Aerospace Industry," *Data Management*, September 1980: 20–21, 27.

Questions

1. Describe the decision support for preparing proposals at Alpha Technology in the 1960s. The 1970s. The 1980s.

2. Would you describe the current system of preparing proposals as being a DSS? Why?

3. What DSS levels exist in the current proposal preparation system? Discuss.

4. Discuss the roles assumed by the organizational personnel in the current proposal preparation system.

Other Readings

Bennett, John L., ed. *Building Decision Support Systems*. Reading, Mass.: Addison-Wesley, 1983.

Bonczek, Robert, Clyde Holsapple, and Andrew Whinston. *Foundations of Decision Support Systems*. New York: Academic Press, 1981.

Carlson, Eric D. "Decision Support Systems: Personal Computing Services for Managers." *Management Review* (January 1977): 4–11.

Donovan, John J., and Stuart E. Madnick. "Institutional and Ad Hoc DSS." *Data Base* (Winter 1977): 79–88.

Keen, Peter G. W. "Adaptive Design for Decision Support Systems." *Data Base* (Fall 1980): 15.

Keen, Peter G. W. "Decision Support Systems: Translating Analytic Techniques into Useful Tools." *Sloan Management Review* (Spring 1980): 33–44.

Keen, Peter G. W., and Michael S. Scott Morton. *Decision Support Systems: An Organizational Perspective*. Reading, Mass.: Addison-Wesley, 1978.

Keen, P. G. W., and G. R. Wagner. "DSS: An Executive Mind-Support System." *Datamation* (November 1979): 117–122.

Sprague, Ralph H., Jr. "A Framework for the Development of Decision Support Systems." *MIS Quarterly* (December 1980): 1–26.

Sprague, Ralph J., Jr., and Eric D. Carlson. *Building Effective Decision Support Systems*. Englewood Cliffs, N.J.: Prentice-Hall, 1982.

Sprague, Ralph H., Jr., and Hugh J. Watson. "Bit by Bit: Toward Decision Support Systems." *California Management Review* (Fall 1979): 60–68.

Watson, Hugh J., Ralph H. Sprague, Jr., and Donald W. Kroeber. "Computer Technology and Information System Performance." *MSU Business Topics* (Summer 1977): 17–24.

Chapter 14

Building a DSS

Learning Objectives

After studying this chapter, you will be able to:

1. Describe how a DSS is created.
2. Discuss the importance of recognition of need when the development of a DSS is being considered.
3. Describe the factors that affect the approval of a DSS.
4. Select the hardware for a DSS.
5. Select the software for a DSS.
6. Discuss the potential building of a DSS.
7. Discuss the components of a DSS.
8. Explain how a DSS is operated.
9. Describe how a DSS evolves.
10. Define the following terms:

decision-making effectiveness
value analysis
champion
problem-oriented language
English-like language
nonprocedural language
"what if" analysis
Monte Carlo (probabilistic) analysis

goal seeking (backward iteration)
DSS data base
DSS model base
strategic models
tactical models
operational models
model building blocks and subroutines

The preceding chapter provided an overview of decision support systems. It discussed important topics such as what a DSS is and how a DSS differs from other types of CBIS, as well as the structure of a typical DSS, the evolutionary way that many DSS are developed, the various levels of DSS, and the role of different organizational personnel in DSS. Although these are important topics, it is also useful to be familiar with some of the details of how a DSS is built. This information is important whether one simply approves the creation of a DSS, is a user of a DSS, or is a DSS builder. The major focus of this chapter is to make you familiar with many of the details of actually building a DSS.

Any CBIS project requires a developmental process. This process consists of the series of interrelated steps that are followed when one is creating a system. The topics in this chapter are presented in roughly the same order as they become important when one is building a DSS. The first step is the recognition of the need for the DSS. Then the DSS must be approved. The hardware and software for the DSS must be selected. Then the DSS is built and operated, and over time it evolves in response to the decision makers' and the organization's needs.

Recognition of Need

The development of any CBIS begins with a recognition of need. A variety of studies have shown that there is a positive correlation between the felt need for a system and the successful implementation of any system that is developed.[1] In the case of most decision support systems, this point is especially important because the system will typically support discretionary users.

Whenever possible, the user should be involved in the development of the DSS because it is virtually impossible for anyone other than the end user to specify the information needed to support semistructured and unstructured decision-making tasks. An involved user is also more likely to become "hooked" on the use of the system than someone who is presented with a completed system. However, there are situations where an end user may not be involved in the developmental process. For example, an institutional DSS may have been developed prior to the current generation of users. In this case, a thorough training experience must substitute for user involvement in the developmental process.

The proposed DSS should be perceived as enhancing decision-making *effectiveness*. Use of the DSS should improve the quality of the decisions that are made. For example, the DSS should improve the promotion decisions made by a marketing manager or the production scheduling decisions of a production manager. This focus is in contrast to efficiency considerations,

---

[1] Michael J. Ginzberg, "Steps Toward More Effective Implementation of MS and MIS," *Interfaces*, May 1978: 57–63.

which are more important to other types of CBIS. *Efficiency* refers to the process of providing the greatest output for a given input.[2] For example, in a transaction processing system, the number of transactions processed per minute is an efficiency concern. Efficiency is less important than effectiveness in a DSS.

Approval of the DSS

A proposed DSS, like any CBIS, should be subjected to an appropriate review before it is approved for development. What is appropriate, however, depends on a number of factors. These factors also influence whether the DSS is approved for development at all. Important factors include:

1. The need for the system.
2. The benefits and costs of the system.
3. The time available for approval.
4. The existence of a champion.
5. The available hardware and software.

In general, the more the DSS is needed, the more likely it is to be developed. In cases of dire need, the DSS may be approved for development without a rigorous review. This was the case with a DSS at the Louisiana National Bank which is discussed in the next chapter.

Before any investment of resources, the benefits and costs associated with a project need to be considered. In the case of a DSS, this is a difficult undertaking because the benefits are hard to quantify. How much is new or better information worth? Because of this difficulty, most decision support systems are justified on an intuitive feeling that the potential benefits justify the costs.[3] Clearly, however, this approach is most acceptable with relatively inexpensive decision support systems. Consistent with this thought is Peter Keen's "value analysis" approach to evaluating a proposed DSS.[4] Keen suggests that when the costs of a DSS are likely to be below a threshold level of about $20,000, one should ask how much the decision maker is willing to pay in order to have the information provided by the DSS. If the value placed on the information exceeds the system's anticipated cost, the DSS should be approved. With more expensive decision support systems, greater efforts should be made to quantify the benefits and costs, even though this may not be entirely possible.

[2] Robert K. Vierck. "Decision Support Systems: An MIS Manager's Perspective," *MIS Quarterly*, December 1981: 36.

[3] Jack T. Hogue and Hugh J. Watson, "Management's Role in the Approval and Administration of Decision Support Systems," *MIS Quarterly*, June 1983: 15–26.

[4] Peter G. W. Keen, "Value Analysis: Justifying Decision Support Systems," *MIS Quarterly*, March 1981: 1–16.

The time available also affects the approval of a DSS. The preceding chapter described a DSS that was developed at Houston Oil and Minerals to analyze a proposed joint venture. Because the decision to be supported by the DSS had to be made in a matter of days, the DSS had to be approved quickly. Sometimes a lengthy, detailed evaluation is not possible if the DSS is to serve its intended purposes.

A champion also affects DSS approval. A *champion* is an individual who supports the development of a system, supplies the organizational clout for its approval, and sees that it is developed. Normally, this person is highly placed in the organization's structure. Most decision support systems have a champion, especially if the system differs considerably from existing applications, requires additional hardware or software, or has wide-ranging organizational implications.

A DSS is more likely to be approved if the required hardware and software are already available in the organization. If the DSS requires either new hardware or new software, the approval process is likely to be more thorough and time consuming. The DSS at Houston Oil and Minerals required no new hardware or software and was quickly approved. The DSS at Southern Railway, which is discussed in the next chapter, required new minicomputers and was carefully studied before approval was given.

Hardware Selection

Intertwined with the approval of a DSS is the determination of what hardware will be used. The major options are a time-sharing network, the organization's mainframe computer, a minicomputer, or a personal computer. Each option offers advantages and disadvantages.

A Time-sharing Network

Companies such as Boeing Computer Services, Tymshare, and Compu-Serve offer national time-sharing networks on which a DSS can be placed. Many companies that already have extensive in-house computing capabilities and staff make use of time-sharing networks. There are several reasons for this practice.

In some instances, better response times can be obtained from a time-sharing network than from in-house computer systems. It is not unusual for companies to experience poor response times when production runs (e.g., accounts receivable and payroll) are scheduled. If the timing of these runs conflicts with the use of DSS, a time-sharing network may be an attractive alternative.

Time-sharing networks offer a variety of capabilities that may be important to the DSS. It is normally possible to use a variety of input–output devices. Most time-sharing networks have an extensive set of software packages, including DSS generators. Because computing is their only business, time-sharing networks tend to keep up with and use the latest hardware and software advances.

A time-sharing network also typically offers a variety of support services. These services include training programs for users, "hotlines" to answer questions, and management consulting services on a contract basis. These services are sometimes easier to obtain from a time-sharing network than to arrange in-house.

The final potential advantage of a time-sharing network is that at a reasonable cost the user can try the DSS approach on a problem or a set of problems and see whether the approach looks promising. If the results are disappointing, relatively little is lost, because the start-up costs have been small.

The major disadvantage of a time-sharing network is cost control. If the DSS is frequently used, the time-sharing costs can become quite high because there is no natural upper limit on them. What frequently happens in this case is that the DSS is brought in-house. The firm buys the required hardware and software and runs the DSS as an in-house application.

Mainframe, Mini-, or Personal Computer

If the DSS is located in-house, a mainframe, mini-, or personal computer might be used. A variety of factors influence the type of computer used. These factors include what kinds of computers are available in-house, the type of decision support that is to be provided, the data needs of the DSS, the computational power that is needed, and the software demands of the DSS.

A major reason for placing a DSS in-house is that the required hardware and software are already available there. In a similar vein, available in-house computer systems influence the placement of the DSS. However, this need not be a limiting consideration. It is not unusual for hardware and software to be purchased specifically for the DSS.

The range of users of the DSS also influences where it is placed. If the system is to support users throughout the organization, a large computer system like an IBM 3081 or CYBER 170 might be needed. On the other hand, if the DSS is to provide decision support for one person, a personal computer like an Apple or an IBM/PC might be used.[5]

The data needs of the DSS also influence where it is placed. Some decision support systems need to draw considerable data from the organization's data base. When this is the case, it may be advantageous to place the DSS on the system where the data base is maintained. However, this may not be as important a consideration as it might first seem. Many personal com-

[5] Richard D. Hackathorn and Peter G. W. Keen, "Organizational Strategies for Personal Computing in Decision Support Systems," *MIS Quarterly*, September 1981: 21–27.

puters are now configured with communications capabilities that allow them to access mainframe or mini-computer data bases. Also, many decision support systems have data needs that differ considerably from what is maintained in existing data bases.

Some decision support systems demand significant computational power, which requires the use of large, fast machines. For example, some linear programming and simulation models require a large number of calculations. However, this has become less of a problem as personal computers have become increasingly powerful. Many OR/MS methods have migrated from mainframe to personal computers.

A final concern is the software that the DSS will use. In general, larger computer systems have a greater variety and number of software packages. However, many DSS software products are now available in personal computer versions with nearly all of the mainframe features intact (e.g., IFPS/Personal, Micro W, and Micro FCS).

Software Selection

An important decision is whether the DSS is to be created by means of DSS tools or a DSS generator. Much of the current excitement about decision support systems is due to the ease with which a DSS can be created with a DSS generator, especially if the DSS is to be of a financial nature. It should be kept in mind, however, that a DSS generator is not a necessity and that many decision support systems have been created without one. The computer-assisted dispatching system at Southern Railway, which is discussed in Chapter 13, is an excellent example of this. Let us first consider the tools that might be used in a DSS and then look at DSS generators.

DSS Tools

The specific tools that go into a DSS depend, of course, on what the DSS is to do. Several tools, however, are quite common and merit discussion. They are programming languages, statistical analysis packages, optimization packages, and data base management systems.

Programming Languages
A variety of programming languages has been used in creating decision support systems. One class of languages is *procedure-oriented languages*, such as BASIC, FORTRAN, COBOL, and PL/1. As the name implies, with these languages the programmer defines the procedure that the computer is to follow. The main advantage of using procedure-oriented languages is that they are widely known and are available on most computer systems. Their major limitation is that they do not contain features that facilitate the creation and the later use of the DSS.

There are always new languages being developed. These languages may still require programmers to describe a procedure for the computer to follow, but features have been included in the languages that make them especially attractive for certain applications. Two relatively new languages that are being used in some decision support systems are APL and PASCAL. APL is especially appropriate for mathematical modeling applications that involve cumbersome mathematical operations such as inverting a matrix. PASCAL has been developed with structured programming in mind and also has useful data handling features.

Problem-oriented languages can also be used with a DSS. A problem-oriented language allows the programmer to describe the characteristics of a problem to be solved rather than a procedure to be followed. A variety of problem-oriented languages has been developed for different types of problems. For example, GPSS is a problem-oriented language used to simulate the behavior of queuing systems.[6] In a GPSS program, the programmer has only to specify the queuing system characteristics, such as arrival times, service times, the number of servers, and the priorities in providing service. The language automatically provides procedures for tasks such as sampling arrival and service times, advancing the simulation through time, gathering data, calculating statistics, and generating reports.

Statistical Analysis Packages

A DSS frequently requires statistical analysis capabilities. For example, regression analysis may be needed to determine the relationship between a dependent and an independent variable. As an illustration, a student health center might employ regression analysis to study the relationship between the demand for service and enrollment at the university. A number of statistical analysis packages, such as SPSS, IMSL, and BMDP, have been developed and are available on many computer systems.[7] In order to use any of the statistical analysis programs in the package, it is necessary only to specify the package and the program and to enter the data according to the specified format. There is no need to specify how the calculations are to be performed, as this logic is preprogrammed.

Optimization Packages

A function of a DSS may be to suggest the best solutions to certain problems, and this procedure may require support from optimization packages. For example, a manager may be interested in investigating the optimal mix of

[6] A variety of problem-oriented languages is discussed in Hugh J. Watson, *Computer Simulation in Business* (New York: Wiley, 1981), Chapter 8.

[7] *Statistical Package for the Social Sciences* (2nd ed.), ed. by N. H. Nie, C. H. Hull, J. G. Jenkins, K. Steinbrenner, and D. H. Bent (New York: McGraw-Hill, 1975); *International Mathematical and Statistical Libraries Manual* (6th ed.) (Houston: International and Mathematical Statistical Libraries, 1977); *Biomedical Computer Programs P-Series*, ed. by W. J. Dixon and M. B. Brown (Berkeley: University of California Press, 1979).

products to produce in light of the contribution to profit that each product makes and the limitations on the available equipment, labor, and raw materials. This particular problem can often be analyzed through linear programming. The analyst develops an objective function (which in this case is the relationship between profit and the quantities of the products produced) and constraint equations (the available equipment, labor, and raw materials). The mathematical formulation of the problem is then entered into a linear programming package such as MPSX.[8] The package performs the laborious calculations required to analyze the linear programming problem and generates output useful to the user, such as, in the current example, the optimal mix of products to produce.

Data Base Management Systems

A DSS requires efficient data handling capabilities. The user frequently must be able to enter new data, update existing data, extract data, analyze data, display data, and present data in reports. For example, in a human resources DSS, the user may need to do things like enter data on recent hires and dehires, analyze the percentage of women in managerial positions, and prepare a report for a government agency. Data handling requirements like these are greatly facilitated by data base management systems such as IDMS, TOTAL, and ADABAS. Data base management systems, which once were available only on mainframe computers, can now be obtained for mini and even personal computers.

DSS Generators

A DSS generator can greatly facilitate the development of a DSS. A DSS generator combines, in a user-friendly package, a set of capabilities that are important to many decision support systems. These capabilities typically include:

- An English-like language.
- Nonprocedural programming.
- Forecasting.
- Statistical analysis.
- Financial analysis.
- Optimization.
- "What if" analysis.
- Monte Carlo (probabilistic) analysis.
- Goal seeking (backward iteration).
- Consolidations.

[8] *IBM Mathematical Programming System Extended—370 General Information Manual* (White Plains, N.Y.: IBM Corporation, 1979), and *IBM Mathematical Programming Systems Extended—370 Primer* (White Plains, N.Y.: IBM Corporation, 1979).

- Data base management.
- Report generation.
- Graphical display.
- Security.

An *English-like language* is one that has a syntax similar to the written and spoken word. The syntax of the language is natural to the user. Although people unfamiliar with computers may question how "English-like" these languages really are, they are more so than most programming languages.

A *nonprocedural language* eliminates some of the restrictions of procedure-oriented languages. The most important characteristic of a nonprocedural language is that programming statements can be sequenced in any order.[9] For example, the following sequence of programming statements would be acceptable in a nonprocedural language.

```
NET WORTH = ASSETS − LIABILITIES
ASSETS = 1000000
LIABILITIES = 800000
```

In calculating the value for NET WORTH, the computer would search out the values for ASSETS and LIABILITIES.

Most DSS generators offer a variety of *forecasting*, *statistical analysis*, and *financial analysis capabilities*. The ability to easily do trend analysis, moving averages, exponential smoothing, Box-Jenkins, means, standard deviations, percentiles, t-statistics, F-statistics, regression analysis, analysis of variance, depreciation, present value, and internal rate of return calculations is common. Figure 14-1 illustrates how a DSS generator can produce a graph of a trend-fit analysis.

Optimization analysis, in the form of mathematical programming, is also available in many DSS generators. The different varieties of mathematical programming may include linear, integer, nonlinear, dynamic, and goal programming.

"What if" analysis allows the decison maker to investigate different scenarios. First, an initial or "base case" situation is described. Then the decision maker might ask, for example, "What would be the impact on profits if sales decrease by 10 percent?" The ability to obtain answers easily to "what if" questions is an important characteristic of DSS generators.

A *Monte Carlo* (or probabilistic) *analysis* permits the decision maker to explore the risk associated with a situation.[10] Appropriate probability distributions (e.g., normal, uniform, and triangular) are specified for the indepen-

---

[9] Sometimes the term also implies that simultaneous equations are automatically detected and solved.

[10] The term *Monte Carlo* refers to procedures for sampling values from probability distributions. This process is random, like the outcomes in the gambling casinos in Monte Carlo, Monaco.

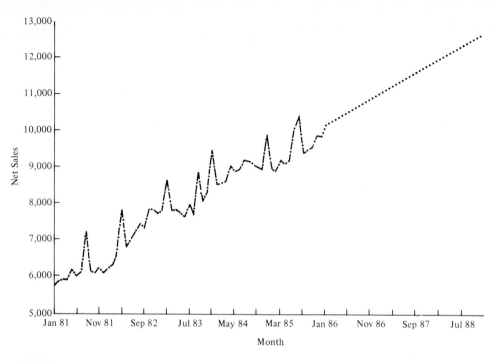

FIGURE 14-1 Actual net sales and a linear three-year forecast. [Source: "Express for Finance," (Waltham, Mass.: Management Decision Systems, Inc.), p. 24.]

dent variables in the model, and their impact on dependent variables is determined by combining the results of repeated samplings from the independent variables. A Monte Carlo analysis might show, for example, the probability that various amounts of millions of dollars of capital might be needed for a new venture. The result of such an analysis is shown in Figure 14-2.

Goal seeking (or backward iteration) is the ability to specify a goal and then determine what value for a variable is necessary in order to achieve the goal. For example, a rate of return of 20 percent may be needed in order for a new product to be approved, and the question might be what market share is necessary in order to achieve this rate of return. Most DSS generators can backward-iterate to a user-specified goal.

Larger organizations normally have multiple product lines, divisions, departments, or other hierarchical structures. This type of situation is illustrated in Figure 14-3. The *consolidation* feature of a DSS generator allows the user to merge data from component parts of the organization into summary information.

Efficient *data management* is important to most decision support systems. Until recently, DSS generators were relatively weak in this area. This situation has changed as vendors have taken one of several possible ap-

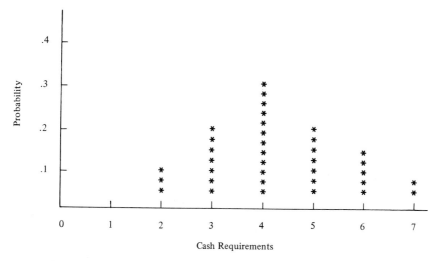

FIGURE 14-2   The cash requirements for a new venture.

proaches. In the case of recently developed DSS generators, vendors have built better data base management capabilities into their products. In fact, the distinctions have blurred between the newer DSS generators with good data base capabilities and the newer data base management systems with good analysis capabilities. Vendors of older DSS generators have responded by developing software products that provide access through the DSS generator to data in corporate data base management systems or, in the case of external data, in a commercial data base (e.g., Chase Econometrics).

Nearly all DSS generators are multidimensional; that is to say, data can be logically organized in multiple ways. Figure 14-4 presents a three-dimensional data base structure that is found in many organizations. Notice that there is a line item dimension (the rows), an organizational dimension (the sections), and a time dimension (the columns). With this data base structure, it is simple, for example, to find the profit of Chicago washers in March 1982.

Many decision support systems generate reports as part of their output. Because formatting a report can be a time-consuming process, most DSS generators have a *report generation* capability that facilitates the preparation of reports.

Decision makers often prefer output in a graphical form. Consequently, nearly all DSS generators can automatically prepare *graphical output,* even in color. Line, bar, and pie charts are all common.

For some decision support systems, *security* is important. Some DSS generators provide security for the data base, the files, the models, and the report definitions.

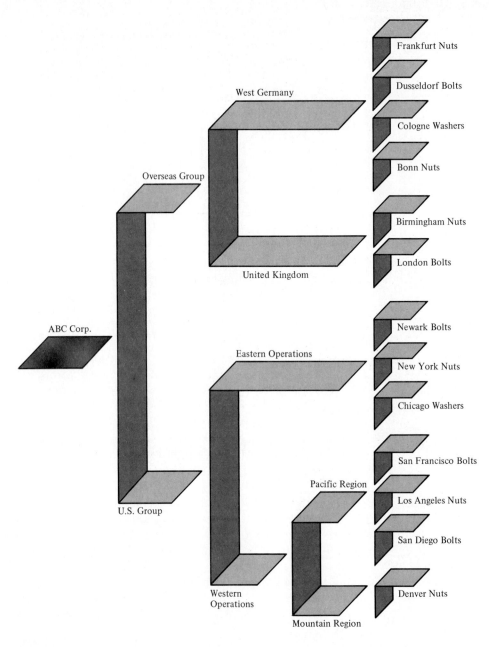

FIGURE 14-3 An organization with multiple operating units. [Source: "System Overview" (Boston, Mass.: FCS-EPS), p. 12.]

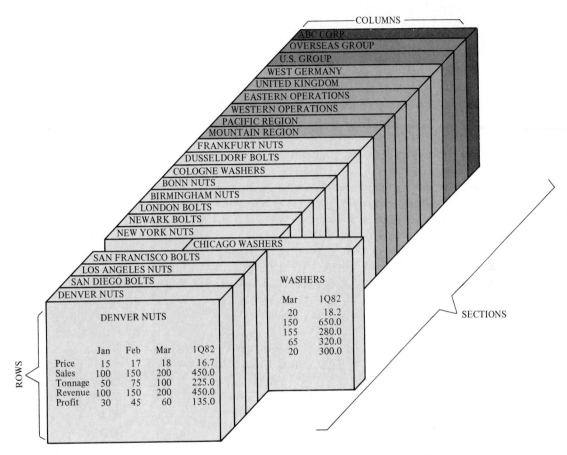

FIGURE 14-4 A three dimensional data base structure. [Source: "System Overview" (Boston, Mass.: FCS-EPS), p. 13.]

IFPS Applied to New-Product Planning

In order to illustrate the power of a DSS generator, we give here an example using IFPS. IFPS is one of the most popular DSS generators in use today, and although the example does not demonstrate all of the capabilities of IFPS, it should give you a feeling for how easily a fairly sophisticated analysis can be performed. Similar capabilities exist with other DSS generators.

The example illustrates new product planning. Assume that a company's marketing research group has prepared the following report on a proposed new product.[11]

It is difficult to assess with certainty how any new product will do. The best that can be done is to quantify the risk. We believe that the proposed new

---

[11] This example is based on a problem in Watson, pp. 290–291.

product has an economically useful lifetime of five years. The total market at the time of introduction should be 500,000 units per year, and this market should grow at a rate of 10 percent per year. At a price of $9 per unit, we believe that the product can capture a significant share of the total market. We believe that the market share can be estimated to be normally distributed, with a mean of 5 percent and a standard deviation of 1 percent.

Production has filed the following report:

At your request, we have prepared probabilistic estimates for the cost of producing the new product. We believe that overhead costs can be described by a triangular distribution with most optimistic, most likely, and most pessimistic costs of $10,000, $12,000, and $15,000, respectively. Unit costs are also believed to be described by a triangular distribution with costs of $6.50, $6.75, and $7.25.

The finance manager feels that the initial investment in the proposed new product can be described by a uniform distribution with lower and upper limits of $90,000 and $100,000. The company uses a 15 percent discount rate when analyzing new product proposals.

Based on this information, the IPFS program shown in Figure 14-5 was prepared. The underlined characters were entered by the DSS builder, and the other characters were displayed at the user's terminal by IFPS. A brief explanation of the IFPS program is provided below.[12]

```
INTERACTIVE FINANCIAL PLANNING SYSTEM — 9.0
ENTER MODELS AND REPORTS FILE NAME
? ANALYZE
FILE ANALYZE NOT FOUND—NEW FILE WILL BE CREATED
READY FOR EXECUTIVE COMMAND
? MODEL
ENTER MODEL NAME
? NPP
BEGIN ENTERING NEW MODEL
```

The user has gained access to IFPS. The name ANALYZE has been given to the file, which will store any models and report definitions. The name NPP has been given to the new product planning model.

```
10 * NEW PRODUCT PLANNING MODEL
```

This is a comment line, indicated by the asterisk.

---

[12] *IFPS User's Manual* (Austin, Texas: Execucom Systems Corporation).

```
INTERACTIVE FINANCIAL PLANNING SYSTEM - 7.0
ENTER MODELS AND REPORTS FILE NAME
? ANALYZE
FILE ANALYZE NOT FOUND-NEW FILE WILL BE CREATED
READY FOR EXECUTIVE COMMAND
? MODEL
ENTER MODEL NAME
? NPP
BEGIN ENTERING NEW MODEL
? 10  * NEW PRODUCT PLANNING MODEL
? 20 COLUMNS 1-5
? 30 INITIAL MARKET=500000
? 40 TOTAL MARKET=INITIAL MARKET, PREVIOUS TOTAL MARKET*1.1
? 50 MARKET SHARE=NORRAND(.05,.01)
? 60 SALES VOLUME=MARKET SHARE*TOTAL MARKET
? 70 GROSS SALES=9*SALES VOLUME
? 80 OVERHEAD=TRIRAND(10000,12000,15000)
? 90 UNIT COST=TRIRAND(6.5,6.75,7.25)
? 100 COST=OVERHEAD+SALES VOLUME*UNIT COST
? 110 NET PROFIT=GROSS SALES-COST
? 120 INVESTMENT=UNIRAND(90000,100000),0
? 130 DISCOUNT RATE=.15
? 140 NDPV=NPVC(NET PROFIT,DISCOUNT RATE,INVESTMENT)
? MONTE CARLO 100
MODEL NPP VERSION OF 03/02/82 -- 5 COLUMNS 13 VARIABLES
ENTER MONTE CARLO OPTIONS
? SEED .5
ENTER MONTE CARLO OPTIONS
? COLUMNS 5
ENTER MONTE CARLO OPTIONS
? FREQ NDPV,NONE
```

FIGURE 14-5   An IFPS program for new product planning.

20 COLUMNS 1-5

The COLUMNS statement indicates that there should be five columns, one for each year.

30 INITIAL MARKET=500000

The initial market is specified as being 500,000 units.

40 TOTAL MARKET=INITIAL MARKET, PREVIOUS TOTAL MARKET*1.1

The total market at the time of product introduction is specified by the value for the initial market, and it increases by 10 percent each year.

50 MARKET SHARE=NORRAND(.05,.01)

A market share is randomly sampled from a normal distribution with a mean of 5 percent and a standard deviation of 1 percent.

60 SALES VOLUME=MARKET SHARE*TOTAL MARKET

The sales volume in units is determined.

70 GROSS SALES=9*SALES VOLUME

The gross sales in dollars are determined.

80 OVERHEAD=TRIRAND(10000,12000,15000)

Overhead expense is randomly sampled from a triangular distribution with most optimistic, most likely, and most pessimistic estimates of $10,000, $12,000 and $15,000, respectively.

90 UNIT COST=TRIRAND(6.5,6.75,7.25)

Unit cost is randomly sampled from a triangular distribution with most optimistic, most likely, and most pessimistic estimates of $6.50, $6.75, and $7.25, respectively.

100 COST=OVERHEAD+SALES VOLUME*UNIT COST

The cost of production is computed.

110 NET PROFIT=GROSS SALES−COST

Net profit is computed.

120 INVESTMENT=UNIRAND(90000,100000),0

The required investment is randomly sampled from a uniform distribution with a lower limit of $90,000 and an upper limit of $100,000. The 0 indicates that the sampled estimate occurs only at time period zero.

130 DISCOUNT RATE=.15

The discount rate is specified as 15 percent.

140 NDPV=NPVC(NET PROFIT,DISCOUNT RATE,INVESTMENT)

A financial analysis capability is used to calculate the net discounted present value for the proposed new product.

<u>MONTE CARLO 100</u>

     IFPS is instructed to perform a Monte Carlo analysis based on 100 iterations.

MODEL NNP VERSION OF 03/02/82 — 5 COLUMNS 13 VARIABLES
ENTER MONTE CARLO OPTIONS
<u>SEED .5</u>

     IFPS requests specifications for conducting the analysis. It is told to use a seed of .5 with the random number generator.

ENTER MONTE CARLO OPTIONS
<u>COLUMNS 5</u>

     Only the fifth (i.e., the last) column is to be output.

ENTER MONTE CARLO OPTIONS
<u>FREQ NDPV,NONE</u>

     The output is to be in the form of a frequency table. Only NDPV is to be output. There are no other specifications for the analysis.

     The IFPS program and analysis specifications result in the output shown in Figure 14-6. At the top of the output is the probability that the net discount present value (NDPV) in year 5 will be greater than the amount indicated. For example, there is a 90 percent chance that it will be greater than $33,667. At the bottom of the output are sample statistics for NDPV, including the mean ($89,485), the standard deviation of the 100 iterations ($45,554), the skewness of the distribution (.2), the kurtosis (peakedness) of the distribution (3.1), and a 10–90 percent confidence interval on the mean ($83,654–$95,315).

     The output options for an IFPS program are greater than those that have been demonstrated. For example, a user-formatted report could have been

FREQUENCY TABLE

PROBABILITY OF VALUE BEING GREATER THAN INDICATED

	90	80	70	60	50	40	30	20	10
NDPV									
5	33667	50664	63191	72732	83720	104612	115117	127403	142933

SAMPLE STATISTICS

	MEAN	STD DEV	SKEWNESS	KURTOSIS	10PC CONF MEAN	90 PC
NDPV						
5	89485	45554	.2	3.1	83654	95315

FIGURE 14-6 Output from the IFPS new product planning model.

```
ENTER POOL OR MODELING LANGUAGE COMMAND
? WHAT IF
WHAT IF CASE 1
ENTER STATEMENTS
? UNIT COST=TRIRAND(7,7.5,8)
? MONTE CARLO 100
ENTER MONTE CARLO OPTIONS
? SEED .5
ENTER MONTE CARLO OPTIONS
? COLUMNS 5
ENTER MONTE CARLO OPTIONS
? FREQ NDPV,NONE
```

FIGURE 14-7   Performing "what if" analysis on the IFPS new product planning model.

generated, a histogram could have been created, and any variable or column in the analysis could have been output. DSS generators tend to have considerable flexibility in their output capabilities.

A powerful capability of a DSS generator is "what if" analysis. In our new product planning example, assume that management is especially concerned about an increase in the unit cost of production. This possibility can be explored by means of "what if" capability of IFPS, as shown in Figure 14-7. The output from this analysis is shown in Figure 14-8. Notice, for example, that the increase in the most optimistic, most likely, and most pessimistic unit cost estimates from $6.50, $6.75, and $7.25 to $7.00, $7.50, and $8.00 results in a decrease in the mean net discounted present value from $89,485 to $20,994.

As has been mentioned previously, "what if" analysis is only one of the capabilities of IFPS and other DSS generators. Typically, there is a capability of doing whatever the user wants—whether it be forecasting, statistical analysis, goal seeking, or any of many other options.

***** WHAT IF CASE 1 *****

FREQUENCY TABLE

PROBABILITY OF VALUE BEING GREATER THAN INDICATED

	90	80	70	60	50	40	30	20	10
NDPV 5	-24380	-14662	-1394	11072	18592	32291	45407	54804	64396

SAMPLE STATISTICS

	MEAN	STD DEV	SKEWNESS	KURTOSIS	10PC CONF MEAN	90 PC
NDPV 5	20994	36972	.3	3.0	16262	25727

FIGURE 14-8   Output from the "what if" analysis in the IFPS new product planning model.

Selecting a DSS Generator

A large number of DSS generators are commercially available. Some of them have been created for personal computers, whereas others are available only on mainframes. Their cost varies from hundreds of dollars to hundreds of thousands of dollars.

Some DSS generators, such as Encore by Ferox Microsystems, Inc., are available only in personal computer versions. Their cost generally runs between $500 and $1,500. They provide a reasonable set of capabilities for developing DSS applications.

Spreadsheets such as VisiCalc and integrated packages such as LOTUS 1-2-3, Symphony, and Framework are also used for DSS work. Their limitation for DSS application development is that common DSS generator capabilities are either not available or are more difficult to use. For example, goal seeking and "what if" analysis are very easy to perform with a true DSS generator but not with other products.

Some DSS generators such as XSIM by Chase Econometrics/Interactive Data Corporation come only in mainframe versions. Their cost runs from $30,000 to over $300,000. They provide a strong set of capabilities for developing DSS applications.

Many vendors now offer mainframe and personal computer versions of DSS generators plus other products that support DSS application development. The personal computer versions may provide a full set or only a subset of the mainframe DSS generator capabilities. For example, IFPS/Personal has most of the capabilities of IFPS but does not allow the user to perform a Monte Carlo analysis. Most of the personal computers and mainframe versions are able to communicate with one another. For example, data may be downloaded to a personal computer from a mainframe or a model may be uploaded from a personal computer to a mainframe. IFPS/Link is a software product that allows any IFPS or IFPS/Personal file to be downloaded or uploaded. Software products are also available to extract data from files on other computer systems and to automatically reformat them for use by the DSS generator. IFPS/DATASPAN does this for IFPS. Products are also available that produce presentation-quality graphics. The IFPS related product that provides this capability is IMPRESSIONIST. More comprehensive modeling capabilities can be obtained through software products such as IFPS/OPTIMUM, which allows the user to ask "What's the *best* solution?" These and other software products offered by Execucom Systems Corporation are described in Table 14-1.

As one is willing to pay more for a DSS generator, its capabilities increase. Table 14-2 presents data on eight popular, comprehensive DSS generators.

When an organization has a DSS generator in-house or has access to one on a time-sharing network, it is likely that the generator that is available will be used for DSS applications. However, this is not always the case, as

TABLE 14-1   DSS Products Offered by Execucom Systems Corporation

Product	Description	Approximate Cost*
IFPS	A mainframe DSS generator	$70,000
IFPS/Personal	A personal computer DSS generator	895
IFPS/Link	Allows IFPS and IFPS/Personal to download and upload files between mainframe and personal computers	5,000
IFPS/OPTIMUM	A mathematical programming enhancement for IFPS that provides best solutions	25,000
IFPS/DATASPAN	Reformats and transfers data from other computer system files to a new IFPS data file	15,000
IFPS/INTERFACES	Provides direct, interactive connections between IFPS and leading general ledger, database, and statistics software packages	6,000–15,000
IFPS/SENTRY	A data entry system that provides an interactive prompting and data validation facility for creating and validating IFPS data files	10,000
IMPRESSIONIST-PC	A presentation-quality graphics package	995
IMPRESSIONIST-MAINFRAME	A presentation-quality graphics package that functions either as a standalone product or interfaces with IFPS/Personal	40,000

*Mid-1985 prices.

evidenced by the fact that some firms have several DSS generators. Some DSS generators are better for certain types of applications than others.

When an organization is in the market for a DSS generator, a three-step selection process is recommended:[13]

1. Compare DSS generators using a checklist of the factors and features that are considered important.
2. Test the most promising DSS generators on typical applications.
3. Ask the users in organizations that are similar to yours what their experiences have been with the DSS generators still under consideration.

[13] A more detailed selection procedure is described in C. Lawrence Meador and Richard A. Mezger, "Selecting an End User Programming Language for DSS Development," *MIS Quarterly*, December 1984: 267–280.

Table 14-2 contains many of the items that would go into a typical checklist, except that an actual checklist would tend to be more detailed. For example, in regard to forecasting capabilities, the checklist should include the specific forecasting methods that will be needed. Unnecessary features should be excluded from the checklist. There are also factors not shown in Table 14-2 that are likely to be important. These include the reputation of the vendor, training programs and their cost and location, and customer services such as user "hot lines" and consulting help. Several promising candidates should emerge from the checklist.

The second step in the selection process is to test the most promising DSS generators on typical organizational applications. A common mistake is to test the DSS generators on problems that are too simple. Sometimes the differences among DSS generators become apparent only with more difficult applications.

The final step is to ask users in other organizations about their experiences with the DSS generators still being considered. Sometimes problems with the DSS generator or the vendor become apparent only after a period of time has passed. The vendors should be willing to supply the names of current users, and an unwillingness to provide this information should be met with concern.

After the three-step selection process has been completed, the organization should have the information on which to base an intelligent choice.

The DSS Builders

After the hardware and the software have been selected, the DSS builders begin their work. The composition of the team can vary considerably depending on the DSS. At one extreme is the situation in which the team consists of one person who ultimately serves as the DSS builder, the intermediary, and the user. This might be the case where the user has a microcomputer with a DSS generator. At the other extreme is the situation in which the team consists of users, management scientists, functional-area staff specialists, and data processing personnel.

Decision support systems are most typically developed by planning departments and functional-area staff groups.[14] They do this in response to their own decision-making needs and to supply management with requested information.

Managers are also involved in the building of a DSS, but the nature of their involvement varies with the organizational level. Top managers participate in generating the idea for the DSS, specifying the information require-

---

[14]Jack T. Hogue and Hugh J. Watson, "Management's Role in the Approval and Administration of Decision Support Systems," *MIS Quarterly*, June 1983: 15–26.

TABLE 14-2 Data on Eight Major DSS Generators

DSS Generator	English-like	Nonprocedural	Forecasting	Statistical Analysis	Financial Analysis	Optimization	"What if" Analysis	Monte Carlo Analysis	Goal Seeking
CUFFS-88	Yes	Yes	Limited	None	Yes	Limited	Yes	Limited	Yes
EMPIRE	Yes	Yes	Yes	Many	Yes	Comprehensive	Yes	Yes	Yes
EXPRESS	Yes	Yes	Yes	Many	Yes	Limited	Yes	Yes	Yes
FCS	Yes	Yes	Yes	Many	Yes	Many	Yes	Yes	Yes
IFPS	Yes	Yes	Yes	Many	Yes	Many	Yes	Yes	Yes
REVEAL	Yes	Yes	Yes	Many	Yes	No	Yes	Yes	Yes
SIMPLAN	Yes	Yes	Yes	Many	Yes	No	Yes	Yes	Yes
XSIM	Yes	Yes	Yes	Comprehensive	Yes	No	Yes	Yes	Yes

DSS Generator	Consolidations	Data Base Management	Report Generator	Graphics Display	Security System	Permanent License	Number of Installations
CUFFS-88	Yes	Yes	Yes	Yes	Limited	$42,000	10
EMPIRE	Yes	Yes	Yes	Yes	No	$45,000 to $60,000	350
EXPRESS	Yes	Yes	Yes	Yes	Yes	$65,000 to $350,000	100+
FCS	Yes	Yes	Yes	Yes	Yes	$74,000 to $167,000	1,000+
IFPS	Yes	Yes	Yes	Yes	Limited	$70,000	1,400+
REVEAL	Yes	Yes	Yes	Yes	Limited	$30,000 to $90,000	Confidential
SIMPLAN	Yes	Yes	Yes	Yes	Yes	$60,000 to $80,000	150
XSIM	Yes	Yes	Yes	Yes	Yes	$300,000	Not available

ments, and final acceptance of the DSS.[15] They play a minimal role in the actual construction of the DSS, testing it, and demonstrating its operation and capabilities. Middle- and lower-level managers tend to be more involved in *all* of the steps in building the DSS. In addition to using decision support systems for their own purposes, middle- and lower-level managers employ them to respond to information requests from upper managerial levels.

CBIS personnel also have a role in building a DSS.[16] They often are part of a development team or serve as a consultant. They also frequently provide the hardware, systems software, and communications capabilities required by the DSS.

The General Structure and Components of a DSS

A DSS has been defined as "an interactive system that provides the user with easy access to decision models and data in order to support semistructured and unstructured decision-making tasks." This definition suggests the general structure and important components of a DSS. There is the *user*, who seeks decision support. There are *data*, which can be accessed directly by the user or can be used as input for processing by the DSS. The data can be conceptualized as being the *decision support system data base*. There are *models*, which provide the system's analysis capabilities. The models can be thought of as being the *decision support system model base*. And finally, there is the *sophisticated software system*, which links the user, the data, and the models together. Figure 14-9, which was first suggested in Chapter 13, shows the relationships among the DSS components.

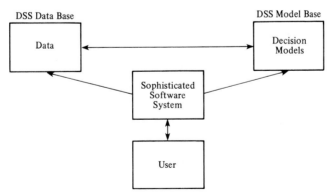

FIGURE 14-9   The general structure and components of a DSS.

[15] Jack T. Hogue and Hugh J. Watson, "Current Practices in the Development of Decision Support Systems," *Proceedings of the Fifth International Conference on Information Systems*, Tucson, Arizona, November 1984: 117–127.

[16] Hogue and Watson, "Current Practices in the Development of Decision Support Systems," 117–127.

Although Figure 14-9 provides a useful first understanding of the general structure and components of a DSS, it is not rich in detail. It does not provide answers to such questions as: What are the dialog options open to users? What data are maintained in the data base? What models are in the model base? Answers to such questions are possible only through a more detailed exploration of the DSS's general structure and components. It should be kept in mind that decision support systems can vary considerably. This point will become clearer when several decision support systems are described in the next chapter.

The Data Base

The data in the DSS data base can include transaction, other internal, and external data, as shown in Figure 14-10.

The *transaction data* come from the organization's TPS. Depending on the needs of the DSS, data from functional areas such as accounting, finance, marketing, production, and personnel might be included. Transaction data are the major source of information about internal company operations.

There are also *other internal data* that might be important to the DSS. Examples include planned dividend rates, forecasts of future sales, the cost of items being out-of-stock, and future hiring plans. Some of these data might be permanently maintained as part of the DSS data base, whereas other data may be entered by the decision maker when the DSS is put into use.

External data are also important to some decision support systems. Examples include industry data, marketing research data, regional employment data, tax rate schedules, and national economic data. These data might come from the U.S. government, trade associations, marketing research firms, econometric forecasting firms, and the organization's own efforts in collecting

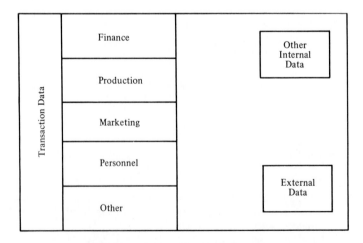

FIGURE 14-10   The DSS data base.

external data. Like the internal data, the external data may be permanently maintained or may be entered at the time the DSS is used.

The management of the data in the data base is important to a DSS. Thought must be given to how the data will be entered, stored, updated, and extracted. As has been mentioned previously, data base management systems, used either as a DSS tool or as a component of a DSS generator, are doing much to facilitate the handling of data.

An interesting question is whether the DSS data base should be a separate entity or a part of the organization's overall data base. Experience has shown that most organizations have fared better by taking the separate data base approach. There are several reasons for this. One is the greater control that one has over a dedicated data base, as there is less need to coordinate efforts with data processing personnel. Also, a DBMS can be selected that fits the needs of the DSS exactly, rather than satisfying overall organizational needs. And finally, many decision support systems do not rely on transaction data as much as one might first think, and the data that are required can be placed in the DSS data base when needed.

The Model Base

The models in the model base supply the analysis capabilities in a decision support system. The models can include strategic, tactical, operational, and model building blocks and subroutines, as shown in Figure 14-11. Each type of model has a potential role in a DSS.

Strategic models are used to support top management's strategic planning responsibilities. Potential applications include company objectives planning, policy planning, plant location selection, environmental impact planning, and nonroutine capital budgeting. Strategic models tend to be broad in scope, with many variables expressed in compressed, aggregated form. The time horizons for the models are expressed in years, as are top management's strategic planning responsibilities. Much of the data required

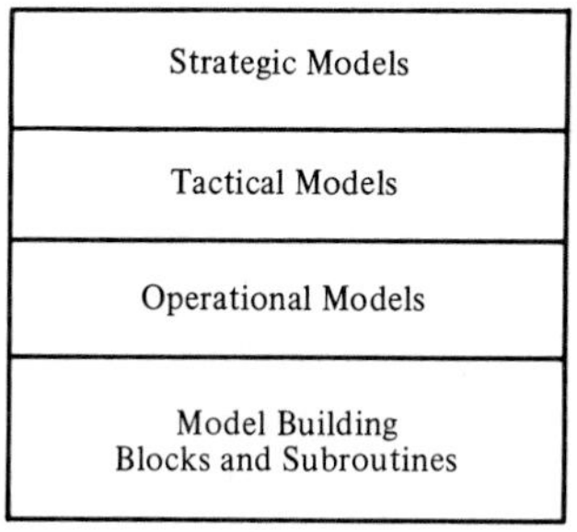

```
+-------------------------------------+
|         Strategic Models            |
+-------------------------------------+
|         Tactical Models             |
+-------------------------------------+
|        Operational Models           |
+-------------------------------------+
|         Model Building              |
|      Blocks and Subroutines         |
+-------------------------------------+
```

FIGURE 14-11   The DSS model base.

by the models is external rather than transaction oriented. The models tend to be of a descriptive rather than of an optimization nature.

Tactical models are employed by middle management to assist in allocating and controlling the organization's resources. Examples of tactical models include financial planning, manpower requirements planning, sales promotion planning, plant layout determination, and routine capital budgeting. Tactical models are usually applicable only to an organizational subsystem, such as production, and there is some aggregation of variables. Their time horizon varies from one month to less than two years. Some external data are needed, but the greatest requirements are for internal data. Some tactical models include optimization capabilities.

Operational models are used to support the day-to-day work activities of the organization. Credit scoring, production scheduling, inventory control, motion and time analysis, and quality control are all potential application areas. Operational models are used by first-line managers to support decision making with a daily to monthly time horizon. The models normally use internal data and often include optimization features.

Strategic, tactical, and operational models can be used to support ad hoc or repetitive decision making. Ad hoc models are used for a one-time-only decision-making task and can be discarded after the decision has been made. The Houston Oil and Minerals example falls into this category of a model which was used only once. Models that are used over and over again become a permanent component of the DSS. The computer-assisted dispatching DSS at Southern Railway, which is discussed in the next chapter, contains models that are used on a continuous basis.

In addition to strategic, tactical, and operational models, the model base might contain *model building blocks and subroutines.* These are the DSS tools that were described previously. They include optimization packages such as those for linear programming, financial analysis packages such as internal rate-of-return analysis, and statistical analysis packages such as regression analysis. They can be stand-alone packages such as BMDP or may be combined in a DSS generator such as IFPS.

The building blocks and subroutines can be used in several ways. They can be used on their own for applications such as data analysis. They can also be employed as component parts of larger models, such as an internal rate-of-return calculation in a financial model. They can be used to determine the variables and parameters in a model as in the use of regression analysis to create a forecasting model. And finally, they can be employed to update models by reexamining the functional relationships used in a model.

Models have not always been as helpful to decision makers as the model builders and users have hoped they would be. There are several reasons for this, and DSS holds the potential for reducing or eliminating several major problems associated with the use of models. One problem is *the difficulty of keeping models up-to-date.* An all-too-common situation has been one of the model builders' creating a model, turning it over to the users, and then moving on to other projects. Because no easy way exists of updating the

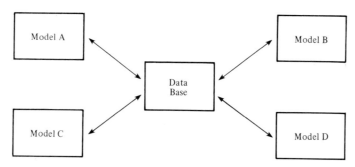

FIGURE 14-12   Integrating models through the data base.

models, over time the models become out of date. Then, one of two conditions occurs, both of which are bad. The first is that the user stops using the model. The second is that the user continues to use the model, but the model's output is no longer valid. With a well-thought-out DSS, the user has the capability of updating the models. The data base contains the data needed to do the updating, and the building blocks and subroutines are available to facilitate the process.

Another major problem with the use of models has been *the lack of integration among models*, which has resulted in the problem of suboptimization. To reduce this problem, models need to be able to "talk" to one another. With a DSS approach to modeling, this integration is potentially accomplished through the data base with the help of the software system. Figure 14-12 shows how this integration takes place. The models feed their output to the data base, which makes the output from each model available to every other model. The software system facilitates the entering and extracting of model output into and from the data base.

The Software Interface

The user interacts with the DSS through the software interface. The importance of this interface has already been discussed along with the DSS data base and model base. It provides the data and model management that are so important in providing effective decision support.

An aspect of the software interface that has not been discussed is the dialog between the DSS and the user. The dialog options that are available should be appropriate for the DSS. Dialog options determine how the DSS is directed and what the DSS provides as output.

A DSS can be directed in several different ways. One approach is to have a menu-driven system. The user simply selects the desired options from a series of menus. This approach is very effective with novice users who need considerable guidance. Another approach is to have a macro command language through which the user directs the system. This approach provides more flexibility but requires the user to be more familiar with the system. Recently, other approaches have been developed. For example, some systems use an input form displayed on a CRT, and the user fills in the form with a light pen. These inputs are then processed by the DSS and the results are displayed.

Output to the decision maker can be provided in a variety of ways. Printed reports, tables, graphical displays, and even voice output are some of the options. A variety of studies have shown that the type of output provided has an impact on the quality of the decisions that are made and on the user's perceptions of the system.[17] It is important to provide output that is appropriate for the users of the systems and for the decisions being supported.

DSS generators provide some flexibility in how they are directed and even more flexibility in the output that is provided. For example, a user can custom-build models or execute models that have already been created and stored. The decision maker can define reports, use preformatted reports, call for tables, or request graphs. Over time, even more flexibility should become available as advances in computer hardware and software continue.

The User

The person who is faced with the problem or the decision that the DSS is designed to support has been referred to as the *user,* the *manager*, or the *decision maker*. These terms fail to reflect, however, the heterogeneity that exists among users of the DSS. There are differences in the positions that the users hold, the way in which a final decision is reached, and the users' cognitive preferences, abilities, and way of arriving at a decision.

A DSS has two broad classes of users: managers and staff specialists. Staff specialists, such as planning analysts, production planners, and marketing researchers, outnumber managers by about a 3-to-2 ratio. Knowing who will actually have hands-on use of the DSS is important when one is designing a DSS. In general, managers expect systems to be more user-friendly than do staff specialists. Staff specialists tend to be more detail-oriented and are more willing to use complex systems in their day-to-day work.

Even within the categories of managers and staff specialists, there are subcategories that are important and that influence DSS design. Managers differ by organizational level, functional area, education, and need for analytic support. Staff specialists differ in areas such as functional area, education, and relationship to management.

In the previous chapter, we discussed the different ways that decisions can be made. Some decisions are made independently by a single decision maker, and others are the result of a group process. In the case of a *single*

---

[17] See, for example, Gary W. Dickson, James A. Senn, and Norman Chervany, "Research in Information Systems: The Minnesota Experiments." *Management Science*, May 1977: 913–923.

decision maker, the DSS provides *personal support,* and personal computers have been very effective in providing this kind of decision support. *Sequential interdependent decisions* require decision makers to make part of a decision and then to pass it on to other decision makers, who make their contributions to the decision. Decision support systems that support sequential interdependent decision making must provide *organizational support.* Capabilities such as access by multiple users throughout the organization and the ability to store and retrieve data, models, and other users' contributions to the decision are important in the provision of organizational support. *Pooled interdependent decisions* are made by a group after interaction and negotiation by group members. A DSS for this type of decision making should provide *group support.*

Users differ in how they arrive at decisions. In the previous chapter, it was pointed out that some decision makers are more rationalistic in their decision making, and that others are more intuitive. A DSS that fails to accommodate these differences is unlikely to be well received. For example, a highly structured DSS that serves an intuitive decision maker with an unstructured decision-making task will not be perceived as being as helpful as a system with more flexibility (i.e., a menu-driven versus a macro command system). Decision makers also differ in their ability to make effective use of different types of analyses. For example, a probabilistic financial planning system would be of limited value to a decision maker who has had no training in or experience with probability concepts. Users also have preferences in the way in which they arrive at a decision. Some are highly autocratic, and others are highly participative. A DSS for an autocratic manager should focus on providing personal support, whereas a participative manager would prefer to have the DSS provide organizational support.

Operating and Evolving a DSS

After a DSS has been built, it is ready to be put into operation. Much has already been suggested about the operation of a DSS. You know how it has been created, about its general structure and components, and especially about the software interface and the user(s). Of some continuing interest, however, might be who actually "pushes the buttons."

Despite efforts to make decision support systems easy to use, many managers, especially top managers, are not hands-on DSS users. There are many reasons for this: poor computer skills, weak typing skills, an unwillingness to take the time and effort to learn how to use the DSS and to operate it, and a preference to have someone else operate the DSS. When an intermediary is used, a staff specialist or a lower-level manager typically assumes this role.

There are advantages to having an intermediary operate a DSS. Because the intermediary normally has better computer skills, is more familiar with the DSS, and uses it more frequently, less time and effort can be devoted to making the system easy to use. Also, an intermediary can suggest analysis options that the DSS can perform and help interpret the output for the user.

By its very nature, a DSS normally evolves over time, but how it changes varies considerably. One possibility is that the DSS may be discarded. This might occur if the DSS fails to be useful or if the DSS was created for a one-time decision and the decision has been made. The latter situation is served by an ad hoc DSS. Another possibility is that the DSS may evolve as more is learned about the decision maker and his or her information needs. This may require minor or even major changes in the DSS. The DSS can also expand in its scope. It can serve more decision makers, additional organizational levels, or a broader range of decisions. It can also go into production use, where it may be used on a regular basis and changes may be made when needed. Institutional DSS are of this type. Clearly, a DSS can evolve in several different ways, depending on the situation.

Summary

It is important to be familiar with some of the details of how a DSS is built, whether one simply approves the creation of a DSS, is a user of a DSS, or is a DSS builder. There is a process that is typically followed when a DSS is created: the need for the DSS is recognized, the DSS is approved for development, hardware and software for the DSS are selected, the DSS builders create the DSS, the DSS is operated, and over time the DSS evolves. Each step in this process has important component parts.

A DSS should be built only in response to a need for the system. The DSS should be created to enhance decision-making effectiveness.

Before a DSS is developed, it must be approved. Factors that affect the approval process for a DSS include the need for the system, the benefits and costs of the system, the time available for approval, the existence of a champion, and the available hardware and software.

Building a DSS involves decisions about the computer hardware to be used. One option is to use a time-sharing network. Other options include personal, mini-, and mainframe computers. Each option offers advantages and disadvantages.

Software must also be selected for the DSS. One approach is to piece the DSS together with DSS tools. The commonly used tools are programming languages, statistical analysis packages, optimization packages, and data base management systems. DSS generators can also be used in the creation of a DSS. They include a variety of capabilities that are important when one is building a DSS. An example has been given of the application of IFPS to new product planning in order to illustrate the use of a DSS generator.

A three-step selection process is recommended when one is choosing a DSS generator. First, potential DSS generators can be initially screened by means of a checklist of important factors and features. Then, the most promising DSS generators can be tested on typical applications. And finally, users of the different DSS generators still under consideration can be asked about their experiences with the generators and the vendors.

After the computer hardware and software are selected, the DSS builders begin their work. Planners and specialized staff personnel are typically the actual builders of a DSS. CBIS personnel may aid in the creation of a DSS and are especially important in providing hardware, systems software, and communications support.

The general structure and components of a DSS include the data base, the model base, the software interface, and the user. The data in the data base can include transaction data, other internal data, and external data. Data base management systems are important to DSS data bases. Many organizations have fared better by keeping the DSS data base separate from the organization's overall data base.

The model base can include strategic, tactical, operational, and model building blocks and subroutines. The strategic models support top management's strategic planning responsibilities. Tactical models assist middle management in allocating and controlling the organization's resources. Operational models support lower management in supervising the organization's day-to-day work activities. Model building blocks and subroutines play an important role in creating and updating the strategic, tactical, and operational models. Model integration is important to a DSS, and it can be achieved through the data base with the help of the software interface.

The user interacts with the DSS through a software interface. The dialog between the decision maker and the DSS includes how the user directs the actions of the DSS and what the DSS provides the user as output.

The users of a DSS can be very heterogeneous. They can be managers or staff specialists; can require personal, organizational, or group support; and can differ in cognitive preferences, abilities, and ways of arriving at a decision.

After a DSS has been built, it is put into operation. Typically, it is operated by a staff specialist, even if the output is to be used by a manager. Over time, the DSS evolves in order to better meet the needs of the decision makers and the organization.

Assignments

14-1. Indicate whether the items listed below are more an indicator of decision-making effectiveness or data-processing efficiency.

    a. Getting faster turnaround times on production runs.
    b. Generating better master production plans.
    c. Improving the evaluations of new product proposals.
    d. Providing a response to more queries per hour.

14-2. Comment on the following position: "The value analysis approach to analyzing the development of a DSS is no approach at all! It permits users to justify the creation of any system they want, almost independent of the dollars and cents involved."

14-3. A DSS can vary from supporting one-time-only decision making to supporting decision making on a continuous basis. How are the approval factors and process likely to differ for these two types of situations?

14-4. Described here are the characteristics of two decision support systems. Based on the available information, make a hardware recommendation. Possible options include a time-sharing network and a mainframe, mini, or personal computer.

    a. The production department needs decision support in production planning and scheduling. The production plan shows, on a monthly basis, what will be produced during the coming year. The production schedule has a much shorter time horizon and shows what will be produced on a daily basis. Both the production plan and the production schedule require data maintained in the organization's data base. For example, the production plan needs to be linked to sales forecasts, and the production schedule needs to be linked to the inventory master file. A variety of people will use the DSS, including first-level and middle management, production planners, and industrial engineers. The DSS will be used on a continuous basis.

    b. Sam Gonzales has a small geological consulting business. He advises his clients on the likelihood of finding oil in areas where they are considering drilling. Over the years, he has developed a set of analytic aids that he uses in performing an analysis. He is interested in creating a DSS in order to perform the analysis that he has been performing manually. He also would like to put some of his personal record-keeping on a computer.

14-5. An affirmative action officer in a large company is considering creating a DSS to help her analyze proposed company personnel policies. The models in the DSS would be of a Markov process type.

$$
\begin{array}{cc}
\text{State Vector} & \begin{array}{c} \text{Transition Matrix} \\ \text{To} \\ C_1\ C_2\ \ldots\ C_n \end{array} \\[2em]
\begin{array}{c} C_1\ C_2\ \ldots\ C_n \\[0.5em] [\,p_1\ p_2\ \ldots\ p_n\,] \end{array} &
\begin{array}{c} C_1 \\ \text{From } C_2 \\ \vdots \\ C_{n1} \end{array}
\begin{bmatrix}
p_{11} & p_{12} & \ldots & p_{1n} \\
p_{21} & p_{22} & \ldots & p_{2n} \\
\vdots & & & \\
P_{n1} & P_{nz} & \ldots & P_{nn}
\end{bmatrix}
\end{array}
$$

A state vector is used to indicate the percentages (p_i's) of people in various categories (C_i's), and a transition matrix is used to indicate the probabilities (p_{ik}'s) of people moving from one category to another. In order to simulate the aggregate movement of employees from one job category to another, the state vector is multiplied by the transition matrix. In addition to analyses of this type, the DSS will also need good data base management capabilities in order to interface with the personnel data maintained in the organization's data base.

a. What DSS tools will this application require?

b. Based on your knowledge of DSS generators, are you likely to find all of the necessary DSS tools for this application in a DSS generator?

14-6. A skyrocket flies upward, explodes, and sends a shower of sparks across the evening sky. Is there an analogous relationship to DSS generators and specific decision support systems? Discuss.

14-7. It has been suggested that DSS generators are English-like and have a variety of analysis capabilities. Even though you have no formal training in IFPS, see if you can identify the purpose and the analysis capabilities in the following IFPS program.[18]

```
MODEL RISK VERSION OF 05/08/79 13:11
1 COLUMNS 1-5
2 *
3 *     INCOME STATEMENT
4 *
5 VOLUME=VOLUME ESTIMATE,PREVIOUS VOLUME*VOLUME GROWTH RATE
6 SELLING PRICE=PRICE ESTIMATE,PREVIOUS SELLING PRICE*1.06
7 SALES=VOLUME*SELLING PRICE
8 UNIT COST=UNIRAND(.80,.95)
9 VARIABLE COST=VOLUME*UNIT COST
10 DIVISION OVERHEAD=15%*VARIABLE COST
11 STLINE DEPR(INVESTMENT, SALVAGE, LIFE, DEPRECIATION)
12 COST OF GOODS SOLD=VARIABLE COST+DIVISION
   OVERHEAD+DEPRECIATION
13 GROSS MARGIN=SALES-COSTS OF GOODS SOLD
14 OPERATING EXPENSE=.02*SALES
15 INTEREST EXPENSE=15742,21522,21147,24905,21311
16 *
17 NET BEFORE TAX=GROSS MARGIN-OPERATING EXPENSE-INTEREST
   EXPENSE
```

[18]This program is adapted from one in *IFPS Tutorial* (Austin, Texas: Execucom Systems Corporation, 1979).

```
18 TAXES = TAX RATE*NET BEFORE TAX
19 NET AFTER TAX = NET BEFORE TAX - TAXES
20 *
21 INVESTMENT = 100000,125000,0,100000,0
22 *
23 RATE OF RETURN = IRR(NET AFTER
   TAX + DEPRECIATION,INVESTMENT)
24 *
25 * DATA ESTIMATES
26 TAX RATE = .46
MONTE CARLO 200
SEED .4
COLUMNS 5
HIST RATE OF RETURN, NONE
```

14-8. Management is interested in obtaining a DSS generator for in-house use. Based on an analysis of potential applications, a number of factors and considerations have been identified as being important in the selection of a DSS generator: It should be English-like and non-procedural; have good forecasting, statistical analysis, and financial analysis capabilities; be able to perform "what if" analysis, goal seeking, and consolidations; have a good data base management system and report generator; provide graphic display; possess an excellent security system; and cost less than $100,000. Using the data provided in Table 14-2, identify one or more DSS generators that meet the stated criteria.

14-9. Review the list of typical DSS generator capabilities that is given in the chapter. If a DSS generator is not used, which of these capabilities would require the involvement of specialists in building the DSS? Who would these specialists have to be?

14-10. Listed here are data that might be needed in a DSS. Indicate whether the data are transaction, other internal, or external data. Where might the data come from?

a. Total industry sales.
b. The firm's market share.
c. The cost of producing the product.
d. The amount of inventory on hand.
e. The amount of the product scheduled for production.

14-11. Listed here are models that might be found in a DSS model base. Indicate whether each model is an example of a strategic, a tactical, an operational, or a model building block or subroutine.

a. A cash flow model for the next month.
b. A trend analysis model.
c. A model of the firm and the industry in which it competes.

    d. A model for evaluating applicants for clerical positions.

    e. A transfer pricing model.

14-12. The most natural way of communicating is through the spoken word. Although some progress has been made in being able to talk to computers, it will be some time before users will be able to communicate with their machines in this way. Why has progress been slow in this area when it has been so rapid in others?

14-13. The chapter suggests that such factors as the nature of the decision and the characteristics of the decision maker influence the design of the output from a DSS. Read Gary W. Dickson, James A. Senn, and Normal Chervanys' article "Research in Information Systems: The Minnesota Experiments." *Management Science*, May 1977, pp. 913–923, and write a report on how the reported findings should influence the design of the output from a system.

14-14. A variety of studies indicates that, in most instances, staff specialists rather than managers operate a DSS. Thinking twenty-five years in the future, do you still see this as being the case? Develop a list of reasons for your position.

CASE   Financial Planning for SRCUS

The Southeastern Regional Credit Union School (SRCUS) is a concentrated educational and training experience designed for people seriously interested in expanding their knowledge of and ability to serve in staff or official capacities in the credit union movement. SRCUS is a three-year, college-level program endorsed by the Credit Union National Association, Inc., and administered by participating state credit union leagues in cooperation with the University of Georgia College of Business Administration and Center for Continuing Education. SRCUS participants spend two weeks of in-residence study in Athens, Georgia, each summer for three consecutive years.

    SRCUS has an academic coordinator who works with the education directors of the sponsoring state credit union leagues in defining SRCUS curriculum, scheduling sessions, selecting and recruiting faculty, administering and teaching in the program, and performing financial planning.

    In the fall of each year, there is a review of the past program, and plans are made for the next year. The curriculum, the faculty, any special problems and concerns, and the overall success of the program are discussed. The revenues and expenses of the program are examined. Revenues come from student tuitions and are directly related to the number of students who attend SRCUS each year. A typical listing of expense items is shown in Table 1.

    SRCUS is not intended to make a profit, but, on the other hand, the sponsoring credit union leagues would like it to break even. There are several ways that this objective can be accomplished. One way is to maintain control over budgeted versus actual expenses. This approach requires accurate cost projections and restraint on unnecessary expenditures. An-

TABLE 1 Expenses Associated with SRCUS

Salaries (UGA faculty)	
UGA faculty salaries	XXX
Academic coordinator's salary	XXX
Staff benefits fees	XXX
Travel expenses	XXX
Honoraria (visiting faculty)	XXX
Housing	XXX
Food service	
Opening-night social	XXX
Coffee breaks	XXX
Banquet	XXX
Lunches	XXX
Gratuities	XX
Photographs	XXX
Duplicating and mailing	XXX
Supplies and materials	XXX
Georgia Center overhead	XXX
Total cost	X,XXX

other avenue is the setting of student tuition. There is a desire to keep student tuition as low as possible and yet to maintain a high-quality, financially viable program. And finally, higher enrollments result in greater revenues. At the annual review and planning session, each state league's education director voluntarily sets a goal for first-year students from his or her state.

The academic coordinator plays an important role in the financial planning and controlling of SRCUS. Each year, he has the responsibility of presenting the actual versus the budgeted costs for the previous year. He is asked such questions as "What costs will change next year?" and "How many students will return for their second and third years of the program?" He is also asked to contribute to the thinking about what tuition should be charged and how many first-year students to try to enroll.

The academic coordinator has been considering creating a DSS to assist in the financial planning for SRCUS.

Questions

1. Is this a reasonable DSS application? Discuss.

2. Describe in detail how you would build a DSS for the application. Be sure to include potential hardware, software, DSS tools, DSS generators, data, models, model building blocks and subroutines, output, building of the DSS, and its operation.

Other Readings

Bennett, John L. *Building Decision Support Systems*. Reading, Mass.: Addison-Wesley, 1983.

Bonczek, Robert H., Clyde W. Holsapple, and Andrew B. Whinston. "Future Directions for Developing Decision Support Systems." *Decision Sciences* 11 (1980): 616–631.

Hogue, Jack T., and Hugh J. Watson. "Management's Role in the Approval and Administration of Decision Support Systems," *MIS Quarterly* (June 1983): 15–26.

Keen, Peter G. W., and Michael S. Scott Morton. *Decision Support Systems: An Organizational Perspective*. Reading, Mass.: Addison-Wesley, 1978.

Sprague, Ralph H., Jr. "A Framework for the Development of Decision Support Systems." *MIS Quarterly* (December 1980): 1–26.

Sprague, Ralph H., Jr., and Eric D. Carlson. *Building Effective Decision Support Systems*. Englewood Cliffs, N.J.: Prentice-Hall, 1982.

Sprague, Ralph H., Jr., and Hugh J. Watson. "A Decision Support System for Banks." *Omega: The International Journal of Management Sciences* 4, no. 6 (1976): 657–671.

Sprague, Ralph H., Jr., and Hugh J. Watson. "Bit by Bit: Toward Decision Support Systems." *California Management Review* (Fall 1979): 60–68.

Thierauf, Robert J. *Decision Support Systems for Effective Planning and Control: A Case Study Approach*. Englewood Cliffs, N.J.: Prentice-Hall, 1982.

Wagner, Gerald R. "Decision Support Systems: The Real Substance." *Interfaces* (April 1981): 77–86.

Chapter 15

Applications
of DSS

Learning Objectives

After studying this chapter, you will be able to:
1. More effectively identify potential DSS applications.
2. More effectively develop DSS applications.
3. More effectively assess the benefits of potential DSS applications.
4. Describe the financial planning system at the Louisiana National Bank.
5. Describe the marketing-mix model known as BRANDAID.
6. Describe the computer-assisted dispatching system at Southern Railway.
7. Describe the DSS for ski area design.
8. Define the following terms:

financial planning system	computer-assisted dispatching
brand manager	train dispatcher
marketing-mix decisions	terrain capacity analysis
aggregate response model	market balance analysis
model calibration	skill balance analysis

Previous chapters have explored the DSS concept and the process and technology used in developing decision support systems. This chapter focuses its attention on *successful DSS applications*. You will learn how several decision support systems function, how they were developed, how they are used, and what their impact has been on decision making and organizational success. These DSS examples should enhance your understanding and appreciation of decision support systems.

The first DSS is a *financial planning system* used by the Louisiana National Bank. The DSS was created in response to a declining profit trend that traditional bank policies had failed to correct. The financial planning system is credited with helping to solve the bank's problems and today continues to be an important source of decision support.

BRANDAID is the next DSS discussed. It is used by marketing managers who are responsible for pricing, promotion, advertising, sales force allocation, and packaging decisions. We will see how BRANDAID was used by a marketing manager in charge of a well-established brand of packaged goods sold through grocery stores.

The next DSS is a *computer-assisted dispatching system* that was developed by Southern Railway. The system shows the current status of trains on color CRTs, allows the train dispatcher to set track switches through the computer, helps to maintain records of train activity, and, most important from a decision support perspective, suggests when trains should meet and pass in order to minimize delays. The dispatching system is relatively new, but the early indications are that it is resulting in significant cost reductions.

The final DSS is microcomputer-based and is used to support *ski area design*. Expert judgment is combined with a number of relatively simple computations to provide information about possible downhill trail and uphill lift design alternatives. The DSS has allowed ski area designers to develop better designs more quickly.

DSS Applications

Before we turn to the discussion of the three decision support systems that are the focal point of this chapter, a few points about DSS applications need to be emphasized. First, it should be kept in mind that a *variety of concerns* can lead to the development of DSS: changing economic conditions, government reporting requirements, competitive pressures, or any of a myriad of other reasons. Second, a DSS *can have many features* such as graphics, data management, and forecasting. Even though we have devoted a considerable amount of time to DSS generators because of their potential role in developing decision support systems, they are not a necessity. They simply make the development of certain types of decision support systems easier. And finally, it should be remembered that there is *virtually an unlimited number of potential DSS applications*. All that is needed is a set of semistructured or

435

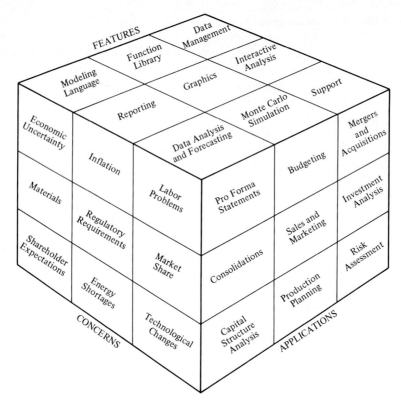

FIGURE 15-1   Concerns, features and applications of DSS. (Source: "EMPIRE®", Applied Data Research, Inc., Princeton, N.J., p. 2.)

unstructured decision-making tasks that might benefit from decision support of an analytic nature. These three aspects of DSS applications—the concern that motivates their development, their features, and their potential range of applications—are illustrated in Figure 15-1.

Financial Planning at the Louisiana National Bank

The *Louisiana National Bank* (LNB) is located in Baton Rouge, the state capital of Louisiana.[1] In 1958, Charles McCoy became the bank's chief executive officer. Under his leadership, the LNB has developed a reputation for innovation. The bank was the first in Baton Rouge to offer credit cards and to install automatic teller machines. Recently, a debit card and a telephone bill

---

[1] This description is summarized from Ralph H. Sprague, Jr., and Ronald L. Olson, "The Financial Planning System at Louisiana National Bank," *MIS Quarterly*, September 1979: 35–46.

paying system have been implemented. Today, the LNB is the largest bank in Baton Rouge with assets in excess of $600 million.

In the fall of 1973, the LNB was facing serious problems. Profits had been declining for over a year. Traditional policies for managing the bank were failing. There was a lack of coordination among decision makers. The bank was slow to react to market and regulation changes.

In response to this deteriorating situation, McCoy designated Gil Urban as corporate planner and charged him with the responsibility of developing a system to help analyze the bank's performance and to support top management decision making. Urban was an excellent choice for this position, because he had extensive banking experience and a personal interest in planning and analysis activities.

The Development of FPS

After an intensive six-week study, Urban began developing the *financial planning system* (FPS). The initial system was designed to produce reports of the type and format that top management had been receiving in the past. Consequently, the transition to FPS went smoothly, and the reports became the focus of discussion and decision making in management meetings. Over time, management's understanding of FPS grew, and the capabilities of the system were refined and expanded.

System Components

FPS has three component parts: data, reports and analyses, and forecasts. Each component plays an important role in the functioning of FPS.

Data
On a monthly basis, summary data from the bank's general ledger accounting system are extracted and entered into FPS. The data are added to a matrix of historical data in which the rows are items in the summary chart of accounts and the columns are time periods. The data base maintains up to 3 years of monthly figures and up to 7.5 years of quarterly figures. The data base also stores twelve periods of forecast data, based on the system's forecasting and simulation capabilities.

Reports and Analyses
Each month, FPS produces a complete set of summary financial statements, including the balance sheet, the income statement, and standard operating reports. Data from the current month are compared with the forecast, the budget, and the actual data for the previous year. A number of special reports are also generated. Of particular importance to the LNB management are the interest rate–volume–mix analysis and the line-of-business-analysis reports.

The latter shows the sources and uses of funds for three major segments of the bank: the retail or customer sector, the public sector, and the commercial sector.

Forecasts

The reports are also forecast twelve months into the future by FPS. Values for the independent variables are entered by management or statistically estimated by FPS with a management override capability. The system contains a built-in linear programming submodel that can be used to optimize earnings with respect to yields, subject to constraints or guidelines defined by management. Forecasts are of a "rolling" or "constant horizon" nature. A forecast of the next twelve months is generated at the beginning of each new month as new data become available. The system can also be used to forecast as far into the future as desired on a monthly or quarterly basis.

Use of the System

FPS is employed in several ways. On the first Tuesday of each month, FPS is used to supply the planning committee with reports and graphs that show the previous month's activity. The planning committee is also given the newly prepared twelve-month forecast.

During the meeting of the planning committee, anticipated changes and pending issues are discussed. Frequently, there are questions and possibilities that need to be explored further at the next meeting after additional runs of FPS. Normally, the planning committee meets twice a month, but in periods of rapid change or when a major set of strategies is under consideration, it meets weekly.

Urban also uses FPS to prepare forecasts for other bank officers who wish to investigate the consequences of possible strategies. The bank officers are interested in the bankwide impact of their decisions because they know that their recommendations and actions will be examined in this context.

Urban also uses FPS on his own initiative. He investigates areas such as the impact of pending changes in money market rates, banking regulations, market trends, and internal policy changes. Urban considers it part of his job to watch systematically for opportunities that will require management action.

FPS also plays an important role in the bank's budgeting process. Each fall, a "grass-roots" budget, as it is called, is prepared. It is composed of about nine thousand data items: one for each budget line item, for each of the cost centers, for each of the twelve months of the coming year. Once the tentative budget is prepared, summaries are then extracted and entered into FPS in the same way that actual data are transferred after the end of each month. FPS is then used to assess the combined impact of the budget estimates, to examine the reasonableness of the estimates compared with top management's judgment, and to search for any inconsistencies in interrelated areas.

Any adjustments of the tentative budget are made through a process of negotiation between top management and the cost center managers. The detailed final budget is approved by mid-December and is then carried in the automated accounting system, which produces monthly budget variance reports for each cost center during the coming year. A summary form of the budget is also stored in FPS for use in summary reports and comparative analyses.

Benefits

The LNB has benefited considerably from the use of FPS. Most important, *it has made the bank more profitable.* Figure 15-2 shows how the bank's profit has grown since late 1974 when FPS was first used to support decision making. As Charles McCoy has said, "I attribute the profit turnaround to our management's creative use of the financial planning system."

The use of FPS has led to *new policies for asset–liability management.* An example of this occurred in 1975 when the government authorized consumer certificates of deposits (CDs) in small denominations for four- and six-year maturities. Many banks hesitated to offer these CDs because of the fear that savers would shift their regular savings to the higher paying CDs. By using FPS, the management at the LNB became convinced that the CDs were an excellent way to obtain long-term funds on which to build their consumer loan portfolio. Consequently, they gave heavy promotion to the CDs, which resulted in increased funds, increased loans, and increased profitability in the retail segment of the LNB's business.

FPS has also provided *a framework, a structure, and a discipline for unified decision making.* Recently, the LNB experienced a growth in credit card loans and decided to sell a large portion of the loans to a New York bank.

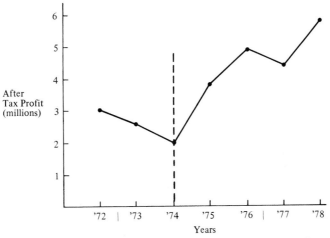

FIGURE 15-2   Profits at the Louisiana National Bank.

TABLE 15-1 Benefits of Using FPS at the Louisiana National Bank

- Increased profits.
- New policies for asset–liability management.
- A framework, a structure, and a discipline for unified decision making.
- Improved reporting and negotiating with bank regulators.
- Faster responses to changes.
- Reduced clerical costs.

Without the convincing analysis provided by FPS, this move would have been strongly opposed by several of the bank's managers because of the bank's history as the leading regional credit card lender.

Reporting and negotiating with bank regulators has been facilitated by FPS. In 1978, management noted that FPS forecast a need for additional capital because of a growing demand for loans. Using FPS, management developed a "balanced growth" plan. This plan called for selling capital debentures instead of capital stock and required the approval of the bank examiners. Not only was the plan approved by the examiners, but the examiners have been subsequently recommending the balanced growth approach to several other banks.

The use of FPS has made it possible to *respond to changes faster*. In March 1978, after several years of liquidity shortages, the LNB was experiencing an average excess liquidity of thirty million dollars a day. FPS forecast, however, that loan growth and deposit shrinkage would create liquidity problems by early fall. Based on this forecast, the planning committee set maximum growth goals for all departments and sold participations in some of the larger loans with good customers. By October, it was clear that the LNB had averted a major liquidity crisis because of the early warning provided by FPS.

FPS produces the normal *monthly reports less expensively* than when they were prepared manually. However, the cost of additional runs to explore alternative plans and assumptions more than consumes this saving. This additional cost does not bother management. As McCoy has said, "FPS clearly paid for itself in helping us generate that first set of strategic plans. Now we don't even think about what it costs, because we couldn't run the bank without it."

Clearly, FPS has resulted in benefits for the LNB. These benefits are summarized in Table 15-1.

Key Factors of Success

A number of factors have led to the successful development and use of FPS at the Louisiana National Bank. A key factor was the *support and involvement of top management*. They requested the system and have been its primary beneficiaries.

TABLE 15-2   Factors Leading to the
Successful Development of FPS at
the Louisiana National Bank

- Top management support and involvement.
- Characteristics of the system's sponsor.
- Organizational environment.
- Transitional development and implementation.
- Unified planning system.

Another important factor was the *characteristics of the system's sponsor.*
Gil Urban was patient, low-keyed, and determined to maintain a low profile.
Although he had the opportunity to build a power base through FPS, he
chose not to do so. Other managers knew this and therefore worked with him
freely.

The bank offered an excellent *organizational environment* for the creation of FPS. There was a need for the system, and the bank had a history of
innovation. Open communications were encouraged, and the system became
a communication vehicle and a framework for unified decision making. Bank
officers have had high morale and pride, which have enabled them to embrace institutional goals over personal goals.

A *transitional development and implementation* approach was used. The
initial version of FPS provided familiar reports and required little additional
understanding. Over time, as trust in the system grew, the system slowly,
patiently, moved managers from the old to new ways of thinking.

And finally, FPS provided *a unified planning system.* It combined three
closely related, but often separated, phases of the planning process: forecasting, analysis, and reporting. FPS allows managers to move from one phase to
another in an easy, integrated manner.

As you can see, the success of FPS at the Louisiana National Bank can be
attributed to a number of factors. These factors are summarized in Table 15-
2. Some of the factors are related to the LNB's management group, others to
the organizational environment, and some to the developmental approach
employed. Each made an important contribution to the success of the LNB's
decision support system.

BRANDAID: A Marketing-Mix Model

A *brand manager* is responsible for marketing decisions about a particular
product sold by a firm. These decisions include what price to charge, how
much to spend on promotion, how to advertise, how sales representatives
should allocate their time, and how to package the product. Collectively,

these are referred to as *marketing-mix decisions*. They are clearly important to the success of a brand.

The effectiveness of marketing-mix decision making is measured in a variety of ways. Clearly, the sales generated by a brand are important. Brand managers are also concerned about the product's market share. Of course, the profit associated with the brand is the bottom-line figure.

Marketing-mix decision making has to consider the environment and actions of competitors. The environment can have a significant impact on sales: just ask any car dealer what effect high interest rates have on new car sales. Many products have a very seasonal sales pattern: Toy sales at Christmas time skyrocket. Consumer markets are competitive. Though companies try to differentiate their brands, the actions taken by competitors usually have an impact and must be considered by brand managers. The problem, then, for brand managers is to make effective marketing-mix decisions for a product selling in an environment that includes competitors.

Its Origin and Function

In the late 1960s, John D. C. Little and others began to address the possibility of providing computerized decision support for marketing-mix decision making. Little's effort several years later resulted in a decision support system called *BRANDAID*.[2] It is a flexible, on-line model and data based system designed to help marketing managers make decisions about price, advertising, promotion, and other marketing variables on the basis of factual data, judgments, and assumptions about how the market works. As will be seen later when its structure is discussed, BRANDAID can be customized for use with different products. Consequently, BRANDAID is not a specific DSS in the strictest sense. It is more of a DSS generator, but not as general purpose as some DSS generators such as IFPS.

Its Structure

The overall structure that BRANDAID envisions is shown in Figure 15-3. The marketing manager is an employee of the manufacturer. He or she makes decisions on product (function and quality), price, advertising, promotion (coupons and samples), and package (appearance and size) that directly affect the consumer. Decisions that affect the retailer are made by the brand manager on price, trade promotion (temporary price reductions and display allowances), salespersons, and package assortment. The retailer affects the

---

[2]This description is based on John D. C. Little, "BRANDAID: A Marketing-Mix Model, Part 1: Structure," *Operations Research*, July–August 1975: 628–655, and John D. C. Little, "BRANDAID: A Marketing-Mix Model, Part 2: Implementation, Calibration, and Case Study," *Operations Research*, July–August 1975: 656–673.

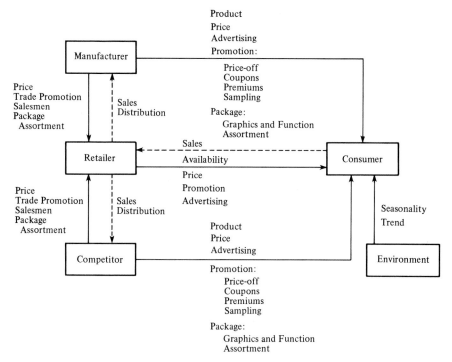

FIGURE 15-3 BRANDAID's overall structure. [Source: John D. C. Little, "BRANDAID: A Marketing-Mix Model, Part 2: Implementation, Calibration, and Case Study," *Operations Research* (July–August 1975), p. 666.]

consumer with decisions on sales availability (shelf space), price, special promotions and display, and sometimes media advertising. Consumer purchases are impacted by the environment, including seasonality and trends in demand. Just as the brand manager's marketing-mix decisions impact the retailer and the consumer, so do the decisions made by competitors. In response to decisions made by the marketing manager, consumers, retailers, competitors, and the influence of the environment, sales flow back up the pipeline, as shown by the dotted line.

BRANDAID employs *aggregate response models*. This means that the output from the models relates decision (controllable) variables to specific sales performance measures. For example, the brand manager can explore through BRANDAID the impact of price changes on market share.

BRANDAID is modular in construction, and individual modules can be added or deleted at will. The major submodels are advertising, promotion, price, salespersons, retail distribution competition, and other influences on sales. The advertising submodel relates the amount spent on advertising to product sales. The promotion submodel covers a wide variety of sales stimulation devices, such as temporary price reductions, premiums, and coupons, and indicates how the pattern of these promotional activities affects sales. The price submodel shows how the price charged by the manufacturer is related to product sales. The salespersons' submodel captures how money spent on salespeople (salary and expenses), the efficiency of the calls, and the quality of the salespeople's calls affect sales. The retail distribution submodel considers the impact on sales of retailer marketing activities such as retail price, retail advertising, availability, quality of shelf position and facings, and number of in-store promotional displays. Another submodel is competition, and it shows how the marketing-mix decisions of competitors can affect the sales of the manufacturer's product. And finally, other influences on sales can be included as submodels. For example, trends and seasonality are often important influences in the environment.

As was mentioned previously, BRANDAID is modular, and not all of the submodels need be employed in a particular application. Some of the submodels are easier to develop than others. For example, the influence of price on sales is easier to model than the impact of retail distribution and competition. Each submodel generates *output* such as that shown in Figure 15-4

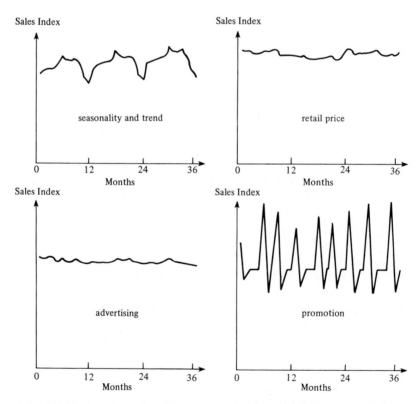

FIGURE 15-4   The output from four BRANDAID submodels when input with company actions and environmental conditions. [Source: John D. C. Little, "BRANDAID: A Marketing-Mix Model, Part 2: Implementation, Calibration, and Case Study," *Operations Research* (July–August 1975), p. 666.]

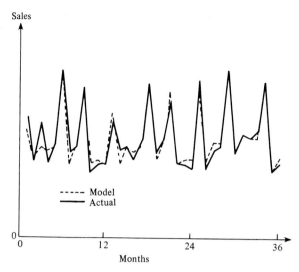

FIGURE 15-5 Tracking BRANDAID's predictions with actual sales data. [Source: John D. C. Little, "BRANDAID: A Marketing-Mix Model, Part 2: Implementation, Calibration, and Case Study," *Operations Research* (July–August 1975), p. 667.]

when *input* with company actions and environmental conditions. Figure 15-4 shows predicted sales (expressed as a sales index) as influenced by seasonality and trend, and decisions on price, advertising, and promotion over the planning horizon. One obtains the combined effect of these factors by multiplying the sales indices generated by the various models. Figure 15-5 shows the result of this multiplication and the tracking of BRANDAID's predictions with actual sales data. In this example, BRANDAID's forecasts are very close to actual sales.

Model Implementation

Experience has shown that the success of BRANDAID in an organizational setting is related to how it is implemented. Little has suggested that *successful implementation* depends on the attitudes and interests of the people concerned. He observed that the best successes have involved:

1. An internal champion who is a senior person on the staff.
2. An appropriate marketing manager who feels comfortable with and sees the opportunities in the project.
3. A models person on location who understands models and computers, believes that they can help, and has a substantial block of his or her own time officially committed to the project.

4. Support from high level executives who display an interest in the project and believe that it has a high potential payoff.

These observations correspond closely with those made by others experienced in developing model-based systems. Perhaps of special interest for DSS is the importance of what Little has referred to as the "models person." This is the "intermediary" and/or "DSS builder" discussed in previous chapters. These are emerging information systems positions that should continue to grow in frequency and importance over time.

In addition to a favorable internal environment for the implementation of BRANDAID, Little has also stressed the importance of an appropriate implementation process. This process includes *introductory* and *ongoing periods*. The steps in each period are summarized in Table 15-3.

Let us consider how the steps in the introductory period can or should be carried out. A *management orientation* can be provided by a one- or two-day seminar for management on marketing models, information systems, and the management sciences in marketing. The *models team* formed should include a marketing manager with decision-making responsibility in the area being modeled (the DSS user); the models specialist who will live with the application, assist in problem formulation, help on data analysis, and perform an educational function for the rest of the team; someone from marketing research with knowledge about the available data; and any other people with skills appropriate to the model's focus. The *initial problem* selected for analysis should be of current concern to the company and be of manageable size. It is best initially to create a small, simple model and to expand it at a later date if warranted. *Calibration* is the process of selecting appropriate model parameters to make the model describe a particular application. It includes the use of judgment, a statistical analysis of historical data, the tracking of model output with actual occurrences to detect deficiencies in the models that need correction, field experiments on actual problems, and the preparation of

TABLE 15-3   The Implementation Process for BRANDAID

Introductory period
- Management orientation.
- Forming a models team.
- Problem selection and formulation.
- Calibration.
- Initial use.

Ongoing period
- Firefighting.
- Tracking and diagnosis.
- Updating and evolution.
- Reuse.

monitoring systems that test whether the model remains valid for its intended purposes. After the model has been calibrated, it is *used* to support decision making on the initial problem.

After the introductory period, BRANDAID goes into ongoing use. It is employed for *firefighting* as unexpected marketing problems occur. New actions are proposed, analyzed by the model, and then carried out. Further *tracking and diagnosis* of the model are conducted as additional sales data become available for comparison with the model's predictions. Based on this tracking and diagnosis and the brand manager's interest in expanding the model's scope, the model is *updated and evolves*. The model is then *reused* for its intended analysis purposes.

A Case Study

BRANDAID has been used in a variety of marketing settings with good results. One reported application has been with a well-established brand of packaged goods sold through grocery stores. The implementation process just described was employed. The models team calibrated and customized the model over a period of about three calendar months, meeting on the average about a halfday per week. Not suprisingly, the initial use of the model revealed deficiencies that required modifications of the model.

On an ongoing basis, the model has been used to analyze price changes, proposed advertising changes, the dropping of a promotion, and its subsequent reinstatement. In each case, the analysis provided by the model has been an input to the decision.

In many cases, the strategies suggested by the model have been used. However, there have also been instances in which other considerations have dictated the ultimate strategy selected.

Information that is counterintuitive is often the most interesting and important output from a model. This type of information was provided one year when the year-to-date sales of the brand were substantially ahead of the previous year, but the model suggested that the brand was in trouble. A promotion had been run in January of the current year but not in the previous year. In March of the current year, there had been a price increase, but its impact was being masked by a large corporate TV special and coordinated promotion in which the brand, among others, had been featured. These conditions led to an unrealistic picture of brand sales. If action had not been taken, brand sales would have dropped substantially as the impact of special promotion and advertising programs faded and the effect of the price increase was seen. Based on the model's analysis, the brand manager proposed additional promotion, a plan that management accepted.

BRANDAID has continued to be used for brand planning and for firefighting. Its use has been expanded to additional brands. This is just one of several companies where BRANDAID has been used for applications involving a wide range of complexity and marketing detail.

Computer-Assisted Dispatching at Southern Railway

Southern Railway provides freight transportation service east of the Mississippi River and as far north as Cincinnati and Washington, D.C.[3] It is a large organization, employing over twenty thousand employees and receiving over $1.5 billion in annual sales revenue. It is now a part of the Norfolk Southern Corporation, the holding company formed by the consolidation of Southern Railway and the Norfolk and Western Railway Company in mid-1982. Southern Railway has been using computers actively since 1954, when they acquired an IBM 705, and computer use has been widespread and growing since that time.

An important part of any railroad operation is *train dispatching*. This activity is performed by a *train dispatcher*, who controls the movement of trains along their routes. It is the train dispatcher who decides what route a train should follow, and when it should be held up to meet opposing trains or to allow following trains to pass. These are important decisions for safety and service reasons, and also for cost reasons, because they affect delays and thus time on the track.

One train dispatcher typically controls the movement over one hundred to five hundred miles of track. Heavily traveled segments often operate under centralized traffic control (CTC), a system in which the dispatcher remotely controls signals and switch settings (into and out of siding tracks) from a console in his office. At the other extreme, where there are no signals in the field (so-called dark territory), the dispatcher controls train movement by issuing written and/or verbal orders by radio to train crews. In all cases, the dispatcher is responsible for safety, for the maintenance of proper records, and for the efficient operation of his territory. Train dispatchers report directly to a chief dispatcher, who, in turn, reports to a division superintendent.

Origin and Development of the CAD System

Southern Railway began investigating *computer-assisted dispatching* (CAD) in 1976.[4] Shortly before this time, a major vendor had installed a new CTC system at an existing office in South Carolina. This new system used a minicomputer and color CRTs to display track diagrams and train locations and to send switch and signal commands, but it provided no computerized decision support and only a few record-keeping capabilities. When the same

---

[3]The authors would like to express their appreciation to Richard Sauder at Southern Railway and to Jack Hogue at the University of Texas at Arlington for providing the documents and other information on which this description is based.

[4]The CAD acronym should not be confused with computer assisted design, as in computer assisted design/computer assisted manufacturing (CAD/CAM).

vendor proposed to further upgrade the system to provide these capabilities, Southern Railway management decided it would be more beneficial to develop a system in-house because the system would be essentially "new ground" for whoever developed it. It was also felt that communication between system users and system developers would be enhanced if the developers were Southern Railway personnel.

The development process for this CAD system was somewhat more traditional than that for many other decision support systems. The specifications for the system were detailed in advance and did not change significantly during the development process. The system was custom-built with DSS tools, as there were no DSS generators appropriate for the application. The initial development utilized quasi-static displays generated on color CRTs to determine acceptable display formats and dispatcher interaction considerations. Next, a prototype system was developed in a simulator environment; dispatchers and other transportation personnel played an integral part in operating the simulator and in finalizing the design of the CAD system. The first working CAD system was installed in mid-1980 in the North Alabama district of Southern Railway's Alabama Division, a 140-mile, high-volume CTC territory. In early 1982, a second CTC territory between Birmingham, Alabama, and Atlanta was added to the system. In mid-1982, the CAD system was expanded to coordinate all Alabama Division dispatching activities, involving over twelve hundred miles of train operation.

Development time was substantial, requiring twelve man years and encompassing nearly five years of elapsed time. The system has improved train operation, reducing train delay 15 percent in the first year of operation, with additional reductions since additional territories were added to the system. Return on investment has exceeded 50 percent. Current plans call for expansion of the CAD system to other divisions of Southern Railway.

System Hardware

The initial CAD system's hardware consisted of two Data General S-130 minicomputers with 128K of internal memory each, supplemented by two twenty megabyte disks. The North Alabama dispatcher operated from a work station equipped with four color CRTs, radio communication equipment, the dispatcher command keyboard, and a separate data input keyboard. Two of the color CRTs were used for track–train display, one was used to input and display train-related information, and the fourth CRT was used to display the meet–pass plan. The dispatcher's command keyboard was used to issue commands to control points in the field. The data input keyboard was used to enter train data.

Hardware for the enhanced and currently operational CAD system consists of a single Data General S-130 minicomputer with a million bytes of internal memory and fifty megabytes of disk storage. This single operation supports three dispatchers and a chief dispatcher. CTC dispatchers utilize a wall-mounted track display and three color CRTs for meet–pass display and data input.

Capabilities of the CAD System

The CAD system has two main subsystems: the dispatch management system (DMS) and the meet–pass system. The features of both DMS and meet–pass are summarized in Table 15-4.

TABLE 15-4   Major Features of the CAD System

- *Train IDs and actual arrival*—Train IDs are shown on color CRTs and are progressed as trains move past control points. Arrival times are automatically shown as the trains pass control points.
- *Automated train-reporting*—This requires the dispatcher to fill in blanks on a CRT. Assumed information (such as the number of cars on a loaded coal train) is maintained in computer files. Function keys on the dispatchers' keyboards generate various marks.
- *Information display and transfer*—A dispatcher can call up any other dispatcher's data base but cannot update this information. Information can, however, be transferred from one territory to another (e.g., information for a train moving from one territory to another).
- *Chief dispatcher information*—The chief dispatcher has his own CRT, which displays train information on any of the dispatcher's territories. This capability reduces the need to interrupt the dispatcher for information.
- *Event log*—The computer maintains all data received from the field, as well as all commands issued by the dispatcher and the computer's own progressive routing module (see below). A chronological log of events can be generated as needed.
- *Permanent records*—Train and movement reports for payroll purposes and mandatory record-keeping are generated daily. Statistical summaries of division operation can be generated on batch reports on request.
- *Progressive routing*—When invoked by the dispatcher, the computer automatically sets signals to maintain cleared routes ahead of all trains until they cannot be progressed further.
- *Routing plan*—The meet–pass plan generated by the computer considers all trains on the territory and those projected to arrive. It then suggests the combination of "meets" and "passes" to minimize delay to all trains (other objectives, such as minimizing the delay to all trains with unequal importance weights for trains, can also be used). It is when the projected arrival at the destination is late that train priorities are generally considered. The dispatcher can modify the plan by forcing meets, by making trains clear up for opposing trains, and by taking track out of service. The plan is continuously updated.

The DMS handles the traditional dispatching activities of the rail system. This system shows the current status of trains on color CRTs, allows the dispatcher to set track switches and signals through the computer, and helps maintain records of train activity.

The second and most interesting subsystem from a decision support perspective is the meet–pass system. Its basic function is to suggest when trains should meet and pass in order to minimize the delay to all trains. The plan is computer-generated by a branch and bound algorithm (a special type of linear programming algorithm). It uses an objective function that attempts to minimize total delay to all trains on the system or projected during the four- to six-hour planning horizon.

The DMS helps formulate the problem by identifying where trains are currently located, when they are projected to come on the system, and what are their physical characteristics. Meet–pass uses the number of cars, tonnage, horsepower, grade, curvature, and speed limit of the track to calculate the expected running time of the trains between control points. This process is dynamic. When a train reaches the next control point, the running time of that train is updated to reflect that arrival time. Other information input by the dispatcher is taken into account by the planning process, such as track out of service, trains in emergency, pickups and setoffs, and train length versus siding length. In addition to these physical characteristics of trains and tracks, such factors as train priority, crew time off-duty, train schedules, and even expected crew performance are part of the data base and can be used in calculating the best plan.

Meet–pass also has a goal-seeking capability. The dispatcher can specify a goal, and the system generates a plan that satisfies the goal. For example, if a train's projected arrival at a destination is late, the dispatcher can ask meet–pass to generate a plan that will increase the likelihood of an on-time arrival for the train.

The CAD system does not fully automate dispatching activities. It only suggests plans that the dispatcher can choose to accept, modify, or disregard. The dispatcher can also use the CAD system to explore the effectiveness of alternative plans. This has proved to be a useful "what if" capability.

A variety of Southern Railway personnel come into contact with the CAD system. Obviously, the dispatchers who operate the system twenty-four hours a day are important users of the system. The chief dispatcher also uses the system. He monitors the CAD system continuously as a means of ensuring that trains will be dispatched effectively. The division superintendent uses the system for status reporting and reviews of previous operation, but use is not continuous, coming about every half hour. The system also generates summary reports on train and dispatching operations for middle management. Parties who have come into contact with the CAD system have been satisfied with it, and this satisfaction has grown as employees have become more familiar with it and enhancements and refinements have been made.

Benefits

The computer-assisted dispatching system has resulted in two major benefits. First, it has *improved record keeping and reporting* on train activity. Dispatchers and management are better able to determine accurately what has happened in the past and what is currently taking place. Second, the system has effected a *decrease in train delays, which results in lower costs.* Figure 15-6 shows average train delays in 1979, before the system was implemented, and in 1980 and 1981, after the system was put in place.

A variety of explanations account for the decrease in time delays. One is the plan suggested by the meet–pass system. About 80 to 85 percent of the time, the meet–pass plan that is generated by the computer is accepted by the dispatcher. These plans have been found to be very effective. Another explanation is that the record-keeping and reporting system has made better data and information available on which to base decisions. A related advantage is that the dispatchers and operations supervisors can function more as a team in trying to determine the best meet–pass plan. Prior to the implementation of the CAD system, operations supervisors did not have ready access to the type of information needed to encourage any kind of group decision making. Another explanation is that the CAD system has caused certain operating policies to be better defined. Prior to the CAD system, the priorities given to certain types of trains were subject to frequent change, which led to inefficiencies. And finally, the CAD system has created an element of competition for the dispatchers and operations supervisors. There is the challenge of trying to develop a plan that is better than the one suggested by meet–pass.

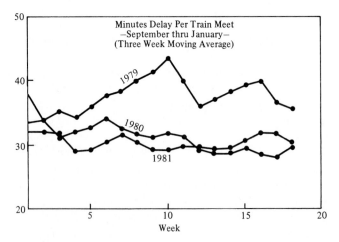

FIGURE 15-6 Average train delays before and after computer-assisted dispatching.

Ski Area Design

The physical design of a ski area is a time-consuming process that requires expert judgment aided by a number of relatively simple calculations.[5] In order to support the design process, a microcomputer-based DSS was created. The DSS saves up to 80 percent of the expert's office design time and helps create a physically and economically balanced design.

The basic physical design of a ski area must balance downhill capacity with uphill capacity. Downhill capacity is expressed as a system of trails cut into a mountain; uphill capacity is represented by a system of lifts to carry skiers from the bottom of the mountain to the top. Ski area design begins with the layout of the downhill trail system.

Terrain Capacity Analysis

The potential trail system is a function of the physical terrain of the mountain. On any mountain there are slopes of varying degrees that can be cut into trails usable by skiers with different skill levels. The steeper the slope grade, the more advanced in ability a skier must be to utilize a trail on that slope. Additionally, there is terrain (e.g., cliffs) that is unusable and terrain that must be left in its original state so that trees and natural formations provide wind breaks and aesthetically appealing mountain scenery separating trails. Although some changes can be made to accommodate a specific trail to a specific-skill-level skier, these changes are small. Basically, a mountain comes with its mixture of potential trails as given to the area design problem. Thus, the potential trail system is devised by a ski area designer physically walking the mountain and then laying out trails on a topographical map. This map layout creates the primary trail system used in the design of the ski area. These data derived from personal inspection and topographical analysis to describe each trail are important data inputs to the DSS.

The initial support provided by the DSS is through the generation of a *terrain capacity analysis*, shown in Table 15-5. This analysis provides the designer with a first look at the total number of skiers that the mountain can handle in a downhill capacity. It combines a set of judgmental decisions with the trail system data to calculate total potential skiers for the area.

Skiers will seek trails by a slope grade related to their skill level. There are seven skills from beginner through expert shown in the column headings of Table 15-5. These skills are related to the trail slope grades. For example, a trail with a maximum grade of 15 percent is categorized beginner, one with a 25 percent grade is considered best for a novice, and so on.

---

[5]This description is taken from David C. Farwell and Ted Farwell, "Decision Support System for Ski Area Design," *Journal of Systems Management*, March 1982: 32–37.

TABLE 15-5 Terrain Capacity Analysis

WINTERSTAR

SKI AREA DEVELOPMENT PLAN
OPTION X
08/03/81

TERRAIN CAPACITY ANALYSIS—SLOPE INVENTORY

ROUTE ID	VERTICAL	LENGTH	WIDTH	% GRADE AVE	TOP	LOW	QUAL	BEGINNER 10%-15% 50.0/ACRE ACRES	SKIER	NOVICE 15%-25% 40.0/ACRE ACRES	SKIER	LOW INTER 25%-35% 30.0/ACRE ACRES	SKIER	INTERMED 30%-40% 20.0/ACRE ACRES	SKIER	HI INTER 35%-45% 15.0/ACRE ACRES	SKIER	ADVANCED 45%-60% 10.0/ACRE ACRES	SKIER	EXPERT 60%+ 10.0/ACRE ACRES	SKIER	PDD TOTAL ACRES	SKIER
1.01	500	3000	100	17	25	8	B	6.9	275														
2.01	500	2800	150	18	30	15	B					9.6	289										
3.01	500	2500	200	20	35	15	A					11.5	344										
4.01	500	2800	150	18	30	15	A					9.6	289										
TOTAL								6.9	275			30.8	922									37.6	1197
5.02	100	750	100	13	15	5	B	1.7	86														
6.02	100	800	150	13	20	5	A	2.8	138														
TOTAL								4.5	224													4.5	224
7.03	900	5500	100	16	25	10	A			12.6	505												
8.03	1000	4800	150	21	35	16	A					16.5	496										
9.03	800	3600	150	22	40	20	A							12.4	248								
10.03	1000	4200	150	24	45	20	A									14.5	217						
11.03	1000	4000	150	25	60	22	B													13.8	138		
12.03	1000	4300	150	23	60	20	A											14.8	148				
13.03	1000	3000	100	20	40	18	A							11.5	230								
14.03	800	4200	100	19	25	15	A			9.6	386												
15.03	400	700	200	57	70	50	B													3.2	32		
16.03	200	350	200	57	60	45	B											1.6	16				
TOTAL										22.3	891	16.5	496	23.9	478	14.5	217	16.4	164	17.0	170	110.5	2416
AREA TOTAL ACRES								4.5		29.2		47.3		23.9		14.5		16.4		17.0		152.7	
AREA TOTAL SKIERS									224		1166		1418		478		217		164		170		3837
PERCENT ACRES								3		19		31		16		9		11		11		100%	
PERCENT SKIERS									6		30		37		12		6		4		4		100%

Source: David C. Farwell and Ted Farwell, "Decision Support System for Ski Area Design," *Journal of Systems Management* (March 1982), p. 33.

Skill also helps determine the number of skiers per acre that a trail can accommodate. The more advanced the skill, the fewer the skiers on a trail. Experts ski fast, covering a large amount of terrain in a short period of time. Their speed demands quick, hard turns on steep slopes with maximum maneuvering room. Beginners, on the other hand, move slowly, making long, sweeping turns to descend the gentler slopes. Thus, in the example, expert and advanced skiers demand a density of 10 per acre, whereas beginners can be accommodated at 50 skiers per acre. Skier density, however, is judgmentally related to more than just skill. Both the geographic location of the ski area and the primary market it serves also bear on density.

In general, expert judgment relates that ski areas in the east, central, and far western United States can be more densely used than areas located in the Rocky Mountain region. This is a matter of snow cover, safety, and skier perception. Eastern skiers are accustomed to, and tolerant of, crowded conditions. Rocky Mountain skiers are used to open slopes relatively free of other skiers. They are dissatisfied with and intolerant of crowded areas. Canadian, Japanese, and European skiers have different perceptions and will be satisfied under different density conditions. Likewise, skiers at an area situated near a large population center designed for weekend recreation will tolerate more crowded conditions than skiers at a remote area designed as a resort destination.

After these factors are considered by the designer, skier density per acre data is entered to the DSS. This judgmental data is also shown in Table 15-5.

The DSS employs menus and question/answer dialogues. The master menu is shown in Figure 15-7. To enter trail data, a 1 is typed, which initiates simple question/answer prompts. Although it is normal to enter trail data sequentially, this is not a requirement. The sort utility will sequence trails by pod, where a pod is a logical grouping of trails with a common base and a common summit.

Winterstar, the example area, has three pods that can be identified on the terrain map, as shown in Figure 15-8. The number of pods is, of course, a function of terrain and each pod tends (though not always) to correspond to an uphill lift system.

Given skier density by skill and trail skill classification, trail length and trail width, the DSS model base calculates the maximum number of skiers by trail, by trail pod, and by skill. The sum of skiers on each trail becomes the downhill terrain capacity of the ski area. A reading of the summary information in Table 15-5 shows that Winterstar can potentially accommodate 3,837 skiers on a 152.7-acre trail system.

Market Balance Analysis

The terrain capacity of a ski area is seldom reached because skiers arrive in a mix of skills dependent on the market population served by the area. Like skier density, the market percent of skiers by skill is a judgmental input. To

```
              TERRAIN CAPACITY ANALYSIS
                 PROGRAM EXECUTION

              TO                          ENTER
      END ALL PROCESSING                  − 0
      ENTER ORIGINAL TRAIL DATA           − 1
      ENTER ORIGINAL LIFT DATA            − 2
      PERFORM AREA BALANCING              − 3
      WRITE TO FILE                       − 4
      COPY EXISTING FILE                  − 5
      PRINT REPORTS                       − 6
      SORT TRAILS AND LIFTS              − 7
      ENTER CODE
      ?
```

FIGURE 15-7   Ski area design master menu. [Source: David C. Farwell, "Decision Support System for Ski Area Design," *Journal of Systems Management* (March 1982), p. 34.]

arrive at this judgment, the designer may survey the market population or sample skiers using competing areas. The market mix judgment is then input to the DSS as a set of goals much like the skier density data.

Figure 15-9 shows that the terrain capacity at Winterstar is not in balance with the potential number of skiers in the marketplace. At ski area saturation (given 3,837 skiers) the marketplace will present too few low-skilled skiers (86 percent capacity beginners, 33 percent capacity novice) and too many intermediate and highly skilled skiers. Since the greatest percent of skiers is in the intermediate skill category, market balancing begins there with a simple calculation.

$$\text{Market Balanced Capacity} = \frac{478 \text{ intermediate skiers}}{0.3 \text{ intermediate total skiers}} = 1{,}593 \text{ total skiers}$$

This calculation shows that if the current design capacity for intermediate skiers is 478 and they represent 30 percent of the market goal, Winterstar has a market balanced capacity of 1,593.

The designer then changes the value for the number of skiers from 3,837 to a number such as 2,000 to reflect the capacity calculation just shown, area access, parking, environmental limits, and so on. The DSS recalculates the number of skiers in each skill category, and the designer can look at the skill balance display shown in Figure 15-10.

The skier density ratio of the skill balance display indicates those skills for which there are too many or too few acres of trails (too much novice at 0.17, too little high intermediate at 1.84). The designer then works with the DSS to create more appropriate ratios. Changes are made to the trail data to reflect the deletion of trails, the addition of trails, and the narrowing or widening of trails to decrease or increase acreage. Continual reference to the skill balance display (Figure 15-10), the topographical map (Figure 15-8), and other displays allows trial-and-error balancing of acreage, skier density, and market by

FIGURE 15-8 A terrain map. [Source: David C. Farwell and Ted Farwell, "Decision Support System for Ski Area Design," *Journal of Systems Management* (March 1982), p. 35.]

skill. When satisfied (balance will seldom be perfect), the designer prints a new terrain capacity analysis.

For Winterstar, an initial balance for 2,000 skiers was obtained by: (1) eliminating B-quality trails 1.01, 2.01, and 5.02; (2) eliminating trail 7.03, which terminates at the summit of the high-density beginner area; (3) widening trails 8.03 and 9.03; and (4) reclassifying the highest grade low inter-

MARKET PERCENT 3837 SKIERS

	STD	GOAL	NUMBER SKIERS GOAL	CURR	RATIO
BEG	.05	.05	192	224	.86
NOV	.10	.10	384	1166	.33
LOW	.20	.20	767	1418	.54
INT	.30	.30	1151	478	2.41
HI	.20	.20	767	217	3.54
ADV	.10	.10	384	164	2.34
EXP	.05	.05	192	170	1.13

FIGURE 15-9   Market analysis display. [Source: David C. Farwell and Ted Farwell, "Decision Support System for Ski Area Design," *Journal of Systems Management* (March 1982), p. 34.]

mediate trail, 8.03, to intermediate. These are all judgmental decisions that were analyzed by the DSS in seconds. A comparison of Figure 15-10, the skill balance prior to trail changes, to Figure 15-11, the skill balance after trail changes, shows that the beginner density ratio rises from 0.45 to 0.73 and there are improvements in the novice and low intermediate ratios. The intermediate ratio has been decreased too much and no change occurs in the higher skills. The changes made are simple, inexpensive ones at this point. More complex and costly changes such as physical grade alteration to move a trail from one skill to another, repositioning of trails, and opening of new slopes can be considered to obtain closer balance ratios in later options.

The ski area design just described, which is called Option A, is presented as a development plan in Table 15-6 when lifts are added. It is a reasonable balance between the downhill capacity of the mountain and the market mix of skiers. Then, given this downhill design, the designer added lift systems, once again drawing on the capabilities of the DSS to balance uphill capability with the aligned downhill capacity and market mix.

SKILL BALANCE 152.7 ACRES

SKILL	ACRES	SKIERS	DEN.
BEG	4.5	100	22.3
NOV	29.2	200	6.9
LOW	47.3	400	8.5
INT	23.9	600	25.1
HI	14.5	400	27.7
ADV	16.4	200	12.2
EXP	17.0	100	5.9
SUM	152.7	2001	13.1

SKIER DENSITY RATIO BY SKILL =

.45		.28		1.84		.59
	.17			1.26	1.22	

FIGURE   15-10   Skill   balance   display.   [Source: David C. Farwell and Ted Farwell, "Decision Support System for Ski Area Design," *Journal of Systems Management* (March 1982), p. 36.]

SKILL BALANCE 127.6 ACRES

SKILL	ACRES	SKIERS	DEN.
BEG	2.8	100	36.3
NOV	9.6	200	20.7
LOW	21.1	400	18.9
INT	46.2	600	13.0
HI	14.5	400	27.7
ADV	16.4	200	12.2
EXP	17.0	100	5.9
SUM	127.6	2000	15.7

SKIER DENSITY RATIO BY SKILL =

.73   .63   1.84   .59
.52   .65   1.22

CAPACITY/DEMAND = .98

FIGURE 15-11 Revised skill balance display. [Source: David C. Farwell and Ted Farwell, "Decision Support System for Ski Area Design," *Journal of Systems Management* (March 1982), p. 36.]

TABLE 15-6   The Ski Area Development Plan: Option A

WINTERSTAR
SKI AREA DEVELOPMENT PLAN
DESIGN CAPACITY—2000 SKIERS   OPTION A   08/03/81

SKI LIFT POD			A	B	C	TOTALS
SKI LIFT TYPE			DOUB	WIRE	QUAD	
LENGTH (FEET)			2550	707	4123	
VERTICAL (FEET)			500	100	1000	
HOURLY CAPACITY			1200	500	2400	
A. VTF/hr. (CAPACITY)		(000)	600	50	2400	3050
	PARAMETERS					
BEGINNER	TRAIL # ..			1		1
	ACRES ...			2.8		2.8
(10%–15%	SKIERS ...	@ 5	%	100		100
GRADES)	DENSITY .	@ 50	/Ac	36		36
	VTF/hr	@ 400	/hr	40		40
NOVICE	TRAIL # ..				1	1
	ACRES ...				9.6	9.6
(15%–25%	SKIERS ...	@ 10	%		200	200
GRADES)	DENSITY .	@ 40	/Ac		21	21
	VTF/hr	@ 900	/hr		180	180
LOW INTER.	TRAIL # ..		2			2
	ACRES ...		21.1			21.1
(25%–35%	SKIERS ...	@ 20	%	400		400
GRADES)	DENSITY .	@ 30	/Ac	19		19
	VTF/hr	@ 1200	/hr	480		480

460 Decision Support Systems

TABLE 15-6 (continued)

WINTERSTAR
SKI AREA DEVELOPMENT PLAN
DESIGN CAPACITY—2000 SKIERS   OPTION A   08/03/81

INTERMED.	TRAIL # ..					3	3
	ACRES ...					46.2	46.2
(30%–40%	SKIERS ...	@ 30	%			600	600
GRADES)	DENSITY .	@ 20	/Ac			13	13
	VTF/hr	@ 1600	/hr			960	960
HI INTER.	TRAIL # ..					1	1
	ACRES ...					14.5	14.5
(35%–45%	SKIERS ...	@ 20	%			400	400
GRADES)	DENSITY .	@ 15	/Ac			28	28
	VTF/hr	@ 1800	/hr			720	720
ADVANCED	TRAIL # ..					2	2
	ACRES ...					16.4	16.4
(45%–60%	SKIERS ...	@ 10	%			200	200
GRADES)	DENSITY .	@ 10	/Ac			12	12
	VTF/hr	@ 2100	/hr			420	420
EXPERT	TRAIL # ..					2	2
	ACRES ...					17	17
(60%+	SKIERS ...	@ 5	%			100	100
GRADES)	DENSITY .	@ 10	/Ac			6	6
	VTF/hr	@ 3000	/hr			300	300
B. VTF/hr. (DEMAND)				480	40	2580	3100
CAP/DEM FACTOR (A/B)				1.3	1.3	.9	1
TOTAL ACRES				21.1	2.8	103.7	127.6
TOTAL SKIERS				400	100	1500	2000
AVERAGE DENSITY				19	36	14	16

Source: David C. Farwell and Ted Farwell, "Decision Support System for Ski Area Design," *Journal of Systems Management* (March 1982), p. 37.

DSS Uses

The DSS allows ski area design alternatives to be analyzed far more quickly than is possible by hand calculations. Table 15-6, which presents design Option A for 2,000 skiers, was developed in one and a half hours. This same analysis would have taken eight hours without the DSS. Once having created

Option A, other options can be investigated in just 15 to 30 minutes. This compares favorably with 2 to 4 hours without the DSS. Because it is so much faster, the DSS makes it feasible to explore more design alternatives.

The DSS has resulted in better ski area designs. A new ski area previously designed was redesigned using the DSS. The DSS allowed the creation of 10 percent more skier capacity, in better balance, with the same physical layout, than the manually completed design. This new option took 15 minutes to create.

The DSS has other potential as well. The DSS is well suited to the creation of phased development plans, which can be balanced not only as to mountain and market but against capital investment and rate of return criteria as well. Phased development planning is possible for both new and existing ski areas. The largest ski area in North America is currently undergoing phased redevelopment planning using the DSS. It has a balanced potential for 130 trails in 16 pods with 30 lift systems serving 23,500 skiers. The DSS is also suited to ski area valuation, since the worth of an area is dependent not only on its present state but also on its potential. The area as it is and the area as it could be are quickly modeled using the DSS.

Summary

A large variety of decision support systems have been developed. The development of a DSS is motivated by one or more concerns. The features of a DSS depend on its intended application.

A finance-oriented DSS is the financial planning system (FPS) at the Louisiana National Bank (LNB). It was developed in the early-to-mid 1970s as a response to the serious problems that the LNB was experiencing. The FPS was developed to help top management with its decision-making responsibilities. The system uses data from the bank's general ledger to prepare reports on current activities, to create forecasts of future conditions, and to perform analyses of interest. A variety of benefits are attributed to the FPS, including increased profits, structure, and discipline for unified decision making; improved reporting and negotiating with bank-regulators; faster responses to changes; and reduced clerical costs. A number of factors have contributed to the success of FPS. These factors include top management support and involvement; the characteristics of the system's sponsor; the organizational environment; the transitional development and implementation of the system; and the capability for unified planning provided by the system.

BRANDAID is a marketing-oriented DSS used to support brand managers in making decisions about pricing, promotion, advertising, sales force allocation, and packaging. It was developed by John D. C. Little in the late 1960s and has been used in a number of organizations. BRANDAID includes several component parts that interact with one another. The component parts are the manufacturer, the retailer, the consumer, the competitor, and the environment. BRANDAID is modular in construction, and the various component parts can be added or deleted at will. Experience has shown that BRANDAID's success depends on how it is introduced into the organizational setting where it is to be used. The implementation process includes introductory and ongoing periods. The introductory period consists of management orientation, the formation of a models team, problem selection and formulation, calibration, and initial use. The ongoing period consists of fire-fighting, tracking and diagnosis, updating and evolution, and reuse. One of the applications of BRANDAID has been to a well-established brand of packaged goods sold through grocery stores.

An operations-oriented DSS is the computer-assisted dispatching (CAD) system created by Southern Railway. It was developed in the late 1970s and is still evolving. Its primary function is to support dispatchers, who must decide when a train should leave the yard, what route it should follow, and when it should be held up to meet opposing trains or to allow following trains to pass. The CAD system was developed by the management science group of Southern Railway over a period of four years. It consists of two main subsystems: the dispatch management system (DMS) and the meet–pass system. From a decision support perspective, the meet–pass system is most interesting. Using a branch and bound algorithm, it suggests optimum meet–pass plans. The initial use of the CAD system has resulted in improved record-keeping and reporting and decreased costs.

A microcomputer-based DSS is being used to support the design of ski areas. It is used in planning the system of trails cut into the mountain and the system of lifts to carry skiers up the mountain. The design process begins with the downhill trail system. The DSS combines a set of judgmental decisions with trail systems data to provide a terrain capacity analysis. The designer uses this information to evaluate the initial set of downhill trail decisions. In an iterative manner, the designer improves on the design with support provided by the DSS. When the downhill trail system design is completed, the uphill lift system design is performed using a similar process.

Assignments

15-1. Four decision support systems were described in the chapter. For each DSS, discuss the data, the models, the software interface, and the user.

15-2. Is the financial planning system at the Louisiana National Bank best categorized as an MIS or a DSS? Why? Is the distinction clear? Why?

15-3. Is BRANDAID best classified as a DSS generator or as a specific DSS? Why? Is the distinction clear? Why?

15-4. Is the computer-assisted dispatching system at Southern Railway best categorized as an MIS or a DSS? Why? Is the distinction clear? Why?

15-5. A DSS supports rather than automates decision making. How is this characteristic exemplified in the DSS for ski area design?

15-6. Decision support systems have the potential for supporting top-, middle-, and lower-management decision making. To what extent is decision making at these levels supported by the decision support systems described in the chapter?

15-7. Decision support systems can be used for ad hoc and continuous decision making. How would you classify the decision support systems described in the chapter?

15-8. Decision support systems have the potential for supporting the intelligence, design, and choice phases of decision making. To what extent are these decision making phases supported by the decision support systems described in the chapter?

15-9. Decision support systems can support independent, sequential interdependent, and pooled interdependent decision making. What kind of decision support is provided by the decision support systems described in the chapter?

15-10. The roles in a DSS include those of the user, the intermediary, the DSS builder, the technical supporter, and the toolsmith. Describe whether these roles were required in the three decision support systems described in the chapter and how they were filled.

15-11. An evolutionary developmental approach is best for most decision support systems. To what extent was an evolutionary approach used with the decision support systems described in the chapter? Do you agree with the approaches that were used? Why?

15-12. The end objective of a DSS is to create organizational benefits. Compare the benefits generated by the decision support systems described in the chapter.

15-13. DSS applications are increasingly being described in journals such as *MIS Quarterly, Management Science, Decision Sciences,* and *Interface.* Review recent issues of these journals and prepare a report on a DSS application that you find.

CASE   The GADS Experience*

From 1970 to 1974, a research group at IBM in San Jose developed one of the first decision support systems. The project centered around a system for geographic allocation of resources and people, and was used both by IBM, to determine, for example, how many reps to put where, when, and how, and by customers, on a test basis. IBM provided the software free— and temporarily—while the customer paid operational costs and provided the data.

One of the most impressive aspects of the Geodata Analysis and Display System— GADS, as it was known—was its proven flexibility. Over 200 people at 17 different organizations used the same version of GADS. And none of them were computer experts.

IBM learned a great deal about end-user problem solving from the GADS project. For one thing, the way organizations do business is very likely to change once automation begins to be applied to decision making. Behavioral studies of the manager and the organization thus become newly important.

For another thing, the nature of decision making itself presented a serious design problem for which traditional systems analysis isn't very well suited. The user interface is one of the least mature aspects of system design.

Also, in order to attack the business user market, the nature of the business would have to be examined. The most obvious finding IBM made along these lines was that decision making is almost entirely unstructured. Managers don't really know how they make decisions, and, on top of that, they don't want to reveal the details of decision making of which they are aware, as these tend to be important specifics.

IBM's DSS research group decided it was necessary to start with the assumption that they didn't know what was needed, and then piece together the answer from the clues. They got the clues by asking simple questions of decision makers: "What do you look at when you are making a decision?" "What do you need to have on hand?" "How do you manipulate these tools?" "What are the standard operating procedures and control procedures you have that you know you want to keep?"

With the answers to these questions, the research group came up with a set of variables that made sense for use in a decision support system. The success of GADS was probably due to the wisdom of this simple analysis.

The significance of the user interface lent weight to two more research directions for IBM. Having discovered that the nonprogrammer user wants a completely interactive system, the importance of a menu-driven system with good display capabilities became obvious. Neither the hardware nor the software available were geared to these characteristics. IBM realized that it was going to have to design a system to really involve the people. Improving the user interface would demand a better terminal.

Any system was also going to require a better language. In an interactive program, screen management—putting up the option or the information, manipulating it, taking it down, and quite possibly keeping it handy for later use—takes up much of the code, about 60%. Because IBM believes the major new application will be interactive, research is being

*Reprinted with permission of DATAMATION® magazine, from Sarah Rolph. "A Study of Decision-Makers," *Datamation*, November 1979: 119. © Copyright by Technical Publ. Company, a Dun & Bradstreet company, 1979. All rights reserved.

done on a language discipline tailored to the heavy use of the display. What is needed is a language that goes beyond the subroutine—coroutines make more sense when a lot of information needs remembering (and only ALGOL and one version of PASCAL use coroutines).

Another important aspect of decision making surfaced in IBM's examination of its successful research effort. The final ingredient of decision making is communication. The social acceptance involved in presenting a decision or solution and the feedback generated from those people the decision involves must be considered part of the process.

Questions

1. GADS is an experimental system that can be used for the geographic allocation of resources and people. Identify potential GADS applications.

2. In this chapter, the financial planning system at the Louisiana National Bank, the BRANDAID marketing-mix model, and the computer-assisted dispatching system at Southern Railway were discussed. Which of these decision support systems is most similar to GADS? Why?

3. An earlier chapter discussed the use of an evolutionary developmental approach for decision support systems. Does IBM's experience with GADS lend credence to this type of development approach? Discuss.

4. Management courses are sometimes viewed as being "soft" or "lacking in specific content." Discuss this viewpoint in light of IBM's experience with GADS.

Other Readings

Belardo, Salvatore, Kirk R. Karwan, and William A. Wallace. "Managing the Response to Disasters Using Microcomputers." *Interfaces* (March–April 1984): 29–39.

Chan, K. H. "Decision Support Systems for Human Resource Management." *Journal of Systems Management* (April 1984): 17–25.

Etgar, M., S. Licht, and P. Shrivasta. "A Decision Support System for Strategic Marketing Decisions." *Systems, Objectives, Solutions* (August 1984): 131–140.

Gerrity, Thomas P., Jr. "Design of Man–Machine Decision Systems: An Application to Portfolio Management." *Sloan Management Review* (Winter 1971): 59–75.

Keen, P. G. W., and G. R. Wagner. "DSS: An Executive Mind-Support System." *Datamation* (November 1979): 117–122.

Keen, Peter G. W., and Michael S. Scott Morton. *Decision Support Systems: An Organizational Perspective.* Reading, Mass.: Addison-Wesley, 1978.

Larreche, J., and V. Srinivasan, "STRATPORT: A Decision Support System for Strategic Planning." *Journal of Marketing* (Fall 1981): 39–52.

Ness, David, and Christopher R. Sprague. "An Interactive Media Decision Support System." *Sloan Management Review* (Fall 1972): 51–61.

Prastacos, G. P., and E. Brodheim. "PBDS: A Decision Support System for Regional Blood Management." *Management Science* (May 1980): 451–463.

Stott, K. L., Jr., and B. W. Douglas. "A Model-Based Decision Support System for Planning and Scheduling Ocean Borne Transportation." *Interfaces* (August 1981): 1–10.

PART VII

THE MANAGEMENT OF CBIS

Up to this point, we have focused on how CBIS help manage the vital resources of an organization. Some of those resources are, or relate to, the CBIS themselves. It is appropriate, therefore, that we devote the remaining chapters of this book to the management of those special resources, the CBIS.

One of the most interesting questions concerning the management of CBIS is *who* will manage them. In Chapter 16 we trace the history of solutions to this problem and examine in some detail current approaches to responsibility for the CBIS function and the organization of the CBIS office. The second major topic of Part VII is the CBIS *life cycle*. The scope of this subject demands two chapters to cover it completely. Chapter 17 deals with the first two life cycle phases, *planning* and *development*, and Chapter 18 addresses the final three phases, *implementation*, *operation*, and *control*.

Chapter 16

Organizational Concepts and CBIS

Learning Objectives

After studying this chapter, you will be able to:
1. Trace the historical evolution of CBIS responsibility.
2. Select an approach to CBIS-office organization based on organizational characteristics.
3. Identify the job positions and responsibilities normally found in CBIS.
4. Structure the CBIS office for selected organizations.
5. Define and use the following terms:

director of CBIS   systems programmer
data base administrator   maintenance programmer
systems analyst   console operator
systems designer   librarian
application programmer   information systems hub

The management function of organizing was identified in Chapter 3 as, in a narrow sense, the structuring of organizational resources. If one were starting a new organization from scratch, two immediate structural questions concerning CBIS would arise: Who is to be responsible for CBIS and how is the CBIS office itself to be organized?[1] There are other organizational implications of CBIS, such as how the number and qualifications of managers in other departments (e.g., marketing) are affected by CBIS, but they are relatively minor compared to the two basic questions.

Responsibility for CBIS

In organizing, the question of who is responsible for CBIS is essentially the same as "where in the organizational structure should the CBIS office be located?" Historically, this question has been resolved on the basis of who was to use the system and which existing organizational entity possessed the expertise to operate such a system. Because traditional relationships often exert a powerful influence on current organization, it is useful to look at the historical evolution of CBIS-office location.

First-Generation Computer Location

Responsibility for computer operations, and later for CBIS, is related to the familiar classification of computers by generations. First-generation computers were direct descendants of special-purpose scientific computers, and early business applications stressed the kind of numerical analysis typical of scientific applications. Because the "number people" in business tended to be in the accounting department, it is not surprising that accounting first became responsible for computer operations, and that payroll, billing, and other accounting applications dominated the early business use of computers. A typical organization chart of the first generation is shown in Figure 16-1.

Second-Generation Computer Location

By the second generation of computers, other considerations began to influence computer location and responsibility. First, departments of marketing, production, and personnel recognized the potential of computers and generated demand for computer resources. Second, greater reliability and easier programming techniques reduced dependence on a few highly trained specialists in the accounting department. As a result, some large organiza-

---

[1] The term *office* is used here generically to include division, directorate, department, or any of the other terms used to describe organizational subdivisions.

470

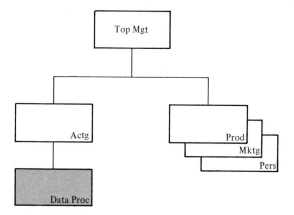

FIGURE 16-1   First-generation computer location.

tions, where the increase in demand for computer services exceeded the increased capacity of second-generation computers, decentralized data processing activities by locating additional computers in other functional departments. In many organizations, however, second-generation computers were adequate to handle all organizational data processing. These organizations simply upgraded the accounting computer, and the accounting department became a data processing service center for the entire organization. The two versions of second-generation organization are depicted in Figure 16-2.

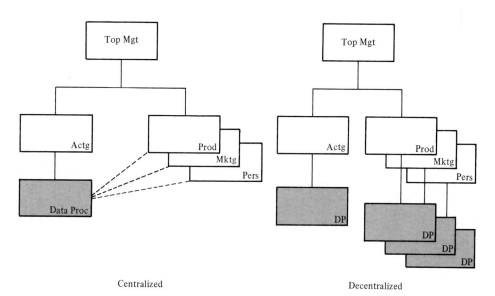

FIGURE 16-2   Second-generation computer location.

Third-Generation Computers and MIS

The nearly simultaneous appearance, in the mid-1960s, of third-generation computer technology and the concept of management information systems had a profound impact on organizational structure. The then vast capacity of third-generation computers and the broad application of information processing to management functions resulted in a happy marriage. MIS concepts of corporate data bases, application bases, and other shared capabilities made enormous demands on hardware, but in most cases, a single computer facility could handle all of an organization's needs. But if centralization was an obvious choice, the assignment of MIS responsibilities was not. Those organizations that had centralized under accounting in the second generation saw no compelling reason to change and, once again, upgraded and expanded their service center concept. The organizations that had decentralized found that functional departments were unwilling to yield their DP activities back to accounting. Accounting would give priority to its own applications, and other users would be slighted, or so the argument went. Whether this was true or not, and the success of many organizations with accounting-based MIS would suggest that it was not, it led to the formation of independent MIS offices. Although it may have been created for the wrong reasons, independent MIS organization has proved to be a more stimulating alternative and has produced more innovative information systems than accounting-based locations. The authors' study of MIS in the late 1970s showed that approximately one half of the organizations had independent MIS offices, about one third still located MIS in finance or accounting, and the remainder, usually specialized governmental organizations, employed other locations.[2] More important, managers of independent MIS reported greater return on investment and greater system performance than did managers of accounting-based systems. The centralized, independent MIS of the third generation is shown in Figure 16-3.

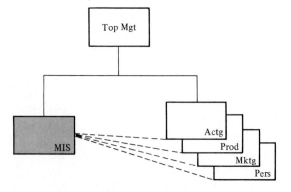

FIGURE 16-3   Third-generation MIS location.

[2] Donald W. Kroeber and Hugh J. Watson, "Is there a *Best* MIS Department Location?" *Information and Management* 2, no. 4 (October 1979): 165–173.

Current Organizational Structure

A few years ago, information systems scholars were ready to wrap up the organization location issue and put it on the shelf with other apparently resolved questions. But once again, technological advances have given managers new options. In particular, advances in data communications and the development of minicomputers and microcomputers have rekindled interest in decentralization. The ring and star distributed systems discussed in Chapter 4 are examples of decentralized systems facilitated by new, fourth generation technology. Because the current alternatives also involve differences in the organization of the CBIS office itself, it is more convenient to examine the two issues together.

Organization of the CBIS Office

Activities in a CBIS office fall into four categories: *administration, systems analysis and design, programming,* and *systems operation.* Administration involves the coordination of the other three activities, data base management, liaison with other departments, and representation of CBIS matters to upper levels of management. Systems analysis and design include the analysis of the existing system and the design of new systems to meet the organization's information needs. In programming, the design specifications are coded into a programming language and are tested and debugged. Finally, systems operation involves the running of programs on computer hardware and the dissemination of the resultant output.

Although these functions are common to all CBIS, they do not always lead to similar organization. Figure 16-4 shows three different approaches to CBIS office organization, and still others are possible.

The CBIS office in Figure 16-4a is organized along activity lines. The separation of analysis and design, programming, and operations is considered a security measure—no one person has access to all of the steps necessary to

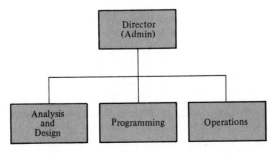

FIGURE 16-4a   Current CBIS organization–
activity orientation.

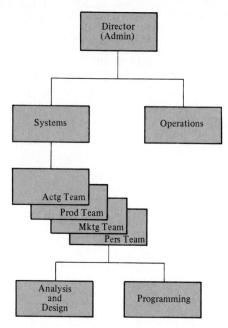

FIGURE 16-4b   Current CBIS organization–project orientation.

defraud the system, and collusion is thought to be more difficult among members of different organizational entities. Organizing for security is particularly important in financial institutions such as banks and insurance companies.

The second organization, shown in Figure 16-4b, employs teams of programmers and analysts and designers organized along project or functional lines. This organization sacrifices some security for the cooperation, understanding, and efficiency that result from a habitual working relationship among the teams and the corresponding functional department heads or project managers. This organization is particularly well suited to heterogeneous or high-technology firms, where CBIS applications tend to be very specialized.

The third variation of CBIS office organization, shown in Figure 16-4c, is based on an increasingly popular belief that new systems development is essentially different from the maintenance of existing systems. At one time, it was almost axiomatic that the best programmer to modify or correct a program was the one who wrote it. The problem with this approach is that programming is a very mobile occupation, and the original programmer may not be around when modifications are required. Also, the increased capacity and speed of contemporary computers make it unnecessary for programmers to employ the statement-saving shortcuts that once made maintenance so difficult for a different programmer. In fact, current techniques of *structured*

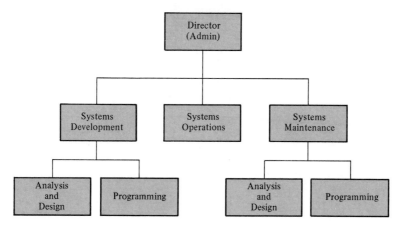

FIGURE 16-4c Current CBIS organization–life cycle orientation.

programming trade brevity and efficiency for format and clarity. Structured programs are much easier for a second programmer to follow, and changes are less likely to bring about undesired results. Consequently, many CBIS offices now treat program change and modification, which can consume up to 80 percent of the total programming effort, as a separate function.

This approach to structuring the CBIS office is sometimes called the *lifecycle* approach because it is based on two important phases of the CBIS life cycle, which is discussed in the next two chapters. It is most applicable where new systems development is particularly difficult or demands rare skills not found in all programmers and analysts. New or less skilled personnel may start in the maintenance division and move on to development if their progress warrants such a move.

CBIS Personnel

Another organizational consideration of CBIS involves the classification of the personnel who work in CBIS, either in the CBIS office itself or in functional departments. Some reference has been made already to administrators, programmers, analysts, and operators. The degree to which these personnel are specialized is, to a large measure, determined by the size of the organization and the extent of its CBIS activities. In a very small organization, the administration of CBIS may be merely an additional duty of another executive, say, the comptroller; programming, analysis, and design responsibilities may be vested in a single person, a programmer-analyst who maintains vendor-supplied software; and the actual operation of equipment may be handled by a few persons who double as data preparation personnel. In very large organizations, the four basic activities may be further broken down into more specialized positions, as shown in Table 16-1, requiring hundreds of persons. This discussion treats activities and subactivities as separate job

TABLE 16-1   Classification of CBIS Personnel

Class of Personnel	Examples
Top management	CBIS steering committee (chaired by VP for services, executive VP, or controller)
Administrators	Director of CBIS Data-base administrator
Systems analysts and designers	Systems analysts Systems designers
Programmers	Systems programmers Application programmers Maintenance programmers
Operators	Console operators Librarians Data preparation personnel
Users	Managers Professional staff Data entry clerks

positions, but it must be remembered that virtually any combination of responsibilities can be devised to meet constraints on the number and capabilities of personnel involved in CBIS.

Administrative Personnel

There is usually one high-level executive responsible for CBIS in an organization. This person could be the chief executive officer but more likely is a vice-president for services, an executive vice-president, or, in those organizations that retain an accounting orientation toward CBIS, the controller or the vice-president for finance. The responsible executive may chair a *CBIS steering committee* that is made up of the heads of user departments (or their representatives) and the *director of CBIS*.

The director of CBIS is the highest ranking CBIS professional in the organization. He or she is responsible for the attainment of the goals and objectives established by the CBIS steering committee. Goals and objectives in CBIS set standards for systems development, operating costs, error rates, security, and timeliness. The director also has normal department head responsibilities for personnel administration, office management, and the budget.

In organizations with central data bases, and even in some without, there is also a position for a *data base administrator* (DBA). The DBA is second in importance only to the director of CBIS and, in fact, may be the deputy director. It is the responsibility of the DBA to standardize data codes, establish the overall schema of the data base, control access to the data base, and maintain the security of the data base.

Systems Analysis and Design Personnel

Systems analysis and design involves two different, but related, tasks. First, someone must analyze the existing system and articulate the need for information and, second, someone must conceive a means of satisfying that need. The responsibility of identifying information requirements rests with a *systems analyst*, whereas the design of a computer-based solution is accomplished by a *systems designer*.

The systems analyst is the more functionally oriented of the two. In fact, the systems analyst may even be a member of the functional department (e.g., marketing, production, or finance) that initiated the request for information.[3] The systems analyst provides liaison between the user and the designer, explaining the capabilities and limitations of the CBIS to the user, and translating the user's request into specific CBIS requirements for the designer. The systems designer then determines the data requirements, the transformation processes that will convert the data into the desired information, and the form and content of the output. Even when this distinction between systems analysts and systems designers is not made, it is a good idea to have in each department a designated point of contact who has some background in CBIS and whose job it is to coordinate functional applications with the system designers.

Programmers

In general terms, programmers translate the English-language statements of systems designers into computer-language statements. *Application programmers* write programs for the basic data processing and MIS applications in the organization, and *systems programmers* write control or service programs.[4] Although there is usually a requirement for some systems programming in every CBIS, more sophisticated systems software, such as compilers, operating systems, and data base management systems tend to be prepared by computer manufacturers or software vendors. In those organizations that separate systems development from systems maintenance, there are also *maintenance programmers*. In general, application and maintenance programmers have similar qualifications.

Operators

Managers using remote terminals sometimes forget that computer *operators* are still necessary. *Console operators* monitor a CRT display unit that gives information on the status of work in progress and requirements for human

---

[3] Systems analysts who are assigned to functional departments are sometimes called *information analysts* to distinguish them from their more data-processing-oriented counterparts in the CBIS office. In this book, we use *systems analysts* generically to include both systems analysts and information analysts.

[4] See the discussion of application and systems software in Chapter 5.

assistance. For example, the CRT may display a list of jobs in queue, the identification of remote users, or the need to load a certain file onto an external storage device. Other operator personnel keep highspeed printers in supply of paper and distribute printer output. A special category of operator, the *librarian*, maintains custody of off-line files, programs, and systems documentation.

Data preparation personnel are frequently classified as operator personnel for the simple reason that they often, in fact, operate keypunch machines, key-to-tape or key-to-disk devices, and other types of data preparation equipment. The role of operators as data preparation personnel has been diminished somewhat by advances in data entry techniques, such as optical character recognition, which require no special data preparation. Also, data preparation personnel are often found in functional departments as opposed to the CBIS office. Of course, the latter point does not mean that they are not CBIS personnel, but it does make them different from most other operator personnel.

Users

Users are perhaps the most important of all categories of CBIS personnel. CBIS exist solely for the purpose of aiding users in the performance of their duties. In the past, users were involved only at the very beginning and very end of systems development. At the beginning of the development process, users participated in the definition of systems requirements; at the end, they participated in training or education sessions on the use of the system and, later, by employing the system in the discharge of their duties. Now, many users, primarily those in the managerial or staff ranks, are becoming increasingly involved in other phases of systems development as well. Involvement of users in the analysis, design, programming, testing, and debugging of CBIS applications has been given the name *end-user computing* in recognition of the differences over more traditional systems development approaches. End-user computing is discussed in detail in Chapter 19.

Not all users of CBIS are managers, of course. Many operational personnel in functional departments use CBIS routinely to enter or retrieve data. When you telephone to advise your insurance company of an address change or to ask your credit card company about a disputed charge, you probably deal with a *data entry clerk* who can call your records out on a CRT terminal, give you the requested information, and post any necessary changes.

The designation of such functional personnel as CBIS personnel has raised some problems in CBIS budgeting. In many cases, clerks and other employees who formerly performed manual tasks now do essentially the same job with the aid of CBIS. But where these persons were once charged to their functional departments, they are now charged to CBIS, thus distorting the true cost of operating the CBIS. CBIS managers must guard against such accounting procedures, especially in organizations that use a profit center concept to evaluate operational efficiency.

Current Organizational Structure: A Second Look

When the variations in CBIS office organization and the placement of CBIS personnel are considered along with the previously mentioned technological advances, there are numerous possible ways to tailor the organizational structure of CBIS to meet the needs of the firm. Instead of attempting an exhaustive listing of combinations, we will use three examples to illustrate the flexibility of CBIS organization.

Figure 16-5 shows the organization of a state division of motor vehicles. Numerous branch offices throughout the state use remote job entry equipment to enter vehicle registration data and to receive titles, license tag renewals, and other output. Terminals in the branch offices are used for inquiries that require no output documents. The CBIS is centralized in the state headquarters because all the branch offices have identical information needs and require access to a common data base. Because of the homogeneous nature of the applications, there is no need to form specialized teams of programmers, analysts, and designers, and a certain degree of security is obtained by the separation of programming, analysis and design, and operations. Other than the users and the data preparation personnel in the branch offices, all CBIS personnel and activities are centralized.

The bank organization shown in Figure 16-6 is quite the opposite of the motor-vehicle-division organization. This bank also has branches but has no

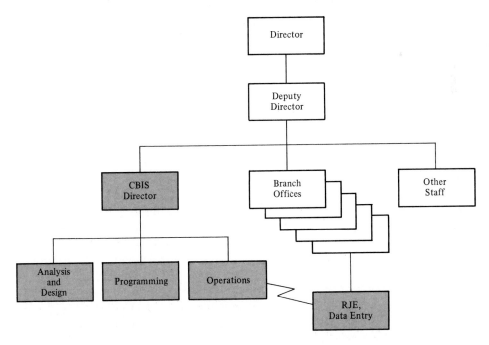

FIGURE 16-5   CBIS in a state division of motor vehicles.

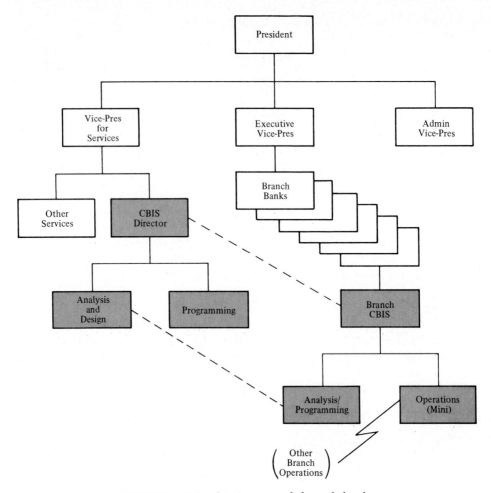

FIGURE 16-6 CBIS in a multibranch bank.

central computer. Instead, each branch has a minicomputer that is part of a ring distributed system. Each branch has a data base of its own accounts and can also make data available to other branches in the ring. The branch CBIS are organized by activity for maximum security and because banking applications are relatively homogeneous. Although the central bank has no computer, it still has a CBIS office. The data base administrator in the central CBIS office must provide for data security and ensure the compatibility of data between branch operations. The central CBIS office also has analysis and programming responsibilities for common applications, such as statement preparation, computation of interest on loans and savings, and credit card accounts. Within the guidelines established by the DBA, branch CBIS offices may design and program applications of purely local interest. For systemwide applications, such as the payroll or the preparation of accounting

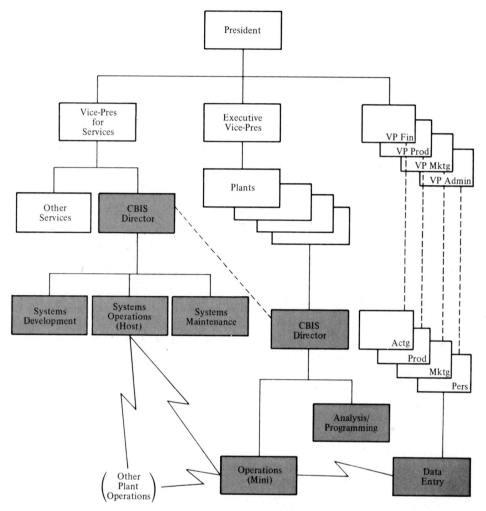

FIGURE 16-7   CBIS in a multiplant manufacturing firm.

statements, the ring system may be made to act as a single large computer through techniques of multiprocessing.

A star distributed system is the best organization for a multiplant manufacturing firm such as the one shown in Figure 16-7. A central CBIS office is responsible for the development, the maintenance, and the operation (on the host computer) of companywide applications such as capital budgeting, financial statement preparation, and resource allocation. The host computer is also the access point to the corporate data base and the application base. Individual plants also have CBIS offices and computer hardware—probably minicomputers. Branch CBIS operations may take several different forms. Locally developed programs may draw on the corporate data base for data, locally originated data may be analyzed with programs from the corporate data base, or both data and programs may be of local origin. In all cases, branch activities are monitored by the central CBIS office to encourage the sharing of programs and data so as to ensure database and application base integrity.

Merger of CBIS Responsibility

The various options we have presented for organizing the CBIS office take into account differences in organizational structure and mission. The recent rise of different types of CBIS has introduced another consideration: How can the total CBIS effort in an organization be coordinated? To what extent, or even *should*, office automation, transaction processing, management information, expert, decision support, and executive information systems be subject to centralized planning and control?

McKenney and McFarlan refer to an "information archipelago" consisting of three "islands of technology"—office automation, data communication, and data processing—and explore the pressures for and against centralization.[5] The pressures they identify are the need for management control, organizational structure, available technology, user demand, costs, the size and expertise of the CBIS staff, and others. Any of these pressures may argue for centralization in one organization and decentralization in another. Although organizational characteristics will ultimately determine the role of the CBIS office, McKenney and McFarlan believe that, over the next few years, most organizations will consolidate policy control over the three "islands" into a single unit. The reasons, they believe, are (1) the costs of technology and the complex evaluation of those costs, (2) similarities in the management skills required of each island, and (3) the need to integrate the technologies of the three islands. Their conclusion calls for an *information systems hub* to control and coordinate the "islands of technology."

Although we have sliced the information systems pie somewhat differently than McKenney and McFarlan, the hub concept and the pressures that argue for it still are applicable. The CBIS model presented in this book could be centrally managed from a hub, as shown in Figure 16-8. Some CBIS might remain under the operational control of staff or functional managers—expert systems, executive information systems, or office automation systems, for example. Others—transaction processing, management information, and decision support systems, perhaps—might well be under the direct control of the information systems office. But all systems would be subject to certain user and hub responsibilities. These responsibilities, again drawn from the work of McKenney and McFarlan, will be described later.

---

[5]James L. McKenney and E. Warren McFarlan, "The Information Archipelago," *Harvard Business Review*, September–October, 1982: 109–19; January–February, 1983: 145–56; and July–August, 1983: 91–99.

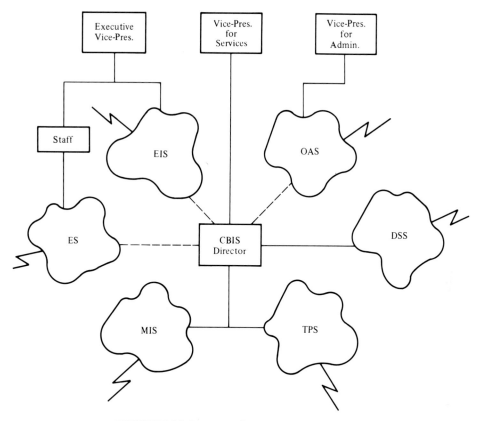

FIGURE 16-8   An information systems hub.

Hub Responsibilities   The information systems hub—the CBIS office in our model—would develop and maintain standards for project control and documentation. However, in recognition of the differences among CBIS, the standards would be flexible. A DSS application, for example, would and should not be held to the same project control standards as those imposed on a transaction processing application. The criteria for the standards would be based on the extent and scope of the application. The personal use of a DSS simply does not demand the same level of control as the organization-wide implications of transaction processing.

Other standards maintained by the hub would include those for telecommunications, programming languages, and the data dictionary. The hub would also maintain an inventory of installed or planned services, recommend preferred suppliers of equipment and services, and examine independent systems (expert systems, for example) for their potential for integration with other systems and/or applications.

User Responsibilities   The hub concept also includes user responsibilities in systems development similar to those found in end-user computing. Under the hub approach, users would *participate* in systems development (as opposed to end-user computing, where they have full responsibility for it). Participation would include involvement in documentation of the support plan, description of network architecture, determination of data base policies, definition of user standards, development of training programs, and the establishment of system security.

CBIS and Organizational Philosophies

An interesting sidelight of the principal organizational issues concerning CBIS is the effect of CBIS on management's attitude toward the centralization of authority and decision making. According to the span-of-control concept in classical organization theory, managers decentralize because of limitations on the number of persons they can supervise. Computers and information systems are capable of providing information for decision making directly to top managers, without the need for intervening layers of management. Would not these intermediate managers become unnecessary? The predictions that CBIS would erode middle management (see Chapter 3) assumed that they would. But it has been shown that middle management is more influential than ever. Do computers and CBIS promote centralization or not?

It now appears that computers and CBIS merely *facilitate* centralization; they do not *cause* centralization. In fact, while this question was being pondered by organization theorists, advances in computer technology that also facilitate *decentralization* were introduced. Although large mainframes, high-speed processing, vast on-line storage, data base management systems, and remote data collection all suggest centralization, minicomputers, microcomputers, and data communications favor decentralization.

Studies have shown that management style plays a much greater role in centralization than does information processing technology. Autocratic managers of the "Theory X" school tend to have little faith in their subordinates and use CBIS to increase their authority. Democratic managers of the "Theory Y" school use CBIS to enhance the creative and innovative talents of their subordinates. Either philosophy can be accommodated by CBIS; indeed, it is management's attitude toward centralization that influences CBIS structure, rather than CBIS influencing the attitude of management. One thing is certain, however: whether decision making is centralized or decentralized, it is enhanced by CBIS.

Summary

CBIS raise two organizational questions: Who is responsible for CBIS activities and how should the CBIS office be structured?

Historically, computers were first placed in accounting departments, and a few CBIS still remain under accounting department control. Today, it is more common to find separate departments of information systems, although many CBIS activities may be carried out in functional departments. Data preparation, data entry, and even systems analysis and design and programming may be performed outside the CBIS office, especially in distributed systems.

The CBIS office itself may be organized according to *activities* (administration, systems analysis and design, programming, and systems operations), *projects*, or the *life cycle* phases of development and maintenance. An activity orientation is viewed as promoting system security; a project orientation fosters good working relationships with users; and the life cycle approach permits CBIS personnel to specialize in either development or maintenance. Recent research into CBIS organization suggests that an *information systems hub* to coordinate the planning and control of CBIS may be a solution to the centralization/decentralization issue in the management of information systems.

CBIS personnel are classified according to the four activity categories: *administrative* (the CBIS director and the data base administrator); *systems analysis and design* (systems analysts and systems designers); *programmers* (application, system, and maintenance); and *operators* (console operators, librarians, and data preparation personnel). *Users* are the most important CBIS personnel, although they are not usually referred to in such terms.

Over the years, it has been argued that computers (and now CBIS) encourage the centralization of authority and decision making in organizations. Although computers may facilitate centralization, recent computer technology also facilitates decentralization. It is the philosophy of management, not computer technology, that determines the extent of centralization in an organization.

Assignments

16-1. Some CBIS are still under the control of the accounting department. Can you explain this placement purely in historical terms, or do you think other factors might be involved? What if the original computer applications had been in marketing—would we find marketing departments in charge of CBIS today?

16-2. The proliferation of microcomputers has caused some consternation among CBIS personnel. What organizational issues are raised when, say, the production department acquires personal computers for its engineering staff?

16-3. Many universities have separate computer facilities for academic and administrative computing. Are any of the CBIS-office organizations in Figure 16-4 appropriate for this situation? If not, what kind of organization would you propose?

16-4. Figures 16-5, 16-6, and 16-7 show the CBIS structure in three different organizations. Prepare such a diagram for an organization that you are familiar with—perhaps your school or your place of employment.

16-5. A small manufacturer of automobile and light truck parts has been sold by its parent company, which previously had furnished all CBIS support. The manufacturer has acquired a Hewlett Packard 3000 minicomputer and has hired you as the CBIS director. Because of budget constraints, you are limited to a staff of four. How will you organize your staff? What skills will you seek in the four people you hire?

16-6. The store managers in a large chain of discount houses used to spend about one half of their time on inventory problems. When the chain implemented a comprehensive CBIS, inventory was managed from the corporate headquarters. The store managers were free to spend more time in supervision and promotion, but the top managers began to get bogged down in operational matters involving inventory. Did this organization centralize or decentralize as a result of CBIS? Would the top management and the store managers be likely to give the same answer to this question?

16-7. Historically, organizations have selected top managers from areas that are currently critical. Thus, production vice-presidents often became company presidents following World War II, marketing managers frequently rose to top management positions in the 1960s and 1970s, and top managers today often have a background in finance. Do you foresee a day when CBIS managers may be in similar demand? What CBIS experience would be *helpful* in top management? What qualifications do CBIS managers *lack* for top management positions?

16-8. Figure 16-8 shows just one possibility for the assignment of responsibilities under an information systems hub. Diagram a hub organization that assigns responsibilities for various CBIS differently.

16-9. The U.S. Department of Defense, which has been a leader in CBIS development, is a strong supporter of centralized CBIS organization. Can you explain this attitude in terms of organizational philosophies?

CASE   Boomer Petroleum—Part II

Dave Fairley finally decided not to push for the centralized development of an expert system for oil prospecting (see Boomer Petroleum—Part I in Chapter 9) and, using an IBM PC, put together a scaled-down version of the system he had in mind. Over a period of several years, Dave and others in the operations division wrote, purchased, and otherwise acquired software of interest to them. They eventually got a form of the oil prospecting system up and running, although data entry was through the keyboard rather than from remote sensors, as Dave originally had envisioned. Perhaps more important, the operations managers found they could use the PCs (by this time they had three) for other tasks, such as report writing with word processing software, production scheduling with electronic spreadsheets, and statistical analysis with various "stat pacs."

In the meantime, Fran Whitecloud, the office manager for Boomer, had convinced Tiny Walker that office automation was "too far out of the mainstream of data processing," as she put it, to be of concern to the accounting department and the information services division. So Tiny did not object when Fran installed a Wang Net for office automation in early 1984. Dave grumbled a bit about Fran "charming" Tiny into agreement, but since he had installed his PCs without even consulting Tiny, he kept his objections to himself.

In December of 1985, Doug Fairley and Tiny Walker retired jointly and with due ceremony. As expected, Dave took over as president effective January 1, 1986. Suddenly Dave's information systems perspective changed. He thought he would still like to use his PC occasionally, but all the data he now needed as president was buried in thick printouts from information services. He had neither the time nor the inclination to key in the data for the analyses he wished to perform. He found the Wang Net convenient, and he liked the idea of leaving messages and coordinating schedules with the Wang terminal, but the Wang, too, fell short of furnishing the data he often felt he needed. The Director of Information Services offered to place a terminal to the main computer in his office, and Dave had to chuckle over the prospect of *three* computer devices at his desk. He recalled the old saying about "trying to drain the swamp when you are up to your hips in alligators" as he contemplated his situation.

Questions

1. Trace the history of information systems management in Boomer Petroleum (you may wish to refer back to Part I of the case) and identify the sources of the problems now faced by Dave. Who is responsible for these problems?

2. What changes would you make in the assignment of responsibility for the various information systems activities in Boomer if you were Dave? Draw an organization chart to reflect the changes you propose.

3. Analyze Boomer's problems in terms of the "islands of technology" in the "information systems archipelago." How could an information systems hub help bridge the islands?

Make a diagram similar to Figure 16-8 to show how an information systems hub could be applied to Boomer Petroleum.

Other Readings

Coleman, Raymond T., and M. J. Riley. "The Organizational Impact of MIS." *Journal of Systems Management* 23, no. 3 (March 1972).

Dickson, Gary W., and John K. Simmons. "The Behavioral Side of MIS." *Business Horizons* 13, no. 8 (August 1970).

Glaser, George. "The Centralization vs. Decentralization Issue: Arguments, Alternatives, and Guidelines." *Data Base* 2, no. 3 (Fall–Winter 1970).

McKenney, James L., and E. Warren McFarlan. "The Information Archipelago," *Harvard Business Review* (September–October 1982; January–February 1983; and July–August 1983).

Patrick, Robert L. "Decentralizing Hardware and Dispersing Responsibility." *Datamation* 22, no. 5 (May 1976).

Reynolds, Carl H. "Issues in Centralization." *Datamation* 23, no. 3 (March 1977).

Tsaklanganos, Angelos A., and Jugoslav S. Milutinovich. "The Impact of the Computer on Organization Structure." *Data Exchange* (November–December 1975).

Wagner, L. G. "Computers, Decentralization, and Corporate Control." *California Management Review* (Winter 1966).

Whisler, T. L. *The Impact of Computers on Organizations.* New York: Praeger, 1970.

Chapter 17

The CBIS
Life Cycle—I

Learning Objectives

After studying this chapter, you will be able to:
1. Recognize the indicators that point up the need for CBIS.
2. State objectives for a CBIS.
3. Identify the factors that deterine CBIS feasibility.
4. Outline a master plan for a CBIS.
5. Select a CBIS design approach.
6. Explain the major steps in CBIS analysis and design.
7. Apply evolutionary development approaches to DSS design.
8. Define the following terms:

CBIS life cycle
technological feasibility
economic feasibility
behavioral feasibility
CBIS project management team
performance standards
milestone schedule
Gantt chart
PERT
top-down approach (to CBIS design)
bottom-up approach (to CBIS design)
total system approach (to CBIS design)

modular approach (to CBIS design)
eclectic approach (to CBIS design)
logical systems design
systems flowchart
programming flowchart
physical systems design
sole source
competitive bidding
RFP
evolutionary systems development

489

The introduction of a new or modified information system into an organization is an event of major consequence, equivalent in impact to the introduction of a new product line, the addition of a new plant, or the reorganization of senior staff responsibilities. Yet many top managers, who would not dream of undertaking these other projects without the most thorough planning and preparation, often avoid involvement when "the information systems people want a new computer."

An information system is a vital organizational resource. Like the product line, the plant, and the organizational structure, it will not last forever. It is conceived and developed under certain environmental conditions, and as those conditions change, it will gradually become outmoded. To keep it alive, management must constantly tend it, cycling through successive iterations of a development process to ensure that the CBIS continues to meet the organization's ever-changing information needs.

In broad terms, the life cycle of a CBIS is no different from the life cycle of any other project. As shown in Figure 17-1, the cycle is initiated by a perceived information need and includes the phases of planning, development, implementation, operation, and control. In this chapter, we address the planning and development phases; the final three phases are covered in Chapter 18.

The similarity between the project life cycle and the management process described in Chapter 3 is not accidental. Management is responsible for the success or failure of a project, and it is logical to adapt the management

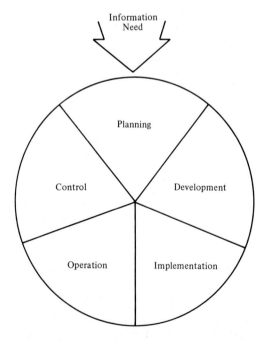

FIGURE 17-1 The CBIS project life cycle.

process to project management. In these final two chapters, we shall further adapt and refine that process to describe the management of a specific project: the introduction of a new or modified CBIS.

The Planning Phase

The ultimate success or failure of a CBIS may well be determined in the planning phase. Although a good plan does not give absolute assurance of a good CBIS, it is extremely unlikely that an efficient CBIS will emerge from a poor plan. The risks associated with a poor CBIS are high indeed; managers can hardly be expected to make correct decisions on the basis of incomplete, untimely, or just plain incorrect information. Given these risks, the decision to introduce a new or modified information system must not be made lightly. It is appropriate, therefore, that planning begin with a thorough evaluation of the need for a new CBIS.[1]

Recognizing the Need for CBIS

The general factors that contribute to the need for CBIS were discussed in Chapter 1: the nature of modern organizations, the current legal and social environment, advancing technology, and the expanding role of management. These factors may be manifested as more specific needs in different organizations. A few examples of such indications of the need for a CBIS, summarized in Table 17-1, will illustrate the point.

TABLE 17-1   Indications of the Need for CBIS

Indication	Example
Complexity	Long-range financial planning, waiting-line simulation
Volume	Banking, insurance transactions
Risk	Space navigation, nuclear power generation
Interdependencies	Coordination between production levels and promotion campaigns
Speed	Military command and control, airline ticket reservations

[1] The cyclical nature of a CBIS project dictates that changes or modifications to an existing CBIS follow the same phases as the introduction of a new CBIS. Since the introduction of a new CBIS is the more difficult undertaking, we will explain the systems life cycle as it applies to a new CBIS; changes are introduced similarly.

The Complexity of Operations

Many organizations have information processing requirements that are virtually impossible without computer assistance. Some of the management science models described in Chapter 7 fall into this category. High-technology industries, firms with a strong commitment to research and development, and many consulting groups have need for CBIS for this reason.

The Volume of Transactions

Other organizations perform relatively simple operations but in such volume as to require computer assistance. Banks, insurance companies, and investment firms are typical of this category.

The Risk Factor

Regardless of the number or complexity of transactions, certain organizations suffer more from errors than others. An error in processing a customer's electricity bill is unfortunate and requires correction, but it is not catastrophic. If the same utility firm errs in dampening its nuclear reactor, the results could be disastrous. The need for the precision afforded by a computer-based information system in such an organization is obvious.

Interdependent Operations

The requirement of exchanging or sharing information among departments in an organization also suggests the need for a CBIS. The manufacturing firm, with finance, accounting, production, and marketing departments all dependent on each other for information, is in this category.

The Requirement of Speed

Sometimes CBIS are required for the sheer speed of their operations. Military command and control systems, which may have only seconds to distinguish an enemy bomber from a commercial airliner, have such requirements. And so does the airline company, which also has only seconds to confirm a ticket reservation before a competing request for the same seat is received.

Objectives of CBIS

Just as managers are guided by organizational goals and objectives in the management process, so CBIS planners must establish goals and objectives for the CBIS. The two sets of objectives are not unrelated. CBIS objectives support organizational objectives, but the former are more specific and, of course, deal with the processing of information. For example, an organizational goal might be to "respond to all orders within three days." This goal may lead to CBIS objectives of "entering all orders into the transaction file within twelve hours of receipt," "furnishing copies of order invoices to finished goods inventory within twenty-four hours of receipt," and so on.

It is important to state CBIS objectives in quantitative terms to facilitate comparison with actual system performance during the control phase. It is also necessary for both the functional and the CBIS staffs to agree on these objectives. There is a natural conflict between these two groups: CBIS personnel need time and other resources to take care of internal operating requirements as well as to satisfy every other department's information needs; the functional staffs just as clearly need the information requested quickly in order to accomplish their primary activities. The dispute must be resolved early, in the planning phase, before irreconcilable differences are permanently built into the system.

Feasibility Studies

Having established the need for a new or modified CBIS and having further identified the specific objectives of the proposed system, CBIS planners must next answer the question, "Can this be done?" Many organizations have established standards for the form, content, and methodology of a feasibility study. Typically, such a study addresses three kinds of constraints: *technological, economic,* and *behavioral* (see Table 17-2).

Technological Feasibility

A CBIS is technologically feasible when the currently available hardware and software can accomplish the objectives of the system. Technological limitations are imposed by the number of remote terminals a computer can accommodate, storage space, access time, computational speed, data base management capabilities, and so forth. Technological feasibility is rarely a problem in commercial applications, although there are still a few scientific applications that push technological limits.

Economic Feasibility

Having been assured by the consulting systems engineer that nothing under consideration is technologically infeasible, the CBIS manager's next question should be, "Yes, but can we afford it?" Again, most firms have standard procedures for evaluating investment opportunities, including the not inconsiderable investment in a CBIS. These procedures usually take the form of a cost–benefit analysis similar to the one described in Chapter 7. A positive net present value or an internal rate of return that exceeds the minimum stan-

TABLE 17-2   Feasibility Studies

Type of Study	Question Answered
Technological	*Can* it be done?
Economic	Is it *cost-effective?*
Behavioral	*Should* it be done?

dard is a signal to proceed. The difficulty in determining the economic feasibility of a CBIS in this fashion lies in estimating the future benefits. Some, like reductions in order processing costs, can be computed. Others, like the goodwill gained from reducing errors, are more subjective. This problem is not unique to CBIS, although it may be less pronounced in other kinds of projects. CBIS planners must resist the temptation to overestimate CBIS benefits in order to justify a new system.

Behavioral Feasibility

Any change in the traditional way of doing things in an organization is going to meet with some resistance, but new CBIS seem to incur more than their share of resentment. It is appropriate, therefore, to ask, "Is all of this worth the trouble that it is going to cause?" For the timid souls who respond, "No," the proposed CBIS project is over. The remainder, hopefully a vast majority, must face the problem of reassuring threatened employees, retraining others, and, regrettably, letting some go. Some displaced employees can be absorbed by attrition, and others can be retrained so that they have new, and perhaps more marketable, skills.

Unfortunately, many of the personnel whose jobs are eliminated by the CBIS—stock clerks, filing clerks, order and billing clerks, and others—simply do not have the qualifications or the motivation to be retrained for the positions created by the CBIS (programming, systems analysis and design and similar jobs). And a few of those who are retrained may still feel a loss of identity in working with the CBIS.

It is doubtful that a CBIS project has ever been rejected solely on behavioral grounds, but the feasibility analysis should be conducted anyway, just to show where such problems will exist and to give personnel and other managers the time to plan how to alleviate these problems when they do occur.

The Master Plan

Assuming that the feasibility is favorable, it is now time to prepare a document to guide the CBIS project through its life cycle. There is no universally accepted format for a CBIS master plan, but there are several topics, shown in the outline in Table 17-3, that tend to be included in most plans.

Objectives

The objectives are the purpose of the project. Even though they have already been established and are known to the CBIS planners, they should be reiterated in the master plan, prominently, as guidelines for all involved. Some examples of systems objectives that support organizational goals were given earlier; others, such as an objective of "holding downtime to 5 percent of total operating time," may be directed at purely CBIS operations.

TABLE 17-3   Outline of a Sample
CBIS Master Plan

  I. Objectives
     A. ....
     B. ....
     C. ....
 II. Organization
     A. Responsible Executive: ...
     B. CBIS Project Management Team:
        1. Chairperson: ...
        2. Members: ...
     C. CBIS Department:
        1. Director of CBIS: ...
        2. Data Base Administrator: ...
        3. ...
III. Resources
     A. Equipment: ...
     B. Personnel: ...
     C. Facilities: ...
     D. Software: ...
     E. Budget: ...
        1. Equipment: ...
        2. Personnel: ...
        3. Maintenance and Supplies: ...
 IV. Control
     A. Milestone Schedule: ...
     B. Progress Reviews: ...
     C. Audit Procedures: ...

Organization

The master plan should outline the organizational changes that will result from implementing the project. The organizational considerations that govern the assignment of CBIS responsibility were discussed in Chapter 16. Even if there are no major organizational changes, and the purpose of the project is merely to modify or upgrade the CBIS, there are certain ad hoc responsibilities not readily apparent on the organization chart. These responsibilities are frequently given to a CBIS *project management team*[2] such as the one shown in Figure 17-2.

Although the CBIS project management team will be constituted differently in different organizations, one important principle should be observed. The chairperson should not have a parochial interest in the system either as

---

[2] Although it may be formed as an ad hoc committee, the CBIS project management team is frequently retained as a permanent *CBIS steering committee* (see Chapter 16) after the CBIS is operational.

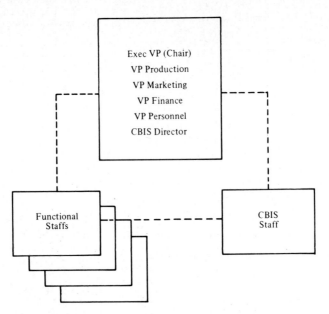

FIGURE 17-2   The CBIS project management team.

the head of a user department or as the head of the CBIS office. It is appropriate for these individuals to serve on the team and for their respective staffs to advise the team and each other, but the chairperson should be someone who is not personally involved and who has sufficient authority to resolve disputes among the users and between the users and the CBIS director.

Resources

Many master plans include at this point an inventory of current resources (equipment, personnel, physical facilities, software packages, and the operating budget) and a list of those additional resources anticipated for the CBIS project. Such an inventory is not a bad idea from the point of view of answering, "Where are we now?" and "Where are we going?" if that is how the inventory is used. Unfortunately, many CBIS project teams view the current resources as constraints that will determine the course of the project. When this attitude is taken in the interest of holding down costs, it is usually a mistake. It is something of an axiom in the computer industry that one can get more computational power for less money by obtaining new hardware than by "adding on" to older equipment. Again, there is nothing wrong with taking stock of one's resources, particularly in the critical area of personnel, as long as that action does not inhibit the development process.

Control Measures

The point has already been made that control begins during planning, where objectives become the standards against which actual performance will be measured in the future. Although such *performance standards* are oriented primarily toward the operation and control phases of the CBIS life cycle, it is also appropriate to establish standards for the development and implementation phases.

The *budget* is one control measure that applies to both the preoperation and the postoperation phases. Expenses are incurred early, with the acquisition of specially skilled development personnel (systems analysts, systems designers, and programmers) and perhaps the services of consultants. Major expenses are also incurred during implementation when the site is prepared, the hardware and proprietary software are acquired, operators are hired, and the conversion to the new system is effected. Personnel expenses carry over into operation, which has other continuing costs for maintenance and supplies. Finally, the audit of the CBIS in the control phase will require even more funds. These costs can get out of hand quickly if they are not strictly controlled by the CBIS project team. As a rough rule of thumb, personnel costs will be between 45 and 55 percent of the CBIS budget, equipment costs (rent or depreciation) between 30 and 35 percent, and other costs (maintenance and supplies) about 15 percent (see Figure 17-3).

Time often becomes a critical factor in a CBIS project, and there are several common methods of exercising control over time during development and implementation. The *milestone schedule*, shown in Table 17-4, provides a calendar of key events and their scheduled dates.[3] Milestone schedules show at a glance whether activities are being completed on time or not, but they offer little additional help.

Personnel

Equipment

Maintenance and Supplies

FIGURE 17-3   The CBIS budget.

[3]Only a few events are shown in Table 17-4 to illustrate a milestone schedule. A real milestone schedule for a CBIS project might contain hundreds of events and cover a period of three to five years. Other scheduling methods are also simplified for illustrative purposes.

TABLE 17-4   Partial Milestone Schedule for a CBIS Project

Date	Milestone
Sept. 1, 198__	Start interviews for systems analysts.
Oct. 1, 198__	Hire systems analysts.
Oct. 15, 198__	Begin information analysis.
Jan. 15, 198__	Complete information analysis.
Jan. 30, 198__	Begin logical systems design.
Mar. 15, 198__	Complete logical systems design.
Mar. 20, 198__	Begin preparation of RFP.
Mar. 30, 198__	Begin detailed systems design.
June 1, 198__	Complete RFP.
June 1, 198__	Start interviews for programmers.
July 1, 198__	Hire programmers.
July 15, 198__	Complete detailed systems design.
July 20, 198__	Begin programming.
Aug. 15, 198__	Receive hardware bids.
Sept. 1, 198__	First progress review.
Sept. 15, 198__	Announce hardware contract.
⋮	⋮
June 10, 198__	Complete conversion to new system.

The *Gantt chart*, shown in Figure 17-4, gives essentially the same information found in the milestone schedule, but in a graphical form. The Gantt chart gives a good pictorial representation of the length of each activity, which activities are being conducted simultaneously, and approximately how far along each activity should be on a given date.

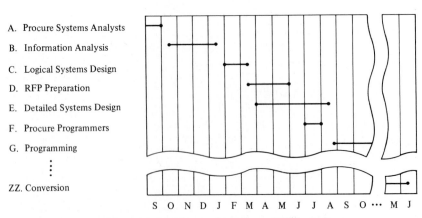

FIGURE 17-4   Gantt chart for a CBIS project.

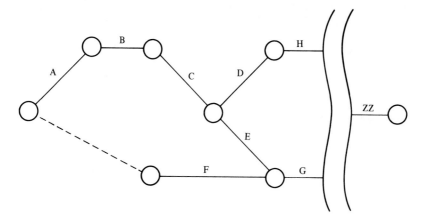

FIGURE 17-5   PERT chart for a CBIS project.

The *PERT* (for "Program Evaluation and Review Technique") network, shown in Figure 17-5, is one of the most powerful project management tools. PERT identifies *critical paths* (sequences of activities that, if delayed, will delay project completion); provides a basis for probabilistic estimates of the project completion time; and, when combined with *CPM* (for "Critical Path Method") techniques, shows how resources can be reallocated to speed up a project or to return a delayed project to its original schedule. The details of how PERT and CPM are used in project management are beyond the scope of this book, but you are likely to encounter them in an operations management or quantitative methods course. If so, keep CBIS projects in mind when you study PERT and CPM.

The Development Phase

The development of a CBIS formally begins when the master plan has been approved by top management, although some preliminary developmental effort is required to ensure proper planning. A tentative system design, for example, must be completed before cost and benefit data can be projected for the economic feasibility analysis. The schedules, too, are dependent on some rough idea of what is to be done during development.

One very important aspect of development, the selection of a design approach, must also be determined during planning. But because it is a major development issue, it is treated here, in the discussion of the development phase, along with the other important activities of systems analysis and design.

Approaches to CBIS Design

CBIS planners usually have a good idea of where they want to go, but they do not always agree on how to get there. There are numerous approaches to designing a CBIS, each with its own relative advantages and disadvantages, to consider before proceeding further with development. The various approaches can be grouped into four categories; a fifth category can be synthesized from the original four. Let us take a brief look at them.

Top-Down Approaches
In *top-down* approaches, the CBIS is designed to support the goals and objectives of the organization as articulated by top management. Information requirements that support top management are considered first. The processing of this information requires as inputs the information needed by middle management, and so on, until basic transaction data are eventually incorporated into the design. Just as objectives themselves are passed down and given added detail at each level in an organization, the CBIS, too, is designed downward, satisfying the information requirements for those refined objectives at each level. For this reason, top-down approaches are also referred to as *objective-oriented approaches*.

The proponents of top-down design argue the logic of supporting organizational goals and point out that the lack of this support is one reason that some top managers are apathetic about present CBIS. Opponents generally acknowledge the need to get top management more involved in CBIS, but they point out that the problem lies in the unique, environmental information needs of top management. These needs are not likely to be satisfied by a top-down approach either, and the needs of middle and first-line managers, who are heavily involved in CBIS, may not be considered fully in the process.

Bottom-Up Approaches
Where top-down is an analytic process of breaking down information requirements into more and more detailed components, a *bottom-up* approach synthesizes the information needed at higher levels from that already being generated at lower levels. Bottom-up design first satisfies transaction processing requirements, then summarizes that data for reports to first-line managers, next analyzes the information in those reports for middle managers, and so on, until all levels are satisfied. These approaches are also classified as *problem-oriented* because they tend to focus on the clearly defined, structured problems typically found at lower levels of management.[4]

---

[4]Some CBIS scholars have labeled bottom-up approaches *evolutionary*, because they tend to follow the historical pattern of CBIS support to successively higher levels of management as CBIS are revised and improved. We avoid that term here because it is more properly used to describe new approaches, discussed later in this chapter, to the development of decision support systems.

Bottom-up design favors the heavy users of CBIS at the middle and lower management levels. If the basic activities of the organization are taken care of, the argument goes, the satisfaction of goals and objectives will follow naturally. Perhaps, but there is still a disenchanted group of top managers not using CBIS because their particular information needs simply cannot be synthesized from transaction data.

Total Systems Approaches

A *systems approach* is one that views the organization as a system in which various resource inputs (labor, material, and capital) are processed into outputs (goods and services). In a systems approach to CBIS design, information is treated as just another resource. All CBIS design alternatives use a systems approach to some extent; a *total* systems approach is an extreme that treats the organization as a single, integrated system to be served by a similar, totally integrated CBIS.

A total systems approach is aesthetically appealing because it provides a convenient, comprehensive model to explain information flows. It also provides for the integration of CBIS applications and the exchange of information between functional departments better than other approaches. The drawbacks of total systems approaches arise when one attempts to use them in the real world. Large, complex, dynamic organizations do not hold still for the five or more years it might take to develop a total CBIS. Consequently, total systems approaches remain theoretical techniques that are rarely used in practice.

Modular Approaches

One can also design an information system on a smaller, more manageable scale by addressing one subsystem or module at a time. The modules are usually designed along the functional lines of finance, accounting, production, marketing, and so on. Since most organizations are structured along similar lines, these methods are sometimes called *organization chart approaches*. Because each module is designed to stand alone, at least until all the other modules are completed, modular approaches are also known as *integrate-later approaches*.

Designing one module at a time places lighter demands on systems development resources, although it usually extends total development time. And if it follows the traditional functional lines, the CBIS is likely to be less disruptive to the organization and more readily accepted by its users. But organization charts do not fully reflect the interactions among departments, and a CBIS designed along functional lines probably will not consider the informal organization and other subtle information flows. Finally, although the intention of integrating later is undoubtedly sincere, the evidence is that this seldom happens. Independent modules soon develop unique characteristics that make them incompatible with other modules, and integration becomes impossible.

An Eclectic Approach

Some CBIS scholars attempt to pass judgment on these approaches, branding some "acceptable" and other "unacceptable." There is no reason, however, that CBIS planners cannot make themselves aware of the pitfalls of the various approaches, and, by careful planning, follow any one with success in a given organization. But an even better solution is to select the best features of each and combine them into an *eclectic* approach.

The outstanding feature of a top-down approach is that it recognizes the needs of a here to fore neglected group in CIBS: top management. Whether one follows the entire top-down route or not, the information needs of top management must be served. If this means refining information normally used at lower levels, fine; do that. If it means obtaining and processing environmental data not used at lower levels, then that must be done also.

A bottom-up approach provides a strong transaction data base and probably lends itself to data base management systems better than the others. An eclectic approach should recognize the fundamental role of transaction processing in organizations and the dependence of supervisory management on that part of a CBIS.

At the present stage of CBIS development, it is still risky to undertake a total systems approach. Yet there is no reason that CBIS planners should not *view* the CBIS as a total system, even though they may not wish to *design* it as such. For example, informational outputs from production should be recognized as necessary inputs for marketing applications, even though the production and marketing applications may not be integrated into a single design. Provisions for this kind of exchange can be made without creating a monster that is impossible to control.

And last, systems theory notwithstanding, there are valid reasons for designing a CBIS that reflects organizational structure. In such a CBIS, problems or changes in one module will have a minimal impact on the overall system. Also, it is easier and more justifiable to run a CBIS as a profit center when its services are rendered along departmental lines. And modules can be implemented as they are produced, without waiting for the entire system to be completed. An eclectic approach can incorporate modular principles and still integrate later successfully if a total systems view is maintained during the development phase.

Systems Analysis and Design

In *analysis*, the current system—the manual system in the case of a new CBIS, or the old automated system in the case of a modification project—is literally taken apart and examined piece by piece, information need by information need. The *design* process is one of assembling a new system that satisfies all these information needs. The actual steps in analysis and design are, of course, considerably more complicated than this simple explanation.

They start, in keeping with the problem orientation borrowed from the bottom-up approach, with an analysis of information needs.

Analysis of Information Requirements

Managers make decisions on the basis of the information available to them. One way to establish information requirements is to examine the decision points in organization activities and to determine what information is required at each one. For example, the decision on how many copies of this book should be printed is based on market demand, price, production costs, storage facilities, interest rates, and competition in the field, to mention just a few factors. If the CBIS is to support the manager who makes this decision, it must provide him or her as much of this information as possible.

Each of the thousands of other decisions made in an organization must be analyzed similarly. Many of the information requirements will be duplicated in different decision situations, an indication of the need to share information, perhaps through a data base management system. The functional staffs should make these requirements known to the project management team through their representatives. But functional managers are sometimes reticent when it comes to voicing their needs, perhaps because of a lack of understanding of just what a CBIS can do for them. It is then incumbent on the systems analysts, who are skilled in both functional and information systems operations, to suggest, prompt, or otherwise draw additional information requirements out of the functional specialists.

Logical Systems Design

The identification of information requirements establishes *what* the CBIS is to do; it is now necessary to define just *how* those information requirements will be satisfied. This step is called *logical systems design* because it reflects the logical relationships among the users, the operators, the equipment, input, output, and processing. It is a deductive process that proceeds from the general to the specific. The general relationships are explained in a *systems flowchart*, such as the one in Figure 17-6, which shows a portion of an ordering subsystem. Systems flowcharts are prepared in close cooperation with the functional users, who provide input on current manual procedures, desired improvement, personnel capabilities, operational requirements, and other matters not generally known to the CBIS staff.

The systems flowchart is user oriented. Because the application is to be automated, the logical system must also be defined with a data processing orientation. Programmers need to know specific relationships, such as those shown in the *programming flowchart* in Figure 17-7. The level of detail in a programming flowchart is geared to the skill and experience of the programmer who will use it. In the extremes, each symbol in the flowchart may result in a single program statement, or the programming flowchart may be only slightly more detailed than the systems flowchart.

The normal flow in a system is from input, through processing, to output.

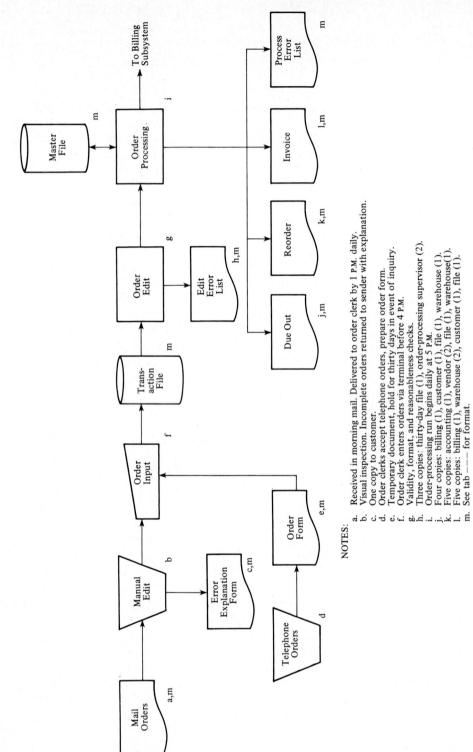

NOTES:

a. **Received in morning mail. Delivered to order clerk by 1 P.M. daily.**
b. Visual inspection. Incomplete orders returned to sender with explanation.
c. One copy to customer.
d. Order clerks accept telephone orders, prepare order form.
e. Temporary document, hold for thirty days in event of inquiry.
f. Order clerk enters orders via terminal before 4 P.M.
g. Validity, format, and reasonableness checks.
h. Three copies: thirty-day file (1), order-processing supervisor (2).
i. Order-processing run begins daily at 5 P.M.
j. Four copies: billing (1), customer (1), file (1), warehouse (1).
k. Five copies: accounting (1), vendor (2), file (1), warehouse(1).
l. Five copies: billing (1), warehouse (2), customer (1), file (1).
m. See tab —— for format.

FIGURE 17-6   Example of a systems flowchart.

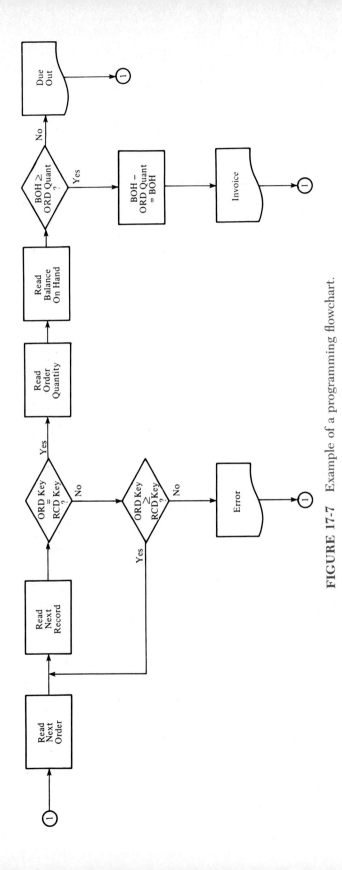

FIGURE 17-7 Example of a programming flowchart.

The design sequence tends to flow backward, from output to input and then to processing.[5]

Output Design   Output design considers the *content*, the *frequency*, the *format*, the *medium*, and the *distribution* of output, as shown in the example in Table 17-5. Content is fairly well established during the information analysis and may be only slightly revised or refined during design. Format treats such matters as column and row headings on reports, spacing, graphic displays, and so forth. Output frequency may be daily, weekly, monthly, or, in interactive systems, continuous. The ouput medium may be paper, preprinted forms, mailers, video displays, or some combination of these and other media. Standard forms, such as the one shown in Figure 17-8, are available to aid in the layout of output, and locally designed forms may be prepared to help organize and collect other output specifications. Finally, distribution instructions tell who is to get the output and, where appropriate, how many copies to make.

TABLE 17-5   Example of an Output Design

Output:	Inventory Status Report
Content:	Date of report. Stock number, description, beginning inventory, quantity shipped, quantity ordered, quantity received, back orders, and balance on hand for each item in inventory.
Format:	Report title: line 3, col. 55–77
	Date: dd/mm/yy, line 4, col. 63–70
	Column headings: line 7,
	STKNUM: col. 10–15
	DESCRIPTION: col. 25–35
	. . . . . .
	BOH: col. 119–121
	Data: lines 9, 11, 13, . . . to last item,
	Stock number: 9999–999, col. 9–16
	Description: X(25), col. 18–42
	. . . . . .
	Balance on hand: 9(4), col. 119–122
Frequency:	Weekly, as of 5 P.M. Friday.
Medium:	4-part, carbonless, 15-pound paper; 132 col; ½-inch green bar
Distribution:	Copy 1: Production manager
	Copy 2: . . .
	Copy 3: . . .
	Copy 4: File

[5] In a *literally* backward design, the sequence would be output, processing, and input. In practice, however, inputs must be known if one is to design processes, and the revised sequence is still referred to as *backward*.

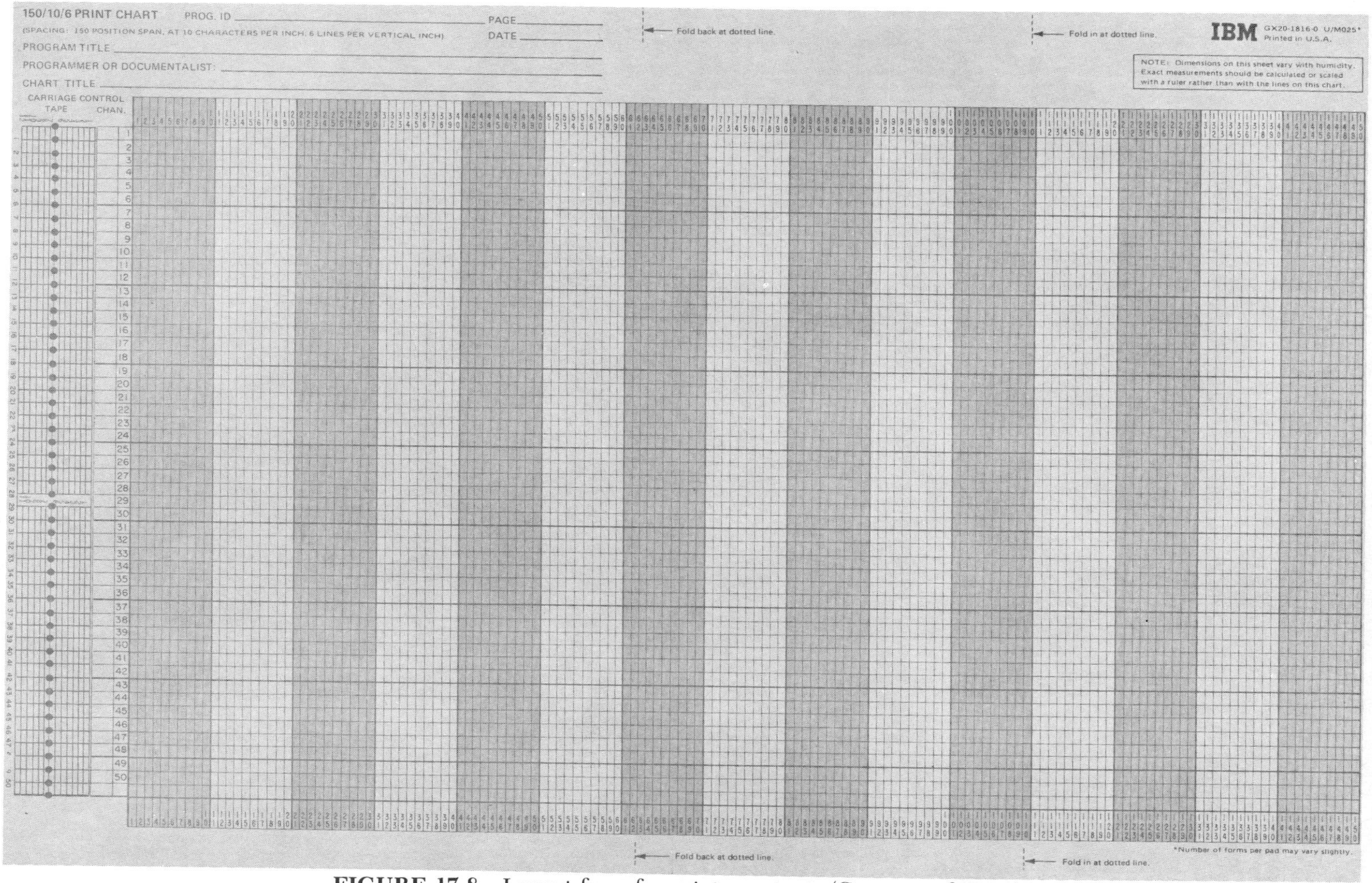

FIGURE 17-8 Layout form for printer output. (Courtesy of IBM.)

507

TABLE 17-6   Example of an Input Design

Input:	Inventory change card
Content:	Date of transaction, stock number, transaction code, quantity
Format:	Date: dd/mm/yy, col. 1–8
	Stock number: 9999–999, col. 9–16
	Code: X, col. 17
	Quantity: 4(9), col. 18–21
Frequency:	Daily, as of 3 P.M.
Medium:	80-column punched card
Source(s):	Shipping orders, order receipts, invoices

Input Design   Input requirements are determined by output requirements. For example, the data *content* section of the input specifications shown in Table 17-6 is clearly related to the output content specifications shown in Table 17-5. The input design considerations are also similar to those for output design, with the exception that input must consider the *source*, rather than the *destination*, of data. Another difference is that input data are frequently collected at shorter intervals than those at which output is produced. An exception to this rule of thumb is found in the transactional processing mode, where input and output occur on a one-to-one basis.

Process Design   Process design establishes the way in which input is converted to output. If we continue the example of a weekly inventory report, one computes an output requirement for the "balance on hand" by adding the quantity received to the beginning inventory and subtracting the total demand for the period. The process must be designed to read the necessary inputs, to perform the required calculations, and to save the answer for inclusion in the output report. A single application, such as the inventory report illustrated here, may involve many processes, each one of which must be specified in the process design stage.

The design of processes can be very routine, as in the inventory report example, or it can be quite complex, as in a marketing research application. Most application programmers could design the inventory report processes with ease, but more complex processes, such as those used in decision support systems, may require the skills of a management scientist. Complex applications also demand greater user involvement to ensure that the processes will actually achieve the intended results. More is said on this subject later.

File Design   It is also necessary during logical systems design to determine the number and type of files required in the system. Considerations of the medium and the organization of application files are discussed in Chapter 8;

the use of data base management systems in lieu of application files is covered in Chapter 6.

Physical Systems Design

The physical system consists of personnel, facilities, hardware, and, in the sense that it is recorded on physical media, software. The design of the physical system includes programming and the selection of hardware. Because programming is primarily a data processing function and, aside from the brief discussion in Chapter 5, outside the realm of this book, we will focus on that part of physical systems design of more concern to management: the selection of hardware.

There are two roads leading to the hardware selection decision. One, *sole source*, is convenient, but it may be more expensive. The other, *competitive bidding*, requires a good deal of effort, but it is probably less expensive.

Sole Source   When an organization has little in-house systems development experience or capability, it may be best to select the computer manufacturer early in the logical systems-design phase. This approach is called *sole source* because the CBIS project management team considers the products of only one manufacturer in the selection of hardware. The choice of the manufacturer may be based on its reputation for service and reliability, on proximity to service facilities, on the recommendation of associates, or on other valid reasons.

The equipment manufacturer usually provides assistance in systems design—around the manufacturer's own equipment, of course. The advantages of this approach are convenience, expert advice, and more efficient utilization of manufacturer-supplied software. The disadvantages are the limitation on available hardware, the operational changes required by the software package, and the automatic exclusion of all other manufacturers—some of whom might have offered better, less expensive alternatives.

Competitive Bidding   When there is a high level of technical expertise already present, or readily available from consultants, an organization is usually better off soliciting competitive bids for its contemplated hardware. Realizing that the contract will probably go to the lowest bidder, computer manufacturers have a strong incentive to propose only the most economic configuration that will get the job done. It is therefore particularly important that the systems specifications, as outlined in the *request for proposal*, or *RFP*, be as complete as possible. The manufacturer is not responsible for capabilities omitted in the RFP or for provisions for growth and expansion.

The specifications in the RFP should include the input volumes and media, the same information for output and files, representative examples of the processing requirements, the data communications requirements, the programming languages to be used, the required delivery date, and the requirements for special capabilities such as graphical displays, data base management systems, and performance monitors. The manufacturer's proposal will recommend a hardware configuration, show how it meets or exceeds the specifications, list other advantages, give a delivery schedule, state the price, and outline the financing arrangements (lease or buy options).

The CBIS committee should conduct a formal evaluation of each proposal and select the best according to previously established criteria. In addition to cost, the committee should consider the capacity for expansion, the availability of software support, compatibility with the existing hardware and software, the manufacturer's reputation for reliability, service agreements, backup support, site preparation requirements, and assistance in training. Many organizations, particularly those in state and federal government, have developed elaborate checklists and grading scales to assign numerical scores to RFPs. Although these methods are helpful, the final choice of hardware is more often made judgmentally rather than by computational techniques.

New Approaches to Systems Development

The project life cycle approach has been employed for many years. It has been used effectively in the development of applications such as order entry, inventory control, and invoicing. In other words, it has been very effective with transaction processing and most MIS applications.

Recently, new approaches to systems development have been suggested. They go by such names as *heuristic development, creative systems design,* and *evolutionary design.*[6] These approaches are better for developing *decision-oriented* applications. These applications are sometimes associated with MIS and almost always with DSS projects. For example, they might be used in the creation of production planning systems, media selection systems, or systems for capital expenditure analysis.

Reasons for the New Approaches

There are several reasons that new approaches are being used to develop decision-oriented applications. These reasons include rapidly changing decision-making environments; uncertainties about management's true information needs; and computer hardware and software advances.

Rapidly Changing Decision-Making Environments
Most observers of the contemporary business world would agree that today's managers are having to make decisions in rapidly changing decision-making environments. A few examples will illustrate this point. The availability of

---

[6]Thomas Berrisford and James Wetherbe, "Heuristic Development: A Redesign of Systems Design," *MIS Quarterly,* March 1979: 11–19. Henry C. Lucas, "The Evolution of an Information System: From Key-Man to Every Person," *Sloan Management Review,* Winter 1978: 39–52.

raw materials can no longer be taken for granted. The prime interest rate continues to fluctuate rapidly. Labor costs continue to increase. Products experience shortened life cycles.

Any decision-oriented application, whether it be MIS or DSS, must accurately describe the decision-making environment if it is to be useful. A difficulty with the project life cycle approach is that the process does not encourage flexibility as the application is being created. To illustrate this point, in many organizations the user is required to "sign off" on the design specifications for the application. This is done specifically to discourage changes. Even if the specifications are appropriate when initially approved, they may no longer be appropriate if the decision-making environment is changing. The development process for decision-oriented application should be flexible enough so that it accommodates changes in the decision-making environment.

Uncertainties About Management's True Information Needs

As early as 1967, Russell Ackoff questioned the assumption that managers always know what information is needed to support their decision-making responsibilities:

> For a manager to know what information he needs, he must be aware of each type of decision he should make (as well as does) and he must have an adequate model of each. These conditions are seldom satisfied.[7]

Subsequent research has shown Ackoff to be correct in his assessment. It is frequently only after a manager has grappled with a decision for a while that his or her information needs become clear.

Computer Hardware and Software Advances

Computer hardware and software advances are making it easier to develop decision-oriented applications in a more flexible manner. Computer terminals, minicomputers, and microcomputers are putting computational power in the hands of the user. Easy-to-use general-purpose languages (such as BASIC), fourth-generation languages (such as FOCUS), and special-purpose languages (such as IFPS, EXPRESS, and EIS) have made computer programming easier. Powerful data base management systems, such as IDMS, Adabas, and System 2000, provide relatively easy access to needed data. And there is a growing core of organizational personnel who know how to put these resources to good use.

Armed with hardware and software advances, today's CBIS specialists are better equipped to create systems in more flexible ways. To illustrate, enthusiasts of the APL programming language talk about the concept of *throwaway code*. The idea is that a program can be so quickly, easily, and

---

[7] Russell L. Ackoff, "Management Misinformation Systems," *Management Science*, December 1967: 8.

inexpensively created, that if the program does not meet the user's needs, it can be thrown away with no great loss. This is the sort of flexibility that is needed when decision-oriented applications are developed.

Evolutionary Systems Development

The new approaches to systems development go by different names, but they have much in common. We have chosen to use the term *evolutionary development* to describe the essence of these approaches. This choice of terminology helps emphasize the evolutionary way in which systems are created.[8]

Evolutionary development requires an exceptionally high level of user involvement. The importance of user involvement has been mentioned before and will be stressed again; however, here we are talking about considerable involvement in all stages of the systems development.

The involvement begins with the user suggesting the decision-oriented application. At this point, the user may be able to provide only an ill-formed specification of the information that is needed. In this period of initial grouping, the systems development group produces a first cut of the output that is needed—a simple model, a dummy report, or a simulated system. The user may even help develop the output. This first cut at the output becomes the basis for a dialog between the user and the development group. Over time, the two groups zero in on the information that is needed. The specifications for the system may never truly be formalized. They evolve over time as the user and the CBIS specialists better understand the decision maker's information needs. As the user contributes to the development of the system and begins to receive benefits from it, he or she becomes increasingly committed to it, and a feeling of ownership is created. At some point in time, the system takes on the capabilities and characteristics that are ultimately needed, and formal documentation of the system begins. The system is never really completed, however, because in an evolutionary system, there is no final product—the system continues to evolve over time. Rather, the system reaches a stage of maturity where changes are less frequent.

Summary

The life of a CBIS can be explained in terms of a five-phase cycle. This chapter covers the first two phases: *planning* and *development*. The remaining phases—*implementation*, *operation*, and *control*—are covered in the next chapter.

[8]The terminology and description presented here are similar to those of Lucas, pp. 44–46.

The planning phase begins with the *recognition of the need* for CBIS. Complex operations, high transaction volume, high-risk operations, organizational interdependencies, and the requirement of speed in obtaining information are all indications that a CBIS is needed. Next, *CBIS objectives* are developed on the basis of organizational goals and objectives. If the implementation of a CBIS is *technologically, economically,* and *behaviorally feasible,* a *master plan* for the CBIS is developed. Master plans for CBIS may take many different forms, but they usually contain the *objectives* of the system, *organizational considerations,* the available *resources,* and *control measures.*

The development phase includes *systems analysis* and *systems design.* In systems analysis, the old system is examined for information needs, and in systems design, a new system is created to satisfy those needs. Systems design is further broken down into *logical* design, in which the general relationships between the systems components are established, and *physical* design, which includes more specific activities, such as programming.

The traditional design and development approaches include *top-down, bottom-up, total systems,* and *modular.* The best features of each approach can be combined into an *eclectic* approach. Recently, particularly in the development of decision-oriented applications, attention has been given to *evolutionary* design approaches, which features iterative interaction between users and systems designers.

Assignments

17-1. Which indications of the need for a CBIS do you think would be present in each of the following organizations?

    a. The Internal Revenue Service.
    b. An automobile manufacturer.
    c. A mail-order retailer.
    d. The RAND Corporation (a high-level "think tank" specializing in government operations).
    e. A construction firm.

17-2. What *CBIS* objectives might arise from the following *organizational* objectives?

    a. Reduce expenses by 10 percent next year.
    b. Answer 90 percent of all customer telephone inquiries during the initial phone call.
    c. Reduce the percentage of defective items produced to 3 percent.
    d. Notify all customers of price and availability changes within five days of the date of change.
    e. Consider vendor reliability in awarding purchase contracts.

17-3. Which type of feasibility might be in question in the following proposed applications of CBIS?

    a. Provide every student in the school of business with a remote terminal to the academic computer.

    b. Conduct all remedial instruction in an elementary school by CAI (computer-assisted instruction).

    c. Pay interest on withdrawn savings up to the hour of withdrawal.

    d. Give a newspaper editor the capability to update a story between editions of the paper.

    e. Include a linear programming model with a capacity of fifty variables and forty constraint equations in a decision support system using personal computers such as the Apple II.

17-4. Refer to Problem 17-3. Now that you have identified the type of feasibility in question, decide which examples are actually feasible. (Use your imagination to fill in any extra details necessary to answer this question, but be sure to identify the assumptions you make.)

17-5. Assume that your university uses a completely manual system of student record maintenance and wishes to develop a CBIS application to maintain student records, distribute grade reports, prepare transcripts, assist in class registration, prepare class rosters, and record grades. Prepare an *outline* of a master plan to accomplish these goals within two years.

17-6. Refer to Problem 17-5. Which approach to CBIS design did you use? Why did you select the one you used? If you did not consciously use one of the five approaches described in the text, which of those do you think is best for this application?

17-7. The CBIS design approaches are generally described with *new* CBIS in mind. Because most organizations today already have some form of CBIS, is it appropriate to apply the design approaches to CBIS *modifications?* Why or why not?

17-8. Prepare a *systems flowchart* for a CBIS inventory application for an automobile parts supplier. Consider the need to fill orders, to reorder, to back-order, to prepare shipping documents (invoices, billing statements, and dues-out), and to generate periodic reports.

17-9. Consider the systems flowchart prepared in response to Problem 17-8. Prepare a *programming flowchart* for the reorder portion of the system.

17-10. Assume that you are the CBIS director for an organization that has outgrown its present computer and wishes to acquire a newer, larger one. Would you seek *competitive bids* or go *sole source?* Why? How would you answer if you were the company president? How would you feel about the situation if you were the customer representative of the manufacturer of the present computer?

17-11. Much has been said and written about managers and operational personnel who feel threatened by computers and CBIS. Some traditional CBIS managers now feel threatened by decision support systems. What can be done to allay their concerns in the way that the fears of the line managers were once put to rest?

CASE   Boomer Petroleum—Part III

As president of Boomer Petroleum, Dave Fairley soon realized that he had to do something about the lack of coordination in computer services. His first step was to move Information Services out of Accounting and form an independent Information Systems Directorate. Within a few weeks, he had hired a Director of Information Systems, Phil Klein. Phil had been a systems engineer with a major computer manufacturer and had had as one of his clients the refinery where Dave had worked prior to coming to Boomer, so Dave felt confident that Phil knew the industry. Dave decided to have Phil report to him directly and gave Phil a free hand to "clean up the mess we got into."

At first, Phil enjoyed both his freedom and his direct relationship with Dave. Soon, however, he discovered that he was having difficulty communicating with the functional managers. His offers to provide information services were generally met with responses such as, "We're getting along fine the way it is now," or "Whatever Dave wants is OK with me." After several months, Phil had not added any new services and, in effect, was simply presiding over those that had been in place when he arrived. At the same time, the functional managers were complaining to Dave that the centralization of information services had denied them control over one of their most important resources—the information they needed to perform their jobs.

"I think we need to get everyone together and clear the air," Phil told Dave. "We need to develop a plan that outlines where we are going and how we are going to get there."

"I agree," said Dave. "Draw up an agenda and I'll call the meeting."

Questions

1. What are the causes of the new problems at Boomer? Who or what is to blame this time?

2. What should be on the agenda Phil is preparing?

3. Use your imagination and Parts I and II of this case to outline a master plan for CBIS development at Boomer Petroleum.

Other Readings

Barnett, Arnold. "Securing User Involvement." *Data Management* (January 1978).

Carrol, Daniel T. "How the President Satisfies His Information Systems Requirements." *Society for Management Information Systems Proceedings* (1976).

Collins, John H. "The Application of the Systems Approach to the Design of Computer-Based Data Processing Systems." *Journal of Systems Engineering* (January 1976).

Courtney, James F. "Evaluating Information Requirements in MIS Design." *Journal of Applied Systems Analysis* 5, no. 2 (1978).

Davis, G. B. "Strategies for Information Requirements Determination." *IBM Systems Journal* (No. 1, 1982).

Gremillion, Lee L. and Philip Pyburn, "Breaking the Systems Development Bottleneck," *Harvard Business Review* (March–April 1983).

King, William R., and David I. Cleland. "The Design of Management Information Systems: An Information Analysis Approach." *Management Science* 22, no. 3 (November 1975).

Kinzer, J. G. "A Model for Systems Design." *Journal of Systems Management* 23, no. 9 (October 1972).

Klein, Robert T., and Ralph Jamaro. "Cost-Benefit Analysis of MIS." *Journal of Systems Management* (September 1982).

McFarlan, Warren F. and James L. McKenney. *Corporate Information Systems Management: The Issue Facing Senior Executives*, Homewood, Ill.: Irwin, 1983.

Munro, Malcom C., and Gordon B. Davis. "Determining Management Information Needs: A Comparison of Methods." *Management Information Systems Quarterly* 1, no. 2 (June 1977).

Rockart, John F. "Chief Executives Define Their Own Data Needs." *Harvard Business Review* (March–April 1979).

Rubin, Martin L. *Introduction to the System Life Cycle*. Vol. 1. New York: Brandon System Press, 1970.

Teichroew, Daniel, and Z. Gackowski. "Structured System Design." *Ideas for Management*. Cleveland: Association for Systems Management, 1977.

Yandav, Surya B. "Determining an Organization's Information Requirements: A State of the Art Survey." *Data Base* (Spring 1983).

Zani, William M. "Blueprint for MIS." *Harvard Business Review* (November–December 1970).

Chapter 18

The CBIS Life Cycle—II

Learning Objectives

After studying this chapter, you will be able to:

1. Distinguish between syntax and logic errors.
2. Discuss the importance of training in the implementation of CBIS.
3. Name and describe the four methods of converting from an old system to a new one.
4. Explain some of the measures necessary to preserve the security and operating integrity of a CBIS.
5. List and explain four types of control measures employed during the CBIS life cycle.
6. Describe the cyclical process of the life of a CBIS.
7. Define and use the following terms:

syntax error	check digit
logic error	progress review
debugging	acceptance test
parallel conversion	post-installation review
phase-in conversion	financial audit
pilot conversion	operational audit
immediate conversion	management audit
data diddling	performance monitor
reasonableness check	software monitor
totals check	

Information systems tend to cycle through phases—planning, development, implementation, operation, and control—in much the same way that management functions describe a cyclical process. The first two phases, planning and development, were covered in Chapter 17. We now conclude our discussion of the CBIS life cycle with an explanation of the final three phases.

The Implementation Phase

The implementation phase is marked by four major activities: site preparation and the installation of hardware,[1] the testing and debugging of software, the training of personnel, and conversion to the new system. It is during this phase that the organization must make the critical, often irreversible, decision to abandon the old system in favor of the new one. It is also the phase during which the organization is most vulnerable to flaws in the design of the new CBIS.

Site Preparation and Installation

In the not too distant past, the installation of a computer implied a major site construction or remodeling job. Today, many small computers need only a clear tabletop and a convenient electrical outlet. In spite of the enormous strides in computer design and construction, the site for a CBIS mainframe computer still needs *some* special attention prior to installation. Computer hardware is still relatively delicate compared with most other industrial equipment and must be located in an environment of controlled temperature, regulated humidity, filtered air, and steady electrical power. The extensive cabling network needed to power and interconnect hardware components is best located under a raised floor for easy access and the prevention of damage. Backup power facilities are needed to guard against the loss or distortion of data in the event of a power failure. And as we shall see, it is often necessary to "harden" computer sites against intrusion or natural disasters.

The user organization is responsible for selecting and preparing the site, but it can usually rely on the computer manufacturer for specifications on the floor space, the cabling, and the environmental requirements of the hardware to be installed. When the site is prepared, the manufacturer performs the actual installation and conducts any necessary electrical checkouts. The manufacturer also runs diagnostic routines to check the systems and the application software furnished with the computer.

---

[1] For this discussion, we shall assume that the CBIS project involves a hardware upgrade, although a modification to an existing CBIS does not necessarily require new or additional hardware.

Testing and Debugging

Whereas manufacturer- or vendor-supplied software can normally be assumed to be free of any significant errors, software developed in-house must be tested thoroughly before it is put into service. If the software is to be available at the time of hardware installation, these tests must necessarily be conducted on other, similar equipment (it is not cost-effective to acquire hardware several months early just to support software testing). The manufacturer may make equipment available for these tests, or the user organization may join a users' group that can make time available for testing as well as for emergency backup of future operations. This kind of cooperation is frequently found among branches of larger organizations—departments of federal or state governments and subsidiaries of large corporations—that operate similar hardware.

The errors sought in testing fall into two categories: *syntax* errors and *logic* errors. Syntax errors are violations of the programming language or the operating system. Misplaced commas, misspellings, the use of reserved words, and other "grammatical" errors fall into this category. Most syntax errors are detected by the checks built into the programming language and are printed in an error listing. Some syntax errors can be tolerated and will not preclude the successful execution of the program, but the more serious ones must be corrected before the program will run.

An error in logic is committed when the programming statements are all valid, but because of some shortcoming in the thinking of the programmer or the systems designer, they do not bring about the intended results. *Adding* the quantity of a customer's order to the inventory balance instead of *subtracting* it is perfectly acceptable to the computer, although it is likely to cause the inventory manager considerable consternation! Logic errors such as this are much more difficult to detect than syntax errors and will show up only under exacting testing.

The best way to test a program is to run data through it and check the output for accuracy. Test or dummy data prepared specifically to exercise all parts of the program provide the most thorough test, but they are difficult to develop and must be checked manually to confirm the computer output. An alternative is to use historical data and to compare the results with those originally obtained with the old system. The shortcomings of this method are that it is not applicable to new applications, and the old input format may not be compatible with the new system.

The detection of errors, be they in syntax or logic, necessitates their correction—a process called *debugging* in CBIS jargon. Syntax errors can usually be corrected by an editing of the incorrect statements, perhaps only with a few simple changes made at a terminal. Errors in logic sometimes force one back into the development phase for further systems analysis, design, and programming to correct the faulty part of the program. In both cases, it is important to retest software after debugging. Seemingly inconsequential changes have a way of producing far-reaching and unwanted results.

Training

Although formal training takes place during the implementation phase, the preparation of personnel for the introduction of a new CBIS really begins much earlier, during planning. The first steps involve assurances of job security and solicitation of user support for the CBIS. The best way to quash the rumors and fears that tend to undermine CBIS support is to keep employees fully informed of the project and the changes it will bring about. Users and other employees at every level should be kept abreast of development progress and encouraged to participate through suggestion programs and by cooperating with systems analysts. Early effort expended by the CBIS project management team in these directions will be well rewarded in the implementation and operation phases.

Procedure Manuals

Another very important prelude to formal training is the preparation of *procedure manuals*. There are two categories of procedure manuals, those for *users* and those for *operators*.

Procedure manuals for users explain how the personnel in functional departments can interface with the CBIS. In some cases, primary job functions may be altered, as they are for clerical personnel, who will perhaps operate terminals and assume data entry responsibilities. For management personnel, the main concern may be how to interpret a certain report, how to request an on-call report, or how to address inquiries to the data base.

The responsibility for preparing procedure manuals for the users lies with the systems analysts—the link between the users and the CBIS in this, the implementation phase, just as in the development phase. The manuals should contain step-by-step instructions for each user activity, samples of relevant input and output documents, and the name of the responsible systems analyst to contact in the event of a problem. For example, a claims clerk in an insurance company might be given a procedure manual that explains how to turn on a CRT terminal, how to sign on with a password that gives access to customer files, how to call up a customer's file with the account number, what the resultant display will look like, and so on, through all possible transactions that the clerk is authorized to initiate.

Operator personnel require different information and must be furnished different kinds of procedure manuals. One kind of procedure manual for operators is prepared in-house and deals with matters peculiar to the CBIS: instructions for the loading of files, the distribution of output, the scheduling of application software, and other production matters. These are *system* manuals and are the CBIS equivalent of standard operating procedures, or SOPs.

A second type of procedure manual for operators deals with the actual operation of the equipment and is furnished by the manufacturer. These *equipment* manuals are completely hardware oriented and explain such mat-

ters as console operation, diagnostic checkouts, trouble indicators, and maintenance procedures.

Training Sessions

Personnel involved in CBIS development become so familiar with the new
system that they sometimes forget how confusing it may be to others who are
less familiar with it. These other personnel—clerks, managers, and even
operators—must be trained to operate and use the CBIS if it is to be successful. Training sessions are normally conducted late in the implementation
phase, just prior to conversion, and they vary according to the classification of
the personnel being trained.

Clerical Training   The personnel involved in data preparation, data entry,
and other clerical duties are best trained in a formal, classroom environment.
Sessions are held during normal working hours, attendance is mandatory,
performance evaluations are conducted at the end of training, and successful
completion is made a matter of record in each employee's personnel file.
There is, however, a question of who should conduct the training: systems
analysts or supervisory personnel.

Because of their involvement in CBIS design and development, systems
analysts are undoubtedly better equipped to conduct clerical training and can
offer more thorough, more authoritative instruction. But the use of CBIS
specialists to conduct training may be intimidating to the trainees and, to
some extent, undermines the position of the supervisory personnel who are
normally looked to for guidance on job-related matters.

On the other hand, supervisors are less knowledgeable on CBIS matters
and must themselves be trained before they can instruct others. But the use
of supervisors in training tends to reinforce the traditional chain of command
in the organization and serves to dispel some of the mystique that invariably
accompanies a new CBIS. In addition, the involvement of supervisors in the
training process places them on the side of the developers in the all-
important commitment to making the CBIS a success. The final decision to
use analysts or supervisors will depend on the complexity of the new system
and the quality of the supervisory personnel.

Management Training   Left to their own devices, management personnel
rarely take the time to attend formal training sessions when, or if, they are
scheduled. In this case, the procedure manuals may be the systems analyst's
sole opportunity to educate management on the use and benefits of the CBIS.
Without formal training sessions, many managers never do become users and
the full potential of the CBIS is never realized. It often requires a decree
from top management to get other managers involved—and then only reluc-
tantly—in CBIS training. A better technique is for top managers to set an
example by their own attendance at training sessions. Not only will subordi-

nate managers be more likely to attend, they will probably be more attentive once they are there.

Unlike for clerical training, the choice of instructors for management training is clear-cut: they should be the systems analysts, who have already developed a working relationship with the functional managers and are familiar with both the managers' information needs and the manner in which the CBIS will satisfy those needs. And those systems analysts who are aware of management's natural aversion to training sessions are forearmed. They will make the sessions short, specific, and directed to the level of their audience. If necessary, separate sessions should be conducted for different functional departments to ensure that only relevant material will be presented. This may strike some as being overly deferential to managerial users, but after all, one major purpose of CBIS is to serve managers, and that cannot be done without a supportive, well-informed, participative management.

Operator Training   Operator personnel are not as likely to experience fear and anxiety over a new CBIS as the users, nor will they encounter the radical job changes that, for example, clerical personnel sometimes face with CBIS implementation. As a result, operator training is less extensive and, in fact, may be carried out "on the job" during the systems tests. To a large extent, operator training consists of a familiarization with any new technology (hardware and systems software) acquired and the new production schedules to be followed. The actual content of CBIS application software is of little consequence to operator personnel.

Training Techniques

The methods of instruction employed in CBIS training vary greatly. The exact mix of instructional techniques in a training program should be selected on the basis of organizational considerations such as the level of the personnel to be trained, the skill and background of the trainees, and the nature of the subject to be taught. Some of the more common techniques, and the conditions under which they are most effective, are described in the following sections.

Tutorials   Tutoring is essentially one-on-one instruction. In the past, tutoring implied a human instructor, but now, the tutor may well be a computer hardware/software combination. Tutorial programs were discussed in Chapter 11 and are quite appropriate for CBIS training when the trainee has sufficient computer literacy to follow simple keyboarding instructions and the number of persons to be trained justifies the rather considerable cost of developing this form of CAI. Programmed tutorials are very effective when the skills to be imparted involve the same device (a microcomputer or a terminal, perhaps) on which the instruction is presented. Airline reservation clerks who already use terminals and who need to be instructed in a new reservation system would be excellent prospects for a programmed tutorial.

The use of human tutors is usually restricted to situations in which the number of trainees is very small (a few senior managers, perhaps) and the material is unstructured. For example, a new DSS capability might involve only a few users whose questions could not be anticipated fully. In this case, a tutor could accommodate the more restrictive schedule of the managers and tailor the instruction to the specific needs of each manager. Senior managers, in particular, are more accustomed to dealing with people than with machines and tend to find this form of tutoring more beneficial.

Small-Group Instruction   Small-group instruction is very similar to the classroom environment found in colleges and universities. The instruction is more formal than it is in tutoring, but there still is an opportunity to question the instructor and to receive some individual attention. Scheduling must be done for the convenience of the majority, so alternative sessions may be required for those who could not attend at the original time. Small-group instruction works well for operational personnel and first-line supervisors whose schedules are more easily arranged to accommodate the training sessions.

Resident Expert   The resident expert is somewhat like an "on-call" tutor. Unless the organization and the CBIS training function is very large, the role of resident expert is usually an additional duty of one of the systems analysts for the specific application. Users or other personnel who need help simply call the resident expert, who will try to resolve the problem over the phone or, if necessary, go to the work site to resolve it. The use of a resident expert is often a second line of training used to complement another form, such as small-group instruction. In a slight variation on this technique, there are also *nonresident* experts available at software firms who can answer questions on commercially prepared software packages.

Built-in Help   Built-in help is similar to a programmed tutorial in that it is a form of CAI, but it is different in that it resides in the application software itself. Built-in help is usually summoned by a few special keystrokes, which produce menus or other opportunities for the user to identify the problem and be instructed on its solution. Built-in help is naturally restricted to those users or other personnel with direct access to the application software. Most commercially prepared, mass-appeal software, such as integrated packages of word processing, spreadsheets, and filing systems, now contain built-in help features.

Conversion

When all applications have been analyzed, designed, programmed, tested, and debugged; when hardware has been selected and installed in a prepared site; and when users and operators have been trained in the procedures required by the new CBIS—then it is time to *convert* or *cut over* from the old to the new system. In spite of all the preparations, however, it is still possible, even likely, for problems to occur when users, operators, data, hardware, and software are all brought together for the first time under live operating conditions. There are several conversion options available to CBIS planners that will reduce this risk of error in the new system.

Parallel Operations

At one time, it was believed that the safest approach to conversion was to run both the old and the new systems simultaneously—in *parallel*—until it was established that the new system was producing results that were "reliable" (i.e., the same as the results of the old system). At that point, the old system was terminated and the new one assumed the primary role. A parallel conversion of a simplified CBIS with only four application modules is shown in Figure 18-1. A real CBIS, of course, would have many more applications.

A parallel conversion is feasible when the new system is little more than an equipment upgrade of the old one, with no new applications. But when new applications are introduced, there is no basis for comparison with the old system. Also, some organizations, such as banks, are reluctant to produce duplicate financial information in spite of all the safeguards against confusion between *live* and *dummy* output. These objections coupled with the increased skill of CBIS personnel and improved hardware reliability, have made the parallel conversion all but obsolete.

Phase-in Operations

A CBIS is *phased in* when the organization converts to one module or application at a time, as shown in Figure 18-2 (again, with a simplified, four-module CBIS). This kind of conversion is most compatible with the modular design approach; the conversion schedule can be timed to coincide with the

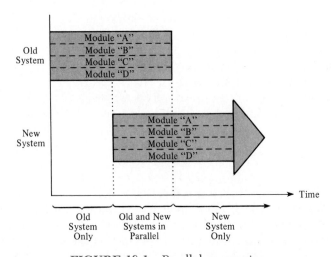

FIGURE 18-1   Parallel conversion.

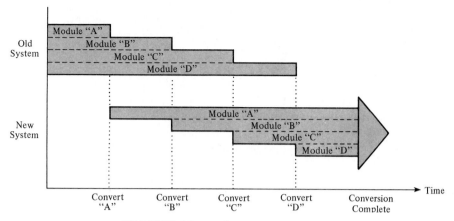

FIGURE 18-2 Phase-in conversion.

scheduled completion of the various modules. The combination of a modular design and a phased conversion makes the most efficient use of a limited CBIS staff, but, as noted in Chapter 17, the development phase will take much longer. There will also be considerable overlap between development and implementation.

A phased conversion also tends to limit the effects of errors to the specific application area of the new module. This advantage is offset, however, by the difficulty of integrating modules that have been introduced over a long period. To alleviate this problem, the most *independent* modules (e.g., billing, general ledger accounting, and inventory record-keeping) should be introduced first, and the more *dependent* modules (financial planning, production scheduling, and other integrated applications) should come later.

Pilot Models

The concept of a *pilot model* is a familiar one in engineering: a small-scale operation is conducted first to confirm that laboratory methods are indeed transferable to the production process, and then full-scale operations may begin. In CBIS conversion, the "small-scale" operation may be a single store in a chain of discount houses, the subscription accounts for one magazine of a large publisher, or any other activity that accurately reflects the "full-scale" operations of the organization. The pilot conversion depicted in Figure 18-3 is for a multiplant manufacturing firm with a single plant acting as the pilot model.

The major advantage of the pilot method of conversion is that it allows the CBIS to be introduced in its entirety, thus fully exercising any integrative features of the system, without jeopardizing information flows in the whole organization. The implementation of the CBIS as a total package, even if only in part of the organization, makes this type of conversion especially appropriate when a total systems-design approach has been used. Of course, if the

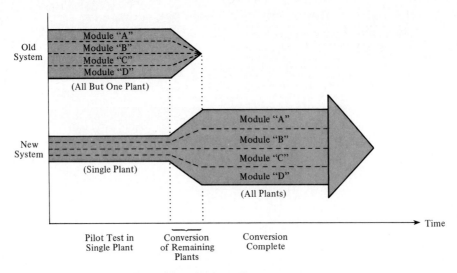

FIGURE 18-3   Pilot conversion.

pilot test is successful, the remainder of the organization can convert in comparative safety.

Immediate Method

Sometimes, the new system is so dramatically different from the old that parallel operations are not feasible, the applications are so extensively integrated that they cannot be phased in, and the organizational structure does not lend itself to a pilot conversion. In these cases, there is no other choice but to convert everything at once—*immediately*—as shown in Figure 18-4. This is frequently necessary in systems dependent on a data base management system where, in order to convert any one application, all of the old

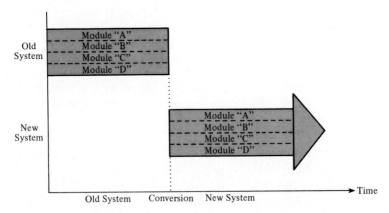

FIGURE 18-4   Immediate conversion.

application-oriented files must be converted to the schema of the data base and they are no longer available for processing under the old system. It may also be necessitated by a total systems-design approach followed during the development phase.

Obviously, the risks are much higher in an immediate conversion, but so are the payoffs if the conversion is successful. Applications dependent on output from other modules are fully operational on conversion, and there is no awkward "in-between" period for users and operators. Immediate conversions may be most appropriate when the CBIS is based largely on vendor-supplied software of proven reliability or when in-house development personnel are highly qualified; in all other cases, the risk of error may be too great for this approach to be recommended.

Planning for Conversion

The factors that argue for one method of conversion over another are known very early in the system life cycle; indeed, they may be organizational characteristics completely beyond the control of CBIS planners. And because conversion methods are related to design approaches (modular design suggests phase-in and total systems design suggests pilot or immediate conversion), the choice of a conversion method should be made concurrently with the selection of a design approach. Both decisions take place during the planning phase and should be incorporated into the master plan.

The Operation Phase

This is essentially a book about the operation of CBIS, and consequently, many operational topics are covered elsewhere. For example, the organization of the CBIS office and the responsibilities of CBIS personnel are covered in Chapter 16, data entry methods are covered in Chapter 4, the way managers use CBIS is addressed in Parts IV and VI, and so on. And because this book takes a managerial approach to CBIS, some operational matters of primary interest to machine room personnel, such as the preparation and use of production run instructions, are not covered at all. But there is one aspect of operations that is of interest to everyone associated with the system: the *security* of CBIS.

The Need for Security

Although the assets of an organization are subject to loss, damage, or destruction from various causes, CBIS tend to be particularly susceptible to these dangers. There are several reasons for the greater vulnerability of CBIS. First, CBIS components are comparatively fragile. Computer hardware can be damaged more easily than, say, the tools on an automobile assembly line, and CBIS data files are positively tenuous compared with most other organizational assets. Second, CBIS are more likely to be the object of hostility on the part of disgruntled workers, protestors, and, recently, even criminals. Finally, trends in the decentralization of CBIS facilities and distributed processing have increased the difficulty of protecting CBIS.

Threats to Security

In order to provide for the security of CBIS, one must first be aware of the nature of the problem: Which components of CBIS are vulnerable? How are they threatened? What is the source of these threats? And how can CBIS be protected from such threats?

Natural Disasters

Some threats to CBIS are obvious and are little different from the threats to other assets. Natural disasters fall into this category. Fires, floods, windstorms, lightning, and earthquakes can occur without warning and destroy or damage hardware, software, and data.

There is little one can do to *prevent* natural disasters, but there is much that can be done to minimize their effects. Hardware, like other valuable assets, should be insured and can be replaced if lost. The disruption to operations that results from the loss of hardware can be minimized if contingency planning has identified available backup facilities—perhaps from the manufacturer, a computer service center, or a users' organization.

Software and data losses are more serious. They, too, can be covered by insurance, but they are unlike hardware in that one cannot go out into the marketplace and replace organizational data or user-developed software. Disaster planning for CBIS must include provisions for backup data and software as well as backup hardware. Many companies maintain off-site, fireproof vaults for storing backup material. This approach is particularly efficient in large, multisite organizations in which the various sites back each other up. Smaller or single-site firms often turn to service centers for backup. Sunguard, a subsidiary of the Sun Oil Company, is an example of a service center that offers both computer backup and vault storage for data and software backup to its customers. Complete backup service such as this typically costs $3,000 to $5,000 per year.[2]

Malfunctions

Natural disasters tend to be catastrophic, but fortunately, they are rare. Malfunctions, on the other hand, usually cause much less damage, but they occur with greater frequency. And worse, whereas CBIS managers are very much aware when disaster strikes, they may be totally unaware that a malfunction is taking place. Malfunctions can occur in hardware as a result of

---

[2] "When Computer Disaster Strikes," *Business Week*, 6 September 1982, 68.

power surges or failures, stray electrical forces (static electricity or the output of nearby electronic devices), the introduction of dirt or other foreign matter into equipment, mechanical wear, operator error, or the inexplicable failure of electronic components. Software also can malfunction, usually because of logic errors, but also because of contamination of the recording medium or stray electrical charges. Although we generally do not speak of "data malfunctions," the proper functioning of CBIS is very much dependent on accurate data, and any inaccuracies among data have the same effect as hardware or software malfunctions.

Hardware reliability is at least partially a function of design and production quality control and, as such, is beyond the control of the user organization. Users can, however, be sure that routine maintenance is performed on schedule, that the machine room is kept relatively free from impurities, that primary power is regulated against surges, that operators are properly trained, and that backup power is available (many computers now contain sufficient emergency battery power to preserve data until backup power can be applied).

Testing and debugging are supposed to ensure software reliability, but anyone who has ever written a computer program knows how an unanticipated combination of events can produce inaccurate results. Liability for CBIS errors is a matter of growing concern for CBIS personnel and has created an expanding market for insurance companies. Three Midwest banks recently sued their data processing service company over software errors that resulted in the overpayment of interest to the banks' customers. One insurance firm, The Hartford, insured only two hundred organizations against CBIS error in 1979 but expected to sell over five thousand such policies in 1982.[3] And malpractice insurance, which until recently was available only to doctors, lawyers, architects, and other professionals, is now available to computer programmers. If software reliability cannot be absolutely *assured*, at least it can now be *insured*. Insurance does not completely solve the problem, of course. Incidental losses, such as not being able to collect accounts receivable if that file is inadvertently destroyed, are still uninsurable. Nor does insurance relieve CBIS managers of their responsibility to eliminate software errors, but it does somewhat soften the blow that can result from such errors.

Criminal Acts

CBIS are doubly exposed to criminal activity: crimes can be, and are, committed both *against* and *with* CBIS. Crimes against CBIS include *malicious* acts such as sabotage and *mischievous* acts such as "data diddling." Crimes committed with the aid of CBIS include fraud, theft, and espionage.

Crimes Against CBIS   In the late 1960s and early 1970s, a few extremists expressed their protest against the war in Vietnam by sabotaging the com-

---

[3]"Insuring Against Computer Foul-ups," *Business Week*, 6 September 1982, 66.

puters of an arms manufacturer and destroying the punched-card records of a local draft office. Although these acts do not seem to have altered the course of the war to any measurable degree, they did point up the vulnerability of CBIS to acts of violence. The results of these acts are much like the results of natural disasters. But although you cannot lock out, say, a flood, you can keep out or at least make entry very difficult for a would-be saboteur.

Hardware can be protected by passive measures, such as by locating the machine room away from normal traffic flows and by "hardening" the site against fire and minor explosions. Active measures include the use of security guards and controlled access—via key, coded locks, or sign-in stations—to hardware locations.

It is more difficult to protect data and software from sabotage, particularly in distributed systems, where there are many points of access to data bases. Data can be protected by the use of passwords, a "read-only" access mode, access limited to specific applications, and the continuous screening of employees who are given access to the system. The last measure is especially important, because many acts of sabotage against data are committed by persons who have authorized access. For example, an employee who is given a one-week termination notice should have his or her access revoked at the time of notification. The revocation of access privileges means that passwords must be changed, a step that should be taken periodically—say, monthly—in any event.

Less serious, but still of major concern, is the threat of data diddling—the *alteration* of data. Numerous cases of data diddling have been traced to teenage whiz-kids who gain access to data bases through communications networks and their home or school computer. Data diddlers rarely have any malicious intent; they do their mischief for the challenge involved without fully understanding the consequences of their acts. The innocent intention of data diddlers is small consolation to the data base administrator who must sort the garbage out of his or her files!

Crimes with CBIS   Those who sabotage hardware gain only some perverse satisfaction from their acts, but those with the ability to sabotage software and data stand to gain much more. The ability to tap into data bases or to modify application software can be used to defraud, steal, or engage in espionage.

Crimes committed with CBIS are much more difficult to detect than those committed against CBIS. Where sabotage leaves wrecked equipment or garbled data in its wake, the clever computer-aided thief can use CBIS technology to cover his or her tracks as well as to perpetrate the crime.

Documented cases of CBIS crime include the now-famous case of the bank employee who diverted fractional cents (the result of rounding) to his own account, a team of race track employees in Florida who printed winning parimutuel tickets on the backup computer, and the California programmer who diverted millions of dollars through electronic funds transfer channels to his numbered Swiss bank account. Less dramatic cases involve a government employee who merely used his agency's computer to maintain records of his stockmarket transactions (thereby "stealing" valuable computer time) and a marketing organization that gained access to its service center's files to obtain the mailing lists of rival firms (a simple case of industrial espionage).

No one knows for certain the extent of such crime, because even those crimes that are detected—and they may be less than 10 percent of the total—are not always reported because they may make the firm appear incompetent, and there is a possibility that others will learn how to duplicate the crime. It has been estimated, however, that the losses to U.S. businesses from CBIS crime may be as high as five billion dollars per year.[4]

Some data need to be protected from illegal access even though their loss or damage might cause no financial harm. For example, personnel files are subject to privacy legislation that prohibits the disclosure of information not only to outsiders but also to users in other functional areas who may otherwise have unrestricted access to the CBIS. Personnel files are also unique in that old backup or "grandfather" files that no longer have value to the CBIS must be given the same protection afforded current files. This is an unusual requirement for most CBIS personnel and one that is easily overlooked if security is lax.

Operating Integrity

Even if natural disasters, malfunctions, and criminal acts were not threats to CBIS, systems managers would still need to take precautions to safeguard data. The very nature of processing—changing, adding, and deleting data—raises the possibility to error. Changes may not be posted properly, incorrect data may be added, or data that should have been saved may be deleted. *Operating integrity* in CBIS deals with elimination of these errors in processing.

The operating integrity of CBIS can be compromised in a variety of ways, the most common being by errors committed during data entry. The old phrase "Garbage in, garbage out" may seem a little worn now, but it is still true. But even if data were perfect, CBIS are still vulnerable to logic errors and rare, but possible, internal processing errors. Any one or a combination of these errors can result in *direct* financial losses, such as overpaying suppliers or underbilling customers, or they can lead to *indirect* losses by providing faulty information to decision makers. A logic error in the computation of a net present value used in financial planning may ultimately be far more costly to an organization than one that, for example, bills a customer a few hundred dollars less than the correct amount.

Some security measures, such as the use of access logs or the maintenance of backup files, also help preserve operating integrity, but other techniques, such as editing or the use of check digits, are strictly error detection

---

[4]Gina Kotoka, "When Criminals Turn to Computers, Is Anything Safe?" *Smithsonian*, August 1982: 117.

methods. We will look briefly at some methods in each category to get a better idea of how systems managers can maintain operating integrity.

Backup Files

If you have an item of extraordinary value—a rare coin, for example—you can protect it by keeping it in a safety deposit box at your bank. But when an item has no *intrinsic* value—the telephone number of a friend back home, for example—you probably would just keep a duplicate copy somewhere.

Data fall into the second category. They have no intrinsic value. They are, after all, only magnetic impressions on a metal oxide or perhaps holes in a card. But CBIS data are unlike your friend's telephone number, which does not change from day to day. Data in CBIS change constantly, thus complicating the procedures for maintaining backup files. The specific approach to backing up data depends on the mode of processing.

Backup in Batch Processing   In batch processing, the old master and transaction files are maintained for at least one cycle to facilitate reconstruction of the current master file should it be damaged—perhaps as it is being used as the old master file in the next cycle (see Chapter 8 for an explanation of batch processing). As an extra precaution, the transaction documents are also saved to permit reconstruction of the old transaction file, should it be damaged as well. As shown in Figure 18-5, this combination of old master file, old transaction file, and transaction documents will cover all backup requirements in a batch system. Of course, the backup files and documents must be stored in a location and a manner that preclude a simultaneous loss of both primary and backup data. A fireproof vault some distance from the processing area would satisfy these conditions.

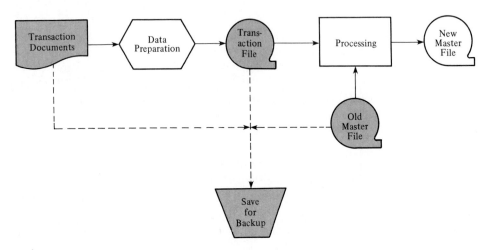

FIGURE 18-5   Back-up in batch processing.

Backup in Transactional Processing   Transactional processing poses a somewhat more difficult problem because the master file is updated continuously and there is no clear distinction between "old" and "new" files. In this case, one can define "cycles" arbitrarily by making periodic copies of the master file. If transaction documents are saved for the most recent "cycle," a new master file can be created at any time from the last copy and the intervening transaction documents. Again, the backup data must be stored separately from the primary data if one is to achieve a reliable backup capability.

Figure 18-6 shows a transactional system in which the master file is copied periodically onto tape, although the medium of the backup file is not important. Of course, if the backup master file is on a sequential access medium such as tape, it is necessary to copy it back onto a direct access medium before resuming processing. Because it is rare actually to use a backup file (just as it is rare for a homeowner to use a fire insurance policy), the slight inconvenience of recopying the file is more than offset by the use of a less expensive medium. There are utility programs available in system software that will copy from disk to tape or tape to disk.

Access Logs

Access logs show the time, date, duration, and user identification of access to CBIS. Increased frequency of access or unusually long access times on the part of a user are cause for suspicion. Exception reports can be prepared to show deviations from past individual usage or from group norms. In most cases, of course, there will be valid reasons for such deviations, but there is also the possibility that they will point to a user who is a real or a potential threat to operating integrity.

Access logs can be either manual or automated. Physical access—to the machine room or the terminal area—is usually recorded manually on sign-in and sign-out sheets at the entrance. Automated logs, maintained by service

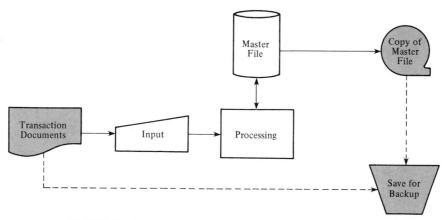

FIGURE 18-6   Back-up in transactional processing.

programs in the system software, record the user identification, the sign-on and sign-off times, and the application software or files accessed.

Originally, access logs were intended to thwart unauthorized access to CBIS. But now, the popularity of distributed processing, the proliferation of terminals and other data entry devices in functional work areas, and the increased use of data communications have made it almost impossible to keep out unauthorized personnel. Nor are unauthorized users likely to use their correct identification—if they even have one—and help the security personnel to locate them. Access logs may tell CBIS managers when unauthorized access has occurred, but they are of little help in apprehending the intruder. As a result, access logs are now used primarily for accounting purposes and for identifying legitimate users who may be inadvertantly threatening CBIS operating integrity. Once identified, these persons can be educated to the proper use of the system.

Error Detection Measures

Errors can be detected at various stages of processing. *Verification* as a means of detecting errors in punched-card input was discussed in Chapter 4. Other input errors can be detected by *editing*. For example, a preprocessing edit of the transaction file for a personnel application might check social security numbers for nine numerical characters. The edit would not ensure that the nine digits used would be the correct ones, of course, but it would screen out gross errors, such as the presence of alphabetic characters or an eight-digit number.

A *reasonableness check* makes sure that the data are within certain reasonable limits, say, $3.50 to $20.00 for the hourly wage rate in a payroll system. In an interactive system, *unreasonable* values—those outside the limits—cause a program interruption and must be verified or corrected by the operator before the program can continue. In other systems, values failing the reasonableness check may be printed on an error listing for correction before a second attempt is made to process them. Reasonableness checks can be employed at any stage in the system—during input, processing, or output. Like editing, reasonableness checks do not ensure accuracy, but they do eliminate gross errors, such as the $10,000 or $15,000 monthly electricity bill we read about every so often.

A *totals check* compares beginning and ending totals—of inventory, for example—with the net change created by all the transactions. Any difference is an indication of an error, probably the loss of one or more transactions during the update process. This is the same principle that we apply to the balancing of our checkbooks: we net out the outstanding checks and the unrecorded deposits and compare the result with the difference between the bank statement and the amount shown in our checkbook. The bank also uses this technique, but in a grander, computer-supported version, to check its daily calculations. As these examples suggest, totals checks are the most appropriate where the data are numerical.

Finally, *check digits* guard against transmission errors that might occur as data are moved internally within the CPU and externally between the CPU and storage devices. A check digit is an extra digit determined by an arithmetic manipulation of numerical data, say, the result of alternately adding and subtracting each digit in a number. In this example, the number 32,754 would have a 7 added to it $(3 - 2 + 7 - 5 + 4 = 7)$ and be transmitted as 327547. Before it is used in processing, the computation of the check digit is repeated and compared with the transmitted check digit. Any difference is an indication that the number was somehow altered during transmission. Of course, the check digit is not part of the number for processing purposes and must be recomputed if the updating process changes the original number.

The Control Phase

Control of CBIS begins during planning and is exercised to some extent in every phase of the CBIS life cycle, just as control is included in each phase of the management cycle discussed in Chapter 3. During planning, control standards are established as objectives of the system, and periodic evaluations of the CBIS are scheduled. One type of evaluation, the *progress review*, occurs during the development phase. Another, the *acceptance test*, takes place during implementation. Shortly after implementation, early in the operating phase, a *post-installation review* is conducted. Periodic *audits* are administered at regular intervals, usually six months or one year, for the remaining life of the system.

Progress Reviews

It would be very unusual for a CBIS project to proceed precisely on schedule in exact conformance to the master plan. More likely, some activities will be delayed, others will proceed more rapidly than planned, new or revised information requirements will precipitate design modifications, and environmental changes will force a restatement of objectives. The purpose of a progress review is to bring these changes to light, to revise the master plan if necessary, and to redirect development efforts when that is required.

Progress is measured by a comparison of the amount of work completed with the amount scheduled for completion using a milestone schedule or Gantt chart (see Chapter 17). Discrepancies are resolved by modification in the schedules or reallocations of development resources. Also, the expenditure of funds is compared with the budget and any necessary adjustments are made. Any changes in either the schedule or the budget must be conveyed to all affected parties.

Deviation from schedules is to be expected and, unless major discrepancies arise, is not a cause for concern. More worrisome are modifications caused by changing information requirements. The CBIS project management team should establish change policies very early and enforce them strictly during development and operation. Once the logical design is completed, any changes desired must be fully justified by the originator and approved by the CBIS project management team. Changes are usually judged more harshly than original proposals, because changes may render some completed work useless and may result in disproportionate expenses. At some point, the CBIS project management team must draw the line on changes and approve only those brought about by environmental conditions beyond organizational control. One exception to this policy occurs in the development of DSS, where changes are more expected than they are in MIS or TPS.

The Acceptance Test

The acceptance test is the final activity before conversion to the new CBIS. In a modular design, there will be an acceptance test for each module, as it is introduced, but a CBIS introduced as a total system must be tested in its entirety.

The acceptance test is a *systems* test, which includes user personnel and must satisfy the CBIS project management team that the CBIS (or module) is ready for implementation. In contrast to testing and debugging, which detect errors in programming only, the acceptance test evaluates user procedures, personnel training, operator procedures, the analysis and design effort, data communications, and every other aspect of the system, including a recheck of the program testing done earlier.

The acceptance test may be designed by CBIS personnel, but it should be conducted by an agency with less personal involvement. The CBIS project management team may form an ad hoc acceptance test team expressly for this purpose. As in all evaluations, there must be clear, quantitative standards for acceptance (or rejection) prior to the test. Error rates, turnaround times, and measures of accuracy provide unambiguous standards for comparison.

The Post-Installation Review

When operation of the new system is *technically* satisfactory—that is, when personnel are achieving the expected speed and accuracy in entering data, all programming errors are corrected, and users are accustomed to the new output—it is time to evaluate the system in *operational* terms. In brief, is the system accomplishing what it was intended to do? This operational test is called the *post-installation review* and is evaluated according to several different criteria.

Cost–Benefit Analysis

The standard for this comparison is the cost–benefit analysis conducted in the economic feasibility analysis, as modified by changes encountered during development. Because it is frequently difficult to place a dollar value on the benefits of CBIS, some organizations treat the CBIS as a *profit center* and "charge" customers (users) for CBIS services. Realistic charges can be developed from a comparison with the fees charged by computer service centers for similar work. In effect, it is as if the user had the choice of "buying" CBIS services, doing without some or all of them, or even going to an outside agency to obtain computer service. In this concept, CBIS "income" is equated with benefits, and the cost–benefit analysis is greatly simplified. This method obviously works best in those organizations already using the profit center concept for other services. Just as obviously, an organization with a fully integrated CBIS cannot really give users the option of not participating in the system. It is inconceivable, for example, that the production department would not participate in the MIS model described in Part IV.

Attitude Surveys

The cost–benefit analysis validates the economic feasibility study; however, it is just as important to validate behavioral feasibility. One way to do this is to survey the attitude of the users toward the CBIS. The design of survey questionnaires is itself a highly specialized skill and may require the assistance of consultants. We need not go into the details of how survey items are constructed. The questions typically address changes in the volume, the quality, the difficulty, and the enjoyment of work as a result of the new system. A well-designed questionnaire will include items that can be validated from second sources, so that differences between actual impact and perceived impact can be determined.

Measurement

Much of the impact of the new CBIS can be measured against and compared with projected standards or past performance. For example, if inventory stock-outs had averaged 3.7 per week prior to implementation of the CBIS and the objective was to reduce this number to 2.5, a new rate of 2.3 represents both an improvement and the meeting or (exceeding) of system objectives. Other measures may be more subtle and more difficult to trace to the CBIS. Certainly, one expects better information to result in better decisions and ultimately in an improvement in some organization-wide measure such as return on investment. But it is difficult to isolate the CBIS contribution to such an improvement.

Audits

Historically, *financial audits* were conducted to provide an independent validation of an organization's financial affairs. The auditing concept was expanded after World War II to include *operational audits* of other, nonfinancial activities. More recently, *management audits* have been directed specifically at management practices. The audit of a CBIS includes some features of each type of audit.

CBIS make an impact on the finances of an organization in two ways: They represent between 5 and 10 percent of the cost of operating the organization, and they are used to maintain the organization's financial records. It is not surprising, therefore, that auditors have had to become skilled in the working of CBIS and that those skills are frequently employed to audit the operation and management of CBIS as well.

Auditors may come from *internal* or *external* sources. The source is not important, as long as the auditor is able to maintain an objective point of view. In a small organization, where the only source of auditors is the accounting department and where the audit must evaluate the performance of the auditors' peers and superiors, objectivity may be lost, and external auditors are called for. Larger organizations may be able to maintain a full-time auditing group that is, for all practical purposes, external to the activities it audits. The financial auditing practice of using external auditors is so well established, however, that many firms that could maintain their own auditing staff still use accounting firms or management consulting groups to audit their CBIS.

Performance Monitors

The auditing of CBIS operations may be facilitated by the use of *performance monitors*. There are two kinds of performance monitors: *hardware monitors* and *software monitors*. Hardware monitors are "black boxes" connected to the computer that keep track of the active and idle time of the various components. For example, a hardware monitor might show that a printer is active 90 percent of the time, whereas the CPU is active only 20 percent of the time. In this situation, hardware efficiency may be improved by the addition of a second printer.

Software monitors are computer programs that record the processing times for application software. Software monitors are used to locate inefficiencies in programming. Software monitors give more specific information than hardware monitors, but they take up memory space, which itself introduces certain inefficiencies. Hardware monitors do not interfere with normal processing, but they cannot reflect on individual programs, because contemporary computers process a number of programs at once under multiprocessing or multiprogramming, and the hardware monitor cannot tell which program is running at any given instant.

The Life Cycle Process

A number of parallels between the management process and the CBIS life cycle have been noted already; one further similarity remains. Like the management process, CBIS exhibit cycles both through and among the five phases, as shown in Figure 18-7.

The initial complete cycle from planning to control has been described in detail; subsequent cycles are initiated when control reveals discrepancies that require a modification of the CBIS. The modification must be planned, developed, implemented, operated, and, of course, subjected to control measures. Even if the CBIS seems perfect—an unlikely event—environmental changes, such as technological advances in hardware and software, will trigger modifications to the system. Although modifications usually do not impact on the whole organization in the way that the initial introductory cycle does, their impact is significant to parts of the organization and they should be managed just as carefully.

There are also incomplete cycles between phases. The need to cycle between planning and development in order to prepare feasibility studies and schedules was discussed earlier. In the same manner, difficulties encountered during implementation may necessitate a return to development, although minor operating difficulties can frequently be resolved by backing up to the implementation phase for further training or by revising of the procedure manuals.

The application of the management process to the CBIS life cycle is just one link between management and CBIS. It is an important one, of course, but one that pales in comparison with the more crucial role of CBIS in support of management and; through management, the whole organization.

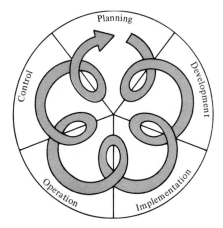

FIGURE 18-7 Loops in the CBIS life cycle.

Summary

The final three phases of the CBIS life cycle are *implementation, operation,* and *control.*

Early in the implementation phase, the site is prepared by the raising of the floor to accommodate cabling, the modification of environmental control equipment to meet the hardware requirements, and the installation of the required security devices. The training of personnel—both operators and users—also begins at this time. After the hardware has been installed, the old system is converted to the new one by running the two in *parallel* for a short time, the *phasing in* of the new system, the testing of a *pilot* model of the new system, or by an *immediate* cut-over.

In this managerial approach to CBIS, the most important aspect of the operation phase is maintaining the *security* of the system. *Physical security* is concerned with the loss, damage, or destruction of the physical components of a CBIS. In general, physical security is achieved by physical means— walls, doors, locks, vaults, and the like—that deny access to CBIS facilities. *Operating integrity* is concerned with the loss or the undesirable alteration of data and software. Operating integrity is also preserved by denial of access and by more subtle means such as passwords and access lists. Because data and software are never *completely* safe, they are generally *backed up* as insurance against loss or damage.

Although control is usually viewed as a separate phase, some control activities take place in every other phase as well: control measures are established during *planning; progress reviews* and the *acceptance test* are conducted during *development;* and the *post-installation review* and *audits* are conducted during the *operation phase.* As in the management cycle, discrepancies discovered during CBIS control are corrected by subsequent iterations through the other phases.

Assignments

18-1. The following BASIC statement was written to compute the standard deviation (*SD*) of a population of *X*s. *SX* and *SX2* have been defined as "the sum of the *X*s" and "the sum of the squares of the *X*s," respectively. *N* is the population size. Find any errors in the statement and identify them as *logic* or *syntax* errors. (You may need to refer to your statistics text to answer this one.)

```
90 LET SD = SQR (SX2 + SX**2/N)/N)
```

18-2. A new CBIS application that allows sales managers to input their estimates of various market and economic variables into a multiple regression forecast of sales is in the final stages of development. Some concern has been expressed about the ability of the sales managers to use this application to its fullest extent. What recommendations would you make for the training of these managers?

18-3. Your university is converting from its locally developed student records system to a commerical package currently used by several other schools in your state. Data from the old system were first copied onto tape, and then the disk files were reformatted for the new system by means of a file conversion program. It is now two weeks before the beginning of a new term. Which conversion method do you recommend and why?

18-4. It was asserted that CBIS are more likely to be targets of sabotage and other intentional acts of violence than are other physical assets. Do you agree? If so, why do you suppose this is the case?

18-5. If you were responsible for the CBIS activities in an organization that produced chemicals, would you be more concerned about crimes committed *against* computers or crimes committed *with* computers? Why? Would your answer change if the organization were an insurance firm instead of a chemical manufacturer? Explain your reasons for answering the way you did.

18-6. In 1970, the U.S. Army implemented a worldwide automated payroll system. In the first month of operation, over 50 percent of the soldiers in one unit in Korea reported an error in their pay. Over 80 percent of the errors were in favor of the government; that is, the soldiers felt that they had been underpaid. Comment on the implementation of this system.

18-7. Access logs give records of entry and exit to computer facilities. Similar records can be maintained to show who (which password account) has accessed data or used application software. Is this procedure likely to stop a person from sabotage? Is it likely to stop a person from theft or fraud? Explain your answers.

18-8. Check digits have been compared with parity bits (see Chapter 4). Explain the analogy implied in this comparison.

18-9. A progress review reveals that problems in the cost-accounting module have necessitated a major redesign of the input for that application, and it is about three weeks behind schedule. What are the implications of these findings? What additional actions might be necessary as a result of the changes made?

18-10. Now that you have answered Question 18-6, you may be interested in knowing that the payroll system in question received exhaustive *acceptance* testing and was implemented following a successful *pilot* test with selected army units. Do these facts in any way suggest the nature of the problem in Korea? What further testing might have helped?

18-11. In a now classic article titled "Management Misinformation Systems," Russell Ackoff described an automated inventory system that cost a company $150,000 per month more than the manual one it replaced, largely because it reordered items *each time* (instead of only the first time) the balance on hand was below the reorder level. What kind of error was committed in the design of this system? Do you think the company in question conducted the four types of control measures recommended in this chapter? Which control measures would have detected this error? Explain how the error would have been exposed in each instance.

Other Readings

Allen Brandt. "An Unmanaged Computer System Can Stop You Dead." *Harvard Business Review* (November–December 1982).

Benjamin, Robert T. *Control of the Information System Development Cycle.* New York: Wiley, 1971.

Boyd, D. F., and H. S. Krasnow. "Economic Evaluation of Management Information Systems." *IBM Systems Journal* (March 1963).

Buss, Martin D. J. "Penny-Wise Approach to Data Processing." *Harvard Business Review* (July–August 1981).

Carlson, Eric D. "Evaluating the Impact of Information Systems." *Management Informatics* 3, no. 2 (April 1974).

Chervaney, Norman L., and Gary W. Dickson. "Economic Evaluation of Management Information Systems: An Analytic Framework." *Decision Sciences* 1, no. 3 (1970).

Ginzberg, Michael J. "Steps Toward More Effective Implementation of MS and MIS." *Interfaces* 8, no. 3 (May 1978).

Herzog, John P. "Systems Evaluation Technique for Users." *Journal of Systems Management* (May 1975).

Lucas, Henry J. "Behavioral Factors in System Implementation." *Research Paper No. 188*, Graduate School of Business, Stanford University, 1973.

Rolefson, Jerome F. "DP Check-Up." *Journal of Systems Management* (November 1978).

Rubin, Martin L. *Introduction to the System Life Cycle.* Vol. 1. New York: Brandon Systems Press, 1970.

Scharen, Laura L. "Improving System Testing Techniques." *Datamation* 23, no. 9 (September 1977).

Senn, James A. "Economic Evaluation of Management Information Decisions Systems." *Proceedings of the American Institute for Decision Sciences* (1974).

Weinberg, Gerals M. *Rethinking Systems Analysis and Design.* Boston: Little, Brown, 1982.

Wolek, Francis W. "Implementation and the Process of Adopting Managerial Technology." *Interfaces* 5, no. 3 (May 1975).

PART VIII

CURRENT CBIS DEVELOPMENTS

The CBIS field is constantly changing. Hardware and software advances, the information requirements of organizations, and the ability of CBIS professionals to use new information technology are just some of the forces that make change a way of life in the CBIS field.

Two years ago when the first edition of this book was published, we felt that the book was up to date in its coverage of CBIS. Although some things have remained largely the same, other developments have taken place that demand consideration in any comprehensive coverage of CBIS. The closing chapter of this book discusses these trends that are well on their way to becoming a permanent part of the CBIS scene.

The chapter opens with a discussion of the fascinating field of artificial intelligence (AI). Robotics, vision systems, natural language processing, and expert systems are major subsets of AI that are considered. Commercial products resulting from AI research are now starting to find their way to the marketplace.

For many years, application development resided solely in the hands of CBIS professionals. This is now changing as more and more end users are developing their own applications. Much of this application development is taking place in information centers. The hows and whys of this trend are discussed.

Few top executives have been hands-on computer users. This is now beginning to change with the appearance of executive information systems. With a few keystrokes, top executives are able to access information that is important to the successful management of their firms. The characteristics and development of executive information are discussed, along with a description of the MIDS system at Lockheed-Georgia.

Computers and computer-related technology are now becoming competitive weapons. A number of examples of CBIS being employed for competitive advantage are presented, as well as a method for identifying when CBIS can be used in this way.

Chapter 19

Current Trends in CBIS

Learning Objectives

After studying this chapter, you will be able to:

1. Discuss artificial intelligence.
2. Describe the use of robots.
3. Discuss vision systems.
4. Describe natural language processing applications.
5. Discuss expert systems.
6. Explain how an expert system is built.
7. Discuss end-user computing.
8. Describe the role of an information center in an organization.
9. Discuss executive information systems.
10. Describe the MIDS system at Lockheed-Georgia.
11. Discuss how CBIS can be used as a competitive weapon.
12. Define the following terms:

artificial intelligence	expert system shell
heuristics	development engine
robotics	inference engine
vision system	backward chaining
natural-language processing	end-user computing
expert system	information center
knowledge engineer	executive information system
protocol method	critical success factors
production rules	strategic grid

Introduction

Exciting changes have been taking place in the CBIS field during the past few years. Some of these changes have already been discussed: personal computers, DSS generators for microcomputers, local area networks, voice mail, and CAD/CAM. These and other developments are having a significant impact on organizations and the people who work for them.

In this closing chapter, we will examine several additional developments. More specifically, we will discuss artificial intelligence and its applications, end-user computing, executive information systems, and the use of CBIS as a competitive weapon. This is a diverse set of topics. However, as is true of almost everything in the CBIS field, they are directly related to computer hardware and software advances, the desire to improve personal and organizational performance, and a growing understanding of how to use computer and related technologies efficiently and effectively.

Artificial Intelligence

It was not long after computers were introduced that people began to explore whether computers could be programmed to think like humans. This interest spawned the field of study now known as *artificial intelligence.*

The first artificial intelligence (AI) investigations were undertaken with no commercial applications in mind. Rather, they were simply studies of the nature of human intelligence.

One of the earliest (mid-1950s) and most famous AI programs was the Logical Theorist developed by Allen Newell and Herbert Simon of Carnegie-Mellon and J. C. Shaw of the Rand Corporation.[1] This program was used to generate proofs of mathematical theorems, including several proposed by Alfred North Whitehead and Bertrand Russell in *Principia Mathematica.* In at least one case, the program provided a more elegant proof than one devised by human mathematicians. Interestingly, no journal wanted to publish a proof thought up by a machine.

Another focus of early AI research was on programs to play complex games such as chess. Unlike simpler games such as tic-tac-toe and checkers, the computer cannot consider all of the possible moves in chess. There are too many moves even for today's fast computers. Rather, *heuristics* (from the Greek word for "discover"), or rules-of-thumb, must be used to reduce the number of possible moves to a subset of the most attractive moves. This is how experts play chess. The primary difference between expert and average chess players is not in the number of moves considered but the number and

---

[1] Joel N. Shurkin, "Expert System: The Practical Face of Artificial Intelligence," *Technology Review*, November 1983: 72–78.

quality of the heuristics employed. Developing chess-playing programs was not an end in itself, but rather an experience for gaining insights into how humans solve complex problems.

Through the 1960s and much of the 1970s, AI remained in research laboratories in leading-edge universities such as Carnegie-Mellon, MIT, and Stanford, often sponsored by Department of Defense funding. Some of the premature projections for AI ultimately resulted in disenchantment as AI research failed to live up to expectations. For example, in a late 1950s article, Herbert Simon predicted that within ten years a chess-playing program would be champion of the world. Instead, it was Bobby Fischer. Today, even though there are excellent chess-playing programs, they cannot consistently beat the grand masters of the game. What was being discovered was that human intelligence is much more complex than originally thought.

Current interest in AI is at an all-time high. Commercial products derived from AI research are finding their way into the marketplace. Dozens of companies such as IBM, Bell Laboratories, Xerox, Digital Equipment, Hewlett-Packard, Schlumberger, and Texas Instruments have investigated heavily in AI research programs. Many AI startup firms, often headed by university researchers, are now working on commercial products. These firms include Teknowledge, Cognitive Systems, Carnegie Group, and Syntelligence. Special-purpose AI computers are now made by Xerox, Symbolics, and Lisp Machines. Optimists are predicting that AI will become a multi-billion-dollar annual business well within a decade.

Despite the current enthusiasm for AI, some observers question whether the optimism is justified. AI has failed to live up to expectations in the past. More has been said about the potential of AI than what currently exists. Only time and the marketplace will tell who is right.

AI is a discipline with many subsets, including robotics, vision systems, natural language processing, and expert systems. Each of these branches on the AI tree of applications is shown in Figure 19-1 and is discussed in following sections.

Robotics

Robots hold a fascination for many people. We grow up reading about them in science fiction books and seeing them on television and in the movies. Most of the more memorable robots, such as R2D2 of *Star Wars* fame, have capabilities far beyond what is currently available. However, the distance between fact and fiction narrows with every AI advance.

Joseph Engelberger, the former president of Unimation, is credited with inaugurating the manufacture of industrial robots in 1963. The use of robots has grown rapidly since then. In the United States, the installation of robots has grown at a rate of 30 percent a year since 1970, when 200 robots were

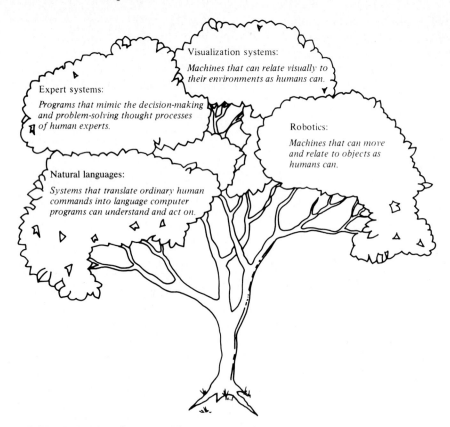

Visualization systems:

Machines that can relate visually to their environments as humans can.

Expert systems:

Programs that mimic the decision-making and problem-solving thought processes of human experts.

Robotics:

Machines that can move and relate to objects as humans can.

Natural languages:

Systems that translate ordinary human commands into language computer programs can understand and act on.

FIGURE 19-1 The AI application tree. [Source: Elisabeth Horwitt, "Exploring Expert Systems," *Business Computer Systems*, March 1985, p. 49. Illustration by Annie Gusman.]

installed, to 1980, with 3,500 robots in place.[2] This growth pattern is not limited to the United States. Even though we are considered the leader in robot technology, Japan is considered the leader in robot application. The British Robot Association estimated that in December 1982, Japan had 13,000 working robots, compared to 6,000 for the United States; West Germany followed with 3,500 working robots, and the United Kingdom had 1,200.[3] United States industry is expected to invest heavily in robots throughout the 1980s. The Congressional Joint Economic Committee predicts that by 1990, there will be 100,000 robots in use in the United States.[4]

Robot applications vary all the way from welding on assembly lines to directing the use of lasers in brain surgery. A *robot* is a machine whose

[2] "GM's Ambitious Plans to Employ Robots," *Business Week*, March 16, 1981: 31.
[3] Keith Rathmill, "The Great Robotics Explosion," *Management Today*, July 1983: 82.
[4] Blake M. Cornish, "The Smart Machines of Tomorrow," *The Futurist*, August 1981: 5.

actions are controlled by a computer. The ability to reprogram the computer provides flexibility in the use of robots.

In a 1983 study, the most frequent uses of robots were found to be, in order:

1. Picking up items and placing them elsewhere.
2. Loading machines with items.
3. Performing repeated tasks such as welding or painting as items pass by on a conveyor belt.
4. Performing repeated tasks such as welding or painting on an intermittent basis.
5. Inspecting items for quality.
6. Assembling parts into a whole.[5]

After thinking about these tasks, it is not surprising to learn that 60 percent of all robots are used in the automobile industry.[6]

Robots offer several advantages over humans, especially in certain jobs. They can work longer hours, do not take coffee breaks, do not go on vacations, do not call in sick, and do not go on strike. They can also work in environments that are unsafe or unpleasant for humans, such as removing white-hot metal from forging furnaces. With the decreasing cost of robots and the increasing cost of human labor, it is estimated by 1987 that human labor costs will exceed those of robots, without taking into account measurable differences in productivity and efficiency.[7]

There has been surprisingly little resistance to the use of robots from labor. There are several reasons that account for this fact. First, some of the jobs lost to robots are not heavily desired by humans. Also, many workers feel that they do not have any choice. Either their company goes with robots or goes out of business because of competition. And finally, and perhaps most importantly, being displaced by a robot does not always mean unemployment. Donald Smith, director of the University of Michigan's industrial development division, expects that 85 percent of the workers displaced will be transferred or retrained within their companies.[8]

The picture for the long-term effects of robots is less clear. As AI research leads to the development of more intelligent robots, new classes of jobs currently performed by humans will be threatened. We can only guess at the changes that this development will cause.

[5]William P. Tassic and Joseph E. Compton, "Robotics: Ramifications for Facilities Planning," *Industrial Development*, September–October, 1983: 4.

[6]"Whatever Happened to R2D2?" *Forbes*, January 3, 1983: 134.

[7]"The Rush for Dominance in Robotics Gains Momentum," *Business Week*, December 14, 1981: 108.

[8]Cindy Skrycki, "Will Robots Bring More Jobs—Or Less?" *U.S. News and World Report*, September 5, 1983: 25.

Vision Systems

Another branch of AI, vision systems, offers the potential for improving the intelligence of robots and for other applications as well. *Vision systems* provide machines with the ability to see. They function using a camera connected to a computer. The image recorded by the camera is divided into many squares, with each square assigned a number, depending on the intensity of its light reflection. The computer then compares the numbers with others in its memory to decide whether the object is, say, a nut or a bolt.

Powerful vision systems are difficult to build. Objects can take on many shapes and forms. Consider a human's face, which may be smiling, frowning, or crying, or a teacup, which may be metal or porcelain and comes in a variety of colors. Most commercially available vision systems are two-dimensional with limited discriminatory power. Many potential applications require three-dimensional vision capabilities. General-purpose vision systems are still many years in the future.

Natural-Language Processing

We hear a lot about various programming languages being "English-like" and computer systems being "user-friendly." The ideal situation, however, would be to communicate with computers in everyday English. *Natural-language processing* is the branch of AI that focuses on providing computers with this capability. Although progress is being made, we are still far away from computers such as HAL in *2001* and *2010*, which hear and speak like a human.

Getting computers to understand a natural language is a difficult undertaking. This was discovered when computers were first introduced and attempts were made to have computers translate material from one language to another. As the story is told, an early researcher asked his computer to translate "The spirit is willing but the flesh is weak," first into Russian and then back into English. The result was "The vodka is good but the meat is rotten."

The fundamental difficulty with natural-language processing is that human speech is fraught with ambiguities, context dependencies, unspoken "common-sense" information, and the beliefs and goals of the speaker. This difficulty results in the man–machine communication problem illustrated in Figure 19-2.[9]

In the upper figure, Person X is expressing an idea to Person Y and is delivering a sequence of words chosen not only for their applicability to his "model" but also for their appropriateness to the listener. The choice of

---

[9]This description is provided in Steven K. Roberts, "Computers Simulate Human Experts," *Mini-Micro Systems*, September 1983: 210.

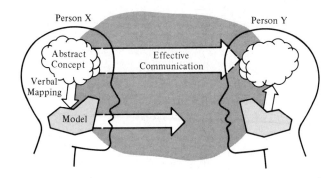

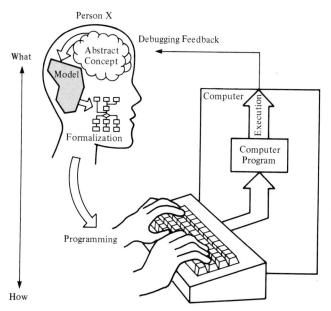

FIGURE 19-2 The man–machine communication problem.
[Source: Steven K. Roberts, "Computers Simulate Human
Experts," *Mini-Micro Systems* (September 1983), p. 210.]

words is based on a shared context, a constantly growing body of knowledge
that links the participants. If Person X is successfully fitting the words to the
context, Person Y can form a corresponding model of the idea and gradually
project it "upward" into abstract conceptual space.

In the lower figure, Person Y has been replaced by a computer. In order
to communicate with the computer, Person X must formalize the model and
express it in a computer language without the benefit of a shared context.
Person X begins with an idea of *what* X wants the computer to do, then dons a
formal intellectual straightjacket to tell it exactly *how*.

Earlier in the book, the evolution of programming languages was discussed using the concept of generations. Machine language was described as the first generation, assembly languages the second, high-level languages such as COBOL and FORTRAN the third, and recently, languages such as FOCUS and IFPS as the fourth. Each generation can be thought of as a movement up the how–what continuum. With higher generation languages, we are better able to tell the computer what we want done and let it decide how to do it.

Having computers recognize the spoken word is more difficult than understanding the typed word. Voice recognition requires the computer to match acoustic signals against a set of electronic templates. This is not an easy task. Many words are difficult to identify because they sound similar to other words. Not all words are pronounced the same way by different people. Some words are pronounced the same way but are spelled differently and have different meanings.

Despite the difficulty of natural-language processing, progress is being made. However, most of the currently available products require that words be spoken slowly and distinctly and confined to a limited vocabulary. Many of the products also require the user to provide his or her pronunciation of words for calibration purposes before the product can be used. Systems of this type are used for placing orders over the telephone, granting employ-

```
IN COBOL:
ON ENDFILE (EMPLOYEE_FILE) GOTO WRAP_UP:
PUT SKIP LIST ('1982 MAY ACT SALES', '1982 MAY EST SALES',
   'DIFFERENCE', '% CHANGE')'
DO WHILE ('1'B);
   READ FILE(EMPLOYEE_FILE) INTO(EMPLOYEE_RECORD)'
   IF EMPLOYEE_RECORD.DEPT = 'MEN'
     : EMPLOYEE_RECORD.DEPT = 'WOMEN'
   THEN DO;
      DIFFERENCE = Y1982_MAY_ACT_SALES - Y1982_MAY_EST_SALES;
      CHANGE = 100* (Y1982_MAY_ACT_SALES - Y1982_MAY_EST
      _SALES)/Y1982?MAY?ACT?SALES;
   PUT SKIP LIST (Y1982_MAY_ACT_SALES, Y1982_MAY_EST_SALES,
      DIFFERENCE, CHANGE);
      END;
   END;
WRAP_UP

IN FORMAL QUERY:
PRINT 1982-MAY-ACT-SALES, 1982-MAY-EST-SALES,
   (1982-MAY-ACT-SALES - 1982-MAY-EST-SALES),
   (100* (1982-MAY-ACT-SALES - 1982_MAY-EST-SALES)/
   1982-MAY-ACT-SALES).
WHERE (DEPT = 'MEN' OR DEPT = 'WOMEN.');

IN NATURAL LANGUAGE:
FOR THE MENS AND WOMENS DEPARTMENTS, COMPARE THE ACTUAL
AND FORECASTED SALES FOR LAST MONTH.
```

FIGURE 19-3 Examples of different data base queries. [Source: Vincent C. Rauzino, "Natural Language Processors," *Computerworld* (September 5, 1983), p. 47.]

ees clearance to make telephone calls, gaining admittance to secured areas, and training air traffic controllers.

As was discussed in Chapter 6, an important advance in data base management systems has been the development of user-friendly query languages. They are now available on micro-, mini-, and mainframe computers and have expanded hands-on computer usage to additional organizational personnel. Two of the more advanced products are Intellect from Artificial Intelligence Corp. and English from Mathematica Products Group. Figure 19-3 shows a data base query in (1) COBOL, (2) a formal query language, and (3) the natural-language Intellect.

The profit potential for companies that create successful natural-language products is enormous. One of the most closely watched efforts is that of IBM and others to develop an office product that accepts voice input and outputs a typed document. At the time of this writing, such products are expected within the year.[10] The potential impact on the office and office personnel is tremendous.

Expert Systems

Geologists were convinced over 60 years ago that a rich deposit of molybdenum ore was buried deep under Mount Tohnan in eastern Washington.[11] But after digging many dozens of small mines and drilling hundreds of test borings, they were still hunting the elusive metal. A few years ago, however, miners hit paydirt. The reason for their success was a computer program called PROSPECTOR, which was developed by SRI, International. Supplied with information ranging from the presence of such materials as magnetite and tourmaline to the location of faults and the presence of magnetic anomalies, PROSPECTOR was able to pinpoint the location of the ore in a small, unexplored area that was ringed by earlier borings and mines.

Programs such as PROSPECTOR that contain the knowledge, experience, and judgment of skilled professionals are commonly referred to as *expert systems* (or *knowledge-based systems*). They solve problems that normally require human expertise. They also serve other expert-type functions such as asking relevant questions and explaining the reasoning behind their problem solutions.

Expert systems date back many years, but have been publicized only recently. As far back as 1965, a conversation at Stanford between Edward Feigenbaum and Joshua Lederberg, a Nobel Prize-winning geneticist, led to research on a computer program that identifies organic compounds by using information provided by mass spectroscopy. With the help of Carl Djerassi, a

---

[10] "Speech System Recognizes 5000 Words," *High Technology*, March 1985: 6.

[11] This description is provided in "Artificial Intelligence Is Here," *Business Week*, July 9, 1984: 54–55.

TABLE 19-1   Expert System Applications

Expert System	Developer	Application
PROSPECTOR	SRI, International	Locates mineral deposits
R1/XSEL-XCON	Digital Equipment	Configures computer systems
ACE	AT&T	Locates faults in telephone cables
Denderal	Stanford University	Determines the structure of molecules from spectroscopic data
DELTA	General Electric	Diagnoses locomotive engine problems
Drilling Advisor	ELF Aquitaine	Recommends how to dislodge stuck drill bits
MYCIN	Stanford University	Produces recommendations for the treatment of blood diseases and meningitis
ONCASYN	Stanford University	Helps doctors keep track of drug therapy for victims of Hodgkin's disease
TAD	Cognitive Systems	Helps in the preparation of income tax returns
Dipmeter	Schlumberger	Helps assess the potential yield of oil and gas fields

professor of chemistry at Stanford, they eventually produced Dendral, the first commercial expert system.

Over the years, other expert systems have been created and used. For example, MYCIN diagnoses certain infectious diseases and recommends appropriate drug therapy. ACE locates faults in telephone cables. DELTA diagnoses locomotive engine problems. These and other expert systems are listed in Table 19-1.

What has led to the current interest in expert systems is not a sudden realization that such systems are possible, but rather, the emergence of computer hardware and software products that facilitate the development and use of expert systems.[12] Recently introduced software includes Personal Consultant from TI, M.1 from Teknowledge, Expert-Ease from Expert-Ease, and Knowledge Engineering Environment (KEE) from IntelliCorp.[13] Many of these products run on personal computers. The consequence of these

---

[12] For a discussion of expert systems development without specialized computer hardware and software, see Hugh J. Watson, *Computer Simulation in Business* (New York: Wiley, 1981), Chapter 9.

[13] Expert system software development tools are described in Paul Kinnucan, "Software Tools Speed Expert System Development," *High Technology*, March 1985: 16–20.

advances is that expert systems no longer remain the sole province of highly trained Ph.Ds with access to large mainframe computers.

Building an Expert System

Expert systems are normally developed by *knowledge engineers.* These are skilled professionals who acquire knowledge from a human expert and embed it in an expert system. They are specialists in getting information from an expert, building the system, and implementing it in its organizational setting. The development of an expert system typically includes the following steps:

1. Identify an appropriate problem.
2. Develop a prototype system.
3. Develop the complete system.
4. Evaluate the system.
5. Integrate the system.
6. Maintain the system.[14]

Let us consider each of these steps in more detail.

Identify an Appropriate Problem

There are several guidelines for selecting a good expert system application.[15] The problem for which the expert system is designed should be solvable over the telephone. Satisfying this requirement ensures that the problem does not require sensory capabilities such as sight and smell, which are difficult to provide as input to a computer. Choose a problem that experts can solve in three minutes to three hours. Choose a problem whose solution requires primarily symbolic reasoning. If the problem requires primarily numerical processing, typical algorithmic computer programs can probably be used. Prefer high-value problems. Expert systems should provide benefits that exceed their costs. Rule out applications where different experts disagree about the correct solution to the problem. Rule out applications where you cannot solve initial problems with a limited subset of the expert's total knowledge. This is the usual "start small" advice for decision support applications.

Develop a Prototype System

The knowledge engineer creates a preliminary, small-scale version of the expert system. This requires that the knowledge engineer work closely with the human expert to understand the problem and how the expert solves it.

---

[14]These are suggested in Frederick Hayes-Roth, "Knowledge-Based Expert Systems— The State of the Art in the U.S.," *Expert Systems: State of the Art Report 12:7,* J. Fox (ed.) (Maidenhead, Berkshire, England: Infotech Ltd., 1984), pp. 52–53.

[15]These steps are suggested in Paul Harmon and David King, "The Engineers Behind Expert Systems," *Computerworld,* March 18, 1985: ID/1–ID/12.

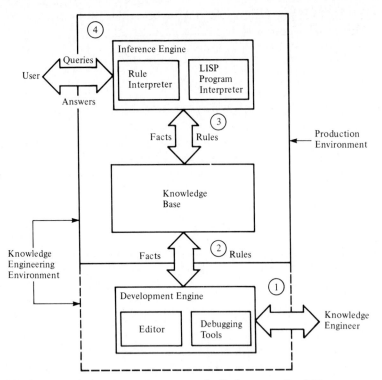

FIGURE 19-4 An expert system shell. [Source: Paul Kinnucan, "Software Tools Speed Expert System Development," *High Technology* (March 1985), p. 17.]

The *protocol method* is typically used for this purpose. The decision maker verbalizes his or her thought processes while performing the decision-making task being studied. The knowledge engineer tape records these sessions so that the facts and processing rules employed by the expert can be identified. In expert systems terminology, the processing rules (or heuristics, rules-of-thumb) are referred to as *production rules*. They typically take an IF–THEN (premise–conclusion) form: IF it looks like a duck, walks like a duck, quacks like a duck, THEN it is a duck.

As has been mentioned, special-purpose software facilitates the development and later use of an expert system. This software can be thought of as a toolkit of development and use capabilities. It is also referred to as *expert system shell*. Figure 19-4 shows the components and use of a shell.

The knowledge engineer takes the facts and rules supplied by the expert and enters them into the *development engine*. This is an interactive front-end program, which makes it easier to enter the facts and production rules and later to debug the expert system. This is shown as (1) in Figure 19-4. These facts and rules form the knowledge base of the expert system: See (2). The knowledge engineer and expert then present test cases to the prototype in order to assess its performance.

Inference engines play an important role in expert systems. They provide the processing capabilities for queries to the expert system. Using their processing logic and the facts and rules in the knowledge base, answers to questions are provided. Inference engines normally use either PROLOG (PROgramming in LOGic) or LISP (LISt Processor). PROLOG tends to be the language of choice for AI work in Europe, whereas LISP is more popular in the United States. An important distinction between the languages is that PROLOG has built-in logic procedures for processing the facts and rules, whereas LISP requires the programming of inferencing procedures. Consequently, Figure 19-4 shows that a LISP-based inference engine includes a LISP program interpreter *and* a rule interpreter.

A variety of procedures can be used for making inferences. A common one is *backward chaining*. With this procedure, the computer is given an outcome (e.g., the patient has a runny nose and a fever) and, by moving backward through the knowledge base, the program determines the diagnosis (e.g., the patient has a cold) and recommends treatment (e.g., take aspirin and stay in bed). Backward chaining is only one mechanism used by expert systems to reach a conclusion. Forward chaining, generate-and-test (i.e., a combination of forward and backward chaining), and semantic networks (i.e., records linked by pointers) can also be used.

Large-scale expert systems that use either LISP or PROLOG consume large amounts of central processing unit time. This has motivated the companies mentioned earlier—Xerox, Symbolics, and Lisp Machines—to produce special-purpose computers that are efficient in running expert systems applications. Much of Japan's frequently mentioned fifth-generation computer project involves the development of AI software and specially designed computers for processing AI applications.

In testing the prototype, the inference engine is used. This is shown in Figure 19-4 as (3). Once the prototype is fully debugged and operating satisfactorily, the knowledge engineer and expert are in an excellent position to assess what will be involved in developing the complete system.

Develop the Complete System

After the prototype has been tested, it is likely to be thrown away, especially if expert systems development tools were used. The replacing system will possibly have altered production rules and inferencing procedures and most likely an expanded set of facts and rules in the knowledge base to handle special cases that were intentionally excluded from the prototype. Attention also turns to the interface between the end users and the expert system. This is seen as (4) in Figure 19-4. The dialog between the user and the system is tailored to include the user's vocabulary and queries that are likely to be made when the system is placed in its production environment. Menus and graphical displays are often included. It is also important for the system to be able to tell why it arrived at a problem solution, because users are normally unwilling to take action on solutions that they do not understand.

Evaluate the System

After the system is completed, it is tested against the performance criteria that were established after the prototyping. Both the knowledge engineer and the expert should be satisfied with its performance. Additional experts may be brought in to try new test cases and to evaluate the system.

Integrate the System

The expert system is then placed in the organizational setting where it will be used. This step includes turning the system over to end users and systems personnel who will maintain it. They must have a thorough understanding of the system and how to fulfill their responsibilities. There may also be a need to interface the system with other data bases, instruments, or other hardware. The system may also be modified to enhance its speed or user friendliness.

A good example of integrating an expert system is provided by Puff, a pulmonary diagnosis system used at the Pacific Medical Center in San Francisco.[16] After Puff was fully tested, it was recoded from LISP to BASIC to improve its efficiency. It was then transferred to a Digital Equipment Corp. PDP-11 computer that was already being used at the hospital. The computer was then connected to a pulmonary measurement instrument. The system functions by having a patient breathe into the pulmonary measurement instrument, feeding the resulting data into the computer, and having Puff create a recommendation for the physician, who takes action.

Maintain the System

After a system is placed in its organizational environment, it must be maintained. An important part of this maintenance is entering new facts and rules into the knowledge base. This task may be performed by systems personnel or may require the skills of a knowledge engineer. Only limited success has been realized in developing systems that "learn" without considerable human intervention. Perhaps one day there will be an expert system with the skills of a knowledge engineer that can develop and maintain other expert systems.

End-User Computing

Historically, application development has been the responsibility of CBIS professionals. Although users have always had an important role in application development, information systems professionals have been largely responsible for the analysis, design, programming, and testing of computer

[16] Harmon and King, p. ID/11.

applications. This is now changing. End users are now developing their own applications. This phenomenon is called *end-user computing.* James Martin, one of the most respected observers of the CBIS scene, calls it "one of the most important trends in DP."[17]

A number of dramatic projections have been made for end-user computing. One study estimated that end-user computing is growing at a rate of 50 to 90 percent per year, whereas another predicted a 400 percent increase between 1983 and 1985.[18] Some think that end-user programming hours may soon exceed those of information systems professionals.[19]

End-user computing offers two significant advantages over formal application development by information systems professionals. No communications or specifications of requirements is needed or performed, since the user develops his or her own application. The application can also be developed in a significantly shorter period of time, because the user can begin application development at any time.

A number of factors have led to the emergence of end-user computing, including the following:

1. Hardware advances.
2. Software advances.
3. The formal application development backlog.
4. Computer literate end users.
5. Organizational arrangements to support end-user computing.

Each of these factors merits discussion.

Hardware Advances

Until the 1970s, computers were not readily available to most organizational personnel. Unless a mini- or mainframe computer was in a person's organizational unit, access to a computer was difficult to obtain. A major breakthrough occurred when computer terminals were introduced. Time on a computer was available even if the user had to work through the complexity of the computer's operating system and with languages that were more difficult to use than those available today.

Another important advancement was the advent of national time-sharing networks offered by companies such as Boeing Computer Services, Tym-

---

[17]Lois Paul, "Martin on Info Center: Take a Broad View," *Computerworld,* March 28, 1983: 20.

[18]John F. Rockart and Lauren S. Flannery, "The Management of End User Computing— A Research Perspective," CISR WP #100, MIT Sloan School of Management, February 1983; "The CRWTH Information Center Survey," *CRWTH News for Better Training,* January 1984: 3–8.

[19]Ronald A. Fink, "The Tilt to End User Programming," *Computerworld,* July 23, 1984: ID/6.

share, and CompuServe. Although these sources of computing power are not inexpensive, they do have a service orientation, offer the latest in software products that facilitate application development, and eliminate any problems with DP over when in-house computers can be used.

The most recent and probably most important hardware advance has been the microcomputer. It has freed end users from virtually all of the restrictions that they experienced previously. They are relatively inexpensive, easy to use, and readily available. For both good and bad, to a large extent they have liberated users from the control of DP.

Software Advances

Some contributions to end-user computing appeared with the availability of application software packages. In the ideal situation, all the user has to do is purchase the package, place it on a computer system, and enter data according to the specified format. In actuality, however, it is seldom this simple. Authorization to purchase the package is not always readily forthcoming. The package often has to be modified to meet the user's needs. Many of the available packages are for transaction processing applications rather than the specialized decision support applications needed by users. Despite these obstacles, application software packages make a contribution to end-user computing.

Fourth-generation languages have also helped. DSS generators like IFPS, EXPRESS, and SYSTEM W make it relatively easy for non-DP personnel to develop sophisticated decision support applications. Data base management systems such as FOCUS, RAMIS, and NOMAD make it relatively easy to query a data base using the query language. More advanced users can even develop their own applications using the data manipulation language.

Microcomputer software has made an especially large contribution to end-user computering. Electronic spreadsheets such as VisiCalc and Super-Calc, data base managers such as dBase III, and integrated products such as Lotus 1-2-3 and Framework have provided users with the tools to develop applications on their own.

The Formal Application Development Backlog

Most organizations have a two- to four-year backlog of approved applications waiting development. This formal backlog is due to shortages of skilled people, the high cost of application development, and the amount of time and effort that must be devoted to maintaining existing applications. Many users have applications that are needed far sooner than what is possible because of the backlog. The solution: Users develop their own applications if at all possible.

Computer-Literate End Users

The day has passed since all of an organization's computer expertise resided in the hands of information systems professionals. In certain areas, some end users know as much or more than the professionals (e.g., the use of microcomputer software). Several developments have contributed to this situation. Colleges are now requiring their graduates to be computer-literate. In particular, most business schools require their students to take coursework in computer concepts, a programming language, microcomputers, microcomputer software applications, and the essentials of systems analysis and design. Many companies run in-house training programs that cover the same topics, except customized to the organization's computing environment. And many people have become proficient on their own, often working with microcomputers and instructional materials at home.

Organizational Arrangements to Support End-User Computing

In the beginning, most information systems groups did not warmly embrace end-user computing. To their way of thinking, the money spent on time sharing, software products, and personal computing was a drain on dollars already in short supply. Less often spoken were concerns about loss of control and job security.

In fairness to CBIS professionals, some of their concerns were and are quite legitimate. For example, because of lack of systems design training and experience, end users often develop applications that are difficult to maintain (e.g., data embedded in a program). End users may not use the appropriate development tool (e.g., a spreadsheet rather than a micro DSS generator). Data may not be handled appropriately (e.g., sensitive data left lying around on a floppy disk.)

Despite the sometimes strong resistance to end-user computing, it has become a force that cannot be stopped. More than one microcomputer has been bought by an end-user department as an "office machine" in order to circumvent restrictions on the purchase of computer hardware. Information systems professionals have been told that they *will* support end-user computing. The current focus of attention in most organizations at the present time is not whether to support end-user computing, but how to do it in the most effective way.

A growing number of organizations are making organizational arrangements to support end-user computing. These changes even include modifications to the organization's structure. Figure 19-5 shows the structure of a

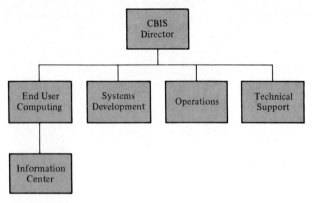

FIGURE 19-5   A CBIS organization supporting end user.

CBIS department in some organizations. It includes a formally chartered group that supports end-user computing.

Information Centers

A highly visible approach to supporting end-user computing is the information center, which is also shown in Figure 19-5. An *information center* can be thought of as "a facility and resources which allow users to carry out their own data processing according to their immediate needs."[20]

The first information center, at least by that name, was begun by IBM Canada in 1974 to satisfy in-house end user computing needs. Because of its success, IBM began promoting information centers to its customers in 1979 and the concept has quickly grown in popularity. A recent survey of 200 Data Processing Management Association (DPMA) members indicated that nearly 60 percent of their companies would have information centers in place by the end of 1984.[21] Table 19-2 presents an interesting description of the birth of information centers.

The typical information center is a physical facility with hardware, software, and support staff. End users come to the information center in order to meet their computing needs. Although information center staff is available to help, application development is the responsibility of end users.

The hardware available in an information center can include terminals, personal computers, or both. The earliest information centers contained only terminals, but as personal computers emerged as an important source of computing power, they have become a part of most information centers.

---

[20]This definition was adopted by a 1984 Share Conference for IBM users. Jean-Pierre Cahier, "Ironing Out Info Center Kinks," *Computerworld*, March 12, 1984: 63.
[21]"Information Centers Gaining," *Computerworld*, February 27, 1984: 5.

TABLE 19-2 And the Information Center Was Born

In the beginning, man created the DP shop. And darkness was upon the face of end users, for there lay between DP man, who spoke a strange tongue, and the users a vast gulf whose waters harbored treachery and foreboding.

And the users would gaze upon the gulf and the kingdom of the DP shop beyond, marveling at its great mysteries and cursing their own ignorance as they waited at the mercy of DP man for new applications.

And DP man observed *it was good*, and the users observed this *stinks*.

And as the hue and cry for more applications rose from the user shore, DP man said, "Let our shops bring forth minicomputers, lots of them, the machines yielding distributed data processing while control is still in our hands."

And the shop brought forth minis and distributed data processing, and DP man was pleased and the users were more pleased than before and Digital Equipment Corp. was *really* pleased.

But few users spoke the tongue of Cobol, and fewer still cared to learn and the vast gulf dividing the two houses again became turbulent.

For account managers demanded an ever-increasing volume of reports because, in the scriptures, it is written that information is a powerful weapon against one's enemies.

And rising executives sought more and prettier computer-generated pictures with which to impress their bosses at meetings.

And there was upon the user shores a new breed of humans, called computer literates, who dared know bytes from bites and did not fear the dark waters of the gulf like their forebears.

And there came Martin, a wizened sage who bestrode the treacherous gulf and observed the rapidly rising tide of dissent, and he observed applications backlogs whose years numbered many.

And the sage looked at the new tools called micros and fourth-generation languages and programs that spoke the forbidden computer tongue called English, heard frequently at the user shore but seldom across the gulf.

And this sage and others like him spoke to DP man in a rising chorus that said, "Yield unto the users tools to create their own applications. Let them dwell in the light of your wisdom, which shall guide them, God willing, in proper use of these tools."

"And remember," said the sages, dangling a tasty morsel in front of DP man, "in time, you'll be rid of the plague of applications backlog."

Let there be the information center.

And the information center was born and it did multiply, and although there was no universal agreement on the DP shores, it is good.

Source: *Computerworld*, September 10, 1984, p. 50.

A variety of software is typically available. End users can program their applications in languages such as BASIC and APL. DSS generators such as IFPS and EIS are often available. Special-purpose statistical analysis languages such as SAS are common. Data base management systems such as FOCUS and RAMIS can be used for queries and application development. Microcomputer software such as WORDSTAR, Lotus 1-2-3, and dBase III are typically available.

An information center normally has a manager and a small staff. Although the information center is a segment of the CBIS organization, its staff should have a user orientation and an understanding of the users' problems and needs. They should have a reasonable technical background, the view of a generalist, and the personal characteristics of patience, flexibility, and creativity. Most information center personnel have a CBIS background, but some come from functional area departments.

The information center staff is normally responsible for the following activities:[22]

- Consulting—helping users define and solve their problems.
- Education—training users to use the hardware and software.
- Technical support—helping users with special hardware, software, communications, and data problems.
- Product evaluation—continuously evaluating new products that may support user needs.
- Marketing—advertising and promoting the information center.
- Resource management—monitoring the effective use of information system resources.
- Administration—running the information center on a day-to-day basis.

The information center is available to all employees but is most heavily used by professionals (e.g., engineers) and specialized staff (e.g., financial planners). The most common applications include generating reports, querying a data base, performing an analysis, and creating graphical materials. These applications are not reducing the formal application development backlog in organizations. Rather, they are attacking what is referred to as the "invisible" backlog. These are applications that end users would like to have developed but have not formally requested. The information center does, however, reduce the number of requests made to information systems professionals for help. It has also improved the image of CBIS in organizations because of its service orientation.

Information centers are likely to become a permanent fixture in most organizations. James Martin predicts that information centers will serve

---

[22]These activities are suggested in Dennis Rielly," Info Center Requires Careful Planning," *Computerworld,* August 22, 1983: 44.

6,000,000 users by 1990.[23] They are another result of hardware and software advances and efforts to use this technology effectively.

Executive Information Systems

Top executives are well known for their unwillingness to be hands-on computer users. Several things account for this. One reason is that many of the responsibilities of top management do not lend themselves to computer support. Much of what top executives do is verbally oriented. They meet with outside publics, go to meetings, communicate decisions that have been made, talk about problems, and the like. Computers have relatively little use in areas such as these.

Another reason is that the available computer hardware and software have not been appropriate for the needs of top executives until just recently. Computer terminals required typing skills that many managers either did not possess or did not want to use because of status concerns or a feeling that it was not how managers should spend their time. The appearance of mouses, touch screens, and function keys has reduced considerably the dependence on typing skills for hands-on computer use. Top executives frequently work with summary data and prefer graphical displays. Only recently have quality graphics software and hardware become available at an affordable price.

Another reason is that most top managers missed the computer generation during their formal education. Many of them have been successful without using computers directly in their work and feel that they can continue to be successful through the remainder of their managerial careers. For these managers to use computers and computer-related equipment, it has to be easy to use and provide information that would otherwise not be available or considerably more difficult to obtain.

In a number of companies, such as Northwest Industries, Merrill Lynch, Wausau Insurance Companies, and Thermo Electron, the situation is changing as some of the barriers are dropping and top executives are becoming hands-on computer users.[24] One form this is taking is the use of personal computers. This phenomenon has been discussed previously. Another form is through the use of a new type of CBIS, sometimes referred to as an executive support system, management support system, or the term that we will use, an executive information system (EIS).

An *executive information system* provides top management with on-line access to information about the firm's current status. This information is easily obtained using a terminal (or PC), which is connected to a host com-

---

[23] Glen Rifkin, "The Information Center: Oasis or Mirage," *Computerworld, OA,* June 15, 1983: 16.

[24] John F. Rockhart and Michael E. Treacy, "The CEO Goes On-Line," *Harvard Business Review,* January–February 1982: 82–88.

puter. A core of up-to-date data is maintained on the mainframe. Both internal and external data are stored. The information provided is often in a graphical format. It is especially appropriate for supporting managements' controlling responsibilities. Some EIS also include projected trends and data analysis capabilities. When this is the case, planning responsibilities are also strongly supported by the EIS. More than any other type of CBIS, executive information systems are used directly by top executives.

The impetus for the creation of an EIS comes from a number of sources. Commonly there is an organizational champion who pushes for its development. There may be a specific business problem or situation that motivates its creation. The EIS may be viewed as a way of making executives more efficient and effective. Its development may be used as a signal to others that information technology should be used in the organization. And as has been mentioned before, advances in computer hardware and software and an increasingly computer-literate management group makes EIS all the more possible.

When designing an EIS, determining the users' information requirements is especially important. A recommended approach is to identify the users' critical success factors (CSF) and then to decide what information provides insights about how well the CSF are being accomplished.[25] *Critical success factors* are those things that the executive feels are most important to being a success in carrying out his or her job responsibilities. For example, a Vice-President for Research and Development might feel that keeping abreast of technological developments is critically important. Potential measures of this factor might include R&D expenditures, the number of trips made by R&D personnel to high technology conferences, and the percentage of R&D personnel taking evening courses at universities (excluding Chinese cooking).

Given this background on EIS, let us consider a specific example. You will see how one company, Lockheed-Georgia, has turned the concepts presented into a highly successful system.

The MIDS System at Lockheed-Georgia

Lockheed-Georgia is a subsidiary of the Lockheed Corporation and is a major producer of cargo aircraft.[26] Over 17,000 employees work at their Marietta, Georgia, plant. Their current major activities are production of the C5-B transport aircraft for the U.S. Air Force, Hercules aircraft for worldwide markets, and numerous modification and research programs.

In 1975, Robert Ormsby, then the president of Lockheed-Georgia, first

---

[25] A discussion of a process for determining an executive's CSF is provided in John F. Rockart, "Critical Success Factors," *Harvard Business Review*, March–April 1979: 81–91.

[26] The authors would like to thank George Houdeshel for providing the information on which this description is based.

expressed an interest in the creation of an on-line status reporting system. This system would largely replace the voluminous printed reports that he and other top executives at Lockheed-Georgia received. He wanted a reduced quantity of data, but with higher quality. Little action was taken for several years as data processing personnel waited for appropriate computer hardware and software technology to emerge. Finally, in 1978, with the appearance of quality color terminals at a price comparable to monochrome terminals, the decision was made to proceed even though the graphics software had to be custom-built.

The responsibility for building the EIS was assigned to a specialized staff department in the finance area. This group was selected because of their past experience in providing top management with data and graphical materials. Bob Pittman, who had considerable Lockheed-Georgia and management information presentation experience, and George Houdeshel, with CBIS experience, were asked to head up the development effort. They took on this task with a small group of specialized staff and CBIS personnel under their direct supervision. Six months later, the first version of the Management Information and Decision Support (MIDS) system was made available for Ormsby's use.

In the beginning, MIDS allowed Ormsby to call up any of 30 displays. Over the years, the number of screens and users has expanded to where MIDS now offers 650 displays for 30 of Lockheed-Georgia's top executives. Efforts are now underway to create subsystems of MIDS for middle management.

In Ormsby's original version of MIDS, a floppy disk with the displays was updated daily and placed in his terminal. As the number of displays expanded and required multiple disks, and more executives received terminals and each needed disks with the updated displays, the MIDS' displays were moved to a mini computer. This change was largely transparent to the users, since the terminals and the displays remained the same. However, to this day the displays are still created and updated off-line on a floppy disk and then transferred to a host computer.

An important consideration in MIDS' design was ease of use. Any display can be called up with a maximum of four keystrokes. Features are included that simplify the accessing of needed information. There are menus that allow users to see what screens are available and how to access them. Figure 19-6 shows the main menu. Each of the areas listed in the main menu is further broken down in additional menus. There is also a keyword index that permits users to find the screens that correspond with descriptive words which are entered by users. An especially interesting feature is user-defined sequences, which allow users to page through a series of displays whose sequence is defined in advance. The sequences are custom-designed for each user and may vary with the area being studied (e.g., key financial figures, production status, the day of the week or month, or any other relevant consideration).

A number of factors contributed to the success of MIDS: the organiza-

```
LOCKHEED GEORGIA CO.

              MIDS MAJOR CATEGORY MENU
        ■ TO RECALL THIS DISPLAY AT ANY TIME HIT 'RETURN-ENTER' KEY.
        ■ FOR INDIVIDUAL CATEGORY MENUS ENTER PROPER ALPHA

A   MANAGEMENT CONTROL              H   HUMAN RESOURCES
      OBJECTIVES;                         CO-OP PROGRAM, EMPLOYEE
      ORGANIZATION CHARTS;                STATISTICS & PARTICIPATION
      TRAVEL CALENDARS
                                      HC  HUMAN RESOURCES CRITICAL ITEMS
B   C-5B ALL PROGRAM ACTIVITIES
                                      M   MARKETING
C   HERCULES ALL PROGRAM ACTIVITIES       ASSIGNMENTS; PROSPECTS;
                                          SIGN-UPS; PRODUCT SUPPORT

E   ENGINEERING & ADVANCED PROGRAMS   MC  MARKETING CRITICAL ITEMS
      COST OF NEW BUSINESS; R & T;
      INTERNATIONAL DEVELOPMENTS      O   OPERATIONS
EC  ENGINEERING CRITICAL ITEMS            FACILITIES & SERVICES;
                                          MANUFACTURING; MATERIEL;
                                          PRODUCT ASSURANCE & SAFETY
F   FINANCIAL CONTROL
      BASIC FINANCIAL ITEMS; COST     FSC  FACILITIES & SERV. CRIT ITEMS
      REDUCTION; FIXED ASSETS; OFFSET; MFC  MANUFACTURING CRITICAL ITEMS
      OVERHEAD; OVERTIME; PERSONNEL    MTC  MATERIEL      CRITICAL ITEMS
                                       QSC  QUALITY & SAFETY CRIT. ITEMS
FC  FINANCIAL CRITICAL ITEMS
                                      P   PROGRAM CONTROL
                                          FINANCIAL & SCHEDULE
G   C-5A GENERAL PERFORMANCE              PERFORMANCE BY PROGRAM

                                      S   SPECIAL ITEMS
```

FIGURE 19-6 The MIDS main menu.

tional champion role played by Ormsby, computer hardware advances, and the efforts of the MIDS staff. The most important factor, however, was the efforts and success in understanding and satisfying the information needs of MIDS' users.

Learning about the users' information requirements was accomplished in several ways. The staff spent considerable time learning about the job responsibilities of the top executives. Secretaries were asked what information was requested and used by their bosses. The top executives were asked what information was most important in carrying out their job responsibilities. Statistics were (and still are) collected automatically by the system on the frequency of use of the various screens by the different managers. Infrequently used screens may be modified or discarded.

MIDS contains information that covers a variety of areas: the calendar of activities for the president of Lockheed-Georgia (now Paul French), the flight schedule for the corporate jet, the production status of C-5B planes being built at the Lockheed-Georgia facility, and employee contributions to Lockheed-Georgia sponsored savings plans. Figures 19-7 and 19-8 show two MIDS displays. The first is for the engineering and advanced programs area. For research, development, and bid and proposal it graphically shows the budgeted and actual amounts. The amounts are also presented in a table. The second figure is for the human resources area. It shows the age distribution of Lockheed-Georgia employees for 1983 and 1984. The graphical display is in

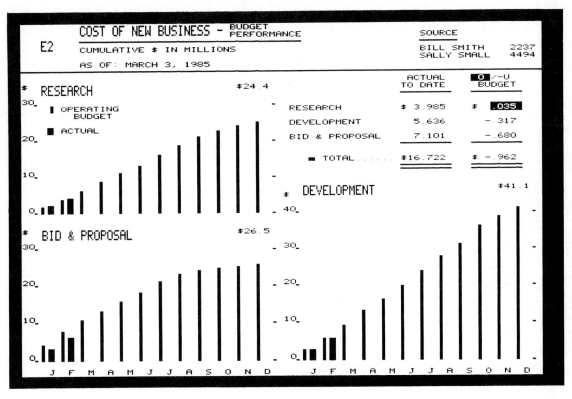

FIGURE 19-7 The MIDS cost of new business display.

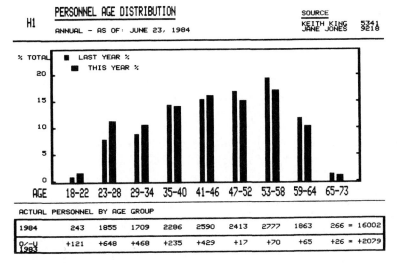

FIGURE 19-8 The MIDS personnel age distribution display.

percentages, whereas the table shows the actual number of employees in 1984 and the change from 1983.

Each screen in the MIDS system is the responsibility of one or more members of the MIDS group. Names and telephone numbers of the responsible person(s) are included on each screen (see the upper right-hand corners of Figures 19-7 and 19-8). The screens are expected to provide interpretations as well as information. For example, if the end-of-the-month cash position is $20M below projections, but the reason for this is that the money is in transit from Saudi Arabia, this information is included as a written comment. Information that needs to be emphasized is presented in red in order to highlight its importance.

The design and maintenance of the screens are critical activities. Users expect the information to be accurate, relevant, timely, complete, and consistent. This responsibility falls on Houdeshel and his staff of nine employees. In addition to extracting data for MIDS from computer-stored data bases, they are constantly obtaining information from telephone calls and published materials.

MIDS has been a very successful system. Although the nature of the system does not lend itself to formal benefit/cost calculations, its frequency of use by top executives and their satisfaction with it are important indicators of success. It has turned several top executives who previously saw no previous role for computers in their job into enthusiastic users.

In its current form, MIDS is exclusively a status-reporting system. There are discussions, however, about enhancements to include projection and analysis capabilities. Despite the appeal of these additions, they will be undertaken only if the system can be kept easy to use and are wanted by the user community.

CBIS as a Competitive Weapon

Organizations are increasingly using CBIS to affect the way they compete. This is a change from when CBIS were used largely for back office support. Now firms are using their CBIS as a competitive weapon, often with telling results. Consider the following examples:

- The Wizzard System provides Avis with information about the location, cost, and performance of its fleet. This helps Avis in its negotiations with suppliers and the service it provides to customers. It gave Avis an advantage over Hertz, National, Budget, and the other car rental firms.
- American Airlines' Sabre and United Airlines' Apollo reservation systems list their flights first when travel agents request information from their computer terminals. When there are many possible flights, being shown first results in additional business.

- Merrill Lynch's innovative Cash Management Account (CMA) provides three appealing services to investors under one umbrella: investment in a Merrill-managed money market fund, cash withdrawal by check or Visa debit card, and credit through a standard margin account. Merrill makes over $60 million per year in CMA-associated fees. It took competitors four years to develop comparable computer-based services.
- When Merrill Lynch decided to offer the CMA, it used BankOne of Ohio rather than a larger New York bank for its computer services. BankOne had positioned itself for this kind of opportunity by expanding its CBIS capabilities beyond its own internal needs and aggressively marketing its computer services.
- Some publishers gained a competitive advantage by quickly using new CBIS technologies to affect the product life cycle and to significantly increase the speed of distribution. For example, in some firms, authors submit their manuscripts on floppy disks or directly with computer to computer communications. The manuscripts are then edited on word processors, typesetting is computerized, and graphics are generated by computers. Promotional materials are distributed using telecommunications.
- Metpath, a large chemical laboratory, has enhanced its customer service by installing computer terminals in doctors' offices and linking them to its laboratory computers. As soon as specimens are analyzed in Metpath's laboratories, the results are electronically transmitted to the doctors' office. This differentiation in service has helped secure the loyalty of physicians, who normally have a tendency to switch from lab to lab in search of lower costs.
- American Hospital Supply offers a broad line of products for doctors, laboratories, and hospitals. It also provides customers with computer terminals for on-line order entry and access to software for applications such as inventory control. American Hospital Supply's customers seldom switch to other suppliers because of these services.
- McKesson is the nation's largest distributor of wholesale products. It developed an information network that tied all of its branch locations to headquarters for ordering, pricing, and tracking of inventories. In this cost-conscious industry, McKesson was able to reduce the number of inventory buyers from 140 to 13.
- Owens Corning Fiberglass helps builders evaluate insulation requirements for new buildings. As long as builders are willing to purchase insulation from the vendor, the service is provided free of charge.

Several factors have led to the use of information systems as a competitive weapon.[27] One factor is improved and less expensive computers and

---

[27] Blake Ives and Gerard P. Learmouth, "The Information System as a Competitive Weapon," *Communications of the ACM*, December 1984: 1193; Robert I. Benjamin, John F.

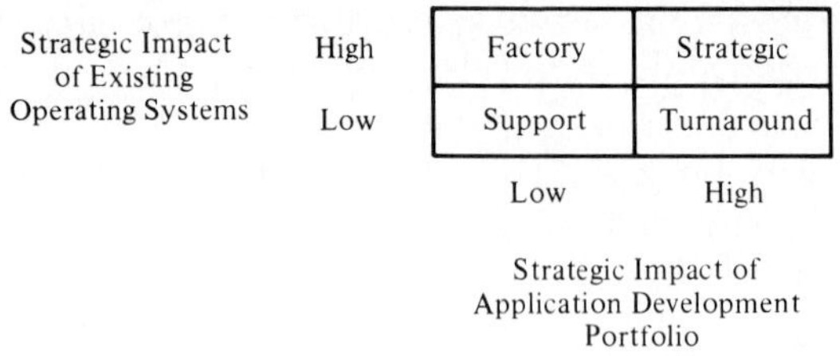

Strategic Impact of Existing Operating Systems	High	Factory	Strategic
	Low	Support	Turnaround
		Low	High

Strategic Impact of
Application Development
Portfolio

FIGURE 19-9   The strategic grid. [Source: F. Warren McFarlan and James L. McKenney, *Corporate Information Systems* (Homewood, Ill.: Richard D. Irwin, 1983), p. 14.]

computer-related technologies. Of particular importance are faster, less expensive computers; larger, less costly computer storage; enhanced, less expensive telecommunications capabilities; and more comprehensive, easier-to-use computer software. Another factor is a challenging business environment. Although business competition has always been intense, it has become more so as it has become global, as seen by the success of the Japanese. And finally, deregulation, especially in the transportation and financial services industries, has resulted in intense competitive pressures. For example, major banks now compete on a nationwide basis through electronic networks.

McFarlan and McKenney have provided a useful way of looking at CBIS as a competitive weapon.[28] Figure 19-9 shows a *strategic grid* where the rows classify organizations on the importance of existing applications and the columns on the potential criticalness of applications under development. The rows and the columns identify cells with characteristics that are important to understanding when CBIS can be used as a weapon.

Firms in the *factory* cell are heavily dependent on their existing applications for the smooth functioning of the organization. Much of their CBIS efforts are directed toward the maintenance of existing applications. New applications under development are unlikely to affect the way the firm competes. Some manufacturing, airline, and retailing firms fall into this category. In these firms, even a one-hour disruption in service from existing applications can have severe operational consequences.

Organizations that fall in the *support* cell are not heavily dependent on existing applications. The firm is able to continue to operate even when data processing breakdowns occur. Also, applications under development are not critical to the firm's ability to compete in the future.

Firms in the strategic cell depend very much on the smooth functioning

Rockart, Michael S. Scott Morton, and John Wyman, "Information Technology: A Strategic Opportunity," *Sloan Management Review*, Spring 1984: 3–4.

   [28] F. Warren McFarlan and James L. McKenney, *Corporate Information Systems* (Homewood, Ill.: Richard D. Irwin, 1983), pp. 14–16.

of existing applications. Their future competitive success depends on the development of new applications. Banks and insurance companies fall into this category.

Organizations in the *turnaround* cell can withstand disruptions to existing applications but are heavily dependent on new applications in order to compete effectively. Some manufacturing firms are described by this cell.

To use the strategic grid, managers should think about the importance of existing and future applications and properly categorize their organization. Those firms in the strategic and turnaround cells should be especially alert to the critical role of future application development. It should be recognized, however, that an organization's cell location can change quickly. Two examples illustrate this point.[29]

Until recently, most banks were located in the factory cell. Existing applications were important for day-to-day transaction processing, but applications under development were unlikely to affect the bank's competitive position. Now many banks have moved to the strategic cell. BankOne, described earlier, is an example of an organization quickly recognizing this change and acting aggressively to take advantage of the opportunity.

In the publishing industry, companies have been in the support cell until recently. Now with the dawn of "electronic publishing," they are moving to the turnaround cell. They may ultimately find themselves in the strategic cell as CBIS becomes a critical element of competition.

Michael Porter's research on industry analysis and the formulation of competitive strategies also provides the basis for a useful way of considering how CBIS can be used for competitive advantage.[30] He identifies five major competitive forces, as seen in Figure 19-10 and listed here:

1. The threat of new entrants into the marketplace.
2. The rivalry among existing firms.
3. The threat of substitute products and services.
4. The buying power of customers.
5. The buying power of suppliers.

Firms wishing to have a competitive advantage should build defenses against these forces and exploit them for their own advantage whenever possible.

McFarlan uses these concepts to develop a way that top management can assess whether CBIS can be used as a competitive weapon.[31] Management must answer five questions. If the answer is "yes" to one or more of the questions, CBIS can be used for competitive purposes.

1. *Can CBIS technology build barriers to entry?* There are really two possibilities here. One possibility is to decrease the likelihood that other firms will undertake the investment in CBIS in order to compete efficiently.

---

[29] Ives and Learmouth, p. 1194.

[30] Michael E. Porter, *Competitive Strategy* (New York: The Free Press, 1980).

[31] F. Warren McFarlan, "Information Technology Changes the Way You Compete," *Harvard Business Review*, May–June 1984: 98–103.

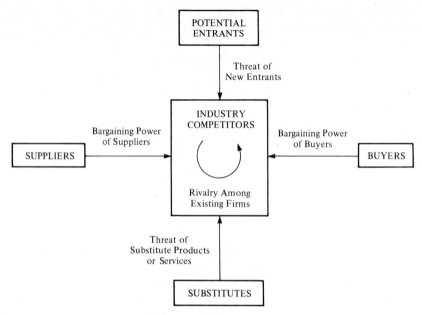

FIGURE 19-10 Forces driving industry competition. [Source: Michael E. Porter, *Competitive Strategy* (New York: The Free Press, 1980), p. 4.]

Metpath is an example of this strategy. In this industry, competitors must also be willing to install computer terminals in doctors' offices in order to compete. The other possibility is that CBIS can break down previous barriers. This is illustrated by banks that offer their services through ATMs. Prior to ATMs, the cost (and banking regulations) of building and operating branch banks served as an entry barrier.

2. *Can CBIS technology build in switching costs?* The focus here is on making it costly for customers to switch to competitors. As customers become more dependent on the CBIS services offered, the less likely they are to switch. They do not want to work with new hardware and software or go back to manual systems. They do not want to test and implement new systems. They do not want to retrain personnel and to develop new procedures. All of these are possible consequences of switching and are costly to the organization. American Hospital Supply is an example of a company that has made it expensive for customers to switch to competitors.

3. *Can CBIS technology change the basis of competition?* Porter has suggested three generic competitive strategies that are applicable here.[32] As applied to CBIS, one strategy is to use CBIS technology to retain or to assume the position of industry leader on the basis of being the *lowest-cost producer*. This strategy was followed by McKesson in reducing its cost of operations. Another strategy is to *differentiate the product or service* offered.

[32] Porter, pp. 34–46.

This approach was taken by Merrill Lynch with its CMA. And a third strategy is specialization in a *niche of a market* by offering unusual product or service features. Owens Corning Fiberglass used this strategy by being willing to determine insulation requirements.

4. *Can CBIS change the balance of power in supplier relationships?* The development of interorganizational systems can give buyers additional power over suppliers. One company has linked its materials-ordering system electronically with its suppliers' order entry system. When the company wants to buy 100 sofas, its computer automatically checks the order-entry system of its primary sofa suppliers and places an order with the one with the lowest cost. The retailer's computer then monitors the supplier's finished goods inventory, production schedule, and other sales commitments to make sure that its order is filled on time. In order to do business with the retailer, suppliers must be part of this interorganizational CBIS.

5. *Can CBIS technology generate new products?* CBIS technology can provide products and services that did not exist previously. The banking industry is an especially good example of this possibility, with ATMs debit cards, electronic bill paying, and other services. There are now electronic grocery stores where customers place their orders by phone and then pick them up at store loading docks or even have the orders delivered. Merrill Lynch's CMA is a product that was made possible by CBIS technology.

Summary

The CBIS field changes rapidly. Many of the changes are related to hardware and software advances, but there are other forces at work, such as competitive business pressures, organizations' information requirements, changes in government regulations, a more computer-literate work force, and enhanced understandings of how to use computer related technologies to improve organizational efficiency and effectiveness.

One recent trend is the appearance of commercial products that are based on artificial intelligence (AI) research. Artificial intelligence is a field of study that strives to develop computer programs that think like humans. Artificial intelligence includes a number of subsets, of which robotics, vision systems, natural-language processing, and expert systems hold the greatest potential for business application.

Robots are machines that are controlled by computer programs. Their use is growing rapidly, especially for jobs that are unsafe or unpleasant for humans and involve highly repetitive physical tasks. Robots also are becoming increasingly cost-effective relative to human labor. In the United States, robots have not received as much resistance from organized labor as one might first think.

Vision systems use a camera and a computer to provide machines with a sight capability. Progress in this area has been slow relative to other AI areas, but it holds great potential, such as for the creation of more intelligent robots.

Natural-language processing refers to communicating with computers much like humans do to one another. This is not a simple task because human communications are fraught with ambiguities, context dependencies, unspoken "common-sense" information, and the beliefs and goals of the speaker. Progress is being made, however, as seen in fourth-generation software, query languages, and speech-recognition systems.

Expert systems solve problems that normally require human expertise. Some of the better known applications are found in geology and medicine. Expert systems are created by knowledge engineers who acquire knowledge (e.g., facts and rules) from a human expert and embed it in a computer program. The development of expert systems has been facilitated by the introduction of software products (e.g., expert system shells), which aid in the creation and use of expert systems.

Historically, application development has been in the hands of CBIS professionals. This is now changing as more and more users are developing their own applications. This change is due to hardware advances, software advances, the formal application development backlog, computer-literate end users, and organizational arrangements to support end-user computing.

The information center is a formal way that many organizations are supporting end-user computing. The typical information center is a physical facility with hardware, software, and support staff. An information center is most heavily used by professionals and specialized staff to generate reports, query a data base, perform an analysis, or create graphical materials.

Executive information systems (EIS) are now used in some organizations by top executives to obtain on-line access to information about the firm's current status. Some EIS also project trends and provide data analysis capabilities. Executive information systems are easy to use (e.g., a maximum of a few keystrokes), include a core of internal and external data, are graphics oriented, and are designed with the executive's critical success factors in mind. The Management Information and Decision Support (MIDS) system at Lockheed-Georgia is a good example of an EIS.

CBIS are now being increasingly used as a competitive weapon, as seen at Avis, American Airlines, Merrill Lynch, Metpath, American Hospital Supply, and other companies. One way of thinking about the importance of CBIS as a competitive weapon is to use the strategic grid, which considers the strategic importance of existing applications and those that are planned for future development. The strategic grid includes four cells—factory, support, strategic, and turnaround—with firms in the strategic and turnaround cells having the greatest opportunity to use their CBIS for competitive advantage. Another way of assessing whether CBIS can be used as a competitive weapon is to ask: Can CBIS technology build barriers to entry? Can CBIS technology build in switching costs? Can CBIS technology change the basis of competition? Can CBIS change the balance of power in supplier relationships? Can CBIS technology generate new products? An answer of "yes" to one or more of these questions indicates an opportunity to use CBIS for competitive advantage.

Assignments

19-1. Alan Turing was a brilliant British mathematician and early computer scientist. He was one of the first to ask whether computers could think. In order to answer this question, he prepared the following test, which is now referred to as Turing's test. The test is to have an interrogator put questions to a computer and a human. If the interrogator cannot distinguish the human's response from the computer's, artificial intelligence has been achieved. Is this a difficult test for an artificial intelligence program to pass? What progress has been made in developing computer programs that pass Turing's test? Discuss.

19-2. Magazines such as *Newsweek, Time, Business Week,* and *Fortune* frequently publish articles on robots. Find a recent article in one of these magazines and write a summary of the use of robots described in the article.

19-3. In order to further illustrate why natural-language processing is challenging, consider the sentence: "I am taking out. . . ." For example, it might be: "I am taking out Claire." Develop a list of sentences with vastly different meanings which begin "I am taking out. . . ."

19-4. Some people predict that expert systems will have their greatest application in areas where semi-difficult decisions are made on a highly repetitive basis. Many banking decisions are of this type. For example, charge card applications have to be processed on a daily basis. The bank officer has to decide whether to issue a charge card, and if so, with what maximum charge limit. Assume that the protocol method has been used with a bank office and the following production rules have been identified.

Rule 1: If credit rating is excellent, then issue a card with a $1,000 limit.

Rule 2: If credit rating is poor, then issue no card.

Rule 3: If credit rating is good and if income is over $20,000, then issue a card with a $1,000 limit.

Rule 4: If credit rating is good and if income is less than $20,000 and if the person is a homeowner, then issue a card with a $1,000 limit.

Rule 5: If credit rating is good and if income is less than $20,000 and if the person is not a homeowner, then issue a card with a $500 limit.

Rule 6: If credit rating is fair and if income is over $20,000, then issue a card with a $500 limit.

Rule 7: If credit rating is fair and if income is less than $20,000, then issue no card.

    a. Prepare a tree diagram that describes how the bank officer makes charge card application decisions. Do you have to assume any production rules in order to handle all possible cases?

    b. What decisions would be made on the following charge card applications:

Kathy S. Blakey, good credit, income over $20,000, not a home-owner.

Daniel P. Thaxton, poor credit, income over $20,000, not a home-owner.

Lynn E. Hughes, good credit, income under $20,000, a home-owner.

19-5. Engineers were among the first end users to do their own application development. Why do you suppose this was the case?

19-6. Some people claim that universities have been running information centers for a long time but under different names. Does your university provide anything similar to an information center? Discuss the similarities and differences. Would you advocate your school moving more to an information center concept? Why or why not?

19-7. Develop a list of characteristics that describe an executive information system. Discuss the extent to which these characteristics are also appropriate for TPS, MIS, OAS, and DSS. Also discuss which of these characteristics apply to the MIDS system at Lockheed-Georgia.

19-8. The MIDS system at Lockheed-Georgia has displays on employee participation in blood drives and employee contributions to company-sponsored savings plans. What critical success factors do you think they are measuring? How good a measure do you think that they are?

19-9. Allen H. Neuharth, President of Gannett Newspapers, devoted much of a year's time to studying the information generation and transmission technologies needed to create the first national newspaper and to transmit it by satellite to seventeen geographically dispersed printing plants. The result is the highly successful *USA Today*. Computers and computer-related technologies make it possible for a 36-page edition to be created, transmitted in eight hours, and printed with full-color quality. To what extent does *USA Today* illustrate building a barrier to entry, building in switching costs, changing the basis of competition, changing the balance in supplier relationships, or generating a new product?

19-10. Read recent issues of publications such as *The Wall Street Journal, Business Week, Forbes,* and *Fortune* to find recent examples of how

CBIS are being used as a competitive weapon. Write a brief description of the examples that you find. Discuss whether the examples illustrate creating barriers to entry, building in switching costs, changing the basis of competition, changing the balance in supplier relationships, or generating new products.

CASE   Peachtree Insurance Company

Peachtree Insurance Company has a network of over 2,000 agents across the United States. The company offers automobile, home, and business insurance. Most of Peachtree's agents have offices in shopping centers and enjoy considerable walk-in business.

As with nearly all insurance companies, Peachtree operates a large data processing facility. This is a necessity because of the customer recordkeeping, billing, claims, and other transaction processing requirements. Just recently Peachtree began installing terminals in agents' offices to provide more timely access to computer-resident data.

Peachtree recently hired Bob Mathews as its new Vice-President for Information Services. One of the reasons that Bob was selected for the position was his interest and past experience in developing decision-support oriented applications. While working for his previous employer, he was instrumental in developing a corporate planning model and a marketing decision support system. Currently, Peachtree has very few applications that support decision making.

Bob has read about expert systems and is wondering if they might have a role at Peachtree. He describes it this way: "We have a lot of repetitive decisions at Peachtree that take a long time to make, are error-prone, and cost us a lot of money. For example, take the way that we make decisions on offering automobile insurance to customers. A customer walks into an agent's office and talks with an agent about obtaining insurance from Peachtree. If this goes well, the customer fills out an application form and is given temporary coverage until the application is processed at the home office in Atlanta. Problems begin right here. Agents are not very good at seeing that forms are filled out completely. Many applications must be sent back to agents for more information. This can slow down the process a couple of weeks. All the while we are giving coverage to someone who we may not want to insure. Finally, a Peachtree automobile insurance underwriter reviews the application and, drawing from the information provided on the form, his or her experience and judgment, and Peachtree's guidelines for making the decision, decides whether or not to extend coverage, and if so, what premiums are appropriate. Once these decisions are made, they are communicated to the agent and customer, and necessary recordkeeping and paper flows begin.

"Why can't we streamline the entire process? When a customer wants automobile or any other kind of insurance, the agent would use his terminal to enter the information required on the application form. We would have a strong front-end edit program to help ensure that all of the required information is provided accurately. Once the information is input, an expert system would make the underwriting decision, which would be transmitted real-time back to the agent's office. If the customer accepts the insurance, the customer master file would be updated with the information that was provided, appropriate documents would be printed at the agent's office, and the customer would sign the required forms. This approach would lead to fewer errors, reduce the time required to make a decision, and allow Peachtree to employ far fewer underwriters."

Questions

1. Develop a list of pros and cons for Bob Mathews' idea.

2. Assume that Bob decides to develop a system along the lines that he described. Develop a comprehensive plan for building and implementing the system. Be very detailed in describing how the underwriting expert system should be created.

3. Discuss whether the proposed system would offer a competitive advantage.

4. What reservations, if any, do you have about developing the proposed system?

Other Readings

"Artificial Intelligence Is Here." *Business Week* (July 9, 1984).

Benjamin, Robert I., John F. Rockart, Michael S. Scott Morton, and John Wyman. "Information Technology: A Strategic Opportunity." *Sloan Management Review* (Spring 1984).

Benson, David H. "A Field Study of End User Computing: Findings and Issues." *MIS Quarterly* (December 1983).

Feigenbaum, Edward A., and Pamela McCorduck. *The Fifth Generation.* Reading, Mass.: Addison-Wesley, 1983.

Hammond, L. W. "Management Considerations for an Information Center." *IBM Systems Journal* (No. 2, 1982).

Hofstadter, Douglas. *Godel, Escher, Bach.* New York: Basic Books, 1979.

Howitt, Elisabeth. "Exploring Expert Systems." *Business Computer Systems* (March 1985).

Ives, Blake, and Gerard P. Learmouth. "The Information System as a Competitive Weapon." *Communications of the ACM* (December 1984).

Martins, Gary R. "The Overselling of Expert Systems." *Datamation* (Fall 1984).

McFarlan, F. Warren, and James L. McKenney. *Corporate Information Systems.* Homewood, Ill.: Irwin, 1983.

McFarlan, F. Warren. "Information Technology Changes the Way You Compete." *Harvard Business Review* (May–June 1984).

Porter, Michael E. *Competitive Strategy.* New York: The Free Press, 1980.

Rockhart, John F., and Michael E. Treacy. "The CEO Goes On-Line," *Harvard Business Review* (January–February 1982).

Appendix A

Flowchart Symbols

Symbol	**Usage**

To show *information* or *data flows*. By convention, arrowheads are not needed to show left-to-right or top-to-bottom flows.

To show a *process*. Brief comments inside the box, such as "COMPUTE PAY," further identify the process.

A general symbol for *input/output*. Specific input/output media may be identified with other symbols.

Punched cards. (Also an example of a more specific input or output medium.)

Paper tape.

A *cathode ray tube* (CRT); usually as an output medium.

A *document* or the output of a printer.

To show an *on-line* storage device.

Symbol	**Usage**
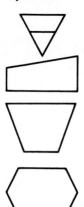	To show an *off-line* storage facility, such as a tape library.
	To show *manual input*, usually by a keyboard device such as a terminal.
	Other *manual operations*, such as the mailing of a bill or the filing of a document.
	To show *data preparation*, such as key punching or coding a mark-sense form.
	To *merge* or combine data or files, especially in a card-oriented system. (Do not confuse with the similar symbol for *off-line storage*.)
◯	A *connector*, used to connect parts of a flow chart when lines are impractical or confusing. Numbers inside the symbol identify matching connectors.
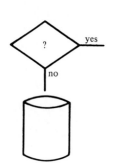	To show a *decision* or *branching operation*. Most commonly, the comment in the symbol will pose a question answerable by "YES" or "NO" to show the branch to be taken.
	A *direct access storage device* (DASD) such as a disk pack; a disk or drum file; the data base.
	Magnetic tape.
	A *data communications link.*
	A *terminal*, in the sense of the beginning or end of a program sequence. The comment "START" or "STOP" may be used in the symbol for further clarification.

Appendix B

Glossary of Terms

Accounting information systems. Information systems that focus exclusively on accounting applications.

Ada. A high-level language named for Ada Augusta, considered by some to be the first woman programmer.

Ad hoc DSS. A decision support system that is developed for an unanticipated, nonrecurring decision-making situation.

Aggregate response model. A model that shows the consequences of different decisions on variables of interest.

Analog model. A physical model that *acts*, but does not necessarily *look*, like the real-world object it represents.

APL (A programming language). A "third-and-one-half"-generation language with excellent data retrieval capabilities.

Application-oriented file. A file, either transaction or master, that is organized for processing with a specific application program.

Application programmer. One who writes application programs, usually in one of the high-level languages such as COBOL or FORTRAN.

Arc. A line connecting two nodes in decision trees, network diagrams, or data structures. In network diagrams: an activity.

Artificial intelligence. The field of study that attempts to program computers to think like humans.

Assembler language. An application programming language in which storage locations and operating instructions are coded with brief combinations of letters and/or numbers and then converted to machine language by systems software called an "assembler."

Audio conferencing. Teleconferencing when there is only voice communications.

Audiographic conferencing. Teleconferencing with voice and graphics capabilities, such as graphic display, facsimile, or freeze-frame video.

Authoring systems. Special-purpose programming languages used to develop computer-assisted instruction.

Automatic hyphenation. A word processing feature that automatically hyphenates a word when the end of a line is reached.

Automated office. A multifunction, integrated, computer-based system that allows many office activities to be performed in an electronic mode. Also referred to as the electronic office or office of the future.

Backward chaining. An inferencing technique used in artificial intelligence in which the computer is given an outcome and it reasons what may have caused the outcome.

Baseband. A communications network with a small bandwidth. Only a limited amount of data can be communicated at a relatively slow speed.

BASIC. *Beginner's All-purpose Symbolic Instruction Code.* An interactive application programming language popularly used

583

with microcomputers. There are both compiler and interpreter versions of BASIC.

Batch processing. The periodic updating of a master file or data base with data from all transactions that have occurred since the previous update.

Behavioral information systems. Information systems designed to gather information about employee perceptions, preferences, and attitudes.

Binary operator. A mathematical expression that separates data into two categories, such as "that which is equal to some value and that which is not," or "that which is greater than some value and that which is not," and so on.

Binary search. A bracketing method of locating a given record in a sequential file packed into a direct access storage device.

Bit. A *bi*nary dig*it;* the presence or absence of an electronic pulse in a designated location within a computer.

Boolean operator. A mathematical expression that classifies data by two or more properties, such as "(both) this property AND that property," "(either) this property OR that property," and so on.

Brand manager. A manager who is responsible for marketing decisions about a particular product sold by a firm. BRAND-AID, which is used by brand managers to support their decision making, is described in the text as a DSS application.

Broadband. A communications network with a large bandwidth. A large amount of data can be communicated quickly by using multiple channels on a single line.

Byte. A group of eight bits, plus a parity bit, usually used to define a single character in a programming language.

Central processing unit (CPU). The hardware component of a computer, consisting of the control unit, the arithmetic and logic unit, and internal storage, that executes programs and manipulates data.

Certainty. A decision-making environment in which the outcomes of future events are known.

Champion. An individual who supports the development of a system, supplies the organizational clout for its approval, and sees that it is developed.

Check digit. An extra digit, derived from the existing digits in a numerical data element, that serves as a check on loss or change or numerical data during transmission.

Choice phase (of decision making). The selection of a particular decision-making alternative.

COBOL. The *Common Business Oriented Language,* developed by CODASYL between 1959 and 1960. COBOL is particularly well suited to file creation and maintenance.

Compiler language. An application programming language in which instructions are written in near-conversational syntax and then converted to machine language by systems software called a "compiler."

Component. The term, in the System 2000 data base management system, that collectively describes the two basic entries: elements and repeating groups.

Computer. An electronic device that can manipulate data according to programmed instructions and make the results available to a user.

Computer-aided retrieval (CAR). A micrographic capability in which the computer assists in the retrieval of documents.

Computer-assisted design (CAD). (Also **computer-aided design**.) An advanced application of computer graphics to aid the design of physical objects.

Computer-assisted dispatching. A computerized system that helps train dispatchers make train dispatching decisions. Computer-assisted dispatching at Southern Railway is discussed in the text as a DSS application.

Computer-assisted instruction (CAI). (Also **computer-aided instruction**.) The use of a computer as a means of delivering instruction.

Computer-assisted manufacturing (CAM). (Also **computer-aided manufacturing**.) The use of computers to control manufacturing machinery.

Computer-based training (CBT). Collectively, the capabilities of computer-assisted instruction and computer-managed instruction.

Computer conferencing. Teleconferencing where the computer is used as the mechanism for communications among the participants.

Computer-managed instruction. The use of computers to create and score tests, maintain grades, and perform other administrative functions associated with instruction.

Computer output microfilming (COM). A micrographics capability where computer-generated output is recorded on microfilm without the generation of a hard-copy source document.

Conference on Data Systems Languages (CODASYL). A conference, now permanent, convened by the Department of Defense in 1959 to develop a standard programming language the result of which, in 1960, was COBOL.

Control program/microcomputers (CP/M). A popular microcomputer operating system.

Control programs. Operating system software that manages the input, output, and storage of data required by application programs.

Critical path. The sequence of activities, as shown on a PERT or Critical Path Method (CPM) network, along which any delay will cause a delay in the completion of the project.

Critical success factors. Those things that an executive feels are most important to being a success in carrying out his or her job responsibilities.

Data. In a CBIS context: unprocessed information; the input to an information-processing system.

Data analysis. The use of a terminal or other on-line input/output device to perform mathematical or statistical analyses of data stored in a data base or master file.

Data base. Collectively, all data files in an organization; the collection of data records in a data base management system.

Data base administrator (DBA). The individual in a CBIS office responsible for establishing data policy and maintaining the security and integrity of the data base.

Data base management system (DBMS). A software or software/hardware combination that maintains data in direct access storage devices and makes them available to application programs or management queries.

Data communications. The movement of data or information by electrical transmission.

Data description language (DDL). The data base management system language used to describe the *schema* and *subschema* of the data base.

Data element. The smallest unit of data that can stand alone and convey information.

Data file. A collection of related data records.

Data management routines (DMR). The portion of data base management system software, comparable to the operating system of a computer, that establishes interface with the storage devices in which the data base is maintained.

Data manipulation language (DML). The data base management system language used to identify and retrieve from the data base data required by an application program.

Data processing. The manipulation of data by a computer to support the recordkeeping and report generation activities in an organization.

Data record. A collection of related data elements.

Data set. The term, in the System 2000 data base management system, to describe a logical collection of data elements analogous to a record.

Debugging. The process of finding and correcting errors in a computer program.

Decision-making effectiveness. The quality of decisions that are made. This is in contrast to data processing efficiency (run times, amount of data stored, number of reports generated).

Decision support system (DSS). An interactive system that provides the user with easy access to decision models and data in order to support semistructured and unstructured decision-making tasks.

Decision tree. A branching diagram of the payoffs and probabilities in a decision situation. Decision trees are particularly useful to analyze multistage decisions.

Design phase (of decision making). The generation and analysis of decision-making alternatives.

Detail reports. Reports that include information on all transactions within the subject matter covered by the report.

Device media control language (DMCL). A specialized language used to assign physical storage space to data in a data base.

Direct access storage device (DASD). A storage device, such as a disk drive, in which any storage location can be accessed directly, without regard to physical sequence.

Distributed systems. A system of electronically linked computers. A *star* system uses a large, central computer while a *ring* system consists only of distributed computers.

DSS builder. A person who assembles the necessary capabilities from DSS tools or a DSS generator to create the specific DSS with which the user/intermediary interacts directly. An organizational role in DSS.

DSS data base. A collection of data used to support a decision support system. It is frequently separate from an organization's overall data base.

DSS generator. A collection of hardware and software tools (programming languages, financial analysis routines, data base management systems) in an easy to use package. Used in the creation of a specific DSS. One of three DSS levels.

DSS model base. A collection of models used to support a decision support system.

DSS tools. A set of hardware and software building blocks (programming languages, financial analysis routines, data base management systems) which are used to create a specific DSS or are incorporated in a DSS generator. One of three DSS levels.

Electronic calendars. The electronic storing of scheduled daily activities.

Electronic filing. The ability to file and retrieve documents in an electronic mode.

Electronic mail. Written (typed) messages that are communicated electronically from a sender to one or more recipients.

Electronic spreadsheet. A matrix of rows and columns in which the cells can be filled with text, numerical values, or formulas involving the values in other cells.

Element. In set terminology: the fundamental unit of a set. In the System 2000 data base management system terminology: a component, comparable to a data element, that has a value and conveys information.

End user computing. The phenomenon of non-data-processing personnel developing their own computer applications.

English-like language. A programming language with a syntax similar to the written and spoken word. A common characteristic of a DSS generator.

Ergonomics. The physiological interaction between man and machine.

Exception reports. Reports that give only information that falls within certain management-defined parameters.

Executive information system. A CBIS that provides executives with easy access to on-line information about a firm's current status.

Expected value. A weighted average; the sum of the products of alternative payoffs weighted by the probability of outcomes; the generally accepted decision criterion under risk.

Expert system. A computer program which has the decision-making capabilities of a skilled professional.

Expert system shell. A software product that facilitates the development and use of an expert system.

Facsimile. The electronic transmission of copies of documents from one location to another.

Feasibility study. A study to determine if a major endeavor, such as developing a new CBIS, is economically, technically, and behaviorally feasible.

Feedback. Output of a system that is used to keep the system under control.

Filing system. Microcomputer software, often integrated with word processors and spreadsheets, with many of the features, but less power and capacity, of data base management systems.

First-generation language. A machine language.

Financial planning system. A system of a financial nature that helps management with its planning responsibilities. The financial planning system at the Louisiana National Bank is described in the text as a DSS application.

FORTRAN. *Formula Translation*, an application programming language particularly well suited to mathematical applications.

Fourth-generation language. An advanced form of a high-level programming language. Fourth-generation languages usually are interpretive, interactive, and oriented toward decision support or data management.

Functional subsystem. In an MIS: the collection of application programs, procedures, information flows, and decision processes to support a specific organizational function, such as production.

Gantt chart. A project management technique in which activities are represented as horizontal lines on a graph which has its horizontal axis labeled in units of time.

Gateway. A communications path between a local area network and external networks.

Goal seeking (backward iteration). Specifying a goal and then determining what value for a variable is necessary in order to achieve the goal. Nearly all DSS generators allow goal seeking to be performed easily.

GPSS (General-purpose system simulator). A high-level, problem-oriented language that simulates waiting lines.

Hardware. The physical components of a computer, such as input devices, the central processing unit (CPU), and output devices.

Hashing. The use of an algorithm for converting the value of a data element into a random storage location. Also called "key transformation."

Heuristics. Rules-of-thumb which are used to reduce many possibilities to ever smaller subsets.

Holism. To view as a whole instead of a collection of parts. Systems are said to be holistic. (Also spelled wholism.)

Host language (DBMS). A data base management system in which the data manipulation language (DML) statements are incorporated into a standard application programming language.

Iconic model. A physical model that *looks* like the real-world object it represents.

Immediate conversion. A technique in which the new system replaces the old system in one sweeping change without phasing or parallel operations.

Independent decisions. Decisions that are made by a single decision maker.

Inference engine. The computer software that provides the processing logic for handling queries to an expert system.

Information analyst. A systems analyst who helps functional users identify information needs and use the CBIS to satisfy those needs.

Information center. A facility and resources that allow users to carry out their own data processing according to their immediate needs.

Inquiry processing. The use of a terminal or other on-line input/output device to obtain limited information from a data base or master file.

Institutional DSS. A decision support system that is used on a planned, repetitive basis.

Integrated packages. Software packages, usually for microcomputers, that incorporate some combination of word processing, electronic spreadsheets, filing systems, graphics, and data communications.

Intelligence. In the decision-making process: the identification of a problem and the collection of input data essential to the solution of the problem.

Intelligence phase (of decision making). A search of the environment for conditions requiring decisions and information to support decision making.

Intermediary. A person who helps a decision maker use a DSS. An organizational role in DSS.

Interpreter language. An application programming language in which instructions are converted to machine language and executed one at a time by systems software called an "interpreter." Many versions of BASIC are interpreter languages.

Inverted tree. A revised tree data structure in which data are placed at different levels to create a desired subschema or simply to show an alternative representation of the data hierarchy.

Key element. An element, usually numerical, in a data record that uniquely identifies the record and facilitates access to it.

Knowledge engineer. Skilled professionals who acquire knowledge from a human expert and embed it in an expert system.

Linear programming. An optimizing technique of management science used when a decision situation can be described with linear equations.

Local area networks. Networks such as Ethernet and Wangnet that serve only a limited geographical area such as a building.

Logic error. A programming error that violates no programming rules but causes incorrect or inappropriate output.

Logical entry. The term, in the System 2000 data base management system, to define a hierarchy of data sets.

Machine language. A binary code of 1's and 0's represented by the presence or absence of an electronic pulse.

Macro flowchart. A general flowchart showing the relationships between users and program modules of a CBIS. The basis for micro flowcharting. Also called a **Systems flowchart.**

Macroinstruction. An instruction, originally in assembler languages, that combined two or more simple instructions. The term *macro* is now used in other contexts, such as the use of a single keystroke in word processing to generate an entire word or phrase.

Magnetic ink character recognition (MICR). A system, used almost exclusively by the banking industry on checks, to read and write stylized characters printed in magnetic ink.

Mainframe. A large computer capable of handling many peripherals and/or satellite computers.

Maintenance programmer. A special category of application programmer whose job it is to make corrections or other changes to application software.

Management audit. A postinstallation check to determine whether or not a CBIS is satisfying the information needs of management.

Management control. A *resource-oriented* function of management usually associated with the middle levels of management.

Management information system (MIS). An organized set of processes that provides information to managers to support the operations and decision making within an organization.

Manager (a user). In the context of a DSS, the person who is faced with the problem or decision. An organizational role in DSS.

Manufacturing resource planning (MRP II). A software package that integrates planning, scheduling, inventory control, forecasting, and other functions that relate to manufacturing.

Marketing-mix decisions. A set of marketing decisions such as what price to charge, how much to spend on promotion, how to advertise, how sales representatives should allocate their time, and how to package the product.

Master file. The basic reference collection of records for a specific application.

Materials requirements planning (MRP). Software that supports the planning of orders for components to be used in a manufacturing process.

Mathematical model. A symbolic model that uses mathematical expressions to describe a real-world object or situation.

Maximax. A decision-making strategy under uncertainty in which an optimistic attitude prevails; to pick the alternative with the greatest *maximum* payoff.

Maximin. A decision-making strategy under uncertainty in which a pessimistic attitude prevails; to pick the alternative with the greatest *minimum* payoff.

Microcomputer. A very small (hand-held or desk-top) computer. Sometimes called a "personal computer."

Micro flowchart. A very detailed flowchart in which each symbol represents a single input, output, or process. The output of systems analysis upon which programming is based. Also called a **Programming flowchart.**

Micrographics. The use of microfilm for the capture, maintenance, retrieval, and display of textual and graphical materials.

Microprogramming. The technique of substituting coded instructions (software) for electronic circuitry (hardware).

Milestone chart. A project management technique in which key events (milestones) are listed with their expected completion dates.

Minicomputer. A small-to-intermediate-sized computer, often with capabilities that exceed those of all but the largest computers of ten years ago.

Model. An abstraction of reality used when the real-world situation represented is too complex, too costly, or too time-consuming for experimentation.

Model building blocks and subroutines. Tools such as optimization, financial analysis, and statistical analysis that can be used to build or to update a specific DSS. They may be combined in a DSS generator.

Model calibration. The process of selecting appropriate model parameters to make a model describe a particular application.

Modem. An acronym for *mo*dulator-*dem*odulator, a data communications device that converts digital data into an analog, such as a modulated sound signal, and back again.

Monte Carlo (probabilistic) analysis. The exploration of the risk associated with a situation through a probabilistic analysis. Nearly all DSS generators allow Monte Carlo analysis to be performed easily.

Multiprocessing. A timesharing technique in which two or more programs are executed simultaneously. Multiprocessing is a hardware feature.

Multiprogramming. A timesharing technique in which programs are executed while the CPU is idle with respect to other programs. Multiprogramming is achieved through systems software.

Natural language processing. The ability to communicate with a computer in an Englishlike manner.

Network data structure. A hierarchical representation of the logical relationships between data in which higher levels may have many branches to lower levels and any lower level may be related to more than one higher level.

Node. In drawing decision trees, network diagrams, or data structures: a circle from which branches or arcs emanate. In network diagrams: an event.

Nonprocedural language. A programming language that allows statements to be sequenced in any order. A common characteristic of a DSS generator.

Nonprogrammable decision. A decision that, because of the nonquantitative nature of the input data or the requirement for subjective evaluation cannot be made computationally. Also called an **Unstructured decision.**

Off-line. Not in direct electronic linkage with the CPU. Off-line storage must be brought on-line by an operator before it can be accessed by an application program.

On-line. In direct electronic linkage with the CPU. On-line storage can be accessed by application programs without operator assistance.

Operational audit. A postinstallation check to determine whether or not a CBIS is performing to the standards against which it was designed.

Operational control. A *task-oriented* function of management usually associated with the lower levels of management.

Operational models. Models used by lower management to support their operational control responsibilities (supervising day-to-day work activities).

Optimize. To select the best possible alternative in a decision-making situation; to **maximize** (profits, income, etc.) or to **minimize** (cost, time, etc.).

Parallel conversion. A technique in which the old or manual system continues to operate for a few cycles as a check on the accuracy of the new system.

Parity. An extra bit added to the binary representation of a character as a check against loss of a bit during transmission. In *even parity*, a bit is added to make the total number of bits in the character even. Similarly, parity can be odd.

Pascal. A power language with excellent mathematical and very good data handling capabilities.

Performance evaluation and review technique (PERT). A network analysis technique used in project management. PERT is particularly helpful in complex, long-range projects such as CBIS development.

Performance monitor. A means, either using software or hardware, of measuring the efficiency of a computer in processing the application programs of a CBIS.

Personal computing. The use of microcomputers to provide personal decision support.

Personnel information systems. (Also **human resource systems** or **human resource management systems**.) Information systems that focus exclusively on personnel or human resource management applications.

Phase-in conversion. A technique in which one program or application at a time is introduced until the old or manual system is eventually replaced with the new system.

Pilot conversion. A technique in which the new system is implemented in a limited fashion—in one plant or in one product line—until it can be determined that the system works and can be implemented organization-wide.

Pilot study. The testing of a system with actual users.

PL/1 (Programming language/1). A high-level language developed by IBM as an answer to the need for a mainframe language that combined the mathematical power of FORTRAN and the data-handling power of COBOL.

Pointer. A data element inserted in a record to show the storage location of the next record to be processed.

Pooled interdependent decisions. Decisions where the decision maker arrives at a decision after negotiation and interaction with others.

Problem-oriented language. A high-level language that requires the programmer only to describe the characteristics of the problem to be analyzed rather than to specify a procedure to be followed.

Production rules. The heuristics used by an expert that are placed in the knowledge base of an expert system.

Production stage. The point in time when a system becomes operational in an organization.

Professional workstation. Systems designed with professionals in mind that combine a variety of office automation capabilities in a single workstation.

Programmable decision. A decision that can be reached by following certain rules that lead to unambiguous results; routine decisions involving quantitative inputs and computational processes. Also called a **Structured decision.**

Programming flowchart. See **Micro flowchart.**

Protocol method. A procedure where an expert verbalizes his or her thought processes while performing a decision-making task in order to understand how the expert arrives at a decision.

Protocols. Technical customs or guidelines that govern the exchange of signal transmission and reception between equipment on a network.

Prototype. An initial test version of a system.

Query language (QL). The data base management system language employed by users at terminals to make inquiries or perform data analyses on data in the data base.

Random file. A file in which records are stored in random locations selected by a hashing or key transformation process.

Real-time processing. The updating of a master file or data base with transaction data in time for feedback to influence the outcome of the transaction; extremely rapid transactional processing.

Reasonableness check. Limits on numerical data, such as pay or an order quantity, beyond which the data will be rejected from processing.

Regression analysis. A statistical prediction technique based on the values of variables related to the predicted variable.

Relational data base. A flat, two-dimensional, tabular representation of the logical relationships between data in a data base.

Repeating group. The term, in the System 2000 data base management system, to identify a number of similar data sets.

Risk. A decision-making environment in which the outcomes of future events are now known, but probabilities can be assigned to those outcomes.

Robots. Machines that can move and relate to objects as humans can.

RPG (Report program generator). A high-level language well suited to the production of formatted reports and the updating of files; used primarily on minicomputers.

Satisfice. To select the first alternative that meets predefined criteria; the decision-making process associated with administrative behavior.

Scheduled reports. Reports that are produced at regular intervals—daily, weekly, etc.

Schema. An overall description of the relationship between data elements in a data base; the data base administrator's view of data.

Scrolling. The process in which an entire display is moved up and down (vertical scrolling) or right and left (horizontal scrolling).

Search and replace. A word processing capability that allows words or phrase-length character strings to be located and replaced.

Second-generation language. An assembler or symbolic language.

Self-contained (DBMS). A data base management system in which a unique language is used for application programming and as a data manipulation language (DML) and/or data description language.

Sequential access storage device (SASD). A storage device, such as a tape drive, in which each record must be read in the physical sequence in which it is stored in order to be accessed by an application program.

Sequential file. A file in which records are stored in the alphabetical or numerical sequence in which they will be processed.

Sequential interdependent decisions. Decisions where a decision maker arrives at part of the decision and passes it on to others for additional decision input.

Serial file. A file in which records, usually transactions, are stored in the order in which they occurred or were recorded.

Server. A computer that allows other computers in a network to share resources.

Simulation. To mimic or imitate a process. When random numbers are used to assign values to process variables, the technique is called *Monte Carlo* simulation.

Software. The symbolic component of a computer system, to include the operating system, the data base management system, compilers, and application programs.

Sort file. A temporary file of transaction records sorted into processing sequence in order to improve the efficiency of processing.

Special reports. Reports for which application software does not exist when the report is requested and must be specially prepared before the report can be produced.

Specific DSS. The system that is used by the decision maker to help in arriving at a decision. The system is designed to support a specific set of decision-making tasks. One of three DSS levels.

Spelling check. A word processing capability that allows documents to be checked for correct spelling.

Strategic grid. A matrix where the rows classify organizations on the importance of existing applications and the columns on the potential criticality of applications under development.

Strategic models. Models used by top management to support their strategic planning responsibilities (setting company goals, establishing company policies).

Strategic planning. An *objective-* or *goal-oriented* function of management usually associated with the top levels of management.

Structured decision. See **Programmable decision.**

Structured programming. An approach to writing application programs according to a specified format or structure to facilitate program maintenance.

Subschema. The relationship among data elements in a data base required for a specific application program; the user's view of data.

Subsystem. A part of a system that is itself a system; the hierarchical level of systems below the one under consideration. A production information system is a subsystem of an MIS.

Summary reports. Reports that use summary measures, such as the mean, the range, or the standard deviation, to describe data in less volume than detail reports.

Supercomputer. A very large computer, frequently one-of-a-kind, marked by extraordinary processing speeds and storage capacities.

Suprasystem. A system made up of other systems; the hierarchical level of systems above the one under consideration. An MIS is a system in the suprasystem of the organization.

Synergism. The systems attribute of the sum being *more* than the total of its parts.

Synonym. A record that, as a result of hashing or key transformation, is assigned to a storage location already occupied by another record.

Syntax error. A programming error that violates one or more rules of the programming language and may prevent the program from being executed.

System. A set of interrelated parts that work together to accomplish some goal or objective.

Systems analysis. The analytical process of determining information needs in an organization and describing an information system to satisfy those needs.

Systems design. An adaptation of the scientific method and other inductive problem-solving approaches that is well suited to the development of *new* systems.

Systems designer. A systems analyst who describes, with flowcharts and other techniques, the programs that will produce information needed by managers.

Systems flowchart. See **Macro flowchart.**

Systems improvement. A deductive approach to correcting deficiencies in *existing* systems.

Systems programmer. One who prepares, frequently in machine language, operating systems, compilers, data base management systems, and other systems software.

Tactical models. Models used by middle management to support their management control responsibilities (allocating and controlling company resources).

Technical supporter. A person who develops additional information system capabilities or components when they are needed as part of a DSS generator. An organizational role in DSS.

Telecommuting. The process of working at home using computer terminals.

Teleconferencing. Conferencing that allows two or more people to communicate electronically from different locations.

Terminal. An on-line input and/or output device, usually with keyboard entry and cathode ray tube (CRT) or typewriter output; a flowcharting symbol for the beginning or end of a program sequence.

Ticklers. Reminders of daily activities that have been scheduled. Electronic ticklers are common capabilities of electronic calendar systems.

Timesharing. The use of a computer system by several users simultaneously.

Toolsmith. A person who develops new technology, new languages, new hardware and software, improves the efficiency of linkages between subsystems, etc. An organizational role in DSS.

Totals check. A verification technique that compares total or net changes after processing to the total or net changes represented by transactions before processing.

Train dispatcher. A person who controls the movement of trains along their routes.

Transaction file. A collection of transactions (additions, deletions, or changes) for the purpose of updating a master file.

Transaction processing. The preparation, editing, sorting, classifying, storing, retrieving, and limited calculating of data for recordkeeping, report generation, and input to managerial activities.

Transaction processing system. A CBIS in which the primary activity is transaction processing.

Transactional processing. The updating of a master file or data base with transaction data as the transactions occur.

Tree data structure. A hierarchical representation of the logical relationships between data in which higher levels may have many branches to lower levels but each lower level is related to only one higher level.

Trend analysis. A statistical prediction technique based on past performance of the predicted variable.

Uncertainty. A decision-making environment in which the outcomes of future events are not known and probabilities of outcomes cannot be assigned.

Unscheduled reports. Reports that can be produced with existing application programs but are not unless specifically requested. Also called *demand* or *on-call* reports.

Unstructured decision. See **Nonprogrammable decision.**

Value analysis. An approach used to evaluate the desirability of creating a DSS. For relatively inexpensive systems, it asks the decision maker to place a value on the information provided by a proposed DSS. If this value exceeds the system's anticipated cost, the DSS is approved. For more expensive systems, more rigorous methods (rate of return) are used to evaluate the decision support system's desirability.

Verification. The process by which data are checked for accuracy; in card input, the keying of data into a *verifier* for comparison to data already punched into the card.

Video conferencing. Teleconferencing with two-way full-motion video combined with two-way audio for a simulation of a face-to-face meeting.

Vision systems. Machines that can relate visually to their environments as humans can.

Voice mail. Spoken messages that are communicated electronically from a sender to one or more recipients.

"What if" analysis. The exploration of the consequences of different scenarios. Nearly all DSS generators allow "what if" questions to be asked and answered easily.

Word processing. The processing of textual materials. Performed by special equipment that facilitates the input, storage, revision, and output of documents.

Word-wrap. A word processing feature that automatically moves text to the next line as the preceding line is completed.

Index

593